Handbook of Historical Archaeology

Handbook of Historical Archaeology

Edited by
Elijah Stevans

STATES
ACADEMIC PRESS
www.statesacademicpress.com

Published by States Academic Press,
109 South 5th Street,
Brooklyn, NY 11249, USA

ISBN: 978-1-63989-260-0

Cataloging-in-Publication Data

Handbook of historical archaeology / edited by Elijah Stevans.
p. cm.
Includes bibliographical references and index.
ISBN 978-1-63989-260-0
1. Archaeology and history. 2. Historic sites. 3. Archaeology. 4. History. I. Stevans, Elijah.
CC77.H5 H57 2022
930.1--dc23

For information on all States Academic Press publications visit our website at www.statesacademicpress.com

STATES
ACADEMIC PRESS

Contents

Preface

In my initial years as a student, I used to run to the library at every possible instance to grab a book and learn something new. Books were my primary source of knowledge and I would not have come such a long way without all that I learnt from them. Thus, when I was approached to edit this book; I became understandably nostalgic. It was an absolute honor to be considered worthy of guiding the current generation as well as those to come. I put all my knowledge and hard work into making this book most beneficial for its readers.

Historical archaeology deals with places, things and issues from the past and present. It primarily uses written records and oral traditions to get knowledge about the same through cultural material. Some of the major sub-disciplines of historical archaeology include classical archaeology or Egyptology and medieval archaeology. The studies conducted under historical archaeology focus on the literate and historical-period societies. It also focuses on the lives of people who have no written records such as working class, slaves and indentured laborers of the historical period. Another form of historical archaeology is industrial archaeology that concentrates on the remains of industries and the industrial era. The topics included in this book on historical archaeology are of utmost significance and bound to provide incredible insights to readers. It presents researches and studies performed by experts across the globe. Those in search of information to further their knowledge will be greatly assisted by this book.

I wish to thank my publisher for supporting me at every step. I would also like to thank all the authors who have contributed their researches in this book. I hope this book will be a valuable contribution to the progress of the field.

Editor

1

THE HANNIBAL ROUTE QUESTION OF 218 BC: A FORENSIC EXERCISE RELATIVE TO HISTORICAL ARCHAEOLOGY

William C. Mahaney

Quaternary Surveys, 26 Thornhill Ave., Thornhill, Ontario, Canada, L4J 1J4, and Department of Geography, York University, 4700 Keele St., Toronto, Ontario, Canada, M3J 1P3
e-mail: arkose41@gmail.com

ABSTRACT

Following a long and protracted survey of all targeted approach routes, cols of passage and exfiltration pathways projected to have been followed by Hannibal and his generals when they crossed into Italy in 218 BC, the physical evidence points to the Col de la Traversette, first identified by Sir Gavin de Beer in the 1960's. The first attempts to identify the route out of a dozen possible transits, focused not only on historical interpretations using the evolution of place names but on physical evidence possibly resident in hearths, alluvial terraces and rock rubble masses along the various approach routes. The primary argument following ten years of investigating every approach route from the Col Agnel in the south to the Col Mt. Cenis in the north, was that if the only blocking rockfall described by Polybius was present below the Traversette col, then mires or fans on either side in France and Italy might contain a record of Hannibal's passage. Beyond their key positions as water sources and foraging areas, the French mire and coalescing alluvial fan sediment in the upper Po, might carry evidence of the ecologic disturbance that could be radiocarbon dated to the Hannibal time line of 2168 cal yr BP or 218 BC. It is this long quest to unlock the Hannibalic invasion route that opened up key areas for historical archaeological exploration. This forensic cross/discipline exercise might serve to highlight a valuable method useful in solving other elusive ancient historical archaeological problems.

Keywords: Hannibalic invasion route; forensic analysis of mire sediment; Po plains; Polybius; environmental

1. INTRODUCTION

The question of the route followed by Hannibal and his army in 218 BC, 2168 cal yr BP (BP=before present, 1950 AD) has rankled and irked historians and classicists for millennia (Freshfield, 1886, 1899; Dodge, 1891; de Montholon, 1905; Wilkinson, 1911; Walbank, 1956, 1990; Brown, 1963; de Beer, 1956, 1967, 1969, 1974; Seibert, 1993) amongst others. No less than seven books were written about the invasion in Hannibal's time (Proctor, 1971), the last known of which (by Silenus, Hannibal's historiographer) was destroyed by the great fire that consumed the library at Alexandria in 300 AD. Since then a number of workers have posited possible routes (Fig. 1), basically dependent upon previous sources including the texts of Livy (trans. de Sélincourt, 1965) and Polybius (trans. Paton, 1922; Scott-Kilvert, 1979), but few have visited the sites in question making their target cols all based on second-hand information. While some have tried to correlate descriptions in ancient texts to the actual landscape and flooding times of rivers (de Beer, 1969), none have coupled the present environment with major topographic features in the ancient texts, let alone searched hearths, likely campgrounds, possible rock-fall impediments to the exfiltration of the mountains. It is the purpose of this summary to outline the thinking that went into trying to elicit an environmental matrix from the ancient texts, one that could be tested against the present landscape, a forensic exercise if you will (Mahaney, 2004, 2008a; Mahaney et al., 2008a, b, c).

Assessing the Hannibalic Route one is faced with countless authorities arguing for one of the three principal routes (Fig. 1) over the other and most key authorities (Proctor, 1971; Lazenby, 1998; Lancel, 1999) opting for the northern route principally because of lower elevation and ease of access. Only de Beer (1967, 1969, 1974), Prevas (1998), and Bagnall (1999) favor the southern route principally because times of flooding, place name matches, and view onto the Po plains closely align with Polybius and Livy. The middle route outlined by Connolly (1981) pitches indecision into Hannibal's thinking that once along the Isère and near Grenoble he would have shifted priority to finding the Col de Genèvre, the most unlikely deviation of travel plans. To enter into this historic mix, a daunting task as it were, required a test of environmental parameters elicited from the ancient texts of Livy and Polybius, forming a matrix of interconnected variables to determine which of the three routes, historic speculation aside, might be closest to the actual route traveled by the Punic Army.

Despite the thinking of some workers that the landscape has changed greatly since the time of Hannibal's invasion, it is clear from environmental summaries published by Sodhi et al. (2006), Mahaney (2008a) and Mahaney et al. (2008a, b, c; 2016a, 2018a) that the landscape we see today, despite many slight modifications by stream erosion and avalanche activity over the last two millennia, is the same as that seen by Hannibal and his army when they crossed into Italia in 218 BC. The landscape was set in place during the Late Pleistocene (the last ice age as it were), the final touches taking place during the Bølling and Allerød interstades that marked the first warming time since the retreat of ice, followed by a cosmic airburst of 12.8 ka (12,800 yrs) that fired the surface leaving a carbonized record in the land surface now resident in paleosols (ancient soils) and rock rinds (Mahaney and Keiser, 2013; Mahaney et al., 2013, 2014, 2016a, 2017d, 2018b). This airburst event, termed the black mat is also defined as the YDB-Younger Dryas Boundary-that marks the transition into a cold period called the Younger Dryas (YD, 12.8-~11.5 ka), a term resulting from earlier pollen work that identified variable pollen concentrations of the cold loving plant (*Dryas octapetala*) in many alpine regions. The distribution of this plant increased during the Younger Dryas event, a glacial resurgence that resulted from a cold time, similar to a nuclear winter, projected to have been caused by the black mat airburst.

The black mat event is known to have affected North, Middle and South America, Greenland, western Europe, Central Asia, (Wolbach, 2018a, 2018b), and is thought to have reached Antarctica (Mahaney et al., 2018c). Its effect on the Western Alps, particularly the area around the Mt. Viso massif was profound, burning the land surface and creating the largest accumulation of soot recorded so far in Western Europe (Allen West, personal communication, 2016). Portions of bedrock and much exposed glacial sediment were carbonized and melted by temperatures topping 2000 °C. The event presumably melted all or most glacial vestiges of the ice age, to be shortly replaced by a resurgence of ice forming during the ensuing nuclear winter which produced revived positive glacial mass balances for more than a millennium.

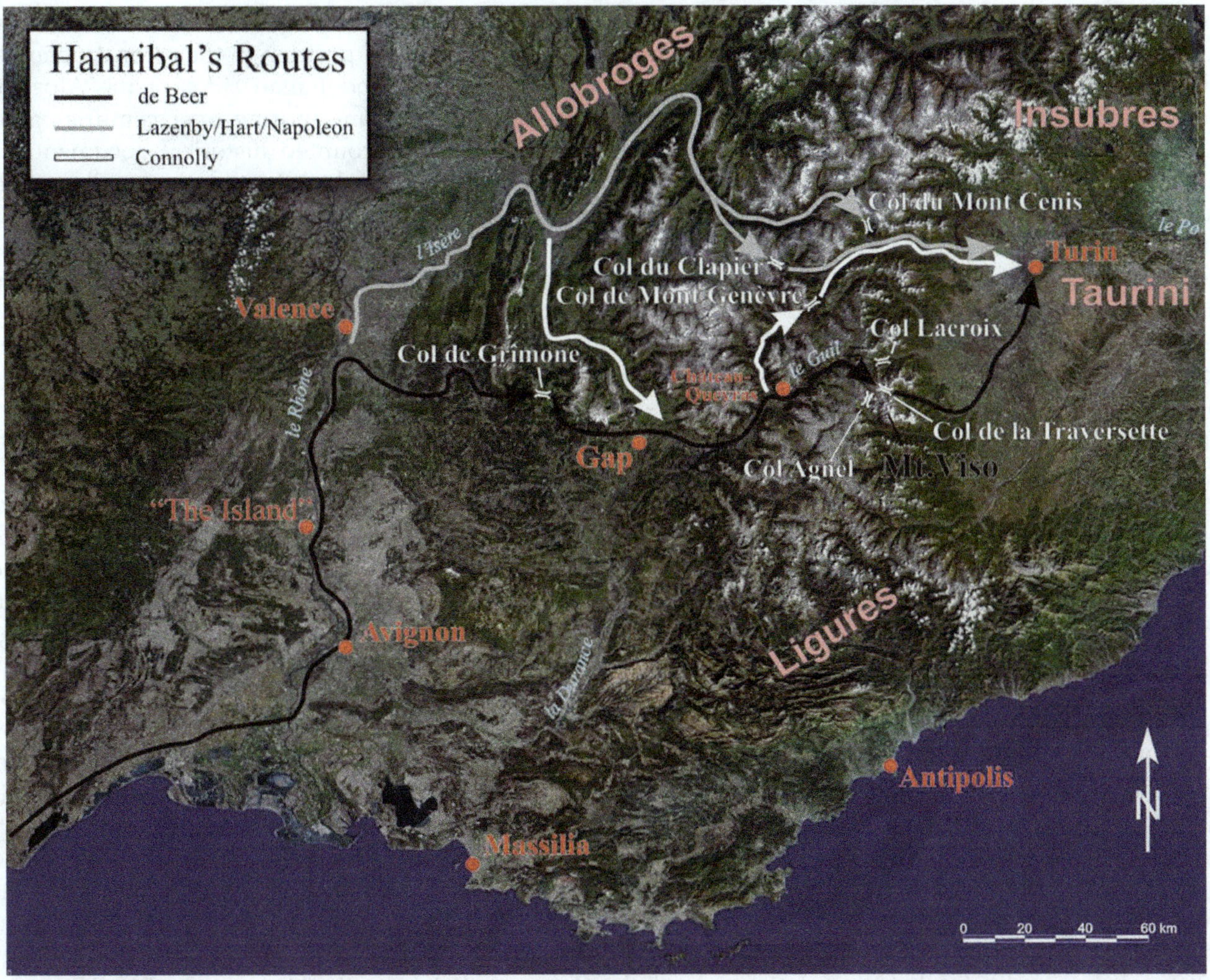

Fig. 1. Invasion routes as proposed by several classicists. Figure reprinted after Mahaney et al. (2017a). Hannibal's Rhône crossing point is not known with certainty but is probably near Arles south of Avignon. The 'Island', Hannibal's resupply point is not known exactly but is probably near present-day Orange. Major tribes - Insubres and Ligures, allied with Hannibal are shown within their nomadic areas; the Taurini refused overtures from Hannibal and were decimated in late 218 BC. The Boii tribe, allied with Hannibal, occupied an area to the east near present-day Bologna.

The YD event lasted for ~1.3 kyr, ending by ~11.5 ka when glaciers worldwide went into recession, nearly disappearing in some cases by the Holocene/Pleistocene boundary (~10 ka). By this time the landscape through which Hannibal passed had been set in place, all further change attributed to minor amounts of air-influxed material into soils and paleosols and mass wasted sediment additions to valley side locations (e.g. the younger rockfall sheet identified by Polybius) in local valleys). Losses of sediment accrued in valleys by stream erosion and development of Holocene terraces only slightly modifying the landscape in the area of the Col de la Traversette. The impediments to exfiltration faced by Hannibal are the very same as exist today on both the French and Italian sides of the Western Alps. It is within this matrix of bedrock and deposits that the search for environmental evidence related to the invasion began in 2002. Starting as a means of matching topographical descriptions and relative changes of elevation mentioned in ancient texts, the study soon morphed into a forensic test requiring the use of methods from diverse disciplines to answer questions related to camping places, foraging areas, deposit impediments, river crossings and other environmental targets as they might have affected time motion analysis of the Punic Army.

Polybius provides us with specific day-indicators of the invasion which allow for a total time travel of five months for the march from New Carthage to the Po plains, with four days from the Rhône crossing to the island, ten days from the island to the beginning of the ascent of the mountains, followed by fifteen days to reach the col. The assumption is that the fifteen days are included in the five months but Polybius is not certain about this. We do not know what Polybius meant by 'ascent of the Alps' as this quote may mean ascent of the Dauphiné Alps or ascent following the debacle in the Combe de Queyras (Mahaney and Tricart, 2008). Taking the Rhône crossing to the island to be approximately 40 km, the next leg to the Col de Grîmone a total of 180 km and allowing for negotiations and resupply efforts with local tribes at Orange to take 2-3 days, it is likely this might consume two weeks. If this is correct then the fifteen days to reach the col would include 105 km-Col de Grîmone to Durance basin, 5 km Durance to Guil catchment, 50 km Guil to Traversette, a total of 160 km and would entail significant time to offset the Durance crossing difficulties, battle in the Combe de Queyras, and reorganization in the upper Guil probably taking six to eight days. The distance from the col to the Po plains is 30 km, the last ten km taken up traveling through a steep gorge.

Of the three routes identified in Fig. 1, both the northern and southern routes are approximately the same distance, only the terrain difference causing a slower rate on the southern leg. The middle route favored by Connolly (Fig. 1) is longer by about 50 km and would have brought the Punic army to within the territory of the Allobroges for a longer period that would have entailed many delays due to engagements relative to the southern route. Putting time distance together for the full route, Polybius gives the distance as 9000 stadia (1597 km). During the first century BC, Strabo calculated 8.5 stadia to the Roman mile which equates to one stadium equal to 177.8 m. The Roman stadium is 0.1778 km, somewhat shorter than an Olympic stade which is 0.184 km or 185 m. Distances were summarized by de Beer (1969) who assumed Strabo's calculations equaled Polybius' distances converted to km's as cited above.

Of all the environmental parameters mentioned in the ancient texts of Polybius and Livy, including: nighttime attack on a col along the approach, snowline elevations, frozen ground (possibly permafrost), long defile below the ascendant col of passage, camping ground near the summit, hearths, view across the Po river plains, rockfall blockade during exfiltration to the Po river, regrouping area on the lee side, the one key element to identifying the route is the large, robust *two-tier rockfall*. All cols of passage have rockfall on the lee side of the Alps but the only pass with a large rubble sheet on the Po river side, one which could have impeded exfiltration, lies below the Col de la Traversette (~3000 m asl). As discussed by Mahaney et al. (2008c, 2010b, 2010c), this is the key element in the route puzzle that has mystified historians and classicists for over two millennia, and the one geomorphic feature as described by Polybius that certifies the southern route identified by Sir Gavin de Beer as the only possible entrance into cis-alpine Gaul transited by the Punic Army in the opening phase of the Second Punic War. Identification of the invasion route hinges on the doublet rockfall (Fig. 2), all other criteria, whether on the land surface or in section below the surface, must occupy a tangential position in the reconstruction on both the French and Italian sides of the Alps. Because most historians writing over centuries about the Punic Wars recounted historical documentation only with little regard to time/motion analysis of the Punic Army, and with scant attention paid to environmental variables recounted here, it is easy to see why belief structures aligned with different groups favored one route over another. This, combined with a lack of ground truthing of routes tied to the ancient literature, led to embedded historical hypotheses lacking any evidence providing an outcome with little chance of finding artifacts that might support a particular route.

Despite other route hypotheses expounded upon by many historians, including mention of routes closer to the Mediterranean coast and others further afield in Switzerland, such as the Great St. Bernard Pass one has to consider Hannibal's prime strategic objective pointed out by Hart (1967)---Linkage with Gallic tribes in cis-alpine Gaul—the Ligurian, Boii, and Insubre tribes with whom Hannibal had established contact prior to the invasion. Travelling too close to the Mediterranean Coast would allow the Romans to maintain contact along the way and travelling north of the Isère River would add to transport time, thus causing delays. Considering that Hannibal had reasonable information from agents sent to contact Gallic tribes in 219, returning to New Carthage (Polybius, III, 34) in spring 218 BC, and as expressed by Polybius, it is reasonable to assume he had knowledge of all major passes leading out of trans-alpine Gaul and that his objective col was the Col de Genèvre at ~2000m asl. Because the Gauls were shadowing him following departure of lowland Gallic cavalry sent from Orange as guides (Polybius III, 50), the Allobroges must have assumed Hannibal's intended crossing target, and realizing they could easily attack and defeat him with his cavalry ineffective in the narrow confines of the pass, they closed up on his rearguard (Polybius III, 52). Thus, with the Allobroges behind and ahead at his col target, either Hannibal or his second-in-command, Maharbal, must have deviated into the Guil River and the gorge (Combe de Queyras) just beyond the Durance/Guil confluence (Fig. 1) as a means of bypassing the Allobroges. Aside from the rockfall on the lee side of the range, no other approach route carries the gorge obstacle described by Polybius and Livy (Mahaney et al., 2010b). In addition to the gorge and rockfall, all other environmental parameters described below line up with arguments presented previously by Sir Gavin de Beer (1956, 1969) and fully support his southern route hypothesis.

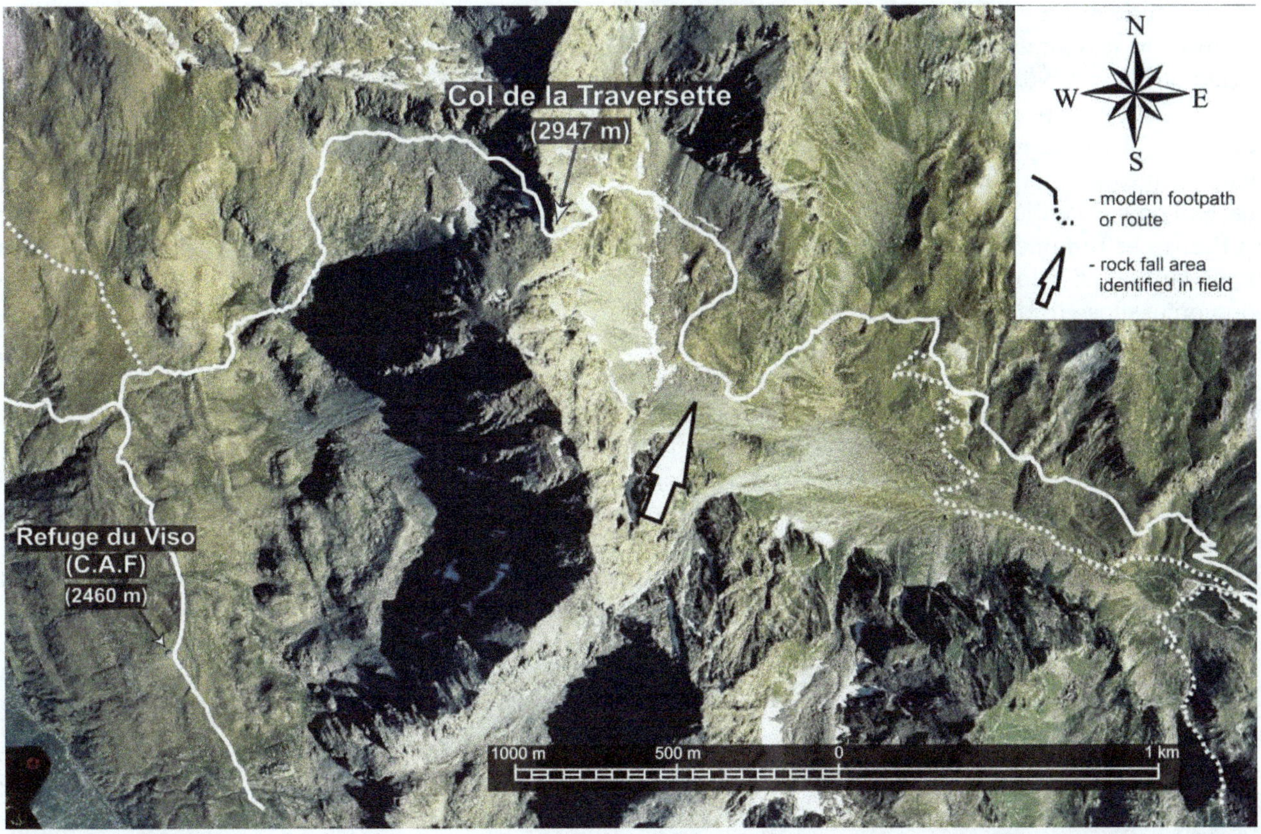

Fig. 2. Traversette rockfall, the main impediment to Hannibal's exfiltration from the Alps. Figure after Mahaney (2008a).

2. REGIONAL BACKGROUND

The regional background to the environmental constraints facing Hannibal and his troops is well explained in several works, notably, de Beer (1956, 1969), Proctor (1971), Lancel (1999), Bagnall (1999), Mahaney (2008a), amongst others. Plunging into the environmental evidence that might be used to target key sites requiring historical archaeological reconstruction has been the prime motivation behind work carried out by Mahaney (2004, 2008a), Mahaney et al. (2007b, 2008c, 2010a, b, 2010b, c, 2014) involved searching through possible reconstructions using methods from several disciplines, including geology, geomorphology, topography, astronomy, ecology, philology, palynology, chemistry, and geochemistry. This differs substantially from other earlier attempts to identify the route, some aimed at naming the route through a local municipality simply to satisfy tourist activity (Proctor, 1971). Others centered on topography and the elevation of local cols supported by previous military strategists, Napolèon for example, that Hannibal had to have used a particular route. Conversely some routes were considered just too difficult for Hannibal to have negotiated steep inclines and narrow ledges to move his animals and soldiers into Italia. Many workers seem to forget or overlook that Hannibal had a standing professional army and that his soldiers were not only capable of rapid movement, they were unencumbered by non-combatants and other non-essential personnel, and were used to movement in mountainous terrain.

Moreover, as previously outlined, the idea that the Hannibalic Army moved through a landscape vastly different from today has been disproven by glacial geological (Mahaney, 2008a; Mahaney et al., 2016a) and cosmic airburst (Mahaney and Keiser, 2013; Mahaney et al., 2018b) studies that show the landscape seen today is essentially the same as that seen by Hannibal and his troops. The only modifications to the land surface result from minor input of aeolian-influxed sediment to soils and paleosols, minor stream incision, and increase in the thickness of mass wasted deposits emplaced in the form of solifluction deposits, debris flows, and rock and snow avalanches. Col elevations have changed little since Hannibal's time mostly with slight tectonic shifts raising height by a few meters.

3. RESULTS AND DISCUSSION

3.1 INITIAL RESEARCH STAGE

Combining expertise as an environmental scientist working in various mountain environments on all continents over several decades, coupled with an interest in classical history, it is not unexpected that Hannibal's invasion over one of the most imposing mountain chains on Earth might pique my interest in focusing on just how and where the invasion was carried out. Hannibal's feat of moving large numbers of troops, support personnel, horses, mules, let alone elephants, across elevations up to 3000 m has few rivals including such figures as Caesar, Belisarius, Charlemagne, Napolèon, even including such modern figures as Rommel in the Alps and the American 10th Mountain Division in the Aleutians. Only Napolèon comes close to the number count of the Hannibalic Army, and he, it seems never ventured close to the 3000 m mark. The question of the route itself has been the driving force of historians and classicists who usually quote each other in constructing 'proofs' of the invasion route, very few ever visiting the approach routes and cols in question. Up to the time of Mahaney (2004, 2008a) no one attempted to target key sites where historical archaeological exploration might reveal artifacts related to the invasion of Hannibal or the later crossing of his brother, Hasdrubal, in 207 BC. Motivation to define the route, some consider to be the great question of antiquity (personal communication, T. Corey Brennan, 2004), seems to lie in the route designation itself, not to target key sites worth historical archaeological exploration. This seems a strange quest to me as given the fact that the Hannibalic Army emerged onto the Po River plains, the route itself of little consequence except that a route designate itself narrows the area of possible archaeological exploration. Moreover, documentation of key sites to explore might lead to the recovery of important information to elucidate the military culture of ancient Carthage. Hence, the environmental targets soon came to carry prime importance in this forensic exercise.

3.2 ENVIRONMENTAL MATRIX

Reading Polybius and Livy, one comes away with a certain briefness attained by both historians describing the invasion, most probably because few could write and most place names were spoken only, maps way off in the future. That Hannibal probably had sketch maps made by his agents who crossed the Alps into northern Italia, it is a given that he probably knew in advance the positions of most major routes, including those that sourced from the Durance and Isère valleys. We may only suppose he had this information but it is certain that being the commander that he was he would not venture forth with an army without knowing his probable route. Most certainly, the only map of the Mediterranean (Strabo, trans. Jones, 1999) made two centuries after the invasion is nearly blank north of Massillia (Marseilles) with a distorted Adriatic oriented nearly east-west (see Mahaney, 2008a, Fig. 2.2). Clearly beyond probable sketch maps and recollections of agents, Hannibal probably fixed on the lowest of all passes across the Col de Genèvre (~2000 m), generally considered a main Gallic artery, later named Pompey's Pass when he led Roman armies into Gaul during the Civil Wars.

If one assumes Hannibal intended to take the Durance route to the Col de Genèvre he would have had to either swing his army eastward from the Rhône to take the Durance north or follow the Rhône to the Drôme confluence stopping near Orange to meet with lowland Gauls whom Polybius (III, 49) affirms he had made a previous arrangement for resupplying his army. Thus, it is highly unlikely that the army would resupply at Orange and trek northward to follow the Isère route and even so, if this route is preferred, one is left wondering where the first mountain pass might be located before encountering the long defile along the final approach route to the high col. Further, if, as Polybius (III, 50) asserts, this first obstacle had to be taken in a night operation, the Gauls abandoning the high pass; the only possible cols are in the Dauphiné Alps—Col de Cabre (1193 m asl) and Col de Grîmone (1318 m asl)—and only the Grîmone pass fits the topographic assessment offered by Polybius (Mahaney, 2008a).

Once across the Col de Grîmone and into the Durance valley with local tribes in tow, Hannibal was faced with mounting obstacles, the followers and the Durance crossing. The followers gave up hostages and cattle but Polybius notes their friendship was uncertain and no doubt his scouts probed both the Guil passage and the Col de Genèvre. We shall never know why Hannibal diverted from the Genèvre to the Guil Valley, but if the Allobroges held the former, it is certain he would have sustained heavy losses trying to force passage. Polybius is certain that Hannibal was with his rear guard (often his position on the trail) making it likely, Maharbal, his second-in-command was with the vanguard and may have made the decision to follow the Guil River. Apparently the army deviated from the Durance following the Guil River into the major defile described by Polybius, an 18-km long gorge with steep cliffs where the army was trapped by an assault on the rear echelons and from the flanks, apparently with the elephant corps and the cavalry up front, Gallic mercenaries in the middle and Hannibal with African and Spanish contingents in the rear. It was the Gauls who got the worst of the assault (Mahaney and Tricart, 2008), which lasted for a day, Hannibal regrouping his troops near a 'certain bare rock' Polybius, III, 53) just inside the gorge entrance. The only large rock thus located is within 2 km of the gorge entrance as described by Mahaney (2008). However as described by Polybius (III, 53), with the flanks unprotected the Allobroges carried out an enfilade attack hurling boulders and other loose debris from the heights onto the soldiers transiting the gorge and with terrifying effect. Because this account is the only one matching the present topography with the ancient texts, it is probable that Hannibal marched from the Drôme to the Durance and into the Guil basin. Following the initial engagement in the lower foothills, the only such large and long gorge is the Combe de Queyras as described by Mahaney (2008a), all other approach routes leading to Mt. Cenis and Col Clapier lacking a long narrow defile (see Mahaney et al., 2008c, 2010c).Putting the two main sources of the invasion together, and considering that Livy never left Padua and wrote 180 years after the invasion, while Polybius followed the invasion 67 years after the event, following interviews with people who, he says, had taken part in events, Polybius' account is preferred. Polybius likely traveled quite possibly with sketches from Silenus in hand, and it is he who provides the most convincing topographic, environmental, and possible stratigraphic information related to the mountain crossing. Whereas the topography is described in general terms by both historians, it is Polybius who provides more detail on the approach defile, snow, frozen ground, view from the col, the rockfall blockage of the exfiltration route and the regrouping area below the rockfall. It is Polybius' rockfall description of a *two-tier rock system* that places him within the ranks of the stratigraphic elite of history as he clearly understood that one deposit was older, the second younger. In translation, at least, he is quoted as interpreting one deposit overlying another, a stratigraphic succession clearly seen even today based on weathering differences displayed on cobbles and boulders in the mass wasted deposits (Mahaney, 2008a; Mahaney et al., 2014).

Polybius was presumably an accomplished military officer but his observation places him within a group of extremely keen interpreters of the landscape. Few, even today, would venture across the Traversette rockfall and recognize two superposed rock deposits distinguished principally on weathering features and soil morphogenesis. Perhaps such weathering features as color and oxidation states of clasts in the two deposits were likely more apparent in Polybius' time than today since the youngest mass would likely have lacked major lichen cover and oxidation effects would have had an age of only a few centuries if the observations of Mahaney (2008a) are correct.

Thus, key environmental parameters comprise an environmental matrix, construed from Polybius and Livy, the former relying on those works available to him from afar including most likely the journals of Silenus who accompanied Hannibal as topographer and scrivener, thin with particulars as they are. These parameters include the following:

First, the crossing of the Durance and decision to follow the Guil River, if made by Marhabal, follows from assessments by Basil Hart (1967) who mentions the unusual authority delegated by Hannibal to Marhabal who often led the vanguard. As previously pointed out, we shall never know who made the decision to tackle the highest route but it is certain that Hannibal did not want to fight the Allobroges (Polybius, III, 52). The defile leading to the high slopes, following a lengthy survey of all possible approach routes (Mahaney et al., 2010b) targets only one candidate, the Combe de Queyras (Mahaney, 2008a), the only gorge with the right length of ~18 km. No other approach route offers the same topographic obstacle with steep walls providing the Gauls with a rock source to be hurled at the Carthaginians (Mahaney, et al., 2010b).

Second, taking snow accumulation into account, assuming the crossing was in October, 218 BC, it is not unusual in the Alps. The snowline was probably similar to today (Neumann, 1992) but a sudden snowfall may have produced melting followed by freezing at the ground/snow interface which would make footing difficult. Such a snowfall might extend as low as 2000 m which indicates the army's first contact occurred above the long defile, most probably near the present Chateau Queyras. It is possible higher up that soldiers slid on sporadic permafrost but this is uncertain as no permafrost was encountered during later investigations (Mahaney et al., 2007a; Mahaney, 2008a). Polybius mentions (III, 54) that following the assault in the defile the time was near the setting of the *Pleiades,* which meant early November. Polybius (Scott Kilvert, trans, 1979) mentions that this could mean even the end of September, 218 BC, but snow could start this early in fall. As pointed out by several authors, including Polybius, the crossing is documented to have occurred at the setting of the Pleiades (Walbank, 1956; Polybius, 1979; Livy, 1965), the astronomical record allowing that the Carthaginians were favored by a "Hunter's Moon" (Full Moon on October 30; Proleptic Julian Calendar, documented by Prof. D. H. Seaquist, University. of Toronto in Mahaney et al. (2008c) which would have provided sufficient moonlight for the descent on the Italian side to have taken place on a twenty-four hour regimen. The moon's elevation above the horizon at the time of transit (about 54 degrees at this site) was the highest for the year, favorable for illuminatiion of the rugged surface and deepening valley of the descent into the upper Po. Nevertheless, single file evacuation of ~20,000 infantry, ~7,000 cavalry (horses plus men), ~10,000 draft horses/mules, ~5,000 handlers and 37 elephants would require an estimated ~200 hr (i.e. 6-8 24-hour days) to clear the col and upper valley, which is within the estimated three days to clear a path through the rockfall (Polybius, III, 55). Whereas we cannot be sure of the troop/animal numbers outside of the elephants, we do know that Hannibal emerged from the mountains with 26,000 soldiers, a figure documented by Polybius (III, 33) from the bronze tablet in the Temple of Hera at Cape Lacinium, a summary considered correct by most modern workers (de Beer, 1969; Lazenby, 1998; Lancel, 1999). Thus, with this number of Carthaginian infantry and cavalry and 37 elephants, it is reasonable to assume his baggage train contained at least several thousand horses and mules for which an unknown number of handlers would be needed. Adding in cooks, artificers, armourers and engineers, the entire army probably numbered (considering losses during the ascent) a number in excess of 26,000 soldiers emerging onto the Po River plains.

Third, regrouping area in the upper valley, unidentified until Mahaney et al., 2017a, 2017b, 2017c, discovered churned-up beds in alluvial mire sediment (Fig. 3) at 2800 m dated to within the Hannibal window of 2168 cal yr BP. These beds (Mahaney et al., 2017a), at approximately ~40 cm depth, with ~15 cm amplitude, contain faecal biomarkers [(5β-stigmastanol and the bile acid deoxycholic acid (DCA)] (Mahaney et al., 2017b) related to horse and mule manure with roundworm eggs and bacteria, the latter belonging to microbe groups of Firmacuties and Clostridia related to gut release from horses and mules (Mahaney et al., 2017b). These findings show the passage of thousands perhaps tens of thousands of animals and potentially humans. Studies of the magnetic susceptibility of sediment within the French mire showed a slight increase in the churned-up beds of several sections (Mahaney et al., 2017c) which may relate either to abnormal concentrations of magnetite or to the presence of weathered artifacts. In any case the mire should be subjected to a metal detection survey and possibly to GPR (ground penetrating radar) investigations. As well, lowland areas behind the Younger Dryas moraines adjacent to the Guil mire should also be subjected to similar surveys.

Fourth, the col from which Hannibal looked across the plains of the Po is one of the main environmental parameters cited by historians. Investigations at all possible crossing places indicate the Traversette col is the only passage which gives a long view, on a clear day nearly to Milan (de Beer, 1969). The two cols adjacent to the Traversette—Col Agnel and Col de la Croix—offer restricted views cross country and do not look down upon the Po plains. Because Polybius definitely targets the Po river plains as the exfiltration point, thus excluding the Dora Riparia leading to the Po from the Clapier and Cenis cols some 50 km to the north. Polybius (III, 54) is said to have called his men to the col and pointed the way toward Rome to reassure them, but he could not have amassed the entire army on any of the cols, and the Col de la Traversette itself could barely hold 100 soldiers, so he must have addressed his key lieutenants not the entire army.

Fifth, the rockfall in question can only be found below the Traversette col, a mass of rubble matching closely to Polybius' estimate of 250 m wide and comprised of two stages of development, one older and the other and upper one younger. While Livy mentions that Hannibal fired the rockfall to heat and split boulders, Polybius is mute on the subject, indicating the firing event never happened. Further, following an extensive investigation of the rockfall surface, clasts embedded in the deposit surface did not reveal any vestige of recent firing, no carbonized material (Mahaney et al., 2008c, 2010b). It appears the rockfall firing episode described by Livy is mere fiction, and more to the point, where and how would wood be obtained as firing material by soldiers close to starvation (Bagnall, 1999) and with timberline far below the rock mass.

Sixth, the regrouping area could lie below any one of a number of possible cols of passage but the likely area below the Traversette is on a bedrock plateau floored with mire and coalescing alluvial fans (Fig. 4) at ~2000 m asl, the latter of which reveal a churned-up bed similar to the alluvial mire on the French side (Mahaney et al., 2018a). That the lee side area has been used for centuries is obvious from a stone house, complete with animal quarters and a urine trough oriented north south, draining onto slopes on the north flank of the Po river and stone walls at around 2250 m used to pen animal stock as described by (Mahaney et al., 2010a).

Seventh, most historic arguments have mentioned Hannibal's famous elephants but few have questioned the ability of elephants to make the journey over the Alps. John Hoyte (Hoyte, 1960) of Oxford University experimented with an elephant crossing Mt. Cenis showing that it was possible and that Hannibal could easily have managed at least the crossing to the north at lower elevation. However, elephants are known to work at high elevations as documented by Mahaney (1990) reaching elevations above 4500 m. Thus, crossing the Traversette col at ~3000 m asl would have been possible although difficult given the narrowness of track in place and lack of forage. The remains of Hannibal's elephants have been found in the Arno terraces near Florence (Romano and Palombo, 2017).

Fig. 3. French mire at 2850 m astride a tributary to the Guil River (see Mahaney et al., 2017c). Areas like this, although scarce, are considered to provide water and forage to Hannibal's projected route into Italia (cis-alpine Gaul). The Younger Dryas moraine and surrounding glacial landscape set in place during the last ice age has been little modified right up to today. Hence, despite claims to the contrary, the landscape viewed by the Punic Army is the same as exists today. Photography by Pierre Tricart.

Eighth, dating the evidence required using *relative* vs. *absolute* methods. *Relative age-dating* methods rely on criteria that relate one topographic/geomorphic entity against another using, for example, height of one terrace over another (ex. Mahaney et al., 2016b), the difference in elevation a measure of the erosion event followed by a deposition (filling process). In other cases, changes in strength of weathering and soil development have been used to establish relative ages in many alpine areas (ex. Mahaney and Kalm, 2013). Also, if different in time the older deposit is expected to carry stronger pedogenesis, that is, a more complex weathering profile compared with the younger deposit. One cannot say for certain what time is involved, only that a soil (e.g. paleosol) in the older terrace represents greater time for development. Also, hearths in deposits that may have been used as bivouacs for a long time may contain stratigraphic evidence belonging to ecologic disturbance, possibly the Hannibal event, and may contain charcoal material that could be dated by AMS C14. Where reported, all soil descriptions follow the Canada Soil Survey Committee (1998) and the USDA (Soil Survey Staff, 1999). All soil and sediment colors reported in the literature are based on the color chips of Oyama and Takehara (1970).

The Traversette rockfall, a case in point, illustrates how surface weathering features (i.e. color of surface clasts) resulting from physical and chemical alteration that distinguishes the two deposits could be used to separate deposits in time (Mahaney et al., 2014). In this case we know the older lobe of debris is >12.8 ka because it contains cosmic material correlated to the black mat event (Mahaney and Keiser, 2013) and the paleosol within can be correlated to Late Glacial (15 ka-12.8 ka) sediment); the younger lobe contains less weathered clastic materials related to weathering and soil development considered to be of middle Neoglacial (~3.0 ka) age; thus the sediment seen by Polybius must be >2.2 ka. Polybius, of course was most likely guided by the color differential which clearly delineated the two deposits on the basis of chemical alteration products (i.e., oxides and hydroxides) and illustrates his extraordinary powers of observation. My interpretation of the rockfall and its importance in the route interpretation was criticized by Kuhle and Kuhle (2012) who favored along with others the northern route via the Col de Clapier, an entrance to cis-alpine Gaul for which there is little supporting evidence (Mahaney, 2008a). The evidence for the Traversette rockfall as the key site supporting the southern route of de Beer (1969) was summarized by Mahaney (2013).

Fig. 4. Upper Po valley, with Pian de Re albergo off to the left, and mire and coalescing alluvial fans showing core and section sites V21, V21A and V21B (in center). Photography and site annotation by Peeter Somelar; figure after Mahaney et al. (2018a). Core and section data from these sites is interpreted in Mahaney et al. (2018a).

To obtain *absolute ages* on materials in this case relies only on radiocarbon (Mahaney et al., 2017a, b, and c), which is used to date relict organic material buried in section. Because the half-life of the ^{14}C isotope is 5710 yrs most of the recovered organic material relevant to solving the Hannibal enigma is well within the first one-half of the first half life decay process, which means that providing there is no contamination of samples one can expect accurate dates with low standard deviations. However, since relevant samples are within ~50 cm depth there is always the possibility of leaching of younger organic carbon downward in section, thus producing younger ages and wider standard deviations. Couple to this, the possibility of ground water influx into older sediment, the addition of younger organic carbon as disolved organic matter may produce the same effect. We may get around this by careful scrutiny of the standard deviations for each date to insure the standard deviation is <3% or approximately ~60 yr or less. The maximum age possible for conventional radiocarbon dates is ~40 kyr; this increases to ~70 kyr for AMS (Accelerator Mass Spectrometry) dates, with somewhat smaller standard deviations for the latter method. All AMS radiocarbon analysis and date assignment follow Bronk Ramsey (2009), Bronk Ramsey and Lee (2013) and Reimer et al. (2013).

An inventory of possible sites for radiocarbon dating along the targeted routes produces alluvial terraces covered with surface soils and buried paleosols, alluvial fans along valley sides, alluvial mires, and possible hearths. In most alpine areas of the world bogs and lacustrine plains often provide a means of obtaining bog-bottom ^{14}C dates which are, at best, minimum ages on organic remains in deposits within which such materials are found. Once a depression is formed it may infill with inorganic sediment for a time (ecesis period), before which recognizable organic remains accumulate which can be dated; hence, the minimum age designated. Lacustrine plains, reacting to lake level fluctuations may contain buried soils that may be dated by ^{14}C but these are not present in suitable positions to add to the Hannibal story. To add hearths to the list requires one to overcome the speculation that requires one to think that Hannibal's army would not pass up a site like this and some assurance that Hannibal actually took the route specified. The same applies to alluvial terraces and with these surfaces the prospect of organic retention is not great which means large samples are required to obtain even minimum organic residue that might be obtained for dating. Alluvial mires, both in the upper Guil and Po catchments, present the best options for dating because water velocities are low and retention of weathered organic sediment is great combining to preserve disturbed sediment beds from some previous episode of bioturbation such as disturbance from a foraging army. In the case of the upper Po drainage the presence of an endangered species of salamander required that all sampling be relegated to alluvial fans away from mire sediments that might have yielded better results both in terms of the physical and stratigraphic evidence (Mahaney et al., 2018a).

Pulling cores and digging sections in alluvial sediment produces planar beds aligned horizontally with the earth's surface so that variance in flow regime and or changes in source sediment produce sorted sediment even in beds with high organic input. Cores of 50-70 mm diameter limit the amount of recovered material for dating and chemical analyses whereas sections produce open faces with widths of 50 cm + allowing collection of material for replicate dating where necessary and higher weight material for laboratory analyses of various kinds. The analyst expects to collect downward from the surface into progressively older beds (shown below in Fig. 5) and if bioturbated (churned-up) beds are encountered such disturbed beds will produce wavelengths and amplitudes of distorted beds with various dimensions, physical evidence normally not seen in cores. In the case of the French vs. the Italian sediment complexes, one might expect the softer French sediment to deform to a greater degree than the Italian coarser sediment, which is approximately what happened. The French sediment sites showed an approximate center of disturbance at 40 cm ± 15 cm amplitude whereas the Italian sites showed disturbance centered at 45 cm ± 10-15 cm in two out of three sites; 60 cm ± 15 cm in the third site. The variation in depth of disturbance is explained by differences in sedimentation rates partly the result of a wetter climate in Italy compared with France.

Aside from the loss of planar beds nearly horizontal to the Earth's surface that is common to mire and alluvial fan deposits (Mahaney, 1990), sediment within the bioturbated beds is commonly much darker (addition of faecal matter and reworked humus) than variegated colors encountered up or down section from the disturbed beds. Common color ranges within the bioturbated beds are: 10YR 1/1, 2/1; 7.5YR 1/1, 2/2, 2,2; to 5YR 1/1,2/1. YR refers to hue, the dominant wavelength, where decreasing color refers to strengthening of the yellow red color. The two numbers that follow refer to brilliance with increasing value from dark to light, and chroma, purity of dominant wavelength, which increases with decreasing white light. Common wavelengths for young sediment such as in the upper Po Valley are 10YR (yellow red) and 2.5Y (yellow), the former for various degrees of weathering and the latter for fresh, unweathered sediment. To use the analogy of a cube to which hue, value and chroma are measured along three edges (Millar et al., 1966), each color notation represents a point in the cube, i.e., the Munsell notation. Within each major hue represented here, a lower value and chroma represent a darker and more carbon-rich sediment. For lithology in the field area, I relied on geological mapping by Tricart et al. (2003).

One of the great assets of working in the Guil and Po valleys rests on the detailed bedrock mapping (Tricart et al., 2003) carried out by Pierre Tricart and his associates from the Institute of Geology, University of Grenoble. Having bedrock control for all sites explored in this area insured that lithologic relationships could be worked out in the laboratory prior to engaging in field work.

Finding the churned-up bed is one part of the task, dating the transition zones to younger beds up section and older planar beds down section, and explaining the greater than 2168 cal yr BP dates within the bioturbated mass still another. The boundaries of the bioturbated mass are so diffuse that the relevant radiocarbon dates may not truly reflect start up and shut down of the bioturbation process even though the two dates should be approximately the same, that is, representative of the x number of days required to produce the bioturbated bed. To further complicate the dating process it is necessary to produce a string of dates from near the surface to approximately the top of the churned-up bed which is a hit or miss proposition as shown in Fig. 5 that relates to section V21A in Mahaney et al. (2018a) where the upper boundary is ~40 cm, the lower boundary at 55 cm but with some variance given the magnitude of disturbance.

3.3 INTERPRETING THE PROOFS

The lead up to the only possible defile along the approach route, the Combe de Queyras, is along either the Drôme River from the Rhône or from the south along the Durance. The southern route of some 150 km from the Durance/Rhône confluence does not lead to a col described by both Polybius and Livy but the Drôme approach does end at the Col de Grîmone in the Dauphiné Alps, the topography of which matches the landscape where Hannibal himself led a night operation to secure passage. These lowland routes have been thoroughly discussed by de Beer (1969) and Proctor 1971), as to likely diversions, but the Drôme route would take Hannibal close to the Col de Genèvre (~2000 m), his likely intended col of passage.

As Hannibal's army approached and crossed the Durance, Hannibal was followed by the Allobroges who threatened his rear echelons (Polybius, III, 52). The question of why the Carthaginians diverted through the Guil valley from the Durance instead of marching towards the Col de Genèvre is uncertain but what is certain is that Hannibal was with the rear guard and the army, often led by Maharbal (Hart, 1967) who, according to Polybius, was informed of other Allobroges massing at the target col. Polybius is on record saying he did not want to fight the Allobroges, so it is possible the order to move through the Combe de Queyras came from Maharbal, Hannibal having his energies directed to the rear. If this is correct, it is odd, if not unusual, that the flanks were not protected adequately because once into the defile presented by the Combe, the Gauls unleashed a ferocious attack that nearly overran the rear of the army (Polybius, III, 53). Because the elephants and cavalry were up front it was the Gallic mercenaries who caught the brunt of missiles and rocks hurled from the high ridges astride the Combe, the result being that Hannibal suffered heavy losses from what appears to be an enfilade attack a tactical maneuver similar to what he himself later used at Trasimene against the Romans in the Apennines (Mahaney and Tricart, 2008), a more modern example coming from Lee's attack on the Union Army at Gettysburg during the American Civil War.

Investigations carried out in the Combe de Queyras over the period 2002-2010 by Mahaney and Tricart (2008) pinpointed unusually large accumulations of boulders and cobbles along and at the base of the northwestern wall with the Guil River to the southeast. It would appear that even in Hannibal's time the approach was to the west of the river but recent flood control efforts may have rearranged some of the rubble deposits, so finding artifacts in this mass would prove difficult and probably impossible.

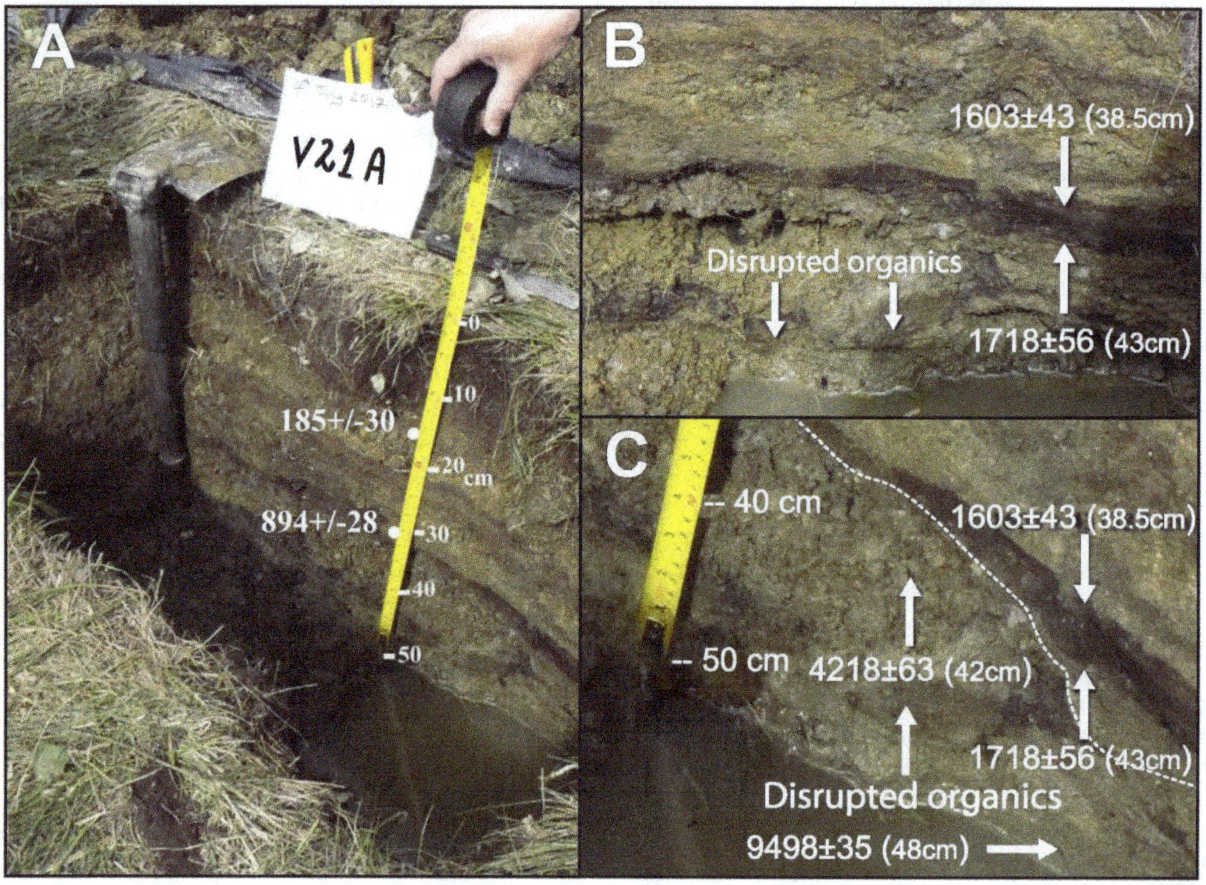

Fig. 5. Radiocarbon dated beds in section V21A showing the age progression from near the surface to approximately ~40 cm depth, the transition from time of normal sedimentation to the onset of massive ecological disturbance, i.e., the churning event. The >2168 cal yr BP dates represent sediment transported into the churned up morass by animals, humans or natural processes such as surface runoff or aeolian influx. Figure from Mahaney et al. (2018a). Color designations for dark to light beds are as explained above.

Following the Guil River toward the high col, the only camping or regrouping place is between 2400 and 2650 m alongside the main drainage and a tributary that passes the G5 alluvial mire sites (Fig. 3) investigated by Mahaney et al. (2017a, 2017b and 2017c). To the south of the G5 sites several low-lying flat lacustrine plains offer some forage opportunities that were likely used by the Punic forces as they reformed following the battle below in the Combe de Queyras. Attempts to section two of these sites to the south of G5 (Mahaney et al., 2017c) produced inconclusive results indicating the ecologically disturbed beds are likely deeper than ~1 m. If, as Polybius (III, 54) indicates, the army camped in snow, some of these depressions were probably used as water sources and even today the main Guil river drains the south side of the valley and would have provided a valuable source of water. More to the point, given the faecal matter and microbe analysis carried out at the G5 site (Mahaney et al., 2018b), which indicates widespread accumulation of animal and presumably human defecation, the entire moraine complex at 2400 to 2600 m asl in the upper Guil Valley is probably laden with metagenomic DNA and fossil faecal matter related to Hannibal's Army.

Reaching the Col de la Traversette at ~3000 m on a clear day, one can see across the Po plains below to some distance, possibly as far as Milan, as de Beer (1969) has stated. The usual view from below the Col de la Traversette is obscured by clouds as illustrated on the cover of *The Warmaker* (Mahaney, 2008b). Other route passages to the north at Col de Clapier and Col de Mt. Cenis have limited views from the summit and all look down upon the Dora Riparia which joins the Po River where Hannibal sortied against the Roman Army of Scipio whence he made contact, first at the Ticinus and latter at the Trebbia before retiring into winter quarters to the south.

The main proof for the Traversette Route is the blocking rockfall at 2600 m, the doublet deposits of such, the oldest lobes dating to at least 12.8 ka because they carry the black mat signature (12.8 ka) seen with microscopic analysis carried out by Mahaney and Keiser (2013) dating the early accumulation of rubble to the Late Glacial and well before Hannibal's time. The younger rubble accumulation that covers nearly three-quarters of the rockfall area is most likely of middle Neoglacial age judging by weathering features and soil morphogenesis that compares favorably with soil research carried out previously by Mahaney (1991). There is no similar rockfall deposit on the lee side of the Alps that would stop an army, only minor accumulations of rock rubble below all other passes (Sodhi et al., 2006).

3.4 ALTERNATIVE HYPOTHESES

Acceptance of the premise of both Polybius and Livy that Hannibal's army foraged in the catchment below the two-tier rockfall for a period of five days, such activity should have ravaged the upper valley and be recorded in the alluvial fan sediment recorded there. Any existing soil would have been ground up and mixed with sediment in situ and imported by animal action. Because the surface soils at all three sites are similar (about 12-cm thickness with A (Ah), C, Cu horizons, classed as Entisols (Soil Survey Staff, 1999) or Regosols (CSSC, 1998), correlation with similar pedons in the upper Guil Valley (Mahaney et al. 2016a) suggests these profiles are young and have been in situ for only two centuries or less. Both soil suites date to the end of the Little Ice Age (less than 170 yr), and their existence further suggests the soils have been protected from flooding that may have occurred since that time. Deeper into the three sections of the upper Po river valley, and the multiple sections of G5 in the upper Guil valley of France, darker beds encountered suggest periodic or aperiodic attempts to produce Histosols or soils with dominant organic compounds relative to inorganic sediment. However, because these organic beds lack oxidized horizons, it appears such attempts, although possibly long-lived in some cases, did not produce pedons.

Alternative testable hypotheses to bioturbation (churning) of sediment caused by Hannibal's Army might be: (1) upper flow regime flooding; (2) earthquake vibration; (3) transhumance; and (4) soil cryoturbation. The upper Po Valley is susceptible to extreme climatic events originating out of the Adriatic, as illustrated in 2008 when excessive precipitation induced intensive mass wasting and flooding in the form of debris flows that inundated valleys and buried deposits up and down the Western Alps from Mt Cenis all the way to the south of Mt Viso (Mahaney et al. 2010a, 2010b). Such flooding events produced well-sorted and stratified sediment successions lacking the mixed-sediment character of the bioturbated beds seen in the French mire and in the upper Po sections described here. Whereas turbulent flooding events are possible and cannot be totally discounted, the available evidence indicates that bioturbation is the process that produced the observed sediment disruption. As reported by Mahaney et al. (2018a), particle size tests on a random collection (n = 6) of small samples taken from the churned-up bed in V21A in the upper Po valley, show extreme variations in texture ranging from coarse sands (sometimes with pebbles) to fine silts and clay with no sorting visible. Water-sorted sediment recovered from alluvial/colluvial fans and lake beds (see Mahaney, 1990) follow the principle of horizontality, that is, beds are parallel with the Earth's surface. Unless disturbed by high-velocity currents, such as extreme flooding that occurs with jökulhlaups etc. or moraine bursts, such bedding is nearly horizontal with the Earth's surface. Exhaustive studies of Holocene alluvial fans on Mt Kenya (Mahaney, 1990) failed to produce distorted bedding despite the presence of active glaciers releasing meltwater during postglacial time.

Freeze–thaw processes in resident soils might produce convoluted beds or horizons which are not parallel in extracted cores or in dug sections excavated in the alluvial fans. Such convolutions usually leave beds or laminae intact, that is, upturned but lacking a disrupted or mixed quality such as is evident in the churned-up beds described here. In any case, heavy snowfall in the Western Alps provides an insulating medium that may counteract freeze–thaw processes in underlying soils (for examples of Cryosols, see Mahaney and Kalm, 2013).

Transhumance might be expected to produce sediment disturbance and it is an activity known to have occurred in the upper Po Valley, as in several Italian valleys, over several centuries, but no record of churned-up or bioturbated sediment exists above the proposed Hannibal beds identified at c.2200 cal yr BP in the subject area. Indeed, while transhumance has been prohibited in the upper Po Valley since the Second World War, the surface soil profiles in resident alluvial fans—V21, V21A and V21B—lack any sign of physical disturbance, which supports similar evidence reported in the upper Guil Valley of France, all this despite the ongoing practice of transhumance occurring every year (Mahaney et al., 2016, 2017a) in the Guil Valley. Linking the churned-up beds in cores and sections in the upper Po Valley with the Hannibal event of 2168 cal BP means there is a time correlation between the churning event and the reconnaissance of the Hannibalic route in the upper Po Valley, Italy's postulated passage of Hannibal. However unlikely, the coeval relation between the churning event and high-resolution dating may relate to some other anthropomorphic event not recorded in history. The churning event may also be partly related to menacing Gallic tribes following Hannibal after the altercation in the 18-km defile, as described by Polybius (Polybius/Scott-Kilvert, 1979, III, 53; surface analysis by Mahaney, 2008a). It remains for DNA analysis to link firmly recovered microbes and helminth parasite eggs with Spanish and/or North African animals.

While extremely sidelined as a probable cause of the churned-up beds, vibrations caused by earthquake activity might be expected to produce dislocated materials but with bed-to-bed or lamina-to-lamina stratigraphy, which is clearly lacking in the disrupted beds of the sediment stack reported by Mahaney et al. (2018a). Similar experiments using vibration tables have illustrated the effects of earthquake activity on sediment sorting (Miyamoto et al., 2007), forcing dislodged sediment into discrete groups. Whereas earthquake activity in the Western Alps is known to be an ongoing process, the deposits under investigation here show little sign of full-scale vibration or neotectonic activity.

Competing routes for the Hannibalic invasion are shown in Figure 1 (Mahaney et al., 2017a), although various other authors (i.e., Guillaume, 1967; Proctor, 1971) have argued for other cols adjacent to the Traversette and Mt Cenis, without linking topographic and geomorphologic evidence to support their claims. Time/motion analyses (Mahaney 2008a) of the northern (Cenis) versus the southern (Traversette) show the Traversette route to be slightly shorter but more rugged over the Traversette pass, longer over the less rugged Mt Cenis. This assumes that Polybius clearly differentiated between the Po plains and the plains adjacent to the Dora Riparia (a northern tributary of the Po River). The only route leading to the Po plains is over the Traversette. All variations between elevations, snowline, presence of frozen ground, long defile on the approach to the mountains and a large rock just inside the defile entrance have been discussed by Mahaney (2008a).

4. CONCLUSIONS

The various stages of reconstructing the Hannibal enigma illustrate just how information buried in the classical literature might be reconstructed to provide an environmental matrix that can be tested using various scientific analyses. In this case, work started with a topographic and geomorphologic base that could be used to provide time/motion analysis to establish movement of the Punic Army, results indicating that of the three proposed routes outlined in Fig. 1, only the middle route is the longest, the northern and southern routes almost identical in time distance but not regarding physical obstacles. The southern route across the highest of all passes with the most rugged terrain would require extra time but just how much is unknown. The battle in the approach defile and construction through the rockfall placed heavy burdens on the army, especially since as Polybius indicates they lost much of their provisions and this must have put a strain on animals, principally upon the elephant corps.

Beyond the initial phase, expertise in a variety of fields was required to put numbers to the allotted time of crossing requiring mathematical/statistical studies and astronomical calculations as to the amount of moonlight, and timing of movement with the hunter's moon. Excavations of mires and hearths required pedological, geochemical, radiocarbon, palynological and microbiological inputs from a variety of co-authors, all of which are listed on numerous papers in reference lists as noted in this paper. While permits were obtained to carry out the geological and biostratigraphic work, no attempt was made to obtain archaeological input beyond what is outlined in various papers. The only artifacts obtained are in the form of microbes and faecal matter obtained from sections dug in sediment piles in various places and from cores taken in similar settings. The main findings of this research affirm the interpretations of Sir Gavin de Beer some decades ago that Hannibal for one reason or another took the highest and most difficult route into Italia across the Col de la Traversette. Indeed, even Polybius is on record saying that Hannibal took the highest route, later named in order of position south of the Col de Genèvre, Hannibal's pass. For the last two millennia, the Traversette has been known as 'Hannibal's Pass' and even during WWII, SOE (Special Operations Executive of British Intelligence) referred to Mt. Cenis as Napoleon's Route, the Traversette as Hannibal's Route in secret documents recently made public (Mulley, 2012).

Polybius is also on record using the phrase—*tas hyperbolas tas anōtatō tōn Alpeōn*—the highest pass of the Alps (personal communication, J. Lazenby, 2007). Thus, whatever your historic theorem of possible or impossible routes, forensic analysis of all environmental parameters in the ancient literature is heavily weighted in favor of Sir Gavin de Beer's southern route across the Traversette. Despite the single file approach off the col to the permanent snowbank above the discarded Italian army barracks at ~2650 m asl, the only route assigned by key environmental parameters is the Traversette negotiated with difficulty by the Hannibalic Army.

ACKNOWLEDGEMENTS

I thank the National Geographic Society (Grant no. 9988-16) for funds to carry out the field and dating part of this research and Lion TV (London) and ZDF (Germany) for filming and allocating funds to Quaternary Surveys during July, 2017. P. Somelar, member of the 2015 and 2017 field teams, was funded also by Estonian Research Council grant PUT1511P. A number of colleagues contributed to this work over the last 15 years and are too numerous to name in full. In particular, I am indebted to Pierre Tricart (Grenoble) for his invaluable assistance in the field and for providing liaison with the Guil Valley Regional Park authority. Chris Allen (Queens University Belfast) and his team provided invaluable microbiological evidence. Brian Kelleher (Dublin City University), and his associates, aided with chemical analyses of samples, and Allen West (Comet Research Group) assisted with advice on Ox Cal radiocarbon dating. Randy Dirszowsky assisted in the field in 2011 and 2017. Marco Rastelli assisted with research permits to carry out field work in the Mon Viso National Park, Italia.

REFERENCES

Bagnall, N. (1999) *The Punic wars*, London, Pimlico.

Bronk Ramsey, C. (2009) Bayesian analysis of radiocarbon dates, *Radiocarbon*, Vol. 51, pp. 337–60.

Bronk Ramsey, C., and Lee, S. (2013) Recent and planned developments of the program OxCal., *Radiocarbon*, Vol. 55(2–3), pp. 720–30.

Brown, J. E. T. (1963) *Hannibal's route across the Alps, Greece and Rome*, Vol.10, pp. 38–46.

Canada Soil Survey Committee, 1998. *The Canadian System of Soil Classification*, 637, Ottawa, Canada, NRC Research Press, pp. 187 (Publ. 1646).

Connolly, P. (1981), *Greece and Rome at war*, London, Greenhill Books.

de Beer, Sir G. (1956) *Alps and elephants*, N.Y., E. P. Dutton.

de Beer, Sir G. (1967) *Hannibal's march*, London, Sidgwick and Jackson.

de Beer, Sir G. (1969) *Hannibal: challenging Rome's supremacy*, N.Y., The Viking Press.

de Beer, Sir G. (1974) *Hannibal: the struggle for power in the Mediterranean*, London, Book Club Associates.

De Montholon, J.F.T. (1905) *Momoires a Sainte Hélène*, v. IV, Paris, Garnier, pp. 277-281.

Dodge, T. A. (1891) *Hannibal*, Boston, Houghton-Mifflin.,

Freshfield, D. W. (1886) The Alpine pass of Hannibal, *Proceedings of the Royal Geographical Society and Monthly, Record of Geography*, Vol. 8 (10), pp. 638–44.

Freshfield, D. W. (1899) Hannibal's pass, *The Geographical Journal*, Vol. 13 (5), pp. 547–51.

Guillaume, A. (1967) Annibal Franchit les Alpes, 218 J.-C., Cahiers de L'Alpe, La Tronche-Montfleury.

Hart, B. H. L. (1967) *Strategy*, London, Faber and Faber.

Hoyte, John (1960). Alpine Elephant in Hannibal's Tracks, Eugene, Oregon, Wiff and Stock, 190 pp.

Kuhle, M., and Kuhle, S. (2012) Hannibal gone astray? A critical comment on W. C. Mahaney et al.: 'The Traversette (Italia) rockfall: geomorphological indicator of the Hannibalic invasion route' (*Archaeometry*, 52, 1 [2010] 156–72), *Archaeometry* Vol. 54, pp. 591–601.

Lancel, S. (1999) *Hannibal*, Oxford, Blackwell.

Lazenby, J. F. (1998) *Hannibal's war*, Norman, University of Oklahoma Press.

Livy (1965) *The war with Hannibal*, transl. A. de Sélincourt, London, Penguin.

Mahaney, W. C. (1990) *Ice on the Equator*, Ellison Bay, Wisconsin, Wm Caxton Press.

Mahaney, W.C. (1991) Later Pleistocene and Holocene glacial chronology at Chamonix and Argentière, French Alps, *Zeitschrift für Geomorphologie,* Vol. 35 (2), pp. 225-237.

Mahaney, W. C.(2004) Geological/topographical reconnaissance of Hannibal's invasion route into Italia in 218 BC, in *Studies in military geography and geology* (eds. D. R. Caldwell et al.), pp. 67–78, Kluwer Academic, Dordrecht.

Mahaney, W. C. (2008a) *Hannibal's odyssey: environmental background to the Alpine invasion of Italia,* Piscataway, NJ, Gorgias Press, , pp. 221.

Mahaney, W.C. (2008b) *The Warmaker.*, Bloomington, Indiana, iUniverse, , pp. 302.

Mahaney, W. C. (2013) Comments on M. Kuhle and S. Kuhle (2012): 'Hannibal gone astray? A critical comment on W. C. Mahaney et al., "The Traversette (Italia) rockfall: geomorphological indicator of the Hannibalic invasion route" (*Archaeometry*, 52, 1, [2010], 156–72}', *Archaeometry,* Vol. 55, pp. 1196–1204.

Mahaney, W.C. and Kalm, V. (2013) Late Holocene paleoclimate and weathering history in the Norra Storfjället Mountains, Sweden, deglacial record and soil stratigraphy, *Geografiska Annaler*, Vol. 95, pp. 145-158.

Mahaney, W. C. and Keiser, L. (2013) Weathering rinds—unlikely host clasts for an impact-induced event, *Geomorphology*, Vol.184, pp. 74–83.

Mahaney, W.C. and Tricart, P. (2008) The unknown Gallic commander: Hannibal's debacle in the Combe de Queyras in 218 BC. Nathanail, C.P., Abrahart, R.G., and Bradshaw, R.P., eds. Military Geography and Geology: History and Technology. U.K., Land Quality Press.

Mahaney, W. C., Miyamoto, H., Dohm, J., Baker, V., Cabrol, N., Grin, E., and Berman, D. (2007a) Rock glaciers on Mars: Earth-based clues to Mars' recent paleoclimatic history, *Journal of Planetary and Space Sciences*, Vol. 55 (1–2), pp. 181–92.

Mahaney, W. C., Milner, M. W., Sodhi, R. N. S., Dorn, R. I., Boccia, S., Beukens, R. P., Tricart, P., Schwartz, S., Chamorro-Perez, E., Barendregt, R. W., Kalm, V., and Dirszowsky, R. W. (2007b) Analysis of burnt schist outcrops in the Alps: relation to historical archaeology and Hannibal's crossing in 218 BC, *Geoarchaeology*, Vol. 22 (7), pp. 799–818.

Mahaney, W. C., Kalm, V., and Dirszowsky, R. (2008a) The Hannibalic invasion of Italia in 218 BC: geological/topographic analysis of the invasion routes, in *Military geography and geology: history and technology* (eds. C. P. Nathanail et al.), pp. 76–86, Nottingham, Land Quality Press.

Mahaney, W. C., Kapran, B., and Tricart, P. (2008b) Hannibal and the Alps: unraveling the invasion route from the geological evidence, *Geology Today*, Vol. 4 (6), pp.223–30.

Mahaney, W. C., Kalm, V., Dirszowsky, R. W., Milner, M. W., Sodhi, R. N. S., Beukens, R., Dorn, R. I., Dorn, R. I., Tricart, P., Schwartz, S., Chamorro-Perez, E., Boccia, S., Barendregt, R. W., Krinsley, D. H., Seaquist, E., Merrick, D., and Kapran, B. (2008c) Hannibal's trek across the Alps: identification of sites of geoarchaeological interest, *Mediterranean Archaeology and Archaeometry*, Vol. 8 (2), pp. 39–54.

Mahaney, W. C., Barendregt, R. W., Carcaillet, C., Tricart, P., Rabufetti, D., and Kalm, V. (2010a) Debris flow burial of ancient wall systems in the upper Po River valley, Italia, *Geology Today*, Vol. 26 (6), pp. 209–15.

Mahaney, W. C., Tricart, P., Carcaillet, C., Blarquez, O., Ali, A. A., Argant, J., Barendregt, R. W., and Kalm, V. (2010b) The Traversette rockfall: geomorphological reconstruction and importance in interpreting classical history, *Archaeometry*, **Vol.** 52, pp. 156–72.

Mahaney, W. C., Kapran, B., Kalm, V., Tricart, P., Blarquez, O., Milner, M.W., Barendregt, R.W., and Somelar, P. (2010c) Hannibal's invasion route: age-old question revisited with new scientific data, *Archaeometry*, Vol. 52, pp. 1096–109.

Mahaney, W. C., Keiser, L., Krinsley, D. H., Pentlavalli, P., Allen, C. C. R., Somelar, P., Schwartz, S., Dohm, J. M., Dirzowsky, R., West, A., Julig, P., and Costa, P. J. M. (2013) Weathering rinds as mirror images of palaeosols: examples from the Western Alps with correlation to Antarctica and Mars, *Journal of the Geological Society*, Vol. 170, pp. 833–47.

Mahaney, W. C., Allen, C. C. R., Pentlavalli, P., Dirszowsky, O., Tricart, P., Keiser, L., Somelar, P., Kelleher, B., Murphy, B., Costa,, P. J. M., and Julig, P. (2014) Polybius's 'previous landslide': proof that Hannibal's invasion route crossed the col de la Traversette, *Journal of Mediterranean Archaeology and Archaeometry*, Vol. 14 (2), pp. 1–20.

Mahaney, W. C., Somelar, P., Dirszowsky, R. W., Kelleher, B., Pentlavalli, P., McLaughlin, S., Kulakova, A., Jordan, S., Pulleyblank, C., West, A., Allen, C.C.R. (2016a) A microbial link to weathering of postglacial rocks and sediments, Mt. Viso area, Western Alps demonstrated through analysis of a soil/paleosol bio/chronosequence. *Journal of Geology*, Vol. 124 (2), pp. 149-169.

Mahaney, W.C., Hancock, R.G.V., Somelar, P., Milan, A.(2016b) Iron and Al Soil/Paleosol Extractions as Age/Environment Indicators: some examples from a catchment in Southern Ontario, Canada. *Geomorphology*, Vol. 270, pp. 159-171.

Mahaney, W. C., Allen, C.C.R., Pentlavalli, P., Kulakova, A., Young, J. M., Dirszowsky, R.W., West, A., Kelleher, B., Jordan, S., Pulleyblank, C., O'Reilly, S., Murphy, B. T., Lasberg, K., Somelar, P., Garneau, M., Finkelstein, S. A., Sobol, M. K., Kalm, V., Costa, P. J. M., Hancock, R. G. V., Hart, K. M., Tricart, P., Barendregt, R. W., Bunch, T. E., Milner, M. W. (2017a) Biostratigraphic Evidence relating to the Age-Old Question of Hannibal's Invasion of Italy: I, History and Geological Reconstruction, *Archaeometry*, Vol. 59, pp. 164-178.

Mahaney, W. C., Allen, C. C. R., Pentlavalli, P., Kulakova, A., Young, J. M., Dirszowsky, R. W., West, A., Kelleher, B., Jordan, S., Pulleyblank, C., O'Reilly, S., Murphy, B. T., Lasberg, K., Somelar, P., Garneau, M., Finkelstein, S. A., Sobol, M. K., Kalm, V., Costa, P. J. M., Hancock, R. G. V., Hart, K. M., Tricart, P., Barendregt, R. W., Bunch, T. E., and Milner, M. W. (2017b) Biostratigraphic evidence relating to the age-old question of Hannibal's invasion of Italy, II: chemical biomarkers and microbial signatures, *Archaeometry* Vol. 59, pp. 179-190.

Mahaney, W.C., Somelar, P., Pulleyblank, C., Tricart, P., West, A., Young, J., and Allen, C.C.R. (2017c) Notes on magnetic susceptibility in the Guil valley alluvial mire correlated with the Punic Invasion of Italia in 218 BC. *Mediterranean Journal of Archaeometry and Archaeology*, Vol. 17, (1), pp. 23-35.

Mahaney, W.C., Somelar, P., West, A., Krinsley, D., Allen, C. C. R., Pentlavalli, P., Young, J. M., Dohm, J.M., LeCompte, M., Kelleher, B., Jordan, S., Pulleyblank, C., Dirszowsky, R., Costa, P., (2017d) Evidence for cosmic airburst/impact in the Western Alps archived in Late Glacial Paleosols. *Quaternary International*, Vol. 438, no. B, pp. 68-80.

Mahaney, W.C., Peeter Somelar, Allen West, Randy Dirszowsky, Christopher C.R. Allen, Tarmo Remmel (2018a) Reconnaissance of the Hannibalic Route in the Upper Po Valley. Italy: Correlation with Biostratigraphic Historical Archaeological Evidence in the Upper Guil Valley of France, *Archaeometry*, doi.org/10.1111/arcm.12405.

Mahaney, W.C., West, Allen, Milan, Alison, Krinsley, David, Somelar, Peeter, Schwartz, Stephane, Milner, Michael W., Allen, Christopher C.R.(2018b). Cosmic impact/airburst on deposits/soils in the Western Alps of the Mt. Viso area, France, *Quaternaria,* Vol. 35 (1) 3–23 .

Mahaney, W.C., Krinsley, D.H., Milner, Michael W. (2018c) Did the black mat/airburst reach the Antarctic: Evidence from New Mountain near the Taylor Glacier in the Dry Valleys. *Journal of Geology*, Vol. 126 (3), pp. 285-305.

Miyamoto, H., Yano, H., Scheeres, D. J., Abe, S., Barnaouin-Jha, O., Cheng, A. F., Demura, H., Gaskell, R. W., Hirata, N., Ishiguro, M., Michikami, T., Nakamura, A. M., Hakamura, R., Saito, J., and Sasaki, S. (2007) Regolith migration and sorting on asteroid Itokawa, *Science*, Vol. 316, pp. 1011–1014.

Millar, C. E., Turk, L. M., and Foth, H. D. (1966) *Fundamentals of Soil Science*, NY, 4th ed, Wiley.

Mulley, Clare (2012) *The Spy Who Loved*, St. N.Y., Martins Griffin, NY, pp. 426.

Neumann, J. (1992). Climatic conditions in the Alps in the years about the year of Hannibal's crossing (218 BC). *Climatic Change*, vol.22, pp.139–150.

Oyama, M., and Takehara, H.(1970), *Standard soil color charts*, Japan Research Council for Agriculture, Forestry and Fisheries, Tokyo, Japan.

Paton, W.R. (1922) *Polybius, The Histories*, Books 3-4, Cambridge, Ma., Harvard University Press, 568 pp.

Polybius (1979) *The rise of the Roman Republic*, trans. I. Scott-Kilvert, pp. 215–29, London, Penguin.

Prevas, J. (1998) *Hannibal Crosses the Alps*. Rockville Centre, NY Sarpedon, , 232 pp.

Proctor, D. (1971) *Hannibal's march in history*, Oxford, Oxford University Press.

Reimer, P. J., Bard, E., Bayliss, A., Beck, J. W., Blackwell, P. G., Bronk Ramsey, C., Buck, C. E., Cheng, H., Edwards, R. L., Friedrich, M., Grootes, P. M., Guilderson, T. P., Haflidason, H., Hajdas, I., Hatté, C., Heaton, T. J., Hoffman, D., L., Hogg, A. G., Hughen, K. A., Kaiser, K. F., Kromer, B., Manning, S.

W., Niu, M., Reimer, R. W., Richards, D. A., Scott, E. M., Southon, J. R., Staff, R. A., Turney, C. S. M., and Van Der Plicht, J. (2013) IntCal13 and Marine13 radiocarbon age calibration curves 0–50,000 years cal BP, *Radiocarbon*, Vol. 55 (4), pp. 1869–87.

Romano, Marco, Palombo, Rita (2017) When legend, history and science rhyme: Hannibal's war elephants as an explanation to large vertebrate skeletons found in Italy, *Historical Biology*, DOI: 10.1080/08912963.2017.1287178 To link to this article: ttp://dx.doi.org/10.1080/08912963.2017.1287178.

Seibert, J. (1993) *Hannibal*, pp. 75–134, Darmstadt, Wissenschaftliche Buchgesellschaft,.

Sodhi, R., Mahaney, W. C., and Milner, M. W. (2006) ToF-SIMS applied to historical archaeology in the Alps, *Applied Surface Science*, Vol. 252, pp. 7140–3.

Soil Survey Staff (1999) *Soil taxonomy*, USDA Agricultural Handbook No. 436, Government Printing Office, Washington, DC.

Strabo, trans. H.L, Jones (1999) Strabo: Geography Vol II. Harvard University Press, Copyright 1923. Strabo's map of the Mediterranean Basin.

Tricart, P., Schwartz, S., Lardeaux, J. -M., Thouvenot, F., and Du Chaffaut, S. A. (2003) Aiguilles-Col Saint-Martin, Carte Géologique de la France, 1:50000.

Walbank, F. W. (1956) Some reflections on Hannibal's Pass, *Journal of Roman Studies*, Vol. 46, pp. 37–45.

Walbank, F. W. (1990) *Polybius*, Berkeley, CA, University of California Press,.

Wilkinson, H. S. (1911) *Hannibal's march through the Alps*, Oxford, The Clarendon Press.

Wolbach, W.S., Ballard, J.P., Mayewski, P.A., Parnell, A.C., Cahill, N., Adedeji, V., Bunch, T.E., Domínguez-Vázquez, G., Erlandson, J.M., Firestone, R.B., French, T.A., Howard, G., Israde-Alcántara, I., Johnson, J.R., Kimbel, D., Kinzie, C.R., Kurbatov, A., Kletetschka, G., LeCompte, M.A., Mahaney, W.C., Melott, A.L., Mitra, S., Maiorana-Boutilier, A., Moore, C.R., Napier, W.M., Parlier, J., Tankersley, K.B., Thomas, B.C., Wittke, J.C., West, A., Kennett, J.P. (2018a) Extraordinary Biomass-Burning Episode and Impact Winter Triggered by the Younger Dryas Cosmic Impact~12,800 Years Ago. 1. Ice Cores and Glaciers. *Journal of Geology*, Vol. 126 (2), pp. 165–84.

Wolbach, W.S., Ballard, J.P., Mayewski, P.A., Parnell, A.C., Cahill, N., Adedeji, V., Bunch, T.E., Domínguez-Vázquez, G., Erlandson, J.M., Firestone, R.B., French, T.A., Howard, G., Israde-Alcántara, I., Johnson, J.R., Kimbel, D., Kinzie, C.R., Kurbatov, A., Kletetschka, G., LeCompte, M.A., Mahaney, W.C., Melott, A.L., Mitra, S., Maiorana-Boutilier, A., Moore, C.R., Napier, W.M., Parlier, J., Tankersley, K.B., Thomas, B.C., Wittke, J.C., West, A., Kennett, J.P. (2018b) Extraordinary Biomass-Burning Episode and Impact Winter Triggered by the Younger Dryas Cosmic Impact ~12,800 Years Ago. 2. Lake, Marine, and Terrestrial Sediments, *Journal of Geology*, Vol. 126 (2), pp. 185-205.

2

EARTHQUAKE LIGHTS IN LEGENDS OF THE GREEK ORTHODOXY

I.V. Florinsky

Institute of Mathematical Problems of Biology, Russian Academy of Sciences, Pushchino, Moscow Region, 142290, Russia
(iflor@mail.ru)

ABSTRACT

Local legends may contain information about real geological events of the past. Earthquake lights (EQL) can occur in the atmosphere over earthquake epicenter areas and adjacent faults before and during quakes. They may look like diffuse airglow, flashes, fiery pillars, and luminous balls. EQL may cause a mystical experience probably due to the influence of their electromagnetic fields on the brain. Subjective perception and interpretation of EQL depend on religious and cultural traditions. We study a stereotype of EQL interpretation in the legends of the Greek Orthodoxy exemplified by the legends about the foundation of two shrines: St. George Monastery near the Cape Fiolent, Crimea and the Panagia Tripiti Church in Aigion, Peloponnese. It is argued that the similar interpretation of EQL observation in the Crimean and Peloponnesian legends were caused by similar natural and economic living conditions of the Greek population in the both regions in the Middle Ages. We also consider some examples of EQL observation took place in other regions and their interpretation in other denominations. Differences and relations between EQL of mechanoelectrical and degassing origin are discussed. Finally, we consider the role of active faults in the production of a mystical experience and sacralization of an affected landscape.

KEYWORDS: Earthquake, seismicity, fault, neurophysiology, legend, religion, mystical experience.

1. INTRODUCTION

Local myths and legends may contain verifiable information about real geological events of the past (Vitaliano, 1973; Bentor, 1989; Piccardi and Masse, 2007). This allows one to conduct research combining expertise and methods of geology, history, archaeology, anthropology, and other sciences. Piccardi (2007a, p. vii) explained the importance of such interdisciplinary studies as follows: "The geological study of mythology and legendary accounts may reveal encoded memories of past geological events, thus providing a reservoir of geological information. On the other hand, it also helps to provide new insight to historical, archaeological and anthropological research, opening a new window on a field traditionally reserved for anthropologists".

Immediately prior to and during earthquakes one may sometimes see diffuse airglow, flashes, glare, and short-lived linear or quasi-spherical luminous objects (e.g., fiery pillars and luminous balls) in the atmospheric boundary layer over quake epicentre areas and adjacent active or reactivated faults. These phenomena are collectively known as earthquake lights (EQL) (Derr, 1973; Papadopoulus, 1999; Thériault et al., 2014). The mechanism of their generation is not completely clear. It is argued that during earthquake preparation processes, the increase of local and regional lithospheric stresses may lead to mechanoelectrical phenomena. In particular, when rocks are mechanically stressed they can cause electric currents due to electron hole charge carriers (Freund et al., 2006, 2007). Prior to relatively strong earthquakes (magnitude > 4), such currents in adjacent faults can cause air ionisation and corona discharges (St-Laurent et al., 2006).

According to the Derr–Persinger hypothesis (tectonic strain theory), EQL formation is connected with the rise of local and regional lithospheric stresses (Persinger, 1976, 1980, 1984; Derr and Persinger, 1986). EQL are frequently observed near active faults and fault-controlled river valleys during minor seismic events (magnitude < 2) days or months ahead of a stronger earthquake. EQL can move along fault lines, probably, due to the redistribution of a lithospheric stress (Persinger and Derr, 1985, 1990a; Derr and Persinger, 1990). As a result, EQL can be observed not only over epicentres, but also over associated active or reactivated faults at a distance of up to several hundred kilometres from an epicentre (Persinger and Derr, 1990b). EQL characteristics, such as colour, size, luminous intensity, and occurrence frequency depend on the local geological situation (i.e., rock magnetic susceptibility), the presence of magnetic anomalies, and topography.

EQL may induce a range of temporary dysfunctions, acute and chronic diseases, and death depending on the observation time and energetic characteristics of EQL and the distance between the EQL and an observer (Persinger, 1983, 1988). This is probably due to the impact of electromagnetic fields of EQL (it is well known that electromagnetic fields may influence an organism - Yakovleva, 1973; Marino and Becker, 1977; Palmer et al., 2006). In certain circumstances, EQL may affect the psyche and probably cause a mystical experience.

Mystical experience is a sort of altered state of consciousness characterized by visual and auditory hallucinations, including apparent contacts with divine or supernatural creatures. These contacts are often accompanied by extreme emotions, such as delight, euphoria, horror, panic, etc. (James, 1902; Maslow, 1964; Tortchinov, 1998; Levin and Steele, 2005). Like other forms of altered states of consciousness, a mystical experience may be both spontaneous and induced (Vaitl et al., 2005). Various accidental and goal-oriented exposures may result in mystical experiences, such as drugs, intoxication, fasting, magnetic and electromagnetic fields, extreme conditions in polar regions, deserts, and high mountains, hypoxia, hyperventilation, physical and emotional overloads, injuries, etc.

In the context of this article, it is essential that a mystical experience may be induced by magnetic fields. For example, numerous experiments have demonstrated that a short (3–5 min) transcranial exposure of the right hemisphere to an extremely low frequency weak magnetic field (0.5–10 Hz, 0.1–5 μT, the signal has a complex pulsed form) evokes an experience of the sensed presence in 80% of the general population (Johnson and Persinger, 1994; Cook and Persinger, 1997; Persinger and Healey, 2002; Booth et al., 2003; St.-Pierre and Persinger, 2006). The sensed presence consists in the feeling or apparent observation of a supernatural creature located near the observer.

EQL are known in all cultures. Subjective perception and interpretation of EQL depend on religious and cultural stereotypes of an individual and society. Sites of EQL watching are becoming places of worship; churches and monasteries are often built in such sites (see examples in Section 3.2). In this paper we study a stereotype of EQL interpretation in legends of the Greek Orthodoxy exemplified by the legends about the foundation of two places of worship: St. George Monastery near the Cape Fiolent, Crimea and Panagia Tripiti Church in Aigion, Peloponnese (Fig. 1).

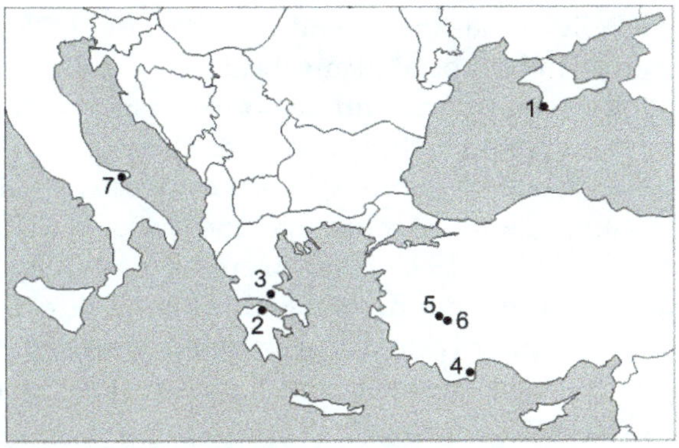

Figure 1. Geographical position of some sites discussed in the paper: 1 - Cape Fiolent, 2 - Aigion, 3 - Delphi, 4 - Chimaera, 5 - Hierapolis, 6 - Colossae, 7 - Monte Sant'Angelo

2. DESCRIPTION OF TWO SITES

2.1 *St. George Monastery near the Cape Fiolent, Crimea*

According to the local legend (Nikon, 1862, p. 7), Greek fishermen were caught by a heavy storm in the sea nearby the Cape Fiolent in the year 891. The storm drove their ship toward sea rocks. They suddenly noticed St. George the Conqueror within a fiery pillar on top of a sea rock. Immediately afterwards the storm subsided. The rescued crew climbed the rock and found an icon of St. George. In memory of this event, a monastery was founded on the steep rocky cliff and the cross was installed on the rock (Figure 2). According to current data, the Balaclavian St. George Monastery was founded no earlier than the late 14th century; the present cross was installed in the post-Soviet period (Tur, 2006, pp. 101–105).

Figure 2. The St. Appearance Rock near the Cape Fiolent, the view from the St. George Monastery

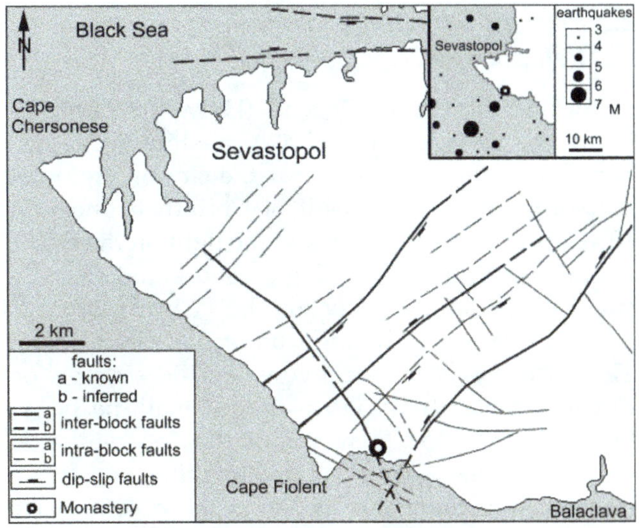

Figure 3. The Cape Fiolent area: faults and earthquakes with magnitudes > 3 from 1927 to 1985 (Borisenko et al., 1982; Borisenko, 1986; modified from Florinsky, 2010, p. 229)

The legend apparently describes the EQL observation and associated mystical experience (Florinsky, 2010, pp. 236–237). Indeed, the local geological environment and regional seismic activity are favourable for EQL occurrence: There are several intra- and inter-block faults on the land in proximity to the monastery (Borisenko et al., 1982) (Figure 3). There are perhaps offshore extensions of the faults and a complex offshore node of their intersection at a distance of 1 km from the monastery. The Cape Fiolent cliffs are composed of volcanic rocks containing magnetite (Pechersky et al., 1991). There are intensive striped magnetic anomalies ranging from 1,200 to -800 nT on the shelf between the Cape Chersonese and the city of Balaclava probably caused by intrusive bodies associated with faults (Gorodnitsky et al., 1967).

The region is marked by the high seismic activity: there is the Sevastopol quake epicentre group located to the southwest of the Cape Fiolent at the distance of 10–30 km from the coast (Borisenko, 1986) (Figure 3). There were EQL cases in the region: fiery flares and pillars in the sea have been seen from the shore from the west to the southeast coasts of Crimea during the 1927 Crimean earthquakes (Nikonov, 2002).

The St. Appearance Rock (Figure 2) is a dome-shaped subvolcanic body composed of keratophyres. It is located in one of the intersections of local faults (Solovyev, 1988). It is known that EQL are often observed above tops of hills (Persinger, 1976). In the case of the apparition of St. George, this rock protruding from the water could play the role of the top of the hill.

2.2 *Panagia Tripiti Church in Aigion, Peloponnese*

According to the local legend (Holy Metropolis of Kalavryta and Aigialeia, 2000), a shipwreck happened at night in the sea near the city of Aigion in the south coast of the Gulf of Corinth in the year 1550. The drowning sailor saw the light on the shore. Swimming to the light, he got ashore and found a small grotto in the slope of the coastal scarp, in which there was a shining icon of the Virgin Mary. The rescued sailor made a vow to build a chapel on this site. Since the grotto was too small, he began building a bit aside. However, on the first night after the work began, the small grotto miraculously increased. It became possible to make a small cave church within the grotto and place there the icon. The present size of the grotto is about 11 × 7 m; its height is about 4 m. The church built around the grotto (Figure 4) acquired its present appearance in the 19th century.

Figure 4. The Panagia Tripiti Church in Aigion; the steep coastal scarp is behind the church

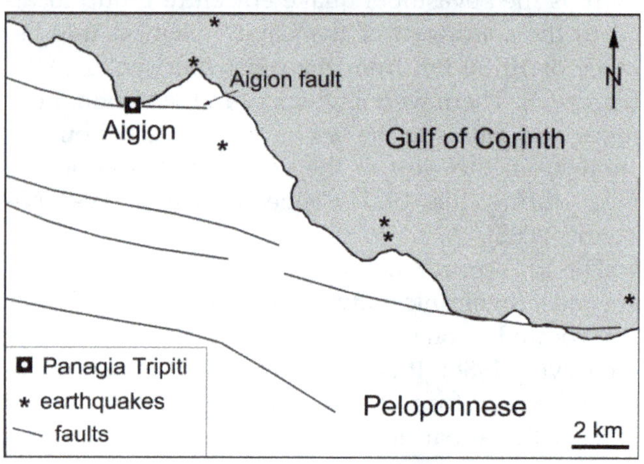

Figure 5. The Aigion area: faults and earthquakes with magnitudes 6–7 from 373 BC to 1995 (Koukouvelas and Doutsos, 1996; Soter, 1999)

We believe that the legend describes the EQL observation and associated mystical experience. Local geological conditions and regional seismic activity are favourable for EQL generation: The Gulf of Corinth Rift is one of the most seismically active Mediterranean regions (Ambraseys and Jackson, 1997). From 373 BC to 1995, there were at least 9 earthquakes with magnitude 6–7 within the radius of 20 km from Aigion (Koukouvelas and Doutsos, 1996) (Figure 5). Local residents on the both sides of the gulf observed EQL (Soter, 1999) during the 1995 Aigion earthquake (magnitude 6.2, the epicentre was in the gulf - Koukouvelas and Doutsos, 1996).

The Aigion fault, topographically manifested and reactivated during this earthquake (Koukouvelas and Doutsos, 1996) (Figure 5), crosses the city and forms the high coastal scarp (Unkel, 2002, p. 32). The scarp is composed of delta conglomerates. The back wall of the Panagia Tripiti Church is based on the steep slope of the scarp (Figure 4), that is, the church and grotto, where the icon was found, are directly located on the fault. The legendary enlargement of the grotto has likely happened due to a small seismogenic collapse of the relatively soft and unstable rocks.

3. DISCUSSION

3.1 *Stereotyped interpretation of EQL in the legends*

One can see almost identical interpretation of the EQL observation in the both legends, the Crimean and Peloponnesian ones. We believe that this is connected with similar natural and economic living conditions of the Greek population in these territories in the Middle Ages.

First, migration and settlement of the Greeks in the basins of the East Mediterranean and the Black Sea generally occurred in terrains with fairly close geomorphological and geological environments, as well as similar geodynamic and seismic situations (Trifonov et al., 2002). We can assume that seismogenic EQL were periodically observed throughout the Greek World.

Second, coastal navigation and fishing was one of the main activities of the Greek population of these territories. Therefore, it was a typical situation when sailors and fishermen caught in a storm in the dark.

A sudden appearance of EQL in the dark over the rocks in the sea or coastal cliffs could really help sailors in orientation. It is clear that sailors could see such an event as a miracle even without possible effects of EQL electromagnetic fields on the brain. If the impact of electromagnetic fields occurred, it was imposed on obvious physical and mental overloads of an organism in conditions of a storm and shipwreck. Such a combined impact of harmful factors could increase a probability for a mystical experience, which context was naturally determined by the Orthodox topics.

After rescuing sailors certainly went to a local church to give thanks to the Lord, to report the incident, and to hear an explanation of a priest. Since an incident described by sailors could be periodically repeated, a priest's explanation could also eventually become stereotyped. In this case, a story of a subjective mystical experience of sailors ('observation' of a saint and/or an icon) could be added to a description of a real event (EQL observation and rescue). Such a stereotypical interpretation could be 'officially' adopted and disseminated by the Patriarchate of Constantinople. Subsequent sacralization of the place of the EQL observation, construction of a chapel, church, or monastery was a matter of time.

3.2 *Other religious interpretations of EQL*

Let us consider some examples of EQL observation took place in other regions (Figure 1) and their interpretation by persons of other denominations.

One of the most famous EQL observations was probably the event described in the Jewish tradition as the apparitions of the Angel and Yahweh to Moses in the burning bush near Mount Sinai (Exodus 3:2–4:17). The Sinai Orthodox St. Catherine Monastery was later founded at this place (Figure 6).

Figure 6. St. Catherine Monastery, the view from Mount Sinai

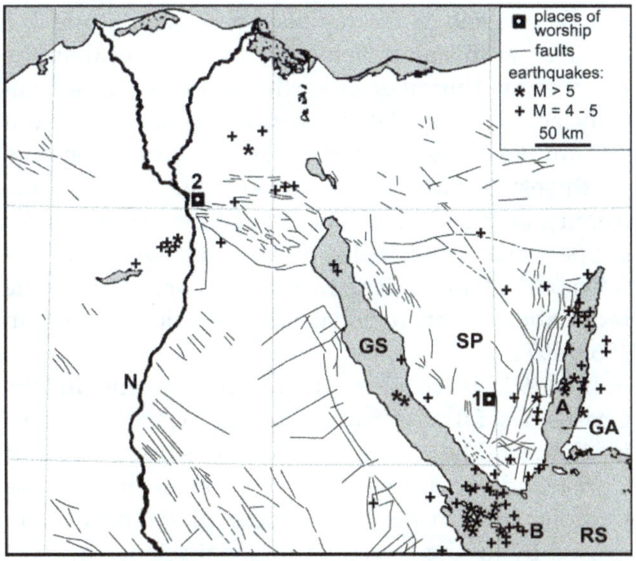

Figure 7. Egypt: faults and earthquakes with magnitudes > 4 from 1900 to 1995 (Egyptian Geological Survey and Mining Authority, 1981; Badawy and Horváth, 1999). 1 - St. Catherine Monastery in Sinai, 2 - St. Mary Church in Cairo. Earthquake epicentre groups: A - near the town of Dahab; B - southward from Sinai. SP - the Sinai Peninsula, N - the Nile, GS - the Gulf of Suez, GA - the Gulf of Aqaba, RS - the Red Sea

Local geological conditions and seismic activity are favourable for EQL emergence. Although the most part of the Sinai Peninsula is aseismic, there is the seismic activity in its edges (Badawy and Horváth, 1999). It is mainly associated with the development of two large extensional tectonic structures, the Gulf of Suez Rift and the Gulf of Aqaba Rift. There is a group of quake epicentres with magnitude 4–5 near the town of Dahab, between St. Catherine Monastery and the Gulf of Aqaba as well as in its waters (Figure 7). The distance from the monastery to these epicentres is 50–80 km. The monastery is located 2 km from a regional topographically expressed north-striking fault, a piece of the fault system associated with the development of the Gulf of Aqaba Rift (Figure 7).

From April 1968 by May 1971, thousands of people belonging to different religions, have seen and filmed luminous phenomena above the Coptic Orthodox St. Mary Church in Zeitoun, Cairo, Egypt (Swann, 1996, ch. 19): relatively large and immobile corona-discharge EQL were interpreted as the Virgin Mary, as well as small fast-moving EQL were interpreted as 'doves'. To commemorate these events, one of the largest Middle Eastern Cathedrals was built in front of St. Mary Church in the late 1970s.

These phenomena were apparently the EQL series caused by a sharp increase of seismic activity in 1969 in the waters of the Red Sea southward from Sinai (Derr and Persinger, 1989), at the junction of two rifts, the Red Sea Rift and the Gulf of Suez Rift (Figure 7). In 1969, 38 earthquakes with magnitude 3–7 occurred in this area that is 10 times greater than the usual annual number of earthquakes in this seismically active zone. Although Cairo is located about 400 km northwestward, there is a system of regional northwest-striking faults between the northern extremity of the Gulf of Suez and Cairo (Fig. 7). We suppose that these faults, being marginal manifestations of the Gulf of Suez Rift, could participate in the redistribution of regional lithospheric stresses in 1968–1971.

In 1992, there were EQL observations at the Greensides' farm near the village of Marmora, Ontario, Canada. They were interpreted as apparitions of Christ and the Virgin Mary. The farm became the Catholic pilgrimage place. These phenomena were caused by (a) the increased regional seismic activity in 1990–1997, and (b) the rise of local lithospheric stresses due to slow flooding of the open pit on the magnetite deposit situated at 2 km from Marmora. Pulsed magnetic field variations with periods of 1–7 s and 10–950 nT amplitudes were measured within the local magnetic anomaly associated with the ore body (Suess and Persinger, 2001).

It is known two Mediterranean legends about the Archangel Michael apparitions in fiery pillars: at Colossae, Turkey in AD 60 (Piccardi, 2007b) and Monte Sant'Angelo, Foggia, Italy in AD 493 (Piccardi, 2005). In the both cases, the phenomena have taken place directly on the local active faults during severe earthquakes clearly described in the legends. This strongly suggests that the legends tell us about EQL observations. The detailed description of the legends and geological settings of the sites can be found elsewhere (Piccardi, 2005, 2007b).

There is a set of phenomena observed in seismically active regions, accompanied by the luminous effects, and interpreted by Catholics as apparitions of the Virgin Mary (e.g., at Lourdes in 1858 and Fátima in 1917 - Swann, 1996). We suppose that these events can be also re-interpreted as EQL.

3.3 *EQL and gas emission*

In Introduction, we mentioned mechanoelectrical hypotheses of EQL generation. However, it is possible that at least a part of EQL are spontaneous combustions of natural gases containing hydrocarbons, which seep from the depths of the lithosphere through faults prior to and during seismic events (Nikonov, 2002). Indeed, short-term manifestations of degassing were recorded prior to and during the 1927 Crimean, the 1993 Patras, and the 1995 Egion earthquakes, such as bubbling of the seawater, significant increase of its temperature, and saturation of its top layer and surface air with hydrogen sulphide (Soter, 1999; Nikonov, 2002).

It is generally possible to obtain a mystical experience because of intoxication by gases (e.g., hydrocarbons, hydrogen sulphide, or carbon dioxide). In the East Mediterranean there are at least three known ancient places of worship which sacralization has been connected with the gas emission, namely: the Hephaestus Temple in Chimaera, Turkey (De Boer et al., 2007; Hosgormez et al., 2008; Etiope et al., 2011), the Apollo Temple in Delphi, Greece (Piccardi, 2000; De Boer and Hale, 2000; Etiope et al., 2006; Liritzis and Castro, 2013), as well as the Apollo Temple (and Plutonium) in Hierapolis, Pamukkale, Turkey (Piccardi, 2007b; Castro et al., 2015). In Chimaera, the landscape sacralization has been associated with the constant burning of dozens of natural gas fires on a vast area of the rocky slope of the Yanartash hill (Figure 8). In Delphi and Hierapolis, trance of pythonesses has been induced by intoxication by gases emanated from cracks in sanctuaries directly located at the local active faults.

Nevertheless, it would be counterproductive to mix EQL of mechanoelectrical and degassing origin. Presumably, there are two types of EQL. It is possible that corona-discharge and fireball EQL, which may occur above faults, can generate fiery pillar EQL by burning gases seeping from these faults.

Figure 8. Chimaera, one of the natural gas fires

3.4 *Faults, EQL, and worship places*

Materials presented indicate a special role of active faults in the production of a mystical experience and sacralization of an affected landscape. Indeed, Piccardi (2001) found that some ancient sanctuaries are directly located on local active faults. He suggested that some sites lying along faults and marked by coseismic surface cracks and gas emission have been interpreted as Hades' Doors and thus worshiped.

The analysis of the statistically representative sample of the Crimean medieval monasteries (104 objects) and geological data demonstrated that almost all shrines are situated along faults of various ranges or at their intersections (Florinsky, 2010). We proposed the hypothesis that particular places are sacralized due to a combination of geoenvironmental factors including (a) regional and local active faults, (b) local magnetic anomalies, (c) regional and local lithospheric stresses, and (d) regional seismic activity. The factors work as follows: There is an increased permeability of the lithosphere along faults and at fault intersections over geological time scales. It creates favourable conditions for development of ore and magmatic bodies generating local magnetic anomalies. Geomagnetic storms modulate the intensity of the geomagnetic field at these anomalies. Prior to earthquakes, the rise of local and regional lithospheric stresses lead to mechanoelectrical phenomena in rocks, which also modulate the intensity of magnetic anomalies and sometimes produce EQL. Local fluctuations of the geomagnetic field and EQL electromagnetic fields influence the brain leading to a mystical experience. All four geoenvironmental factors are rather stable in time and space. This provides an opportunity to produce repeated mystical experiences at a particular site, which eventually becomes a place of worship (Florinsky, 2010).

4. CONCLUSIONS

Subjective perception and interpretation of EQL depend on religious and cultural traditions. The similar interpretation of EQL in the legends originated in two regions, Crimea and Peloponnese, situated quite far from each other, were caused by similar natural and economic living conditions of the Greek population in the both territories in the Middle Ages.

The results show that the application of geological and neurophysiological expertise to the analysis of local legends allows one to reconstruct past events associated with seismic activity. On the one hand, this can help in regional geological researches, on the other - provides additional opportunities for historical, anthropological, and religious studies.

Notice that we analysed certain aspects of the geoenvironmental impact on the human psyche and behaviour, which have a significant influence on the culture and society. The results cannot be used to evaluate the hypothesis of the existence of God, and are not intended to 'revise' sacred texts.

ACKNOWLEDGEMENTS

The author thanks D. Ryan (Tile Films, Dublin, Ireland) for the invitation to participate in the filming of the documentary "Sacred Sites of the World" and the idea to analyse EQL interpretation in the Greek Orthodox legends as well as O.N. Tynyanova ('Space and Time' Journal, Moscow, Russia) and V.L. Syvorotkin (Department of Petrology, Lomonosov Moscow State University, Russia) for discussions.

REFERENCES

Ambraseys, N.N. and Jackson, J.A. (1997) Seismicity and strain in the Gulf of Corinth (Greece) since 1694. *Journal of Earthquake Engineering*, Vol. 1, 433–474.

Badawy, A. and Horváth, F. (1999) Seismicity of the Sinai subplate region: kinematic implications. *Journal of Geodynamics*, Vol. 27, 451–468.

Bentor, Y.K. (1989) Geological events in the Bible. *Terra Nova*, Vol. 1, 326–338.

Booth, J.N., Koren, S.A. and Persinger, M.A. (2003) Increased proportions of sensed presences and occipital spikes with 1- and 10-msec. point duration of continuous 7-Hz transcerebral magnetic fields. *Perceptual and Motor Skills*, Vol. 97, 951–952.

Borisenko, L.S. (1986) Geological criteria of seismic activity in Crimea. *Seismological Researches*, No. 9, 38–48 (in Russian, with English abstract).

Borisenko, L.S., Novik, N.N., Tikhonenkov, E.P. and Chebanenko, I.I. (1982) Tectonic features of the southwestern part of the Crimean Mountains in the context of the problem of seismic hazard forecast. *Tectonica i Stratigrafia*, No. 23, 11–16 (in Russian).

Castro, B.M., Liritzis, I. and Nyquist A. (2015) Oracular functioning and architecture of five ancient Apollo Temples through archaeoastronomy: novel approach and interpretation. *Nexus Network Journal*, doi:10.1007/s00004-015-0276-2.

Cook, C.M. and Persinger, M.A. (1997) Experimental induction of the "sensed presence" in normal subjects and an exceptional subject. *Perceptual and Motor Skills*, Vol. 85, 683–693.

De Boer, J.Z. and Hale, J.R. (2000) The geological origins of the oracle at Delphi, Greece. In: McGuire, W.J., Griffiths, D.R., Hancock, P.L. and Stewart, I.S. (Eds.), *The Archaeology of Geological Catastrophes. Geological Society London Special Publications*, Vol. 171, 399–412.

De Boer, J.Z., Chanton, J. and Zeitlhöfler, M. (2007) Homer's Chimaera fires (SW of Antalya/Turkey); burning abiogenic methane gases; are they generated by a serpentinization process related to alkalic magmatism? *Zeitschrift der Deutschen Gesellschaft für Geowissenschaften*, Vol. 158, 997–1003.

Derr, J.S. (1973) Earthquake lights: a review of observations and present theories. *Bulletin of the Seismological Society of America*, Vol. 63, 2177–2187.

Derr, J.S. and Persinger, M.A. (1986) Luminous phenomena and earthquakes in Southern Washington. *Experientia*, Vol. 42, 991–999.

Derr, J.S. and Persinger, M.A. (1989) Geophysical variables and behavior: LIV. Zeitoun (Egypt) apparitions of the Virgin Mary as tectonic strain-induced luminosities. *Perceptual and Motor Skills*, Vol. 68, 123–128.

Derr, J.S. and Persinger, M.A. (1990) Geophysical variables and behavior: LXIII. Quasi-experimental evidence of the tectonic strain theory of luminous phenomena: The Derby, Colorado earthquakes. *Perceptual and Motor Skills*, Vol. 71, 707–714.

English Standard Version Bible with Apocrypha (2009) Oxford, Oxford University Press.

Etiope, G., Papatheodorou, G., Christodoulou, D., Geraga, M. and Favali, P. (2006) The geological links of the ancient Delphic Oracle (Greece): a reappraisal of natural gas occurrence and origin. *Geology*, Vol. 34, 821–824.

Etiope, G., Schoell, M. and Hosgörmez, H. (2011) Abiotic methane flux from the Chimaera seep and Tekirova ophiolites (Turkey): understanding gas exhalation from low temperature serpentinization and implications for Mars. *Earth and Planetary Science Letters*, Vol. 310, 96–104.

Florinsky, I.V. (2010) Sacred places and geophysical activity. In: Florinsky, I.V. (Ed.), *Man and the Geosphere*. New York, Nova Science, 215–255.

Freund, F.T., Takeuchi, A. and Lau, B.W.S. (2006) Electric currents streaming out of stressed igneous rocks – a step towards understanding pre-earthquake low frequency EM emissions. *Physics and Chemistry of the Earth*, Vol. 31, 389–396.

Freund, F., Salgueiro da Silva, M.A., Lau, B.W.S., Takeuchi, A. and Jones, H.H. (2007) Electric currents along earthquake faults and the magnetization of pseudotachylite veins. *Tectonophysics*, Vol. 431, 131–141.

Egyptian Geological Survey and Mining Authority (1981) *Geologic Map of Egypt*, scale 1 : 2,000,000. Cairo: Egyptian Geological Survey and Mining Authority.

Gorodnitsky, A.M., Maljauvkin, A.M., Ushakov, C.A. and Shreider, A.A. (1967) The method and some results of the hydromagnetic survey of the north-eastern part of the Black Sea. *Moscow University Bulletin, Series Geology*, No. 6, 57–59 (in Russian).

Holy Metropolis of Kalavryta and Aigialeia (2000) *The Sacred Shrine Panagia Tripiti*. URL: http://users.otenet.gr/~imka/mains/shr-trypiti_en.html

Hosgormez, H., Etiope, G. and Yalçin, M.N. (2008) New evidence for a mixed inorganic and organic origin of the Olympic Chimaera fire (Turkey): a large onshore seepage of abiogenic gas. *Geofluids*, Vol. 8, 263–273.

James, W. (1902) *The Varieties of Religious Experience: A Study in Human Nature*. New York, Longmans.

Johnson, C.P. and Persinger, M.A. (1994) The sensed presence may be facilitated by interhemispheric intercalation: relative efficacy of the Mind's Eye, Hemi-Sync Tape, and bilateral temporal magnetic field stimulation. *Perceptual and Motor Skills*, Vol. 79, 351–354.

Koukouvelas, I.K. and Doutsos, T.T. (1996) Implications of structural segmentation during earthquakes: the 1995 Egion earthquake, Gulf of Corinth, Greece. *Journal of Structural Geology*, Vol. 18, 1381–1388.

Levin, J. and Steele, L. (2005) The transcendent experience: Conceptual, theoretical, and epidemiologic perspectives. *Explore*, Vol. 1, 89–101.

Liritzis, I., and Castro, B. (2013) Delphi and cosmovision: Apollo's absence at the land of the Hyperboreans and the time for consulting the oracle. *Journal of Astronomical History and Heritage*, Vol. 16, 184–206.

Marino, A.A. and Becker, R.O. (1977) Biological effects of extremely low frequency electric and magnetic fields: A review. *Physiological Chemistry and Physics*, Vol. 9, 131–147.

Maslow, A.H. (1964) *Religions, Values, and Peak Experiences*. Columbus, Ohio State University Press.

Nikon, Archimandrite (1862) *The First Class Balaclavian St. George Monastery*. Chernigov, St. Elias Monastery (in Russian).

Nikonov, A.A. (2002) The 1927 Crimean earthquakes: unknown phenomena in the sea. *Priroda*, No. 9, 13–20 (in Russian).

Palmer, S.J., Rycroft, M.J. and Cermack, M. (2006) Solar and geomagnetic activity, extremely low frequency magnetic and electric fields and human health at the Earth's surface. *Surveys in Geophysics*, Vol. 27, 557–595.

Papadopoulus, G.A. (1999) Luminous and fiery phenomena associated with earthquakes in the East Mediterranean. In: Hayakawa, M. (Ed.), *Atmospheric and Ionospheric Electromagnetic Phenomena Associated with Earthquakes*. Tokyo, Terra, 559–575.

Pechersky, D.M., Didenko, A.N., Safonov, V.A., Tikhonov, L.V. and Tselmovich, V.A. (1991) Petromagnetic and palaeomagnetic characteristics of the Middle Jurassic volcanism in the Mountain Crimea. *Bulletin of the Academy of Sciences of the USSR, Geologic Series*, No. 3, 85–104 (in Russian).

Persinger, M.A. (1976) Transient geophysical bases for ostensible UFO-related phenomena and associated verbal behavior? *Perceptual and Motor Skills*, Vol. 43, 215–221.

Persinger, M.A. (1980) Earthquake activity and antecedent UFO report numbers. *Perceptual and Motor Skills*, Vol. 50, 791–797.

Persinger, M.A. (1983) Geophysical variables and behavior: IX. Expected clinical consequences of close proximity to UFO-related luminosities. *Perceptual and Motor Skills*, Vol. 56, 259–265.

Persinger, M.A. (1984) Geophysical variables and behavior: XVIII. Expected perceptual characteristics and local distributions of close UFO reports. *Perceptual and Motor Skills*, Vol. 58, 951–959.

Persinger, M.A. (1988) Geophysical variables and behavior: LIII. Epidemiological considerations for incidence of cancer and depression in areas of frequent UFO reports. *Perceptual and Motor Skills*, Vol. 67, 799–803.

Persinger M.A. and Derr, J.S. (1985) Geophysical variables and behavior: XXIII. Relations between UFO reports within the Uinta Basin and local seismicity. *Perceptual and Motor Skills*, Vol. 60, 143–152.

Persinger M.A. and Derr, J.S. (1990a) Geophysical variables and behavior: LXI. UFO reports in Carman, Manitoba and the 1975 Minnesota quake: evidence of triggering by increased volume of the Red River. *Perceptual and Motor Skills*, Vol. 71, 531–536.

Persinger M.A. and Derr, J.S. (1990b) Geophysical variables and behavior: LXII. Temporal coupling of UFO reports and seismic energy release within the Rio Grande Rift System: discriminative validity of the tectonic strain theory. *Perceptual and Motor Skills*, Vol. 71, 567–572.

Persinger M.A. and Healey, F. (2002) Experimental facilitation of the sensed presence: possible intercalation between the hemispheres induced by complex magnetic fields. *Journal of Nervous and Mental Disease*, Vol. 190, 533–541.

Piccardi, L. (2000) Active faulting at Delphi, Greece: seismotectonic remarks and a hypothesis for the geologic environment of a myth. *Geology*, Vol. 28, 651–654.

Piccardi, L. (2001) Fault-related sanctuaries. *American Geophysical Union, Fall Meeting 2001*, abstract #U52B-03.

Piccardi, L. (2005) Paleoseismic evidence of legendary earthquakes: the apparition of Archangel Michael at Monte Sant'Angelo (Italy). *Tectonophysics*, Vol. 408, 113–128.

Piccardi, L. (2007a) Preface. In: Piccardi, L. and Masse, W.B. (Eds.), *Myth and Geology. Geological Society London Special Publications*, Vol. 273, vii–viii.

Piccardi, L. (2007b) The AD 60 Denizli Basin earthquake and the apparition of Archangel Michael at Colossae (Aegean Turkey). In: Piccardi, L. and Masse, W.B. (Eds.), *Myth and Geology. Geological Society London Special Publications*, Vol. 273, 95–105.

Piccardi, L. and Masse, W.B. (Eds.) (2007) *Myth and Geology. Geological Society London Special Publications*, Vol. 273.

Solovyev, I.V. (1988) Bajocian volcanic structure of the Cape Fiolent (south-western Crimea). *Kiev University Bulletin, Series Geology*, No. 7, 42–49 (in Russian).

Soter, S. (1999) Macroscopic seismic anomalies and submarine pockmarks in the Corinth–Patras rift, Greece. *Tectonophysics*, Vol. 308, 275–290.

St-Laurent, F., Derr, J.S. and Freund, F.T. (2006) Earthquake lights and the stress-activation of positive hole charge carriers in rocks. *Physics and Chemistry of the Earth*, Vol. 31, 305–312.

St.-Pierre, L.S. and Persinger, M.A. (2006) Experimental facilitation of the sensed presence is predicted by the specific patterns of the applied magnetic fields, not by suggestibility: re-analyses of 19 experiments. *International Journal of Neuroscience*, Vol. 116, 1079–1096.

Suess, L.A. and Persinger, M.A. (2001) Geophysical variables and behavior: XCVI. "Experiences" attributed to Christ and Mary at Marmora, Ontario, Canada may have been consequences of environmental electromagnetic stimulation: implications for religious movements. *Perceptual and Motor Skills*, Vol. 93, 435–450.

Swann, I. (1996) *The Great Apparitions of Mary: An Examination of Twenty-Two Supranormal Appearances*. New York, Crossroad.

Thériault, R., St-Laurent, F., Freund, F.T. and Derr, J.S. (2014) Prevalence of earthquake lights associated with rift environments. *Seismological Research Letters*, Vol. 85, 159–178.

Tortchinov, E.A. (1998) *Religion of the World: Experience of the Transcendence (Transpersonal States and Psychotechnique)*. St. Petersburg, Peterburgskoe Vostokovedenie (in Russian, with English summary).

Trifonov, V.G., Soboleva, O.V., Trifonov, R.V. and Vostrikov, G.A. (2002) *Recent Geodynamics of the Alpine–Himalayan Collision Belt*. Moscow, Geos (in Russian, with English summary).

Tur, V.G. (2006) *Orthodox Monasteries in Crimea in 19th – early 20th Centuries*. 2nd rev. enl. ed. Kiev, Stilos (in Russian).

Unkel, I. (2002) *Europäische Erdbebenzone Golf von Korinth: Geologisch-hydrogeologische Untersuchungen in der Region Aigion, im Umfeld der kontinentalen Tiefbohrung AIG 10 (NW-Peloponnes, Griechenland)*. Diploma thesis. Karlsruhe, University of Karlsruhe.

Vaitl, D., Birbaumer, N., Gruzelier, J., Jamieson, G.A., Kotchoubey, B., Kübler, A., Lehmann, D., Miltner, W.H.R., Ott, U., Pütz, P., Sammer, G., Strauch, I., Strehl, U., Wackermann, J. and Weiss, T. (2005) Psychobiology of altered states of consciousness. *Psychological Bulletin*, Vol. 131, 98–127.

Vitaliano, D.B. (1973) *Legends of the Earth: Their Geologic Origins*. Bloomigton, Indiana University Press.

Yakovleva, M.I. (1973) *Physiological Mechanisms of the Action of Electromagnetic Fields*. Leningrad, Medicina (in Russian, with English abstract).

3

ISLAMIC POTTERY PRODUCTION IN EASTERN SICILY (10th-11th CENTURIES): PRELIMINARY ARCHAEOMETRIC DATA ON LOCAL AND IMPORTED PRODUCTS FROM PATERNÒ (SICILY)

Michelangelo Messina[1], Lucia Arcifa[2], Germana Barone[3], Claudio Finocchiaro[3], Paolo Mazzoleni[3*]

[1]University of Catania, Department of Humanities, Piazza Dante, 32, 95124, Catania (Italy), michelangelomessina91@gmail.com
[2]University of Catania, Department of Educational Sciences, Via Biblioteca , 4, 95124, Catania (Italy) l.arcifa@unict.it
[3]University of Catania, Department of Biological, Geological and Environmental Sciences, C.so Italia, 57, 95129 Catania (Italy). pmazzol@unict.it, claudio.finocchiaro@gmail.com

*Corresponding author: Paolo Mazzoleni (pmazzol@unict.it)

ABSTRACT

From the 9th to the 11th century, Sicily has been part of the Islamic oecumene, the *dār al-Islām*. Up until now, very few studies have been carried out on the centres of pottery production of this period, and most of them concern the Emiral capital of the isle, Palermo.
The archaeometric data obtained with chemical and minero-petrographic analyses on Islamic pottery found in Paternò – a town situated in the southwestern slope of Mt. Etna – has provided a certain number of issues of very important matter. The selection of the samples has been made among the archaeological finds coming from the excavation near the church of Cristo al Monte, on the hilltop, which represented the inner part of the medieval *madīna*.
The mineralogical and chemical characterization of the ceramic body has been attained using optical microscopy on thin sections and X-ray fluorescence respectively, in order to define the probable provenance of each sample. Further information of technological matter has been provided using X-Ray diffraction on powdered samples, which furnishes mineralogical data useful to hypothesise the firing temperatures: the main task attained on this issue was the focus on the self-slipped ware with salted water, one of the main technological class in Islamic Sicily. Finally, energy dispersive X-Ray fluorescence was adopted for a preliminary investigation of pigments used to decorate the lead glazed pottery. The issues related to both the local and imported pots – the latter represented almost completely by Palermo's products – provided some important historical and archaeological information about the means of Sicilian pottery production during this important period.

KEYWORDS: Pottery production, Eastern Sicily, glazed pottery, Islamic archaeology

1. INTRODUCTION AND HISTORICAL BACKGROUND

The Islamic period of medieval Sicily is little known from a historical point of view for different aspects, especially in its archaeological perspective. While the number of studies for the western part of the isle - and for the Emiral Capital of Palermo in particular - is growing (Nef and Ardizzone, 2014), there are still a lot of shadows for the most important cities in Central and Eastern Sicily. The characterization of ceramics of the 10th-11th centuries found in Paternò (Catania) is inspired by the need of a wider comprehension of the material culture for those territories that remained, for a longer period, a frontier zone (*ṯaġr*) between the *Dār al-Islām* ("The house of the *Islām*") and the imperial oecumene of Constantinople.

Islamic troupes arrived in Sicily following Asad Ibn al-Furāt, an important malikī jurist who guided the beginning of the *ğihād* against the isle under the banners of the Aghlabid Amirs of Ifrīqiya (modern Tunisia) in 827 C.E. (Nef, 2011). After the major conquests of Agrigento (828) and Palermo (831), a time of periodic confrontation between Muslim and imperial forces occurred, along the roads between the two sides of the island and around the fortified *kastra* (Nef and Prigent 2013, Arcifa, 2013). From the 9th to the 11th century, Eastern Sicily was the main theatre of war, and occasionally capitulations of cities took place: Enna (859), Syracuse (878), Taormina and Rometta (902 and 962-4) are just a few examples (Fig. 1). Since 916 C.E., Islamic Sicily passed under the rule of the Shiite Caliphate of the Fatimids (Pellitteri, 1997).

For Catania and Paternò, the chroniclers did not furnish a certain date of surrender or fall after siege. In particular, Paternò is a town situated on the southwestern side of Mt. Etna, and the written sources did not have historical remarks about it, except for the important citation of this centre among the "cities" (*mudun* sing. *madīna*) of Islamic Sicily. According to this list of the Arab geographer al-Muqaddasī (X century), a "city" (*madīna*) is the capital of an administrative department (*iqlīm*), an information that needs to be better evaluated in its territorial dimension (al-Muqaddasī, 1991).

The medieval documents about Paternò's territory record the presence in this area of a *Murum Marabotti* (Garufi, 1913) and of the *Rocca que dicitur de Maraboto* (Ardizzone, 1927), related to some *sepolturae sarracenorum*[1]. These terms could witness the existence of a *ribāṭ* in Paternò, i.e. a military-religious institution widely spread along the border zones of the *Dār al-Islām* in this period (Picard and Borrut, 2003). This fascinating hypothesis needs to be ascertained with archaeological data.

A certain number of archaeological excavations took place on the hilltop of *Baṭarnū*, the so-called "Collina Storica". Along the northern wall of the Bianchi's Graveyard joined to the church of Cristo al Monte, the Superintendence to the Cultural Heritage of Catania (dir. L. Maniscalco) found a hydraulic complex consisting of a semi-circular cistern that was replenished with rainwater by built canals and terracotta pipes, or *qawādīs* (sing. *qādūs*, Fig. 8), an Arabic term that remained in the Sicilian dialect (*catusu*). The archaeological evidences detected at the moment show the implantation of these buildings during the 10th century, after a long period of abandon of the hilltop. Since then, two Islamic phases have been detected: the main building phase is datable between the 10th and the very beginning of the 11th century (Phase IV); probably during the central decades of the 11th century, these structures collapsed, as recorded in a series of destruction and abandon layers (Phase V, Arcifa, Messina in press.).

In this context, this archaeometric study aims to give new important data for the study of the production of Islamic pottery in Sicily. In fact, the state of the research in this topic is still unripe even if some Sicilian centers of production have already been recognized in the past by archaeometric tools: Palermo (Giarrusso and Mulone, 2014), which was the Islamic capital of the isle during these centuries; Siracusa (Ben Amara et al., 2009), which represented the main Byzantine city until its conquest in 878; Mazara del Vallo (Molinari, 2010), Agrigento (Alaimo and Giarrusso, 2007) and Piazza Armerina (Alaimo et al., 2010). Unfortunately, the archaeometric data presented in these papers - consisting almost exclusively of petrographic features - do not allow a comparison among these centers of production, and for the most part of them a more extensive and multivariate analysis needs to be done.

A further perspective has also a socio-economic and historical importance: starting a study on the productive landscape of a frontier zone represents an opportunity to better understand in what senses - negative and positive - urban and rural sites were affected by a "never-ending holy war" (*ğihād dā'im*, al-Muqaddasī, 1991).

2. EXPERIMENTAL

2.1 Materials

For what concerns the Islamic Sicilian pottery, five main technological classes can be distinguished: i) self-slipped ware with salted water (SSW); ii) lead-

[1] Translations: "The wall of the Marabouts", the "so-called Maraboto rock" and "muslim tombs".

glazed ware (LGW), which was provided of a light-coloured surface as well as with a SSW treatment in the first firing process, in order to furnish a white base for the metal oxides used as pigments (Cuomo Di Caprio, 2007); iii) painted ware (PW); iv) cooking ware (CW); v) common ware (Com. W., Table 1).

The painted ware of this period is characterized by different kinds of banded motifs, for which a chrono-typological differentiation has been proposed (Arcifa, 2010): a loop motif characterized the amphorae during the middle-byzantine period (late 8th-9th century) and was still widespread between Sicily and Southern Italy until the mid-11th century (Raimondo, 2002, Arthur and Leo Imperiale, 2015). Other kinds of decorations were depicted in transport amphorae produced between Palermo and Western Sicily: the sinusoidal line characterizes the earliest products (end 9th-beginning 10th century), which was substituted by oblique and parallel strokes during the 10th century (Nef and Ardizzone 2014). The surface of the PW could be whitened with a SSW treatment (i.e., sample PCM 25/42).

In order to achieve a certain characterization of these different products and their provenance, fourteen samples have been selected from the abovementioned Paternò archaeological excavation (Par. 1, PCM). Furthermore, three kiln wastes for self-slipped (PCM 25/35), lead-glazed (PCM 25/36) and painted (PCM 25/42) ware have been analysed as reference samples for local production. Finally, with the aim to compare the data of some products supposed of Palermo and North Eastern Sicily, we studied two samples representative of Palermo's common (Pa1) and lead glazed ware (Pa2) and two samples of common (TF1) and painted ware (TF2) from Taormina.

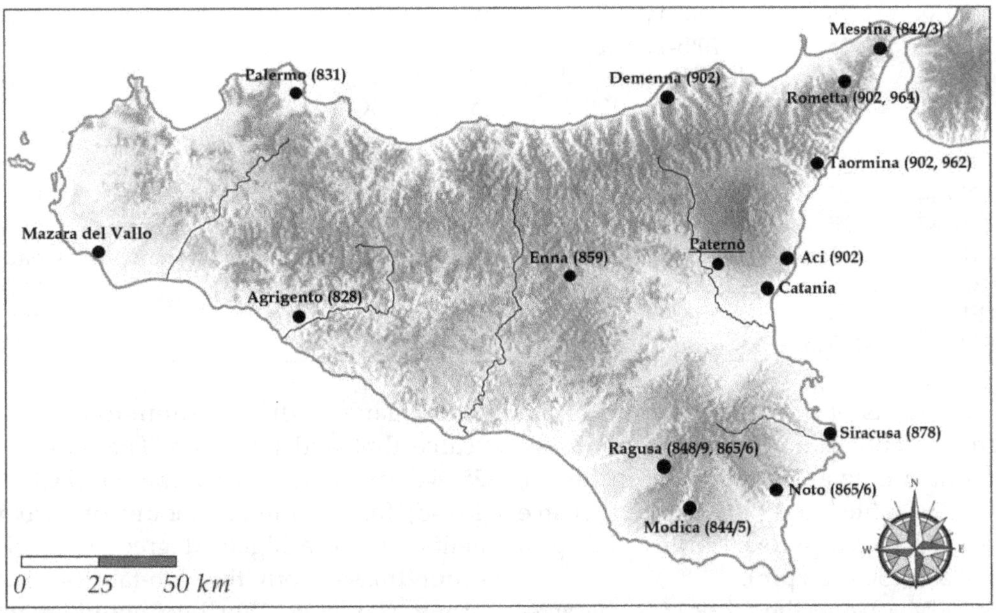

Figure 1. Main Sicilian towns and their date of conquest (CE) by the Islamic power during the 9th-10th centuries.

2.2 Methods

Once catalogued and prepared, the samples were analysed at the laboratory of the Department of Biological, Geological and Environmental Sciences at the University of Catania, using the following analytical methods: i) optical analysis with a polarized-light microscope (OM); ii) mineralogical analysis with X-ray diffraction (XRD) using a SIEMENS D5000, with Cu-kα radiation and Ni-filter; iii) chemical analysis of bulk with wavelength dispersive X-ray fluorescence (WDXRF), carried out using a Philips PW 2404/00 spectrometer, and of glassed surface with energy dispersive XRF (EDXRF) Bruker Tracer IV SD. The combination of these complementary analytical techniques allowed us to suppose their provenance, as well as to raise some important technological issues linked to the different classes.

The main task of this paper, in which a preliminary report of a research still in progress is presented, is the proposition of a multidisciplinary approach for the characterization of Sicilian Islamic pottery in general, in order to improve the chemical and petrographic data about the ceramic productions of this period, which remains mostly unknown - especially for the Eastern part of the isle. Earlier Islamic pottery analysis has been reported (Al-Shorman & El-Khouri, 2013; Amiri et al., 2013; Sarhaddi-Dadian et al., 2015).

3. RESULTS AND DISCUSSION

3.1 Petrographic analyses

Using the optical microscope on thin sections, a total number of eight fabrics has been detected (Fig. 2).

Samples of fabric A show a scarcely micaceous groundmass, with dominant quartz (grain size: 50-500 µm), minor amounts of plagioclases, pyroxenes and very scarce amphiboles and volcanic rock fragments. The latter mainly show a porphyritic texture with plagioclase phenocrysts. Metamorphic rock fragments are also very scarcely represented. It is possible to distinguish the sub-fabric A1 (PCM 14/2, PCM 14/3, PCM 25/35, PCM 25/36, PCM 25/38), characterized by minor amount of medium-fine grains than the samples of the sub-fabric A2 (PCM 25/42, PCM 25/43).

Table 1. Sampling and methods applied. SSW = self-slipped ware with salted water, CW = cooking ware, LGW = lead glazed ware, PW = painted ware.

Sample	SU	Chronological context	OM	XRF-WDS	XRF-EDS	XRD	Tech. Class
PCM 14/2	14	10th-11th cent.	X	X		X	SSW
PCM 14/3	14	10th-11th cent.	X	X		X	SSW
PCM 19/4	19	10th-11th cent.	X	X		X	CW
PCM 25/35	25	10th-11th cent.	X	X		X	SSW
PCM 25/36	25	10th-11th cent.	X	X	X	X	LGW
PCM 25/37	25	10th-11th cent.	X	X	X	X	LGW
PCM 25/38	25	10th-11th cent.	X	X		X	PW
PCM 25/39	25	10th-11th cent.	X	X		X	PW
PCM 25/40	25	late 9th-early 10th?	X	X		X	PW
PCM 25/41	25	9th-early 10th?	X	X		X	PW
PCM 25/42	25	10th-11th cent.	X	X		X	PW/SSW
PCM 25/43	25	9th-11th cent.	X	X		X	PW
PCM 25/44	25	10th-11th cent.	X	X	X	X	LGW
PCM 25/45	25	10th-11th cent.	X	X	X	X	LGW
Pa1	Ref. Sam.	10th-11th cent.	X	X		X	Com. W.
Pa2	Ref. Sam.	10th-11th cent.	X	X	X	X	LGW
TF1	Ref. Sam.	mid-9th cent.	X	X		X	Com. W.
TF2	Ref. Sam.	mid-9th cent.	X	X		X	PW

The fabric B consists of one single sample (PCM 25/41), which presents a micaceous groundmass, with medium-fine quartz as predominant inclusion, common micas (biotite and muscovite), scarce feldspars and very scarce pyroxenes (50 - 125 µm) and carbonate clasts (50 - 250 µm).

The sample PCM 19/4 of the fabric C is characterized by a scarcely micaceous groundmass, with coarse grains of dominant plagioclases and volcanic rock fragments with porphyritic and in some cases vesicular texture, scarce (< 5%) quartz, amphibole and metamorphic rock fragments. These petrographic features suggest a Mt. Etna production area (Barone et al., 2010).

The fabric D (PCM 25/37) has a scarcely micaceous groundmass, without coarse inclusions, and a fine fraction formed by dominant quartz and scarce carbonate clasts, very scarce pyroxenes, feldspars and micas.

The fabric E samples show a homogeneous fossiliferous groundmass with carbonate clasts as dominant medium-coarse to medium-fine fraction, common quartz with a medium-to-fine grain size and scarce flint and feldspars. The sub-fabric E2 (PCM 25/44) distinguishes by the E1 (PCM 25/39, PCM 25/45) for the minor amount of carbonate components, due to a higher degree of vitrification of the groundmass. Both the sub-fabrics show abundant brown clay clots. Worth of note is that the Palermo reference samples (Pa1 and Pa2) belong to the fabric E.

The fabric F (PCM 25/40) are quite similar to the fabric E samples, but the dominant inclusions are formed by quartz characterized by different size and shape.

The reference samples from Taormina have different petrographic features: the fabric G (TF1) shows a scarcely micaceous groundmass with dominant coarse-to-medium grain size metamorphic rock fragments (500–2000 micron), scarce micas and quartz and very scarce amphiboles, feldspars and pyroxenes. The fabric H (TF1) is fine grained, with inclusions formed by quartz, micas, calcite and pyroxenes.

Figure 2 – microphotographs of representative samples for each Fabric (from A to H). (crossed nicols).

The petrographic observations allow us to give some preliminary hypothesis about the production sites of the studied pottery. The fabric A samples probably represent the most significant Paternò local production since the kiln wastes analyzed (PCM 25/35, PCM 25/36, PCM 25/42) belong to this fabric. The sample PCM19/4 (fabric C) represents one of the local cooking ware, produced adding volcanic rock fragments to the clay. On the contrary, the pottery of fabric E is supposed to be representative of the Palermo manufacture, as suggested by the close similarity with the reference materials and with literature data (Giarrusso and Mulone, 2014). The fabric F is similar to the Palermo samples, but it could derive from other centers of production in Western Sicily (probably Agrigento, Alaimo and Giarrusso, 2007). Finally, regarding the sample PCM25/37 of fabric D, it is not possible to suppose the site of production on petrographic basis. The Taormina fabrics (G and H) both showed very different features with respect to the other groups.

3.2 Chemical analyses

Even if the amount of samples still prevents a significant statistics, chemical data (tables 2-3) confirmed the main petrographic groups (A and E) due to the following features: 1) samples of fabrics A and B have high SiO_2 amounts (average 60.65 wt%), CaO contents from 8.2 to 11.8 % and, among the trace elements, higher V abundances; 2) the samples belonging to the fabric E present lower SiO_2 content (and high CaO and Sr; 3) fabrics C, D and F (a single sample for each one), show different chemical compositions from the samples of the previous groups.

The biplot diagrams of the first two principal components, calculated using major and trace elements, are reported in Fig. 3 and Fig. 4, respectively. On the whole, the multivariate analysis allows us to confirm the petrographic observations. Samples belonging to fabric A are plotted in a restricted area that may be related to local production as stated by petrography, joined to the only sample of fabric B, probably representing another production from Northeastern Sicily. Regarding the Paternò samples of fabrics E, they have chemical composition close to the reference specimens from Palermo, thus suggesting this provenance.

The chemical data for fabric C, D and F do not allow us to constrain the production center, since they do not show chemical and petrographic similarities with the reference materials such as Taormina samples (fabrics G and H).

3.3 X-ray diffraction and the self-slipped surface technology

The mineralogical data (Table 4) permit some considerations about the production of some technological classes. With the exceptions of few samples, all the studied potteries are characterized by the presence of newly-formed Ca-silicates and by absence of calcite and clay minerals. However, these features, suggesting high firing temperature, seem related to the light surface on pottery due to the addition of seawater or salt to the clay and/or the water during the forming procedure (Cuomo di Caprio, 2007, Bonifay, 2004). According to Barone et al. (2012), the addition of NaCl decreases the temperature of formation of Ca-silicates, as well as the decarbonation apex and the amount of Fe forming hematite, the latter representing the main cause of the bleaching effect.

The XRD data of the samples with thick whitened layer (PCM14/3, PCM25/35, PCM25/36, PCM 25/44) showed high anorthite and diopside abundances. On the contrary, the samples in which the white layer is thin (PCM14/2, PCM25/45, Pa2, Fig. 5) have no Ca-silicates or only low amount of Gehlenite. These cases could suggest that the mineralogical composition of the SSW samples - i.e. the amount of the silicates of higher temperature - was probably affected by presence of salt, and not necessarily by the attainment of high firing temperatures (750°C; Barone et al., 2012, contrarily to what reported in the previous literature, > 850-900°C; Ben Amara et al., 2009). In this scenario, the variability in thickness of the whitened layer and mineralogical composition may be related to different factors: the abundance of NaCl in the system; the duration of the phase of reducing atmosphere at the end of the firing process; the peak of temperature achieved in the kiln; etc. In fact, the most homogeneous white surface is obtained when this firing process does not get to a too much high vitrification, i.e. with a lesser amount of Ca-silicates. The data will be improved, especially by a wider range of firing experiments, which also include the possibility of an experimental archaeology program attained in some kilns still existing in the Paternò territory. Nevertheless, these data suggest that the NaCl effects cause not only the appearance of a white surface on pots, but also a sensible decrease in the firing temperatures needed to obtain a good final product. The best light surfaces do not require high temperatures, thus possibly representing a very important technological feature in the production of those pots that required two cooking processes - the lead glazed pottery. NaCl represented a good way in economizing fuel during the "cottura a biscotto" (first firing process), producing a good white surface capable of standing out the colors of Sicilian glazed potteries from the Islamic period up to the 13th-14th centuries in some Proto-majolica productions (Cuomo Di Caprio and Fiorilla, 1992).

Regarding the samples without whitened layer (PCM 25/38, PCM 25/40, PCM 25/41 and PCM 25/43), we can suppose, on the basis of XRD data, high temperature firing processes (900-950°C), while in PCM 25/39, Pa1, TF1 and TF2 the presence of calcite testifies low firing temperatures (650-750°C).

On the whole, the discussed firing temperatures are in accordance with other Sicilian Islamic pottery productions. For Agrigento amphorae and their supports (600-800°C) as well as for cooking pots (600-700°C), very low temperatures were suggested, while for pots with a light surface that sometimes turns to a patchy greenish yellow, higher temperatures have been proposed (Alaimo and Giarrusso, 2004, 2007). For the Palermo pottery, with no surface treatments and glazed ware, similar variations in the firing yield were supposed (Giarrusso and Mulone, 2014), according to the relation between the remaining carbonate granules and the voids generated by their decarbonation.

Tables 2-3. Chemical data: major, minor (wt %) and trace (ppm) elements.

Sample	Fabric	SiO_2	TiO_2	Al_2O_3	Fe_2O_3	MnO	MgO	CaO	Na_2O	K_2O	P_2O_5	L.O.I.
PCM 14/2	A1	63.324	0.759	13.17	5.019	0.09	2.02	8.217	1.472	2.853	0.256	2.82
PCM 14/3	A1	61.15	0.841	14.024	5.632	0.084	2.38	10.178	1.948	2.667	0.226	0.87
PCM 19/4	C	53.997	1.188	18.781	7.028	0.127	2.713	10.048	1.584	2.844	0.779	0.91
PCM 25/35	A1	60.258	0.855	14.623	5.422	0.083	2.482	10.756	1.498	2.853	0.26	0.91
PCM 25/36	A1	58.013	0.809	15.225	4.916	0.079	2.592	11.872	1.464	2.69	0.291	2.05
PCM 25/37	D	46.651	0.921	14.555	4.697	0.063	3.158	20.344	0.922	2.182	0.527	5.98
PCM 25/38	A1	59.925	0.873	14.779	5.482	0.089	2.511	9.274	1.175	3.024	0.258	2.61
PCM 25/39	E1	51.672	0.783	13.867	5.142	0.097	1.498	15.785	0.282	2.25	0.554	8.07
PCM 25/40	F	54.315	0.742	13.539	4.682	0.104	3.135	14.277	0.805	2.684	0.528	5.19
PCM 25/41	B	62.343	0.935	13.53	5.844	0.086	2.242	8.261	0.86	2.957	0.342	2.6
PCM 25/42	A2	63.211	0.912	14.469	5.877	0.097	1.807	8.926	1.365	2.735	0.34	0.26
PCM 25/43	A2	58.695	0.875	14.86	5.389	0.095	2.533	10.462	1.037	2.938	0.837	2.28
PCM 25/44	E2	52.59	0.772	13.146	5.58	0.084	1.576	18.205	0.962	1.907	0.209	4.97
PCM 25/45	E1	54.73	0.801	13.434	5.396	0.093	1.622	15.763	0.842	2.095	0.333	4.89
Pa1	E1	49.5	0.778	13.558	5.262	0.09	1.737	17.026	0.262	2.105	0.253	9.43
Pa2	E1	50.715	0.776	13.286	5.157	0.094	1.763	16.815	0.847	2.021	0.476	8.05
TF1	G	62.33	0.766	16.523	5.409	0.095	1.479	2.21	1.745	3.766	0.507	5.17
TF2	H	46.261	0.693	14.491	4.158	0.101	2.886	13.905	0.738	3.988	0.35	12.43

Sample	Fabric	Sr	V	Cr	Co	Ni	Zn	Rb	Y	Zr	Nb	Ba	La	Ce	Pb	Th
PCM 14/2	A1	372	118	93	11	40	90	89	21	210	13	374	48	84	18	8
PCM 14/3	A1	398	114	111	12	44	81	86	28	222	16	341	53	107	11	9
PCM 19/4	C	931	198	103	18	47	120	92	29	237	31	627	78	113	18	10
PCM 25/35	A1	368	138	114	12	47	87	95	28	239	18	393	55	89	8	10
PCM 25/36	A1	276	137	110	10	49	71	57	25	151	6	329	50	101	6976	100
PCM 25/37	D	627	142	142	10	65	99	80	35	225	21	336	58	119	2946	40
PCM 25/38	A1	481	141	116	11	48	113	103	29	229	17	359	50	102	20	8
PCM 25/39	E1	659	91	96	18	54	99	82	29	263	15	240	51	112	21	9
PCM 25/40	F	600	126	107	16	57	114	90	22	209	13	350	45	80	18	8
PCM 25/41	B	405	126	111	12	46	105	99	30	320	17	394	55	111	21	9
PCM 25/42	A2	388	146	121	13	48	87	99	31	289	20	378	51	104	10	10
PCM 25/43	A2	408	139	115	11	48	113	98	24	223	15	404	49	104	22	8
PCM 25/44	E2	388	105	100	16	54	87	60	27	222	10	224	57	116	3664	49
PCM 25/45	E1	493	104	96	18	55	93	71	36	255	15	248	58	107	6092	74
Pa1	E1	340	89	93	19	53	107	72	28	235	14	265	53	89	26	10
Pa2	E1	462	93	94	14	56	91	65	35	247	13	381	45	110	6570	82
TF1	G	188	107	67	11	39	88	113	25	197	18	863	50	93	392	15
TF2	H	258	113	84	10	48	115	126	24	138	13	764	45	78	35	11

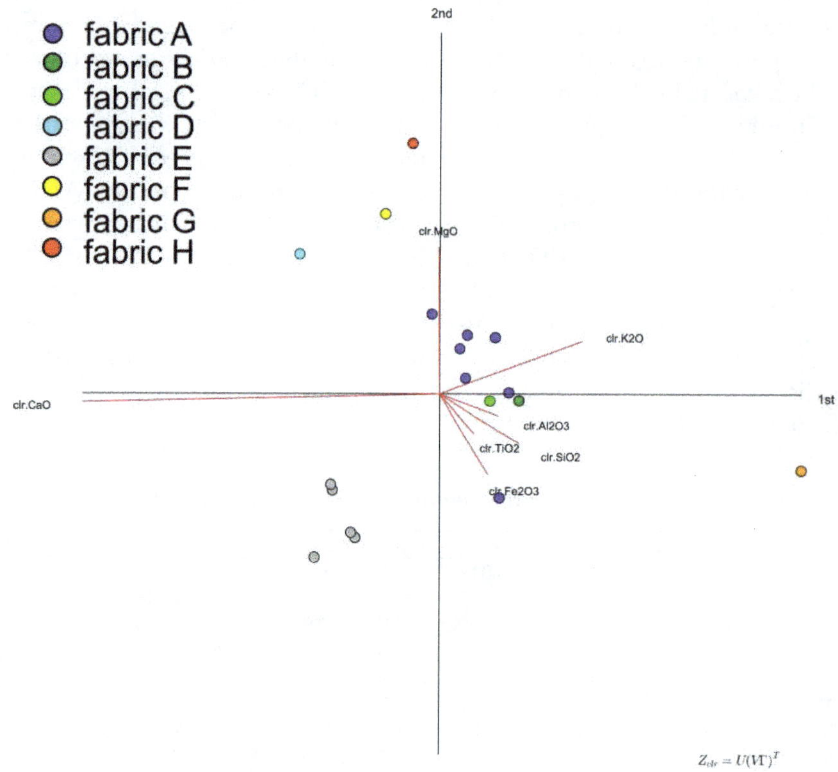

Figure 3. Biplot representation of PC1 and PC2 of major elements explaining the 92% of the total variance.

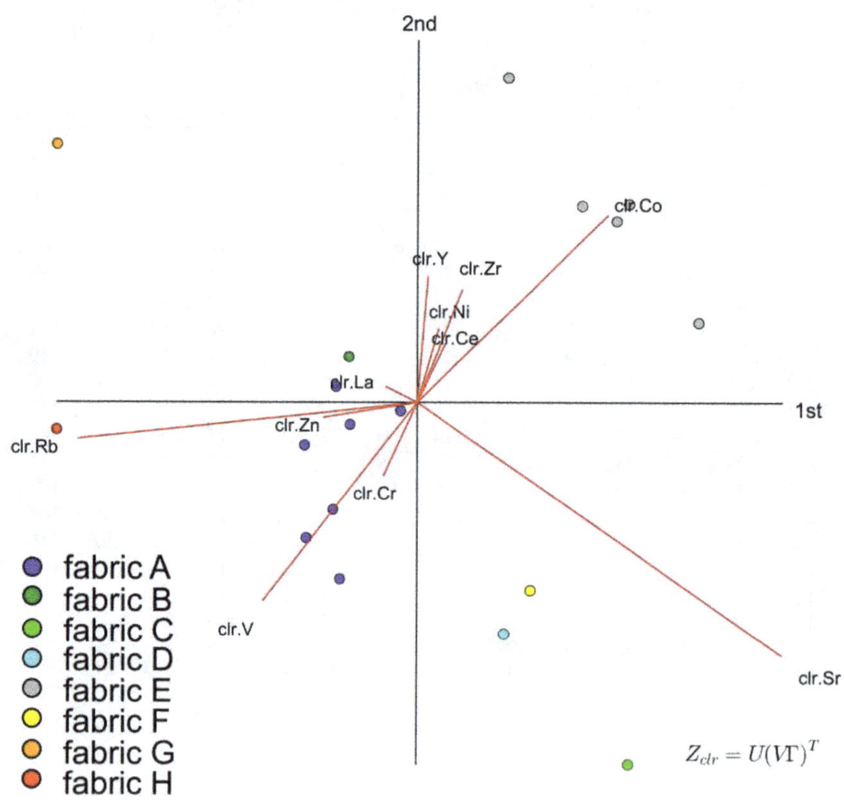

Figure 4. Biplot representation of PC1 and PC2 of minor elements explaining the 60% of the total variance.

*Table 4. Mineralogical results (XRD) and ceramic body of the cited samples. Qz = Quartz, Ab = Albite, Di = Diopside, Micr = microcline, An = anorthite, Hm = Hematite, Gehl = Gehlenite, C Min = Clay minerals, Cc = Calcite; XXX = very abundant, XX = abundant, X = scarce, tr = trace. SSW = self-slipped ware with salted water, CW = cooking ware, LGW = lead glazed ware, PW = painted ware, * indicate the pottery with whitened surface.*

Sample	Fabric	Qz	Ab	Di	Micr	Mica	An	Hm	Gehl	C Min	Cc	Tech. Class
PCM 14/2	A1	XXX	X		X	X						SSW *
PCM 14/3	A1	XXX		X	X	X	XX					SSW *
PCM 19/4	C	XXX		X		X	XX	X	X			CW
PCM 25/35	A1	XXX		XX	X		XX	X				SSW *
PCM 25/36	A1	XXX		XX	X		XX					LGW *
PCM 25/37	D	XXX		XX			XX	X	X			LGW *
PCM 25/38	A1	XXX		X			XX	X				PW
PCM 25/39	E1	XXX	Tr							XX	XX	PW
PCM 25/40	F	XXX		XX	X		XX		X			PW
PCM 25/41	B	XXX		X	X		XX	X				PW
PCM 25/42	A2	XXX		XX			XX					PW *
PCM 25/43	A2	XXX		X	X		XX	X				PW
PCM 25/44	E2	XXX		X			XX	XX				LGW *
PCM 25/45	E1	XXX		X			X	XX	XX		X	LGW *
Pa1	E1	XXX			X				X	X	XX	Com. W
Pa2	E1	XXX						XX	X	XX	XX	LGW *
TF1	TF1	XXX	XX		XX					XX		Com. W
TF2	TF2	XXX	XX		XX					XX	XX	PW

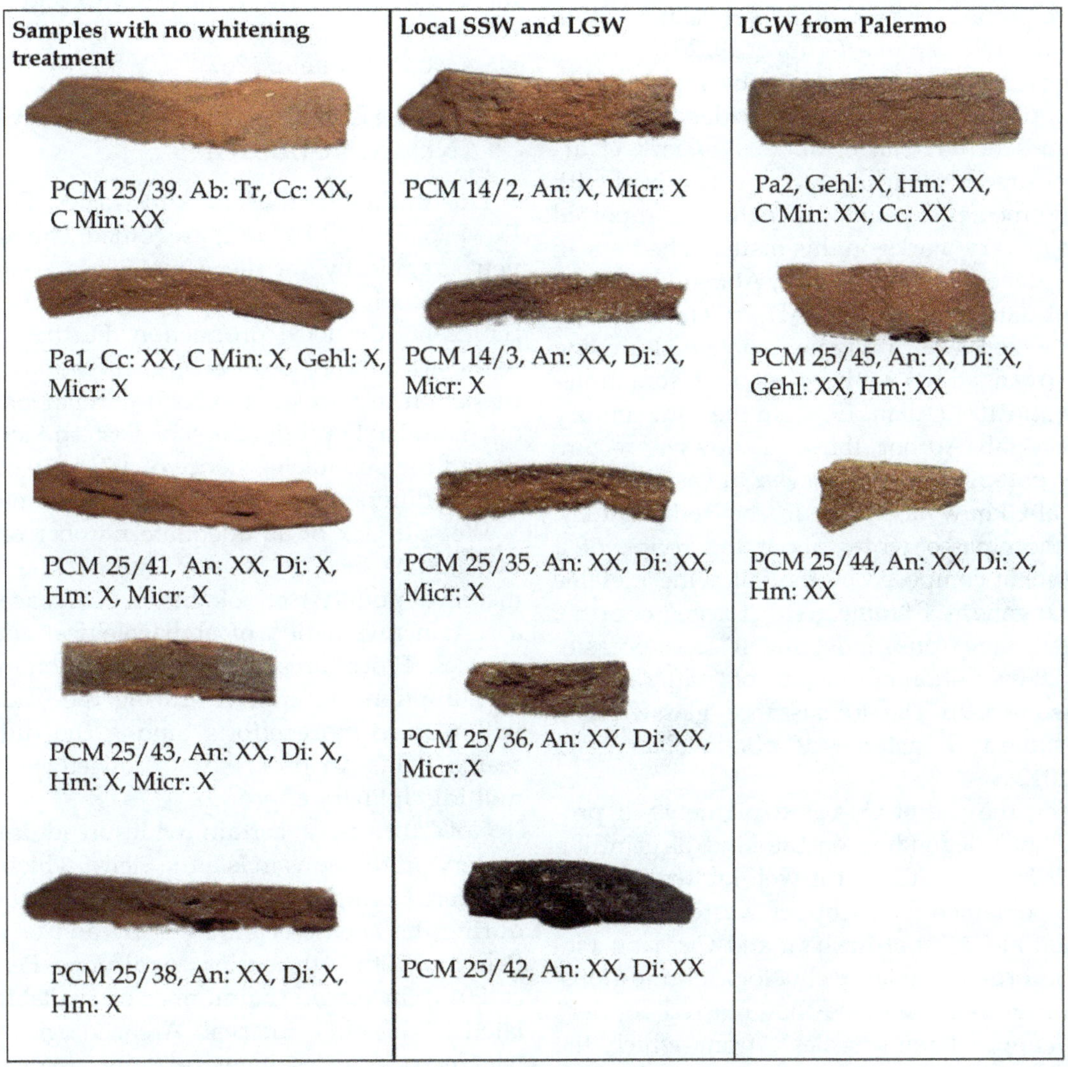

Figure 5. Ratio between whitened layer and amount of Ca-silicates.

3.4 *pXRF on glaze and pigments*

pXRF-EDS spectra have been collected on glazed surfaces. Furthermore, a wide usage of medieval sources about the glazed pottery production is proposed, with the aim to obtain a picture of the relationships existing among raw materials, craftsmen and productive networks. The chemical characterization of the pigments used for the polychrome decoration under the lead glaze (Figs. 6-7) may be summarized as follows:

- Each spectrum is dominated by the lead peaks, an evidence that confirms the technology of the glassy coating as a Pb-based glaze;
- The measure on brown pigments has shown also the peaks of manganese (Mn) and iron (Fe);
- Copper seems to be widespread on the glaze, but the green pigment displays a higher peak related to smaller ones of zinc (Zn) and sometimes tin (Sn). The use of Cu-rich pigments in Sicilian glazed pottery it is also reported in Caltagirone ceramics, dated between the 13th and the 18th century (Crupi et al., 2010).

Dark brown pigments, obtained by grinding Mn and Fe rich phases, are particularly widespread since ancient times (Colomban et al., 2001, Clark et al., 1997). The usage of manganese variously mixed with iron for the medieval palettes of potters is reported in the few literary works on this matter. The Persian potter and alchemist from Kashan, Abū al-Qāsim (its manuscript dates back to 1301 AD), refers about the *muzarrad*, which was a pigment obtained mixing *maġnisiya* (manganese) with cobalt and sometimes iron, in a ratio 10:1 (Allan, 1973). In the 14th century Cairo, the Arab Author Ibn al-Ukhuwwa recommends the potters to use the *maġnīz* in vases decoration (Ibn al-Ukhuwwa, 1976). In the 16th century, Cipriano Piccolpasso writes about the recipe of a brown pigment composed by the following metallic parts: 1 manganese, 1 "rame arso" (roasted copper), 6 "rena" (silicates from sands) and 10 lead, occasionally with the addition of one part of "zaffera nera" (Piccolpasso, 1879). The Renaissance glassworkers used the same raw materials to obtain black glass (Moretti, 2012).

Regarding the use of Cu-based pigments, it provides two hues depending on the kind of grinding process (Grifa et al., 2016). It is well known that the green color obtained from copper wastes is widely spread. Abū al-Qāsim al-Kashānī and Cipriano Piccolpasso recorded similar technological traditions. The Persian author mentions the "roasted copper" and the "copper hammerscales", from which the oxidation furnish the green pigment, as well as the yellow pigment derives from the roasted iron (Allan, 1973); the term *tūbān*, reported in the list of Ibn al-Ukhuwwa, refers to the pigment obtained from the copper oxidation (Ibn al-Ukhuwwa, 1976). Similarly, Cipriano Piccolpasso, more than two hundreds year later, says: "Take some old copper pieces and put them in the half of a pot or something else, and cook them as we will say, until the copper roasts. The best roasted copper - Dioscoride refers - is the red one, that once grinded looks like cinnabar" (Piccolpasso, 1879). The reference to the Greek author could probably explain the similarities among these traditions as far as time and space.

The presence of copper, zinc and a small amount of tin in the spectra could testify that among the "old copper pieces" there could also be some brass and bronze pieces. This hypothesis is supported also by the Renaissance glassworkers that called "Orpello", "Tremolante" and "Canterello" the brass foils, melted in order to obtain an intense green glass (Moretti, 2012). Furthermore, some partnerships between glassworkers and metal smiths are registered among the documents of the Geniza (Cairo, Egypt), probably due to the provision of raw materials used for glass works (Goitein, 1967).

4. ARCHAEOLOGICAL CONSIDERATIONS AND CONCLUSIONS

Due to the fact that the kiln wastes (PCM 25/35, PCM 25/36, PCM 25/42) are joined, chemically and petrographically, in the same fabric A with some other samples, we can propose that this ensemble represents the local production. Further researches will clarify the reasons behind the additional differentiation in two sub-fabrics, the relationships with other probable productions of Eastern Sicily (Fabric B) and the possible existence of a "group of ateliers" among different and more or less close centers.

We still lack of an adequate number of archaeometric data in order to start writing the history of medieval pottery technologies in Sicily, as well as of a certain revaluation of archaeological and written sources. Procedures of production, commerce and consumption of ceramics during the Middle Ages will require more efforts among the different research fields, in order to acknowledge a valuable multidisciplinary approach.

Nevertheless, a certain widespread interest for pottery productions in Islamic Sicily, which products circulated along the shores of Central Mediterranean during the apex of Fatimid Sicily and of its capital Palermo (10th-11th century, Ardizzone, Pezzini, Sacco 2015), increased the number of available data related to this time interval. Archaeological and archaeometric studies have partially characterized at least five centers of production: the *madīna Ṣiqilliya* (Palermo), Mazara del Vallo (Molinari and Valente,

1995, Molinari, 2010; 2012), Agrigento (Bonacasa Carra and Ardizzone, 2007), Piazza Armerina (Alaimo et al., 2010, Pensabene et al., 2014, Alfano et al., 2015) and Syracuse (Fiorilla, 2009, Ben Amara et al., 2009). To this list, we can now add Paternò, that is probably just one of the different centres of production around Mt. Etna, which products seem to have competed with Palermo's pots especially at the end of the Islamic period, as witnessed by certain archaeological finds in Southern Italy (Arthur, 1986, pp. 546-547, Fig. 1.4 e p. 554. Molinari, 1995, p. 194). However, the ceramic records studied for this archaeological site suggests two more reflections linked to the documentary and literary data.

We found that between the beginning and the end of the Islamic phase in Paternò (Phases IV and V, 10th-beginning of the 11th century and throughout the 11th century, respectively), the widest local production is constituted by the whitened pots, tiles, bricks and pipes (Fig. 8, Table 8.1). Considering that all the local glazed pottery and part of the cooking and painted wares were provided with a light surface, we can imagine that the craftsmen widely used one of the main local raw materials: clay and salt from the Salinelle, surrounding the northern and eastern sides of the hill. This fact is remarkably related to some medieval documents – which date from the 12th century onwards - testifying that at least one area of production was closely related to the main monuments of the hilltop. Among the wells donated by the local lords (Henry and his son, Simon Aleramico), a *cretazzu* in the nearby of the Church of S. Leonardo is registered (Ardizzone 1927, pp. 37-38). Even if this term probably needs more philological insights, C. Ardizzone possibly related it to the *stazzuni* (i.e., an area of production containing a built kiln) painted in the "*Pianta di Paternò, e terre concesse dal Conte Henrico alla Chiesa di Giosafat*", drawn and written in the 16th century when the priory of S. Mary of Giosafat entered into the properties of the monastery of S. Nicolò l'Arena in Catania (Fig. 8.2). The view depicted the north-western of the suburbs (*propre Castrum* in the documents). We can reasonably assume that the main area of production - equipped also with sources for the water supply (Fig. 8.3) – could be situated in this zone, since the most important related evidences have been found in the northern slope of the hill, where we can see the rest of the *stazzuni* depicted in the 16th century. The geological features of this territory fit with an important archaeological find that well testifies a glazed pottery production in the nearby: a fragment of a kiln bar with a significant drop of glaze (Fig. 8.1). Future characterizations of the clay sediments from the Salinelle, as well as further archaeological prospections and excavations, will provide accurate details on this productive landscape.

Another important datum derives from the percentages of Palermo's glazed products during the first Islamic period (Phase IV of the archaeological excavation north of Cristo al Monte church, *supra*): almost the entire lead glazed ware records of the UUSS related to this phase (10th-early 11th century) come from the Emiral Capital of Sicily (Table 8.2). This important remark not only fits well with the studies about the distribution of Palermo's products along the coasts of the Central Mediterranean (Fig. 10.1), but the kind of pottery – almost totally bowls and plates, with a few amphorae (Fig. 10.2) - that circulates even suggests an interesting philological interpretation of an Arabic text. In fact, the Arab geographer Ibn Ḥawqal has described, in his *Ṣūrat al-arḍ*, the markets (*aswāq*, sing. *sūq*) of this *madīna* and among the merchants and craftsmen he reports a "group" (or "community", *ṭā'ifa*, Raymond, 1997; Geoffroy, 2000) of *ġaḍā'iriyyūn*. Such a term could be translated with "manufacturer of porcelain-like translucent dishes" (Goitein, 1967, pp. 110-111, Shatzmiller, 1994, pp. 117-118) – as inferred from the word *ġaḍā'ir* (sing. *ġaḍār*, *ġiḍār* and *ġuḍār*), which means "plates", *scutella* (Dozy, 1881, vol. 2, p. 216, Fili, 2003, pp. 401, 404-406) and also to the other recurrance of this kind of craftsman along the *dār al-Islām* for the same period. This short passage (Ibn Ḥawqal, 1992, p. 114), which will deserve more attention in the future, seems to suggest that during the visit of the geographer in 973 AD, an important number of artisans were engaged in the production of these particular products.

Such a high-specialized industry should not be surprising: the documents of the Geniza testify that an enormous numbers of craftsmen of different kinds (over 450: Goitein, 1997, Shatzmiller, 1994) operated in the sector of ceramics, which seems to have known this kind of specialization.

Further multidisciplinary researches will have to better focus on the production procedures of the different artisans, the channels of communications in which their products circulated and their consumptions, keeping in mind this peculiar aspect of the pottery industry in the Islamic world.

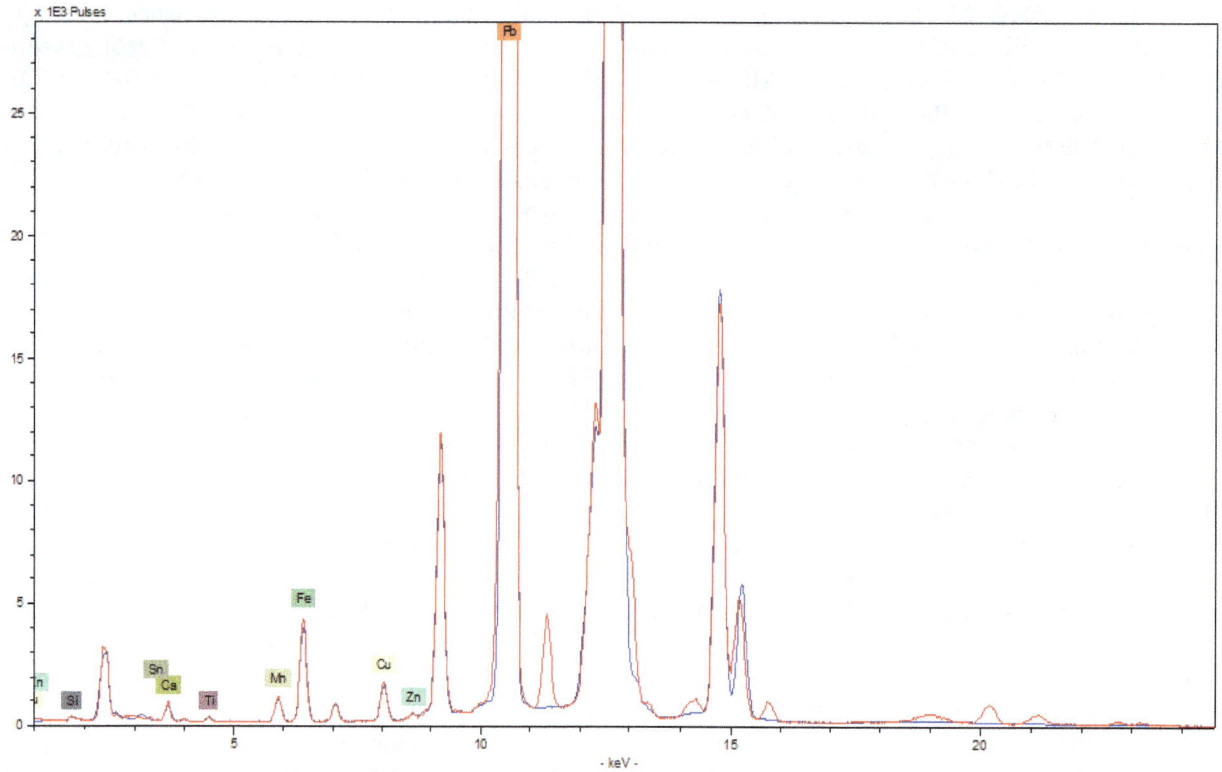

Figure 6. XRF-EDS spectrum of brown pigment on sample Pa2.

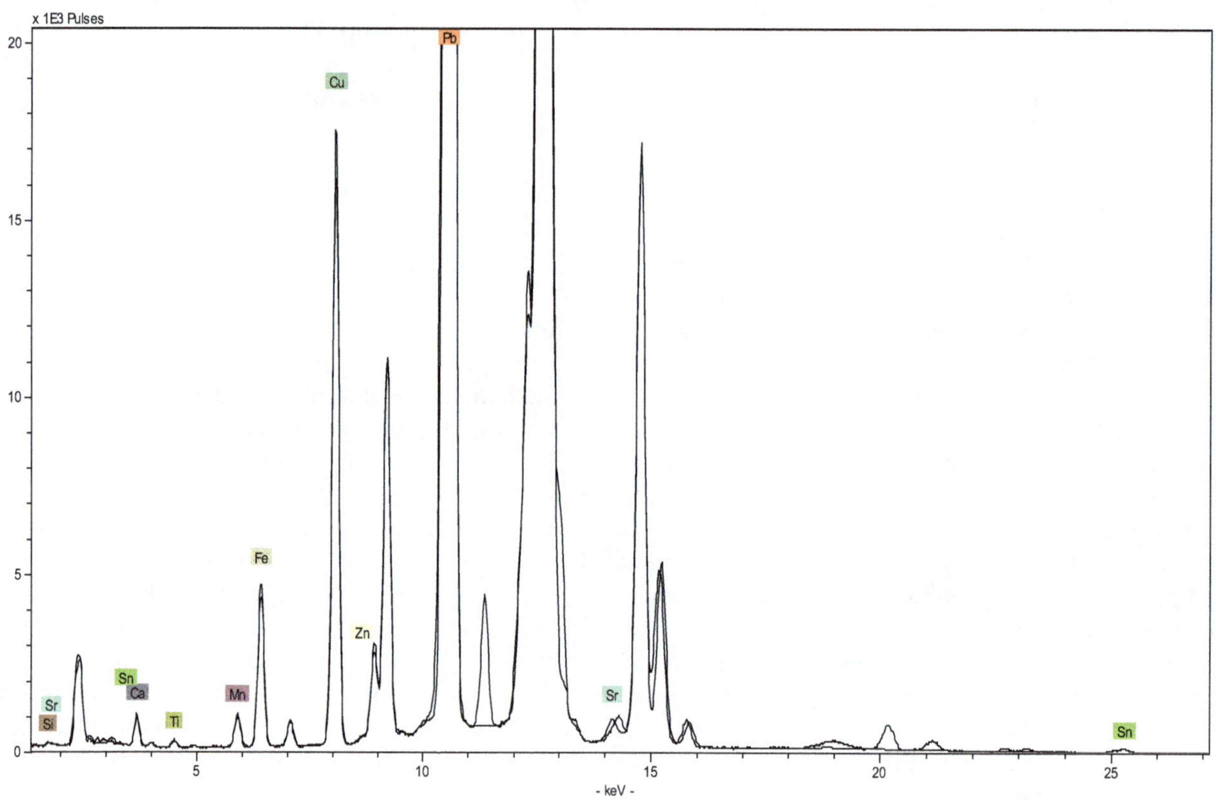

Figure 7. XRF-EDS spectrum of green pigment on sample Pa2.

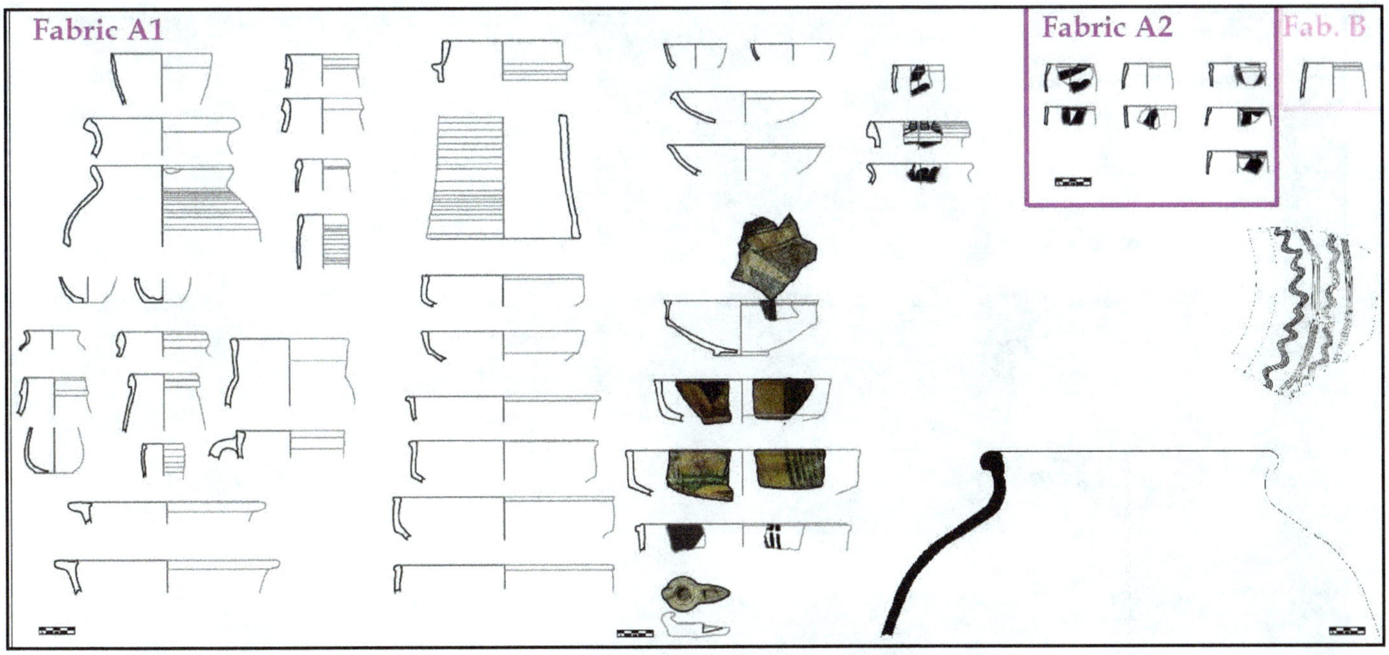

Figure 8. Local products (Fabric A1-A2) and probable Eastern Sicilian importations (Fabric B). The impressed jar at the bottom right drawn by S. Arrabito.

Table 8 - Ceramic records for the Islamic phase of the excavation at the church of Cristo al Monte.

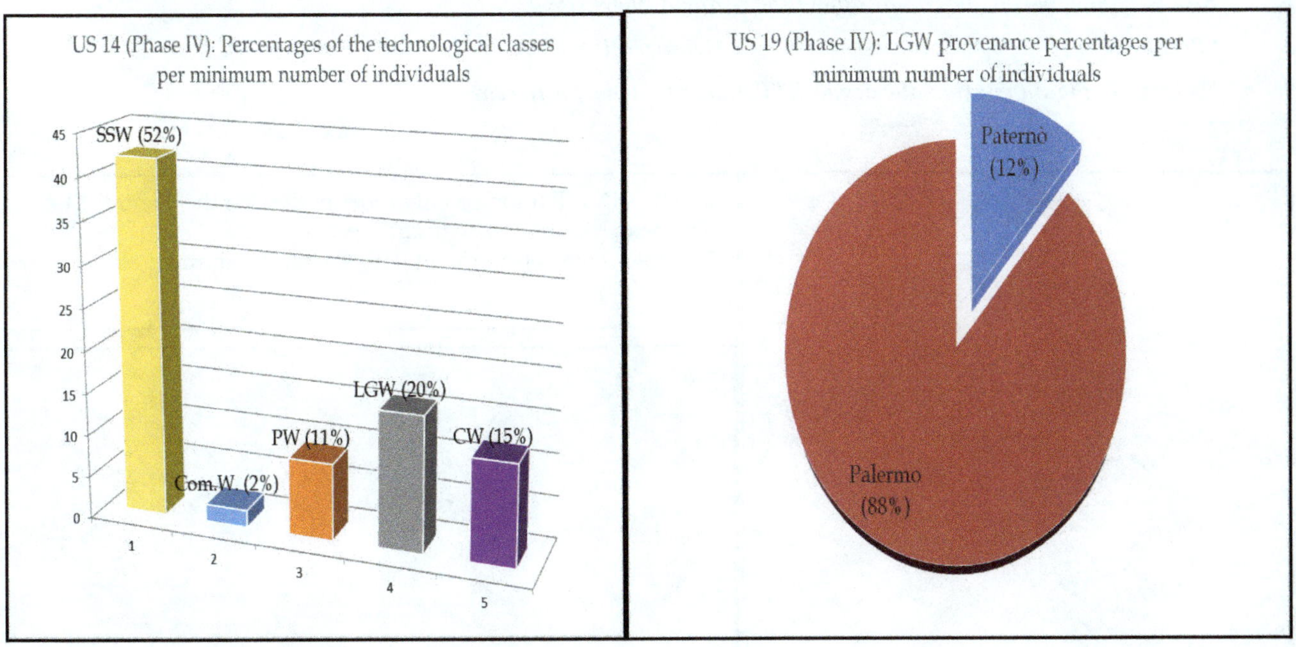

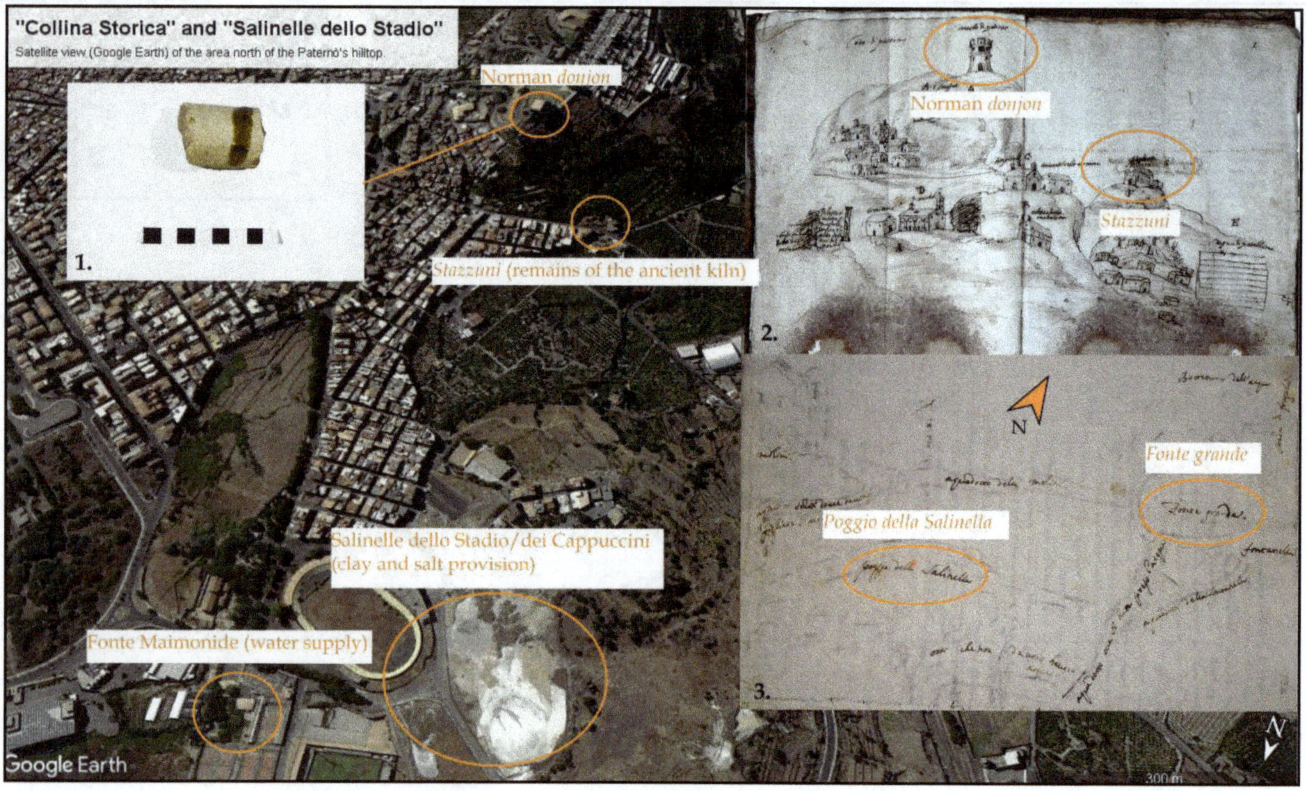

Figure 9. Probable production area in the northern slope of the hilltop of Paternò:

1. *Kiln bar found during the restoration of the Norman tower (1980's).*
2. *"Pianta di Paternò, e terre concesse dal Conte Henrico alla Chiesa di Giosafat", 16th century.*
3. *"Schizzo di pianta relativo alle acque di "Fontana Grande", 18th century*[2]*.*

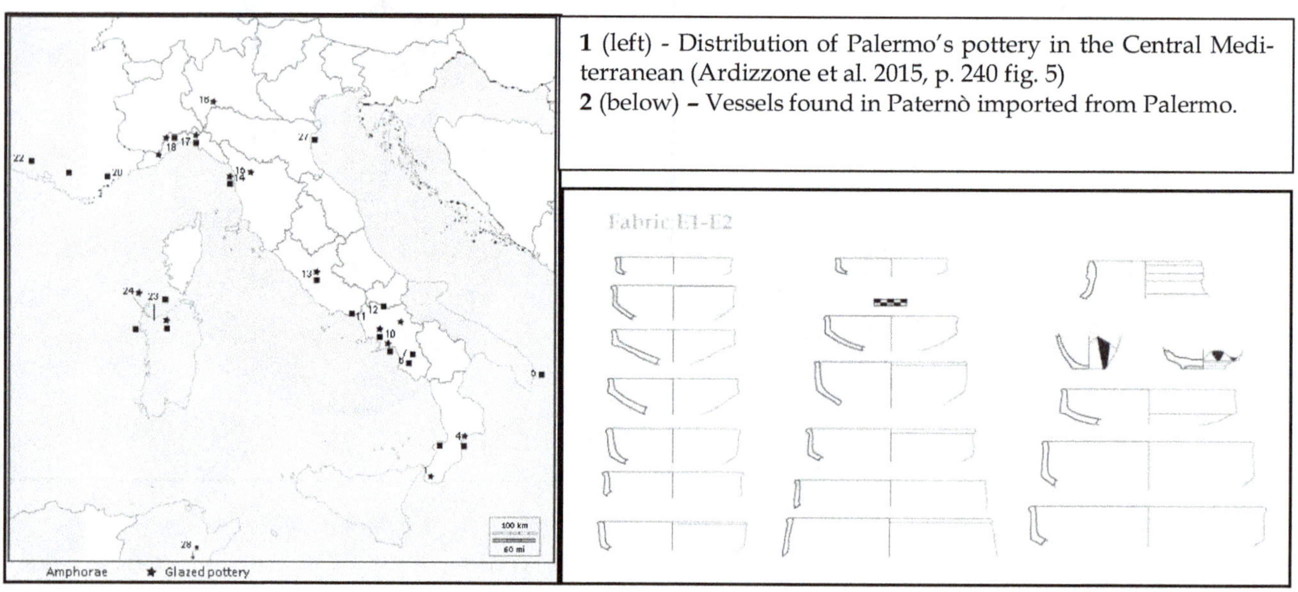

Figure 10. Palermo's products between Paternò and the Central Mediterranean.

[2] These and other interesting cartographic evidences, preserved in the Archivio di Stato of Catania, are available for free on the following site: http://www.ascatania.beniculturali.it/index.php?it/192/indice-delle-piante-topografiche.

REFERENCES

Allan, J.W. (1973), Abū 'l-Qasim's Treatise on Ceramics, *Iran*, vol. 11, pp. 111-120.

Alaimo, R., Gasparini, E., Giarrusso, R., Maggiore, G., Pensabene, P. (2010) Produzione ceramica nell'insediamento medievale presso la Villa del Casale di Piazza Armerina, in *Piazza Armerina. Villa del Casale e la Sicilia tra tardo antico e medioevo*, P. Pensabene (ed.), Roma, "L'Erma" di Bretschneider, pp. 39-60.

Al-Shorman, A.A and El-Khouri, L (2013) Archaeometric characterization of the Byzantine and Umayyad pottery at Barsinia, north Jordan. *Mediterranean Archaeology & Archaeometry.* Vol.13, No.2, 207-220.

Alaimo, R., Giarrusso, R. (2004), Indagini mineralogiche petrografiche su materiale ceramico medievale rinvenuto a Palermo in via Torremuzza, appendix to Pezzini E., Ceramica di X secolo da un saggio di scavo in via Torremuzza a Palermo, in *La ceramica altomedievale in Italia*, Patitucci Uggeri S. (ed.), Firenze, All'Insegna del Giglio, pp. 372-374.

Alaimo, R., Giarrusso, R. (2007) Caratterizzazione mineralogico-petrografica dei reperti ceramici, in *Agrigento dal Tardo Antico al Medioevo. Campagne di scavo nell'area della necropoli paleocristiana. Anni 1986-1999*, R. M. Bonacasa Carra, and F. Ardizzone (ed.), Todi, Tau Editrice, pp. 409-425 e Tavv. XXI-XXIV.

Alfano, A., Carloni, C., Pensabene, P. (2015) Produzione e circolazione presso l'insediamento medievale della Villa del Casale, in *Atti del VII Congresso Nazionale di Archeologia Medievale (Lecce, 9-12 settembre 2015)* P. Arthur, M. L. Imperiale (ed.), Firenze, All'Insegna del Giglio, vol. 2, pp. 218-222.

Amiri, M, Kouhpar, S.M.M, Neyestani. J, Nadushan, F.K (2013) Comparative study of a pottery sample from Sasanian Islamic sites of Fars and Siraf. *Mediterranean Archaeology & Archaeometry.* Vol.13, No.2, 2013, pp. 89-101

Arcifa, L. (2010) Nuove ipotesi a partire dalla rilettura dei dati archeologici: la Sicilia orientale, in *La Sicile de Byzance à l'Islam*, A. Nef, and V. Prigent (ed.), Paris, De Boccard, pp. 15-49.

Arcifa, L. (2013), Romaioi e Saraceni intorno all'827. Riflessioni sul tema della frontiera, in *La Sicilia del IX secolo tra Bizantini e Musulmani,* Modeo, S., Congiu, M., Santagati, L. (ed.), Caltanissetta 2013, pp. 161-181.

Arcifa, L., Messina, M. (c.d.s.) La frontiera arabo-bizantina in Sicilia orientale (IX-XI secolo): per uno studio dei modi di produzione, circolazione e consumo della ceramica, in *Atti VIII Congresso Nazionale di Archeologia Medievale*

Ardizzone, C. (1927) I *diplomi esistenti nella Biblioteca Comunale ai Benedettini: regesto*, Catania, Aurora 1927.

Ardizzone, F., Pezzini, E., Sacco, V. (2015) The Role of Palermo in the Central Mediterranean: the Evolution of the Harbour and the Circulation of Ceramics, *Journal of Islamic Archaeology*, vol. 2.2, pp. 229-257.

Arthur, P. (1986) Appunti sulla circolazione della ceramica medievale a Napoli, with an appendix of D. Williams, in *La ceramica medievale nel Mediterraneo occidentale. Atti del III Congresso Internazionale organizzato dal Dipartimento di Archeologia e Storia delle Arti dell'Università degli Studi di Siena e dal Museo delle Ceramiche di Faenza*, Firenze, All'Insegna del Giglio, pp. 545-554.

Arthur, P., Leo Imperiale, M. (2015) Le ceramiche di età bizantina (tardo VII-XI secolo), in *Apigliano. Un villaggio bizantino e medievale in terra d'Otranto. I reperti*, Arthur, P., Leo Imperiale, M., Tinelli M. (ed.), Apigliano Parco Archeologico, Editrice Salentina, pp. 35-46.

Barone, G., Belfiore, C. M., Mazzoleni, P., Pezzino, A., Viccaro, M. (2010) A volcanic inclusions based approach for provenance studies of archaeological ceramics: application to pottery from southern Italy, *Journal of Archaeological Science*, vol. 37, pp. 713-726.

Barone, G., Mazzoleni, P., Spagnolo, G., Aquilia, E. (2012) The transport amphorae of Gela: a multidisciplinary study on provenance and technological aspects, *Journal of Archaeological Science*, Vol. 39, pp. 11-22.

Ben Amara, A., Schvoerer, M., Fiorilla, S., Cilia Platamone, E., Thierrin-Michael, G., Delerue, S. (2009) Est-il possible de déterminer la provenance de céramiques glaçurées à décor vert et brun (Xe-XIe siècles) mises au jour en Sicile?, in *Actas del VIII Congreso Internacional de cerámica medieval en Mediterráneo (Ciudad Real-Almagro, 27 febbraio-3 marzo 2006)*, J. Zozaya, M. Retuerce, M. Á. Hervás, A. de Juan (ed.), Ciudad Real, Asociación Española de Arqueología Medieval, Vol. 1, pp. 207-214.

Bonacasa Carra, R. M., Ardizzone, F. (2007), *Agrigento dal Tardo Antico al Medioevo. Campagne di scavo nell'area della necropoli paleocristiana. Anni 1986-1999*, Todi, Tau Editrice 2007.

Bonifay, M. (2004) *Études sur la céramique romaine tardive d'Afrique*, 1301. BAR-IS, Oxford.

Clark, R. J. H., Curri, L., Henshaw, G. S., Laganara, C. (1997) Characterization of Brown-Black and Blue Pigments in Glazed Pottery Fragments from Castel Fiorentino (Foggia, Italy) by Raman Spectroscopy, X-Ray Powder Diffractometry and X-Ray Photoelectron Spectroscopy, *Journal of Raman Spectroscopy*, vol. 28, pp. 105-109.

Colomban, P., Sagon, G., Faurel, X. (2001) Differentiation of antique ceramics from the Raman spectra of their coloured glazes and paintings, *Journal of Raman Spectroscopy*, vol. 32, pp. 351-360.

Cuomo Di Caprio, N. (2007) *Ceramica in archeologia 2. Antiche tecniche di lavorazione e moderni metodi di indagine*, Roma, "L'Erma" di Bretschneider.

Cuomo Di Caprio, N., Fiorilla, S. (1992) Protomaiolica siciliana: rapporto preliminare sulla "Gela ware" e primi risultati delle analisi di microscopia ottica, *Faenza*, vol. 78, pp. 7-60.

Dozy R. (1881) *Suppléments aux Dictionnaires arabes*, Leiden, Brill, 2 voll.

Fili, A. (2003), Quelques aspects de la céramique médiévale d'après les textes arabes, in *Actas das 3.as Jornadas de Cerâmica medieval e pós-medieval. Métodos e resultados para o seu estudo*, Tondela, 28-31 October 1997, Câmara Municipal de Tondela, pp.391-406.

Fiorilla, S. (2009), Primi dati sulle produzioni ceramiche di Siracusa. Ceramiche dall'area del tempio di Apollo, in *Actas del VIII Congreso Internacional de cerámica medieval en Mediterráneo (Ciudad Real-Almagro, 27 febbraio-3 marzo 2006)*, J. Zozaya, M. Retuerce, M. Á. Hervás, A. de Juan (ed.), Ciudad Real, Asociación Española de Arqueología Medieval, Vol. 1, pp. 193-206.

Garufi, C.A (1913) Per la Storia dei secoli XI e XII. Miscellanea diplomatica IV. I de Parisio e i de Ocra nei contati di Paternò e Butera, *Archivio Storico per la Sicilia Orientale*, X, pp. 346-373.

Geoffroy, E. (2000), "ṭā'ifa", s.v. in *The Encyclopedia of Islam*, vol. X, PJ. Bearman, Th. Bianquis, C. E. Bosworth, E. Van Donzel, W. P. Heinrichs (ed.), Leiden, Brill, pp. 116-117.

Giarrusso, R., Mulone, A. (2014) Caratterizzazione mineralogico-petrografica di campioni ceramici provenienti da Castello - S. Pietro, dalla Chiesa della Gancia (Palermo) e da Castello della Pietra (Castelvetrano), in *Les dynamiques de l'islamisation en Méditerranée centrale et en Sicile: nouvelles proposiions et découvertes recentes*, A. Nef, F. Ardizzone (ed.), Roma-Bari, Ècole française de Rome, Edipuglia 2014 pp. 191-195.

Goitein, S.D. (1967), *A Mediterranean society. The Jewish communities of the Arab world as portrayed in the documents of the Cairo Geniza. Vol. I Economic foundations*, Berkeley-Los Angeles-London, University of California Press.

Grifa, C., Cavassa, L., De Bonis, A., Germinario, C., Guarino, V., Izzo, F., Kakoulli, I., Langella, A., Mercurio, M., Morra, V. (2006) Beyond Vitruvius: New Insight in the Technology of Egyptian Blue and Green Frits, *Journal of the American Ceramic Society*, vol. 99, pp. 3467-3475.

Houel, J. (1977) *Viaggio in Sicilia e a Malta*, G. Macchia, L. Sciascia, G. Vallet (ed.), Palermo-Napoli, "Storia di Napoli e della Sicilia" Società Editrice.

Ibn al-Ukhuwwa (1976) *Ma'ālim al-qurba fī aḥkām al-ḥisba*, ed. M. M. Sha'bān, Cairo, al-Hay'a al-Miṣriyya al-'Āmma li-l-Kitāb.

Ibn Ḥawqal (1992) *Ṣūrat al-arḍ*, Beirut, Dār Maktaba al-Ḥayāt.

Molinari, A. (1995) La produzione e la circolazione delle ceramiche siciliane nei secoli X-XIII, in *Actes du 5ème Colloque sur la Céramique Médiévale en Méditerranée Occidentale*, Rabat, pp. 191-204.

Molinari, A. (2010) La ceramica siciliana di età islamica tra interpretazione etnica e socio-economica, with an appendix of Cassai D., in *Piazza Armerina. Villa del Casale e la Sicilia tra tardo antico e medioevo*, P. Pensabene (ed.), Roma, "L'Erma" di Bretschneider, pp. 197-228.

Molinari, A. (2012) La bottega del vasaio di Mazara, in *Islam in Sicilia. Un giardino tra due civiltà. Archeologia dell'Islam in Sicilia*, A. Bagnera (ed.), Gibellina, Assessorato Regionale al Turismo Sport e Spettacolo - Fondazione Orestiadi, pp. 36-37.

Molinari, A., Valente, I. (1995) La ceramica medievale proveniente dall'area di Casale Nuovo (Mazara del Vallo) (seconda metà X/XI secolo), in *Actes du 5ème Colloque sur la Céramique Médiévale en Méditerranée Occidentale*, Rabat pp. 416-420.

Moretti, C. (2012) La pratica chimica dei vetrai del Rinascimento. La preparazione delle materie prime (I Parte). Introduzione e descrizione dei procedimenti, *Rivista della Stazione Sperimentale del Vetro*, 42-4, pp. 24-39.

Nef, A. (2011) Comment les Aghlabides ont décidé de conquérir la Sicile, *Annales Islamologiques*, vol. 45, pp. 191-211.

Nef, A., Ardizzone, F. (2014), *Les dynamiques de l'islamisation en Méditerranée centrale et en Sicile: nouvelles proposiions et découvertes recentes*, Roma-Bari, Ècole française de Rome, Edipuglia 2014.

Nef, A., Prigent, V. (2013), Guerroyer pour la Sicile (827-902), in *La Sicilia del IX secolo tra Bizantini e Musulmani,* Modeo, S., Congiu, M., Santagati, L. (ed.), Caltanissetta 2013, pp. 13-39.

Pellitteri, A. (1997) *I Fatimidi e la Sicilia (sec. X). Materiali per uno studio sulla Sicilia thaghr e terra di gihād con particolare riferimento a fonti ismaelite dell'epoca,* Palermo, Centro Culturale al-Farabi.

Pensabene, P., Alfano, A., Carloni, C., Ventura, M. (2014) Note preliminari sulla ceramica di età islamica prodotta ed importata alla Villa del Casale di Piazza Armerina (EN), in *Atti XLVI Convegno Internazionale della Ceramica (Savona, 24-25 maggio 2013),* Albisola, Centro Ligure per la Storia della Ceramica, pp. 307-312.

Picard, C., Borrut, A. (2003) Rābata, Ribāt, Rābita: une institution à reconsidérer, in *Chrétiens et Musulmans en Méditerranée médiévale (VIIIe-XIIIe siècle). Échanges et contacts,* N. Prouteau, Ph. Sénac (ed.), Poitiers, Centre d'études supérieures de civilisation médiévale, pp. 33-65.

Piccolpasso Durantino, C. (1879) *I tre libri dell'arte del vasajo,* G. Vanzolini (ed.) third edition, Pesaro, 1879.

Raimondo, C. (2002) Nuovi dati sulle produzioni ceramiche nella Calabria altomedievale: il caso del castrum bizantino di Santa Maria del Mare, *Archeologia Medievale,* vol. 29, pp. 511-541.

Raymond, A. (1997) "ṣinf", s.v. in *The Encyclopedia of Islam,* vol. IX ed. C. E. Bosworth, E. Van Donzel, W. P. Heinrichs, G. Lecomte, Leiden, Brill, pp. 644-645.

Sarhaddi-Dadian, H, Ramli, Z, Nik Hassan Shuhaimi, Nik Abdul Rahman & Mehrafarin, R (2015) X-Ray diffraction and X-ray fluorescence analysis of pottery shards from new archaeological survey in south region of Sistan, Iran. *Mediterranean Archaeology and Archaeometry,* Vol. 15, No 3, pp. 45-56.

Shatzmiller, M. (1994), *Labour in the Medieval Islamic World*, Leiden, Brill 1994.

4

VERIFYING THE RELIABILITY OF HISTORICAL SOURCES THROUGH A MINERALOGICAL AND PETROGRAPHIC APPROACH: THE CASE OF THE "BLACK-GREEN STONE" FROM THE MESSINA CATHEDRAL (SICILY, ITALY)

G. Sabatino[1*], M. Di Bella[1], S.Quartieri[1], A. Giuliano[2], F. Italiano[3], G. Marcianò[1], A. Tripodo[1], D. Romano[1]

[1]*Dipartimento di Scienze Matematiche e Informatiche, Scienze Fisiche e Scienze della Terra, University of Messina, Viale G. d'Alcontres 31, 98166 S. Agata, Messina*
[2]*Museo Regionale di Messina, Viale della Libertà 465, 98121 Messina*
[3]*Istituto Nazionale di Geofisica e Vulcanologia, Sez. Palermo, Via Ugo La Malfa, 153, 90146 Palermo, Italy*

Corresponding author: Giuseppe Sabatino (gsabatino@unime.it)

ABSTRACT

The aim of this work is obtaining information on the provenance of some very peculiar green (or black-green) stones used both as façade and floor decorations in the Messina Cathedral. Historical sources and available literature data suggest that these materials could belong to the amphibolite of the Peloritani Mountains. In order to verify the true provenance, some stone samples were studied through various analytical methods (SEM-EDS, XRPD, XRF). The investigated specimens resulted to be metabasites showing pseudomorphic and vein textures, with relicts of olivine replaced by serpentine - forming a mesh textures - and orthopyroxene mostly altered to bastite. Pseudomorphic minerals are serpentine (lizardite and chrysotile), magnetite, amphibole (tremolite-actinolite series) and chlorite (talc-chlorite). These results demonstrate that the analysed green stones cannot belong to the amphibolite outcrop of the Peloritani Mountains. Otherwise, they show mineralogical and petrographic features very similar to those of "verde Calabria", a rock typology largely exposed in the Northern Calabria area - belonging to the ophiolitic series - and widely used in the last century as building material.

KEYWORDS: Messina Cathedral, green decorative stones, amphibolites, petrography, Calabrian ophiolitic series

1. INTRODUCTION

During the past centuries, several historic buildings of the Messina town - as well as of some villages in the province - were widely decorated using a typical black-green stone. Important examples are visible in the façade decorations of the Messina Cathedral (Figures 1a and b). After 1908 Messina earthquake, remains of collapsed historical buildings (Fig. 1c) were saved and transferred in a vast area next to a silk factory, right out the city centre (named Filanda Mellinghof). In the same area, the City Regional Museum was then built after some decades. From these remains - coming from different known locations and provided by the Museum authority - some stone samples used for floor and façade decorations (XIIIth - XIVth century) were selected for this study, in order to define their origin provenance.

Figure 1. a) Messina Cathedral today; b) Particular of the decorative rows; c) Image of Messina Cathedral after the 1909 earthquake

The Historical Notary Archives of Messina and Palermo retain several documents reporting legal transactions and purchasing of decorative stones. Some examples are reported in the following.

1- Legal transaction 1494-1500. "... in lu quali autarectu sia unu pavimentu a scaccheri di petri russi et nigri di Zaffaria..." and then " ... lu quali pavimentu divi esseri laboratu di petri russi di Tauromena, di nigri di Zaffaria et marmuri ..." Order for a chess-like floor and a small altar made with reddish stone from Taormina and black stones from Zafferia.
2- Legal transactions 1540-1550. "Messina 30-11-1546, pagati 27 Tarì ... a mastro Salvo di Rugeri, alias Gallo di Zaffaria. Sonno per portari petri nigri di Zaffaria, iuxta lu ordini et misura, chi li havi dato mastro Dominico Vanello, capo mastro scarpellino per la fruntera di nostri matri ecclesia ...". This transaction reports the date of the order – given to the artisans Salvo di Rugeri and Gallo from the Larderia and Zafferia Villages - for providing "black stones" for the building of the main Church façade.
3- "Messina 22-12-1550"...unza 1.12, pagati per comandamento di lo ditto mastro di opera Angilo di Rugeri, alias Gallo di Zaffaria. Etso per prezo di novanta pezi di petra nigra a gr. 9 per uno, stimati per mastro Bastiano Fiorentino et mastro Leonardo Carrara, mastri Scarpellini, approbato per lo m.co Jo. Angelo Montursulo, capomastro scultori di la ecclesia: quali petri hanno servir per lo pavimento, che si fa in la nostra matri ecclesia ... pagati per lo banco di Ansaluni unsa 1.12 ..." In this transaction, dated a couple of years after the first quoted one, a reference is made to stone workers - who followed the florentine architect Montorsoli (known to work in the Church in that period) - using the mentioned stones for the floor decorations of the Main Church.

These documents indicate, as material provenance, the quarries located in the nearby of the Larderia Village (Peloritani Mt., about 8 km South of Messina) and in the close Zafferia Village, where metamorphic amphibolitic rocks belonging to the Aspromonte Unit outcrop.

Moreover, in two previous studies performed by Stagno and Zipelli (1985) and Principato and Triscari (1999), the black-green stone used in many façade and floor decorations was classified as an "amphibolite" from the Peloritani Mountains.

To verify the reliability of the historical sources and to provide more precise information on this decorative material, we carried out an archaeometrical characterization of four stone fragments through a multidisciplinary approach, involving petrographic, mineralogical and chemical analysis.

1.1 HISTORY OF THE MESSINA CATHEDRAL AND FINDINGS IN SAID PROVINCE OF THE INVESTIGATED STONES

The most impressive historical evidence here discussed is the Messina Cathedral (XIIIth - XIVth century). The foundation of this church is probably dated to the Norman Roger II. The official consecration took place on September 22th, 1197 in the presence of Emperor Henry VI. From ongoing research, it seems that at the time of the consecration, the Cathedral was not completed, either in the structural and decorative parts.

Many interventions were made - since the middle of the '500 - by the Florentine architect Giovanangelo Montorsoli (pupil of Michelangelo), who, according to some documents, worked on the main façade and to some of the floor decorations. The façade (Fig. 1a) - originally decorated in the XIV cent. and completed in the XVII cent. – presents now about 20 rows of a geometric inlay decoration performed with black-green stones embedded in a Carrara white marble support (Fig. 2 a-e), alternating with reddish Mesozoic limestones coming from a quarry near Taormina (50 Km to the South) (Bottari 1929).

A wonderful geometric mosaic originally covered the entire Cathedral floor, but it was destroyed during the 1908 earthquake (Triscari 2010). After this event, a new floor was built. The present one (Fig. 2c-d-e-f) was made in 1945-47, after the heavy damages following the anglo-american bombing of the town occurred on June 1943. For the same reason, the original twenty façade marble inlay decoration rows were reduced to only nine (Fig. 1a and b) and subsequently reconstructed with the original marble fragments. The original recovered portions - both of the floor and of the front wall decoration - are still preserved in the Regional Museum of Messina and attributed to this church on the basis of recent artistic/historical studies (Giuliano 2012). Messina Museum also preserves some fragments of the wall and floor decoration - apparently coming from the Cathedral - with fantastic animal figures, probably dated XIIIth or beginning of XIVth century (Giuliano 2015; Fig. 2e).

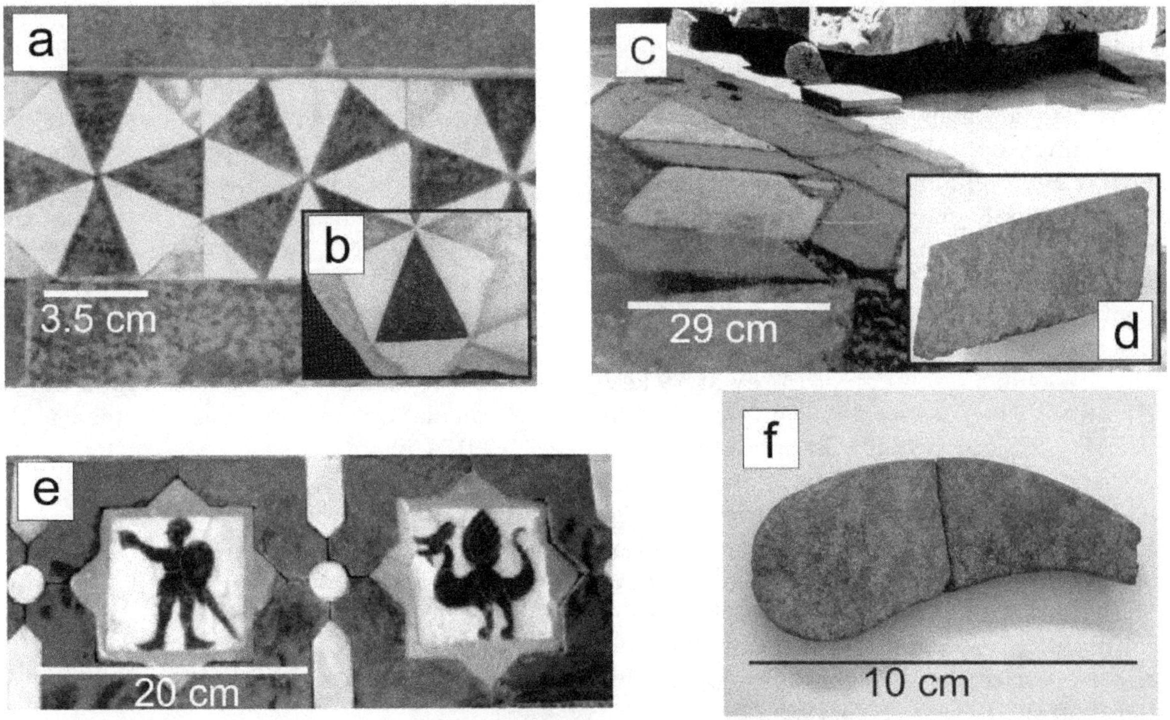

Figure 2. a) Geometric inlay decoration in black-green stones embedded in a Carrara white marble from the façade and b) particular; c-d) portion of a decorative band from the original floor; e); fragments of wall/floor decoration with fantastic animal figures; f) ornament from the façade

In the Messina Museum collections and deposits, fragment specimens coming from other unknown sites are preserved, together with an impressively large jar (about 60 cm high) entirely excavated in a single block of this supposed "amphibolite" and probably originally exhibited in the Cathedral.

The peculiar black-green stone was also largely used for the floor decoration of the S. Francesco all'Immacolata Church, built in 1254. Also this floor was destroyed during 1908 earthquake, but the preservation of the original materials allowed its partial reconstruction. Nowadays, the church floor is formed by at least the 30% of the original decorations.

No further uses of this black-green stone are known in the Messina area or in the surrounding, except for part of a geometric floor decoration of the main Church of Casalvecchio Siculo (about 30 km South of Messina), dated before the XVIIth century (Di Bella et al. 2010).

As clearly evident from this introduction, the only information on the provenance of this black-green stone derives from historical documents of financial transactions (payments for the provided materials and for the performed works) and by the archaeological research conducted by the Regional Museum of Messina. However, no specific archaeometric data are available. This work aims at filling this gap by providing mineralogical and petrographic evidence, essential for ascertaining the true provenance area of this building material.

2. SAMPLES AND ANALYTICAL METHODS

The decoration specimens from the Messina Cathedral (Fig. 2) were provided by the Regional Museum of Messina. Specifically:

- sample MC1: from the Cathedral façade decorations (Fig. 2a, b)
- sample MC2: from the Cathedral façade decorations (Fig. 2e)
- sample MC3: tile from the floor (Fig. 2c-d)
- sample MC4: decorative frieze (Fig. 2f).

To minimize the damage, a small piece of each sample was extracted from the rear surface of the fragments. From each fragment, the corresponding thin section was made to perform petrographic and Scanning Electron Microscopy-EDS (SEM-EDS) investigations. Small portions of the three samples (MC2, MC3, MC4) were powdered to perform X-ray Powder Diffraction (XRPD) analyses, whereas the triangular decorative tile MC1 was not powdered and directly analyzed, due to its small size. Bulk composition was determined for all the samples measuring major and some trace elements concentration by X-ray Fluorescence (XRF) analysis. Analytical investigations were performed using the instruments of the CERISI Geochemical Laboratory, the Earth

Sciences Laboratory and the Diffractometric Laboratory of the University of Messina.

Specifically:

a) Petrographic analyses were performed by polarizing optical microscopy, to define texture and preliminary mineral composition;

b) Micro-textural and compositional analyses were made by an ESEM-FEI Inspect-S electron microscope coupled with an Oxford INCA PentaFETx3 EDX spectrometer, a Si(Li) detector equipped by a ATW2 ultra-thin window with a resolution of 137 eV at 5.9 keV (Mn Kα1). The spectral data were acquired in ESEM (Environmental Scanning Electron Microscope) conditions at a working distance of 10 mm, with an accelerating voltage of 20 kV, counting time of 60 s, count rate of approximately 3000 cps with dead time below 30%. The results were processed by INCA Energy software. This software uses the XPP matrix correction scheme developed by Pouchou and Pichoir (1984, 1985).

c) X-ray powder diffraction analyses were carried out using a BRUKER D8 ADVANCE diffractometer, with Cu Kα radiation, on a Bragg-Brentano theta-theta goniometer equipped with a SiLi solid-state detector Sol-X. Acquisition conditions are 40 KV and 40 mA. Scans were performed typically from 2 to 80 degrees 2ϑ, with step size of 0.02 degrees 2ϑ, with a counting time of 1 second. Observed peak positions were matched against the ICDD-JCPDS database. The data analysis was performed using EVA software. The raw diffraction scans were stripped of Kα2 component, the background was corrected and the digital data were smoothed with a Fourier digital filter. The observed peak positions (Fig. 4) were matched against the ICDD JCPDS database.

d) Chemical analyses were performed by wave length dispersion XRF spectrometry (WDXRF), measuring major, minor and trace elements with a Bruker model S8 Tiger setup (Bruker 2015a, b). The excitation source was a Rh tube at 4 kW. The power and the current intensity were changed according to the analyzed element and their amounts, in order to avoid detector saturation. The concentrations of major and minor elements were calculated through the software package GEO-QUANT M, an accurate method for measuring 11 elements using more than 20 certified materials as standards in the calibration process (Bruker 2015a, b). The software GEO-QUANT T was used for the calculation of the trace elements (Bruker 2015a, b).

3. RESULTS

3.1 Messina Cathedral stones

From the macroscopic point of view, the studied rock samples are dark-green to greyish-green in colour, and are characterized by the peculiar presence of swarthy patches and a schistose structure. Petrographic investigations reveal different degrees of pseudomorphic serpentinization. Colourless to pale-green serpentine replaces olivine, forming polygonal mesh texture arranged as an irregular network among olivine relics, and filling cracks within olivine porphyroclasts. The samples show mainly pseudomorphic to relict-granular texture, with minor portions characterized by nematoblastic structure (Fig. 3 a-b-e-f). The main parageneses include serpentine, relicts of olivine and pyroxene, with variable amount of amphibole, chlorite, talc and opaque minerals.

The mineralogical analysis of the four samples provided evidence for the presence of clinochlore, tremolite, clinochrysotile, lizardite, forsterite, and talc (Fig. 4). The amounts of these phases in the studied samples - determined by Rietveld method and expressed in weight % - range as following: clinochlore (60.5 - 31.1 %), tremolite (12 - 31 %), clinochrysotile (11 - 32 %), lizardite (6 - 17 %), forsterite (0 - 5 %) and talc (0.9 - 1.8 %).

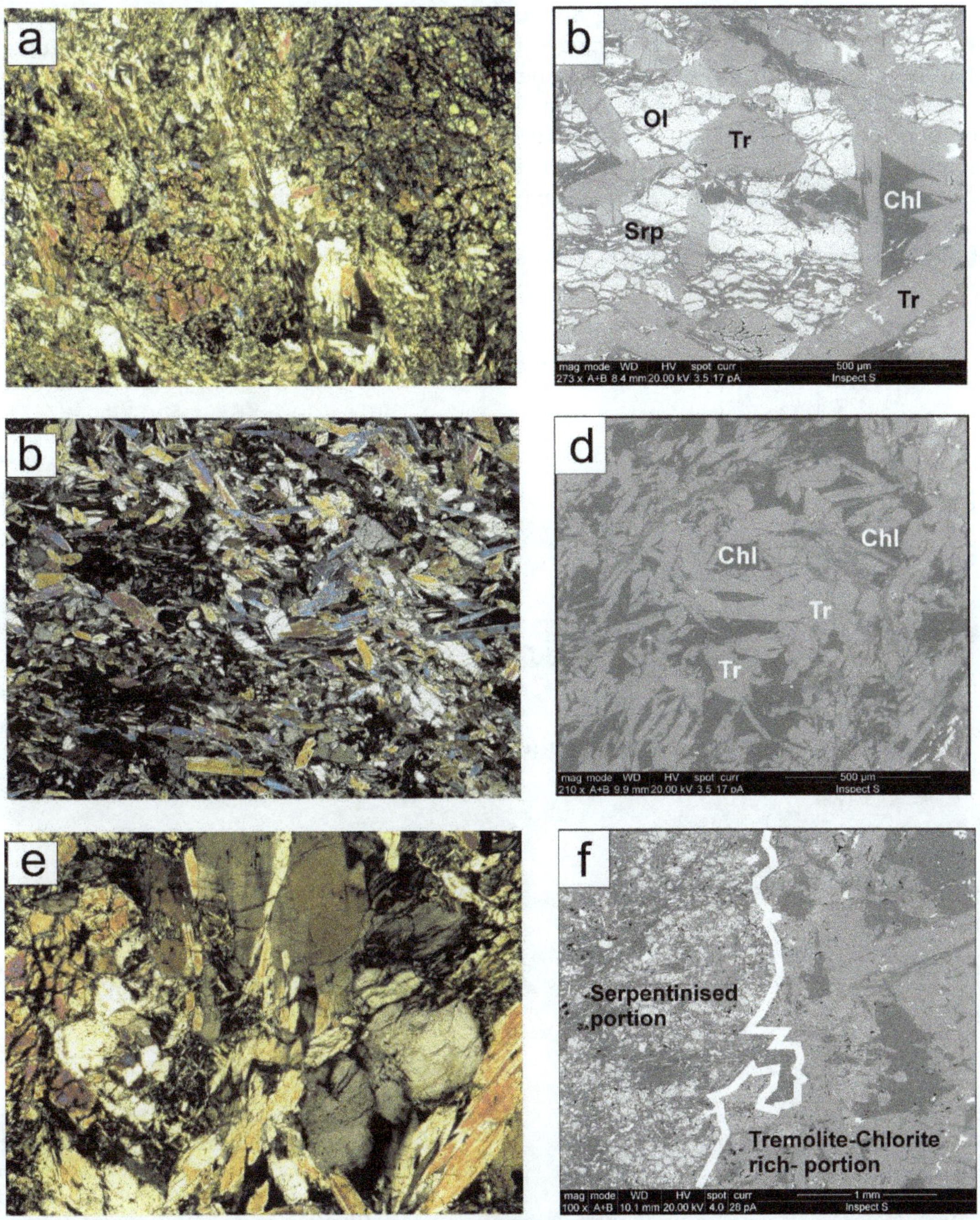

Figure 3. Crossed polar light photomicrographs of the representative structures of the studied stone samples (a-c-e) and SEM-EDS images of some selected area (b-d-f). In details: (a, b) serpentinized micro-domains displaying pseudomorphic to relict-granular texture; (c, d) tremolite- and chlorite-bearing micro-domain; (e, f) contact between the two different types of micro-domains.

The characteristic dark speckles visible on the hand specimens represent the serpentine-rich areas characterized by mesh texture juxtaposed to nematoblastic amphibole- and chlorite-rich portions. In particular, hetero-granular *olivine* is in colourless dismembered relict crystals. SEM-EDS analyses (Tab. 1) show forsterite-rich compositions (~ 80% Fo). The grains are pseudomorphically replaced by meshwork isotropic serpentine (Fig. 3a-b). The replacement starts along the crystal boundaries and proceeds inwards. *Serpentine* group minerals occur as the polymorphs lizardite and chrysotile, as evidenced by XRPD analysis (Fig. 4). Minor amounts of *orthopyroxene* grains appear deeply replaced by "bastite". *Amphibole* is in randomly oriented stubby-prismatic to long-prismatic colourless nematoblastic crystals (Fig. 3c-d), that - based on the optical features, the chemical composition (Table 1) and the XRPD data (Fig. 4) – can be classified as tremolite. Its composition is better defined using the relative amphibole classification diagram (Meeker et al., 2006) reported in Fig. 5a. *Chlorite* forms small-sized colourless and irregular flakes (Fig. 3c-d), having anomalous brown interference colours, usually arranged in close spatial association with the serpentine minerals. It is Mg-rich (Mg# = 0.94) and compositionally defined as clinochlore. On the relative classification diagram (Hey 1954; Fig. 5b) its composition falls in the talc-chlorite field. *Magnetite* is the most common opaque mineral phase and is produced as a consequence of olivine serpentinization. It forms small irregular grains frequently scattered in the rock, mainly among serpentine and chlorite minerals. Chemical data indicate a chromium enrichment (Table 1). Among the opaque minerals, also abundant Ni-rich sulphides grains were found (Table 1). Calcite veins occur rarely.

Overall, the chemical, mineralogical and petrographic data suggest that the studied stones may be classified as serpentinized ultramafic rocks.

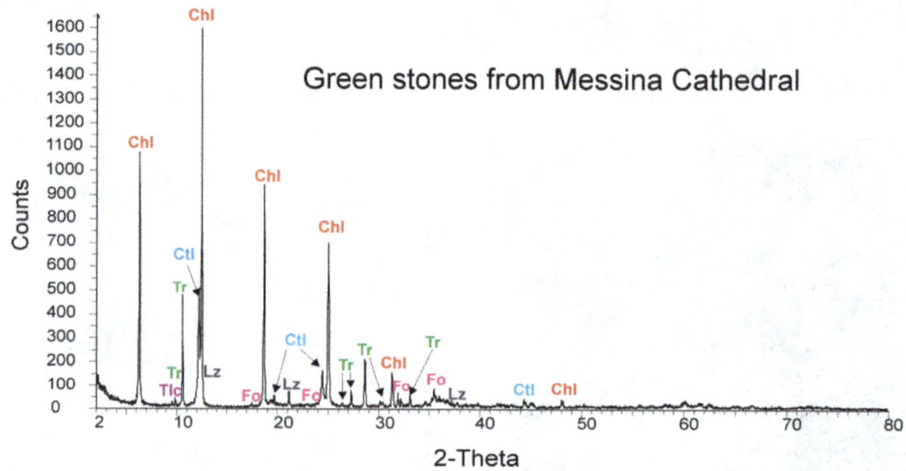

Figure 4. X-ray powder diffraction pattern representative of the analyzed green stones.

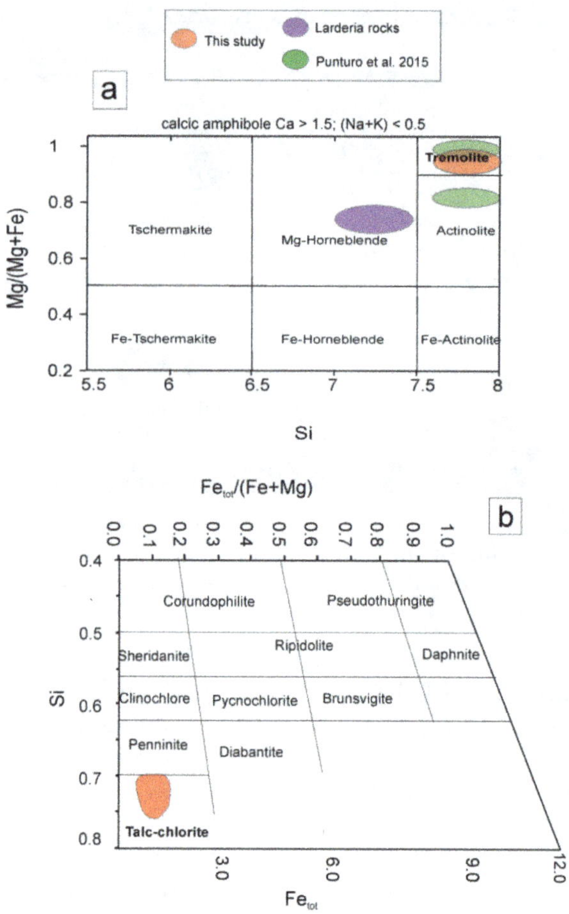

Figure 5. Classification of analyzed amphibole after Leake et al. (1997) (a) and chlorite according to Hey (1954) (b) - For comparison, the areas of the amphibole from Larderia amphibolites and from the Calabrian serpentinites (Punturo et al., 2015) are also drawn.

Table 1 - Chemical data (SEM-EDS) of amphibole, chlorite and olivine present in the studied green-stone specimens.

	AMPHIBOLE				
SiO_2	59.72	58	60.4	58.1	58.4
TiO_2	0.88	1.61	0.63	0	0.44
Al_2O_3	3.75	4.75	3.6	1.87	1.14
FeO	24.23	25.7	23.9	4.09	4.61
MgO	11.43	9.98	11.5	25.7	25.3
CaO	0	0	0	9.77	10.2
Total	100	100	100	100	100
Si	7.963	7.77	8.04	7.78	7.81
Al^{IV}	0.037	0.23	0.04	0.22	0.18
Tot.	8	8	8	8	7.99
Al^{VI}	0.101	0.02	0.14	0.08	0
Ti	0	0	0	0	0.04
Mg	4.816	4.98	4.73	4.92	4.96
Fe	0.083	0	0.13	0	0
Tot.	5	5	5	5	5
Mg	0	0.14	0	0.21	0.08
Fe	0.335	0.53	0.27	0.46	0.52
Ca	1.633	1.43	1.64	1.4	1.46
Tot.	1.968	2.11	1.91	2.07	2.06
Mg#	0.91	0.94	0.92	0.96	0.92
Group	Calcic	Calcic	Calcic	Calcic	Calcic
Subgroup	Tr-Ac	Tr-Ac	Tr-Ac	Tr-Ac	Tr-Ac
Name	Tr	Tr	Tr	Tr	Tr

	CHLORITE				
SiO_2	44.16	42.73	42.12	45.15	41.97
Al_2O_3	12.83	13.35	14.87	9.23	14.58
Cr_2O_3	0	0.57	0	0.47	0.6
FeO	6.75	6.87	7.04	8.11	6.62
MgO	34.22	35.31	34.57	36.25	35.58
CaO	2.03	1.17	1.4	0.79	0.65
Total	100	100	100	100	100
Si	7.28	7.064	6.96	7.487	6.92
Al	2.493	2.601	2.896	1.804	2.835
Cr	0	0.075	0	0.062	0.078
Fe^{2+}	0.931	0.95	0.973	1.125	0.913
Mg	8.41	8.702	8.516	8.962	8.752
Ca	0.359	0.207	0.248	0.14	0.115
Tot.	19.474	19.598	19.592	19.58	19.618
Group	chlorite	chlorite	chlorite	chlorite	chlorite
Name	Clino-chl	Clino-chl	Clino-chl	Clino-chl	Clino-chl

	OLIVINE				
SiO_2	43.2	42.3	42.8	43.1	42.3
FeO	15.8	17.4	16.9	18.6	19.2
Al_2O_3	0.93	0.72	0.55	0.97	0.87
MgO	39.7	39.3	39.2	37.3	37.6
CaO	0.44	0.36	0.59	0	0
Total	100	100	100	100	100
Si	1.13	1.1	1.11	1.12	1.1
Al	0.03	0.02	0.02	0.41	0.42
Fe2	0.34	0.38	0.37	1.45	1.46
Mg	1.54	1.52	1.52	0.03	0.02
Ca	0.01	0.01	0.02	0	0
Tot.	3.05	3.04	3.04	3.01	3.01
End Members					
Fo	81.8	80.1	80.5	78.1	77.8
Fa	18.2	19.9	19.5	21.9	22.3

	Ni-rich SULPHIDES		
MgO	9.39	9.27	21.71
Al_2O_3	0	1.24	14.45
SiO_2	14.51	13.77	2.17
SO_3	40.59	36.91	24.31
CaO	1.93	1.36	2.54
FeO	16.23	22.78	31.46
NiO	17.36	14.69	3.38
Total	100	100	100

	Cr- rich MAGNETITE		
MgO	17.35	19.23	9.25
Al_2O_3	1.83	0	0
SiO_2	19.45	20.07	8.67
CaO	1.04	0	0.5
TiO_2	1.65	0	2.23
V_2O_5	0.87	0	0.93
Cr_2O_3	10.49	4.47	5.52
FeO	47.32	56.23	72.9
Total	100	100	100

3.2 ASPROMONTE-PELORITANI UNIT AND THE AMPHIBOLITES FROM LARDERIA

The Peloritani Mts. constitute the Sicilian portion of the Calabria–Peloritani Arc, a tectono-metamorphic edifice characterized by a complex folded geological structure, where several metamorphic units are recognized (Bonardi et al. 1976; Messina et al. 1995, 1997). The locality of Larderia, indicted in the historical sources as the provenance quarry area of the green building stones, belongs mainly to the Aspromonte Unit. This Unit consists of amphibolite-facies metamorphic rocks, mainly represented by paragneiss, migmatitic paragneiss and augen gneiss, with minor marble and amphibolite, diffusively intruded by late Variscan granitoid plutons. In the same area, sporadic outcrops of the Mela Unit are also exposed, consisting of a poli-metamorphic basement represented mainly by paragneiss and micaschist, with subordinate meta-mafic rocks and silicates marble. It must be underlined that no outcrops of serpentinitic tremolite-bearing rocks occur in the Peloritani Metamorphic Units, because the origin of these rocks is linked to a different/peculiar evolution process.

Some mafic rocks from Larderia and Zafferia localities, belonging to the Aspromonte metamorphic Unit (Peloritani Mts.), were collected for this study and analysed through SEM-EDS and XRPD (Fig. 6).

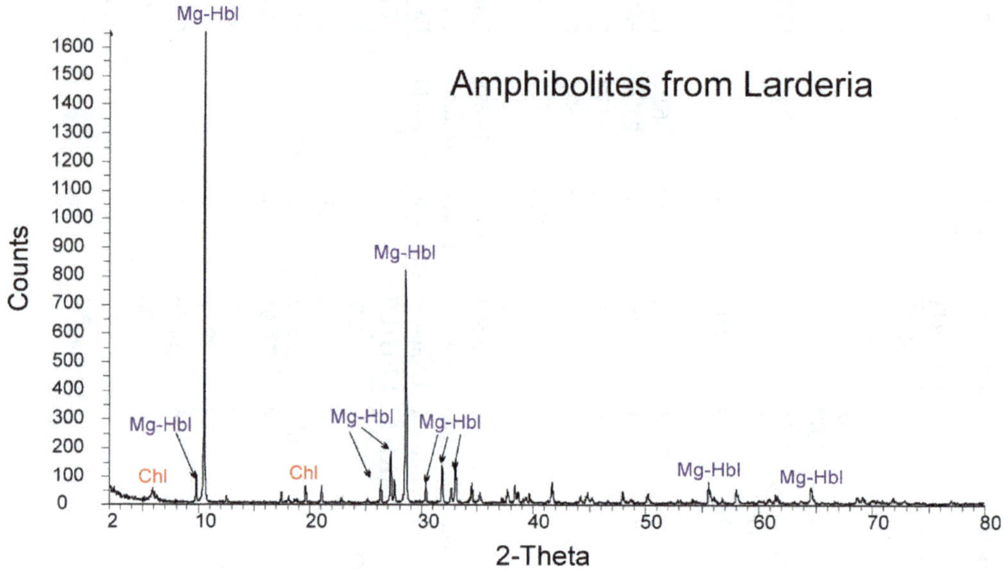

Figure 6. X-ray powder diffraction pattern of amphibolite sample from Larderia

The samples show dark green colour, foliated structure and fine to medium grain-size. They result to be amphibolite or metahorneblendite, composed by prevalent granoblastic to nematoblastic green Mg-hornblende (95%), minor chlorite, rare plagioclase, and titanite (3%), magnetite and zircon as accessory minerals. These mineralogical and petrographic features are not compatible with those of the studied ornamental stones.

4. DISCUSSION

All the previously reported information about the metamorphic rocks from the Larderia area - and in general from the Aspromonte Unit and Peloritani Mts. metamorphic units - points towards different compositional and structural features with respect to those of the green stones here studied.

Differently, we suggest that our samples could derive from the Calabrian ophiolite sequences of the Calabrian Peloritanian Arc (Fig. 7). Indeed, similar rocks - commercially known as "pietra verde" ("green stone") or "Verde Calabria" - are very abundant in the Sila Piccola and Catena Costiera, and have been extensively used in the past as building and decorative materials. The terms "green stone" or "black-green stone" include two lithotypes: serpentinite and metabasite associated in ophiolitic sequences, both having been quarried and used as construction material (Rodolico 1946). The quarrying district "Verde Calabria", with its main sites in the territory of the villages of Conflenti, Martirano, Decollatura and Gimigliano (South-Eastern Sila Piccola; Punturo et al. 2004, 2015), and in the Mt. Reventino area (South-Western Sila Piccola), constituted an important economic reality linked to the extraction and processing of green stone since prehistoric times (Punturo et al. 2004, 2015; Zakrzewska et al. 2008). The most famous "green stone" masons worked in Delianuova (Calabria) until a few decades ago.

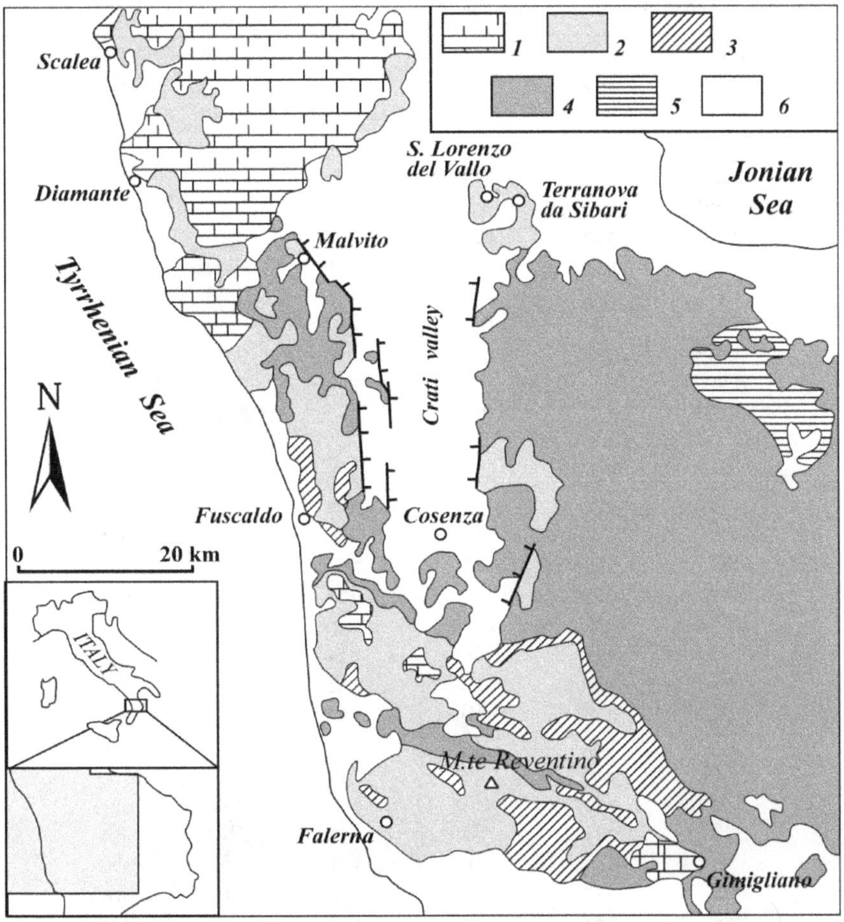

Figure 7. Geological sketch map of the northern sector of the Calabrian-Peloritani Arc (after Punturo et al. 2004). 1) Apennine Units Complex; 2) Ophiolite Units; Continental Crust Units; 3) Castagna Unit; 4) Calabride Units; 5) sedimentary cover of the Calabride Units; 6) Liguride Complex of the Calabrian-Lucanian boundary; 7) Miocene-Oligocene sedimentary sequences

These green stones show remnants of the original protogranular texture, which has been inherited from their harzbugitic-lherzolitic protoliths. The mineral assemblage of serpentinite from Mt. Reventino Area - where the quarries are located – is mainly made of serpentine group minerals ± magnetite ± tremolite-actinolite ± chlorite ± Cr-spinel. The serpentine group minerals and small magnetite grains completely replace former olivine and orthopyroxene crystals and appear as pseudomorphic aggregates with typical net-like and mesh-textures. Different dilatation vein systems filled by serpentine group minerals crosscut the rock. Orthopyroxene grains appear deeply replaced by "bastite", whereas clinopyroxene is present as millimetric grains or inclusions within rarely preserved holly-leaf shaped Cr-spinel of peridotitic origin, that, in most cases, are almost completely retrogressed to magnetite and chlorite (Punturo et al. 2004, 2015). These features of the ultramafic serpentinitic rocks from the Calabrian ophiolitic sequence are therefore in agreement with those of the ornamental stones here studied. Furthermore, based on the literature data of Punturo et al. (2004, 2015), we can better define the compatibility of our samples with the rocks of the ophiolitic sequence, particularly in terms of mineral chemistry of the amphibole tremolite (Fig. 5a) and of the trace element signature. For this purpose we considered high field strength elements (HFSE; Table 2), which are rather immobile during weathering, hydrothermalism and metamorphism (Wood et al. 1979; Bienvenu et al. 1990). In particular, the plots Ti *vs* V and Nb/Y *vs* Ti/Y of Fig. 8 report the fields of the Calabrian-Lucan metabasites (Spadea 1979), the M. Reventino-Gimigliano Unit serpentinites (Spadea 1979) and the samples studied by Punturo et al. (2004). On these plots we also reported the XRF data (Table 2) of the studied green stones (red stars). As one can see, the samples from the Messina Cathedral are chemically comparable to the "Pietra Verde" coming from the historical quarries of S. Mango D'Aquino and Mt. Reventino (Calabria, Italy) studied by Punturo et al. (2004).

Table 2 - X-ray fluorescence data for major (%) and trace elements (ppm) in the studied green stones.

Samples	MC1		MC2		MC3		MC4	
Oxides %		***se**		***se**		***se**		***se**
SiO_2	40.95	0,26	40.94	0,28	42.87	0,28	41.16	0,28
TiO_2	1.34	1,26	1.77	1,23	1.59	1,84	1.48	1,12
Al_2O_3	4.61	0,92	3.56	0,92	3.4	1,02	3.87	1,02
Fe_2O_3	10.99	0,13	6.79	0,15	7.14	0,14	7.99	0,15
MnO	0.19	1,47	0.17	1,6	0.15	1,65	0.17	1,71
MgO	28.14	0,25	36.1	0,21	36.18	0,21	33.69	0,21
CaO	5.27	0,46	0.69	1,56	0.36	1,91	2.1	1,84
Na_2O	0.48	9	0.57	9,67	0.42	9,5	0.67	8,7
P_2O_5	0.01	0,9	0.01	0,9	0.01	0,9	0.01	0,9
L.O.I.	8.99		9.96		7.67		9.4	
Total	100.97		100.56		99.79		100.54	
Trace elements (ppm)								
Y	9	3,04	10	3,55	12	3,41	9	5,67
Nb	7	4,74	7	7,68	8	7,14	6	8,89
La	19	8,1	16	8,4	18	8,4	17	8,4
Ce	40	15,8	21	16,7	30	16,4	18	16,3
Cr	3068	0,23	3373	0,17	3559	0,21	2633	0,22
Ni	1226	0,25	1228	0,2	1342	0,2	1565	0,2
Rb	4	7,17	3	7,16	3	9,42	4	7,12
Ba	15	4,8	12	17,2	16	25,2	14	22,2
Pb	14	0,97	10	5,87	9	7,06	12	6,31
Th	10	10,3	6	16,6	6	17,6	7	16,8
Sc	22	4,48	24	3,12	24	3,73	23	3,66
V	188	0,72	190	0,73	205	0,9	198	0,95
Co	117	0,34	81	0,42	97	0,4	94	0,41
Sr	9	6,58	5	4,71	7	6,82	8	6,33
Zr	40	0,83	24	0,53	20	0,6	38	0,74
Zn	77	1,18	35	1,64	38	1,79	45	1,9

*se = standard error evaluated with the Poisson's Law ($\sigma_N = \sqrt{N}$), it includes error of concentration, preparation and calibration.

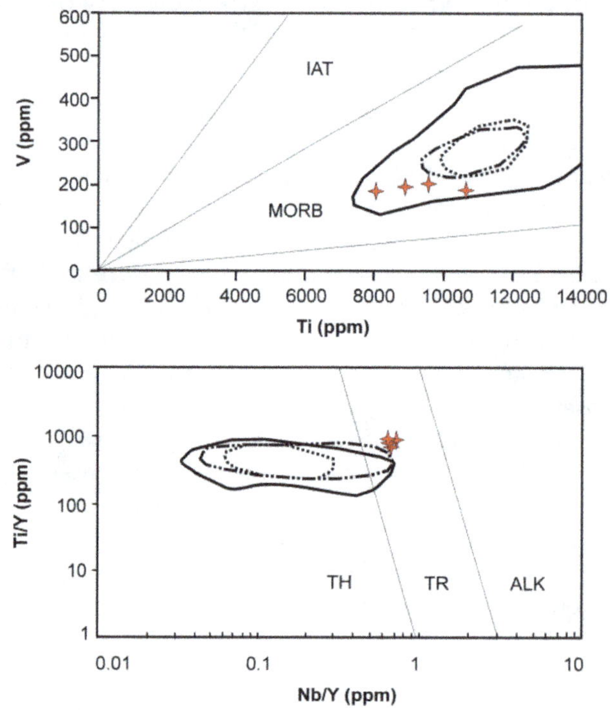

Figure 8. Ti vs V and Nb/Y vsTi/Y plots after Punturo et al. (2004). On the diagram the following fields are represented: Calabrian-Lucan metabasites (continuous line) (Spadea, 1979); M. Reventino-Gimigliano Unit serpentinites (dashed line) (Spadea, 1979); samples studied by Punturo et al. (2004) (dotted line).The red star represents the XRF composition of the green-stone samples analysed in the present work.

5. CONCLUSIONS

The investigated specimens of the "green stones" used for decorating the façade and the floor of the Messina Cathedral resulted to be metabasites showing pseudomorphic and vein textures, with relicts of olivine replaced by serpentine - forming a mesh textures - and orthopyroxene mostly replaced by bastite. The pseudomorphic minerals are serpentine (lizardite and chrysotile), magnetite, amphibole (tremolite-actinolite series) and chlorite (talc-chlorite).

The results of this chemical, mineralogical and petrographic study bring into question the reliability of some historical documents that - concerning the provenance of this decorative and building material – indicate the region of the medium-high amphibolite facies metamorphic rocks present nearby the Sicilian Zafferia and Larderia villages. The presence of a historical decorative handicraft and of a quarrying activity in the nearby of these villages is not questioned. However, our data suggest that the most reliable provenance region is the famous Calabrian "Green Stone district" where, since prehistoric times, serpentinites and metabasites associated in an ophiolitic sequence have been quarried and used as construction material.

ACKNOWLEDGEMENTS

The authors are grateful to the various Directors of the Messina Regional Museum for providing the samples, allowing the entrance in the Museum repositories and for the useful collaboration and discussion. Thanks are also due to Prof. Maurizio Triscari (University of Messina, now retired) and Prof. Rosolino Cirrincione (Catania University) for the useful suggestions. This research exploited the analytical facilities of the Laboratory of Geochemistry of "CERISI" (Progetto Centro di Eccellenza Ricerca e Innovazione Strutture e Infrastrutture di grandi dimensioni – Cod. PONa3_00422, European Regional Development Fund) in Messina.

REFERENCES

Bienvenu, P., Bougault, H., Joron, J.L., Treuil, M. and Dmitrief, L. (1990) MORB alteration: Rare earth elements/ non rare earth hygromagmaphile element fractionation, *Chemical Geology*, Vol. 82, pp. 1-14.

Bonardi, G., Giunta, G., Liguori, V., Perrone, V., Russo, M. and Zappetta, A. (1976) Schema geologico dei Monti Peloritani, *Boll. Soc. Geol. It.*, Vol. 95, pp. 49-74.

Bottari, S. (1929) Il duomo di Messina, Messina-

Bruker (2015a) Product overview: advanced analytical solutions.

Bruker (2015b) XRF lab report - S8 TIGER plus GEO-QUANT M.

Di Bella, M., Giuliano, A., Sabatino, G. and Triscari, M. (2010) Peculiar medieval floor decorations and artefacts from the town of Messina. In proceedings of A.I.Ar. Meeting, Pavia, February, Italy, pp 15-18.

Giuliano, A. (2012) Una significativa novità sulle origini del Duomo di Messina in *"Archivio Storico Messinese"* n. 93, Messina 2012.

Giuliano, A. (2015) Il ritrovamento dell'antica soglia del Duomo di Messina ed altro ancora. In: "IV Corso di aggiornamento per insegnanti e guide turistiche" Museo Regionale di Messina, 11 febbraio 2015.

Hey, M.H. (1954) A new review of the chlorites. *Min. Mag., Vol.* 30, pp. 1-277.

Leake, B.E. et al. (1997) Nomenclature of amphiboles: report of the subcommittee on amphiboles of the international mineralogical association, commission on new minerals and mineral names, *The Canadian Mineralogist*, Vol. 35, pp. 219-246.

Compagnoni, R., Giacobbe, A. and Russo, S. (1995) Pre-Alpine poly-metamorphism in a new thrust sheet of the Calabrian-Peloritan Arc: Mela Unit. In: Proceedings of SIMP, Meeting, Venezia, September, Italy 1995; Vol. 14, pp. 225-226.

Messina, A., Giacobbe, A., Perrone, V. and De Francesco, A.M. (1997) The Mela Unit: a new medium-grade metamorphic unit in the Peloritani Mts. (Calabrian-Peloritan Arc, Italy), *Boll. Soc. Geol. It.*, Vol. 115, pp. 1-16.

Principato, A. and Triscari, M. (1999) Tappeti marmorei pavimentali in provincia di Messina. In: Proceedings of F.I.S.T., Meeting, Bellaria, Italy, Vol. 22, pp. 314-316.

Pouchou, J.L., Pichoir, L. (1986) Les éléments très légers en microanalyse X – Possibilités des modèles récents de quantification, *J. Microsc. Spectrosc. Electron.*, Vol. 11, pp. 229-250.

Pouchou, J.L. and Pichoir, L. (1984) Possibilités d'analyse en profondeur à la microsonde électronique, *J. Microsc Spectrosc Electron*, Vol. 9, pp. 99-100.

Punturo, R., Fiannacca, P., Lo Giudice, A., Pezzino, A., Cirrincione, R., Liberi, F. and Piluso, E. (2004) Le cave storiche della "Pietra Verde" di Gimigliano e Monte Reventino (Calabria): studio petrografico e geochimico, *Boll. Acc. Gioenia Sc. Nat., Vol.* 37, pp. 35-57.

Punturo, R., Bloise, A., Critelli, Catalano, Fazio and Apollaro (2015) Environmental Implications Related to Natural Asbestos Occurrences in the Ophiolites of the Gimigliano-Mount Reventino Unit (Calabria, Southern Italy), *Int. J. Environ. Res.* , Vol. 9, pp. 405-418.

Rodolico, F. (1946) Le pietre delle città di Italia. Ed. Le Monnier. Italy, Firenze.

Spadea, P. (1979) Contributo alla conoscenza dei meta basalti ofiolitici della Calabria settentrionale e centrale e dell'Appennino Lucano, *Rendiconti della Società Italiana di Mineralogia Petrologia*, Vol. 35, pp. 251–76.

Stagno, F. and Zipelli, C. (1985) Risorse naturali del territorio messinese utilizzate in passato. Le "pietre nere" (petri nigri) delle fasce nel prospetto del Duomo di Messina. In *Atti Acc. Peloritana Pericolanti,* pp. 63-23.

Triscari, M. (2010) Georisorse del costruito a Messina: una storia di 25 secoli e l'abdicazione ai calcestruzzi armati. In: Accademia Nazionale delle Scienze, "La ricerca scientifica dopo il terremoto siculo-calabrese del 1908" Scritti e documenti, XLIII, pp.164-191, Tip. Della Pace Roma. Italy.

Zakrzewska, A.M., Capone, P.P., Iannò, A., Tarzia, V., Campopiano, A., Villella, E., Giardino, R. (2008) Calabrian ophiolites: dispersion of airborne asbestos fibers during mining and milling operations, *Periodico di Mineralogia*, Vol. 77, pp. 27-34.

Wood, D.A., Joron, J,L, and Treuil, M. (1979) A re-appraisal of the use of trace element to classify and discriminate between magma series erupted in different tectonic settings, *Earth and Planetary Sciences Letters*, Vol. 45, pp. 326-336.

5

THE PORTRAIT ART DURING THE BYZANTINE PERIOD, JORDAN

Mohammad Nassar[1]

The University of Jordan, Faculty of Arts and Design, Amman, Jordan

(mohammadnassar@hotmail.com)

ABSTRACT

The Madaba city has two main locations are included art of portraits in mosaic pavements from Byzantine period. The first one is in Church of the Virgin Mary and the second from in the Hippolytus hall both located in the central of the Madaba City. The study examines a selection of visual arts, such as human portraits and human portraits represent of the Goddess in order to detect certain important aspects of ancient society in Jordan from the Byzantine era. The study found that the respective artist was able to implement his drawings on those floors in accordance with the principles and rules relating to the technical work. This led to a highlighting of the aesthetic side of these works, although there are some portraits was destroyed of the churches in the region. Additionally, the artist was able through these portraits to give an idea of some show beliefs that existed before the advent of Christianity in the region. These drawing of the portraits are an important historical document of members of Byzantine society, especially given the scarcity of records documenting daily life during this period.

KEYWORDS: Madaba, Church, Virgin Mary, Hippolytus hall, human portraits, Portrait, mosaic, Madaba, Byzantine.

[1] This research was accomplished during the sabbatical year

1. INTRODUCTION

The visual arts play an important role in highlighting daily life in societies in generally. It can also be applied to ancient societies; particularly those dating back to the prehistoric period beginning with drawings such as were implemented on cave walls. Drawings have played an important role in highlighting the social, economic and cultural development of ancient societies, particularly given the lack of written material relating to those aspects; hence the decision to study art of portraits drawings prevalent during the Byzantine era in Jordan so as to get an idea regarding Byzantine society at the time. In addition to providing information regarding the community's technical progress, through their technical analysis, these drawings provide a witness to daily life in the community.

Amongst the art of portraits in mosaic pavements from Byzantine period is one found at Madaba. The latter occupies a geographically important site in central of Jordan, 30 km south of Amman and included also three locations: Mount Nebo, Uyun Musa and Mukhayyat). A History of area as part of the Arab province, comes through the writings of the Romans and the Byzantines philosophers, like Roman Ptolemaic and Byzantine Asitvans (Spijkerman 1978, 180). Madaba was visited by many travelers, they describe the plan of the city, including Tristram, Schumacher, Musil, and Father Manferdi (Tristrm 1873, 311; Schumacher 1895, 113; Manfredi 1899, 150; Musil 1907, 329, 330, 332-333). The city of Madaba during the Byzantine period, were fully active in religious architecture in order to spread the Christian religion in the region that was part of the province of Arab (Devreesse 1940, 220). The writings that appeared in the floors of churches in Madaba and the surrounding area indicate that Madaba was very important in religious architecture and wide and that the oldest known church history up to now is the Church of Saint George in Nebo, dated to AD 535/536 and then we find many other churches after. This study deals with the historical aspect of the region during the Byzantine period, based on which we have an understanding of the technique used in carrying out the drawings. (Table 1).

2. THE TECHNIQUES USED IN THE MOSAIC FLOORS

We first consider the technique used in the pavements' construction. As is usually the case with large mosaic pavements, each has a bed composed of several layers. The first consists of soil, a compacted layer of local red earth. On top of this is a layer of small round pebbles packed closely together and covered with a layer of ash and lime mortar. This smooth bed covered the whole area, to a thickness of 13 cm. A layer of wet lime plaster, on average 1 cm. thick, was spread over it. This was done in stages, area by area, and the mosaicist had to work before the plaster dried. Normally, the mosaicist would draw outlines of the composition in red or black. He would then start laying the tesserae into the wet plaster. The tesserae were usually cubes 1 cm. square, cut from local limestone, basalt, jasper, or oil shale. Sometimes glass tesserae were used in order to achieve brighter colours, such as green, blue, and gold (Neal 1976, 241; Piccirillo 1986a, 40; Ling 1994, 77-89; Nassar and Al-Muheisen 2010; Nassar and Turshan 2011; Al-Muheisen and Nassar 2012; Nassar 2013; Nassar and Al-Muheisen 2013; Al-Muheisen and Nassar 2014; Nassar 2015; Nassar and Sabbagh 2016)). Much the same technique (without glass tesserae) was used for the floors of the locations of study in Madaba area.

3. THE PORTRAIT: DESCRIPTION AND ANALYSIS

The art of portrait (bust) of the visual art and implemented on raw materials and various technologies, such as murals painting, sculpture, mosaics and other. The art Portrait in general of ancient arts, which could artist that employed in the formation of his art, and it seems that this kind of art has its roots in the centuries old, and one of the oldest forms in Jordan is found at the site of Ain Ghazal, which goes back to the Neolithic period (Rollefson 1984, 185-192; Grissom 2000, 25-45). Portrait and formed through three forms of models either full or half or human heads, and can identify shapes Portrait here busts carried out on the floor mosaic in the Byzantine period. Portrait on the art of mosaics, ~~it seem~~ appeared in the Roman period, for example, Bust-Portrait Ponoma Goddess of Autumn/ the Season Mosaic at Cirencester in Corinium Museum, England, which dates to late second century AD (Russell 1986, 243-266; Ling 1998, 13, Fig. 5). The study shed spotlight on the Byzantine busts - portraits that appeared on some floors mosaic in Jordan and Madaba as a model. At the begging we will to describe the bust-Portrait, A which is subject of the study and then analysis symbolically and technical to know how to progress by artist byzantine, also we know there were influents or effects, whether classical or local. Can be classified of the bust-Portrait that found in the floors of churches Madaba into two main for the description and analysis of the symbolic and analysis of Art: the portrait represents the shapes humanity and the other represents the Goddess, In the beginning, the study descriptions for each section and then will allocate titles in terms of the analytical study is the analysis art.

4.1 PORTRAIT - BUST (MAN).

The Portrait carried out on the floors of some Byzantine churches in Jordan, for example, there is an example of a great portrait busts of bearded man from the Chapel of the Priest John at Mount Nebo - Mukhayyat, which dates to 565 AD (Saller and Bagatti 1949; Piccirillo 1989, 176-200; 1997, 66, Pl. 216). Here, the man came amid of the simple frame, the colors are read and black, while the man wearing a tunic colored in red, black, gray and white. The cover of the robe has two broad red stripes (tunica laticlavia) and a red clock. Head is cover by simple halo came in a circular motion, and black colored gray; his beard and mustache and tinted black and brown, eyes large and wide, broad nose to the end.

Figure 1 Portrait-bust (Man) /Mount Nebo

4.2 PORTRAIT - BUST OF WOMAN

It seems that the beginning of the speared pictures with Women in portrait was executed on the mosaics found in the National Archaeological Museum in the city of Naples in Italy, dated to between the end of the first century BC and the beginning of the first century AD (Dunbabin 1999, 72, Fig. 8). There are some locations in Jordan included a Woman bust Portrait, for example, on the floor of the Chapel of the Priest John at Mount Nebo-Mukhayyat (Fig. 2), which dates back to 565 AD (Saller and Bagatti 1949; Piccirillo 1989, 176-200; Piccirillo 1997, 66, Pl. 217). The Portrait came amid a simple square frame, colored black shale and dark red, which represents a woman wearing a dress tunic, colored white, black and gray. The mantle colored in red, pink and yellow; while connects to the top with bond circular colored in yellow and black like the ring, hair long was a wreath and a crown of pearls colored in yellow, earrings round shape. It is also a pearl, surrounded by a halo white and black; the face of portrait is round with a wide brown eyes.

Figure 2 Portrait - Bust of Woman/ Mount Nebo

Such Portrait found in the Archaeological Museum Naples National in Italy, but here was the oldest, dated to the end of the first century B.C. and the beginning of the first century AD (Maiuri 1953, 98, 99; Ling 1998, 124, Fig. 88; Dunbabin 1999, 80, Plate 8).

4.3 PORTRAIT REPRESENT OF THE GODDESS

The portrait of the goddess it seem is appeared in the floor mosaics during the Greek period, we find one example from Greece is found in the floor of dining room (room 9) at Eretria, which dates to middle fourth century BC. (Ling 1998, 21, fig. 11). Here, the goddess of Dionysus, god of the grape harvest is riding a leopard. The identity of the gods in Greek, Roman and Byzantine period, the goddess appeared on some of the mosaic floors in the city of Madaba, such as the goddess of the sea (Thalassa), goddess of Tychy luck and happiness when the Greeks and Romans, the gods Terra (goddess of agriculture). Also, we find bust Human portraits represent of the Goddess such as four seasons ((spring, summer, autumn and winter)).

4.4 PORTRAIT - BUST OF THALASSA

Portrait -bust of a woman represent of Thalassa (the Goddess of the sea), was found on the floor of the church The church of the Apostles in Madaba (Fig. 3) dated to 578 AD (Lux 1968, 106-129; Piccirillo 1997, 38, 106; figs. 78, 80), which represents part of a woman who came amid a broad drop came in a circular motion like a medal 2.20m tinted from the outside and yellow painted brick, either from within any part of another colored painted oil painting, white and gray and frameworks between the Greek inscription.

Figure 3. Portrait - Bust of Thalassa, Madaba

The portrait of the goddess of the sea out amid the waves of water, with her left hand she holds a ship's oar, colored black brick, and yellow, while raising her right hand in greeting and bracelets adorn the wrist, arm, head round shape and hair here came a long hanging on the shoulders loose rising from the sea waves, eyes wide and black, and the face oval shape. Surrounding the goddess scene of the water included a number of the fishes; there are two fish shark and jellyfish. The colored fishes painted oil painting, brick and gray, while we find right side of the goddess picture sea monster colored green and dark red, while, we find the scene is generally carried out on a white background.

The Portrait of Thalassa goddess is rear in the Byzantine era, it seems we find three examples in the world during the Roman and Byzantine period we can compare with those found in Jordan, but we find some examples included a depicted with two wings on her head such as found in Antioch in Asia Minor and Jaen Museo arqueologico Museum in western province. While in Arabian province they had come without wings. It seems that this scheme appears only in western Provinces. The portrait of the goddess of Thalassa was found in Syria (Fig. 4), which dating back to the fifth and sixth centuries A.D (Eraslan 2015a, 6, fig. 11).

Figure 4. Portrait - Bust of Thalassa, Syria

The Thalassa similar to those found in the Apostles Church, but through here appeared of the head it seem a crown decorated with geometrical motif and the eyes more wide. Also, here raising her lift hand in greeting and bracelets adorn the wrist, arm, head round shape, while in case of the Apostles Church is raising her right hand. In addition, she holds a ship's oar came diagonally, while those found in Apostles Church came stand over the waves of water. Finally we see here one lobster claw, while in case of the Apostles Church we find two lobster claws.

Figure 5. Portrait - Bust of Thalassa, Antioch

One example from Asia Minor was found in the floor of the Room B (Yakto Complex) at Antioch (Fig. 5), which dates back to the third quarter of the 5th century A.D (Levi 1947, 323-325; Cimok 2000, 248, 249; Eraslon 2015a, 5, fig. 10; 2015b, 454-462, Fig. 7). Through here, the head of Thalassa cames with twin lobster claws and she holds a ship's oar (paddle) in the right hand came diagonally resemble those found in Syria, while a dolphin in the lift hand.

Also Eros is riding dolphins, while the different fishes rising from among the waves of water. Additionaly, we see here one lobster claw, while in case of the Apostles Church two lobster claws.

Finally, we find one example from western Province, in Spain at Jaen Museo arqueologico Museum (Fig. 6), which dates to the second half of the 4th century A.D (Eraslan 2015a, 5, fig. 9). Here, the Thalasa head came as a lobster claws, while, the wheel on her shoulder together with Cetus. It seems the hands disappeared beneath the waves, whereas the right had of Portrait of Thalassa goddess at the church of the Apostles is over the waves. Additionally, she holds a ship's oar (paddle) came diagonally over the waves, while, in case of the church of the Apostles the paddle is stand over the waves. The colors are resemble in the two locations.

Figure 6. Portrait - bust of Thalassa goddess, Spain

4.5 PORTRAIT - BUST OF TERRA (GE)

The bust of portrait of the woman represent of Terra or Tellus, Gaia or Ge (the goddess of the Earth) is on the floor of the upper Chapel of the Priest John at Khirbat al- Mukhayyatt (Fig. 7), which dates to 565 AD (Saller and Bagatti 1949, 100; Piccirillo 1986b, 38, Fig. 51; 1997, 174, Pl. 226; Merrony 1998, 468; Figueras 2000, 273, Fig. 6). Here, the portrayed bust of Terra came amid scrolls of acanthus leaves; wearing a tunic and above the mantle; the head adorned with a crown of fruit such as apples, grapes; hair are covered with this crown; the face oval shape, eyes big and wide, there is a pearl necklace in the neck, carrying in her arms a basket of fruits such as grapes and melons. The Greek inscription ΓΗ is on head sides of the Portrait. The colors here seem clear, but in general can take advantage of colors found in the church, a dark red color, dark green and white background.

Figure 7. Portrait - bust of Terra (Ge) Khirbat al-Mukhayyatt

Ther are two examples also from Madaba area, both of which are similar to those found in the upper Chapel of the St John. The first one is on the floor of the first row of acanthus scrolls of the nave at the Church of Saint George at Mount Nebo (Fig. 8), dating to the AD 535/536 (Saller and Bagatti 1949; Piccirillo 1989, 203-224; 1997, 178, Pl. 244, 251). Here, the head Terra goddess is damage and surrounded by acanthus scroll leaves; wearing a strip tunic and a necklace. Her two hands to present fruits which fill it seem a cloth which was filled with a melon, grapes, pomegrantes and apples. The colours are red, dark red, green, dark green, black, brown, yellow, dark yellow and white bakground.

Figure 8. Portrait- bust of Terra (Ge) Mount Nebo

The second one is on the floor of west of the nave at the Church of Bishop Sergius at Umm al- Rasas (Fig. 9), which dates to AD 587/588 (Piccirillo 1987, 177-239; 1989, 273-282; 1997, 234, Pls. 365, 368). We see here, the Terra goddess is came as a full- length, while in case of others came as a bust. Also, the part of the head of Terra goddess is damage it seem by iconoclasts. The goddess wearing a long sleevless tunic with a decorative band around the neck, and tied at the waist with a knotted girdle, has dropearrings and a crown of fruits; the upper part of the her left arm is adorned with a large bracelet. She hold the corners of a large cloack in her hands, filled with grapes pears, apples and pomegrantes. The colours are red, dark red, green, dark green, black, brown, yellow, dark yellow and white bakground.

Figure 9. Portrait of Terra (Ge), Umm al- Rasas

Additionally, The Portrait of Terra goddess is appeared in southern Joran era during the Byzantine period, on the floor of the south aisle of the Petra Church (Fig. 10), which dates to 447AD (Bruennow and Domaszewsski 1904-9, 329, 393; Roussin 1985, 271; Piccirillo 1997, 334; Waliszewski 2001, 257, Pl. 8.2b; Hachlili 2009, 179, Pl. 12.1a). Here, the Terra goddess came in this case as a part of a group containing the four Seasons; the Terra goddess through here is damage, we find only the part of the head with Greek inscription ΓΗ. The colours are red, dark read and white background.

Figure 10. Portrait - bust of Terra (Ge), Petra

There are the Portrait of Terra is also known from the west bank on the floor of the El-Maqerqesh mosaic at Beit Jibrin (Fig. 11), dating from the (Vincent 1922, 259-281; Avi-Yonah 1932, 146, No. 23; 1981, 283-382, Pl. 49; 1997, 197; Hachlili 2009, 179, Pl. 8.2b). Here, the Portrait of Terra with a crown, dressed in a tunic and holding fruit in her sash.

Figure 11. Portrait of Terra (Ge), Beit Jibrin

The Portrait of Terra is also known from the northern part of the levent, there are two examples from Antioch Museum, both smilar to those found in the upper Chapel of the Priest John. The first exmple is on the floor of the House of Ge and the Sasons (Fig. 12) dating from the second and the third cenutry (Donceel-Voûte 1995, 97, fig. 9). Here, the sash with fruit very smilar to those found in the upper Chapel of the Priest John. Also, we find the Terra goddess through here is damage, we find only the part of the head with Greek inscription ΓΗ. The colours are red, dark read and white background.

Figure 12. Portrait of Terra (Ge) Antioch

The second example also from the Antioch Museum was found on the floor of the House of Ge and the Seasons (Fig. 13), dating from the second and the third cenutry AD (Donceel-Voûte 1995). Here, the goddess wearing a tunic; the head adorned with a crown of fruit such as apples smilar to those found in Jordan examples such as the Chapel of the Priest John. We see beside right shoulder her stands a cornucopia (horn of plenty) brimming with fruits of the earth; hair here came a long hanging on the shoulder; while the face round shape and the eyes big and wide. The Greek inscription ΓΗ is on head sides of the Portrait. The colors here seem clear, but in general can take advantage of colors found in the church, a dark red color, dark green and white background.

Figure 13 Portrait of Terra (Ge) Antioch

4.6 PORTRAIT - BUST OF TYCHE

The goddess of Tyche is meaning in the Greek luck or chance and it seems appeared as a image in Athenian Amphora, which dates to the fifth centery BC.,while we find image of the goddess of Tyche during the Hellenistic period came as sculpted of Tyche from a marble (Tyche of Antioch) Roman copy in the Vatican Museum at Rome, dating to 300 BC. (Pollitt 1986, 3, Fig. 1). It sems the oldest Portrait of Tyche in the mosaic pavement appeared during the Roman period in the floor of the Brantingham Tyche Mosaic in East Yorkshire, England, which dates dates to the middle of the fourth century AD. (Halkon 2013, Pl. 36; Ottaway 2013; Smith 2005, 30). The most of the Portraits of the Tyche goddess are came with four seasons (Spring, summer, Autumn and winter) like found in the Hippolytus Hall at Madaba City.

4.7 PORTRAIT - BUST OF TYCHE (SPRING)

Portrait- bust of Tyche goddess (Fig. 14) representing the spring is in the floor of the Hippolytus Hall at Madaba, which dates to the first half of the sixth century AD (Piccirillo 1982, 373-408; 1997, 66, Pl. 26), it is carried out scrolls and gods on the floor of colored black shale and brown, wearing a dress is simple colored white. The head is covered with a crown came in the form of geometric is a came as a turreted crown, colored red dark and light brown. The face of the goddess is oval shape, eyes big and wide, while the hair here came a long held around the forehead with ribbon, colored red and dark red; it is holding a cornucopia in her left arm included a presence of a cluster of grapes colored in red dark red and white.

Figure 14 Portrait-Bust of Tyche (spring), Madaba

4.8 PORTRAIT - BUST OF TYCHE (SUMMER)

The Portrait of Tyche goddess representing the Summer and here also came to mosaic floors of the Hippolytus Hall at Madaba - border of the east panel (Fig. 15), which dates to the sixth century A.D. (Piccirillo 1982, 373-408; 1997, 66, Pl. 13) these gods is through this summer, we find the center of the coil from acanthus leaves, colored white, yellow, gray, olive or dark green. Here, carried out scrolls and gods on the floor of colored black shale and brown, wearing a dress is simple colored white embossed lines longitudinal simple, a two presentations on both sides of the garment, colored red dark and light, whereas there are lines in the middle of the dress but less offer compared with lines and side here colored in yellow. And stuck her left hand a cornucopia with a bundle of wheat colored in yellow and white. The head is covered with a crown came in the form of geometric is a came as a turreted crown and color of the crown in red dark and light brown, white, hair curly and colored painted oil shale, brown, red light and dark, and white, eyes are big, colored brown, neck is a long.

4.9 PORTRAIT - BUST OF TYCHE (AUTUMN)

Portrait- bust of Tyche (Fig. 16) representing the Autumn (Piccirillo 1982, 373-408; 1997, 66, Pl. 27) Image of the gods Tychy is also like the previous pictures, but there are also some minor differences, for example, dress code here was decorated with lines of simple causal colored dark green, was the lines on the chest and shoulders, also find that the torch is unlighted as is the case in the previous picture. . The head is covered with a crown came in the form of geometric is a came as a turreted crown, colored red dark and light brown. The face of the goddess is oval shape, eyes big and wide, while the hair here came a long held around the forehead with ribbon, colored red and dark red; it is holding a cornucopia.

Figure 15 Portrait-Bust of Thche (summer), Madaba

Figure 16 Portrait-Bust of Tyche (autumn), Madaba

4.2.3.4 PORTRAIT - BUST OF TYCHE (WINTER)

Portrait-bust of Tyche representing of winter (Fig. 17), here are similar to the previous picture also from the same site, but there are some differences, it seems here that the goddess holds in her left hand a cornucopia with torch. This indicates that winter balloon was colored red, yellow, gray and white. (Piccirillo 1982, 373-408; 1997, 66, Pl. 14). The dress is found here more than the simplicity of dress before, but here was decorated decoration crow step on both sides of the garment and on the shoulders, this type of decoration spread widely on the floor mosaic in Byzantine churches, for example is on floor of the Church of Saint John at Gerasa, dating to 531 AD (Piccirillo 1997, 244, Pl. 410). It seem, the head is elongation more than the previous image, the crown took the same design as previous, but the colors here where we find some change in the color yellow is dominant, while in the former crown color red is the one who prevailed.

Figure 17 Portrait-Bust of Tyche (winter), Madaba

The Portrait of Tyche goddess is rear in the Byzantine era, it seems we find three examples in the world during the Roman and Byzantine period we can compare with those found in Jordan, we find one example from the West Bank, is on the floor of the semicircular exedra (Sigma) Paladius Street at Scythopolis (Beit She'an) (Fig, 18), at Israel Museum, Jerusalem, which dates to the dated to AD 507 (Tsafrir and Foerster 1997, 130, Fig. 42; Figueras 2000, 279, Fig. 12; Lewin 2005, 99).

Figure 18. Portrait-Bust of Tyche, Scythopolis

Through here, the Portrait came amid a medallion, colored black and white background, which represents a young woman wearing a dress tunic with circular bond same as found on the floor of Chapel of the Priest John at Mount Nebo-Mukhayyat, colored black, red, gray and white background. Also, we find here, the head is covered with a crown came in the form of geometric is a came as a turreted crown (form of a city wall with towers) similar to those found on the Hippolytus Hall, colored black, red and dark red. The face of the goddess is oval shape, eyes big and wide, while the hair here came a long held around the forehead with ribbon, colored red and dark red; in her hands she holds a cornucopia filled with fruit and a palm growing out of the horn is a cross. The goddess of Tyche Mosaic is known from two earlier examples in England and Greece. The first is one in the floor of the Brantingham Tyche Mosaic in East Yorkshire, England (Fig. 19), which dates to the middle of the fourth century AD. (Halkon 2010, Pl. 36; Ottaway 2013; Smith 2005, 30).

Figure 19 Portrait-Bust of Tyche, England

Here we find that the bust portrait of Tyche also came amid a medallion, colored white, gray and dark red background with saw motif, which represents a woman wearing it seem a simple tunic, colored white, gray and dark red. The head is covered with a crown came in the form of geometric is a came as a turreted crown (form of a city wall with towers) similar to those found on the Hippolytus Hall and the other examples, colored black, grey, dark red and white back ground. Also, here, the face of the goddess is oval shape, eyes big and wide, while the hair here came a long held around the forehead, colored red and dark red. A Tyche is usually seen with a cornucopia, or horn of plenty, but unfortunately this clinching piece of evidence would be on the left shoulder - the very part of the center piece that has been lost. The second is one in the floor of the third Room at island of Kos, Greece (Fig. 20), dating to the first half of the fifth century AD. (Brouscari 1977, 68, 72, Figs, 3- 5, 9). Through her, the Portrait of the goddess of Tyche is enclosed in a medallion with row of spindles and pairs, while case of the image of Tyche at Hippolytus Hall came a medallion of acanthus levees of. She wearing a dress a light colored chiton covering the upper part of her chest and right arm and a dark colored himation is crossing her chest and covering her left arm. Also, we find here in her right hand she is holding a cornucopia with grapes and pomegranates. Her head a crown with cameo ornament and her hair falls in waves on her back.

Figure 20. Portrait-Bust of Tyche, Kos, Greece

5. ARTISTIC ANALYSES OF THE DRAWINGS

The analysis of the drawings found on the mosaic floors pavements has an important role in our knowledge of the extent to which artists used certain elements and the criteria governing works of art. Correspondingly, we study these images as found on the drawings executed on the mosaic floors in certain churches in Jordan, such as reflect the daily life of peasants during the Byzantine era.

Lines: The lines are the basic elements in the artwork. They have an important role in building a work of art; we find this is same wonderful role exists in nature. As we note, lines come in all forms, whether a simple straight line, or in as curved lines, italics, refractor parallels, orthogonal lines, and so forth. Through a descriptive study of the drawings, we have shown that many fonts were used by the artists in drawing scenes of daily life from the Byzantine era.

Curved lines: The artist was able to form from these lines many motifs, particularly in images representing scenes of daily life, especially where plant elements are concerned. These curved lines emerge prominently in some of the sub-branches of the twigs and the leaves of the acanthus leaves (Figs.7, 9, 14 - 17). We also find that knife forms came use curved lines (figs.7, 9, 14 - 17).

Semi-circular lines: Semi-circular lines are used in the formation of many motifs. Most of them are found in the scrolls as parts of acanthus leaves (figs.7, 9, 14 - 17).

Circular lines: Circular lines are employed by the artists in the pictures; these lines can be seen in the formation of the scrolls acanthus leaves (figs.7, 9, 14 - 17). In addition, we find that circle scrolls made up of acanthus leaves are used as borders for the images on some of the floor mosaics. Additionally, the artists use circular lines in drawing some of the armor worn by some of the farmers and soldiers as protection against the animals they are trying to catch.

Sharp or broken lines: Sharp lines are an important type of line employed by the artist in creating these scenes, and are evident in the forms of twigs and leaves. They appear on the acanthus leaves (figs.7, 9, 14 - 17).

The form: The form is one of the important elements governing works of art. It is no less important than fonts and others elements. It constitutes an important aspect of works of art. Here, the artists employed Portraits of Human and goddess with scenes of daily life on mosaic pavements, such as peasants and animals used in agriculture, also images of hunting. These are well distributed in these decorative circles. The artists used scrolls of twigs, grapes and acanthus leaves in the design as well; these are explained through the images of farmers and animals.

The Texture: The texture played an important role in shaping artistic works. Here, texture was determined through the use of lines and contrast between surfaces so as to create a sense of texture. The scenes representing daily life as found on the mosaic floors are of polished stones, which give a sense of texture beautifully. The role of texture is evident with all of the drawings. Shadow and light: Shadow and light depend mainly on the color. We find here that good colors have emerged, ranging from light to dark, and with differences generally delineated by lines. In this way, the artist was able to create the sensation of three dimensions. The scenes depicted here indicate a strong knowledge of how to use color and to distribute it, which helps to highlight shadow and light effectively.

The space: we find that the artists don't make much use of space in these scenes, which feature distributions of motifs of plants interspersed with the images of humans and animals very little space exists between them, and what vacuum there is here is deliberate. This is also what distinguishes these drawings that were executed on mosaic floors during the Byzantine era.

Unit: Here we find a significant degree of unity, whereby the artist was able to form a thread between the different parts of the drawings and form of them a single unit in a consistent manner. This indicates the Byzantine artist's ability to distribute multiple motifs in a coherent and logical way. He creates the sense of a single unit through the distribution of motifs involving the rolls of twigs, vine leaves and acanthus in a coherent manner; the same is evident with his images of human, animal, which exist inside the scrolls. He employed the idea of integration with respect to the decorative elements so as to create a sense unity in this work of art.

Balance or equilibrium: We find that the balance in nature evident in these images is wonderful; the artist benefitted from this balance, and he certainly emphasized it in his art. We see this in these drawings; the artist expressed this balance through his paintings, and sought to gain access to a configuration of an integrated professional, combining the old distribution of elements and units with a consistency and in a manner demonstrating the relationship between each and with the surrounding spaces. They included most of the spaces and surfaces. This balance is also evident in the implementation of decorative units. Particular forms of scrolls and the content of human and animal elements suggest to the viewer a sense of psychological wellbeing, indicating the experience and broad access enjoyed by the artist during the Byzantine era.

Rhythm: The rhythms of the important elements in these works were employed in a coordinated manner on the mosaic floors, and are reflected in the scenes of daily life. Among the elements the artist uses for inspiration are rhythm and repetition. This rhythm is highlighted through the repetition of scrolls of twigs and acanthus leaves. Additionally, the artist used a gradient, both with respect to colors and shapes; continuity of domains is evident in the scrolls.

***Sovereignty*:** The role of color in the drawings that appear on the mosaic floors in the scenes of daily life is strong. In these works, it is clear, for example, that the artist focused on images of humans, goddess and visibility, as evidenced in the scrolls of acanthus leaves and twigs. Thus, we find that the artist, in these drawings, found it necessary to pay attention to certain, important elements for instance, that of sovereignty played an important role and was employed in order to highlight the aesthetics.

6. DISCUSSION & CONCLUSION

We have investigated the portrait that appeared on the mosaic floors in some churches in Jordan during the Byzantine era. Diversity of decoration to the mosaic floors, living elements, including human, plant elements, including the leaves and twigs and the fruits of grapes and pomegranates, has shown that diversity at the artistic taste of the aesthetic of the artist. Additionally, the artist was drawing some of the topics of his paintings of everyday life from Greece mythology dealing with them closely, such as his portraits, including in those scenes a few neighboring areas that were thus compared to these scenes. This means that the artist in the Byzantine Jordan was aware of the realization of the daily life through drawning on the mosaic floors. Focused on where the artist was and did we notice that his drawings were well-thought according to this place. The artist adopted the style to repeat some of the motifs and in particular implemented the picture scrolls of daily life, so that the humanitarian side echoes inside the forms of plant and shell items. Here, we tried to highlight the images that are an important part of the topic dealt with through these drawings. Artist's interest of the decorative motives, for example, the images, whether human drawn within the frames of the grapes, acanthus leaves along with fruits and flowers, we find that the artist has dealt with carefully to give the landscape's aesthetic. The influences came from the size of culture and cultural heritage that prevailed in the region, especially under the Roman influence and this is what we observe in motifs, such as scrolls of twigs, leaves and fruits of grapes and acanthus, which was prevalent earlier in the Art and Architecture, in Roman times, particularly in the Decapolis cities; benefited from the art of the Byzantine artist.

TABLE 1 Type and place of the portraits under study

Figure No.	Type of Portrait	Place of the Portrait
Fig. 1	PORTRAIT – BUST (MAN).	Mount Nebo – Mukhayyat
Fig. 2	PORTRAIT – BUST OF WOMAN	Mount Nebo – Mukhayyat
Fig. 3	PORTRAIT – BUST OF THALASSA	Madaba
Fig. 4	PORTRAIT – BUST OF THALASSA	Syria
Fig. 5	PORTRAIT – BUST OF THALASSA	Antioch
Fig. 6	PORTRAIT – BUST OF TERRA (GE)	Spain
Fig. 7	PORTRAIT – BUST OF TERRA (GE)	Mount Nebo – Mukhayyat
Fig. 8	PORTRAIT – BUST OF TERRA (GE)	Mount Nebo – Mukhayyat
Fig. 9	PORTRAIT – BUST OF TERRA (GE)	Umm al- Rasas
Fig. 10	PORTRAIT – BUST OF TERRA (GE)	Petra
Fig. 11	PORTRAIT – BUST OF TERRA (GE)	Beit Jibrin
Fig. 12	PORTRAIT – BUST OF TERRA (GE	Antioch
Fig. 13	PORTRAIT – BUST OF TERRA (GE	Antioch
Fig. 14	PORTRAIT – BUST OF TYCHE (SPRING)	Madaba
Fig. 15	PORTRAIT – BUST OF TYCHE (SUMMER)	Madaba
Fig. 16	PORTRAIT – BUST OF TYCHE (AUTUMN)	Madaba
Fig. 17	PORTRAIT – BUST OF TYCHE (WINTER)	Madaba
Fig. 18	PORTRAIT – BUST OF TYCHE	Scythopolis
Fig. 19	PORTRAIT – BUST OF TYCHE	Yorkshire
Fig. 20	PORTRAIT – BUST OF TYCHE	Kos

REFERENCES

Avi-Yonah M. (1932) Mosaic Pavements in Palestine, *QDAP* II: 136-181

Avi-Yonah M. (1981) *Art in Ancient Palestine*. Jerusalem.

Avi-Yonah M. (1993) Mosaics at El-Maqerqesh, in E. Stern (ed.), *The New Encyclopedia of Archaeological Excavations in the Holy Land. Jerusalem*. Vol I: 197-198.

Brouscari, E. (1997) The Tyche of Cos on a mosaic from a late Antique house in Cos. Pp. 65-77

S. Isger and B. Poulsen (eds) *Patron and Pavements in late Antiquity*. Odense University Press.

Bruennow, R. and Domaszewski, A. (1904-1909) Die Provincia Arabia. 3 vols. Strassburg.

Cimok.F. (2000) *Antioch Mosaics*. İstanbul: A Turizm.

Devresse, R. (1940) *Les anciens évêchés de Palestine». Mémorial Lagrange*. Paris, Librarie Lecoffre

Donceel-Voûte, P. (1995) Syro-Phoenician mosaics of the 6th century, in R. Ling, (ed.), *Fifth International Colloquium on Ancient Mosaics*. Ann Arbor, MI. Part 2: 88-100.

Dunbabin , K. (1999) *Mosaics of the Greek and roman World*. Cambridge, Cambridge University Press.
Eraslan, S. (2015a) Tethys and Thalassa in Mosaic. Art, *Art-Sanat* 4: 1-13
Eraslan, S. (2015b) Oceanus, Tethys and Thalssa Figures in the Light of Antioch and Zeugma Mosaics. *The Journal of International Social Research*. Vol. 8. 37: 454-462.
Figueras, P. (2000) Motivos paganos en nnosaicos cristianos y judíos de Oriente: problemática e interpret ación (I) Espacio, Tiempo y Forma, Serie II, Historia Antigua, t. 13: 261-296
Grissom, C. (2000) "Neolithic statues from 'Ain Ghazal: construction and form" *American Journal of Archaeology* 104: 25-45.
Hachlili, R. (2009) *Ancient mosaic pavements: themes, issues, and trends*. Leiden, Koninlijke Brill.
Halkon, P. (2010) Britons and Romans in an East Yorkshire Landscape, UK, *Bollettino di Archeologica on Line I, Volume speciale E, E10, 3: 24-40.*
Levi, D. (1947) *Antioch Mosaic Pavements*, Princeton: Princeton University Press.
Lewin, A. (2005) *The Archaeology of Ancient Judea and Palestine,* Paul Getty Museum
Ling, R. (1994) Against the technique, in Fifth international Colloquium on Ancient Mosaics, *Journal of roman Archaeology*, Part one, supplementary series 9, 77- 88.
Ling, R. (1998) *Ancient Mosaics*. London: Princeton University Press.
Lux, U. (1968) Die Apostel-Kirche in Madaba. *zeitschrift des deutschen Palästina-Vereins* 84: 106-129.
Manfredi G. (1899) "Piano generale delle antichità di Madaba", *Nuovo Bullettino di Archeologia Cristiana* 5, 149-170.
Merrony, M. (1998) The Reconciliation on Paganism and Christianity in the Early Byzantine Mosaic Pavements of Arabia and Palestine. *Liber Annuus* 48: 441-482
Musil, A. (1907) *Arabia Petraea, i, Moab, Topographischer reisebericht*, Wien, Alfred Hölder.
Al-Muheisen, Z., and Nassar, M., 2012. The Second Church at Yasileh in Jordan and its Mosaics, *Greek, Roman, and Byzantine Studie*s 52.4: 661-683.
Al-Muheisen, Z., and Nassar, M. (2014) Geometric Mosaic Pavements at Ras ed-Deir, Jordan. *Greek, Roman, and Byzantine Studies* 54: 87-104.
Nassar, M., and Al-Muheisen, Z. (2010) Geometric Mosaic Pavements of Yasileh in Jordan, *Palestine Exploration Quarterly* 142.3: 182-198.
Nassar, M. and Turshan, N. (2011) Geometrical Mosaic Pavements of the Church of Bishop Leontios at Y amun (Northern Jordan). Palestine Exploration Quarterly, vol. 143, no.1: 41-62
Nassar, M., and al-Muheisen, Z. (2013) Geometric Mosaic Ornament at Khirbet al-Bediyeh, Jordan. *Greek, Roman, and Byzantine Studies* 53: 551-609.
Nassar, M. (2013) The Art of Decorative Mosaics (Hunting Scenes) from Madaba Area during Byzantine Period (5th-6th c. AD)., *Mediterranean Arhaeology and Archaeometry*, Vol. 13, No 1, 67-76.
Nassar, M. (2015) The Geometric Mosaics at Qusayr Amra in Context. *Greek, Roman, and Byzantine Studies* 55: 414–430
Nassar, M. and Sabbagh, A. (2016) The Geometric Mosaics at Khirbat Mar Elyas: A Comparative Study. *Greek, Roman, and Byzantine Studies* 56: 528–555.
Neal, D. (1976) Floor mosaics, in D. Strong and D. Brown (eds), *Roman Crafts*. London: Gerald Duckworth &Co. Ltd, 241-252.
Ottaway , P. (2013) *Roman Yorkshire: People, Culture and Landscape*. Blackthorn Press
Piccirillo, M. (1982) La chiesa della Vergine a Madaba. *Liber Annuus* 32: 373-408.
Piccirillo, M. (1986a) *Byzantine Mosaiken aus Jordanien, trans. H. Buschhausen*, Wien, Amt der NEO Landeregierung Verlag.
Piccirillo, M. (1986b) «La cité de Nébo», *Le Monde de la Bible* 44: 30-39.
Piccirillo, M. (1987) Le iscrizioni di Um er-Rasas - Kastron Mefaa in Giordania, I (1986 - 1987). *Liber Annuus* 37: 177- 239.
Piccirillo, M. (1989) Chiese e Mosaici di Madaba. documentazione grafica a cura di P . Eugenio Allita. Jerusalem - Milan.
Piccirillo, M. (1997) *The Mosaics of Jordan.Amman*, American Center for Oriental Research
Pollitt, J. (1986) *Art in the Hellenstic Age*. Cambridge: University Press.
Rollefson, G. (1984) "Early Neolithic statuary from 'Ain Ghazal (Jordan)" *Mitteilungen der Deutsche Orient-Gesellschaft* 116: 185-192
Rowe, A. (1930) *The Topography and History of Beth Shean*. Philadelphia
Saller, S. and Bagatti, B. (1949) The Town of Nebo (Khirbet el - Mekhayyat). With a Brief survey of other Ancient Christian Monuments in Transjordan. Jerusalem.

Schumacher, G. (1895) "Madaba" *zeitschrift des deutschen Palästina-Vereins* 18: 113-125.

Smith, D. (2005) *Roman mosaics at Hull*. 3rd edition revised by Martin Foreman. Hull.

Spijkerman, A. (1978) *The Coins of the decapolis and Provincia Arabia, with Historical and Geographical Introductions* by M. Piccirillo, Jerusalem

Tristram, H. (1873) *The Land of Moab: travels and discoveries on the east side of the Dead Sea and the Jordan*. New York, Harper and brothers.

Tsafrir, Y. and Foerster, G. (1997) Urbanism at Scythopolis-Bet Shean in the Fourth to Seventh Centuries. *Dumbarton Oaks Papers*,Vol. 51:85-146 Published by: Dumbarton Oaks, Trustees for Harvard University.

Vincent, L-H. (1922) Une villa Greco-romaine a Beit Djebrin, *Revue biblique* 31: 259-281

Waliszewski, T. (2001) Mosaics, in T.Z. Fiema et al. (eds), *The Petra Church*, Amman: 219-270.

6

THE DEVELOPING CRAFT OF BONE TOOL TECHNOLOGY AT CHALCOLITHIC TELEILAT GHASSUL, JORDAN

B. AbuHelaleh[1], S. Bourke[2], U. Thun Hohenstein[3]

1. *Petra College for Tourism and Archaeology, Al Hussein Bin Talal University, 71110 Ma'an, Jordan.*
2. *NEAF, SOPHI, A14, University of Sydney, Sydney, Australia.*
3. *University of Ferrara, Department of Humanities, Corso Ercole I d'Este 32 – 44121 Ferrara, Italy*

Corresponding author: bellal.abuhelaleh@gmail.com

ABSTRACT

The Late Neolithic and Chalcolithic site of Tuleilat Ghassul is located on the northeastern corner of the Dead Sea and was occupied throughout the Fifth Millennium BCE. It is the type-site of the Ghassulian culture and, covering 20 hectares, is one of the largest Chalcolithic sites in the southern Levant. This paper analyses the worked bone objects from Hennessy's (1967-77) and Bourke's (1994-99) Sydney University excavations at Ghassul, currently stored in the Salt, Amman Citadel and Yarmouk University museums in Jordan. The aim is to investigate the production methods and describe specific form/function combinations of worked bone tools at Ghassul and to contextualize the assemblage through comparative analyses with contemporary artefacts recovered in Jordan.

Results display a variety bone objects categories like pointed tools, spatulas and decorated objects. Stereomicroscopic analysis documents different production processes on bone objects surfaces. Bone objects at Teleilat Ghassul illustrate the development of bone crafting during Chalcolithic period.

KEYWORDS: Ghassul, Jordan, Bone objects, Chalcolithic, Teleilat Ghassul

1. INTRODUCTION

Teleilat Ghassul has long been famous for its nearly unbroken sequence of occupation throughout the Fifth Millennium BCE, spanning the transition from the Late Neolithic into the Early Chalcolithic in its earliest phases, and then the full span of the Ghassulian Chalcolithic culture. First excavated by the Pontifical Biblical Institute (1929-38, 1959-60), and then by the University of Sydney (1967-77, 1994-99), the sequence begins with two phases of single-room Late Neolithic semi-subterranean roundhouse dwellings, followed by eight phases of rectilinear multi-room Chalcolithic period occupation (Hennessy, 1982; Bourke, 2008).

The Ghassul sequence reveals major changes to subsistence and material culture over the course of the near-millennium long sequence of Chalcolithic occupation, culminating in the 'Classic' Ghassulian assemblages of the last three phases (Hennessy Phases A-C). Archaeozoological analyses by Mairs (Mairs, 2009) and archaeobotanical analyses by Meadows (Meadows, 2005) revealed that significant changes in economic activities, including aspects of 'secondary products revolution' - more specifically the development of wool fiber production and dairying, donkey domestication, the use of deep plough and field rotation practices, the domestication of the olive and the increased utilization of other fruit along with more productive cereals (Bourke 2002, 2008) – occurred during the second half of the Fifth millennium BCE, (Bourke et al., 2001, 2004). In material cultural terms, the diversification of the Ghassulian material assemblage over time, featuring a greater range of items, many carefully crafted from exotic materials, becomes ever more elaborate. One feature of the later Ghassulian horizons is the production of figurative polychrome wall paintings, such as the PBI 'Star', 'Bird', 'Notables' and Hennessy's 'Procession' (Drabsch and Bourke, 2014), which together draw attention to the development of elaborate public cult practices, in the service of an emerging elite.

A variety of bone objects found within the site during previous archaeological excavation were preserved in Jordanian Museums. Thirty-four of these were awls, spatulas, and decorated objects. We are looking to apply Archaeozoological analysis to understand the production methods and describe specific form/function combinations of worked bone tools.

2. BONE OBJECTS

Bone tools from Teleilat Ghassul came from the collections in the Amman Citadel Museum, Salt Archaeological Museum and Yarmouk University Archaeological Museum. 34 bone objects which can be found in the bone objects sample were studied. Unfortunately, there was no access to raw material or production debitage as it is no longer preserved or stored in museums or by the Jordanian Department of Antiquities. It's possible that some bone artifacts assemblages were removed to be studied outside Jordan, which may limit our understanding of the production process.

3. METHODOLOGY

Bone tools categories have been classified based on a variety of scientific characteristics and methodologies. We considered the local production need for bone tools and the variety of demands by ancient societies. Classification was undertaken based on the shape and size of the bone tools. This lead to a better understanding of the categories of bone tools (Abuhelaleh et al., 2015; Beyries, 1987; Choyke and Schibler, 2007; Cristiani, 2008; D'Errico, 2001; Gebel et al., 2017; Karasneh, 1989; Nielsen, 2009; and Yerkes et al., 2003).

There is no particular scheme that can be applied simply to Jordanian bone tools due to the scarceness of published data for the Chalcolithic period. But data from published Chalcolithic and Neolithic sites in the Near East were compared. (Abuhelaleh et al., 2015; Garfinkel and Horwitz, 1988; Gebel et al., 2017; Karasneh, 1989; Nielsen, 2009).The previous study by Mairs L. D., who divided bone objects from Teleilat Ghassul in three categories (Points, shuttels, Rods/'Spacers'), was also considered (Mairs, 2009).

Our research recognizes the change of human demands and society, organization through Neolithic to the Chalcolithic. Although animal resources related to the diversity of environments surrounded through Neolithic and Chalcolithic periods (Abuhelaleh et al., 2015; Barone, 1980; Becker, 2013; Choyke and Schibler, 2007; Karasneh, 1989; Nielsen, 2009).

Archaeozoological and taphonomic analysis weredone by the use of Leica EZ4 HD stereomicroscope in order to document all anthropic modification on bone tools surfaces and also to distinguish butchering processes from production traces. Data collected from bone tools were used to reconstruct technologies, steps of production and the possible ancient use for each category (Camps-Fabrerm, 1990; Choyke and Schibler, 2007; Cristiani, 2008; Bertolini and Thun Hohenstein, 2017; D'Erricoa, 2001; Martin, 1999).

Osteological analysis was applied on bone tools by the use of animal skeletal collection to classify bone tools sources and past human manipulation of animal species from the surrounded environment (Boessneck et al., 1963; Martin, 1999; Schmid, 1972).

4. CATEGORIES

Based on bone tools typology, the tools were classified into three main categories; 1. Pointed bone tools, 2. Spatulas, 3. Decorated tools (Fig. 1). Bone tools categories contain subdivision categories related to specific production, final shapes and size.

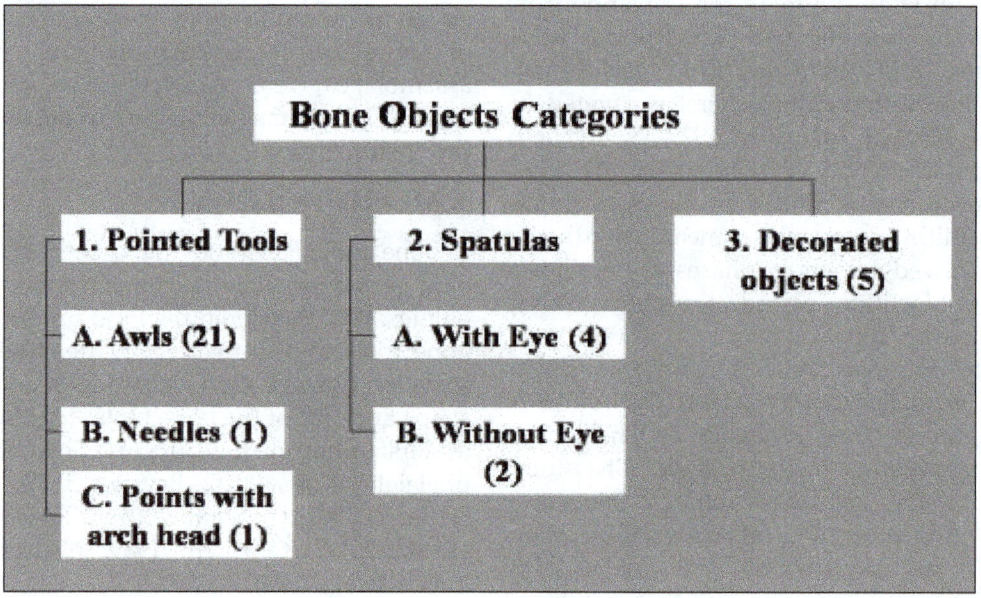

Figure 1: Scheme of bone objects categories from Teleilat Ghassul

4.1. Pointed tools

In this category bone tools were classified into three types; the first type is Awls: 21 awls were found and present two subdivision categories between short and long awls. One of the awls contains semi dental modification on both lateral sides from dorsal view (Fig. 2). Most of the awls are in good preservation conditions. It was found that only 5 awls have a complete proximal head. Most of the awls are made from the metapodial portion from middle to distal side. While few others are made from the middle shaft of long bones. There were fractures on the proximal side in most of them, and this could happen during the use of tools. Anthropic modification was noted on the surface of bone tools. Longitudinal scraping on ventral and dorsal surfaces was covering most surfaces. It shows the use of heavy tools to shape surface. There was a record of the use of retouch stone tools in this process.

It was also noted that short awls have wide size compared to the small thickness of long awls. Thickness of short awls could be related to use of complete middle shaft of the bone. Instead of the use half of shaft in long awls.

One of the awls contains semi dental modification on both lateral sides from dorsal view. The dental view has thickness of bone without sharp head. This awl has similar proximal head shape of short thick awls. This object is made from the proximal to the middle shaft of the radius bone belonging to a medium animal size.

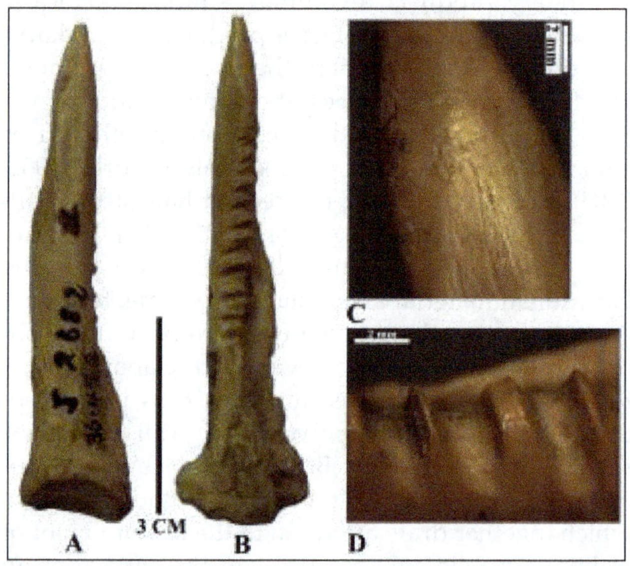

Figure 2: Bone object N. J2682, dental awl; A: Frontal view of left lateral side, B: Dorsal view of left lateral side, C: view of longitudinal and perpendicular scraping on proximal portion by Stereomicroscopy, D: view of lateral side of dental modification by Stereomicroscopy.

The second type is Needles. Small size needle with piercing on proximal portion were found (Fig. 3). Needle has an external arch shape on proximal portion, surrounding the piercing. Diameter of inside circle is 2.2-2.4 mm, which makes it as a unique shape different from known other needle from other prehistoric sites in Jordan. Needle has a reddish brown color which could be related to burning of bone to increase its hardness. We noted a circular and parallel scraping on proximal portion. Other longitudinal scraping was documented on middle to distal of shaft surface.

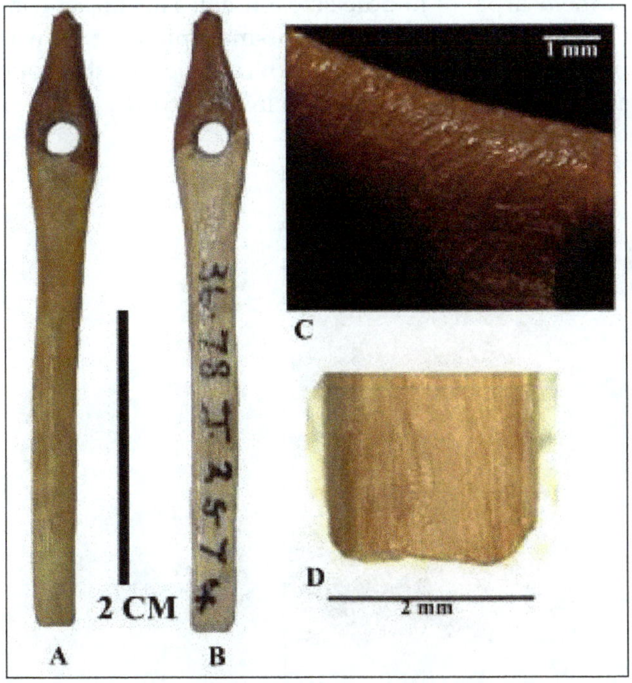

Figure 3: Bone object N. J2574, Needle with piercing; A: Frontal view, B: Dorsal view, C: perpendicular scarping in circular direction (Stereomicroscopy photo), D: view of longitudinal scraping on distal portion (Stereomicroscopy photo).

The third type is point with an arched head: only one arched head object was found. It was produced from the middle shaft of the long bone from a large animal. On proximal surface from front view; we note a variety of scraping directions. It could be related to work with course and hard surface. While we documented on dorsal view a parallel inclined scraping on both lateral sides of object. This type of modification could be related to cutting and smoothing the object.

4.2. Spatulas

Six Spatulas fabricated from large animal ribs were found. There are two subdivisions of these categories. First; four spatulas with piercing. Mairs suggested the name of this category as shuttles (Mairs, 2009). The piercing was made from both surfaces and the proximal edge was polished. Object J.2581 has a broken part of pierced circle on distal portion, which can be as a result of production fail or broken during use of tool (Mairs, 2009). Abrading technique was used to smooth distal portion (Fig. 4).

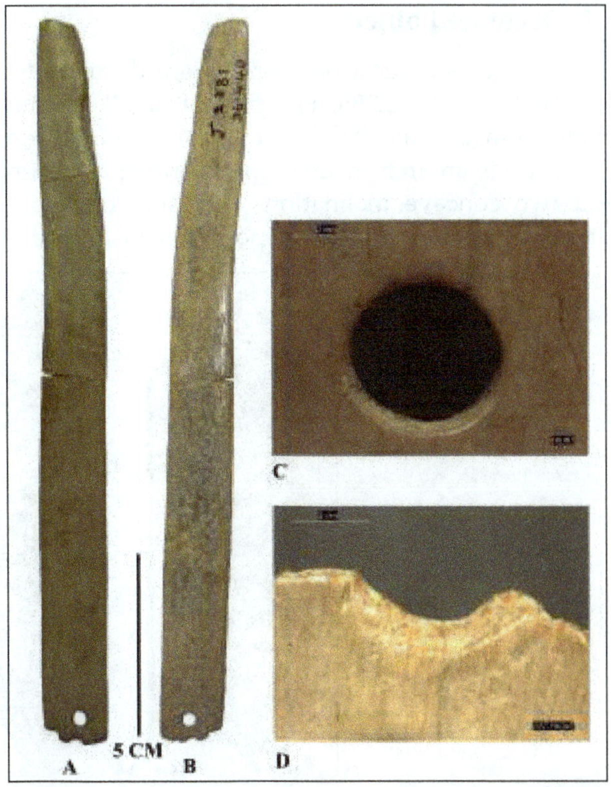

Figure 4: Bone object N. J2581, Spatula with piercing; A: Frontal view, B: Dorsal view, C: view of piercing border from frontal view (Stereomicroscopy photo), D: view of broken piercing on the border of distal portion (Stereomicroscopy photo).

The second category contains two spatulas; the first one is a broken proximal portion of spatula while the second one is uncompleted. The distal portion was broken.

In this category, human used to cut ribs in two symmetrical half long the shaft axes, in order to get thin spatulas. In general, all spatulas are thin and have a length that is more than 150 mm and the surfaces were smoothed by stone tools in longitudinal direction.

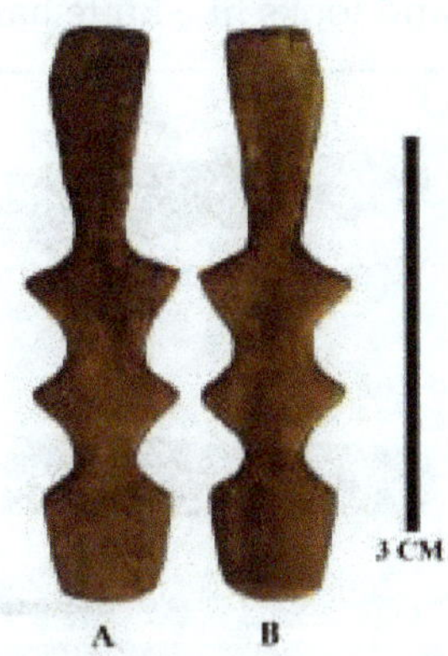

Figure 5: Bone object N. J.2355, Decorated pendant; A: Frontal view, B: Dorsal view.

4.3. Decorated objects

Five objects made from bones were documented. The first object (J.2355, Fig. 5) is a small pendant made from the middle shaft of a large animal long bone. It has an arch inclination on proximal portion and two concave inclinations to inside from both lateral sides and the distal portion has a straight edge. The object has a reddish brown color due to light burning.

The second object (J. 2563, Fig. 6) is middle shaft of metacarpal of middle size animal. This object contains on the dorsal side two small piercing. It was pierced by drilling on the external side of the bone and the hole could be used to insert a cord.

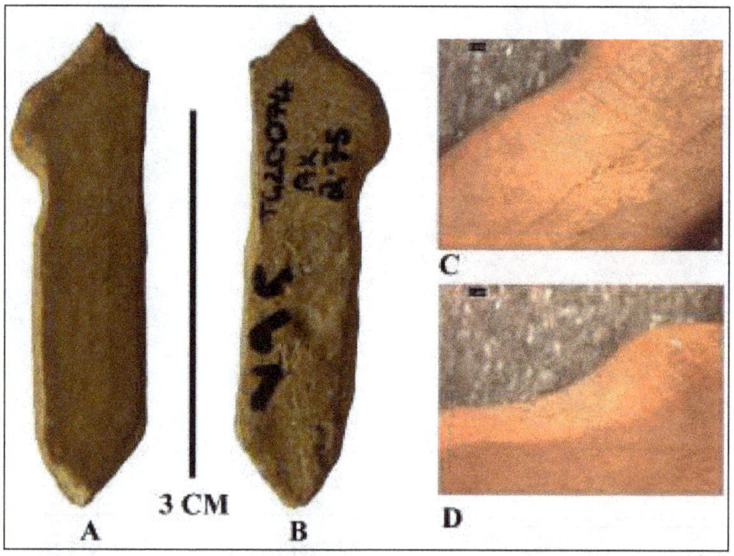

Figure 6: Bone object N. TG 20074, Decorated bone; A: Frontal view, B: Dorsal view, C: unsystematic perpendicular cut marks on frontal surface (Stereomicroscopy photo), D: view of perpendicular scraping on left lateral side (Stereomicroscopy photo).

Third object (J. 2359) is a broken portion of a vertebra with piercing made by drilling from both sides. The size suggests that it belonged to large animal. The remainder of the tool is not present and, therefore, its purpose is uncertain.

The fourth object (TG. 20074) is a small decorated bone that can be connected to another part of decorated object or a tool. This object made from a large animal bone and has been smoothed using an abrading technique and there are a variety of perpendicular cut marks on the surface and parallel perpendicular scraping on lateral sides. The object is 46 mm long, complete and looks like knife handle.

The last object (J. 2353, Fig. 7) is a perforated bone with 11 pierced 'eyes'. These were made by drilling from both sides and are not completely symmetrical. Between each piercing, there are parallel perpendicular lines on both sides of the object, produced by sawing. The object is 100.1 mm long and the piercings are close to equidistant at 7.3 mm. It is made from the shaft of a large animal long bone. It has been smoothed on the lateral sides at both ends but no other modification has been was found. This object was mentioned by Scham and Garfinkel as perforated rods (Scham and Garfinkel, 2007).

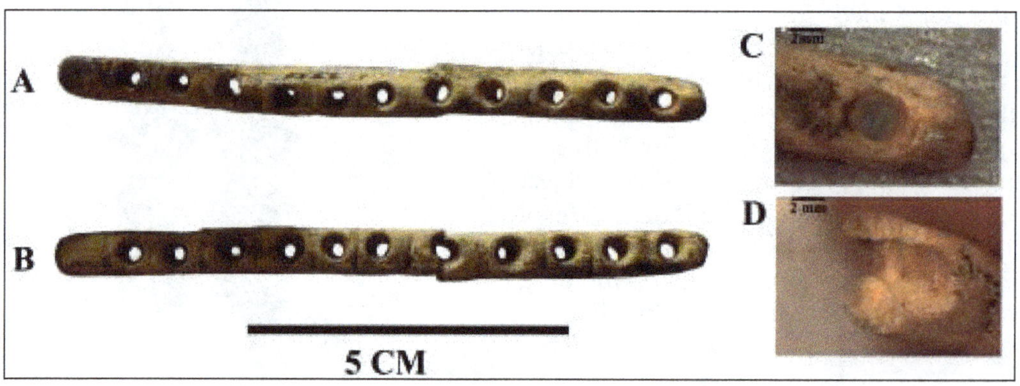

Figure 7: Bone object N. J. 2353, perforated bone; A: Frontal view, B: Dorsal view, C: view of piercing and smoothing by abrading technique on left side (Stereomicroscopy photo), D: view of internal surface of piercing hole number 7 (Stereomicroscopy photo).

5. ANTHROPIC MODIFICATION

Based on the analysis of each category by using a stereomicroscope, a variety of common anthropic modification, that represent various manipulations of bone tools surface, were noted.

On pointed objects, cut marks located on articulation portions of bone and connected to disarticulation of carcass, were noted (Fig. 8).

Most of the awls contain longitudinal scraping on surfaces. This seems to be as a result of cleaning of the ventral and dorsal surfaces. Circular cut marks on the proximal portion which could be related to using of tools were documented. Also on proximal and middle portions of the pointed tools, soft polishing was observed. While on distal portion smoothing of articulation by abrading technique was noted.

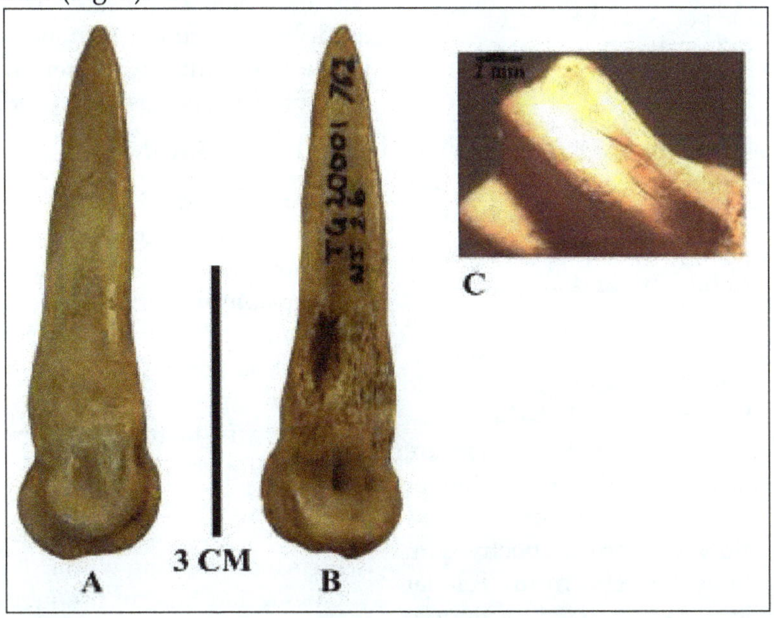

Figure 8: Bone object N. TG 20001, Short awl; A: Frontal view, B: Dorsal view, C: view of distal portion of the metapodial bone show cut marks during disarticulation of bone and smoothed lateral side by abrading technique (Stereomicroscopy photo).

Spatulas surfaces seem to be smoothed by use, so many of anthropic manufacturing marks are polished or canceled. But we document perpendicular and unsystematic scraping on the surfaces. Abrading technique is clear to be used on distal portion of spatulas. No burning on the spatulas surfaces was noted.

Some objects have coloured surfaces ranging from reddish brown to black but none seems to be highly burned (Fig. 9). Most of the pointed bone tools surfaces were preserved and manufacturing modifications are still evident on their surfaces.

Fractures on bone tools in many cases happen due to natural modification of site. Proximal head of pointed tools was preserved only in four cases. While the rest of bone points have ancient fractures which seem to be related to using of tools. Most of the spatulas were well preserved even they are thin and have a long shaft.

On pointed tools with an arch head proximal portion, small fractures from percussion were documented due to use of these tools with hard surfaces. Also on the proximal portion, a variety of unsystematic perpendicular scraping was observed.

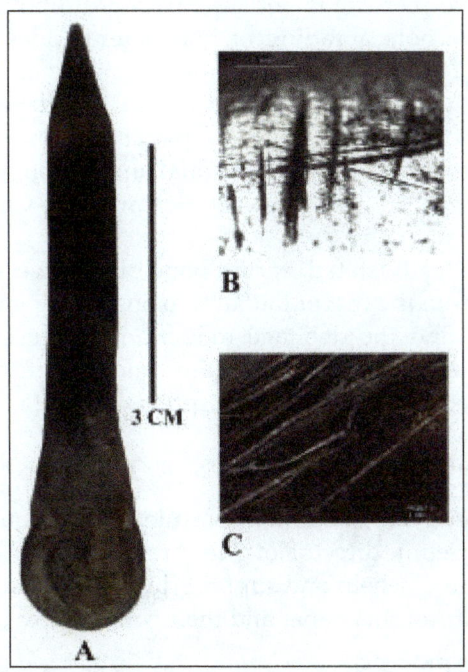

Figure 9: Bone object N. J. 8146, Burned short awl; A: Frontal view, B: View of perpendicular scraping on longitudinal cut marks, C: view of proximal portion show parallel scraping (B, C; Stereomicroscopy photo).

6. DISCUSSION

Pointed tools are the most represented in bone tools categories. The use of pointed tools has continued to dominate in daily working from the Neolithic period. Archaeozoological analysis noted circular traces on the proximal portion of awls. This could be related to the use for perforating leather and fur, these traces were found in many case studies during Neolithic and Chalcolithic periods like Baidha, Ba'ja, Ain Ghazzal, Basta, and Tell AbuSuwwan (Abuhelaleh et al., 2015; Garfinkel and Horwitz, 1988; Gebel et al., 2017; Karasneh, 1989; Nielsen 2009).

In spatulas categories, four pierced spatulas were documented. These modifications indicated the clear appearance of new daily activity within the site that could be related to weaving activity. The possible use of these tools to produce baskets was reduced due to the small thickness and long proportion of spatula. This can't support hard movements during production of baskets. Spatulas during Neolithic period were made of the longitudinal half of large size animal ribs. But Teleilat Ghassul spatulas are thinner in width and thickness, and they are longer than Neolithic ones.

Piercing became a main and interesting activity in producing decorated bone objects from Teleilat Ghassul. Other possibility was suggested by Bourke to use perforated rods object as raw bone to produce beads. But from the microscopic photo, it was observed that pierced entrances extended to outside. And also piercing is not systematic from both sides. And we note abrading of both lateral sides of the object. These results reduce the possibility of using it to produce beads. Also, we would like to mention that perforated rods with 11 piercing are made onlong bone from large size animal and not on ivory as mentioned in the work of Scham and Garfinkel (2007).

As already stated, earlier bone objects were separated from the rest of faunal remains, making it difficult to find the debitage reduction sequence to increase data about production technique. But comparing bone tool with Neolithic published data, a similarity of bone tools typology and anthropic modification was recognized. Also metapodial bones and zeugopodial bones were mainly utilized as a raw material to produce pointed tools. Human groups in Teleilat Ghassul kept bone shafts with epiphysis as handle of awl and also produced two type of awl: long and short awls.

We noticed also the use animal bones from different ages of carcasses. Awls were made from subadult to adult animal's bones. Other categories can't be classified due to the removal of articulation portions of the bones used to produce objects.

7. CONCLUSION

Samples studied from Teleilat Ghassul site were well preserved and they present a variety of categories showing the development of bone crafting during Chalcolithic period.

Piercing became more developed and controlled during this period. This can be seen in pierced needle, spatulas and perforated rod. It can present one of the art features of bone industry during Ghassulian period.

Pierced spatula with their specified typology can be used only to handle soft tissue. It could be a clear evidence of weaving within Tuleilat Ghassul site.

Ghassulian human used domesticated animal and wild animals from the surrounded environment as sources of raw material to produce bone objects. Some samples from awls show theuse of sheep and goat to produce awls. While spatulas and decorated objects belong to large size animal bones.

Awls shaped in two dimensions between long and short shaft. This indicated more specialization and crafting demand of daily works. It's possible to use more short and thick awls to elaborate leather/fur from large size animal. While long and thinner awls can be used to elaborate leather/fur from medium size animals.

Decorated object style reflects different art and ritual ideas within Teleilat Ghassul site. Particularly there is no repeating of these objects between all bone object that came from this site.

ACKNOWLEDGEMENTS

We would like to thank Department of Antiquitie-Jordan and Yarmouk University, director of Amman Citadel Museum, director of Salt Archaeological Museum and director of Yarmouk University Archaeological Museum, for help and support during the study. We would also like to thank Dr. John Winterburn for reading drafts of this paper and their constructive editing and feedback.

REFERENCES

Abuhelaleh, B., Al Nahar M., Thun Hohenstein, U., Berruti, G. L. F. and Cancellieri E. (2015) Experimental Study of Bone Artifact Manufacture from the Neolithic site Tell Abu Suwwan (PPNB-PN), Jordan. Adumatu, Vol. 32, pp. 7-20.

Barone, R. (1980) Anatomia comparata dei Mammiferi domestici. V1: osteologia. Edizione italiana a cura di Bortolami Ruggero. Edagricole.

Becker, C. (1991) The analysis of mammalian bones from Basta, a Pre-Pottery Neolithic site in Jordan: Problems and potential, *Paléorient*, Vol, 17, N.1, pp. 59–75.

Bertolini M., Thun Hohenstein U., (2017), Bevel-ended tools on large ungulate ribs during the Bronze Age in northern Italy: Preliminary result of functional and experimental analyses. *Quaternary International,* Vol. 427, pp. 253-267.

Beyries, S. (1987) Variabilité de l'industrie lithique au Moustérien: approche fonctionnelle sur quelques gisements français. BAR International, Oxford, Archaeopress Series, England 328.

Boessneck, J., Müller, H. and Teichert, M. (1963) Osteologische Unterscheidungsmerkmale zwischen Schaf (Ovis aries Linné) und Ziege (Capra hircus Linné). *Kühn-Archiv,* Vol. 78 N. 1/2, pp. 1–129.

Bourke S. (2008) The Chalcolithic Period, in: In: Adams R, editor. Jordan: An Archaeological Reader, London, pp. 109-160.

Bourke S., Zoppi U., Hua Q. and Gibbins S. (2004) The End of the Chalcolithic Period in the South Jordan Valley: New 14C Determinations from Teleilat Ghassul, Jordan. *Radiocarbon*, Vol. 46, N. 1, pp. 315-323.

Bourke, S. (2002) The Origins of Social Complexity in the Southern Levant: New Evidence from Teleilat Ghassul, Jordan. Palestine exploration quarterly, Vol. 134, pp. 2-27.

Bourke, S. (2007) The Late Neolithic/Early Chalcolithic Transition at Teleilat Ghassul: Context, Chronology and Culture. *Paléorient* Vol. 33, N. 1, pp. 15-32.

Bourke, S. (2008) The Chalcolithic period. In: Adams R, editor. Jordan: An Archaeological Reader. London, Equinox, pp. 60-109.

Bourke, S., Lawson, E., Barbetti, M. and Zoppi, U. (2001) The Chronology of the Ghassulian Chalcolithic Period in the Southern Levant: New 14C Determinations from Teleilat Ghassul, Jordan. *Radiocarbon* Vol. 43 N. 3, pp. 1217-1222.

Bourke, S., Lovell, J., Seaton, P., Sparks, R., Meadows, J. and Mairs, L. (2007) Preliminary report on a Fourth Season of Excavation by the University of Sydney at Teleilat Ghassul, Jordan 1999, ADAJ Vol. 51, pp. 35-80.

Camps-Fabrer, H. (1990) i hes typologiques e l in ustrie osseuse prehistorique. Cahier III: Poincons, pointes, poignards, aiguilles. Aix-en-Provence, Universite de Provence.

Choyke, A. and Schibler, J. (2007) Prehistoric Bone Tools and the Archaeozoological Perspective: Research in Central Europe. In C. S Pierre and R. B. Walker (eds), Bones as tools: current methods and interpreta- tions in worked bone studies, Society for American Archaeology, Meeting 2007, *BAR International Series*, Oxford, pp. 51-65.

Clutton-Brock J. (1979) The Mammalian Remains from the Jericho Tell, *Proceedings of the Prehistoric Society,* Vol. 45, pp 135-157.

Cristiani, E. (2008) Analisi funzionale dei manufatti in materia dura animale del Riparo Dalmeri (Altopiano della Marcesina, Trento). *Preistoria Alpina*, Vol. 43, pp 259-287

D'Errico F., Henshilwood C. S. (2007) Additional evidence for bone technology in the southern African Middle Stone Age. *Journal of Human Evolution*, Vol. 52: 142-163.

D'Errico F., L.R. Backwell, and L.R. Bergerb. Bone tool use in termite foraging by early hominids and its impact on our understanding of early hominid behavior. *South African Journal of Science*, Vol. 97, pp. 71-75.

Dabsch B. and Bourke S. (2014) Ritual, Art and Society in the Levantine Chalcolithic: The 'Processional' wall painting from Teleilat Ghassul. *Antiquity*, Vol.88, pp. 1081-1098.

Drabsch, B. and Bourke, S. (2014) Ritual, art and society in the Levantine Chalcolithic: the 'Processional' wall painting from Teleilat Ghassul. Antiquity Publications Ltd, *Antiquity*, vol. 88, pp. 1081–1098.

Garfinkel, Y. and Horwitz. L. (1988) The Pre-Pottery Neolithic B Bone Industry of Yiftahel, Israel. *Paléorient,* Vol 14, N. 1, pp. 73–86.

Gebel H.G.K., Benz M., Purschwitz C., Kubíková B., Štefanisko D., al-Souliman A.S., Tucker K., Gresky J. and Abuhelaleh B. (2017) Household and Death: Preliminary Results of the 11th Season (2016) at Late PPNB Ba'ja, Southern Jordan. *NEO-LITHICS* Vol 17, N. 1, pp. 18-36.

Hennessy J. (1982) Teleilat Ghassul and its place in the archaeology of Jordan. *Studies in the History and Archaeology of Jordan*, Vol. 1, pp. 55-58.

Karasneh W. (1989) Bone artefacts from Basta, Ain Ghaza and Wadi Shoeb. MA thesis, Yarmouk University.

Martin L. (1999) Mammal remains from the eastern Jordanian Neolithic, and the nature of caprine herding I steppe. *Paléorient,* Vol. 25, N.2, pp. 87-104.

Meadows J. (2005) Early Farmers and their Environment: Archaeobotanical Research at Neolithic and Chalcolithic Sites in Jordan. PhD Thesis, La Trobe University.

Nielsen P. (2009) Worked bones in Pre-Pottery Neolithic B (PPNB) from southern Levant. Master thesis. University of Edinburgh.

S. Bourke, Zoppi U., Q. Hua & S. Gibbins (2004) The end of the chalcolithic period in the south Jordan valley: New 14C determinations from Teleilat Ghassul, Jordan. *Radiocarbon,* Vol. 46, N. 1, pp. 315-323.

Scham S. and Garfinkel Y. (2000) Perforated rods - new Chalcolithic ivory type. *BASOR N.* 319, pp. 1-5. Schmid E. (1972) Atlas of animal bones for prehistorians, archaeologists and quaternary geologists. Elsevier Publishing Company, London.

Yerkes R. W., Barkai R., Gopher A. and Bar Yosef O. (2003) Microwear analysis of early Neolithic (PPNA) axes and bifacial tools from Netiv Hagdud in the Jordan Valley, *Israel. Journal of Archaeological Science,* Vol. 30, pp. 1051-1066.

7

EXTREME PHYSICAL PHENOMENA DURING THE TROJAN WAR

S. Papamarinopoulos[1], P. Preka-Papadema[2], K. Gazeas[2], P. Nastos[3], and K. G. Kiriakopoulos[4]

[1]*Faculty of Geology, University of Patras, GR 26504, Rio Patras, Greece*
[2]*Section of Astrophysics, Astronomy and Mechanics, Faculty of Physics, National and Kapodistrian University of Athens, University Campus, GR 15784, Athens, Greece*
[3]*Laboratory of Climatology and Atmospheric Environment, Faculty of Geology & Geoenvironment, National and Kapodistrian University of Athens, University Campus, GR 15784, Athens, Greece*
[4]*Laboratory of Mineralogy and Petrology, Faculty of Geology & Geoenvironment, National and Kapodistrian University of Athens, University Campus, GR 15784, Athens, Greece*

Corresponding author: Kosmas Gazeas (kgaze@phys.uoa.gr)

ABSTRACT

The Homeric Epic, Iliad, describes the Trojan War's events during a period of only seven days around Patroclus' death. These events are initiated after Athena's appearance as a shooting star. During this period, the poet describes in detail various physical phenomena, which attributed to the gods. Zeus' thunderbolts in a clear sky, 'divine' screams, a fallen thunder stone inducing odor of sulphur, sporadic yellow, red and dark clouds appearing out of nowhere, red droplets are falling from the sky, river Xanthus is flooding and turns into red, Hephaestus' 'flames' ignite fires, whereas seismic activity and raising of the sea level are recorded. The above phenomena can be explained as a consequence of the local weather's circumstances and landscape peculiarities, as well as due to the partial solar eclipse's manifestation, which occurred during the same period. We analysed all these descriptions in detail and we concluded that an intense astronomical phenomenon like a meteor shower including some fireball's explosions is indicated by the poet, in parallel with the Trojan War's combats. This is in accordance with the mythological account of a comet's appearance during Troy's fall, because meteor showers produced by the remnants of the comets, when they approach to the Sun.

KEYWORDS: Iliad, Odyssey, meteors, bolides, fireballs, eclipses, seismoacoustic coupling, seismotectonic activity

1. INTRODUCTION

The Homeric Epic, Iliad, describes the Trojan War's events during a period of only seven days, approximately one or two months before Troy's conquest, althought the Trojan War lasts for ten years according to the Homeric epics. During this period of seven days, the following events take place: a) the departure of Achilles from the battle and the Achaeans' total defeat in the war, as well as the killing of Achilles' friend, Patroclus, by Hector (described in *four days*) b) Achilles' return in the battle and Hector's killing by him (described in *one day*) c) Achilles pays tribute to Patroclus' death and offers Hector's body to Priamus (described in *two days*). Homer does not mention in Iliad the period in association with Achilles' death neither Troy's conquest.

The epic starts presenting the Greeks and the Trojans tired from the calamities of the war. The warriors decided to stop the war by setting the two opponents over Helen's fate, Menelaus and Paris, to fight in a duel. They proposed that whoever was the winner he would take Helen and the armies will have to be retreated. The duel was performed and Menelaus won. However, the goddesses Hera and Athena had different opinion. They wanted the war to start again. Zeus accepted their will and sent Athena in the battle field. Indeed, Athena flew from Olympus as a *glitter star emanating infinite sparks* and appeared in the battle field. The glitter star phenomenon was *visible* under the *daylight*, because the battles' were conducted *only* during the *day*. The latter means that the heavenly body was *very bright*. It did not touch the ground and it did not erupt. It had only an *exceptional brightness*. Homer mentions that heavenly phenomena were known to the sailors which they were the sky's excellent observers because they used to watch the heavenly bodies as navigation's guides.The warriors *'interpreted'* this exceptional heavenly phenomenon as divine 'sign'. It was *Athena's personalization* as she arrived in the battle field (Il.4.73-80):

''Ὣς εἰπὼν ὄτρυνε πάρος μεμαυῖαν Ἀθήνην, βῆ δὲ κατ' Οὐλύμποιο καρήνων ἀΐξασα. οἷον δ' ἀστέρα ἧκε Κρόνου πάϊς ἀγκυλομήτεω ἢ ναύτῃσι τέρας ἠὲ στρατῷ εὐρέϊ λαῶν λαμπρόν· τοῦ δέ τε πολλοὶ ἀπὸ σπινθῆρες ἵενται· τῷ ἐϊκυῖ' ἤϊξεν ἐπὶ χθόνα Παλλὰς Ἀθήνη, κὰδ δ' ἔθορ' ἐς μέσσον· θάμβος δ' ἔχεν εἰσορόωντας Τρῶάς θ' ἱπποδάμους καὶ ἐϋκνήμιδας Ἀχαιούς.'

'So saying, he stirred on Athene, who was already eager, and down from the peaks of Olympus she darted. Just as the son of crooked-counseling Cronos sends a star to be a portent for seamen or a wide army of warriors, a gleaming star, and from it the sparks fly thick; so darted Pallas Athene to earth, and down she leapt into their midst; and amazement came on all who saw her, on horse-taming Trojans and well-greaved Achaeans'

Papamarinopoulos (2008) mentioned this scene and he wondered whether this was a *comet's* description. Indeed, there was a mythological reference of Electra, Dardanus' mother and Troy's founder, which was presented flying in the sky with *her hair flowing freely in it*, during Troy's conquest (e.g. Stagiritis, 1815). Electra's appearence as a heavenly body has a good similarity with a *comet's manifestation* according to the author. However, the Iliad's battle events occur only within seven days, just one or two months *before* Troy's conquest. During these days, Homer described Athena's brief appearance as a 'sparking star'and not Electra's appearence as a 'comet'. Morover, it is known that a comet is usually visible for either hours or days, and therefore it can be observed for a long time.

Athena's rapid behavior is understood from the phrases *'κατ' Οὐλύμποιο καρήνων ἀΐξασα'* (from the peaks of Olympus she darted*)* and *'ἤϊξεν ἐπὶ χθόνα Παλλὰς Ἀθήνη'* (so darted Pallas Athena to earth*)*. The word *'ἀΐξασα'* originates from the verb *'αἴσσω'* which means *hurl* or *move fast*. In other words, Athena *hurled* from Olympus to the Troad, like a fast *'gleaming star, and from it, sparks fly thick'*. Also, the phrase *'κὰδ δ' ἔθορ' ἐς μέσσον'* is interpreted as *'and down she leapt into their midst'. The verb 'ἔθορε' is past tens of the* verb *'θρώσκω'* and it has the prefix *'κατά'* in front of it. This means *'she jumped downwards'*. With this phrase, Homer describes Athena's appearance, with respect to the observer's horizon in the Troad, as suddenly hurled from the *Olympus,* and as such, was fast moving descending from a *higher* elevation (*κατά+ἔθορε* which becomes *κὰδ δ' ἔθορε*) to a *lower* one.

If Athena's appearance was a comet's description, meaning that it has reached such a low altitude with respect to the ground, the Trojan War would have finished immediately due to the Troad's plain unprecedented catastrophe. Such a very fast appearance of a *'sparking star'* in the sky matches well with the shooting star's manifestation; some of the brightest shooting stars, can be visible during daylight. A subcategory of shooting stars is characterized as *earthgrazers* and is described as follows: 'Earthgrazers are long, bright shooting stars that streak overhead from just below the horizon. They often display colorful halos and long-lasting trails. Earthgrazers are so distinctive because they follow a path nearly parallel to the ground, depending on the observer's location and his view with respect to the horizon' (www.spaceweather.com). The above description fits well with the behavior of an earthgrazer shooting star. They appear in low altitude above the horizon and moves horizontally in the upper atmosphere near to horizon offering to the observer the illusion as almost touching the ground. Consequently, a 'sparking star-earthgrazer shooting star' appeared in the daylight compelling all the warriors to be amazed by the heavenly visitor.

This is another astrophysical phenomenon which is described in the Homeric Epics (Theodosiou et al, 2011) and it is attributed to Zeus according to the prevailing theological ideas of prehistoric antiquity. The latter means that god Zeus has the responsibility of everything falling from the sky including *meteors, shooting stars,* besides the known *thunders.* Indeed, Papamarinopoulos et al (2013) indicated that a meteor shower described in the Odyssey and three *'Zeus' type thunders'* occurred in an otherwise clear sky. These thunders were not of atmospheric origin but they were three big and bright eruptive meteors. One of them was accompanied by a meteorite's impact on the ground. In the Iliad, the clear description of the shooting star which sent by Zeus, confirms the above reference in the Odyssey.

Apart of the previously mentioned phenomenon Patroclus' death coincides with another astronomical phenomenon, *a solar eclipse,* as it is proposed by Henriksson (2012) and Papamarinopoulos et al. (2014). The proposed, by the authors, dates for this solar eclipse are 11 June 1312 B.C. (Gregorian calendar) and 6 June 1218 B.C., respectively. Both publications indicated that the first scene, on the Achilles shield, describes Troy's sky during the solar eclipse's manifestation. The referred constellations in this scene marked the solar eclipse's position in the sky.

It is noticeable that *the above mentioned solar eclipse* is followed by another observed *solar eclipse ten years after* which is described in detailed in Odyssey, as indicated firstly by Heraclitus of Pontus (Allegories, 75, 1, 1-9, 3). Schoch (1931), Papamarinopoulos (2008) and Baikouzis and Magnasco (2008) proposed the date of 16 April 1178 B.C. for the Odyssey's eclipse. However, Papamarinopoulos et al (2012) proposed the date 30 October 1207 B.C., after taking into account all the text's details such as the climate conditions, agricultural and bucolic scenes, the long-lasting nights, Laertes' type of life in the field and the described astronomical phenomena (observation of specific constellations all the night, the *'ὀψὲ δύων Βοώτης*-late set Bootes' period (see also Aratus of Soli, Phaenomena and Diosemeia, 579-585) and the visibility of planet Venus in the east before sunrise). All of them were not compatible to the spring but to the autumn. Moreover, the two proposed solar eclipses of 6 June 1218 and 30 October 1207 B.C. (proposed for the eclipses described in Iliad and Odyssey respectively) have a time separation of ten years. On contrary, Henriksson's proposed solar eclipse does not satisfy the Homeric text (see Papamarinopoulos et al. (2014)).

Table 1: Display of the War's years and Odysseus' return

1227-1226 B.C.	Trojan War's 1st year
1218-1217 B.C.	Trojan War's 10th year
1208-1207 B.C.	Odysseus' return to Ithaca, twenty years after his departure

* Every Homeric 'war year', as a time period, is counted between two successive spring or/and summer periods, because wars were not conducted in the winter.

We additionally mention, that through-out the prehistoric and historic period of Greece there was not a unanimous calendar for both the Achaean Kingdoms and city states. Table 1 presents this *common period,* mentioned by Homer, which is not depended on any particular prehistoric calendar but it was connected only with the activities during *the Trojan War.* It is also known that the battles were not conducted during the *winter.* Consequently, the *war's activities 'year', as a time period,* started during the spring or in the summer and ended in the next successive *season.* According to Papamarinopoulos et al. (2014), the *1st year* of Trojan War was between *1227-1226 B.C.* and the *10th year* was between *1218 and 1217 B.C..* Moreover, according to Calchas, Agamemnon and Odysseus (Il.2.328-330, Il.2.134-138, and Il.2.295-296), the events described in Iliad occurred *at the beginning* of the *10th* year of the Trojan War. Consequently, the general *war's activities* and *Troy's conquest* occurred in the *spring/summer* of 1218 B.C.

According to the description of Achilles' shield, the first scene presents the constellations which surrounded the celectial location of the solar eclipse, as indicated by Henriksson (2012) and Papamarinopoulos et al. (2014). Homer also poetically describes the hero's shield (Il.19.373-398) as the *Moon-Μήνης* ('from which went out afar a gleam as of the moon'), Achilles in his panoply as the *Sun-ἠλέκτωρ Ὑπερίων* (*'And behind him stepped Achilles armed for battle, gleaming in his armor like the bright Hyperion'*) and his helmet as a *shooting star-ἀστὴρ ὡς ἀπέλαμπεν* (*'it shone like a star, the helmet with crest of horsehair, and around it waved the plumes of gold'*).

Achilles' *helmet* and his hair are described by the poet, as a *sparking star ('ἀστὴρ δ' ὣς ἀπέλαμπεν').* His *hair,* in particular, is presented, as *thick braids of gold ('πυκνές χρυσές πλεξούδες') wiggling* around as *the sparks of the shooting star.* The description of Achille's helmet and shield, in *combination,* remind us the spectacular shooting star, which appeared *three days before* Patroclus' death and signaled the commencing of the war. This astronomical event eventually led to Patroclus' death. Moreover, Homer presents Achilles with his new *armour* as the *Sun* and calls him *ἠλέκτωρ Ὑπερίων (Elector-Hyperion=Sun).* The bright solar disc is Achilles' body, dressed with his shining panoply.

It is *shadowed,* however, by his *shield* existing *in front* of him. Homer calls that *shield* deliberately Moon (*μήνης = Moon).* The *Sun,* Achilles, is covered by the *Moon,* his *shield.* In other words the observed solar eclipse's phenomenon is presented symbolically (Figure 1).

Figure 1. (Top): Partial solar eclipse, observed from Embu, Kenya by one of the authors (K. Gazeas) on 15 January 2010. (Middle): Achille's modern statue in Kerkyra Island is shown. Homer mimicked the phenomenon on Achilles by calling his new shield-moon-and his new shining panoply-sun.The shield-moon-is in front, of Achilles-the sun-, as in the statue. Homer's emphasis in Achilles' shining panoply, as the sun, illustrates the sun's visibility due to the partial solar eclipse, observed obviously in the Trojan battle. The poet also mimicked Achilles's shining new helmet with his 'golden' wiggling hair in the air, as a sparking star. (Bottom): A large fireball hurtles to Earth during the annual Geminid meteor shower. The picture was taken by Wally Pacholk from the Mojave Desert area near Victorville. (Daily Mail, December 2009 http://fireballs-eteorites.blogspot.gr/2009/12/december-2009.html).

Homer *allows* the *mimesis* of these *phenomena,* the shooting star and the solar eclipse to be *'visible'* again in the minds of his readers who listen or read his poem. He does it, by combining these *unique astronomical* phenomena into one person, the *unique warrior Achilles*. These phenomena were impressive in the minds of the early years' observers. They are both, focused on Achilles because they are associated, with Patroclus' loss, his friend. The first is the amazing shooting star which signaled the war's beginning leading to *Patroclus' death*. The second occurred *at the peak of the drama,* described in the Iliad; the death of his beloved friend *coincided* with the *solar eclipse*. After these two consecutive events, Achilles enters the battle field, ready to take revenge.

During the seven days of the epic, several more phenomena are described, in addition to those mentioned above. Zeus' thunderbolts occurred in a clear sky and 'divine' screams were heard engulfing the warriors in terror. A thunderbolt with the sulphuric odor impacted the ground. Dark, yellow and red clouds appearred locally out of nowhere, sometimes connected with odor. 'Red droplets' were falling from the sky, Xanthus River's waters were flooding and turned red, Hephaestus' 'flames' were falling from the sky, while tremors and rising of the sea level were recorded.

In this paper, we try to identify and analyse the epic's descriptions, having in mind what Plutarch (Fragmenta 157), the Delphic priest wrote: 'The *old physical science* for both, the Greeks and the Barbarians is *natural logos* hidden deeply within myths and theology'. In other words we shall search to find 'the old physical science' and the phenomena related with it, which are presented *hidden deeply* behind *divine* interventions. Athena's *divine* interference in the battlefield, for instance, was a myth by poetic allowance. However, it contains a true physical event, an exceptionally bright *earthgrazer shooting star*.

2. BRIEF DESCRIPTION OF THE PHENOMENA

In the Iliad, five references of *Zeus' thunders* are described. However, according to Homer's description, the weather conditions do not match with any kind of storm. During the first day, a cool north wind is described (Il.5.697-698), while the next days are characterized by very hot atmospheric conditions and calmness (Il.10.570-575, Il.11.621-622, Il.11.642, and Il.11.811-812). Only at the sixth day the weather changes to NW direction (Il.23.194-195). While battles are carried out, there is no reference of any storm. In addition, it is known that the battles did not take place during the winter. During spring and summer, storms may sporadically occur in the area of Troad. Moreover, the dates for the Iliad's events as proposed by Henriksson (2012) and Papamarinopoulos et al. (2013) correspond to a typical warm summer.

Three more passages describe events, in which '*sudden moving clouds*' accompanied by strong '*divine screams*', appeared. There are two additional descriptions with similar characteristics, which present further complexity. The first event is the red droplets, falling from the sky and the appearance of a red cloud. The second event exhibits the flooding of Xanthus' River, the changing of its waters' color into red and the warriors' feeling of the ground tremors.

All these events, including Athena's appearance like a shooting star, are tabulated in sequence, as they are presented in the Homeric text and shown in the Table 2 (A, B and C).

3. PHENOMENA PROCEEDING PATROCLUS' DEATH

During the day in which Athena appeared as a *shooting star* (number 1, Table 2A), Mars roared few hours later '*as nine or ten thousand warriors*', because Athena injured him. The latter spreads terror in the armies, (number 2, Table 2A). Simultaneously, Mars *engulfed* himself with a '*black darkness*' as fire does, producing hot air and black smog. This strong powerful sound like a prolonged 'roar', with smog's appearance fits well with a '*fireball's breakage*'. Homer seems to associate Mars' manifestation (fireball's breakage) with Athena's appearance, as a shooting star, connecting the latter with Mars' 'wound' (Il.5.859-867):

ὁ δ' ἔβραχε χάλκεος Ἄρης ὅσσόν τ' ἐννεάχιλοι ἐπίαχον ἢ δεκάχιλοι ἀνέρες ἐν πολέμῳ ἔριδα ξυνάγοντες Ἄρηος. τοὺς δ' ἄρ' ὑπὸ τρόμος εἷλεν Ἀχαιούς τε Τρῶάς τε δείσαντας· τόσον ἔβραχ' Ἄρης ἆτος πολέμοιο. Οἵη δ' ἐκ νεφέων ἐρεβεννὴ φαίνεται ἀὴρ καύματος ἐξ ἀνέμοιο δυσαέος ὀρνυμένοιο, τοῖος Τυδεΐδῃ Διομήδεϊ χάλκεος Ἄρης φαίνεθ' ὁμοῦ νεφέεσσιν ἰὼν εἰς οὐρανὸν εὐρύν.

Then brazen Ares bellowed loud as nine thousand warriors or ten thousand cry in battle when they join in the strife of the War god; and trembling came over Achaeans and Trojans alike, and fear took hold them; so mightily bellowed Ares insatiate of war. Just as a black darkness appears from the clouds when after heat a blustering wind arises, so to Diomedes, son of Tydeus, did brazen Ares appear as he went among the clouds to broad heaven.

Table 2A: Homeric scenes and proposed physical events which are including within 1st to 4th days.

number	number of day	described event/passage	proposed physical event
1	1st day	Athena's appearance like an exceptional bright star emanating infinite sparks (Il.4.73-86).	*Appearance of an earth grazer bright shooting star in the Troad.*
2	1st day	Mars was injured by Athena and his scream was terrible. The armies were in terror. He left covered in a dark cloud (Il.5.859-866).	*Fireball's breakages and trajectory of its debris.*
3	2nd night	Zeus' thunders cause terror among the Achaeans.They make libations to Zeus.	*Fireball's breakages*
4	3rd day	Zeus' thunder originated from Ida mountain. It blazed flash into the warriors who were dazzled and terrified (Il.8.75-77). Zeus hurled a white thunder, from Ida mountain, and let it to crash on the ground in front of the horses emitting flame and releasing sulfur. The horses bolted and the charioteers were panicked (Il.8.133-136).	*Two almost simultaneously scrap bolide's explosions directed from Ida Mountain to the Troad. In the second case, a burning meteorite smelling sulphur crashed on the ground.*
5a	4th day at dawn	Zeus sent Eris to the Achaeans' ships-she holds a war's portent screaming terribly (Il.11.3-12). Immediately after that, *simultaneously*, Athena and Hera hit the ground (Il.11.45-46). Zeus roused an evil agitation and he trickled blood drops from the sky (Il.11.52-54).	*A bolide's remnant impacts on the ground, somewhere near the ships. The produced dust grains from the bolide's dissintegration are mixed with the early morning's moisture due to the very hot day. The mixture being in condensation falls down as red drops. The colour depends on the bolide's chemical composition.*
6	4th day	God Poseidon from mount Samos peak of Thrace arrived in Troad. The high mountains and the woodland are trembled (Il.13.10-19). Poseidon's terrible scream equally in intensity as Ares' scream in the first day was heard (Il.14.147-151). Hera moves quickly from Lemnos and Imbros, clothed in mist and arrived to Lectum (opposite to Lesbus). The topmost forest trembled beneath her feet. (Il.14.281-285). Hera climbed to Ida's peak, Gargaron, and Zeus covered it with a gold thick cloud (Il.14.342-345, 350-351). The sea surged up to the huts and ships of the Achaeans (Il.14.392).	*A fireball's breakages whose heard in the Troad. Its debris' trajectory was visible above Imbros island as a mist cloud leading toward Lectum (from West to South) and reach Gargaron (Ida's peak). The fireball's remnants appeared as a golden cloud on Ida's mountain peak. Simultaneously, an earthquake occurred and it was felt in the entire region of Asia Minor's coast. A typical consequence of a submarine epicentre is the sea's surging up to the beach.*
7	4th day	Zeus thundered from Ida Mountain answering to Nestor's prayer (Il.15.377-378).	*Fireball's breakage in Ida Mountain.*

Table 2B: Homeric described scenes and proposed physical events around Patroclus's death

number	number of day	described event/passage	proposed physical event
5b	4th day at noon	For the second time, Zeus trickled red drops (Il.16.458-459).	*This is a continuation of the phenomenon previous described in 5a. The difference with it is the solar eclipse's occurrence at noon. During the solar eclipse, the temperature is drastically reduced and the moisture is increased. As a consequence the remaining remnants of the bolide fall dawn as red drops.*
5c	4th day at noon	Zeus sends Athena like a red cloud (mist) in the battlefield. This mist sits on the ground (Il.17.543-552).	*These conditions mentioned above assist the red grains (see 5a and 5b) to pill up in the atmosphere and to fall dawn on the battlefield as reddish fog during the maximum phase of the solar eclipse.*
8	4th day at noon	Zeus covered Ida Mountain with clouds and he thundered with lighting from it (Il.17. 593-596).	*Bolide's explosion*
9	4th day at noon	Achilles stead above the trench and Athena set around his head a golden cloud with a gleaming flame. Also, the goddess strengthen Achilles' scream. The horses scared and the charioteers panicked (Il.18.184-229). The sun had set prematurely due to Hera ((Il.18.239-240).	*A fireball's impact on the ground caused a fire. A golden dust cloud containing the remnants of the fireball was emanated in the atmosphere. The flame from the fire is engaged by the dust cloud. The golden cloud and the fire's smog caused the darkening of the atmosphere and the warriors thought that the sun set prematurely.*

During the second night, after the *'sparking star's appearance'* while Achaeans enjoy a rich dinner, they hear Zeus' thunders and they gave explanations among themselves that it was a bad omen (number 3, Table 2A). They were afraid and made libations to Zeus (Il.7.478-479):

'παννύχιος δέ σφιν κακὰ μήδετο μητίετα Ζεὺς σμερδαλέα κτυπέων· τοὺς δὲ χλωρὸν δέος ᾕρει …'

'And all night long Zeus, the counselor, devised them evil, thundering terrifyingly. Then pale fear seized them…'

These very strong sounds *without lightnings* were experienced at night by the warriors, who, in turn, got frightened and thought that they came from a *distant ongoing storm.* But in this case they would have seen the lightning prior to the thunder. Homer, however, does not mention any lighting in the text. Only Zeus's 'bangs' are described. Thus, the phenomenon has no meteorological origin. It can be easily explained as a breaking of a fireball at some distance from the Achaeans's camp. In any case we know that Zeus was responsible for 'thunders' of either meteorological or astronomical origin. Such a case justifies the fear of warlords and their libations to Zeus, as it is an unusual phenomenon and not a usual storm.

During the dawn of the third day (Il.8.1-2), Zeus arrived on mountain Ida's peak, in order to have a better look of the Trojan War's battlefield (Il.8.47-52). The latter has an altitude of 1774 m and is located southwards, 58 km away from Troy's plain. Zeus had his throne on the mountain's peak named Γάργαρον-Gargaron (Il. 3.276, Il.3.320, and Il.8.48). At the same day, at noon (Il. 8.66-68), when the Sun was at its higher position in the sky while crossing the local meridian (*'Ηέλιος μέσον οὐρανὸν ἀμφιβεβήκει'-the sun had bestrode mid heaven*), Zeus *thundered* from Mount Ida and *flashed* in the battlefield. The war chiefs and all the chariots were dazzled by the brilliance of the event and run away in panic (number 4, Table 2A). Immediately, Zeus *thundered again* from Mount Ida and threw a *thunderbolt* before Diomedes' horses, which were got scared from the *fire and the odor of sulfur*. Diomedes and Nestor fled away with their chariots in terror. The description is as follows (Il. 8.75-77 and Il. 8.133-170):

'αὐτὸς δ' ἐξ Ἴδης μεγάλ' ἔκτυπε, δαιόμενον δὲ ἧκε σέλας μετὰ λαὸν Ἀχαιῶν· οἳ δὲ ἰδόντες θάμβησαν, καὶ πάντας ὑπὸ χλωρὸν δέος εἷλεν…'βροντήσας δ' ἄρα δεινὸν ἀφῆκ' ἀργῆτα κεραυνόν, κὰδ δὲ πρόσθ' ἵππων Διομήδεος ἧκε χαμᾶζε· δεινὴ δὲ φλὸξ ὦρτο θεείου καιομένοιο, τὼ δ' ἵππω δείσαντε καταπτήτην ὑπ'ὄχεσφι…. τρὶς μὲν μερμήριξε (Τυδεΐδης) κατὰ φρένα καὶ κατὰ θυμόν τρὶς δ' ἄρ' ἀπ' Ἰδαίων ὀρέων κτύπε μητίετα Ζεὺς'

'Then himself he thundered aloud from Ida, and sent a blazing flash into the army of the Achaeans; and at the sight of it they were struck with wonder and pale fear seized them all… He thundered terribly and let fly his white lightning-bolt and down before the horses of Diomedes he hurled it to earth; and a terrible flame arose of burning sulphur and the two horses seized with terror, shrank back beneath the chariot… Thrice he wavered in mind and heart and thrice from the mountains of Ida Zeus the counselor thundered.'

This entire event had a direction toward south, with respect to the battlefield, *originating* from Mount Ida. It is known that lightning and thunderbolt occurs only during a storm. However, the scenario of a storm, occuring during the battle, must be rejected, as *it is not mentioned by Homer.* Moreover, the fresh smell in the air after a thunderstorm is caused by ozone, which is naturally created near the ground by lightnings. Lightning is also known to produce nitrogen oxides within thunderstorms. These chemicals can react with other elements in the presence of sunlight, to produce ozone (Pfister et al., 2008; Ryu and Jenkins, 2005). In our case the thunderbolt stroke in broad daylight and produced odor of sulfur within the battlefield.

Consequently, Zeus's particular thunderbolt has not a meteorolical origin. The possibility of a nearby volcanic eruption as responsible for the sulphur's odor, it is not supported from past geological studies. The last volcanic eruption in North and South Aegean Sea and at North West Asia Minor is dating back thousands of years (Cagatay et al, 2015 and Ballengee et al, 2015).

Table 2C: Homeric scenes and proposed physical events within the 5th day

number	number of day	described event/passage	proposed physical event
10a	5th day (dawn)	Participation of all the gods in battle (Il.20.20-25, Il.20.75). Ares' and Athena' mixed divine screams are heard in various parts all over the Troad (Il.20.48-53). Zeus thundered on the sky, Poseidon shook the earth, the boats and Troy's city and god Aides screams terribly.	*A fireballs' breakage occurs above the Troad. A strong earthquake accompanied by an underground's roar is occurred.*
10b	5th day	An impenetrable cloud covered Poseidon and other gods near Hercules' wall (Il.20.149-150). Also, Hera spread a thick mist near to the Xanthus' River ford (Il.21.6-7).	*A meteors' cloud with their remnants occurred in Hercules' wall and near to Xanthus' River ford.*
10c	5th day	Xanthus' river flow was blocked by many *dead bodies* and clogged the River's ford. The river's water flow flooded the plain (Il. 21.218-307). The river's waters turn red color like blood (Il.21.326).	*The earthquake changes the flowing river in front of the Xanthus' River ford caused the river's swelling. This can be happened due to landslides of slopes river and/or to deflection of water from the normal flow. As a consequence, the plain was flooded. The waters' red color is the result of the sediment's shuffling in the river's bottom and of the dead bodies'* blood.
11	5th day	Hera screamed and said to Hephaestus to manifest much flame. She said to gods Zephyrus and South to rouse from the sea a fierce blast in order to push the Hephaestus' flames in the Troad plain. The flame burned everything in the plain and heated the river's waters (Il.21.328-382).	*Dissolution of a bolide over the Aegean Sea and close to Troad's coastline. The strong southwest wind, a blast wave, pushed two flaming debris toward the plain and Xanthus River. The fragment's falling caused extensive fire.*

On the other hand, the bolides explode into the atmosphere with loud strokes and light. When a bolide remnant (meteorite) strikes on the ground could produce odor of sulfur, depending on the bolide's chemical structure (Kaplan and Hulston, 1966, Ebel, 2011). The odor of sulfur originates from ferrous sulfuric oxides, which is one of the possible components of the meteorites e.g troilite which is a rare iron sulfide mineral (FeS). Troilite is among the minerals found in samples of the meteorite that struck Chelyabinsk in Russia on February 15th, 2013 or in the Canyon Diablo meteorites, which have been found around the Barringer Crater (Meteor rim in Arizona, USA (Figure 2, top). Thus, we conclude that a bolide exploded in the atmosphere originated from Mount Ida's direction. A burning part of the exploded meteor reached in the battlefield, while the flashing and the sulfur's odor of the bolide's remnant (meteorite) caused panic in the army.

4. PHENOMENA THAT OCCURRED ON PATROCLUS' DAY OF DEATH

Poseidon was watching the battle from the peak of mountain Samos of Thrace (Il.13.10-40). That day Poseidon decided to help Achaeans; he came down from the mountain and went to Achaeans' camp (Il.13.31-33). Although his presence encourages the Achaeans in the battle, the Trojans are victorious.

Figure 2. (Top): Yellow meteorite: Canyon Diablo iron meteorite fragment (IAB) 2641 gr. (Bottom): Red meteorites: Eucrite, Polymict Breccia, Fell October 1960 Western Australia, (http://www.meteorite-times.com/Back_Links/2006/June/Meteorite_of_Month.htm).

As the Achaeans'leaders are going to ask Achilles' assistance, Poseidon roared as nine or ten thousand warriors (number 6, Table 2B). His roar was similar with Mars' roar, which was heard few days ago. It seems that a similar phenomenon as in Mars' case occurred, i.e. a new fireball broke in the atmosphere and a strong prolonged sound was heard. The description is as follows (Il.14.147-151):

'...Ὣς εἰπὼν μέγ' ἄϋσεν ἐπεσσύμενος πεδίοιο. ὅσσόν τ' ἐννεάχιλοι ἐπίαχον ἢ δεκάχιλοι ἀνέρες ἐν πολέμῳ ἔριδα ξυνάγοντες Ἄρηος, τόσσην ἐκ στήθεσφιν ὄπα κρείων ἐνοσίχθων ἧκεν.'

'...So saying, he shouted mightily as he sped over the plain. As loud as nine thousand warriors, or ten thousand, cry in battle when they join in the strife of the War god, so mighty a shout did the lord, the Shaker of Earth, send out from his breast.'

The emerged cloud with fireball's fragments was not observed over the entire battlefield; because the big meteor flied somewhere near to the Trojan plain. Indeed, almost simultaneously with *Poseidon's scream*, Hera, being 'covered' by a *kind of mist*, departed from Lemnos and Imbros islands and arrived to cape Lectum, opposite to Lesbos Island, at the foot of the Mount Ida (Figure 3). This description illustrates the fireball's breakage as it appearred over Imbros Island. The fireball's fragments are contaminated with meteoritic particles in powder-size grains (rich in iron, sulfur etc) producing a contrail along the fireball's path. They are all advected within the *atmosphere* which is *Hera's usual personification* with a direction from Imbros Island *southwards*, i.e. towards Lectum, opposite to Lesbos Island (Il.14.281-285).

'...τὼ βήτην Λήμνου τε καὶ Ἴμβρου ἄστυ λιπόντε ἠέρα ἑσσαμένω ῥίμφα πρήσσοντε κέλευθον.Ἴδην δ' ἱκέσθην πολυπίδακα μητέρα θηρῶν. Λεκτόν, ὅθι πρῶτον λιπέτην ἅλα· τὼ δ' ἐπὶ χέρσου βήτην, ἀκροτάτη δὲ ποδῶν ὕπο σείετο ὕλη.'

'...they left the cities of Lemnos and Imbros and clothed about in mist went out speeding lightly on their way. To many-fountained Ida they came, mother of wild beasts, to Lectum, where first they left the sea; and they went on the dry land and the topmost forest quivered beneath their feet.'

Wind's direction was *opposite* to the direction which fireball's fragments initially had. The Homeric text gives detailed information on this, since at that day Zeus left 'heaven' and settled himself on the mountain Ida's peak, before Poseidon's appearence in the battlefield. His arrival must be at around 10:00-10.30 in the morning because it occurred after *'the woodcutter's lunch time'* (Il.11.84-90). After that, Homer describes a *sandstorm*, originating from Ida's mountain (*southward* of Troy's battlefield) with direction toward the Achaeans camp (*north or north-west* with respect the battlefield). The sandstorm covers the Achaeans' ships with a lot of dust (*'ἐπὶ δὲ Ζεὺς τερπικέραυνος ὦρσεν ἀπ' Ἰδαίων ὀρέων ἀνέμοιο θύελλαν, ἥ ῥ' ἰθὺς νηῶν κονίην φέρεν- And Zeus who hurls the thunderbolt roused from the mountains of Ida a blast of wind that carried the dust straight against the ships'*, (Il.12.252-254)). The northward motion of the sandstorm indicates airflow towards the same direction, while the fireball's fragments moved towards the opposite direction.

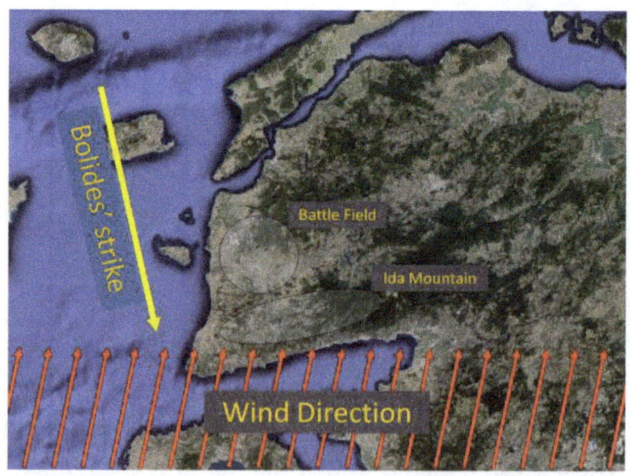

Figure 3: A bolide strikes over Imbros Island with southward direction towards Lectum (opposite to Lesbos Island). The produced particle cloud, like a mist, also moves southwards due to its initial kinetic energy. As the motion brakes down due to atmospheric friction, the southern wind takes place and directs the motion northwards. The cloud's momentum against the existing southern wind decelerates up to cape Lectum, which is located in the feet of Mount Ida, and then it turns northwards.

We note that the particle cloud, *like a mist*, moves southwards due to its initial kinetic energy. As the motion brakes down due to atmospheric friction, the already mentioned southern wind takes place and directs the motion northwards (see Figure 3). The cloud's momentum against the existing southern wind decelerates up to cape Lectum, which is located on the feet of Mount Ida, and then it turns northwards. The mist which includes the bolide's remnants, after the turning, appears as a 'gold cloud' (Il.14.343-345) on Ida's mountain peak.

According to the text, goddess Hera is decided to '*mislead*' Zeus in order to help Poseidon. From this reason Hera from mount Olympus arrived in Lemnos and together with god Hypnus departed from Lemnos and Imbros islands to Mount Ida's peak (Gargaron). Hera met Zeus who asked her to be '*bedded in love*'. The goddess was willing but she was afraid that everybody could see them, on the mountain's peak: *Ἴδης ἐν κορυφῇσι, τὰ δὲ προπέφανται ἅπαντα'-'on the peaks of Ida and everything is plain to view'* (Il.14.332). Then Zeus covered the mountain peak with a 'thick golden cloud' (Il.14.343-345):

'…τοῖόν τοι ἐγὼ νέφος ἀμφικαλύψω χρύσεον· οὐδ' ἂν νῶϊ διαδράκοι Ἠέλιός περ, οὗ τε καὶ ὀξύτατον πέλεται φάος εἰσοράασθαι.'

'…With such a cloud shall I enfold you, a cloud of gold. Through it not even Helios could discern us, though his sight is the keenest of all for seeing.'

The official English interpreter gives the impression to the reader, that Zeus covered only Hera and himself with the cloud by saying '*shall I enfold you*'. However, in some phrases earlier in the text (Il.14.332), Hera clearly says that the *peaks* of Ida Mountain are *visible* to everybody and not *only herself* in particular. Consequently Zeus responding to Hera's request covered from *all possible* sides the mountain's peak. This is exactly the meaning of the verb '*ἀμφικαλύπτω*' and not '*enfold*'. The word's power '*ἀμφι*' means that every side on the mountain's peak has the *same property* as its corresponding antidiametric side. In other words the entire mountain peak is fully covered and hence is invisible from all directions. The initial mist, originating from Imbros Island, reached Mount Idas' peak. It is the fireball's remnants which were driven by the air. The cloud's thickness was such that, it did not allow the sun's rays to penetrate it. It fully covered the peak and got a *golden (yellow) color*. The color depends on the chemical composition of the fireball. We note that the meteorite *on the ground* of another fireball had an odor of sulfur (see section 2). The latter had also a characteristic yellow color.

We mention to the reader that Homer characterizes Mount Ida having many fountains (Il.14.307 '*πολυπίδακος Ἴδης*'). In the text the word spring ('*πηγή*'), which means simply flowing water from the ground, is not used. On the contrary the word many fountains ('*πίδακες*') from which water were ejected from the ground upwards is used. It is understandable that when water is ejected upwards due to pressure, as the fountain does, it comes back to the ground like glistering dew drops, as exactly it is described in the text (Il.14.350-351):

'…ἐπὶ δὲ νεφέλην ἕσσαντο καλὴν χρυσείην· στιλπναὶ δ' ἀπέπιπτον ἔερσαι.'

'…and were clothed about with a cloud, fair and golden, from which fell drops of glistering dew.'

We also note that this particular mountain peak is called 'Gargaron' whose name means gurgling water, even in modern Greek grammar.

Moreover, the above mentioned golden thick cloud had *a pleasant smell* according to the text ('*ἀμφὶ δε θυόεν νέφος ἐστεφάνωτο- and about him (Zeus) a fragrant cloud was wreathed*', (Il.15.153)). Even if we accept that the chemical composition of the fireball was iron sulphide, it did not retain the sulfur's odor because of the prevailing conditions on Ida's mountain peak, in which the following plants existed: grass, lotus, crocus and hyacinth (Il.14.347-349). The combination of the odors of these fresh plants in a watery environment due to the existence there, of many *nature made fountains*.

Later, as the Achaeans are fighting close to their ships, against the advancing and victorious Trojans, Nestor *prayed* to Zeus and the latter *responded* with a *thunder* originating, once more, from Ida Mountain ('*μέγα δ' ἔκτυπε μητίετα Ζεύς…- Zeus the counselor thundered aloud*', (Il.15.377-380)). The clouds covered fully the mountain's peak, they are dense and golden, and offer a pleasant smell. From *these* properties we conclude that they are not stormy clouds (number 7, Table 2A). Although Homer describes a very hot day, these particular clouds do not fit with the *cumulonimbus clouds*. These are associated with *thermal thunderstorms*, expected in the hot hours of the day, following intense heating at the ground (Metaxas et al. 1999, Nastos et al. 2002, Nastos et al. 2014). In addition, there wasn't any reference for *lightening*. If this '*thunder*' was connected with a meteorological phenomenon, there should have been a preceeding lightening which is exhibited *always* before the thunder. Consequently, the above mentioned Zeus' thunder is one more meteoric phenomenon (fireball's breakage).

During the afternoon hours of the same day, the Achaeans retreated *near their ships* hunted down by the Trojans. The Sun was still well above the horizon, while Achilles was going to the trench, in order to be seen and scare the Trojans (Il.18. 197-201). In this Homeric battle scene, Achilles has already passed *the trench* and he was on the *defense wall's top*, having the ships in his front and the plain in his back, (Il.18.148-150 and Il.18.198). Another *thick golden cloud* and a big fire with *bright flame reaching the sky* were visible from the direction of Troy's plain, on Achilles' back (number 9, Table 2B). The phenomenon was accompanied by *strong sounds* personalized as Achilles' *terrible screams*. The flame and the strong sounds are poetically associated with goddess Athena and Achilles (Il.18.203-229) too.

'...ἀμφὶ δ' Ἀθήνη ὤμοις ἰφθίμοισι βάλ' αἰγίδα θυσσανόεσσαν, ἀμφὶ δέ οἱ κεφαλῇ νέφος ἔστεφε δῖα θεάων χρύσεον, ἐκ δ' αὐτοῦ δαῖε φλόγα παμφανόωσαν... ὡς ἀπ' Ἀχιλλῆος κεφαλῆς σέλας αἰθέρ' ἵκανε. στῆ δ' ἐπὶ τάφρον ἰὼν ἀπὸ τείχεος....ἔνθα στὰς ἤϋσ', ἀπάτερθε δὲ Παλλὰς Ἀθήνη φθέγξατ' ἀτὰρ Τρώεσσιν ἐν ἄσπετον ὦρσε κυδοιμόν.... ἀτὰρ καλλίτριχες ἵπποι ἂψ ὄχεα τρόπεον· ὄσσοντο γὰρ ἄλγεα θυμῷ. ἡνίοχοι δ' ἔκπληγεν, ἐπεὶ ἴδον ἀκάματον πῦρ δεινὸν ὑπὲρ κεφαλῆς μεγαθύμου Πηλεΐωνος δαιόμενον· τὸ δὲ δαῖε θεὰ γλαυκῶπις Ἀθήνη.'

'...and around his mighty shoulders Athene flung her tasseled aegis, and around his head the fair goddess set thick a golden cloud, and from the man made blaze a gleaming flame. ...so from the head of Achilles went up the gleam toward heaven....There he stood and shouted and from afar Pallas Athene called out, but among the Trojans he roused unspeakable confusion....And the fair-maned horses turned their chariots backward, since they saw woe in their hearts. And the charioteers were stricken with terror when they saw the unwearied fire blaze terribly above the head of the great-hearted son of Peleus; for the goddess flasing-eyed Athene made it blaze.'

The scene describes a flaming fireball, which broke loud and a meteorite's piece fell on the ground, close to inflammable materials and caused fire. The remnants *as a golden (yellow) cloud* appeared over Achilles' head *in projection*. The common properties of the early clouds in comparison with this scene, as well as the yellow color on Ida Mountain's peak, imply the common chemical composition and origin of all these fireballs. Moreover, this particular cloud's appearance had an effect in the sky (Il.18.239-241): *'Ηέλιον δ' ακάμαντα βοώπις πότνια Ηρη πέμψεν επ' Ωκεανοίο ροάς αέκοντα νέεσθαι. Ηέλιος μεν έδυ-Then was the unwearyingly Sun sent by ox-eyed queenly Hera to return, unwilling, to the stream of Ocean. So the sun set'*. The thick dust cloud, transported by the air (Hera), covered the sunlight and it gave the impression that the sunset occurred *earlier* than his normal time.

5. RED DROPLETS AND A RED CLOUD

Zeus *at dawn* of the forth day (Il.11.1-14 and Il.11.50) sends Mars' sister and comrade, Eris (Strife), to the Achaeans' ships. Eris was extended up from the sky down to earth (*'ἥ τ' ὀλίγη μὲν πρῶτα κορύσσεται, αὐτὰρ ἔπειτα οὐρανῷ ἐστήριξε κάρη καὶ ἐπὶ χθονὶ βαίνει -'She first rears her crest only a little, but then her head is fixed in the heavens while her feet tread on earth'*, (Il.4.439-445)). She had in her hands *'πολέμοιο τέρας (a portent of war)'*, standing between the ships and screaming loudly (*'ἤϋσε θεὰ μέγα τε δεινόντε ὄρθι - she uttered a great and terrible shout a shrill cry of war'*. Eris' voice was heard in the entire Achaeans' campus and their ships. In other words, a terrible scream was heard from one edge of the battle field all the way to the other, accompanied with a war's celestial symbol (*'τέρας'*). The warriors heard the scream, awakened suddenly and they began to prepare for the war (number 5a in Table 2A). Then, goddesses Athena and Hera (Il.11.45-46) honored Agamemnon, King of Mycenae, with a big stroke (*'γδούπος'*), like a body falling on the ground (Il.11.45-46):

'...ἐπὶ δ' ἐγδούπησαν Ἀθηναίη τε καὶ Ἥρη τιμῶσαι βασιλῆα πολυχρύσοιο Μυκήνης...'

'...Athene and Hera thundered, doing honor to the king of Mycenae...'

The interpreter describes the word *'εγδούπησαν'* which means *'hit the ground'* as *'thundered'*. This is not correct, however, because the thunder is associated with a meteorological phenomenon and not with the sound of falling body on the ground. The Homeric passage seems to describe the appearance of a bolide in the sky (*'πολέμοιο τέρας'*), giving details about its trajectory (*Eris extended between sky and earth*), its explosion (*Eris' scream*) as a celestial and loud phenomenon. A large part of this bolide fell on the ground with a strong sound (*'γδούπος'*). The warriors did not see any lighting coming from the bolide, since they were sleeping in their tents and woke up abruptly, exactly to this strong sound.

Simultaneously, Zeus caused a *'bad disruption'* in the air and *'blood' droplets* from the sky fell on the ground, as an omen of many men's death (Il.11.52-55):

'...ἐν δὲ κυδοιμὸν ὦρσε κακὸν Κρονίδης, κατὰ δ' ὑψόθεν ἧκεν ἐέρσας αἵματι μυδαλέας ἐξ αἰθέρος...'

'...The son of Cronos roused an evil din and down from on high out of heaven he sent dew drops dank with blood...'

We consider that this atmospheric disruption can be produced by the dissipation of the soil's dust and the bolide's fragments, due to a creation of an impact crater, with high velocity upwards in the atmosphere.

Another explanation of this *'bad disruption'* could be a dust devil (tornado). However, studies on tornadoes over the wider area of Greece (Nastos and Matsangouras 2010, Matsangouras et al. 2014, Nastos and Matsangouras 2014) have revealed that, on one hand, tornado's monthly variability depicts a maximum during automn and on the other hand, tornadoes are pre-frontal extreme phenomena (thunderstorm). There is no report of a nearby thunderstorm mentioned by Homer. Also the described extremely warm weather conditions do not fit with the autumn climatic conditions, in which one expects high propability of tornado's occurrence. Moreover, tornadoes most commonly develop during the warm time of the day, as more than 75% of all cases occur during 08:00–15:00 hours UTC with a maximum at 12:00 hours UTC. Following Homer's description this atmospheric phenomenon occured early in the morning. Consequently *Zeus' air disruption* can not be explained or compared with a tornado.

Another approach is to think that a *Saharan red dust cloud* was transported to the North East Aegean Sea and fell as the dawn's moisture (*'blood'droplets*). Such a hypothesis, although attractive, is also rejected because the Saharan episodes are common in East Mediteranian Sea during late winter and *very* early spring. They occur when strong southern air mass flows towards north direction and is adverted from Saharan regions towards the Aegean Sea (Barkan et al. 2005, Antoine and Nobileau 2006, Kaskaoutis et al. 2008, Nastos 2012). The duration of these dust events is usually 1-2 days, since the depressions favoring them, while they move quickly and attenuated. Specifically, during spring, the *Sharav* cyclones carry Saharan dust towards the Eastern Mediterranean, while in summer the most intense activity occurs in the central part. By the end of summer a low pressure system over the Balearic Islands drives the dust plumes towards the Western Mediterranean (Meloni et al. 2007). On the other hand, Saharan episodes are associated with an *extensive cloudiness* that covers a whole area over Eastern Mediterranean. This is generated by the presence of the depression and the uplift of water vapor from the sea. Such a southern air flow associated with cloudy weather is not documented in the Iliad. Instead, the description fits well with sunny days and heatwave conditions. Also, a Saharan episode is not associated with any atmospheric disturbance, as the described Zeus' *atmospheric disruption*.

An alternative scenario could be that the *'blood' droplets* could be caused by ash's red constituents from a possible nearby volcanic eruption. However, we know from detailed geological studies in Greece and in Asia Minor that there is not any near or distant volcanic activity during the 12th and/or the 13th century B.C. since no ash deposit has been ever found in drilled cores collected in either the Hellespont, Black Sea or in the Troad itself, in this time period. Consequently, we conclude that the *'blood'droplets* do not have a volcanic origin.

Another interpretation of the *red* drops phenomenon is that it could be caused by the Haematococcus Pluvialis, unicellular green algae which produces astaxanthin, a type of *red* pigment ketocarotenoide, with major antioxidant properties. This kind of algae has a complex life cycle changing several cell forms, depending on the environmental conditions (Elliot, 1934). Under environmental stress, it appears morphological cell changes, characterized by *red* color, reaching the ground as *red* droplets, in case of a rain episode (Guerin et al., 2003; Guerrero et al., 1999). The geographical distribution of *Haema*tococcus Pluvialis is widespread, since it appears in wetlands of North America and the coasts of European Atlantic Ocean, while it is worth noting its absence over the wider area of Mediterranean (Martinez-Silva, 2011). A recent paper by Fernández-Lozano et al. 2015 analyzes a rare *red rain* event in Spain during autumn 2014. The authors came to the conclusion that *Haema*tococcus Pluvialis was transferred by strong western winds blowing over Iberian Peninsula from the Atlantic Ocean, since there is not any sign of Pluvialis in the nearby lakes the day after the rain event. Taking into consideration the aforementioned assumption, the case of *red rain droplets* caused by *Haema*tococcus Pluvialis should be excluded, since, to the best of our knowledge, it has not ever been reported in the Eastern Mediterranean.

We have rejected all other possible exlpanations for the *'blood droplets* and we have pointed out that the bolide's explosion is poetically described as the Eris' appearence and scream, while Athena and Hera hit the ground. We conclude that the *'blood' droplets'* are connected with the bolide's explosion with the following mechanism: At dawn, a big bolide intersected the atmosphere with a terrible sound *('Eris' scream'*) and impacted on the ground *('ἐπὶ δ' ἐγδούπησαν Ἀθηναίη τε καὶ Ἥρη - Athene and Hera thundered')*, producing a crater from which the soil and the fragments of the bolide were ejected upwards (*'εν δε κυδοιμόν ώρσε κακόν Κρονίδης- The son of Cronos roused an evil din'*). Powder-like grains, produced by the remnants of the bolide's explosion, can act as condensation nuclei. The increased humidity during dawn, as well as the event's proximity to the sea, combined with the pre-existing condensation nuclei, could result in *'blood'droplet's* precipitation. The red color of the droplets is characteristic for the iron-oxides and their chemical compounds (e.g. *haematite*) and clay's minerals, which are consisted a common chemical composition of the meteors (Figure 2b, bottom). In addition, *red-colored nitrogen oxides* can be produced, as the bolide causes chemical reaction between the existing elements.

In addition to the morning's events which were analysed above, new similar events are presented later, during the solar eclipse's manifestation. In an earlier paper, Papamarinopoulos et al. (2014), have presented analytically the solar eclipse's occurrence and progression (solar eclipse's start time is 14:10

LT). At *noon* (Il.16.777-780), when Patroclus engaged in fighting with Sarpedon (5b, Table 2B), Zeus sprinkled the battlefield with *'blood' droplets* (Il.16.459):

'αἱματοέσσας δὲ ψιάδας κατέχευεν ἔραζε'
'he shed bloody rain drops on the earth'

Earlier in our text, we had interpreted the dawn's fall of *'blood' droplets* as a result of a high humidity. But now, the fall of *'blood' droplets* happened during *hot atmospheric conditions at noon* (Il.10.572-575, Il.11.621-622, Il.11.642-643, Il.11.811-812, Il.12.385-388). It is known that a sudden decrease in the atmospheric temperature occurs during a solar eclipse. As a consequence of *temperature drop, humidity rises*, as shown in Figure 4. These conditions, in combination, most likely interpret the *'blood' droplets*, due to condensation process on the *red grains* that have remained in the atmosphere, due to the bolide's explosion in early morning. The lack of a blowing wind allowed the morning's *red grains* to remain in the atmosphere. Thus, these *red droplets* have the same explanation as the early morning's ones, under the extreme conditions of the solar eclipse. Figure 5 presents a simulated representation of the atmospheric conditions during the partial solar eclipse (with a magnitude of 75%) of 6th of June 1218 B.C. (see Papamarinopoulos et al, 2014), as it could be observed from the wider area of Troy. The diagram utilizes measurements similar to those in Figure 4, but decreased by a factor of 75% and adjusted accordingly for afternoon hours, in order to mimic atmospheric changes during the partial eclipse in Troy. This Homeric scene following by a reference of a 'kind of darkness' at noon, after Sarpedon's dead (Il.16.567-568), fits well with the time period between 14.30-14.45 LT of Figure 5.

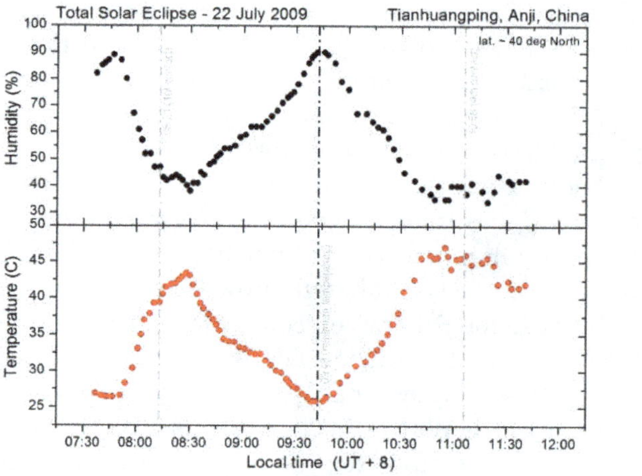

Figure 4. Local atmospheric conditions change during a solar eclipse, as the upper atmosphere cools down and this is transferred gradually on the ground. In parallel, humidity rises as a consequence of temperature drop. The diagram above shows actual measurements during the total solar eclipse, which occured on 22 July 2009 in Tianhuangping, China (from K. Gazeas' observation).

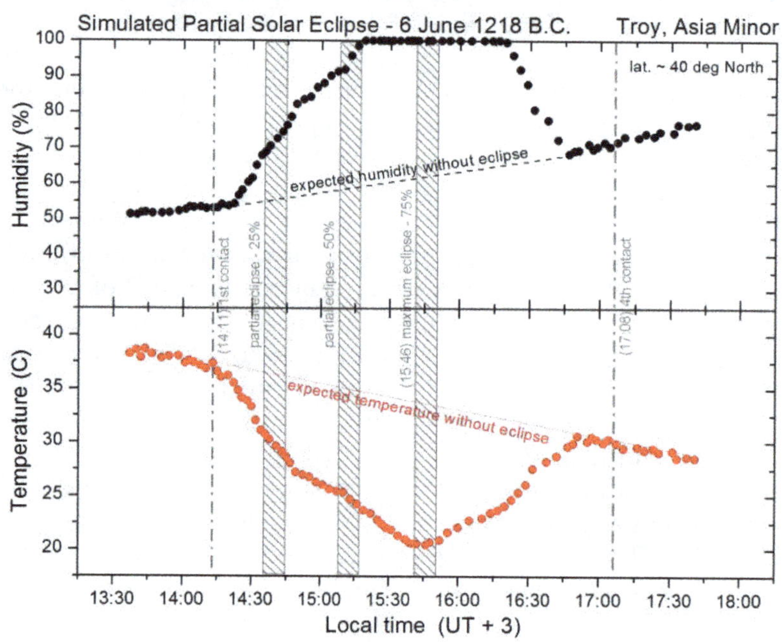

Figure 5. The diagram shows a simulated representation of the atmospheric conditions in the area of Troy during 6 June 1218 B.C., using as a guide the actual measurements from Figure 4 but decreased by a factor of 75%. In addition the actual values are multiplied by an additional factor which represents the temperature drop as the daylight deminishes and temperature drops during evening times. When 25% of the solar disk is covered one may notice a temperature drop but it is very rare. Usually human senses detect temperature drop when 50% of the solar disk is covered. This is connected with illumination changes, which start being obvious in the environment even for an unaided eye. For the next 30 minutes the eclipse moves from 50% to 75% when the temperature drops significantly and humidity rises to maximum.

After the fall of the *'blood' droplets'*, Hector and Patroclus got engaged in fighting (Il.16.760-761) and Patroclus was killed by Hector (Il.16.786-810). According to the description about the solar location (Il.16.777-780), it is indicated that the time has been advanced toward *late noon*. Then, Achaeans and Trojans began fighting around the dead Patroclus' body and 'another kind of darkness' at noon is described by the Homeric text (Il.17.269-270, see also Il.17.366-376). The scene fits well with the time around 15:15-15:30 LT, according to Figure 5. While they continue to fight, in order to obtain Patroclus' dead body, Zeus sends Athena like a *red cloud* (5c, Table 2B) in the battle field (Il.17.543-552):

'…ὣς ἣ πορφυρέῃ νεφέλῃ πυκάσασα ἓ αὐτὴν δύσετ' Ἀχαιῶν ἔθνος, ἔγειρε δὲ φῶτα ἕκαστον'

'…so Athene wrapping herself in a dark-shimmerring cloud entered the throng of the Danaans and roused each man.'

This *deep red cloud* (personalized by Athena) did not stay in the sky but it *landed* on the battlefield between the fighters. We note that the interpreter did not pay attention to the word *'πορφυρέη- porphyra'* which in Greek means *deep red*. He does not characterize the cloud as *deep red*, but as 'dark shimmering cloud'!

The red cloud could be produced by the *red grains* (*'blood' droplets*), which remained in the atmosphere since early morning, acting as condensation cores. The existence of these grains in the atmosphere in combination with the steep humidity rise and temperature drop, due to the solar eclipse, produced a deep red cloud, which fell over the battlefield, giving the impression of a *mist*.

We mension that, just a little earlier, *there is not a single cloud* either on the plain or on the mountains (*'νέφος δ' οὐ φαίνετο πάσης γαίης οὐδ' ὀρέων'-on all the earth and the mountains was no cloud seen')*, according to the Homeric text (Il.17.366-376). Almost simultaneously with the *red cloud's falling* on the battlefield, Zeus who was always on Mount Ida's peak, *fully covered* the mountain with clouds (number 8,Table 2B) and *lightened and thundered*: *''Ιδην δὲ κατὰ νεφέεσσι κάλυψεν, ἀστράψας δὲ μάλα μεγάλ' ἔκτυπε -enfolded Ida with clouds and lightened and thundered mightily'*, (Il.17.594-596). It seems that the mist spread over a large area and all the Mount Ida covered by the haze. One more bolide's explosion directed from the Mount Ida has occurred.

A few minutes later, being close to the solar eclipse's maximum phase, Ajax shouts in agony that it is impossible to see anything (Il.17.643-647). Ajax's *complete divisibility* is explained due to the *combination* of the red cloud's landing in the battlefield just minutes earlier than the eclipse's peak (~15:40 LT, see Figure 6) and the resulted significant darkening of the eclipse itself at 15:45 LT (solar disk's obscuration of 75%) according to Papamarinopoulos et al. (2014). The divisibility period lasted only for a few minutes, because immediately Zeus (Il.17.648-650):

'…αὐτίκα δ' ἠέρα μὲν σκέδασεν καὶ ἀπῶσεν ὀμίχλην, ἠέλιος δ' ἐπέλαμψε'

'…immediately scattered the darkness and drove away the mist and the sun shone on them'

Zeus acted *twice* at that time; he scattered the *darkness* and drove the *mist*. In other words, the *two different phenomena* which in combination produced the complete divisibility-the *solar eclipse's effect* and the *red cloud-haze*-were completely vanished. Then, *'ἠέλιος δ' ἐπέλαμψε'-the sun shone'*. The Sun're-shone' is used and not simply 'shone', because the verb 'to shine' means *'λάμπω'*, whereas the Homeric verb ἐπιλάμπω' meaning that the Sun did not shine for some time and then it *shone again*.

6. SEISMIC ACTIVITY

In Section 4, we refer to the Homeric description (Il.13.17-19) about Poseidon, who came from Thrace, while the mountains and the woods were trembling beneath his feet and he arrived to the Troad (*'τρέμε δ' οὔρεα μακρὰ καὶ ὕλη ποσσὶν ὑπ' ἀθανάτοισι Ποσειδάωνος ἰόντος - And the high mountains and the woodland trembled beneath the immortal feet of Poseidon as he went)*. In addition, when Hera and Hypnus arrived in Cape Lectum, opposite to Lesbos Island, the woods were trembling too under their feet (*'Τὼ δ' ἐπὶ χέρσου βήτην, ἀκροτάτη δὲ ποδῶν ὕπο σείετο - and they went on the dry land and the topmost forest quivered beneath their feet'* (Il.14. 281-285)). These two phenomena occurring sequentially in the same morning, with a relatively short interval between them, could be interpreted as two distinct geophysical events, which seem to have local earthquake's characteristics. They are distributed along Asia Minor's west side towards the Aegean Sea. Almost simultaneously, the sea's level rise reached the Achaeans' ships and tents ('ἐκλύσθη δὲ θάλασσα ποτὶ κλισίας τε νέας τε *Ἀργείων -the sea surged up to the huts and ships of the Argives'*, (Il.14.392-393)). This activity, in connection with the two seismic events, is similar with a small tsunami's performance. The entire presented information indicates a sub-marine epicentre with a shallow depth. We note that all three places, which are connected with tremors, located on the well known active North Anatolian Active Fault System (Figure 6).

The next day, after Patroclus' death, early in the morning, terrible screams by Athena and Mars are heard in all Troy's plain (number 10a, Table 2C). Simultaneously, a terrible strong thunder from Zeus (*'δεινόν δε ἐβρόντησε… ὑψόθεν' - terribly thundered… from on height*) was heard and an earthquake produced by Poseidon was felt (*'Ποσειδάων ἐτίναξε γαῖαν ἀπειρισίην - Poseidon caused the vast earth to quake'*). Mountains, the plain, Troy's city, the Achaeans ships were all shaken severely (Il.20.45-65). Even Hades screamed (*'he leapt from his throne and cried aloud'- δείσας δέ εκ θρόνου ἆλτο καὶ ἴαχε'*) from his underground palace, being scared that the ground will open from above, due to the intense earthquake. We should mention again that just in the previous day, two more weak seismic events accompanied by tsunami waves were also occurred. During this day, almost 24 hours after the first two weak earthquakes, a very strong earthquake was felt throught-out the plain, from the Hellespont to Ida Mountain.

Trifonov (2010) indicated that in Troy VI layer's walls, there was evidence of a seismic damage (Figure 7). The existence of seismic activity does not mean necessarily that these seismic events correspond to the seismic event decribed by Homer. The high seismicity of the entire region is compatible with traces of seismic events, recorded in various Troy's layers, which have occurred in various time periods.

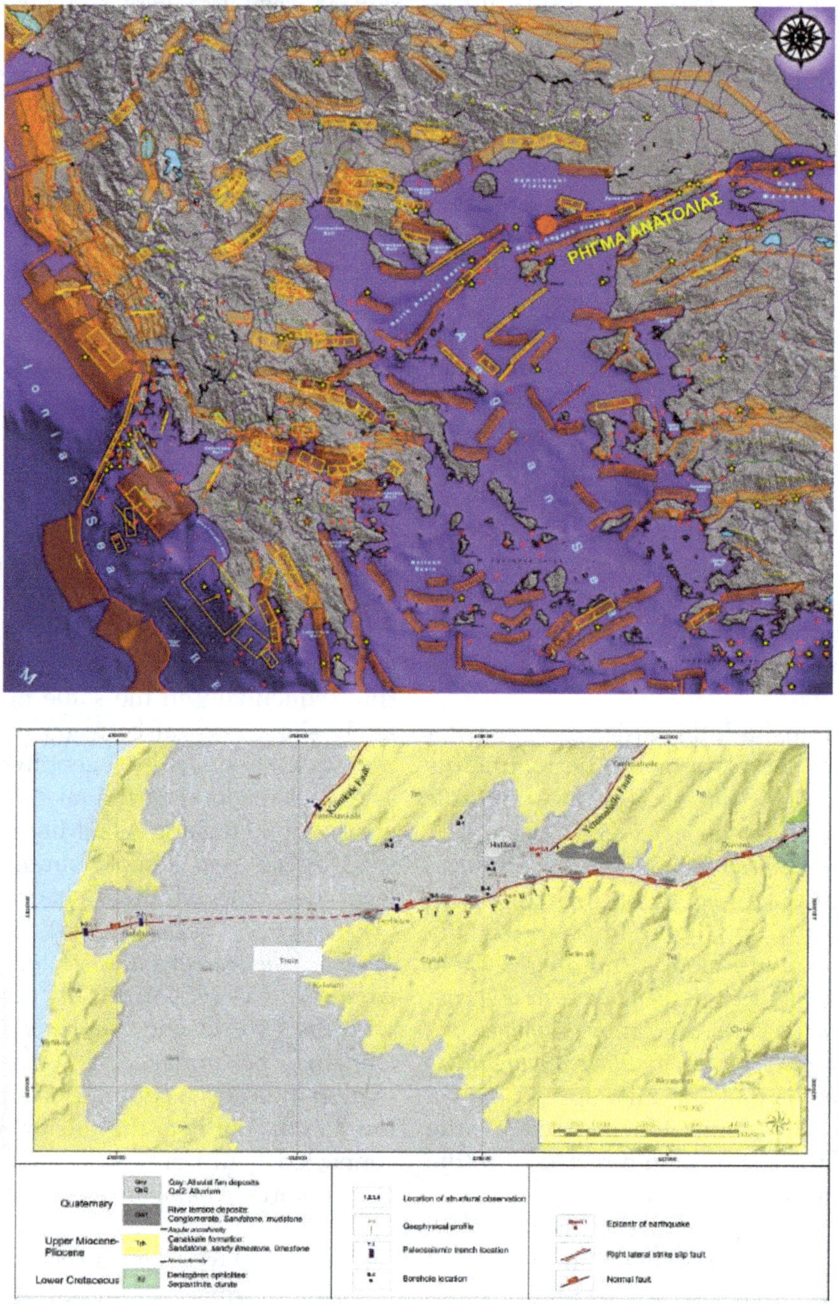

Figure 6. a) The gridded map of the geological faults in the wider Aegean area. (Papanikolaou, I.D. and Papanikolaou, D.I. (2007). Seismic hazard scenarios from the longest geologically constrained active fault of the Aegean. Quaternary International 171-172, 31-44. b) Troy's fault is passing through Troy's site. It is an extract from the paper published by Kurcer et al (2012).

Figure 7: a. Break in anti-seismic constructions in the eastern part of Troy's VI walls constructed by 'Poseidon' himself during Laomedon's kingship (Troy VIh layer) in accordance to Iliad and the Greek mythology. b. The clockwise rotation of the Palace VIM (southern part of Troy's VI layer. c. The counter clockwise rotation of the wall in the Roman epoch (southwestern part of the Troy IX layer). The two seismic rotational motions in clock and anticlockwise directions of adjacent constructions of Troy's VI and IX layers respectively demonstrate deformations by different seismic events, (after Trifonov, 2010).

Kurcer et al. (2012) attempted to interprete the visible seismic damages in Troy's walls shown in Figure 7 carrying out extensive field work on the so called 12 km Troy fault (Figure 6). The team's rational is based on palaeoseismic evidences, *excavated* along the Troy fault, passing through *ancient* Trojan territory, and also in C-14 datings carried out on samples from chronological datings taken from drillings at different depths from Troy's fault too. They concluded that the visible damages, on Trojan walls are not due to *ground differential motion* but they are due to past seismic events originating from different faults and *not from the main Troy fault itself.* The authors followed the formula introduced by Pavlides and Caputo, (2004), concluded also that the so called Troy fault is not responsible for any seismic activity until 1190 B.C. They attributed the damages in Trojan walls in other active faults, in Biga Peninsula or/and from Gaziköy-Saroz regions which represent the north branch of North Anatolian Fault System.

As they admit in their research, they could not reach a bigger depth in the Tevfikiye trench due to the found by them free water horizon. If they had reached some meters or so deeper than the depth, which they have stopped, they *might have found* evidence of an earthquake which had occurred on the Trojan layer VIh, and/or the 'Homeric' earthquake occured one or two months before Troy's conquest, which occured in 1218 B.C. according to Papamarinopoulos et al. (2014).

Exactly due to the high seismicity of this region, in accordance with the Greek mythology and the Iliad as well, the strong walls of (layer VIh) Troy's Acropolis that withstand the strong earthquakes were built *so strongly* by *'Poseidon'* himself *during Laomedon's kingship.* The resistance to earthquakes of these Acropolis' walls, of course need an 'engineer' as capable as 'Poseidon', the so called in Iliad 'ενοσίχθων'-κοσμοσείστης (the world's shaker), since 'Poseidon' was the god of the earthquakes and of the waters too.

This strong earthquake which deformed the constructions of Troy VIh layer is dated *after* 1300 B.C. (Troy VIa-VIh, c.1700-1250 B.C., (Fields, 2004)), in accordance to the archaeological studies. No human remains have been found in the debris produced by this earthquake. It seems that people left in time without taking away their belongings and the same people came back and rebuild the city using the debris produced by the previously mentioned earthquake. They rebuild it fastly and careslessly, placing the new buildings within the Acropolis, with dense stucture.

Probably they did, under military threat. This new 'rebuild' city is Troy VIIa layer. From the conducted studies, there is no cultural void between Troy VIIa and VIh layers, because the found objects are similar. Troy VIIa layer extends over a small period, maybe within one human generation (~30 years). It is totally destroyed by fire and it is replaced by Troy VIIb layers (Troy VIIa-VIIb2, c.1250-1050 B.C., (Fields, 2004)).

Blegen (1963) indicated that Troy VIIa layer is the Homeric Troy, because the archaeological findings led to a regime under emergency, maybe even under siege. The fact that other supporting findings of the siege have not been found is due to the complete destruction of the layer VIIa by the builders of the layer VIIb. Further destructions of VIIa and VIIb have occurred by the new successive building activities, from that period until the Roman times. One needs to add that further catastrophes have occurred in VIIa and VIIb layers by Schliemann and other excavators, because architectural remains were removed and the recording of the obtained data did not follow the typical modern procedures. This has as the consequence that some findings got lost for ever and some others produced confusion.

In accordance with the Greek mythology before the *known* Homeric *Trojan War* against the Trojan King Priamus, there was another war, conducted by Hercules and the fathers of the heroes of the *known Trojan War* against the Trojan King Laomedon, who was Priamus' father. *Young Priamus* was witnessed the first Trojan War and became Troy's King, as Laomedon's successor. The latter has been killed by Hercules. The second *known* (Homeric) Trojan War had the Achaean King Agamemnon of Mycenes and the *old now Trojan King Priamus* as leaders of the Greeks and the Trojans respectively. It seems that after the first Trojan War, there was always the military threat of a second war and this was the cause of the fast and careless, dense structure building, *within the Acropolis,* after the earthquake which destroyed Troy VIh layer.

We mentioned earlier in the text that the strong Trojan (layer VIh) walls were built by *'Poseidon'* himself *during Laomedon's kingship.* However, Laomedon refused to pay and Poseidon sent a monster to do damages on the plain, according to the Greek mythology. Hercules killed this monster, but again Laomedon refused to pay. This was the reason of the first Trojan War. Consequently, the strong *Troy VIh* was the *layer corresponding* with the *Laomedon's Kingdom.* We also note that the Troy VIh layer presents *earthquake's destruction* and the successive, culturally similar, *Troy VIIa layer presents fire's destruction.* This evidence is in accordance with the second (Homeric) Trojan conquest, in which the *Acheans burned the city.* The Troy VIIa was the Priamus's Kingdom. The Homeric descriptions of seismic activity took place one or two months before Troy's second fall.

7. PHENOMENA OF THE NEXT DAY AFTER PATROCLUS' DEATH DAY

The next day, after Patroclus' death, starts with terrible screams by Athena and Mars, a terrible strong Zeus' thunder and an intense earthquake, produced by Poseidon (see previous section). After these events, Poseidon, Hera and the other gods withdrawn in Hercules' wall (Il.20.149-150) and they covered themselves by an opaque cloud (*'ἄρρηκτον νεφέλην'- impenetrable cloud*). Hercules' defensive antiflood wall was situated close to Hellespont, against the Poseidon's monster (see the previous section). It was protecting Troy's plain, as it was at that time period. We interpret these phenomena as a *bolide's explosion* which occured in some distance from the Troad. It is known that the sound of the Tunguska bolide's explosion, in 1908, was heard at a distance of 800 km from the epicenter of the event, without seeing any light (Rubtsov, 2009). Also, in the Homeric text no light is described during this explosion. Its fragments and powder-sized grains (number 10b, Table 2C) caused the appearence of an opaque cloud.

After the strong earthquake's occurrence and during the battle's progress, Achilles has pushed the Trojans near to the ford (*'πόρος'*) of Xanthus River (Il.21.1). Part of the Trojan army is within the river, whereas the rest of the army retreats to the plain toward the city. At that moment *'Hera spread before them (the retreating part) a thick mist to hinder them'- 'ἠέρα δ' Ἥρη πίτνα πρόσθε βαθεῖαν ἐρυκέμεν',* (Il.21.6-7). This thick mist is a second appearance of the cloud's remnant produced by the previously mentioned bolide's breakage which was transferred by the *atmospheric air (personalized by Hera)* to the plain (number 10b, Table 2C). Achilles is now in combat with the Trojans in Xanthos River's waters *at the ford,* while he had killed several enemies. According to the text, the dead bodies were so many that they obstructed the river's flow towards the Hellespont (Il.21.213-221). As a consequence, the river's waters flood the plain, pushing dead bodies outwards. The turbulent waves reached Achilles, who was trying to run within the flooded plain (Il.21.234-300). The water's impetus and quantity is quite large and Achilles' life is in danger (number 10c, Table 2C). The *ford ('πόρος')* was positioned northwest to Troy's city, near to Ilus' tomb (Il.14.433, Il.21.1, Il.24.349-351, and Il.24.692-693). Obviously, the river narrows in this area, which was near Troy, serving as the passage from and towards the city. Probably, the strong earthquake rearranged the river's path, by inducing landslides in its slopes. The latter in combination with the existence of many dead bodies in the river's ford blocked the river's flow in that narrow passage, resulting in flooding of the plain.

Then the text describes that river *Xanthus,* whose name means *blond,* changes his color into deep red (*'πορφυρέον'*), while it is still flooding and rushing. The interpreter *again* misses entirely the waters' redness by saying simply 'dark flood'! The waters' red color is attributed by Homer to the bodies' blood (Il.21.324-327):

'...Ἦ καὶ ἐπῶρτ' Ἀχιλῆϊ κυκώμενος ὑψόσε θύων μορμύρων ἀφρῷ τε καὶ αἵματι καὶ νεκύεσσι. πορφύρεον δ' ἄρα κῦμα διιπετέος ποταμοῖο ἵστατ' ἀειρόμενον, κατὰ δ' ᾕρεε Πηλεΐωνα'.

'...he spoke and rushed tumultuously on Achilles raging on high and seething with foam and blood and corpses. And the dark flood of the heaven-fed river rose towering above him and was about to overwhelm the son of Peleus.'

The red color may be caused by stirring of sendiments of the river's bed together with what fell from the slopes and the blood of dead bodies as well. However, after a short time, the strong water's flow cleared and the normal flow of the river restored. Homer's notification that the event will last temporarily is given as information to Achilles by the 'gods Athena and Poseidon' which intervene and confirm to Achilles that the river will be soon calm (Il.21.292): *'ἀλλ' ὅδε μὲν τάχα λωφήσει, σὺ δὲ εἴσεαι αὐτός'- 'he will soon cease and you yourself will know it'.*

According to the Homeric text, the two rivers, Xanthus-Scamander and Simoes, which flow northward, towards the Hellespont, they are connected at some point (*'ἀλλ' ὅτε δὴ Τροίην ἷξον ποταμώ τε ῥέοντε, ἧχι ῥοὰς Σιμόεις συμβάλλετον ἠδὲ Σκάμανδρος - but when they had come to the land of Troy and the two flowing rivers where the Simois and the Scamander join their streams'*, (Il.5.773-776)). This connection point must be southwards of Xanthus' river ford, because the flooding occured only there. The flood phenomenon does not include Simoes. For this reason, although Xanthus *'invited'* Simoes to flood by adding water from his springs in order both to kill Achilles, Simoes did not *'respond'* (Il.21.311-314). Furthermore, if we assume that a submarine earthquake or a submarine landslide had occurred in the Hellespont and caused a tsunami, it would have simultaneously produced a reversal of both the rivers' flows and it would have flooded the entire plain. A tsunami would have destroyed the ships and the camp itself. No battles could be performed in the flooded plain. Consequently, the normal continuity of the battle would have stopped.

The question which rises here is 'if the described earthquake is related or not with the bolide's explosion' because there are seismic waves which are generated by the sonic blast wave assosiated with the meteor (Angin and Haddon, 1987). When a bolide enters the atmosphere at hypersonic velocities, it produces a ballistic shock wave, within a narrow *Mach Cone*. The induced pressure wave propagates an almost cylindrical wave front. Additional shock waves with quasi-spherical wavefronts can also be produced by the bolide's fragmantation. These shock waves propagate through the atmosphere and could be detected as infrasound waves. These infrasounds impinge the earth's surface with sufficient energy to induce a measurable seismic signal (Edwards et al. 2007). Indeed, Le Pichon et al. (2013) recorded infrasounds in sensors of the Conprehensive Nuclear Test Ban Treaty (CNTBT) associate with the Chelyabisk bolide's explosion (2013). According to Tauzin et al. (2013), in the case of Chelyabinsk event, there are fine seismic records of Rayleigh waves (Figure 8), produced by the coupling of ground motion with the incident shock wave, which was caused by the main sonic blast that it is associated with the observed damages and injuries. These Rayleigh waves were recorded in 4000 km distance away from the focal point of the bolide's explosion.

Additionally, Vasilyev, N.V. (2004) mentions that the two seismic stations placed at Irkutsk Magnetographic and Meteorogical observatory recorded the Tugunska seismic event produced by a bolide's explosion. There are references that have shown simultaneous seismic records with magnitudes ~M5 and ~M4, in connection with the Chelyabinsk and Tunguska bolides' explosions respectively. After the presented analysis, one can not exclude the coupling between the Homeric seismic event and the bolide's explosion.

When Xanthos River overflooded the field and Achilles was in danger, *Hera screamed* fearing for Achilles' life. Another *'sound'* was heard in the atmosphere as *divine voice, (Il.21.328,' Ἥρη δὲ μέγ' ἄϋσε'-but Hera cried out*). Hera asked Hephaestus to manifest much *flame* in order to burn the trees and inflame the river until her herself told him to stop (Il.21.333-341). The flame's origin was from a southwest direction with respect to Trojan field, from Aegean Sea side and was coupled by a terrible gale, a fierce blast:

'...ἀλλ' ἐπάμυνε τάχιστα, πιφαύσκεο δὲ φλόγα πολλήν.αὐτὰρ ἐγὼ Ζεφύροιο καὶ ἀργεστᾶο Νότοιο εἴσομαι ἐξ ἁλόθεν χαλεπὴν ὄρσουσα θύελλαν, ἥ κεν ἀπὸ Τρώων κεφαλὰς καὶ τεύχεα κήαι φλέγμα κακὸν φορέουσα· σὺ δὲ Ξάνθοιο παρ' ὄχθας δένδρεα καῖ', ἐν δ' αὐτὸν ἵει πυρί...ἀλλ' ὁπότ' ἂν δὴ φθέγξομ' ἐγὼν ἰάχουσα, τότε σχεῖν ἀκάματον πῦρ'

'...manifest much flame, but I will hurry and rouse from the sea a fierce blast of the West Wind and the white South Wind that will utterly consume the Trojan dead and their battle gear, spreading on the evil flame. And you along the banks of Xanthus burn up his trees and set him about with fire ... when I call to you with a shout then stay your unwearied fire.'

We interpret this phenomenon as a *strong shock wave (χαλεπήν ὄρσουσα θύελλαν- fierce blast)* accompanied by a fiery body, a meteorite *('φλόγα πολλήν' - much flame)*, which had been produced by a low altitude flying bolide's explosion (*Hera' scream*), over Aegean Sea (number 10d, Table 2C). Homer further describes the *fiery gale's* results. This incident burnt the plants and bushes close to Xanthus River and evaporated fully the previously flooded plain close to the river's ford ('πόρος'). Moreover, a second flaming meteorite falls on the river, producing bubbling and eddies and tormented the river's life forms (Il.21.342-345 and Il.21.349-361):

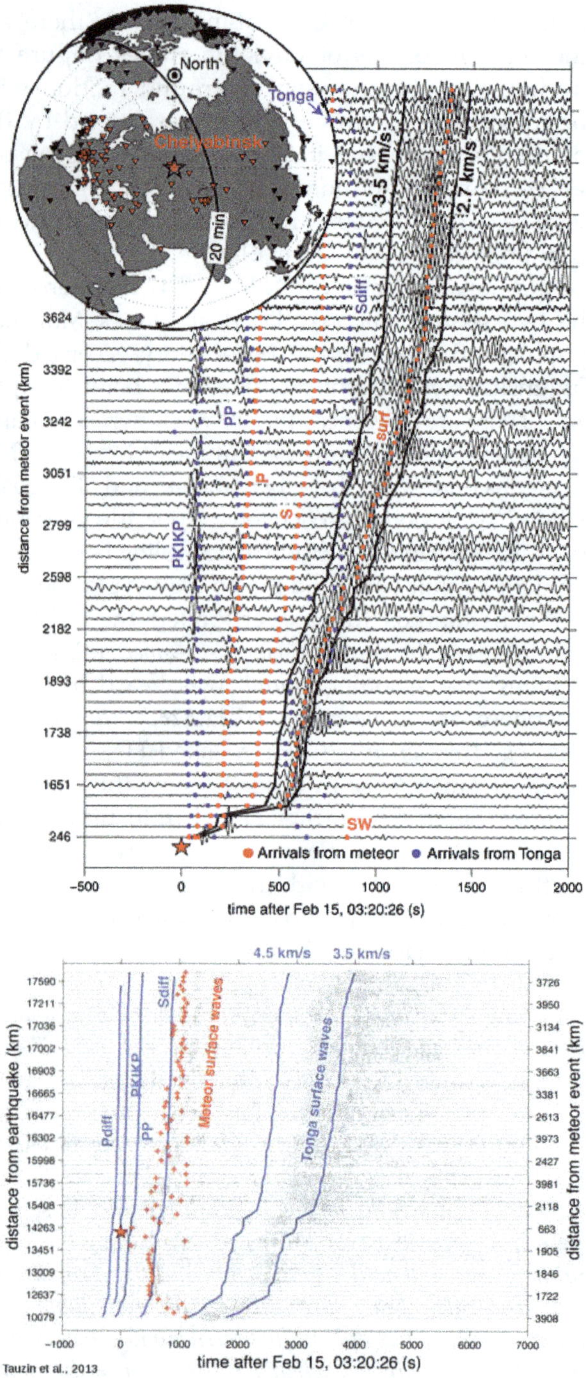

Figure 8. (top) Vertical component seismograms for stations located within ±4000 km from the city of Chelyabinsk. Body waves (PKIKP, PP, and Sdiff) from the Tonga earthquake are indicated with blue dots. The gray curves delineate inferred Rayleigh waves associated with the Chelyabinsk meteor. Predicted travel times for P, S, surface waves, and shock waves (SW) induced by the meteor event are indicated with red dots. The map at the top left shows the location of the city of Chelyabinsk (red star) with all broadband seismological stations within 4000 km (red triangles) and away (black triangles). (bottom) Temporary arrivals of seismic waves associated with Chelyabinsk meteor event (15 Feb. 2013) on which waves from the Tonga earthquake are superimposed. B. Tauzin, E. Debayle, C. Quantin, N. Coltice, 2013, Geophys. Res. Lett., 40, 3522–3526.

'Ἥφαιστος δὲ τιτύσκετο θεσπιδαὲς πῦρ. πρῶτα μὲν ἐν πεδίῳ πῦρ δαίετο, καῖε δὲ νεκροὺς πολλούς...πᾶν δ' ἐξηράνθη πεδίον, σχέτο δ' ἀγλαὸν ὕδωρ.'

'Hephaestus made ready wondrous blazing fire, first on the plain was the fire kindled and began to burn the dead, the many dead...and all the plain was dried and the bright water was stayed.'

'ὃ δ' ἐς ποταμὸν τρέψε φλόγα παμφανόωσαν. καίοντο πτελέαι...τεῖροντ' ἐγχέλυές τε καὶ ἰχθύες οἳ κατὰ δίνας, οἳ κατὰ καλὰ ῥέεθρα κυβίστων ἔνθα καὶ ἔνθα πνοιῇ τειρόμενοι πολυμήτιος Ἡφαίστοιο. καίετο δ' ἶς ποταμοῖο ἔπος...'' οὐδ' ἂν ἐγὼ σοί γ' ὧδε πυρὶ φλεγέθοντι μαχοίμην....' Φῆ πυρὶ καιόμενος, ἀνὰ δ' ἔφλυε καλὰ ῥέεθρα.'

'And then against the river he turned his gleaming flame. Burned were the elds...tormented were the eels and the fishes in the eddies and in the fair streams they plunged this way and that sorely tormented by the blast of Hephaestus of many wiles. Burned too was the mighty river...nor will I fight you ablaze with fire as you are...So he spoke, burning with fire and his fair streams were seething'

The Homeric expression *'πυρὶ καιόμενος-burning with fire'*, gives the impression that Xanthus River was in flames itself. In reality the river's bubbling, the life forms' discomfort and the plants' burning in both the river's sides, gave the optical illusion to a distant observer that the river itself was in flames.

This phenomenon did not last long, due to Hera's 'command' to Hephaestus, to extinguish his fire:

''Ἥρη, αὐτίκ' ἄρ' Ἥφαιστον προσεφώνεεν...Ἥφαιστος δὲ κατέσβεσε θεσπιδαὲς πῦρ, ἄψορρον δ' ἄρα κῦμα κατέσσυτο καλὰ ῥέεθρα'

'Hera immediately she spoke to Hephaestus... Hephaestus quenched his wondrous blazing fire and once more the wave rolled along the fair streams' (Il.21.377-382).

Hera's personification as the atmospheric air, associated with the blast wave's propagation, coupled with Hephaestus' flame (meteorites) seized to function.

8. CONCLUSIONS

We analysed fully some Iliad's descriptions of physical phenomena covered by devine interventions, taking into account that the *old physics* was *hidden* within *mythos* and *theology*, as mentioned by Ploutarch. Additionally, we take into account that in Plato's time, the *logos* was the *historic event* and the *mythos* was divided into *the genuine tradition* and the *fabricated one (Tim.26.e.4-5, Resp*.377.b.6). However, in the Homeric text, according to Homeric Dictionary of Krousios and Seiller (Pantazidis, 1888) and Mitropetrou (2012), *mythos* signified speech, oration, narrative, dialogue, custom, command, advice, suggestion, opinion, the issue of speech, conversation, logical argument etc. (e.g. see Il.12.80 (*'μῦθος ἀπήμων'-prudent words),* Od.1.358-359 (*'μύθος δ' ἄνδρεσσι μελήσει πάσι- but speech shall be men's care, for all*), Od.17.153 (*'εμείο δε σύνθεο μύθον'- but hearken to my words),* Od.21.67 (*'αὐτίκα δὲ μνηστῆρσι* ***μετηύδα*** *καὶ φάτο μῦθον - at once she spoke among the suitors and said*), Od.21.70-71 (*'οὐδέ τιν' ἄλλην μύθου ποιήσασθαι ἐπισχεσίην ἐδύνασθε'-nor could you find any other plea to urge*) etc)). The corresponding verb is 'μυθέομαι' means 'speak' or 'say'. Later, in the advancing centuries, the meanings of mythos and logos are changed. Consequently, in Iliad, the old physics (the physical phenomena) was hidden behind theology (devine interventions) and mythos signify the genuine tradition; oral tradition, by disseminating speech.

We initially recognized many *physical events* as different 'divine' interventions attributed to *'gods and godesses'.* However, after highly detailed multi-scientific analysis, we concluded that the main source of these physical events was *a very strong meteor shower*, which contained bolides' explosions, fireballs' breakages and meteroid's impacts on the ground. Also, *two seismic activities* within a two day time period are described. The first was a typical earthquake produced by a known seismotectonic mechanism, whereas the second seems to be a rear case of an earthquake produced by a seismoacoustic coupling between the infrasounds of a supersonic blast in the atmosphere and the production of *P, S, Love* and *Rayleigh* waves (Figure 8) on the ground. Such an event was recently recorded in Chelyabinsk (2013) and analysed by Tauzin et al (2013). We note that these *events* coexisted with *a solar eclipse* which have been described by Henriksson (2012) and Papamarinopoulos et al. (2014). The *red cloud's appearance* during the solar eclipse's maximum phase is interpreted absolutely, taking into account the specific existing climatic conditions during the solar eclipse (sharp temperature drop with simultaneous humidity rise) and the remaining fragments of a bolide in the atmosphere.

It is worth to notice that Homer has chosen to describe only this specific 7-day time period around the Patroclus' death, out of the entire 10-years period of the war. This does not include the Acheans' principal hero, Achilles' death, or the conquest of Troy by Dourian Horse. Therefore we reach the unavoidable conclusion that this happened just because of all these 'extreme' physical events occurred in that week. And it was natural for the observers of that prehistoric period to attribute these 'extreme' physical events in 'divine' activities.

ACKNOWLEDGEMENTS

We express our gratitude to Professor Lilian Karali and Professor E.Lekkas of the University of Athens for multiple discussions and advices given by them in connection with questions, which rose during our analysis of the Homeric text. We also feel grateful to Dr. K. Kalachanis for his usefull comments and corrections in the ancient Greek text and translation.

DEDICATION

We dedicate this paper to Emeritus Professor Stephanos A.Paipetis, from Kerkyra Island, of the University of Patras in Greece the scientist who first started the study of Homer's Epics, worldwide, from the standpoint of Science and Technology, an excellent researcher with international impact, an analyst of myths, poetry and a pure student of the Universe's enigmas a person with a unique sense of humor.

REFERENCES

Anglin, F. and Haddon, R. (1987) Meteoroid sonic shock-wave generated seismic signals observed at a seismic array, *Nature*, vol. 328, pp. 607-609.

Antoine, D. and Nobileau, D. (2006) Recent increase of Saharan dust transport over the Mediterranean Sea, as revealed from ocean color satellite (SeaWiFS) observations, *Journal of Geophysical Research*, vol. 111, D12214, doi:10.1029/2005JD006795.

Baikouzis, C. and Magnasco M.O. (2008) Is an eclipse described in the Odyssey? *Proc. Natl. Acad. Sci.U.S.A.*, vol. 105(26), pp. 8823-8828.

Balengee, S. J. A., Kuehn, S. C., Anastasakis, G., Piper, D. J. W. and Pe-Piper, G. (2015) Holocene to Pleistocene Tephrochronology of eleven marine sediment cores from the Aegean Sea, *Geological Society of America, SE Section*, At Chattanooga, TN (Abstract from a conference paper).

Barkan, J., Alpert, P., Kutiel, H. and Kishcha, P. (2005) Synoptics of dust transportation days from Africa toward Italy and central Europe, *Journal of Geophysical Research*, vol. 110, D07208, doi:10.1029/JD006795.

Blegen, C. (1963) *Troy and the Troyans*, London: Thames and Hudson.

Çağatay, N., Wulf, S., Sancar, Ü., Özmaral, A., Vidal, L., Henry, P., Appelt, O. and Gasperini, L. (2015), The tephra record from the Sea of Marmara for the last ca. 70 ka and its palaeoceanographic implications, *Marine Geology,* vol. 361, pp. 96–110.

Ebel, D. S. (2011), Sulfur in extraterrestrial bodies and the deep earth, *Reviews in Mineralogy and Geochemistry,* vol. 13 (1), pp. 315-336.

Edwards, W., Eaon, D., and Brown, P. (2007) Seismic observations of meteors: Coupling theory and observations, *Rev. Geoph.*, vol. 46, pp. 1-21.

Elliot, A. (1934) Morphology and life history of Haematococcus pluvialis, *Arch. Protistenk,* vol. 82, pp. 250-272.

Fernández-Lozano, J., Guillén-Oterino, A., Gutiérrez-Alonso, G., Abel-Flores, J. and Pérez-Turrado, J. (2015). Presencia de Haematococcus pluvialis (Flotow, 1844) en la provincial de Zamora (Haematococcaceae), *Bol. R. Soc. Esp. Hist. Nat. Sec. Biol.*, vol. 109, pp. 103-109.

Fields, N. (2004) *Troy c. 1700-1250 BC,* Oxford: Osprey Publishing book.

Henriksson, G. (2012) The Trojan War dated by two solar eclipses, *Mediterranean Arhaeology and Archaeometry,* vol. 12(1), pp. 63-76.

Heraclitus of Pontus, (1962), *Allégories d'Homère, Les Belles Lettres,* Paris.

Guerin, M., Huntley, M.E. and Olaizola, M. (2003) Haematococcus astaxanthin: applications for human health and nutrition, *Trends in Biotechnology,* vol. 21, pp. 210-216.

Guerrero, M.G., Rodriguez, H., Vargas, M., García-González, M., Campo, J.A.d., Moreno, J. and

Kaplan, R. I. and Hulston, R. J. (1966) The isotopic abundance and content of sulfur in meteorites, *Geochimica at Cosmochmica Acta,* vol. 30 (5), pp. 479-496.

Kaskaoutis, D.G., Kambezidis, H.D., Nastos, P.T. and Kosmopoulos, P.G. (2008) Study on an intense dust storm over Greece, *Atmospheric Environment* , vol. 42 (29), pp. 6884-6896.

Le Pichon, A., Ceranna, L., Pilger, C., Mialle, P., Brown, D., and Herry, P. (2013) 2013 Russian fireball largest ever detected by CTBTO infrasounds sensors, *Geophy. Res. Lett.*, doi: 10.1002/grl.50619.

Kurcer, A., Chatzipetros, A., Tutkun, S.Z., Pavlides, S. Ozden, S, Syrides, G. Vouvalidis, K., Ulugergerli, E., Ozkan, A. and Ekinci, Y. L. (2012) *An Assessment of the Earthquakes of Ancient Troy, NW Anatolia, Turkey,* in Tectonics-Recent Advances, p. 171-200, Ed. E. Sharkov.

Martínez-Silva, A.S. (2011) Evaluación del crecimiento celular y de los pigmentos obtenidos de la microalga Haematococcus pluvialis (CHLOROPHYTA: VOLVOCALES) cultivada en diferentes medios. *Centro de Investigación en Ciencia Aplicada y Tecnología Avanzada. Instituto Politécnico Nacional.,* México, D.F., p. 103.

Matsangouras, I.T., Nastos, P.T., Bluestein, H.B. and Sioutas, M.V. (2014) A climatology of tornadic activity over Greece based on historical records, *International Journal of Climatology,* vol. 34 (8), pp. 2538-2555.

Meloni, D., di Sarra, A., Biavati, G., DeLuisi, J.J., Monteleone, F., Pace, G., Piacentino, S. and Sferlazzo, D.M. (2007) Seasonal behavior of Saharan dust events at the Mediterranean island of Lambedusa in the period 1999-2005, *Atmosheric Environment,* vol. 41, pp. 3041-3056.

Metaxas, D.A., Philandras, C.M., Nastos, P.T. and Repapis, C.C. (1999) Variability of precipitation pattern in Greece during the year, *Fresenious Environmental Bulletin,* vol. 8, pp. 001-006.

Mitropetrou, H. (2012). The Origins of the Greek Geomythology through the Cosmogonies, Theogonies and the Cycle of Hercules. Doctorate thesis, University of Patras.

Nastos, P.T., Philandras, C.M. and Repapis, C.C. (2002) Application of Canonical Analysis to Air Temperature and Precipitation Regimes over Greece, *Fresenius Environmental Bulletin,* vol. 11(8), pp. 488-493.

Nastos, P.T. and Matsangouras, J.T. (2010) Tornado activity in Greece within the 20th century, *Advances in Geosciences,* vol. 26, pp. 49-51.

Nastos, P.T. (2012), Meteorological Patterns Associated with Intense Saharan Dust Outbreaks over Greece in Winter, *Advances in Meteorology,* vol. 2012, Article ID 828301, doi:10.1155/2012/828301.

Nastos, P.T., Matsangouras, I.T. and Chronis, T.G. (2014) Spatio-temporal analysis of lightning activity over Greece - Preliminary results derived from the recent state precision lightning network, *Atmospheric Research,* vol. 144, pp. 207-217.

Nastos, P.T. and Matsangouras, I.T. (2014) Analysis of synoptic conditions for tornadic days over Western Greece, *Natural Hazards and Earth System Sciences,* vol. 14(9), pp. 2409-242.

Pandazidis, I. (1888) *Homeric Dictionary,* Ed Konstandinidis, Athens, Greece (in Greek).

Papamarinopoulos, St. P. (2008) A comet during the Trojan War? *Science and Technology in Homeric Epics,* Paipetis S.A. (Ed.), Springer Science, pp. 341-356.

Papamarinopoulos, St. P., Preka-Papadema, P., Antonopoulos, P., Mitropetrou, H., Tsironi, A. and Mitropetros, P. (2012) A new astronomical dating of Odysseus' return to Ithaca, *Mediterranean Arhaeology and Archaeometry*, vol. 12(1), pp. 117-128.

Papamarinopoulos, St. P., Preka-Papadema, P., Antonopoulos, P., Mitropetrou, H., Tsironi, A. and Mitropetros, P. (2013) The anatomy of a complex astronomical phenomenon described in the Odyssey, *Mediterranean Arhaeology and Archaeometry*, vol. 13(2), pp. 69-82.

Papamarinopoulos, St. P., Preka-Papadema, P., Mitropetros, P., Antonopoulos, P., Mitropetrou, H. and Saranditis, G. (2014) A new astronomical dating of the Trojan War's end, *Mediterranean Arhaeology and Archaeometry*, vol. 14(1), pp. 93-102.

Pavlides, S. and Caputo, R. (2004) Magnitude versus faults' surface parameters: quantitave relationships from the Aegean, *Tectonophysics*, vol. 380 (3-4), pp. 159-188.

Pfister, G. G., Emmons, L. K., Hess, P. G., Lamarque, J. - F., Thompson, A. M. and Yorks, J. E., (2008) Analysis of the Summer 2004 ozone budget over the United States using Intercontinental Transport Experiment Ozonesonde Network Study (IONS) observations and Model of Ozone and Related Tracers (MOZART-4) simulations, *Journal of Geophysical Research*, 113(23), art. no. D23306.

Rubtsov, V. (2009) *The Tunguska Mystery*, Astronomer's Universe, Springer.

Ryu, J.-H. and Jenkins, G.S. (2005) Lightning-tropospheric ozone connections: EOF analysis of TCO and lightning data, *Atmospheric Environment* 39(32), pp. 5799–5805.

Stagiritis, A. (1815), *Ogygia or Archaeology*, Wien (1817) , (in Greek).

Schoch, C. (1931) Die säkulare Accelaration des Mondes und der Sonne, *Astronomische Abhandlungen,Ergänzungshefte zu den Astronomischen Nachrichten*, Band 8, B2, Kiel.

Tauzin, B., Debayle, E., Quantin, C. and Coltice, N. (2013) Seismoacoustic coupling induced by the breakup of the 15 February 2013 Chelyabinsk meteor, *Geoph. Res. Lett.*, 40, pp. 3522-3526, doi:10.1002/grl50683.

Theodosiou, E., Manimanis, V.N., Mantarakis, P. and Dimitrijevic, M.S. (2011) Astronomy and Constellations in the Iliad and Odyssey, *Journal of Astronomical History and Heritage*, 14/1.

Trifonov, V.G. (2010) *Tectonic and climatic rhythms and the development of society*, in Man and the Geosphere, Ed. Florinsky I.V., 2010 Nova Science Publishers, pp. 257-305.

Vasilyev, N. V. (2004) The Tunguska Meteorite: A space phenomenon of the summer of 1908, Moscow, *in Russkaya Panorama*, p. 86.

Translation: Homer Iliad Books 1-12 and Books 13-24, translated by Murray A. T., revised by Wyatt.W.F, Loeb Classical Library, Harvard University Press 1999 (second edition).

8

THE HANNIBAL ROUTE CONTROVERSY AND FUTURE HISTORICAL ARCHAEOLOGICAL EXPLORATION IN THE WESTERN ALPS

W.C. Mahaney

Quaternary Surveys, 26 Thornhill Ave, Thornhill, Ontario, Canada, L4J1J4 and Department of Geography, York University, 4700 Keele St., N. York, Ontario, Canada, M3J 1P3.

Corresponding author: W.C. Mahaney arkose41@gmail.com

ABSTRACT

If we are ever to find artifacts related to Hannibal's invasion of Italia the actual col route needs to be identified with certainty so that specific sites such as hearths, army bivouac/regrouping areas and other topographic features described in ancient texts are brought into focus. Some of the key environmental features include a gorge along the approach route, bivouac area near the summit of the Alps, and a blocking rockfall on the lee side of the range, amongst others. Strange that Kuhle and Kuhle (2012, 2015) provide a rebuttal of the Traversette Pass blocking rockfall (for location see Fig 12.1, Mahaney, 2008) as the route Hannibal followed into Italia when all evidence points to the one rockfall, a massive topographic feature described by Polybius nearly 2200 years ago. They present various quibbles over various translations of Polybius by no end of authors over the last two millennia, excellent photographs of various passes, but with the Traversette Col and major landforms misplaced on Fig. 1, and mention of fieldwork without offering any field evidence of any kind that might lead to historical archaeological exploration. Yet, it is clear from any author translating Polybius' *Histories* that Polybius did indeed see the rockfall mentioned in all ancient texts and he clearly understood the deposit to be a substantial mass, a two-tier event, that is, older and younger deposits superimposed on one another. Kuhle and Kuhle quote Walbank (1990) as a prime author who disputed translations of Polybius (Scott-Kilvert, 1979) etc. saying the topographic situation and time lines were inventions by others. What then, if one were to go to Paton (1922) revised by Walbank and Habicht (2010), only to find that the translation of the rockfall encounter runs parallel with Scott-Kilvert's translation, the one favored by Mahaney (2008, 2013).

KEYWORDS: Hannibalic Wars; Traversette Rockfall; Polybius' *Histories*; Search for historical archeological evidence.

1. INTRODUCTION

Every municipality in Transalpine France would like to claim ownership of Hannibal's invasion route into Italia in 218 BC, such a quest compelling Dennis Proctor to research the question (Proctor, 1971). Similarly, nearly every ancient historian/classicist who has studied the Second Punic War has waded into the controversy of 'which route' did the great captain follow (see Fig. 1), seemingly because the 'great route' is sometimes referred to as the 'great question of antiquity', (T Corey Brennan, Rutgers University, personal communication, 2005). The idea of the 'great question' was discussed by Mahaney (2008) and in other co-authored papers with colleagues, the conclusion being that great question or not, the main emphasis lay with the possibilities for historical archaeological exploration and recovery of artifacts once the invasion route was identified. Such recovery would help explain the culture of ancient Carthage. The prime difficulty up to now has been the proclivity of authors to argue for one route over another on the basis of photographic evidence (Kuhle & Kuhle, 2015), assessment of topography too difficult for animals and humans, philological discussions of place/river names, almost all without any attempt at actual field investigations to search for the rockfall in question, possible hearths, sporadic permafrost, defile along the approach route, and regrouping area as identified by Polybius. The only possible rockfall in question, is that identified and discussed by Mahaney (2008), and Mahaney et al. (2007; 2008a, b; 2010a, b, c; 2014), that lies below the Col de la Traversette, in the upper Po River catchment.

Given the description provided by both Polybius and Livy, the location and composition of the rockfall is an integral part of the invasion route forensic effort to link it with suspected hearths and foraging areas on both the proximal (French) and distal (Italian) sides of the Alps. Recent excavations in an alluvial mire at ~2600 m asl (Fig. 2) on the French side in the upper Guil River catchment (Mahaney et al., 2016a, 2016b) point to a significant link between probable foraging/watering areas on the inbound leg of the invasion, the legendary rockfall [landslide in Scott Kilvert (1979) and Paton (1922)], and regrouping area on the lower slopes on the lee side of the Alps (Mahaney, 2008). The first recovered artifacts from the alluvial mire include a churned-up bed in several cores and sections and increased organic matter within the bioturbated sediment, all radiocarbon dated to 2168 cal yr BP (218 BC) (Mahaney et al., 2016a), and all documenting a mass animal deposition termed the MAD beds. Moreover bacteria endospores, a single fossil tapeworm egg linked to equine species, and bile acids linked to horses and mules (Mahaney et al., 2016b) complete the artifact recovery, where, perhaps, for the first time bacteria serves as an artifact. The geomorphological and biological evidence presented in these findings point to the passage of large numbers of animals, perhaps tens of thousands, at precisely the time of the invasion. Moreover, susceptible magnetic measurements taken from churned-up beds in three sections show spikes in Fe, although with magnetization numbers overall reflecting the water soaked reducing environment of the mire, which correlates with the geochemical and palynological evidence.

Slight differences of the blocking rubble mass (Fig. 3) on the lee side of the Alps are presented in both translations (noted above) of the Hannibalic invasion of Italia—Scott-Kilvert and Paton--but the essentiality is that Hannibal encountered a massive rockfall, a doublet comprising two deposits, one older and one younger, an impediment to the passage of horses, mules and elephants. A further essentiality is that there is only one rockfall on the lee side of the Alps with the mass and the necessary couplet of deposits to match Polybius' description and it is located between 2600 and 2350 m asl below the Col de la Traversette (~3000 m asl). Rockfalls below all other possible passes—Col du Agnel, Col de la Croix, Col de Genèvre, Col du Clapier, Mt. Cenis (Fig. 1)--are now and were during Hannibal's time insubstantial, hardly of sufficient mass to block even modern tourists. Polybius' identification of the Traversette rockfall presents an answer to the question of the invasion route location as Sir Gavin de Beer pointed out several decades ago. It is now incumbent upon archaeologists to carry out exploration of this landmark and other nearby likely hearths/foraging areas to determine if artifacts can be recovered, stratigraphically tied to 2168 calibrated ^{14}C yr BP, the time of the invasion (see Mahaney et al., 2016a for details on the radiocarbon chronology). What is urgently needed on the French side of the range is a ground penetrating radar (GPR) survey of the G5 mire at ~2600 m elevation.

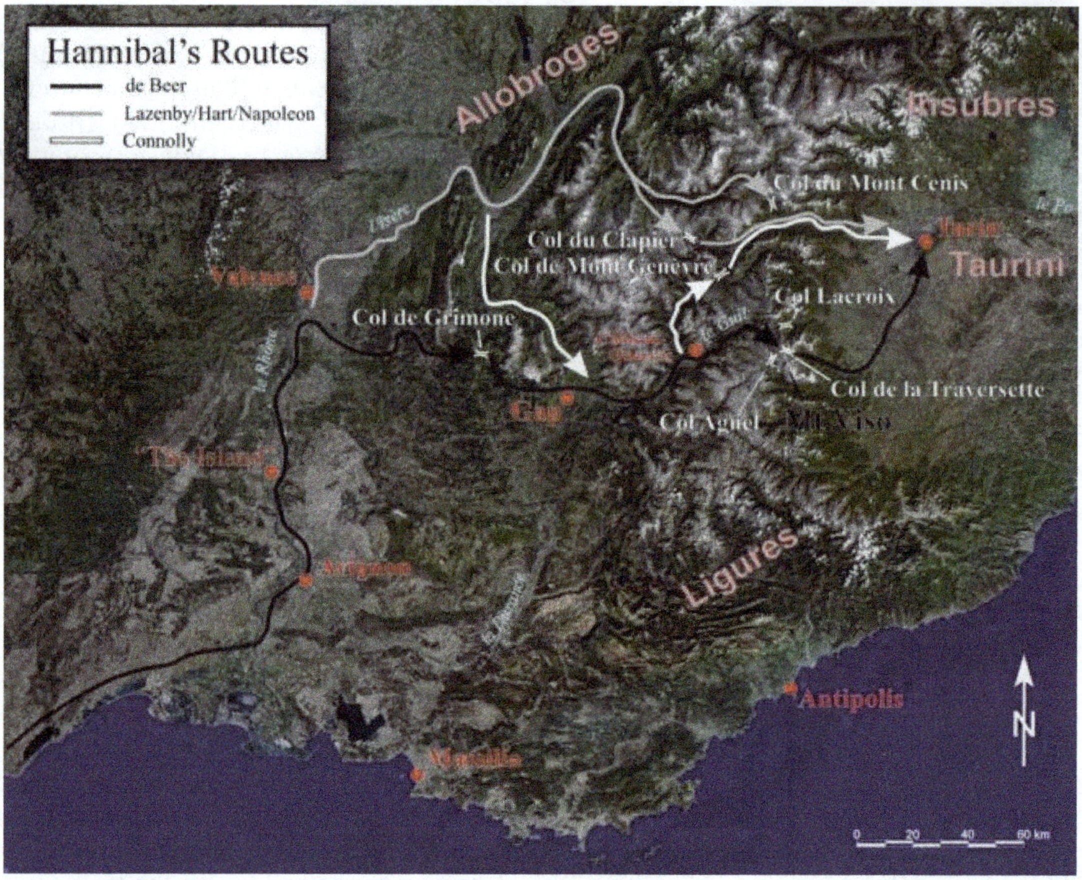

Fig. 1. Satellite map annotated with the main invasion routes of the Second Punic War as proposed by different authorities over the last two centuries. The major cols are listed from south to north with the Col de al Traversette (3000 m) called Hannibal's col since antiquity. Tribes, e.g. Allobroges, are located in approximate cis-and trans-alpine areas. Satelllite image courtesy of USGS, JPL, NASA. Reprinted from Mahaney (2008).

The Kuhle & Kuhle (2012, 2015) dispute over the rockfall, its existence and the route should have led them to come forth with some hard evidence (other than photography and odd mismatched quotations) as to why another route is preferred, and in the absence of such evidence, there is hardly any need to continue with quotes from authors purporting to show why the Traversette is not the route in question. Surely these authors must know that even weak belief structures require more than mere quotes from authorities most of whom have never visited sites along the proposed routes, much less the cols in question, let alone set about to do any significant field work to prove their assertions. Claiming to rely on firsthand accounts as Kuhle &Kuhle (2015) have done should discount Livy as he had only access to Polybius and presumably Silenus' account of the invasion, the latter source presumably destroyed in the great fire of the library in Alexandria, 300 AD. Polybius being the only reliable firsthand written account of the invasion route makes all other sources at best second and third-hand renditions of the event, and accordingly, highly questionable (see Lancel, 1999 on this).

2. HISTORICAL RECORD

The historical record quoted by Kuhle & Kuhle (2015) from Livy (trans., de Sélincourt, 1972) and Polybius (trans., Scott-Kilvert, 1979) is more or less correct with the exception of what is interpreted by Scott-Kilvert (1979) with regard to Polybius. However, Scott-Kilvert's (1979) translation of Polybius is little different from W.R. Paton's (1922) translation, only the odd word phrasing-landslip vs landslide-presenting differences between the two translations. Essentially, both Scott-Kilvert and Paton (the latter revised by F.W. Walbank and C. Habicht, 2010) describe the descent from the pass along steep cliffs whereupon the narrowness of the path made further progress with the elephants and pack animals impossible. Paton's translation thus, 'a previous landslip having carried away about one and a half stades of the face of the mountain and a further landslip having recently occurred.' Compare this translation with Scott-Kilvert's (1979) interpretation (Polybius states, Book III, 54): 'A previous landslide had already carried away some 300 yards of the face of the mountain, while a recent one had made the situation still worse' and it is clear Hannibal faced a rubble mass through which he could not possibly proceed with horses and elephants, although his infantry could pass toward the lower slopes. Both translations use the term 'face of the mountain', that is, the bedrock source area above the rubble mass making up the 'landslide' or 'landslip.' All of this, including mention of rubble (cf. rockfall) has been fully reiterated by countless historians and need not be re-discussed here. Clearly the Traversette rockfall, a two-tier deposit from two mass wasting events, is the blocking mass Polybius described. If mention of 'landslip' is to be construed as the bedrock sliding plane of transported mass wasted sediment as Kuhle & Kuhle (2015) assert, one would have to imagine Hannibal's engineers cutting through bedrock, as there is no near-horizontal sliding plane of rock blocking anyone's progress below any of the possible transit cols. With the Traversette case, and because of the steep cliffs, there is no possibility of bedrock blocking the army, only rubble sourced from near vertical cliffs along the Italian/French border producing the rockfall mass.

Fig. 2. G5 mire site in the upper Guil Valley at ~2600 m, the upper reach of the 'Faito', common name for the north spur of the drainage. The Younger Dryas (YD) moraine lies astride the alluvial outlet and documents a readvance of ice during the last stage of the last glaciation (Late Glacial). The YD follows the YDB (Younger Dryas Boundary) dated to 12.8 ka, time of a local cosmic airburst identified over this area of the Western Alps (see Mahaney and Keiser, 2013 and Mahaney et al., 2013, 2016c) for a detailed assessment in both the upper Guil and upper Po catchments. Photography by Pierre Tricart (Université de Grenoble).

Fig. 3. Projected trail followed by Hannibal's army from the Guil River to the west across the Col de la Traversette to the blocking rockfall in the upper Po River catchment. Reprinted from Mahaney (2008).

The interpretation of Kuhle & Kuhle (2015) that 'landslip' in translation (Paton, 1922) of the ancient texts reveals only rock for Hannibal's Army to pass suggests the mass wasted sediment sped off down the mountain to some undisclosed resting place, hardly a logical argument, as gliding planes lie upslope and underneath a mass wasted deposit, the latter responding to gravity and friction coming to rest downslope. It is disingenuous to argue that on the basis of translation variations - landslip vs. landslide - that Hannibal was forced to forge a trail through rock as opposed to rubble and even so rubble is what both Polybius (III, 54) and Livy (XXI, 37) recount as the two-tier blocking mass. Even Livy's translator identifies the transit col as the Traversette (Livy, de Sèlincourt, 1972, p. 60) based on his reading of the ancient text. Since it was Polybius who identified the blocking mass, and who had to have been present given his identification of the two-tier event that produced the landform, most historians take his version over that of Livy who recounts heating of rock to remove obstacles, presumably boulders as one would not heat bedrock expecting any comminution of material. As Lancel (1999) mentions, one has to consider Coelius Antipater's (contemporary of Polybius, work now lost—see Lazenby, 1998, p. 261) influence on Livy, more or less a 'distorted mirror' and probably all originating from Silenus. Polybius is **mute on the firing event** which probably indicates it never took place (Mahaney, 2008). However, the nature of the terrain is such that no 'landslip' (that is a shear surface) plane exists below the Traversette, only steep cliffs and couloirs that act to provide source material for numerous rockfall and talus deposits. Moreover, the translation of ἀπορρῶγος from Polybius, meaning 'precipitous cliff or abyss; or landslip in the sense of something fallen away' describes the descent from the Traversette Col exactly, and 'landslip' (Paton, 1922) is synonymous with landslide (Scott-Kilvert, 1979) with or without a shear bedrock plane exposed in the proximal position, upslope from a settled mass of rubble. Even if bedrock were an obstacle, Hannibal's engineers would have constructed a route around or over it.

Figure 1 in Kuhle & Kuhle (2015) mixes locations of the Traversette Col and the rockfall and incorrectly assigns a glacial origin to what is clearly a mass wasted deposit. Thus, the mention of fieldwork, sadly lacking in Kuhle & Kuhle (2015), has led to misidentification of pertinent topographic features. For the proper location of the Col de la Traversette, the reader is referred to Mahaney (2008), in particular to Fig. 12.1 for the topography and elevation of the col, and Fig. 8.10 for the geology. As for the soil cover in mass wasted deposits, one would expect such after millennia of subsidence and repeated re-ballasting of the path through the upper rockfall (see Mahaney, 2008), and with subsidence the rockfall today does not look as robust a feature as it did in Polybius' time.

As previously argued by Kuhle & Kuhle (2012), they believe there is no mention of a landslide/rockfall in the various translations of Polybius, yet as noted above Scott-Kilvert (1979) uses the term 'landslide', which is better termed rockfall (Mahaney, 2008), given the random orientation of coarse clastic debris in the Traversette deposit and the lack of any sliding plane upslope from the deposit. Surely Kuhle & Kuhle must know that landslides result from mass wasting processes and involve removal and deposition of sediment from a higher to a lower position. To argue that Hannibal's starving troops had to cut a path through rock rather than re-ballast or strengthen a path through a rockfall simply belies any of the various translations, either that of Scott-Kilvert (1979) or of Paton (1922). Both translations speak of a two-tier event, either two landslides or two land masses (the latter, i.e. 'landslips'). Polybius' description of the two-tier event was probably based on the character or state of the two deposits at the time: one, the younger, with fresh, un-pitted, nearly lichen-free clasts, sediment lacking any appreciable soil cover, the other, older, with darker (oxide/hydroxide-rich clasts), lichen covered even ~2200 yr ago and carrying sporadic soil cover (Mahaney et al., 2014). The very fact that Polybius distinguished the two deposits, *the only such two-stage rockfall deposit on the lee flank of the Alps*, speaks to his understanding of landscape.

Alternatively, it is possible Polybius could have coupled the two-tier event to trim lines in the bedrock, all mica schist at this locality and similar to almost all other passes, but identification of such, given the ease with which schist weathers would have been as difficult in his time as now. During various expeditions to survey the route from 2002 on, attempts were made by me to try to identify trim lines in the cliffs above the Traversette rockfall but without success. Hydrolization and oxidation of the bedrock is rapid enough to overprint fresh bedrock so that middle Neoglacial (~3 ka) and Late Glacial (13-15 ka) surfaces, have by this time taken on the same or similar colors. In Polybius' time the younger rockfall deposit would have been very fresh looking compared with the older Late Glacial deposit. Age control on the older rockfall lobes comes from identification of a cosmic airburst/impact that most certainly correlates with the black mat event or the YDB (Younger Dryas Boundary) of 12.8 ka (Mahaney and Keiser, 2013; Mahaney et al., 2013).

As outlined in Mahaney (2008), the geologic/geomorphologic character of every major pass from the Col Agnel to Mt. Cenis, was assessed with respect to difficulty of access and exfiltration, the result being that only the Col de la Croix proved to be relatively impossible, the inbound and outbound track itself of no particular advantage to Hannibal attempting to reach the Po River country. If Kuhle & Kuhle (2015) prefer the Col du Clapier as Hannibal's main transit pass into Italia, there is neither a rockfall to block passage, nor any need for Hannibal's engineers to cut rock forging a path to the Dora Riparia (not the Po), and Polybius (Paton, 1922; III, 56) is definite Hannibal was intent on reaching the Po plains.

Paton's translation of Polybius states the great general's assessment of the width of the rockfall as equivalent to 1.5 stades, one stade being 0.1778 km. Calculation of the width as amounting to 0.3 km or 300 m is close to the present width of the Traversette rockfall as measured by Mahaney (2008) and more or less equivalent to Scott-Kilvert's (1979) figure of 300 yards quoted above.

I cannot imagine that any presentation of google images or crisscrossing discussions from Polybius and Livy et al. as presented by Kuhle & Kuhle (2015) adds anything but further obfuscation to the history. However, if the southern route of Sir Gavin de Beer is to be discredited by Kuhle & Kuhle, they should at least bring in the entire environmental matrix from the ancient literature, such as the defile on the approach march (de Beer, 1967, 1969; Mahaney, 2008, 2008b), the presence of sporadic permafrost/firnpack (de Beer, 1969; Mahaney, 2008), place names in north-south order (Mahaney, 2008), the rockfall (Mahaney et al., 2008a, b; 2010a, b, c; 2014) and the regrouping area in the upper Po River (Mahaney, 2008; Mahaney et al., 2010b).

It is strange indeed, that with Kuhle & Kuhle's (2015) focus on the rockfall 'enigma', that no mention is made of the firing event heralded about in the ancient texts, the absence of evidence for which is well documented in Mahaney (2008) and in (Bagnall, 1999; Mahaney et al., 2007, 2010a, c; 2014). Furthermore, the one lone, small rockfall below the Col du Clapier (Sodhi et al., 2006) is the only fired deposit below any of the major cols of passage on the lee side of the Alps, the fired clasts sampled and analyzed as described in Mahaney et al. (2007). The unweathered state of this deposit and lack of lichens and any soil development indicates the deposit is of relatively recent age (<100 yr) and quite possibly was fired by road crews clearing a path to a hydro station in the upper valley (see Sodhi et al., 2006, for chemical analysis of the fired rock). The rockfall firing event most probably originated in the original text of Silenus who accompanied Hannibal on his invasion of Italia, and is purely an imaginary invention, for which there is no evidence in the form of carbonized rock in the Traversette rockfall (Mahaney, 2008).

The statement (Kuhle & Kuhle, 2015) make that: 'on the Traversette it is the first ~80 m of altitude towards the Italian side that is particularly difficult, such that even mules cannot master it (Fig. 1, '3')' is particularly revealing, and underscores my previous statement, as to why visitation to field sites is so important. It is not the first 80 m of the descent that is most difficult, as anyone who has trod the path will tell you, but the last ~50 m just above the old unmanned Italian army barracks immediately above the rockfall. Kuhle & Kuhle go on to explain: 'It is for this reason that in the 15th Century a tunnel—unique for a pass in the Alps—was bored through rock in order to enable caravans to avoid the upper pass region. In fact, the tunnel was put in place because of the winter snow, not to make it easier for travelers and animals to transit the pass (Pierre Tricart, personal communication, 2015). Even today, workers from the Refuge du Viso (CAF, France) and the Rifugio Giacoletti/Mon Viso, Italia are often obliged to remove snow from the Col de la Traversette to allow tourists and trekkers to transit the pass itself (not the lower slopes). Even a fresh fall of snow in 218 BC, as described by both Livy and Polybius, would not have stopped the invading Punic Army despite the slippery ground etc. After all, Hannibal's troops and animals got across the pass and down to the rockfall impediment, and according to many authors, in nearly record time.

The argument proposed by Kuhle & Kuhle (2015) that the Traversette exfiltration is too difficult belies the physical state of Hannibal's army with personnel hardly the equal of the average modern male. These were professional soldiers as Paton (1922) states, men used to long hard treks, and who would have been equal to the task of cresting the Traversette and descending into the Po River valley. As for the elephants, the trail down out of the Traversette would have been negotiable, just as *Loxodonta africana* [much larger beasts compared with Syrian elephants (*Elephas maximus*) used by Hannibal] are known to have traversed the much higher (~4700 m asl) and steeper slopes of Mt. Kenya (Mahaney, 1990, 2008).

3. CONCLUSIONS

While discussions of the Hannibalic route, and various episodes connected with the invasion of Italia of 218 BC, continue to titillate and rouse enthusiasm of many as to how an army the size of Hannibal's could pass over the Alps without leaving a trace, most previous interpretations of the historic literature on the subject have done little to identify the correct route. The first attempts to analyze climate (Neumann, 1992) during the invasion, flood times for rivers (de Beer, 1969), and weather controlling movement at sea and on land (Proctor, 1971) provided a step in the right direction. Mahaney (2004, 2008) constructed an environmental matrix—permafrost/firnpack, elevation, approach defile, hearth locations, rockfall, foraging areas, regrouping area--out of the ancient texts and analyzed each environmental factor against each major col concluding that the original assessment of the projected southern route, thought to have been used by Hannibal by Sir Gavin de Beer, was correct. Even with elevations imprecisely known at the time, Polybius's (trans. 1979) description of the invasion route strongly suggests the Traversette as the crossing point into the peninsula, an inference supported by Varro's mention in *De Re Rustica* (quoted by Proctor (1971)) of the passes in geographic order from north to south—'Hannibal's Pass' lying south of the Col de Genèvre. Moreover, reference to Varro's mention of the five cols, including Hannibal's Col as the highest, is quoted in Servius' commentaries translated in Savage (1934). Polybius also used the phrase, *tas hyperbolas tas anōtatō tōn Alpeōn*, 'the highest pass in the Alps' (John Lazenby, personal communication to WCM, 2007; Lazenby, 1998, p. 45).

All environmental evidence, firnpack/sporadic permafrost, defile on the approach march, blocking rockfall and grassy regrouping area on the lee side point to the Traversette as the transit col, and reinforce the notion that if another route is preferred, one needs to circumvent the evidence presented in ancient texts to prove it. Even then with artifacts in hand, one would need to prove they did not originate from Hasdrubal's invasion of 207 BC ending with his destruction by Roman legions at the Metaurus River.

While no artifacts have been recovered to date, the Guil-Po valleys and the Traversette rockfall are prime targets upon which to focus future historical archaeological explorations by someone with a license to carry out the research. The objective ought to be on actual field analysis not a rehash of ancient literature without corroborating field evidence. For example, the analysis of ballast in the Traversette rockfall roadway (Mahaney, 2008), ancient walls in the upper Po regrouping area (now buried by debris flows in 2008; Mahaney et al., 2010b), excavation of a single un-cemented dwelling/station and grave on a bedrock bar (~2250 m asl) overlooking the upper Po valley, foraging areas in the Guil and Po valleys and analysis of rockfall in the Combe de Queyras, the latter the probable defile where Hannibal lost considerable men under attack from the Allobroges (Mahaney, 2008).

Of all the pundits assessing the various Hannibalic routes through the Alps, and this includes some notable historians/classicists aside from de Beer (1969), such as, Brown (1963), Connolly (1981, Cottrell (1992), Dodge (1891), Hart (1967), Seibert (1993), Lazenby, (1998), Prevas (1998), Wilkinson (1911) to name a few, none have had Hannibal cutting through solid rock, a bedrock shear plane (as it were-'landslip') to forge a path down out of whatever high pass was picked as the point of entry. None, outside of Paton (1922), have mentioned a 'landslip,' although Cottrell mentions a huge boulder, just how huge is left to the imagination of the reader. In any case future work will eventually lead to the recovery of artifacts and these will, in all likelihood, originate in one or more localities in the Guil and upper Po valleys. Recent finds of physical sedimentary evidence in the form of a bioturbated bed in an alluvial mire in the Guil River catchment, dated precisely to 2168 cal yr BP (218 BC), have been recovered along with bacteria endospores and tapeworm eggs from horses, have been reported recently (see Mahaney et al., 2016a, 2016b).

ACKNOWLEDGEMENTS

This work was funded by Quaternary Surveys, Toronto.

REFERENCES

Bagnall, N. (1999) *The Punic Wars*, Pimlico, London.

Brown, J. E. T. (1963) Hannibal's route across the Alps. *Greece and Rome*, **10**, 38–46.

Connolly, P. (1981) *Greece and Rome at war*, Greenhill Books, London, 320 pp.

Cottrell, L. (1992) *Hannibal enemy of Rome*, Da Capo Press, New York.

de Beer, G. (1967) *Hannibal's march*, Sidgwick and Jackson, London.

de Beer, G. (1969) *Hannibal*, The Viking Press, New York.

Dodge, T. H. (1891) *Hannibal*, Houghton Mifflin, New York.

Hart, B. H. L. (1967) *Strategy*, Penguin, London.

Kuhle, M. and Kuhle, S. (2012) Hannibal gone astray? A critical comment on W. C. Mahaney *et al.* (2010), 'The Traversette (*Italia*) rockfall: geomorphological indicator of the Hannibalic invasion route', *Archaeometry*, **54**, 591–601.

Kuhle, M., Kuhle, S. (2015) 'Lost in translation or can we still understand what Polybius says about Hannibal's crossing of the Alps—a reply to Mahaney [Archaeometry, 55 (2013), 1196-1204, *Archaeometry*, 57, 759-771.

Lancel, S. (1999) *Hannibal*, Blackwell, Oxford, 241 pp.

Lazenby, J. F. (1998) *Hannibal's war*, University of Oklahoma Press, Norman, OK.

Livy, trans. Aubrey de Sélincourt, (1972) *The war with Hannibal*, Penguin, London.

Mahaney, W. C. (1990) *Ice on the Equator*, Wm Caxton Ltd., Ellison Bay, WI.

Mahaney, W. C. (2004) A geological/topographical reconnaissance of Hannibal's invasion route into Italia in 218 bc, in *Studies in military geography and geology* (eds. D. R. Caldwell, J. Ehlen, and R. S. Harmon), 67–78, Kluwer Academic Publishers, Dordrecht.

Mahaney, W. C. (2008) *Hannibal's Odyssey: environmental background to the alpine invasion of Italia*, Gorgias Press, Piscataway, NJ.

Mahaney, W. C. (2013) Comments on M. Kuhle and S. Kuhle (2012): 'Hannibal gone astray?', *Archaeometry*, **55**, 1196–204.

Mahaney, W.C., Keiser, L. (2013) Weathering rinds-unlikely host clasts for an impact-induced 478 event. *Geomorphology*, 184, 74-83.

Mahaney, W. C., Milner, M. W., Sodhi, Rana, Dorn R. I., Boccia, S., Beukens, R. P., Tricart, P., Schwartz, S., Chamorro-Perrez, E., Barendregt, R. W., Kalm, V., and Dirszowsky, R. W. (2007) Analysis of burnt schist outcrops in the Alps: relation to historical archaeology and Hannibal's crossing, *Geoarchaeology*, **22**, 797–816.

Mahaney, W. C., Kapran, B., and Tricart, P. (2008a) Hannibal and the Alps: unraveling the invasion route from the geological evidence, *Geology Today*, **4**(6), 223–30.

Mahaney, W.C., Kalm, V., Dirszowsky, R., Milner, M.W., Sodhi, R.N.S., Beukens, R., Dorn, R., Tricart, P., Schwartz. S., Chamorro-Perez, E., Boccia, S., Barendregt, R.W., Boccia, S., Krinsley, D.H., Seaquist, E.R., Merrick, D., Kapran, B. (2008b) Hannibal's trek across the Alps: identification of sites of geoarchaeological interest. *Journal Mediterranean Archaeology and Archaeometry*, **8**, (2), 39-54.

Mahaney, W. C., Tricart, P., Carcaillet, C., Blarquez, O., Ali, A. A., and Barendregt, R. W. (2010a) Hannibal's invasion route: age-old question revisited with new scientific data, *Archaeometry*, **52**, 1096–109.

Mahaney, W. C., Barendregt, R. W., Carcaillet, C., Tricart, P., Rabufetti, D., and Kalm, V. (2010b) Debris flow burial of ancient wall systems in the Upper Po River Valley, Italia, *Geology Today*, **26**(6), 209–15.

Mahaney, W. C., Kapran, B., Kalm, V., Tricart, P., Carcaillet, C., Blarquez, O., Milner, M. W., Barendregt, R. W., and Somelar, P. (2010c) The Traversette rockfall: geomorphological reconstruction and importance in interpreting classical history, *Archaeometry*, **52**, 156–72.

Mahaney, W.C., Keiser, Leslie, Krinsley, D.H., Pentlavalli, P., Allen, C.C.R., Somelar, P., Schwartz, Stephane, Dohm, James M., Dirzowsky, Randy, West, Allen, Julig, P., Costa, P. (2013) Weathering rinds as mirror images of palaeosols: examples from the Western Alps with correlation to Antarctica and Mars. *Journal of the Geological Society*, Lyell Volume, doi: 524 10.1144/jgs2012-150.

Mahaney, W.C., Allen, C.C.R., Pentlavalli, P., Dirszowsky, R., Tricart, P., Keiser, L., Somelar, P., Kelleher, B., Murphy, B., Costa, P.J.M., Julig, P. (2014) Polybius's 'previous landslide': proof that Hannibal's invasion route crossed the col de la Traversette, *Journal Mediterranean Archaeology and Archaeometry*, **14**, (2), 1-20.

Mahaney, W. C., Allen, C.C.R., Pentlavalli, P., Kulakova, A., Young, J. M., Dirszowsky, R.W., West, A., Kelleher, B., Jordan, S., Pulleyblank, C., O'Reilly, S., Murphy, B. T., Lasberg, K., Somelar, P., Garneau, M., Finkelstein, S. A., Sobol, M. K., Kalm, V., Costa, P. J. M., Hancock, R. G. V., Hart, K. M., Tricart, P., Barendregt, R. W., Bunch, T. E., Milner, M. W. (2016a) Biostratigraphic Evidence relating to the Age-Old Question of Hannibal's Invasion of Italy: I, History and Geological Reconstruction, *Archaeometry*, doi: 10.1111/arcm.12231.

Mahaney, W. C., Allen, C. C. R., Pentlavalli, P., Kulakova, A., Young, J. M., Dirszowsky, R.W., West, A., Kelleher, B., Jordan, S., Pulleyblank, C., O'Reilly, S., Murphy, B.T., Lasberg, K., Somelar, P., Garneau, M., Finkelstein, S. A., Sobol, M. K., Kalm, V., Costa, P. J. M., Hancock, R. G. V., Hart, K. M., Tricart, P., Barendregt, R. W., Bunch, T. E., Milner, M. W. 2016b. Biostratigraphic Evidence relating to the Age-Old Question of Hannibal's Invasion of Italy: II Chemical biomarkers and microbial signatures. *Archaeometry*, doi: 10.1111/arcm.12228.

Mahaney, W. C., Somelar, P., Dirszowsky, R. W., Kelleher, B., Pentlavalli, P., McLaughlin, S., Kulakova, A., Jordan, S., Pulleyblank, C., West, A., Allen, C.C.R. (2016c) A microbial link to weathering of postglacial rocks and sediments, Mt. Viso area, Western Alps, demonstrated through analysis of a soil/paleosol bio/chronosequence. *Journal of Geology*, 124, 149-169.

Neumann, J. (1992) Climatic conditions in the Alps in the years about the year of Hannibal's crossing 218 bc, *Climatic Change*, **22**, 139–50.

Paton, W.R. (1922) *Polybius, The Histories*, Books 3-4, Harvard University Press, Cambridge, Ma., 568 pp.

Polybius, trans. I. Scott-Kilvert (1979) *The rise of the Roman Empire*, Penguin, London.

Prevas, J. (1998) *Hannibal crosses the Alps*, Sarpedon, Rockville Centre, NY.

Proctor, D. (1971) *Hannibal's march in history*, Oxford University Press, Oxford.

Savage, J.J.H. (1934) The manuscripts of Servius' commentary on Virgil. *Harvard Studies in Classical Philology*, **45**, 157-204.

Seibert, J. (1993) *Hannibal*, 75–134, Wissenschaftliche Buchgesellschaft, Darmstadt.

Sodhi, R., Mahaney, W. C., and Milner, M. W. (2006) ToF-SIMS applied to historical archaeology in the Alps, *Applied Surface Science*, **252**, 7140–3.

Walbank, F. W. (1956) Some reflections on Hannibal's Pass, *Journal of Roman Studies*, **46**, 37–45.

Walbank, F. W. (1990) *Polybius*, University of California Press, Berkeley, CA.

Wilkinson, H. S. (1911) *Hannibal's march through the Alps*, Oxford at the Clarendon Press, Oxford, UK.

9

LITHIC INDUSTRIES OF THE AEGEAN UPPER MESOLITHIC

A. Sampson[1], J. K. Kozlowski[2], M. Kaczanowska[3]

[1]*University of the Aegean, Laboratory of Environmental Archaeology, Rhodes, Greece*
[2]*Jaggiellonian University, Krakow, Poland*
[3]*The Polish Academy of Arts and Sciences, Krakow, Poland*

Corresponding author: *(adsampson@rhodes.aegean.gr)*

ABSTRACT

Recent research at Areta in the northern side of Chalki Island (Dodecanese) has revealed an enormous quantity of lithics of the Mesolithic period. It is the first time that such an old settlement is located in the area of the Dodecanese, thus extending to the southeast of the Aegean the already known Mesolithic network of sites and creating a sea route from Cyclades to Dodecanese. Apart from the Melian obsidian, there is great abundance of obsidian from Yali of Nissiros used for making tools despite its poor quality. The last few years' surveys of the Aegean University discovered an extensive Mesolithic site at the southern part of Naxos that follows the usual model of Mesolithic occupation with the selection of sites very close to the sea. The types of tools in both sites exhibit a number of analogies with the sites of the Aegean Mesolithic such as Maroulas in Kythnos and Kerame 1 in Ikaria. Dissimilarities between the above-mentioned inventories result first of all from the fact that different raw materials were exploited. Despite of the missing absolute dates, the regularity and increase of geometrical tools, and the presence of other microlithic forms may suggest that the lithic industry of both sites represents a later phase of the Aegean Mesolithic. The lithic industry of the Upper Mesolithic resembles with the lithic repertory of the aceramic level X of Knossos showing an origin from the Aegean and not from the East.

KEYWORDS: Chalki, Areta, Naxos, Roos, Knossos, obsidian, microliths, Melos, Yali

1. INTRODUCTION

The last two decades, Mesolithic sites have been excavated around the Aegean Basin such as Cyclops Cave in the Northern Aegean, Maroulas in Kythnos (Cyclades) and Kerame 1 in Ikaria resulting a flourishing Aegean Mesolithic culture. Moreover, a network of sites was located in Kythnos, Ikaria and eastern Peloponnese (Runnels 1996, 2001, 2009) showing a dense occupation mainly on coastal areas.

The common stone industry of Ikaria and Kythnos, as well as the transportation of the obsidian from Melos and Yali to different parts of the Aegean lead to the assumption that sea routes had existed at least since the 9th mill. BC. Smaller sea routes could have existed among the islands of the central and southern Aegean serving for the distribution of Melos and Yali obsidian to the Mesolithic centers. The new Mesolithic site in Chalki Island was responsible for the transfer of Melian obsidian to the Dodecanese while Naxos stands in the course of the voyage from Ikaria to Melos.

Until now, the choice of inhabitation in small islands is related to the interest in key positions belonging to a network of sea routes and suitable for fishing. The large settlement in the island of Chalki (Sampson 2010) constitutes a stop in the SW Aegean suggesting routes to Crete and Cyprus (Sampson 2014, 2015). The advantages of this location are the safe mooring bay and the proximity to the cave. The island would have offered several food sources meaning vegetables or animals. The high density of surface findings is greater than those of Kerame 1 in Ikaria and Roos in Naxos while it suggests intense activities for quite a while.

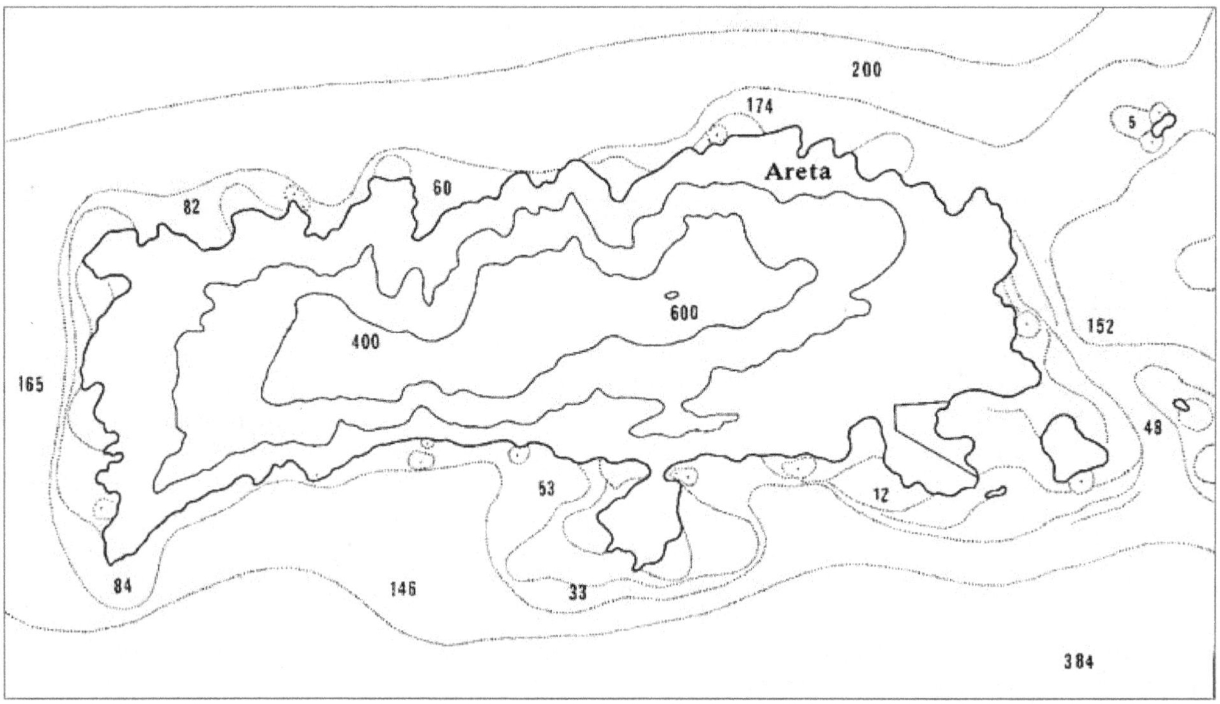

Figure 1. Map of Chalki Island

2. THE MESOLITHIC SITE OF ARETA, CHALKI

Chalki is a small island of the Dodecanese region, 35 nautical miles west of the city of Rhodes (Fig. 1). The island is rocky and mountainous covering an area of 32 sq. km and consisting almost exclusively of limestone. The length of the island is 4 km from west to east. It has been estimated (Vernicos 1986) that on the island there are four types of land cover and land use: 1) plains containing «Older Fill» (10%), 2) slopes of mountains with soil (35%), 3) rocky slopes with little soil (45%) and 4) rocky peaks, inaccessible even to pasture goats (10%). A few caves have been found mainly in the northern part of the island as well as a few dolines. Few valleys and some natural basins contain more than 6m backfill (Older Fill, Bintliff 1977), derived from erosion of the Pleistocene. A natural cut by erosion on the beach of Pontamos shows several phases of sedimentation of an Older Fill with an iron oxide composition and different sized materials. Within this there is a layer of aeolianite, a soft sandstone from the cementation of dunes (Rachham & Vernicos 1991).

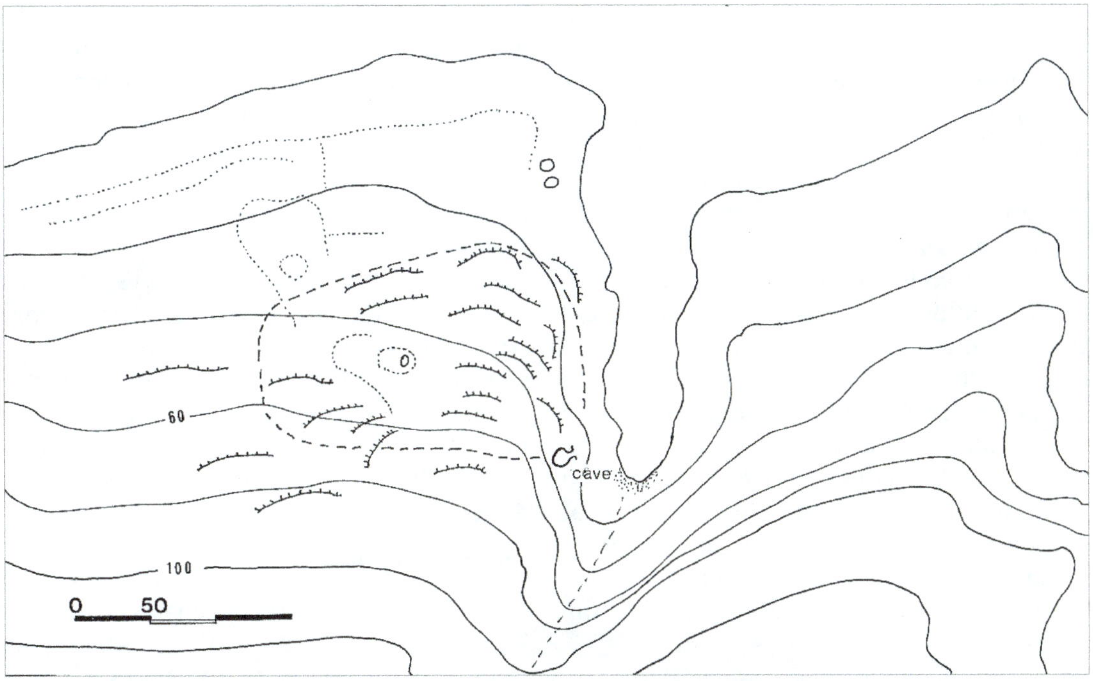

Figure 2. Areta in Chalki. Topographical map (--- boundaries of scattered artifacts).

An episode of great erosion in historical times, called the Younger Fill (Bintliff 1977), was observed in several parts of the island such as the saddles under the village of Kastro and Antramassos. In the latter material, pottery of historical times was found coming from the eroded terraces that existed on the slopes above it. The soils of the Younger Fill are composed of tenuous *rendzinas*. The rainfall is much less than that of Rhodes (400-450mm per year), probably because the mountains of the island are not so high as to pull the rainfall and the orientation from west to east is a further handicap.

Although Chalki today is one of the most naked islands in the Aegean preserving a variety of vegetation of plants or trees in very small numbers but representative of the Aegean. Pine remnants and dense vegetation of shrubs exist on the eastern and northern side of the island (Pefkias, Kania). Information from old residents speak of significant vegetation in the past by conifers and fruit trees. The maquis vegetation is represented by lentisks (*Pistacia lentiscus*) and cedars on the northeastern side of Chalki. In Pampakies there is also a dense vegetation of "fides", a kind of cedar (Juniperus phoenicea). Cypresses, pines and other trees were used in the past to build ships and houses, so apparently there was an exploitation of woodlands.

Vernikos and Racham (1991) believe that the naked environment of Chalki is not due to human intervention and grazing of animals but to natural factors that were active during the Pleistocene. The environment of the island may have never been very different in ancient times than today.

Figure 3.Areta, Chalki. View from the north

Areta is a very remote area located in the northern part of the island, at a point where a deep fjord-like bay is opened that ends in a small sandy beach (Fig. 2, 3). Near the beach, a well collects fresh water from the deep gorge. In a flat area to the west, a large wall was built in the past near the rocky beach in order to keep the soil for crops. However, the erosion today is huge caused by the rain and the action of the waves leaving little soil between the rocks. Terraces for crops and two threshing floors show the capacity of agricultural production in this area.

At higher levels many terraces have preserved the minimum soil between the rocks. These are very limited places where the locals till the first half of 20th century could have planted barley and legumes. In all those terraces in an extensive area measuring 25000 sq. m., enormous quantities of obsidian artifacts have been collected. The probability of the existence of Mesolithic architectural remains is small because the last centuries, major interventions have taken place in the whole area due to intense cultivation activity. A cave divided in three partitions is located in the gorge above the small beach. Today it's no longer used as a pen, but in 2010 there were accumulated into this huge amounts of sheep wool. Obviously, this cave should have been used by the Mesolithic occupants of the area, however the thick layer of manure prevents the surface survey.

2.1 The Lithic Artifacts

The inventory numbered 769 artifacts that are fairly homogeneous in respect of raw materials and techno-morphological features.

Raw materials

Among raw materials obsidian predomina-tes, of which most artifacts were made (Fig. 4). The inventory contained dark obsidian with white inclusions originating from the island of Yali (of which 41.8% of artifacts were made) and dark-grey transparent obsidian from the

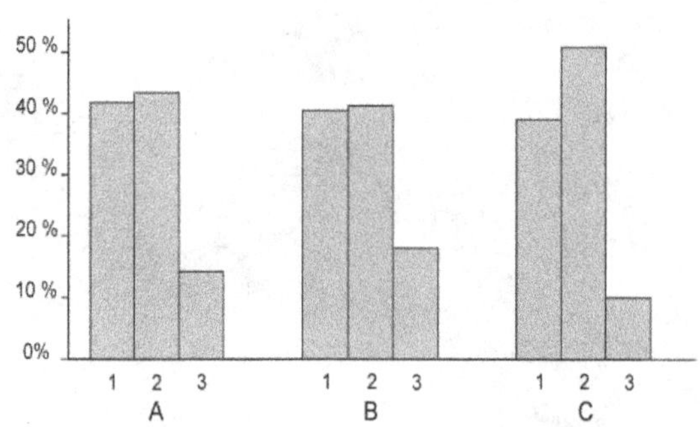

Figure 4. Areta. Raw materials structure: A - general, B - only flakes, C - chips. 1 - obsidian from Yali, 2 - Melian obsidian, 3 - siliceous rocks.

island of Melos, represented by 43.4% of artifacts. The presence of Melian obsidian was confirmed at numerous Mesolithic sites of the Aegean Sea (e.g. at Kythnos - Sampson *et al.* 2010; Youra - Kaczanowska, Kozłowski 2008; Ikaria - Sampson *et al.* 2012) as well as on its western coast (e.g. at Franchthi - Renfrew, Aspinall 1990) and eastern coast (e.g. Cukurici Höyük - Horejs 2012). The presence of both obsidian from Melos and from Yali at Chalki confirms the functioning of a network of contacts and seafaring skills of the inhabitants of this site. The distance from Chalki to Yali is about 70 km in a straight line while to Melos about 200 km. Seafaring in the Aegean Sea was easy due to the existence of chains of islands stretching along Anatolian coast and, latitudinal, across the Aegean Sea (Sampson 2015). Obsidian was arriving Chalki in the form either of concretions or of initial cores. Apart from obsidian, small pebbles of two types of siliceous rocks were exploited, namely: brown-reddish opaque flint (10.1%) and grey transluscent flint (4.1%). Moreover, one core from radiolarite and two artifacts from other siliceous rocks were discovered.

Inventory structure

The inventory structure is provided on Fig. 5. When compared with other Mesolithic sites in the Aegean (e.g. Maroulas), the site at Chalki shows a distinctly lower index of flakes - even when chips are added to this group. Both at Maroulas and at Kerame 1 in Ikaria flakes (together with chips) constituted more than a half of the inventory, whereas at Chalki the proportion of flakes, splinters and chips together is 49%. On the other hand, the tool index at Chalki is higher (17.9), while at Maroulas or Kerame 1, it is about 10%. It seems, that Chalki was a short-term camp set up by a group that arrived with its own store of raw materials (which is evidenced by the high proportion of cores - 10%), while the on-site working of raw materials played a minor role. Possibly, some retouched tools were also brought to the site.

MORPHOMETRICS

The inventory from Chalki can be defined as microlithic. The size of cores, blanks and tools reaches up to 34 mm at most, while it should be added that only two artifacts reach the maximum size. The length of flaking faces of cores is between 13 and 27 mm. These specimens are well-exhausted thus in the initial stage they could have been somewhat larger. The most numerous group includes cores with the flaking surfaces between 14 to 19 mm; flake dimensions are similar (Fig. 6). Nearly the half of all tools were made from blanks between 14 and 19 mm long (Fig. 6). It should be emphasized that flakes longer than 19 mm are more numerous (31%) than tools of similar size (26%). This fact corroborates a hypothesis that some slightly larger cores also existed in the initial stage of reduction, or that some worked pieces were brought to the site from elsewhere. Blanks from Chalki are smaller than the flakes from Maroulas, the length of which is in the interval of 9 to 81 mm, or from the site of Kerame 1 in Ikaria where blank size reaches as much as 59 mm. At the two latter sites the larger specimens were made from local raw materials - quartzites and quartz at Maroulas and quartz at Kerame 1. When artifacts from extralocal obsidians are compared no difference in size between the sites is observed.

CORES

The inventory provided 77 cores and fragments. Almost half of the specimens were made of obsidian from the island of Yali (43 specimens). Relatively high was the proportion of cores from brownish flint (12 specimens). The cores represented all the stages of reduction. Initial cores were fairly numerous (13 spec.- 16.8%), and included hyper-microlithic cores measuring 14-16x14-18x8-16 mm. Reduction of initial cores was restricted to only one or two removals. In this group only one specimen was made of Melian obsidian, three specimens of obsidian from Yali, three from brown flint, and one from radiolarite. Among initial cores, there were as well slightly larger specimens as well, flaking surfaces of which were between 22 and 17 mm long, produced from larger flakes mainly of obsidian from Yali. No preliminary preparation was registered in the group of initial cores, except from the platform.

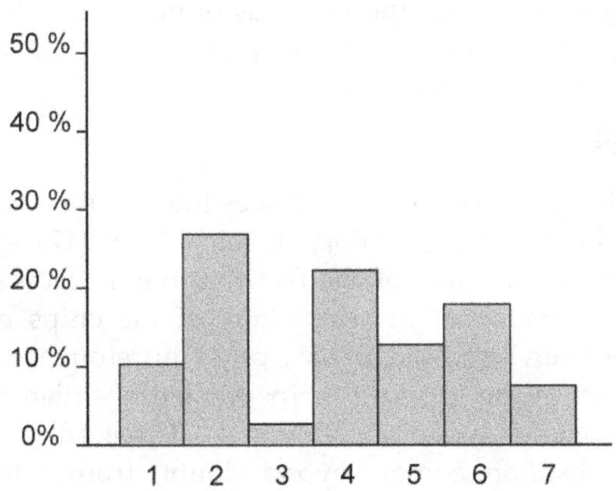

Figure 5. Areta. Inventory structure: 1 - cores, 2 - flakes with splinters, 3 - blades, 4 - chips, 5 - splintered pieces, 6 - tools, 7 - undetermined fragments.

The remaining cores are predominantly single-platform cores in an advanced stage of reduction (24 spec.). The flaking surfaces of these cores are located in the narrower face of a concretion (Pl. I 1, 2); preparation usually extends onto sides (Pl. I 3). Reduction was carried out until a core was totally exhausted, and in the final stage became flat (Pl. I 4, 5). Sometimes, attempts were made to detach blanks from flat cores using splintered technique (Pl. I 5). Cores with a rounded flaking surface were relatively rare (Pl. I, 1). These cores had oblique platforms that gave an

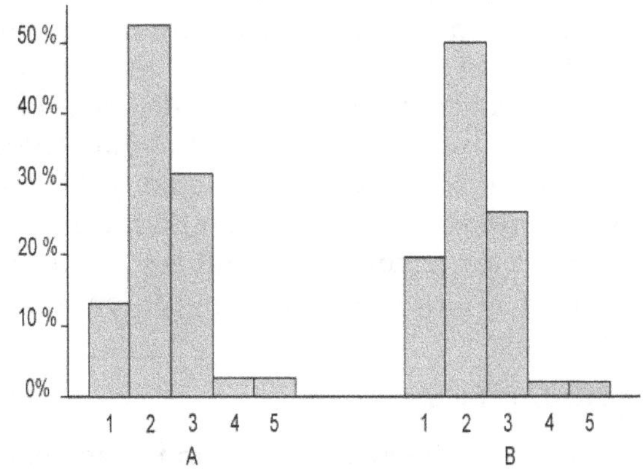

Figure 6. Areta. Length of: A - flakes, B - tools. 1 - <13mm, 2 - 14-19mm, 3 - 20-25mm, 4 - 26-32mm, 5 >32mm

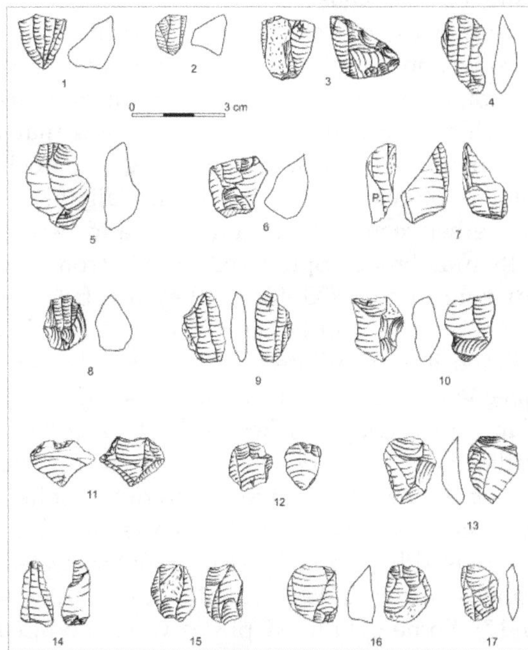

Plate I. Areta: 1-10 - cores, 11-1- splintered pieces

acute angle making blank removals easier. The operations of platform rejuvenation and retrimming were also used.

Except for single-platform cores, double-platform specimens were also found (6 spec.). These were not classical double platform cores with a common flaking surface and alternate reduction from two platforms, but - rather - cores with the orientation changed to the opposite (Pl. I 6). Just as in the group of single-platform cores specimens made on flakes were also present (Pl. I 7).

In the final stage of reduction of polihedral cores the location of platform was changed several times in order to better exploit a raw material nodule. The result was a kind of multiplatform specimen with random reduction (5 spec.)

As far as one third of all cores is concerned, they have been preserved as fragments in a degree that made their attribution impossible (26 spec.). Although in the material collected from the site surface flakes are predominant, yet the flaking surfaces of a number of cores show blade scars (Pl. I 1, 3, 4, 7-9) or blade-flake scars (Pl. I 5, 10). These cores were made from both: good quality Melian obsidian and obsidian from Yali with poor cleavage from which blade removal was difficult, or from siliceous rocks. The blade scars appear on small specimens.

SPLINTERED PIECES

Ninety eight splintered pieces and fragments account for 12.7% of the inventory. Thus, the component of splintered technique is higher than at the site of Maroulas where splintered pieces are 8.5%, and nearly twice as high as at Kerame 1 where the proportion of splintered pieces is only 5.6%. A high component of splintered technique is typical of sites where difficulties occur in raw materials procurement. The most numerous group includes splintered pieces of obsidian from Yali (52 spec.). They are between 11 to 22 mm long and between 7 and 18 mm broad. Splintered pieces from Melian obsidian are fewer (33 spec.); they are between 13 and 25 mm long, and between 6 and 22 mm broad. The dimensions of splintered pieces from brown flint (10 spec.) and grey-brown siliceous rock (3 spec.) are similar. Frequently, flakes (Pl. I 11, 12, 13), sporadically also blades (Pl. I 14), were worked using splintered technique. Moreover, splintered pieces were made from residual cores or small, flat concretions (Pl. I 15, 16). Some bipolar, two-sided specimens are entirely covered with splinter scars (Pl. I 17). Some splintered pieces were modified by retouch into tools, as a rule into denticulated-notched tools, occasionally into backed pieces. Less often, splinters were also retouched into tools (4 specimens).

FLAKES

Flakes together with splinters constitute the most numerous group of artifacts, although their proportion is lower at Chalki than at other Mesolithic sites of the Aegean. Most specimens have been preserved as fragments. The raw materials structure is provided in Fig. 4. Flake length is between 12 and 32 mm, width between 10 and 25 mm, and thickness between 2 and 10 mm. Comparison of flake size from the two types of obsidian (from Melos and Yali) shows that flakes from Melian obsidian are slightly larger (the most numerous group includes flakes about 20 mm). Sporadically dorsal cortex is present. Majority of flakes show dorsal pattern, usually unidirectional. Almost one third of flakes from Melian obsidian shows scars perpendicular to the flake axis which – in this case – is related to change of orientation rather than to core preparation. Probably the knapper wished to fully exploit a nodule of raw material with good cleavage.

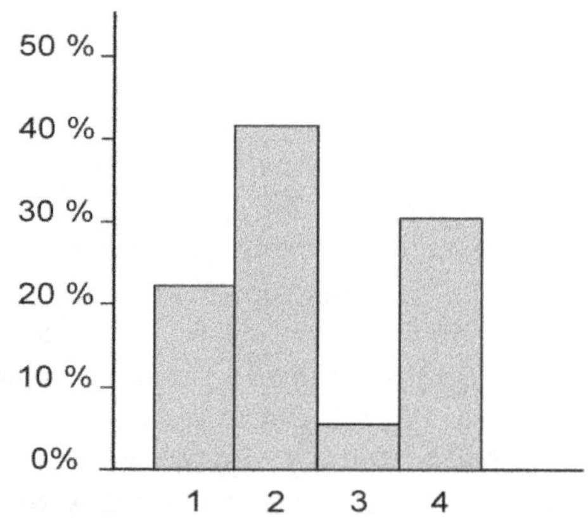

Figure 7. Areta. Butt types of flakes: 1 – unprepared butts, 2 – formed by single blos, 3 – faceted butts, 4 – linear and punctiform butts

As already mentioned, core preparation is modest. This is confirmed by the analysis of flake butts which are predominantly unprepared or formed by a single blow, while specimens with a facetted butt are few (Fig. 7). Because the series of flakes with preserved butts is too small, the methods of blank detachment from the cores made on various raw materials cannot be reconstructed.

Chips

The group of chips, i.e. flakes that are less than 14 mm long in the inventory, is fairly large (171 spec.). However, in view of the fact that the artifacts from Chalki are small in size, many of the chips could have been used as blanks, or as unretouched tool inserts. In the group of chips Melian obsidian has a conspicuous ascendancy (Fig. 4). Three chips from this obsidian come, beyond doubt, from retouch. This means that tool-reutilization – although to a small extent – must have taken place at the site.

Blades

Blades (20 spec.) are merely 2.6% of the inventory. Most are broken specimens; only four blades were complete. Blade width is between 9 and 15 mm, and the maximum length could have been slightly more than 30 mm. Blades are predominantly from Melian obsidian; as many as 16 blades out of 20 were made from this raw material. Some blades show micro-retouch on the edges; this does not attest their function as tools but could have been the effect of post-depositional processes. It is also likely, that some, more regular specimens could imply a younger (Neolithic) intrusion.

2.2 *Retouched tools (Pl. II-IV)*

The collection included 138 retouched tools that in respect of raw materials, techno-morphology and measurable attributes represent a homogeneous assemblage. Only two tools could be a younger intrusion, namely: a dihedral burin on a regular blade and a backed piece on a blank split off from a tool with surface retouch. Among the raw materials, obsidian has a decided ascendancy: from Melos - 95 specimens, and from Yali - 34 specimens. Siliceous rocks are represented by 9 specimens from chert or brown flint. Most retouched tools are hypermicrolithic or microlithic (between 5 to 25 mm); specimens up to 35 mm (among perforators) occur sporadically.

End-scrapers (9)

All the end-scrapers are microlithic. They are made on flakes with oblique dorsal pattern (Pl. II 1-3), or on short blades (Pl. II 4), or blade-flakes (Pl. II 5). All the specimens are with weakly rounded fronts shaped by steep retouch. An end-scraper is with bilateral, steep retouch (Pl. II 6); an end-scraper shows damage on one edge, probably post-depositional (Pl. II 4).

Burins

The only burin is a dihedral medial specimen shaped on a regular blade (the preserved fragment is 2.7cm long; the proximal part is broken off), made from Melian obsidian (Pl. II 7). The small size and regular blank indicate that this burin could be a Palaeolithic or Neolithic admixture.

Backed pieces (13)

All the backed pieces are microlithic. The most numerous are angulated backed pieces made on bladelets (Pl. II 8-10), or with a convex or arched back (Pl. II 11–13). Two specimens are hypermicrolithic, one of them has inverse retouch (Pl. II 12). Straight backed pieces on bladelets are represented by two specimens with very steep retouch (Pl. II 14, 15) and two fragments (Pl. II 16, 17). Backed pieces on splintered pieces had partially retouched back (Pl. II 18, 19). A straight backed piece was made on a blank detached from a tool with surface retouch; possibly this is a Neolithic admixture (Pl. II 20).

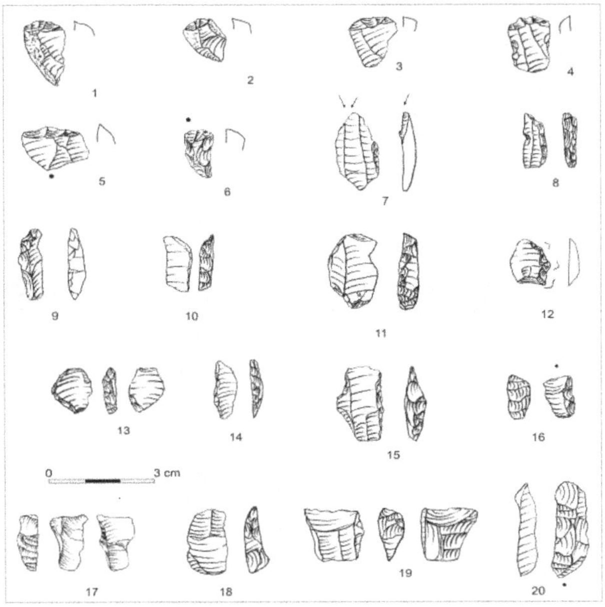

Plate II. Areta. 1-20 – retouched tools

Geometrical inserts (5)

Inserts with double truncations include: rectangles (2 spec.), trapezes (2 spec.), and an irregular rhomb (1 spec.). The items are between 6 and 17 mm long. The rectangles were made on regular bladelets: one has parallel truncations with alternate retouch (Pl. III 1), the other has a thick proximal truncation and a thinner distal truncation, both shaped by obverse retouch (Pl. II 16, 17). One trapeze on a regular bladelet has truncations shaped by alternate retouch: the proximal truncation is thicker, the distal is thinner (Pl. III 3). The other trapeze, made on a sub-crested blade, has truncations shaped by alternate retouch (Pl. III 4). An irregular rhomb was made on a regular bladelet, with truncations shaped by obverse retouch (Pl. III 5).

Truncations (13)

Most frequent are specimens with an oblique distal truncation made on fairly broad bladelets with a preserved proximal part (Pl. III 6,7), possibly very short (Pl. III 8, 9) or even hyper-microlithic (Pl. III 10, 11). Three specimens (Pl. III 6, 7, 9) are with straight truncations. One specimen has a narrow straight truncation and bilateral retouch (Pl. III 13). Also occur a specimen with an oblique truncation and lateral retouch made on a flake (Pl. III 14) and another with straight truncations and lateral retouch (Pl. III 15, 16). The specimens are between 8 and 20 mm long.

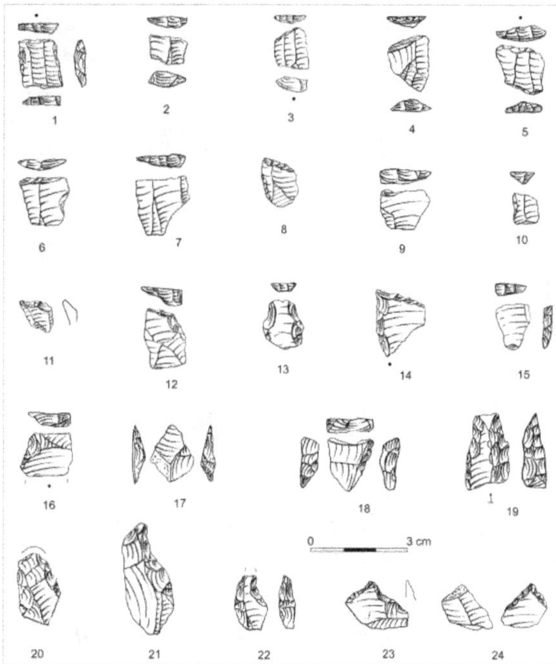

Plate III. Areta. 1-24 – retouched tools

Other microliths (2)

To the other microliths are reported: a point with two convergent blunted backs made on a flake (Pl. III 17), and a triangle on a fragment of a bladelet with two convergent blunted backs and a straight base (Pl. III 18).

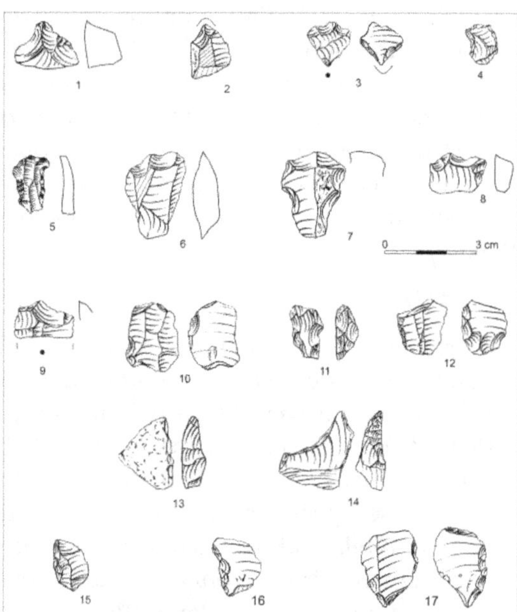

Plate IV. Areta. 1-17 – retouched tools

Perforators and becs

In this group belong 23 perforators and becs (atypical perforators), the length of which is up to 37 mm and 13-17 mm, respectively. The group of typical perforators consists of a specimen with a straight tip shaped on the one edge by bidirectional steep retouch, and on the other by semi-steep obverse retouch (Pl. III 19), two specimens with asymmetrical tips shaped by semi-steep retouch (Pl. III 20, 21), and a microlithic specimen on a bladelet (Pl. III 22).

Atypical perforators are represented by numerous microflake specimens: a) with broad tips shaped by fine obverse retouch (Pl. III 23), b) shaped by inverse retouch (Pl. III 24), c) by Clactonian notches (Pl. IV 1, 2), d) a double specimen on a short flake, with the distal point shaped by Clactonian notches and the proximal end shaped by inverse micro-retouch (this specimen is strongly smoothed by use-wear, Pl. IV 3), e) a specimen on a hypermicrolithic flake with the lateral point shaped by semi-steep retouch (Pl. IV 4), f) a bladelet with bilateral retouch and with a similar lateral point (Pl. IV 5). Some of these specimens have been preserved as fragments.

Notched-denticulated tools (49)

The group of notched-denticulated tools is characterized by relatively small blanks no more than 30 mm long and 17 mm broad. The blanks are made by parallel, convergent, opposite and perpendicular dorsal pattern. Sporadically, partial cortical surfaces occur. Specimens with transversal retouch (Pl. IV 6, 7) and others with transversal and lateral retouch (Pl. IV 8-10) are most frequent. Some specimens present bilateral (Pl. IV 11) or proximal (Pl. IV 12) retouch. Some of the specimens have been preserved as fragments.

Side-scrapers

Four fragments of lateral side-scrapers were found: a fragment on a tile of Yali obsidian (Pl. IV 13), two side-scrapers on flake fragments with centripetal scars (Pl. IV 14), and a side-scraper on a splintered piece. All the specimens are with high, steep retouch.

Retouched flakes (18)

One specimen was shaped by lateral obverse retouch on a small splinter (Pl. IV 15), and another on a splintered piece. Other specimens were shaped on flakes and flake fragments by transversal, lateral retouch, inverse or obverse (Pl. IV 16), and proximal-lateral retouch also inverse (Pl. IV 17).

2.3 THE SIGNIFICANCE OF TOOLS FROM CHALKI WITHIN THE "AEGEAN MESOLITHIC"

The series of retouched tools from Chalki exhibits a number of analogies with the island sites of the Aegean Mesolithic, notably with Maroulas in

Kythnos (Sampson *et al.* 2010) and Kerame 1 in Ikaria (Sampson *et al.* 2012). At Maroulas and Kerame 1 the proportion of retouched tools is about 10%, thus it is lower than at Areta. The dissimilarities between the above-mentioned inventories result first of all from the fact that different raw materials were exploited. At Areta there are no artifacts (also tools) from quartz or quartzite, while tools from siliceous rocks (chert, flint) are only 8.1%. At Maroulas quartz accounts for 43.5% of the inventory, quartzite for 2.4%, and siliceous rocks (white patinated flint) 11.9%. Although at Kerame 1 the proportion of quartz is small (about 3%), siliceous rocks (first of all white patinated flint) constitute nearly a half of the inventory. This was caused by the fact that in Kythnos and Ikaria quartz was locally available like, additionally, in Ikaria siliceous rocks. Despite the various frequencies of tools from obsidian at the sites in question (Areta - more than 90%, Maroulas - nearly 50%, Kerame 1 - 25%), as well as of tools from obsidian from Melos and Yali, the measurable attributes of tools from these raw materials are within the same modes of size.

The frequency of the various tool types too, shows fairly important differences, in spite of techno-morphological similarities of types of blanks and retouch. End-scrapers that at Areta account for 6.5% of the inventory, at Maroulas are 17.9%, and at Kerame 1 16.8%. In respect of morphology the end-scrapers at Areta are short blade and flake specimens; similar end-scrapers were registered at Kerame 1 (Sampson *et al.* 2012, Pl. 5:1, 2, 5, 14) and Maroulas (Sampson *et al.* 2010, Pl. XII 14–16, XIII 14). At Maroulas, hypermicrolithic specimens also occur (Sampson *et al.* 2010, Pl. XIV 11–16) just as at Areta where only one burin was found, the ascription of which is anyway uncertain; burins in the Aegean Mesolithic are relatively rare while their proportion at Maroulas is 1.2% and Kerame 1 only 0.7%.

Backed pieces are a permanent stable component of assemblages of the Aegean Mesolithic. Their average index is about 10 (at Areta - 9.4, at Kerame 1 - 10.8) and only at Maroulas it is low - 3.1%. At the three sites in question, backed pieces are with a straight back (Maroulas - Sampson *et al.* 2010, Pl. XVII 25–29, Kerame 1 - Sampson *et al.* 2012, Pl. 11:1, 3), with an arched back (Maroulas - Sampson *et al.* 2010, Pl. XVIII 3–6, Kerame 1 - Sampson *et al.* 2012, Pl. 11:4–7), or with an angulated back (Maroulas - Sampson *et al.* 2010, Pl. XVII 30–35, Kerame 1 - Sampson 2012 *et al.* Pl. 12:9). There are no major differences between the sites in respect of blanks or type of retouch.

Truncations, too, are a stable element of the Aegean Mesolithic. Their proportion oscillates from 5% at Kerame 1, 8.3% at Maroulas, to 9.4% at Areta. In respect of morphology these are specimens on blade like flakes or on bladelets with straight or oblique truncations (Maroulas - Sampson *et al.* 2010, Pl. XVII 8, 9; Kerame 1 - Sampson *et al.* 2012, Pl. 10:7–11), sometimes hypermicrolithic (op. cit. Pl. 12: 12–17). At the sites of the early Aegean Mesolithic, such as Maroulas, dated at the first half of the 9th millenium BC, double truncations are recorded (Sampson *et al.* 2010, Pl. XVII 12–14, Sampson *et al.* 2012, Pl. 11:1, 2). However, at Areta double truncations are more numerous (3.6%) representing more regular geometrical forms such as rectangles, rhombs and trapezes. Possibly, this suggests that Areta represents a later phase of the Aegean Mesolithic. The presence of other microlithic forms at Areta (Pl. 37, 38) could provide an additional argument in support of this hypothesis.

In all the assemblages discussed here, the component of perforators and atypical perforators (becs) is fairly high (Areta - 16.6%, Maroulas - 15.8%), Kerame 1 - 18.6%). These are typical blade perforators (Maroulas, Sampson *et al.* 2010, Pl. XV 5, Kerame 1 - Sampson *et al.* 2012, Pl. 10: 2, 3) which are less numerous, while more numerous are the atypical flake perforators (becs), sometimes shaped by Clactonian notches; hypermicrolithic atypical specimens also occur as at Maroulas (Sampson *et al.* 2010, Pl. XV 12–16) and Kerame 1 (Sampson *et al.* 2012, Pl. 7:13–19).

As far as denticulated or notched tools are concerned, the differences in the frequency of these tools between the sites under discussion are conspicuous. The proportion of denticulated or notched tools is particularly high at Areta; however this does not seem to reflect functional differences between the sites, but, rather, it is the effect of differing raw materials, first of all a much higher proportion of obsidian at Areta. The edges of obsidian pieces were more easily damaged primarily by post-depositional agents (although some damage could be use-wears). At the sites with a greater presence of quartz, flint or quartzite the edges of artifacts were more resistant to damage.

Standard location of retouch is not registered at Areta either, although transversal and lateral-transversal retouch is predominant. At all the sites of the Aegean Mesolithic side-scrapers are recorded, although their proportion is small (Maroulas - 7.4%, Kerame 1 - 3.7%, Areta - 2.9%). At the three sites in question side-scrapers are relatively the largest tools, made on flakes, possibly on splintered pieces with lateral retouch.

Retouched flakes are numerous at the sites of "Aegean Mesolithic". Their proportions are: Areta - 13%, Maroulas - 16.9%, and Kerame 1 - 22.8%. Comparison of frequencies shows that a higher proportion of quartz and siliceous rocks correlates with a higher proportion of retouched flakes, which were rarely made from obsidian. Retouched flakes are presented with irregular, usually semi-steep, lateral or lateral-transversal retouch. Sometimes, splintered pieces have marginal retouch.

The inventory from Areta does not contain macrotools or macrochoppers that are present at Maroulas and at Kerame 1. This situation, too, can be accounted for the exploited raw materials: obsidian was unsuited for this type of tools.

Figure 8. Roos, Naxos

Figure 9. Roos beach from the west

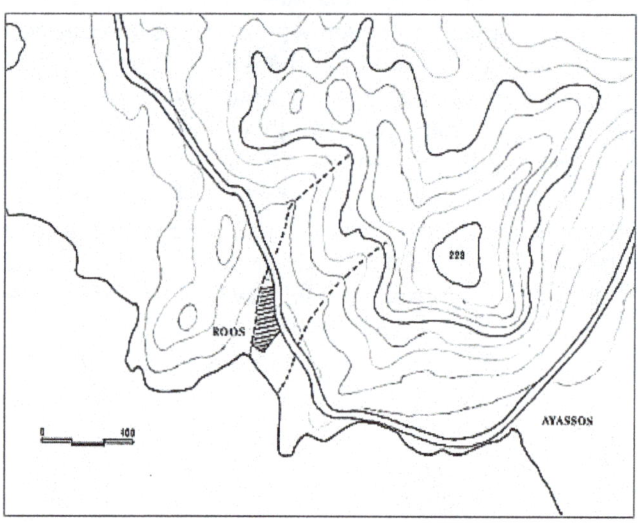

Figure 10. Roos, Naxos. Map of the area

3. THE SITE OF ROOS, NAXOS

The research of the Aegean University in Naxos at the southern side of the island revealed a large quantity of lithics of the Mesolithic period showing an extended installation (Sampson 2010, 85; 2016). The surface findings, plenty of Melian obsidian and white flint, show that the settlement, of more than 20000 sq. meters, lies next to a river with deep watercourse which flows into the sea. The choice of location follows the usual model of occupation of Mesolithic settlements meaning the proximity to the sea (Fig. 8-10). During the survey for the collection of the surface findings, the whole area was divided in five sectors (Fig. 11). Naxos is the largest island of the Cyclades with many dietary sources and other sites of the same period are expected. An additional reason for attracting Mesolithic settlers was the existence of an extensive quarry of white flint at Stelida (Seferiades 1983; Sampson 2006; Carter et al. 2015).

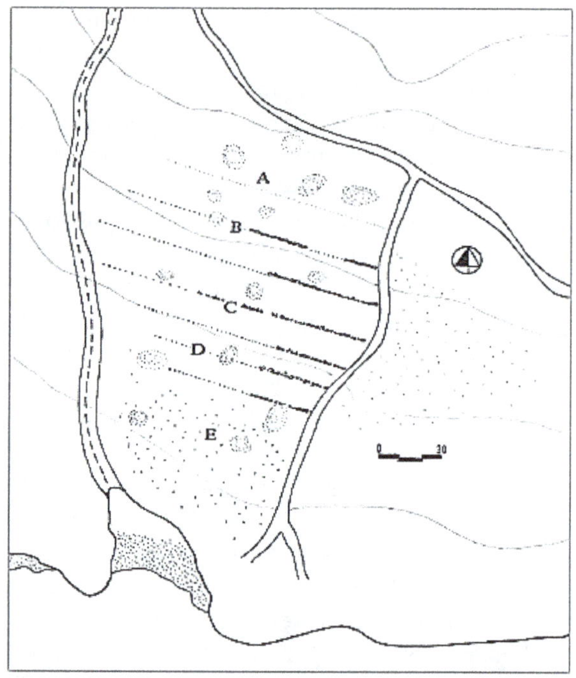

Figure 11. Roos. Topographical map of the site

3.1 The lithic artifacts

The total number of artifacts amounts to 180. The most numerous group are flakes and scaled pieces (71 specimens - 39.4%), followed by tools (29 specimens-16.1%), splintered pieces (26 specimens - 14.4%), and chips (26 - 14.4%). It is worth noticing that only one core (0.5%) was recorded.

Raw materials

The most represented material was obsidian (Table 2), which may have originated from the island of Melos. It is worth noticing that obsidian artifacts at Roos are comprised primarily of blades and splintered pieces (84.6% of splintered pieces are made from obsidian). These splintered pieces were not used as cores, because scaled pieces were made into tools extremely rarely (1 case only).

The provenance of white patinated flint (Table 2) remains uncertain: in fact, these may be artifacts made from different raw materials which were given a similar look by the white patina, or white variants of chert from the Stelida region in Naxos (Carter et al. 2015). The precise identification of these raw materials would only be possible by means of mineralogical and chemical analysis.

Quartz (Table 2) is a common rock occurring in the tabular form. It is not particularly good knapping material, but due to being common and easily available, quartz was used relatively often.

Cores

A characteristic of the Roos inventory is the lack of cores, except for one small (28x29x9 mm) flat double platform core from obsidian. On its back side, the core has unidirectional scars running transversally to the core's orientation. They suggest that the stage of double platform reduction was preceded by its exploitation as a single platform core with parallel scars (Pl. V 1).

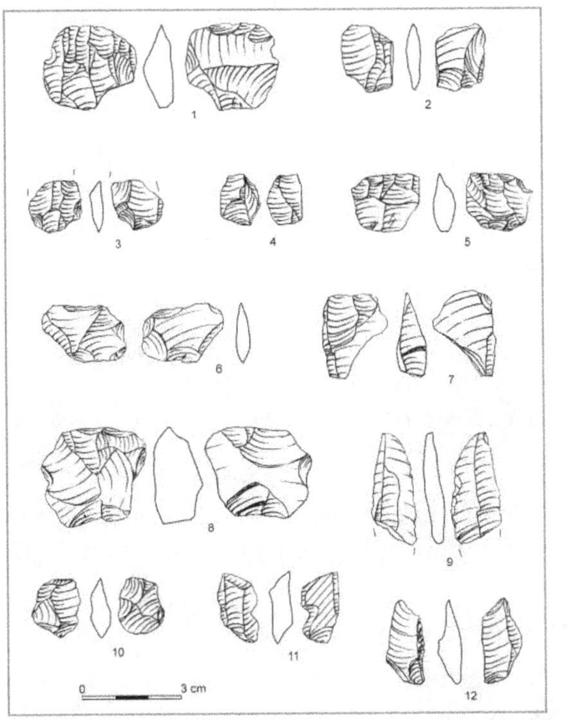

Plate V. Roos. Splintered pieces

Splintered pieces (26 specimens)

Splintered pieces make up 14.4% of the inventory, which indicates that the splinter technique was the predominant method used for the production of microlithic flake and blade blanks. Splintered pieces could also have been used as tools, which resulted in the fragmentation of some of these artifacts (7 fragments among 26 splintered pieces). The vast majority of splintered pieces are made of obsidian; only 3 pieces are made of white patinated flint and 2 of quartz.

Splintered pieces are bipolar and bifacial, and are covered with scars from flake removals (Pl. V, 2-6) so that it is not always possible to determine whether they were made from thermal fragments, tablets, flakes (Pl. V, 7,8), and only exceptionally from a blade (Pl. V,9). There is only one quadripolar splintered piece (Pl. V, 10) in the assemblage. Some of the splintered pieces bear scars from blade removals (Pl. V, 11, 12; VI, 1-3), which suggests they might have been used as bladelet cores. The same function had probably specimens with para-burin scars on the narrower sides (Pl. V, 7; VI, 4).

Only one initial splintered piece was made on the mesial part of a regular mediolithic blade from white patinated flint, with lateral retouch (Pl. VI 5).

Flakes and scaled pieces

There were 71 flakes and scaled pieces, which account for 39.4% of the entire assemblage. Most of them are made from obsidian (45 specimens - 63.4%), 15 flakes are made from white patinated flint, 10 from quartz, and one from a flint covered with a patina of a beige color. Flakes vary in size from 11-42mm in length, 11-30mm in width, and 2-12mm thick. Quartz flakes are the largest, while those made from obsidian are the smallest. There were only 8 scaled pieces identified, which is surprising given the large number of splintered pieces known from the site. On the other hand, the splintered pieces are very small and this may have led to the classification of some of the scaled pieces as chips. Scaled pieces are smaller than flakes, with the length ranging from 11 to 14 mm. Perhaps, two obsidian pieces resembling burin spalls are also the products of splinter technique.

Flakes most often have butts formed with a single blow (9) or natural (6). Pieces with prepared (4) and dihedral (2) butts are known, too, while flakes with punctiform and linear butts are relatively few (2). Unlike blades, among which no cortex pieces were recorded, the discussed group included both initial flakes (4) and flakes with lateral (1) and distal (2) cortex; however, there was only one obsidian specimen among them, the rest being made from white- or beige-patinated flint (5) or quartz (1).

On their dorsal sides, flakes most often bear scars from removals parallel to the flake's axis. Transversal scars, indicative of the change in core orientation rather than of core trimming, were recorded in 6 cases. In addition, there were 3 flakes with negatives of opposed removals and 3 more with concentric scars, the latter perhaps connected with core trimming. It cannot be excluded that, analogically to blades, the collection of flakes from Roos include some younger admixtures, but they are extremely difficult to identify.

Chips

There were 26 chips identified, most of which (17 pieces or 65.4%) were made from obsidian. Quartz chips come second, while those made of white patinated flint are the least numerous group. The relatively low percentage of chips made of white patinated flint, lower than the share of this raw material in the entire Roos assemblage, suggests that it may have reached the site in the form of finished products.

Blades

Twenty blades were identified, including 3 complete forms. The percentage of blades in the whole of the Roos assemblage is relatively high and amounts to 11.1%, while in other sites in the Aegean islands it was much lower, reaching only 1.9% in Maroulas, and 1.4% in the Kerame 1 in Ikaria. The share of blades in the layer linked with the initial Neolithic in Knossos was below 10%. This relatively high representation of blades in Roos may stem from:

a) The presence of artifacts of another chronology (probably Neolithic) in the site.

b) The site being occupied by groups representing other Mesolithic traditions, similar for example to the one known from layers 3 and 5 at Klissoura Cave 1 in Argolid (Koumouzelis et al. 2003).

c) The attribution of the Roos materials to other phases of the Mesolithic, probably younger than Maroulas and Kerame 1 dating to the early or mid-9th millennium BC.

Taking into account that the Mesolithic with the "blade tradition" originates from local Late Palaeolithic industries developing in continental Greece rather than in the littoral zone, and that Mesolithic assemblages known thus far from the islands represent the "flake tradition", the first of the above hypotheses seems to be the most likely.

Blades are exclusively made of obsidian. Complete specimens vary from 24 to 26 mm in length and from 10 to 12 mm in width. Most of the fragmentarily preserved blades probably had similar dimensions, as they are typically 10-12 mm wide. Only two blades are distinctly larger (of 18 and 20 mm in width). The blades come from single platform cores in the advanced stage of reduction, as their dorsal surfaces show no traces of cortex. Among the 9 blades in which the butt survived, 4 had the butt formed with a single removal, 2 had facetted butts and 2 other natural butts. One blade has punctiform butt. The blades' edges are parallel or converging, and the scars on their dorsal sides are from blade removals only. Not all the blades are regular as two have twisted profile. It is worth noticing the presence of a proximal fragment of a regular sub-crested blade, probably being a Neolithic admixture.

3.2 Retouched tools (Pl. VI-VII)

End-scrapers

Four specimens are included in this category of tools: distal fragment of blade end-scraper made from obsidian (Pl. VI, 6), short end-scraper made on obsidian blade (Pl. VI, 7), end-scraper on obsidian blade with irregular distal retouch and lateral notches (Pl. VI, 8), fragment of a short end-scraper on flake from white-patinated chert (Pl. VI, 9).

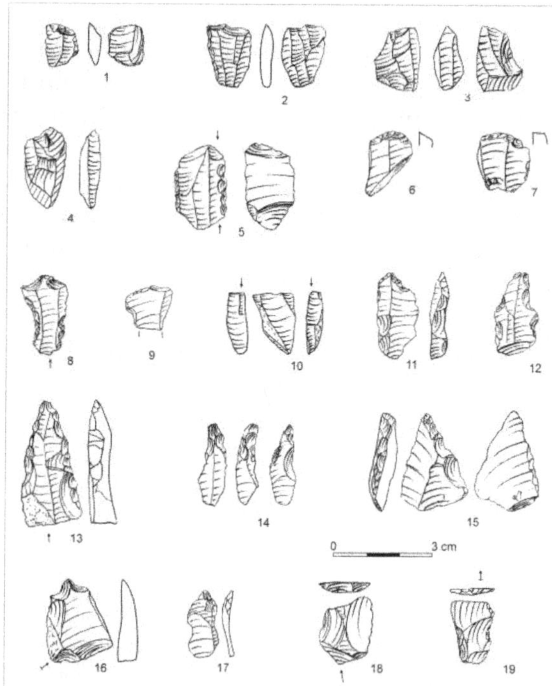

Plate VI. Roos. 1-5 splintered pieces, 6-19 retouched tools

Burin

A double burin on a snap made on the fragment of an obsidian splintered piece was found (Pl. VI, 10).

Perforators/becs

They include one atypical perforator on obsidian blade, retouched in the proximal part (Pl. VI, 11), atypical perforator on obsidian blade with lateral notches (Pl. VI, 12), perforator on macroblade from white patinated chert (Pl. VI, 13), atypical alternate perforator on a thick blade from white patinated chert (Pl. VI, 14), alternate perforator on a flake from white patinated chert (Pl. VI, 15), and atypical bec on the flake from white patinated chert (Pl.VI, 16).

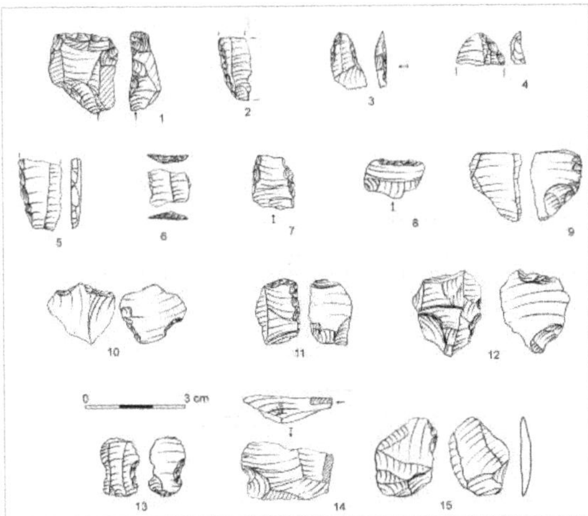

Plate VII. Roos. Retouched tools

Retouched truncations

Four specimens are included in this category of tools: obliquely retouched truncation on the irregular obsidian bladelet (Pl. VI, 17), obliquely retouched truncation on the obsidian flake from core preparation or change of orientation (Pl. VI, 18), transversally retouched truncation of the obsidian flake from the change of orientation on the core (Pl. VI, 19), retouched truncation+ single blow burin on a thick obsidian blade like flake (Pl. VII 1).

Backed pieces

Four specimens were uncovered: obsidian backed blade, slightly convex (Pl. VII, 2), fragment of the convex backed obsidian blade, transversally broken as a result of the pressure on the lateral edge opposed to the blunted back, with irregular retouch or micro-scars from the use (Pl. VII, 3), distal end of the obsidian backed blade (or segment) (Pl. VII, 4), proximal part of the slightly convex regular backed blade from white patinated chert (Pl. VII, 5).

Trapezes

Two specimens were found: trapeze on the regular obsidian blade with both truncations abruptly retouched (Pl. VII, 6) and atypical trapeze on the obsidian blade-like flake; truncations were formed on lateral edge of the flake (Pl. VII, 7).

Retouched flakes

Four specimens have been uncovered: small obsidian flake with distal retouch (Pl. VII, 8), fragment of obsidian blade-like flake with flattish lateral inverse retouch (Pl. VII, 9), flake from the change of core orientation with lateral-distal retouch, made from white patinated chert (Pl. VII, 10), obsidian splinter with obverse lateral/distal retouch and thinning of the proximal part (Pl. VII, 11).

Notched-denticulated tools

Three specimens are included in this category of tools: obsidian flake from the change of core orientation with inverse distal and proximal notches (Pl. VII 12), obsidian bladelet with bilateral alternate notches (Pl. VII 13), fragment of the obsidian flake with transversal Clactonian notch, made from white patinated chert (Pl. VII 14).

Other

Fragment of a bifacial tool (or splintered piece) made from white patinated chert (Pl. VII, 15).4.

DISCUSSION

The general tool composition at Areta does not diverge from other sites of the Aegean Mesolithic, such as Maroulas in Kythnos (Sampson et al. ed. 2010) or Kerame 1 in Ikaria (Sampson et al. ed. 2012) (Table 2). Similarities can be demonstrated to the inventory from Roos (also a surface collection), and to some degree also to the aceramic (X) level in Knossos (Kaczanowska, Kozłowski 2011). All the mentioned sites are distinguished by the high percentage of denticulate tools with notches and retouched flakes. The small differences observed may reflect the different functions of the tools at the sites, although one cannot rule out that they may be chronological and cultural markers. The appearance of tools made on regular blades (e.g. trapezes and retouched blades) may point to a later chronological phase.

The most numerous group of tools at Roos includes perforators, which at Maroulas make up 15.5% of the inventory and are completely absent in layer X at Knossos. The second most numerous group at Roos contains retouched flakes and denticulate tools with notches, which are the most frequent tool forms at Maroulas and Kerame 1. At Roos, the frequency of backed and truncated pieces, which in Maroulas and Knossos (layer X) account for 1/5 of all tools, is similar to that of retouched flakes and denticulate tools. Among the very few trapezes at Roos (two pieces), one is made on a very regular blade with symmetrical truncations (Pl. VII 6), which differs from the atypical trapezes (being in fact doubled truncated pieces) known from Maroulas (Sampson et al. 2010, Table 95: 21, 22). The discussed specimen and similar tools from Areta incline us to suppose that the Roos and Areta inventories represent a later phase of the Aegean Mesolithic, during which an expansion of this culture to the southern Aegean and Crete seems to prevail. The location of more sites, in the future, on islands of Southern Aegean could give new perspectives on this hypothesis.

In recent survey at Stelida (Carter et al. 2015), several Mesolithic artifacts have been collected, mostly belonging to the early phase of the Aegean Mesolithic (denticulates, retouched flakes, end-scrapers, atypical perforators, truncated bladelets and convex backed bladelets).

The implements typical of the late phase of the Mesolithic, mentioned in Stelida, are not illustrated.

Table 1. Major tool categories in Aegean Mesolithic sites

Site	End-scrapers (%)	Burins	Perforators	Microliths (backed pieces, truncations, trapezes)	Retouched flakes	Denticulated - notched tools	Retouched blades	others
Ikaria	16,8	0,7	18,8	16,8	23,5	19,5		3,9
Maroulas	17,9	1,2	15,9	8,3	16,9	25,9		13,9
Knossos	4,2			19,4	44,6		12,7	19,1
Chalki	6,5	0,7	16,6	14,4	13,4	35,5		12,9

Table 2. Raw material in Roos

Raw material	N	%
Obsidian	129	71,6
White patinated flint	31	17,2
Quartz	19	10,5
Beige patinated flint	1	0,5
Total	180	99,8

ACKNOWLEDGMENTS

Thanks are due to the NCN (Polish National Research Centre) -grant no 2015/19/B/HS3/00477- for financial support of this research. We also thank the archaeologists Tonia Tsourouni for the editing of the text and Konstantina Davri for the editing of the illustration, as well as Dr. Vagia Mastrogiannopoulou for her contribution in the surface survey and the location of the Roos site in Naxos.

REFERENCES

Bintliff, J. L. (1977) *Natural environment and human settlement in Prehistoric Greece, based on original fieldwork*, vol. I, II, B. A. R., International Series, Oxford.

Carter, T., Contreras, D., Doyle, S., Mihailovic, D., Moutsiou, T., Skarpelis, N., (2015)The Stelida Naxos Archaeological project: new data on the Middle Palaeolithic and Mesolithic Cyclades, *Antiquity* 341.

Kaczanowska, M., Kozłowski, J.K. (2011) Lithic industry from the aceramic levels at Knossos: an alternative approach, *Eurasian Prehistory*, 8, 1-2, 67-88.

Koumouzelis, M., Kozlowski, J. K., Kaczanowska, M. (2003) Mesolithic finds from Cave 1 in the Klissoura Gorge, Argolid, in N. Galanidou and C. Perlès (eds), *The Greek Mesolithic, Problems and Prespectives*, British School at Athens, Studies 10, 113-122.

Rackham, O. (1982) Land-use and the native vegetation of Greece, in Bell M. and Limbrey S. (eds), *Archaeological Aspects of Woodland Ecology*, B. A. R. International Series 146, 177-197.

Runnels, C. N. (1996) The Palaeolithic and Mesolithic remains from the Berbati-Limnes survey, in B. Wells and C. Runnels (eds), *The Berbati-Limnes Archaeological Survey 1988-1990*, Stockholm, 23-35.

Runnels, C. N. (2001) The Stone Age of Greece from the Palaeolithic to the advent of the Neolithic, in T. Cullen (ed.), *Aegean Prehistory. A review*, AJA, Supplement 1, 225-255.

Runnels, C. N. (2009) Mesolithic sites and surveys in Greece: A case study from the Southern Argolid, *Journal of Mediterranean Archaeology* 22, 1, 57-73.

Rackham, O. and Vernicos, N. (1991) On the ecological history and future prospects of the island of Chalki, in A.T. Grove, J. Moody and O. Rackham (eds), *Crete and the South Aegean Islands. Effects of changing climate on the environment*. Geography Department, Univ. of Cambridge, 347-361.

Sampson, A. (2006) *Prehistory of the Aegean. Palaeolithic, Mesolithic, Neolithic.* Atrapos ed. Athens.

Sampson, A. (2008) *The Cyclops Cave on the island of Youra, Greece. Mesolithic and Neolithic networks in the Northern Aegean Basin. Intra-site analysis, Local Industries, and Regional Site Distribution,* Vol 1, INSTAP Academic Press, Philadelphia.

Sampson, A., Kaczanowska, M., Kozłowski, J. K. (2010) *The prehistory of the island of Kythnos (Cyclades, Greece) and the Mesolithic settlement at Maroulas*. Kraków, Polish Academy of Arts and Sciences.

Sampson, A. (2010) *Mesolithic Greece. Palaeoenvironment, Palaeoeconomy, Technology*, ed. Ion, Athens.

Sampson, A. (ed. 2011) *The Cyclops Cave on the island of Youra, Greece. Mesolithic and Neolithic networks in the Northern Aegean Basin, vol. II: Dietary resources and Palaeoenvironment*. INSTAP Academic Press, Monograph Series, Philadelphia.

Sampson, A., Kaczanowska, M., Kozłowski, J. K. (2012) *Mesolithic occupations and environments on the island of Ikaria, Aegean, Greece,* Monograph in Folia Quaternaria, Krakow.

Sampson, A. (2014) The Mesolithic of the Aegean Basin, in C. Manen, T. Perrin, J. Guillaine (eds), *The Neolithic transition in the Mediterranean*, Errance, 193-212.

Sampson, A. (2015) The Aegean Mesolithic. Environment, Economy and Seafaring, in A. J. Ammerman and T. Davis (eds), *Island Archaeology and the Origins of Seafaring in the Eastern Mediterranean,* Proceedings of the Wenner Gren Workshop held at Reggio Calabria, 2012 *Eurasian Prehistory*, 11 (1–2): 63–74.

Sampson, A. (2016) An extended Mesolithic site in Naxos, *Mediterranean Archaeology and Archaeometry* vol. 16, No 1, 269-271.

Seferiades, M. (1983) Une centre industriel préhistorique dans les Cyclades: Les ateliers de debitage du silex de Stelida (Naxos), in *Les Cyclades, Materiaux pour une étude de Geographie Historique,* Univ. de Dijon.

Vernicos, N. (1986) Chalki in the Dodecanese, Working Papers for the Seminar On Upgrading Chalki's Natural Environment: Social and Economic, Univ. of the Aegean.

10

COROPLASTIC ART IN SICILY: AN INVESTIGATION ON PROVENANCE AND MANUFACTURING TECHNOLOGY OF GREEK ARCHITECTURAL TERRACOTTAS FROM GELA (ITALY)

G. Barone[1], P. Mazzoleni[1], S. Raneri[1], G. Spagnolo[2], A. Santostefano[2]

[1] *Department of Biological, Geological and Environmental Sciences, University of Catania, C.so Italia 57, 95129 Catania, Italy*
[2]*Department of Ancient and Modern Civilizations, University of Messina, Polo Universitario Annunziata, 98168 Messina, Italy*

Corresponding author: Paolo Mazzoleni (pmazzol@unict.it)

ABSTRACT

In the 6th and 5th centuries B.C., Gela (Italy, Sicily) was one of the most important production centres of architectural terracottas in the Mediterranean basin. Nevertheless, few archaeometric data are actually available in scientific literature on this interesting artifacts class.

Here we report an archaeometric characterization of Geloan coroplastic materials. In particular, an investigation on finest architectural terracottas found in dumps archaeological contexts in Gela has been carried out with the aim at identifying the distinctive features of the production and the manufacturing techniques. The group of samples includes various remarkable architectural elements: painted sima and geison fragments, and acroteria specimens.

Information about provenance, fabric features, technology and manufacturing techniques have been obtained by performing petrographic (OM), mineralogical (XRD) and chemical analyses (XRF). Moreover, as most of the identified petrographic fabrics have revealed the presence of volcanic temper, EDS chemical analysis have been performed on clinopiroxenes, being the latter ones an effective tool for provenance attributions. Finally, an analytical characterization of the painted polychrome decoration has been carried out by using Scanning Electron Microscopy coupled with Energy-Dispersive Spectrometry (SEM-EDS) and micro Raman spectroscopy.

The obtained results allow us to define, for the first time, the technological features of the Geolan architectural terracottas production, opening new perspectives in the study of the coroplastic art in archaic Sicily.

KEYWORDS: Roof revetments, coroplastic art, Sicily, Gela, terracottas, archaic age

1. INTRODUCTION

In the archaic and classical period, Greeks usually protected the wooden roofs of the monumental buildings with terracotta revetments. Along with acroteria on top of the roofs, these revetments had also the function of decorating the temples.

According to scholars, Gela (Italy), an important Greek colony founded in the early 7th century B.C. on the Southern coast of Sicily, was one of the main centres of production of architectural terracottas in the Mediterranean basin in the 6th and 5th centuries B.C., since a large amount of very refined roof revetments and acroteria fragments have been found in the city. The archeological interpretations also suggest that, at the beginning of the 6th century B.C., the Geloan artisans (or at least the Syracusan ones) invented a specific style of roof revetment, today know as "Sicilian system", which quickly became very popular in Sicily and (Wikander, 1986; Winter, 1993). In fact, during the 6th century B.C., this system was employed in the temples of both Gela and Syracuse, as well as in the famous Treasury of Gela in the Panhellenic sanctuary of Olympia (Schleif and Süsserott, 1944; Mallwitz, 1972; Mertens-Horn, 1990; Heiden, 1995). On the other hand, the hypothesis of high-specialized local workshops of architectural revetments and decorations at Gela accords well with the clear archaeological evidences of a local rich production of potteries (Adamesteanu, 1954, 1956a; De Miro and Fiorentini, 1983) and terracotta figurines (Sguaitamatti, 1984; Uhlenbrock, 1988; Spagnolo, 2000).

The "Sicilian" roof revetment system was characterized by specific features as the profile of its architectonical elements and the painted decorative patterns (Wikander, 1986; Winter, 1993). Its main component was the so-called "Geloan" sima, which was placed both on the long sides of the roof (lateral sima) and on all the three sides of the gable (raking and horizontal sima). This sima was formed by an upper part with a cavetto profile (always decorated with a painted leaf- pattern) and a roll and a lower fascia, provided with tubular waterspouts on the long sides of the temple. The second component of the "Sicilian system" was the geison revetment plaque, usually decorated with a painted guilloche-pattern. Disc and palmette acroteria, or fine acroterial statues (mostly horsemen, sphinxes and other winged figures), usually located on the ridgepole and at the corners of the roof, enriched and completed the decoration of the Sicilian temples (Danner, 1997).

As mentioned above, the archaeological excavations at Gela have brought to light numerous fragments of architectural terracottas, the most significant of which come from the acropolis area of Molino a Vento and from the dumps of Giardino Calì and Madonna dell'Alemanna. Many scholars have published several of these findings (Bernabò Brea and Carta, 1949-1951; Adamesteanu, 1953, 1956b, 1958; Adamesteanu and Orlandini, 1956, 1960, 1962; Orlandini, 1954, 1956, 1958; Castoldi, 1998; De Miro and Fiorentini, 1976-1977; Ferrara, 2009; Greco, 2009). However, so far they have not gone beyond the traditional methodological approach, only based on the morpho-typological and stylistic classification of the artifacts, and they have not verified the assignment of the products to Geloan artisans. Indeed, contrary to the researches performed, for example, on the Etruscan and center-Italic architectural decorations (Lulof 1996; Rescigno and Sampaolo, 2005), no archaometric investigations have been carried out on the terracottas from Gela. The unique example available in literature is represented by the study performed on few specimens from the Treasury of Gela at Olympia (Lang and Mommsen, 2006).

Therefore, our research aims to fill this gap by investigating the provenance, the sources of supply of raw materials and the manufacturing technology of this remarkable class of artifacts thought a multi-methodological archaeometric approach.

For this purpose, a group of sima, geison and acroteria fragments, found at Gela and deposited in the local Archaeological Museum, has been examined. The specimens, datable in the 6th century B.C., come from two important archaic sanctuaries areas, namely from the dump context found in 1957 in the GiardinoCalì area, in the western part of the acropolis (Orlandini, 1968), and from the dump context excavated in 1951 on the hill of Madonna dell'Alemanna, to the north of the Greek city (Adamesteanu, 1956b) (Figure 1).

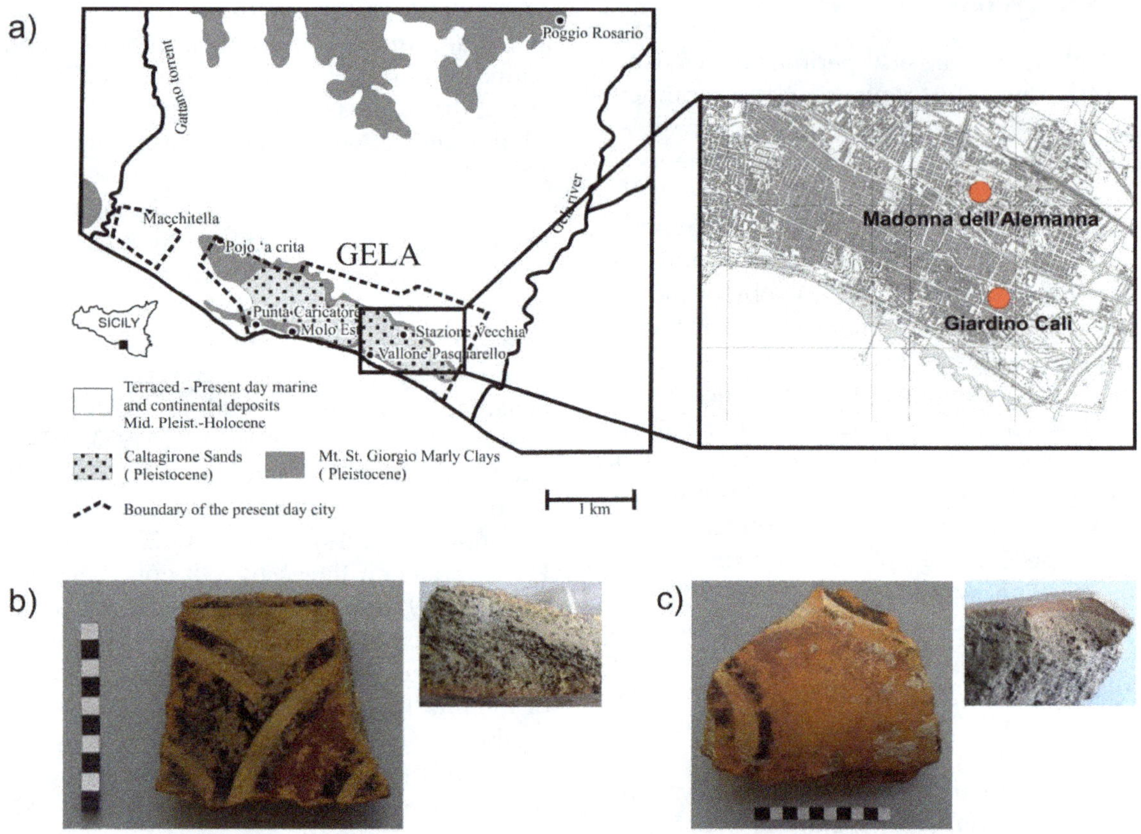

Figure 1. Geographical localization of Giardino Caliand Madonna dell'Alemanna in the city of Gela and geological setting of the area (from Barone et al., 2012). Pictures of (b) geison fragment (GETCA 3) and (c) acroterion fragment (GETCA 10), as examples of the analyzed specimens with painted decoration.

2. EXPERIMENTAL

2.1 Materials

Twenty samples of fine architectural terracottas have been analyzed: fourteen specimens from the dump of the Giardino Calì area (labeled as GETCA 1-14), and six specimens from the dump of Madonna dell'Alemanna (labeled as MDA 1-6) (Table 1).The samples mainly include "Sicilian" roof friezes, namely geison revetment plaques and "Geloan" sima, as well as a sima of "a mantello" type and three fragments of acroterial statues. On the surface, almost all the samples from Giardino Calì site retain traces of the painted decoration.

As regards the morphology of the profile and the decorative patterns, the sima and geison specimens are more or less comparable with the already published friezes from the sanctuary of the acropolis of Molino a Vento (Bernabò Brea, 1949-1951; Greco, 2009). The only exception are GETCA 1-5 and 11-13 samples from Giardino Calì, which belong to a geison revetment of unknown type, probably related to a larger and maybe older temple. The ceramic paste of all the samples from the Giardino Calì shows homogenous features, with numerous coarse and medium grained inclusions (1-1.5 mm). The ceramic paste does not have a homogeneous color, because of the considerable thickness of the wall of the specimens. In detail, the color mainly ranges from reddish yellow (Munsell 5YR 6/6 - 7/6; 7.5YR 7/6) or red (Munsell 2.5YR 5/8 - 6/6 - 6/8) near the surface, and from pale yellow (Munsell2.5Y 6/6 - 7/4; 5Y 6/3 - 7/3 - 7/4) or gray (Munsell 10YR 5/1) in the inner core. Except the above-mentioned larger geison revetment, the other samples show some traces of a very thin depurated clay slip of slightly lighter color. The acroterial statues fragments (GETCA 9, 10 and 14) have the same coarse clay paste of the friezes, but their surface is always covered by a thick highly depurated clay slip, which was useful to model the figures.

Regarding the typological and decorative appearance, the samples from the Madonna dell'Alemanna area are quite similar to those from the Giardino Calì area (and to those from Molino a Vento), even if different technical features can be recognized. In fact, in order to have a sampling set as comprehensive as possible of the artifacts used in the temples of the city of Gela during the archaic period.

Table 1.Macroscopic features of the studied architectural terracottas along with information on samples: ID, inventory number, typological classification and color of clay paste based on the Munsell Soil Color Charts (MI: Munsell index, Munsell, 2000).

Site	Sample ID	Inventory number	Type	Macroscopic features
Giardino Calì	**GETCA 1**	2647	*geison*	Compact clay paste with coarse and medium grained volcanic inclusions. Core: 5YR 6/6 (reddish yellow). Surface: 2.5YR 6/8 (light red)
	GETCA 2	2668	*geison*	Compact clay paste with coarse and medium grained volcanic inclusions. Core: 5YR 7/6 (reddish yellow). Surface: 2.5YR 6/8 (light red).
	GETCA 3	2530	*geison*	Compact clay paste with coarse and medium grained volcanic inclusions. Core: 5Y 7/3 (pale yellow). Surface: 5YR 7/6 (reddish yellow).
	GETCA 4	2539	*geison*	Compact clay paste with coarse and medium grained volcanic inclusions. Core: 5Y 7/4 (pale yellow). Surface: 7.5YR 7/6 (reddish yellow). Painted decoration (black).
	GETCA 5	2464	*geison*	Compact clay paste with coarse and medium grained volcanic inclusions. Core: 5Y 7/4 (pale yellow). Surface: 10YR 7/3 (very pale brown.
	GETCA 6	2098	*"Geloan" sima*	Compact clay paste with coarse and medium grained volcanic inclusions. Core: 2.5YR 6/6 (light red). Surface: 2.5YR 6/8 (red). Painted decoration (black).
	GETCA 7	2377	*"Geloan" sima*	Compact clay paste with coarse and medium grained volcanic inclusions. Core: 5Y 6/3 (pale olive). Surface: 5YR 7/8 (reddish yellow). Painted decoration (black).
	GETCA 8	2758	*sima of "a mantello" type*	Compact clay paste with coarse and medium grained volcanic inclusions. Core and surface: 5YR 6/6 (reddish yellow).
	GETCA 9	2879	*acroterion*	Compact clay paste, with coarse and medium grained volcanic inclusions. Core and surface: 5Y 6/4 (light reddish brown). Painted decoration (black).
	GETCA 10	2802	*acroterion*	Compact clay paste, with coarse and medium grained volcanic inclusions. Core: 10YR 5/1 (gray). Surface: 5YR 6/6 (reddish yellow). Highly depurated clay slip. Painted decoration (black and red).
	GETCA11	/	*geison*	Compact clay paste with coarse and medium grained volcanic inclusions. Core: 5Y 7/3 (pale yellow). Surface: 5YR 7/6 (reddish yellow). Painted decoration (black and creamy white).
	GETCA12	/	*geison*	Painted decoration (red).
	GETCA13	/	*geison*	Compact clay paste with coarse and medium grained volcanic inclusions. Core and surface: 2.5Y 6/6 (olive yellow). Painted decoration (black).
	GETCA14	/	*acroterion*	Compact clay paste with coarse and medium grained volcanic inclusions. Core and surface: 2.5Y 7/4 (pale yellow). Painted decoration (black, red and creamy white).
Madonna dell'Alemanna	**MDA1**	/	*"Geloan" sima*	Compact clay paste with small and medium grained white inclusions. Core and surface: 7.5YR 7/4 (pink).
	MDA2	/	*geison*	Compact clay paste with small and medium grained white inclusions. Core: 10YR 6/1 (gray). Surface: 7.5YR 7/6 (reddish yellow).
	MDA3	/	*geison*	Compact clay paste with small and medium grained white inclusions. Core: 5Y 7/4 (pale yellow). Surface: 7.5YR 7/6 (reddish yellow)
	MDA4	/	*geison*	Compact clay paste with small and medium grained white inclusions. Core and surface: 7.5YR 7/6 (reddish yellow).
	MDA5	/	*geison*	Compact clay paste with small and medium grained white inclusions. Core: 10YR 5/1 (gray). Surface: 7.5YR 7/6 (reddish yellow).
	MDA6	/	*"Geloan" sima*	Compact clay paste with small and medium grained white inclusions. Core: 2.5Y 7/4 (pale yellow). Surface: 7.5YR 7/6 (reddish yellow).

Among the architectural terracottas from Madonna dell'Alemanna we have intentionally chosen the only specimens with a clay paste much more depurated and compact than the others, and without coarse inclusions. This technical peculiarity is probably due to the different size of the roof revetments; in fact, the selected fragments have a thinner wall than the other terracottas, likely belonging to smaller friezes, namely to minor sacred buildings.

The surface of almost all samples from Giardino Calì dumps is painted with the typical archaic colors, i.e. black, red and creamy white, which have been analyzed in order to investigate the composition of the pigments and the firing technique. According to the macroscopic examination, the three colors appear directly applied on the ceramic surfaces, without any base slip (similar to that documented, for example, on the painted antefixes from Gela: see Castoldi, 1998). In some cases, there are traces of engraved preparatory drawings (Winter, 1993).

2.2 Methods

Petrographic (OM), mineralogical (XRD), chemical (XRF and SEM-EDS) and spectroscopic (μ-Raman spectroscopy) analyses have been performed on the studied samples.

In order to characterize the artifacts in terms of texture, groundmass and inclusions, a selection of representative samples have been analyzed in thin section by optical microscopy, using a polarized transmitted light microscope Nikon Eclipse E400 POL. The mineralogical composition of specimens has been determined by means of X-ray diffraction using a Siemens D5000 instrument, with Cu Kα radiation, 40 kV, 30 mA and Ni filter. Randomly oriented powders have been scanned from 2° to 45° 2θ, with a 0.02° 2θ step size and a counting time of 3 s per step. Chemical data have been obtained by means X-ray fluorescence (XRF) spectrometry (PHILIPS PW 2404/00) on powder-pressed pellets; total loss on ignition (LOI) was gravimetrically estimated after overnight heating at 950 °C. Chemical data were treated with the statistical methodology mainly based on the log-ratio technique introduced by Aitchison (Aitchison, 1986) and employed in order to avoid the constant sum problem. The centred log-ratio transformation (clr) of data is applied as follows: $x \in SD \rightarrow y = \ln (xD / gD (x)) \in RD$, where x is the vector of the D elemental compositions, y is the vector of the log-transformed compositions, $xD = (x1, x2, \ldots, xD)$ and $gD(x) = (x1 \bullet x2 \bullet \ldots \bullet xD)1/D$. This operation transforms the raw data from their constrained sample space, the simplex $Sd(d = D - 1)$, into the real space Rd, in which parametric statistical methods can be applied to the transformed data. Subsequently, the clr-transformed data set was explored by biplots, a graphical representation of variables and cases projected on to principal component planes. Both the clr-transformation and the biplot calculations were obtained by using CoDaPack (Thió-Henestrosa and Martin- Fernandez, 2011), a compositional software that implements the basic methods of analysis of compositional data based on log-ratios.

Additionally, scanning electron microscopy (SEM-EDS) measurements have been performed in order to investigate chemical composition of the volcanic inclusions of some analyzed samples. Data have been collected using a Tescan Vega LMU scanning electron microscope, equipped with an EDAX NeptuneXM4-60 micro-analyzer, characterized by an ultra-thin Be. Measurements have been carried out by using spot mode analysis on polished thin sections, with 20 kV accelerating voltage and 0.2 nA beam current.

Finally, the painted decorations have been investigated through chemical (SEM-EDS) and spectroscopic analyses, in order to obtain information on colors composition and technological features. In particular, micro-Raman spectra have been acquired with a Raman Jasco NRS-3100 apparatus, equipped with a microscope with x10, x20 and x100 objectives, by using a laser excitation source at 785 nm; laser power has been controlled by means of a series of density filters, in order to avoid heating effects. Depth resolution was set to few micrometers by means of a confocal hole. The system has been calibrated using the 520.7 cm-1 Raman band of silicon before each experimental session.

3. RESULTS

3.1 Minero-petrographic analyses

Petrographic analyses on thin section have been performed on a representative selection of studied samples with the aim at characterizing texture and mineralogical composition, following the scheme proposed by Whitbread (1995). Three different fabrics have been recognized (Figure 2), mainly characterized by fossil-rich and micaceous groundmass, with and without volcanic inclusions.

In detail, Fabric A (specimens GETCA2 and GETCA8; Figure 2.a) is characterized by fossil-rich groundmass and volcanic inclusions. The vughy microstructure is due to single-double space distributed vugs and vesicles, the latter one partially preferred oriented (in GETCA8). The groundmass is quite homogeneous and fossil-rich, with scarce micas in GETCA8. The color is mainly brownish and the optical activity is from medium (GETCA2) to low (GETCA8). The inclusions (c:f = 40:60) are mainly represented by coarse-grained and polimodal volcanic rock fragments and by quartz, plagioclase and pyroxene. Amorphous phases are also present, red in color and with altered edges.

Fabric B (specimens GETCA4 and GETCA7; Figure 2.b) is characterized by a more heterogeneous micaceous groundmass and volcanic inclusions. The vughy microstructure exhibits open spaced vugs and vesicles, the latter one preferential oriented. The groundmass, from yellowish to yellow-brownish in color, is very heterogeneous; therefore, it is probably the result of the mixture of two different clay sediments (micas-rich and mica-poor). It also exhibits low/medium-low optical activity. Inclusions (c:f = 30:70) are characterized by coarse grain sized volcanic rock fragments, and minor amount of quartz, plagioclase pyroxene and altered feldspars. Amorphous phases are present, both red and black, mainly characterized by evident altered edges.

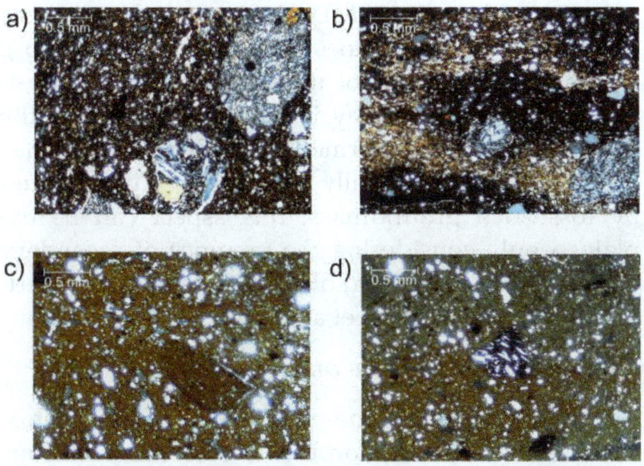

Figure 2. Microphotographs of samples representative of the petrographic fabrics recognized by thin section analysis: (a) GETCA 8, (b) GETCA 7, (c) MDA 5, and (d) MDA 3.

Finally, Fabric C (specimens MDA1-MDA6; Figure 2.c-d) is characterized by fossil-rich and micaceous groundmass with chamotte inclusions. The vughy microstructure is due to (in order of abundance) channel, vugs, vesicles, mainly open spaced; preferred oriented vesicles can be observed in samples MDA1 and MDA2. The groundmass is mainly from brown-yellowish to brown-reddish in color and exhibits a medium-low optical activity, high only in MDA5. It is also homogeneous, with fine quartz and mica (scarce in MDA6) and microfossil molds, with re-crystallized calcite. Inclusions (c:f = 10:90), subangular in shape and mainly exhibiting a bimodal grain size distribution (unimodal in MDA4, MDA, MDA6), are characterized by dominant fine-grained chamotte (scarce in MDA2), quartz, plagioclase and rare metamorphic quartz in MDA5. Amorphous phases are also present, mainly reddish-black in color. Noteworthy is that the sample MDA3 exhibits the same textural features of the other MDA specimens, except for the presence of volcanic inclusions (small fragment of volcanic rocks, glass, plagioclase and pyroxene).

In order to obtain information on firing temperature, for the evaluation of which the groundmass optical activity can be also used as supporting data, semi-quantitative mineralogical analyses have been carried out by means X-ray diffraction method. In fact, as it is well known (Cultrone et al., 2011; Maggetti, 1982; Riccardi et al., 1999), the presence of specific mineralogical phases in archaeological ceramics are suitable to esteem firing temperature.

In particular, in Ca-rich clays, chemical reactions between minerals in the clay allow the newly formation of Ca-silicates phases as gehlenite, anorthite and diopside, indicative of high firing temperature (about 850-900 °C); of course, neither anorthite nor diopside can be used for temperature esteem when related to tempers composition. In the case of poor-Ca clays, the absence of carbonates does not allow the formation of Ca-silicate and changes are mainly related to textural features, with the only transformation of low-T phases in high T-phases; however, some minerals can be used as temperature indicators, as phyllosilicates and hematite (Cultrone et al., 2001). In fact, in XRD patterns of Ca-poor clay materials, a gradually reduction of peaks intensity of phyllosilicate due to dehydroxilization of clay minerals and an increase of peaks related to hematite can been observed with the increasing of firing temperature.

Table 2. Mineralogical data of the studied samples. For GETCA samples, the semi-quantitative XRD results are reported for both total bulk and only groundmass. Qtz = Quartz; CM = clay minerals; Cal = calcite; Ab = albite; An = anorthite; Di = diopside; Hem = Hematite; Pl = plagioclase; Gh = gehlenite; Ms = muscovite. The number of (+) is related to the mineralogical phase abundance; tr = trace.

Sample ID	*Bulk/groundmass*	*Qtz*	*Cal*	*An*	*Ab*	*Di*	*Hem*	*Gh*	*CM*	*Ms*
GETCA1	Total bulk	+++		++	+	+	+	tr	tr	
GETCA1	groundmass	+++	tr	tr		tr	++	++	tr	
GETCA2	Total bulk	+++		++		+				+
GETCA2	groundmass	+++	tr-	tr		tr		tr		
GETCA3	Total bulk	+++		++		+	tr	tr	tr	
GETCA3	groundmass	+++	tr	tr		tr	+	+	+	
GETCA4	Total bulk	+++		++		+				+
GETCA4	groundmass	+++	tr	tr	++	tr	+	tr		

GETCA5	Total bulk	+++		++		+	tr	tr	tr	
GETCA5	groundmass	+++	tr	tr		tr	+	+	tr	
GETCA6	Total bulk	+++		++		+	tr	+	tr	
GETCA6	groundmass	+++	tr	tr		tr	+	+	tr	
GETCA7	Total bulk	+++		++		++	tr	tr		
GETCA7	groundmass	+++	tr	tr		tr	+	+	tr	
GETCA8	Total bulk	+++		+	+					
GETCA8	groundmass	+++	tr	tr		tr	+	tr	tr	
GETCA9	Total bulk	+++	tr	++		++	+	tr	tr	
GETCA9	groundmass	+++	tr	+		+	+	tr	tr	
GETCA10	Total bulk	+++	tr	++		+	tr	tr	tr	
GETCA10	groundmass	+++	tr	+		tr	+	tr	tr	
MDA 1	Total bulk	+++	++	+		+	+	tr	+	
MDA 2	Total bulk	+++	++	+		+	+		+	
MDA 3	Total bulk	+++	tr	++		++	+	+	+	
MDA 4	Total bulk	+++	tr	++		+	+	+	+	
MDA 5	Total bulk	+++	tr	+		+	+		+	
MDA 6	Total bulk	+++	++	++		++	+	+	+	

In consideration of the presence of volcanic rock fragments, and plagioclase and pyroxene as inclusions, in samples labeled as GETCA, XRD analyses have been carried out on both total bulk and on the only groundmass, the latter one obtained by gently crushing samples in agate mortars and separating magnetically the volcanic inclusions. The semi-quantitative data obtained by the analysis of X-ray patterns are reported in Table 2. On the basis of the obtained data and the information gained from the optical activity features of analyzed materials, it is possible to assess an overall medium-high firing temperature for both the set of studied architectural terracottas (namely GETCA and MDA).

In detail, in GETCA samples, the analysis of XRD patterns related to the only groundmass allows to highlight the presence of newly formed minerals as anorthite, diopside and gehlenite, that suggest a firing temperature of about 850-950 °C, according to the medium-low optical activity observed in thin sections. Similar mineralogical composition has been obtained for samples labeled as MDA, in which the presence of hematite, anorthite, and diopside can be considered indicators of medium-high firing temperatures (850-950 °C, in accordance with the medium-low groundmass birefringence). Exception is represented by sample MDA3, in which the presence of volcanic inclusions does not allow to esteem firing temperatures because of its mineralogical composition. Finally, noteworthy is that, in some cases, the coexistence of newly formed minerals and calcite has been observed, especially in samples characterized by fossil-rich groundmass; this aspect can be explained only considering the presence of secondary calcite due to circulation of Ca-rich solutions in burial conditions (Cultrone et al., 2014).

3.2 Chemical analysis on pyroxenes

According to Barone et al. (2010), the petrochemical characterization of the volcanic inclusions may allow obtaining useful information on the provenance of archeological artifacts in terms of sources of supply of raw materials. In particular, as clinopyroxenes keep the original composition unaltered, their chemical composition can unambiguously discriminate volcanic products belonging to distinct magmatic provinces.

Table 3. Average compositions and relative standard deviations of pyroxenes from each analysed sample.

Oxide wt%	*GETCA 4 (n = 14)*		*GETCA 2 (n = 16)*		*GETCA 7 (n = 13)*		*GETCA 8 (n = 3)*		*MDA 3 (n =2)*	
	Mean	*St. Dev.*	*Mean*	*St. Dev.*	*Mean*	*St. Dev.*	*Mean*	*St. Dev.*	*Mean*	*St. Dev.*
SiO_2	51.01	1.36	50.59	1.44	51.67	1.58	50.81	0.72	50.27	1.45
TiO_2	1.19	0.49	1.15	0.41	0.93	0.52	1.25	0.16	1.37	0.36
Al_2O_3	3.65	0.93	4.21	1.38	3.30	1.36	4.19	1.03	4.73	1.02
Cr_2O_3	0.18	0.10	0.39	0.45	0.40	0.36	0.12	0.02	0.14	0.11
FeO	7.96	1.12	6.86	1.60	5.95	1.73	7.00	0.45	7.98	0.70
MnO	0.31	0.08	0.25	0.10	0.26	0.09	0.25	0.10	0.27	0.10
MgO	14.97	1.07	15.04	1.41	16.03	1.68	15.10	0.24	14.46	1.03
CaO	19.94	0.61	20.26	2.58	20.90	0.51	20.57	0.45	20.00	1.15
Na_2O	0.60	0.11	0.49	0.14	0.44	0.14	0.54	0.01	0.65	0.08
K_2O	0.20	0.14	0.13	0.04	0.14	0.06	0.16	0.04	0.13	0.04

On the basis of the aforementioned, from the studied architectural terracottas exhibiting volcanic inclusions (Fabric A and B, as well as sample MDA3, belonging to Fabric C), 48 pyroxenes have been selected and analyzed; the average compositions are listed in Table 3.

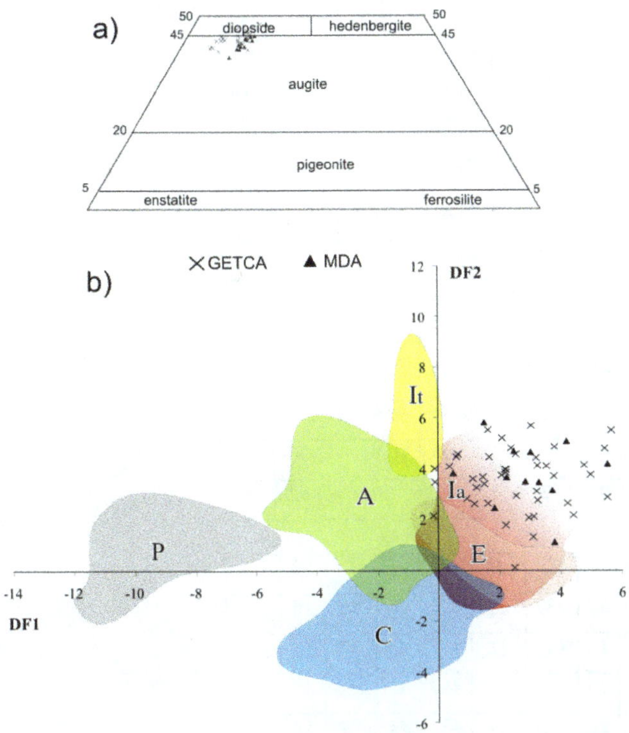

Figure 3. (a) Classification diagrams (Morimoto et al., 1988) of pyroxenes from volcanic inclusions in GETCA and MDA3 samples, and (b) DF1 vs. DF2 diagram showing the correspondence between clinopyroxenes from volcanic rocks and those from terracottas samples. It = Hyblean tholeiites; Ia = Hyblean alkaline basalts; E = Mt. Etna; A = Aeolian Arc; P = Pantelleria Island; C = Campanian province.

The preliminary classification of the analyzed pyroxenes has been made according to Morimoto et al. (1988); the obtained results (Figure 3.a) allow to highlight a quite homogeneous sub-calcic compositions; in fact, the analyzed pyroxenes mainly fall in fields from diopside to augite. The statistical analysis of pyroxenes obtained by plotting chemical data on the DF1 vs. DF2 diagram proposed by Barone et al. (2010) (Figure 3.b), in which the different populations of southern-Italy and Sicilian volcanic products are clustered into clearly distinguishable groups, shows that the inclusions identified in the Geloan architectural terracottas have a strong affinity with the products of southeast Sicilian magmatic provinces (Iblean alkaline basalts and Mt. Etna products, small overlapped in the pyroxenes discrimination diagram). Therefore, this result suggests these areas as possible source of supply of the raw materials employed in the Geloan revetments manufacture.

3.3 Geochemical data

Ceramic materials are usually characterized by two main components: the plastic fraction, consisting in the clay sediments employed in the manufacture of the artifacts, and the aplastic one, due to aggregates, that can be included in the original sediment or even intentionally added by artisans to the mixture for technical aims. From the chemical point of view, the composition of the whole ceramic artifact is therefore the sum of the geochemical features of both clays and inclusions. In this perspective, in order to investigate aspects as the provenance of the artifacts, the contribute of possible intentionally added inclusions in changing the geochemical compositions of clays has to be considered. Therefore, on the basis of the above mentioned, in this study, chemical analysis by XRF have been performed on the only groundmass of the samples with the aim at obtaining the chemical composition of the solely clay sediments and integrating these data with the provenance information gained from the chemical analysis of pyroxenes in volcanic inclusions. Only in this way, the possibly common or different geographical source of both plastic fraction and aggregates can be verified.

The chemical composition of terracottas samples obtained by XRF on the groundmass fraction is reported in Table 4. The results suggest a quite homogeneous composition for the overall studied samples; however, some differences in term of major and trace element abundances between the two sets of architectural terracottas (namely GETCA from Giardino Calì and MDA from Madonna dell'Alemanna) can be inferred. In particular, GETCA samples exhibit higher contents of Fe_2O_3, TiO_2 and Co than MDA ones; on the contrary, these latter ones are characterized by higher levels of Ni.

The statistical treatment of data allows better highlighting the differences in geochemical features between the two sets of materials, as well as obtaining additionally information on the provenance of the clayey sediments.

In fact, data have been compared with reference groups consisting in several ceramics and clayey raw materials of certain Geloan provenance (Aquilia et al., 2012; Barone et al., 2012), and with ceramics and clays from Siracusa (Barone et al., 2014) and Lentini (Barone et al., 2005). The selection criterion of the reference groups used to compare the terracottas is based on the similarity between petrographic features of studied materials and other Sicilian archaic artifacts, as well as on the results obtained from chemical analysis of pyroxenes, indicating the Iblean magmatic province as source of the volcanic aggregates.

Table 4. Chemical composition of the analyzed samples. Major element are reported in wt%, minor elements in ppm.

Sample ID	SiO_2	TiO_2	Al_2O_3	Fe_2O_3	MnO	MgO	CaO	Na_2O	K_2O	P_2O_5
GETCA1	57.89	0.96	15.09	6.93	0.09	2.11	12.55	1.57	2.32	0.49
GETCA2	58.31	0.98	14.97	7.26	0.09	2.20	11.69	1.71	2.22	0.56
GETCA3	57.19	0.95	14.93	6.77	0.09	2.39	13.59	1.61	2.09	0.39
GETCA4	57.36	0.95	14.69	6.74	0.09	2.35	13.73	1.64	2.11	0.35
GETCA5	58.34	0.87	14.03	6.26	0.08	2.37	14.29	1.61	1.83	0.31
GETCA6	58.53	0.92	14.06	6.65	0.09	2.15	13.50	1.42	2.34	0.33
GETCA7	58.65	0.84	14.17	6.33	0.08	2.22	13.89	1.25	2.23	0.34
GETCA8	59.69	0.90	14.38	6.17	0.08	1.85	12.73	1.37	2.51	0.30
GETCA9	61.08	0.72	13.84	5.57	0.08	2.11	13.45	0.94	1.99	0.22
GETCA10	59.56	0.90	14.63	6.47	0.08	2.03	12.18	1.48	2.31	0.35
MDA1	62.80	0.81	12.91	5.32	0.11	2.29	12.27	0.79	2.37	0.33
MDA2	61.72	0.86	12.94	5.58	0.10	2.31	12.97	0.80	2.53	0.18
MDA3	61.06	0.89	13.56	5.68	0.07	2.72	12.80	1.10	1.96	0.16
MDA4	60.67	0.92	13.66	5.70	0.10	2.75	12.43	0.92	2.61	0.26
MDA5	62.82	0.86	13.05	5.13	0.08	2.39	12.04	0.91	2.56	0.16
MDA6	62.90	0.80	12.36	4.99	0.08	2.96	13.11	1.03	1.62	0.16

Sample ID	Sr	V	Cr	Co	Ni	Zn	Rb	Y	Zr	Nb	Ba	La	Ce	Pb	Th
GETCA1	632	80	71	24	28	53	65	28	232	29	475	44	86	16	7
GETCA2	444	80	66	23	34	51	44	12	149	11	454	48	97	13	6
GETCA3	615	82	67	25	29	53	59	26	226	30	419	47	118	15	7
GETCA4	604	79	67	27	31	59	56	26	225	29	436	45	94	14	9
GETCA5	668	75	70	23	31	53	49	27	228	24	368	38	92	11	6
GETCA6	588	78	62	24	32	57	63	27	226	26	421	38	78	15	9
GETCA7	559	73	70	23	31	52	67	28	236	24	344	40	91	19	8
GETCA8	579	82	66	25	30	49	60	27	219	23	355	33	83	14	7
GETCA9	222	65	79	18	43	46	33	6	101	n.d.	264	30	77	3	n.d.
GETCA10	598	80	63	25	28	49	64	28	230	24	423	35	88	17	8
MDA1	677	94	88	14	37	91	72	24	270	16	659	44	66	18	9
MDA2	603	100	90	11	42	87	84	24	227	17	378	31	74	18	9
MDA3	436	104	89	7	49	71	40	27	161	6	341	35	65	0	8
MDA4	495	93	92	8	50	72	50	30	144	3	592	46	86	17	8
MDA5	348	91	76	6	47	64	35	15	105	1	373	38	71	12	6
MDA6	354	76	66	4	43	56	20	18	146	2	377	28	57	13	6

The biplot of Figure 4 shows a good accordance between GETCA and MDA samples, and the Geloan ceramics and clays. In the case of samples exhibiting volcanic inclusions from the southeast Sicilian magmatic provinces, the results clearly neglect the expectations, as they also group with Geloan reference materials. This result suggests an overall local production of the analyzed specimens, claiming a different provenance of clays and aggregates used in the manufacture of GETCA terracottas.

3.4 Painted decoration characterization

The analytical characterization of the painted decoration, representative of the different colors observed on GETCA samples (see Table 1), have been obtained by performing both chemical and spectroscopic analyses. In detail, SEM-EDS measurements, performed by using spot mode analysis on small chips drawn from the painted surfaces, have allowed obtaining quantitative data about the chemical composition of the pigmenting agents along with eventual components related to deterioration processes. The average chemical composition of the analyzed samples, expressed as weight percentage (wt%), is reported in Table 5.Regarding black surfaces, the color is due to the presence of manganese oxide; on creamy white surfaces, silica, calcium and alumina (in order of abundance) have been detected; finally, red surfaces are characterized by iron oxides. It is worth of note that on some surfaces (for example on the GETCA7 sample), chloride and sulfate have been also detected, interpretable as deterioration products.

In order to obtain in-depth information on pigmenting agents, micro-Raman non-destructive and non-invasive analyses have been carried out on the painted surfaces. The analysis of Raman spectra (Figure 5.a) have allowed to identify pyrolusite (strong band at about 640 cm^{-1} ascribed to Mn-O stretching mode; Sepúlveda et al., 2015), meta-kaolin (Frost, 1997) and haematite (226, 292, 410, 496, 611 cm^{-1}; Zoppi et al., 2008) as pigments for black, creamy white and red, respectively.

As regards the firing behavior, taking as reference the assumptions recently made in a multidisciplinary study on some archaic architectural terracottas from Capua (Rescigno and Sampaolo, 2005), we have also verified the possibility that the Geloan artisans have performed one or more firing phases to obtain the different colors. In fact, according to that study, the artifacts from Capua would have been fired twice (the first time at high temperature, with diluted base colors; the second time at a lower temperature, with the complete polychrome decoration), or, more probably, in a single firing cycle, but with a skillful alternation of oxidizing and reducing atmosphere in order to achieve the colors red and black from pigments consisting of iron oxides.

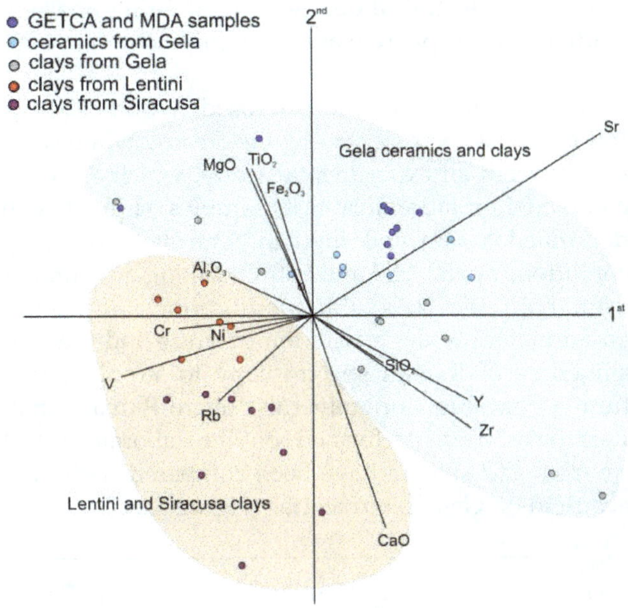

Figure 4. Biplot of the two principal components.

Table 5. Semi-quantitative average chemical composition (wt%) of pigment layers (black, red and creamy white) in studied samples obtained by EDS analyses.

	Black layers				*Red layers*		*Creamy layers*
	GETCA4	*GETCA 7*	*GETCA 11*	*GETCA 13*	*GETCA 12*	*GETCA 14*	*GETCA 11*
Na_2O	0.8			0.5±0.3	0.5±0.3	0.4	
MgO	2.0 ±0.5	2.2±0.8	2.7±0.4	3.6±0.5	1.0±0.2	2.7±0.8	5.7±4.0
Al_2O_3	7.8±1.0	7.3±2.0	8.3±0.6	12.2±3.6	8.7±2.5	9.4±1.1	**10.1±4.9**
SiO_2	17.9±4.7	29.4±8.5	29.5±3.8	29.8±14.6	23.9±2.6	31.0±7.3	**58.7±12.6**
SO_3		14.1±5.7					
Cl_2O		0.8±0.1					
K_2O	0.9±0.1	1.0±0.6			1.6±0.8	0.5±0.2	2.0±1.1
CaO	4.6±1.5	21.7±6.0	11.6±4.3	5.3±1.2	3.6±2.1	10.9±0.4	**15.5±6.1**
TiO_2	0.7±0.4	0.5±0.2				0.5±0.1	1.1±0.2
MnO	**24.4±3.3**	**7.0±0.2**	**15.3±2.0**	**16.3±3.0**			
FeO	41.0±4.4	18.7±2.0	32.7±5.5	32.4±9.7	**60.6±7.9**	**44.5±6.9**	6.9±4.4

Effectively, according to the macroscopic observation, there are no traces of any diluted base color in our samples and the creamy white color looks applied in the decorative patterns as well as the other two colors, which means that the artisans have not used it as a slip. Therefore, for Gela specimens we can exclude the hypothesis of two different firing phases.

Moreover, the detection of Mn-based pigment in black color suggests very interesting implications in this regard. In fact, contrary to the use of iron oxides, which during firing needs two different atmosphere conditions (oxidizing and reducing, respectively) in order to produce the colors red and deep black, the use of manganese oxides allows to obtain stable black hue also in an oxidizing atmosphere and with firing temperature about 950 °C. Therefore, by employing this technical device, a single firing phase in oxidizing atmosphere was just enough to obtain both colors.

A confirmation of the proposed hypothesis - in this case, however, regarding the creamy white color -comes from an experimental study, which we have conducted on laboratory tests samples, slipped with depurated kaolin and fired in controlled oxidizing conditions at 750, 850 and 950°C. Taking advantages from both the structural modifications of kaolin-based materials along with temperature and the sensitiveness of Raman spectroscopy to supply structural information on minerals, micro-Raman analyses have been performed on the laboratory test samples and spectra have been compared with data acquired on Geloan terracottas (Figure 5.b).

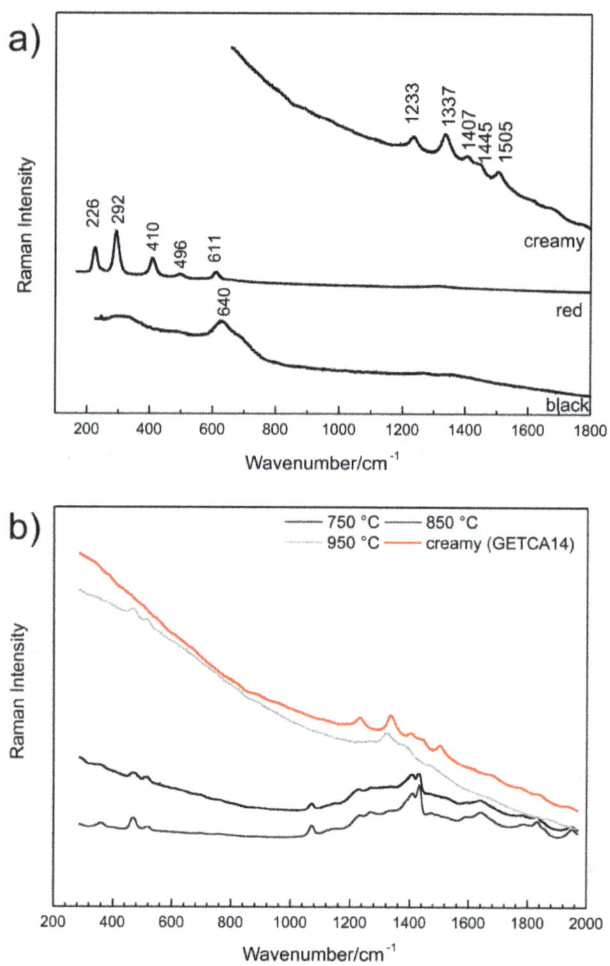

Figure 5. μ-Raman spectra collected on (a) black, red and creamy white surfaces, and on (b) laboratory samples slipped with kaolin and fired at different temperatures along with spectra collected on GETCA 14 sample for comparison.

The obtained results suggest a good spectral matching between the creamy white surfaces and the test samples fired at 950 °C. It is of great interest that the temperature esteemed on the basis of spectroscopic data acquired on painted decorations are in agreement with the firing T_{max} suggested by the mineralogical composition of the ceramic bulk; in this sense, it can be assumed a single firing phase for the manufacture of both terracotta and decoration.

4. DISCUSSIONS AND CONCLUSIONS

All the analyses performed on the Geloan architectural terracottas have provided very interesting results, filling a gap in the current archaeological and archaeometric literature on this important class of artifacts.

First, according to our investigations, all the studied specimens seem to have been manufactured in Gela, because the petrographic and chemical characteristics of the ceramic bulk show a good agreement with the published data on local raw materials and locally produced ceramics. The slight differences in chemical composition between the two set of samples from Giardino Calì and that from Madonna dell'Alemanna may be due to the use of distinct local sources of clay supply. In all cases, we can assign to Gela this production of high quality architectural decorations, confirming with laboratory data a hypothesis so far only supported by archaeological arguments.

The analyses have also provided significant information concerning the manufacturing technology. In particular, in the samples from Giardino Calì, the petrographic investigations have revealed an abundant presence of intentionally added temper of non-local provenance. The specimens are in fact characterized by coarse-grained volcanic inclusions, which are absent in the clay sources within the territory of Gela (see Figure 1). The chemical analyses performed on the pyroxenes have indicated their strong affinity with the products of southeast Sicilian magmatic provinces (Iblean alkaline basalts and Mt. Etna products). Therefore, we can hypothesize that the Geloan artisans imported the volcanic material from neighbouring areas and added it to the clay paste in order to improve the production process. Indeed, they surely knew that the presence of numerous coarse inclusions reduces the plasticity of clay, thus making the artifacts more resistant during the drying and firing phases and limiting the risk of cracks or deformations. But, why to choose volcanic materials of non-local provenance? Probably because the artisans had experienced that these materials ensured a better performance in the case of large size and painted artifacts of exceptional value, as the architectural terracottas from Giardino Calì. Conversely, in the case of smaller size or even undecorated roof revetments, it was not necessary to use a very coarse clay paste with a specific added temper, as demonstrated by the results of the analyses on the architectural terracottas from Madonna dell'Alemanna. Indeed, these terracottas, belonging to smaller size revetments, therefore to minor sacred buildings, are characterized by absence of volcanic inclusions.

Regarding the painted decoration, both chemical and spectroscopic analyses have given relevant data on the composition of colors and on the firing behaviour. For red and black colors, the use of iron oxides and pyrolusite, respectively, has been identified, while depurated kaolin has been detected in the creamy white color. The use of manganese oxides in order to obtain the black color, as well as the spectroscopic evidences on the kaolin, strongly suggest a single firing phase in oxidizing atmosphere at about 900-950 °C for the manufacture of both ceramic bulk and painted decoration.

In conclusion, the archaeometric approach applied to the study of the Geloan architectural terracottas can be considered a starting point for a more comprehensive interpretation of the numerous archaeological issues related to the coroplastic production in Sicily during the archaic age. Thanks to the availability of these new analytical data and the definition of the manufacturing characteristics of the Geloan production, future studies on roof revetments from other Greek colonies in Sicily could be approached in the prospective of providing a detailed overview on the various manufacturing traditions as well as unveiling the local coroplasts "techne".

REFERENCES

Adamesteanu, D. (1953) Coppi con testate dipinte a Gela. Archeologia Classica V, 1-9.

Adamesteanu, D. (1954) Uno scarico di fornace ellenistica a Gela. Archeologia Classica VI, 129-132.

Adamesteanu, D. (1956°) Via Dalmazia. Scoperta di una fornace greca arcaica. Notizie degli Scavi X, 277-281.

Adamesteanu, D. (1956b) Madonna dell'Alemanna. Scoperta di una nuova area sacra. Notizie degli Scavi X, 382-392.

Adamesteanu, D. (1958) Nuove antefisse dipinte di Gela. Archeologia Classica X, 9-13.

Adamesteanu, D., Orlandini, P. (1956) Gela. Scavi e scoperte 1951-1956. Notizie degli Scavi X, 203-401.

Adamesteanu, D., Orlandini, P. (1960) Gela. Scavi e scoperte 1951-1956. Notizie degli Scavi XIV, 67-246.

Adamesteanu, D., Orlandini, P. (1962) Gela. L'acropoli di Gela. Notizie degli Scavi XVI, 340-408.

Aitchison, J., 1986. The statistics analysis of compositional data. Chapman and Hall, London, UK.

Aquilia, E., Barone, G., Mazzoleni, P., Ingoglia, C. (2012) Petrographic and chemical characterisation of fine ware from three Archaic and Hellenistic kilns in Gela, Sicily. Journal of Cultural Heritage 13, 442-447.

Barone, G., Mazzoleni, P., Aquilia, E., Barbera, G. (2014) The Hellenistic and roman Syracuse (Sicily) fine pottery production explored by chemical and petrographic analysis. Archaeometry 56, 70-87.

Barone, G., Mazzoleni, P., Spagnolo, G., Aquilia, E. (2012) The transport amphorae of Gela: a multidisciplinary study on provenance and technological aspects. Journal of Archaeological Science 39, 11-22.

Barone, G., Lo Giudice, A., Mazzoleni, P., Pezzino, A., Barilaro, D., Crupi, V., Triscari, M. (2005) Chemical characterization and statistical multivariate analysis of ancient pottery from Messina, Catania, Lentini and Siracusa (Sicily). Archaeometry 47, 745-762.

Barone, G., Belfiore, C.M, Mazzoleni, P, Pezzino, A, Viccaro, M. (2010) A volcanic temper based approach for provenance studies of archaeological ceramics from Southern Italy. Journal of Archaeological Science 37, 713-726.

BernabòBrea, L., Carta, R. (1949-1951)L'Athenaion di Gela e le sue terrecotte architettoniche. Annuario della Scuola Archeologica Italiana di Atene XXVII-XXIX, 7-102.

Castoldi, M. (1998) Le antefisse dipinte di Gela. Contributo allo studio della pittura siceliota arcaica, Milano.

Cultrone, G., Rodriguez-Navarro, C., Sebastian, E., Cazalla, O., De la Torre, M.J. (2001)Carbonate and silicatephasereactionsduringceramicfiring. Eur J Mineral. 13, 621–34.

Cultrone, G., Molina, E., Arizzi, A. (2014) The combined use of petrographic, chemical and physical techniques to define the technological features of Iberian ceramics from the Canto Tortoso area (Granada, Spain). Ceramics International 40, 10803–10816.

Danner, P. (1997) Westgriechische Akrotere, Mainz amRhein.

De Miro, E., Fiorentini, G. (1976-1977) Gela: scavi dell'acropoli 1973-1975. Kokalos XXII-XXIII, II, 1, 430-447.

De Miro, E., Fiorentini, G. (1983) Gela protoarcaica. Annuario della Scuola Archeologica Italiana di Atene LXI, 53-104.

Ferrara, B. (2009) Acroteri a Gela alla luce delle nuove acquisizioni. In *Deliciae Fictiles IV,* Lulof, P., Rescigno, C. (Eds.), Oxford, pp. 464-476.

Frost, R.L (1997) The structure of the kaolinite minerals - a FT-Raman study. Clay Minerals 32, 65-77.

Greco, G. (2009) Per una revisione delle terrecotte architettoniche di Gela In *Deliciae Fictiles IV,* Lulof, P., Rescigno, C. (Eds.), Oxford, pp. 446-455.

Heiden, J. (1995) Die Tondächer von Olimpia. OlympischeForschungen XXIV.

Lang. M., Mommsen, H. (2006) Neutronenaktivierungsanalysenzur Herkunftsbestimmungdes Dachesdes Geloer Schatzhauses in Olympia In *Archäometrie und Denkmalpflege,* Hahn, O., Stege, H. (Eds) Jahrestagungander Staatlichen Akademie der Bildenden Künste, Stuttgart, pp. 166-168.

Lulof, S. (1996) The ridge-pole statues from the late archaic temple at Satricum, Amsterdam.

Munsell, A.H. (2000) Munsell soil color chart. Gretag, Macbeth, New Windsor.

Maggetti, M. (1982) Phase analysis and its significance for technology and origin In *Archeological Ceramics,* Olin, J.S., Franklin, A.D. (Eds.), Washington, Smithsonian Inst. Press, pp. 121–33.

Mallwitz, A. (1972) Olympia und seineBauten, München.

Mertens-Horn, M. (1990) Archaische Tondächer Westgriechischer Typologie in Delphi und Olympia. Hesperia 59, 235-248.

Morimoto, N., Fabries, J., Ferguson, A.K., Ginzburg, I.V., Ross, M., Seifert, F.A., Zussman, J., Aoki, K., Gottardi, G. (1988) Nomenclature of pyroxenes. Mineral. Petrol 39, 55–76.

Orlandini, P. (1954) Le nuove antefisse sileniche e il loro contributo alla conoscenza della coroplastica siceliota. Archeologia Classica VI, 251-266.

Orlandini, P. (1956) Altre antefisse sileniche di Gela. Archeologia Classica VIII, 47.

Orlandini, P. (1958) Nuovi acroteri a forma di cavallo e cavaliere dall'acropoli di Gela, in: Scritti in onore di Guido Libertini, Olschki, L.S., (Ed.), Firenze, pp. 117-128.

Orlandini, P. (1968) Topografia dei santuari e documentazione archeologica dei culti. Rivista dell'Istituto di Archeologia e Storia dell'Arte XV, 20-66.

Rescigno, C., Sampaolo, V. (2005) Appunti sull'impiego del colore sulle terrecotte architettoniche capuane. Mediterranea II, 133-163.

Riccardi, M.P., Messiga, B., Duminuco, P. (1999) An approach to the dynamics of clay firing. Appl Clay Sci. 15, 393–409.

Schleif, H., Süsserott, H.K. (1944) Grossgriechische Dachterrakotten. Das Schatzhaus von Gela. OlympischeForschungen I, 83-110.

Sepúlveda, M., Gutiérrez, S., Vallette, M.C., Standen, V.G.. Arriaza, B.T., Cárcamo-Vega, J.J. (2015) Micro-Raman spectral identification of manganese oxides black pigments in an archaeological context in Northern Chile. Heritage Science 3, 1-6.

Sguaitamatti, M. (1984) L'offrante de porceletdans la coroplathiegéléenne. Mainz amRhein.

Spagnolo, G. (2000) Le terrecotte figurate dall'area della stazione vecchia di Gela e i problemi della coroplastica geloa nel V sec. a.C.. Quaderni di Archeologia Università di Messina 1, 179-207.

Thio-Henestrosa, S., Martın-Fernandez, J.A. (2005)Dealing with compositional data: the freeware CoDaPack. Math Geol. 37, 773–93.

Uhlenbrock, J. P. (1988) The Terracotta Protomai from Gela. A Discussion of Local Style in Archaic Sicily, Roma.

Whitbread, I. K. (1995) Greek Transport Amphorae: A Petrological and Archaeological Study, Fitch Laboratory Occasional Paper, 4, The British School at Athens.

Wikander, Ch. (1986) Sicilian Architectural Terracottas. A Reappraisal, Stockholm.

Winter, N. (1993) Greek Architectural Terracottas from the Prehistoric to the End of the Archaic Period, Oxford.

Zoppi, A., Lofrumento, C., Castellucci, E.M., Sciau, P. (2008)Al-for-Fe substitution in hematite: the effect of low Al concentrations in the Raman spectrum of Fe_2O_3. Journal of Raman Spectroscopy 39, 40-46.

11

OBSIDIAN DEPOSITS FROM NORTH-WESTERN IRAN AND FIRST ANALYTICAL RESULTS: IMPLICATIONS FOR PREHISTORIC PRODUCTION AND TRADE

Akbar Abedi[1], Bahram Vosough[2], Mehdi Razani[1], Masoud Bagherzadeh Kasiri[1], Daniel Steiniger[3], Ghader Ebrahimi[4]

[1]*Archaeometry Department, Tabriz Islamic Art University, 51385/4567, Tabriz, IRAN*
[2]*Geology Department, Payam-e Noor University, Tabriz, IRAN*
[3]*Deutsches Archäologisches Institut, Eurasien Abteilung, Berlin, GERMANY*
[4]*Archaeology Department, Mohagegh Ardabili University, Ardabil, IRAN*

Corresponding author: akbar.abedi@tabriziau.ac.ir

ABSTRACT

New studies on prehistoric obsidian artifacts and their provenance have been published by Iranian and international researchers during recent years, which showed, that some obsidian tools might have come from an unknown source located in Iran (perhaps Sahand or Sabalan Mountains). The aim of this paper is to discuss recently discovered obsidian sources in north-west Iran. After a brief introduction of recent obsidian studies in Iran the paper addresses some recent filed work and the geochemical analyses of samples from these surveys (from Tajaraq near Miyaneh and Ghizilja near Bostababad in the Bozghoosh Mountains) by using portable ED-XRF analysis. The results suggest that three major obsidian groups can be distinguished, which are classified as group A and B of Tajaraq besides a single group of Ghizilja. The implications of the new results are discussed along with actual limitations and future research directions.

KEYWORDS: Obsidian Deposit, Tajaraq, Ghizilja, North-West IRAN, portable ED-XRF, Prehistoric Sites

1. INTRODUCTION

Obsidian is one of the most important raw materials for tool making that was used from the Paleolithic to the Iron Age in NW Iran (Abdi, 2004). The color of obsidian ranges generally from green and green-grey to black, brown, red and pink. It is translucent at the edges and in thin sections and also completely transparent, glass like, colorless obsidian tools are known. (Reedy, 2008: 9; Gourgaud, 1998). Although there is a variety of minerals, inclusions and products of re-crystallization and weathering, found in obsidian thin sections under the microscope, almost none of these could be used successfully for provenance studies. Therefore, the chemical analysis of obsidian is the standard method for provenance studies of archaeological artefacts (Reedy, 2008: 9; Gourgaud, 1998).

In general, obsidians are divided into three main groups, based on the chemical composition and mineralogy of the geological source magma within which they occur. These three groups are alkaline, calc-alkaline and per-alkaline. Besides the main components, there are trace elements that make it possible to identify different sources. Different magmas in the same volcanic area can have different geochemical fingerprints, so after the sampling of each of these sources the artefacts can be attributed to the studied obsidian outcrops. (Glascock et al., 1998).

Regarding the high number of the obsidian samples found in NW Iran and western Asia, at well-known sites during the last century, many questions about their origin have been raised. More precisely, it has to be asked, if the extremely large number of obsidian tools in most prehistoric sites of NW Iran has been imported or if were they were possibly made of local (up to now unknown) sources? The answers to these questions will be very influential on the interpretation of regional and trans-regional trade mechanisms in the light of so called obsidian exchange networks, connecting adjacent regions such as Anatolia and the Caucasus.

With a focus on these research questions, a field campaign with the intention to find local obsidian sources was carried out by some of the authors in September 2016. This survey, at its first step, led to the identification of an obsidian source around the village of Tajaraq, Miyaneh, located in the Bozqush Mountains, which, as the first identified source of obsidian in Iran, could play an important role the discussions mentioned above.

The geological background of NW-Iranian obsidian deposits can be described in the framework of regional structural zoning models. The studied area is located in western Alborz-Azarbaijan zone (Nabavi, 1976), with widespread and linear Tertiary magmatism in the Urmiyeh-Dokhtar magmatic belt, north of the Lut desert and central Iran, and the western Alborz-Azrbaijan structure. Most of the magmatism seems associated with the active subduction of the oceanic crust of the Neotethys below the Central Iran plateau (Berberian and King, 1981; Alavi, 1991; 1994-1996; Shahabpour, 2004). The acid magmatism is a synchronous phenomena and resulted in very similar chemical compositions of volcanic and plutonic rocks (calc-alkaline to high potassium calc-alkaline, alkaline and shoshonite series).

Based on another model proposed by Moayyed (Moayyed, 2001 and 2002), the Urmiyeh-Dokhtar Tertiary age magmatism, besides the northern block of the Lut and Central Iran, as well as the western Alborz of Azarbaijan, haves no relation to the active subduction of the Neotetes oceanic crust but should be related to the post collisional arc magmatic processes.

2. HISTORY OF OBSIDIANS PROVENANCE STUDIES IN NORTHWEST IRAN

Renfrew and his colleagues have initiated obsidian studies in the Middle East and Iran. With the advent of obsidian studies in relation to trade and exchange in the Neolithic period in the whole Near East, some typical Iranian sites, such as Tepe Sarab and Goran in Kermanshah, Tepe Ali Kosh of Dehloran, etc. have been investigated and analyzed and provided the required background for the future studies on obsidian. These studies continued from the 1960s to the 1970s, but as in the other parts of the Near East, they suffered a long interruption from the 1980s to the early 21st Century. Again, from around 2000, after excavations in obsidian rich sites by Iranian archaeologists, a broad academic collaboration was established between Iranian scholars and researchers from out-side Iran, which led to a joint scientific research up till now. In the northwest of Iran, due to its proximity to the obsidian sources of East Anatolia and the Cauca-sus (and probably local sources too), the percentage of obsidian tools obtained is much higher than in other parts of Iran. So far, valuable studies have been carried out by various researchers in the area. Most of the studies that were carried out by Renfrew and his col-leagues since the 1960s, have revealed the Anatolian (Lake Van Basin) and Armenia deposits (Lake Sevan Basin), as the source of obsidian tools from Iran. Considering the fact that during the sixth to the third millennium B.C. (Neolithic to Bronze Age period), there have been many cultural and trade connections with these regions, they have been trying to figure out how these communications were in detail (Renfrew, 1969; 1977; Renfrew and Dixon, 1976; Wright,

1969; Renfrew et al., 1966; Mahdavi and Bovington, 1972).

Burney was the first who mentioned the possible existence of local obsidian sources in NW-Iran, dis-cuss-ing the excavations carried out in the Neolithic layers of Yanik Tepe (Burney, 1964). But without any sup-port from chemical analyses or the geological record of distinct obsidian outcrops, this was not much more than a reasonable assumption, consider-ing the abundancy of obsidian tools at Yanik Tepe. Since the Sa-hand Mountain is very close to Yanik Tepe, Burney referred to it as a possible resource and origin of the obsidian from Yanik Tepe (Burney, 1964: 56-57).

The provenance of prehistoric artefacts is one of the main topics in archaeometry, since it provides the background for the investigation of trade routes, the way in which raw materials were provided for ancient societies, and how inter-regional communi-cation networks evolved. In the case of the prove-nance of obsidians from the northwestern regions of the country, long-distance trade trough different parts of West Asia and the Middle East can be recon-structed (Chataigner et al., 1998). Based on the re-sults obtained at previous and recent studies (Ren-frew et al., 1966, 1969, Dixon et al., 1968, Cann et al., 1968, 1969, Renfrew, 1969, 1970, Dixon, 1976; Ren-frew and Dixon, 1976; Blackman, 1984; Williams-Thorpe, 1995; Chataigner et al., 1998; Liritzis, 2002; Frahm, 2010; Liritzis and Zacharias, 2011; Liritzis and Stevenson, 2012; Düring Bleda and Gratuze, 2013; Chataigner and Gratuze, 2014a-b;), the only obsidian sources discovered in the Middle and the Near East are at present located in the Anatolia and the Caucasian region and most of the laboratory in-vestigations have revealed the origin of all obsidian arte-facts from ancient sites originate from these two regions. But amongst some of the samples, in partic-ular samples from Iranian sites, there are some arte-facts whose original source cannot be defined as their chemistry differs distinctively from the well-known sources of Anatolia and the Caucasus. Irani-an re-searchers have tried to define some candidates for local obsidian sources (Khademi et al,. 2007; Ghorabi et al., 2009; Khademi et al., 2010), but in most cases, these samples did not belong to real geo-logical out-crops but were surface finds. Also these findings have not been published yet in a detailed way, so they cannot be definitely confirmed or de-nied by referring to these documents alone. Amongst these, a study by Niknami and his col-leagues on material from around Miyaneh and the mountains of Bozgush seemed the most promising (Niknami et al., 2010; Abedi, 2015). The identification of some real obsidian outcrops in the region of Tajaraq (Bozgush Mountains near Miyaneh), and at Ghizilja (near Bostanabad), both in the East Azarbai-jan province, presented in the following, can provide a sound base for a new focus in research on obsidian resources in Iran.

3. MATERIALS AND METHODS

3.1. GEOGRAPHICAL LOCATION OF TAJARAQ (BOZGUSH MOUNTAINS, MI-YANEH)

The region of investigation (N 37° 73' 58" - E 47° 68' 38") is located c. 1.5 km south of the village of Tajaraq, Kandovan area (20 km aerial distance, northeastern part of the district), near the city of Mi-yaneh, in the province of East Azarbaijan, north-western Iran (Figs. 1 and 2.1).

In terms of regional morphology, this area is lo-cated in one of the most violent areas of the Azarbai-jan region. High mountains, deep valleys and mean-drous, massive landslides. Relatively plain water rivers such as Germi Chay and its sub branches have given this area a very disparate and disconnected visage. However, the region of investigation at this study has not too rough, mostly hill-like cliffs. The altitude of the site exceeds 2150 m above sea level. This region has a mountainous climate with moder-ate summers and very cold winters and the snowy summits are a spectacular characteristic of the area. The humidity level in the region is high and this, from the viewpoint of human geography, means plenty of water for agriculture and horticulture, re-sulting vast gardens and agricultural farms in the region, especially around the Tajaraq village. The small village of Tajaraq is located north of the obsid-ian outcrop.

3.2. GEOLOGY OF THE SITE (TAJARAQ)

The territory of Azarbaijan in northwestern Iran in-cludes the provinces of Zanjan, Ardabil, plus East and West Azarbaijan. Due to the diversity of geolog-ical evolution and the complexity of the structural setting of different rocks, the lack of sufficient geo-logical studies provokes often different and contra-dictory views about it. This zone is classified in the Alborz-Azarbaijan zone, the Gorgan-Rasht zone and the Khoy-Mahabad zone (Fig. 2.1). Iran's crustal thickness map (Dehghani and Makris, 1983) show the increasing of crustal thickness in eastern parts of Azarbaijan (west coast of the Caspian Sea towards the Talesh Mountains and Ardebil province) up to 45 Km based on geophysical (gravimetric) data. The maximum thickness of the crust is seen in Azarbaijan in its central part, near the mountains of Moro and Mishoo, which reaches 48 kilometers.

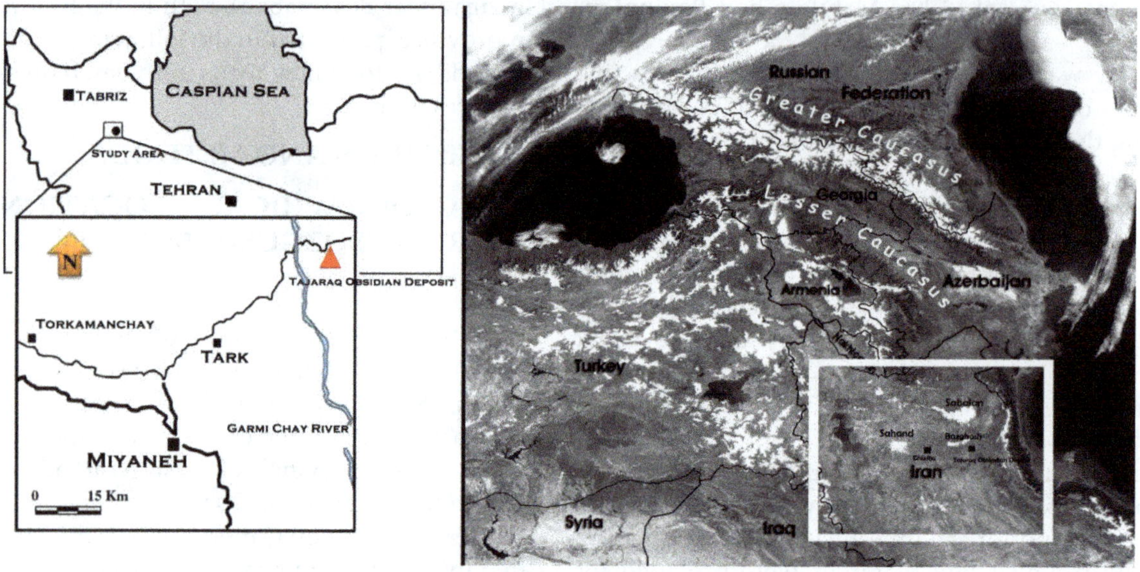

Figure 1. Geographical location of the study area and the Tajaraq deposit of obsidian in Miyaneh, and Ghizilja, East Azarbaijan province, NW IRAN

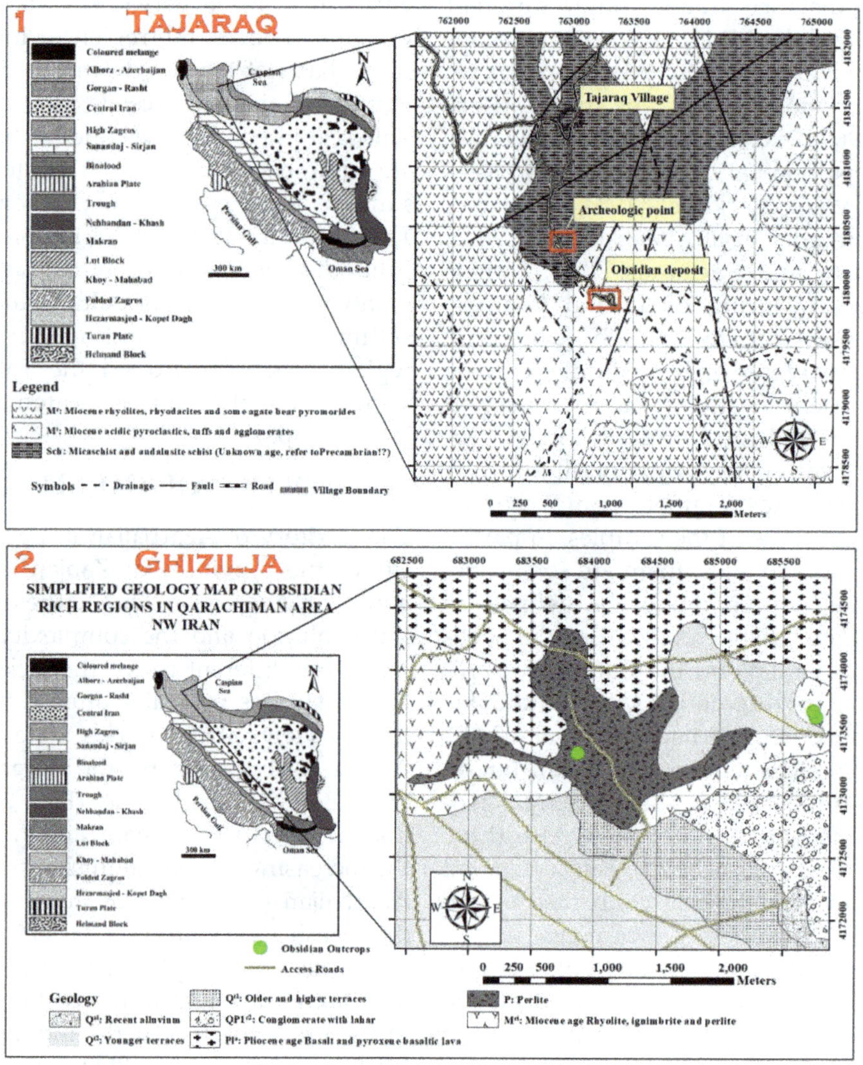

Figure 2. Simplified geological map of Tajaraq district (after Behrouzi and Amini, 1992) and its location on the Iranian tectonic zoning map (after Nabavi, 1976)

The oldest deposits in the territory of Azarbaijan and in the Miyaneh region belong to Precambrian and has been exposed in different parts often along faults and uplifts. In the east of the Bozgusuh Mountains and along the Germi Chay River, Ney Baghi and Sari Qomish villages, a relatively large outcrop of metamorphic rocks with andalusite, cordierite, amphibolite and forsterite schists besides wollastonite marble and metadiabase characteristics have been reported. On these units, different geological formations from the early Paleozoic torecent ages can be seen in the Middle, South, and Eastern parts of Bozgoush. The most important geological event in this region is magmatism, or more precisely, Alpine phase volcanism from Eocene to Quaternary, which causes the formation of the most important geological events in the region, the formation of Bozgoush Mountains in the Eocene and the Chehel Noor Mount in the Miocene (Aghanabati, 2004).

According to the 1: 100,000 scale Sarab geological map quadrangle (Behrouzi et al., 1992), the major units exposed in the visited area are (Fig. 2.1): Schist (old metamorphic attributed to Precambrian composed of mica schist, andalusite schist and marble). Miocene age pyroclastic (Mt) are deposited on the above mentioned metamorphics after a great unconformity as light colour acidic tuff, lapilli stone and agglomerates. This unit is the host of the obsidian reserves in Tajaraq region with NW-SE/SW bedding status. Finally, the violet-hepatic brown color rhyolite-rhyodacite- devitrified pyromerides (Fig. 2.1) are observable in this region. The obsidian reserve is located in a pyroclastic unit as dispersed lenses in a horizon of variable-thickness (Fig. 3). The actual thickness of the obsidian rich pyroclastic horizon in this area is between 1 to 10 m and the boundary of the host rocks with the obsidian black lenses in this region is completely sharp (Fig. 4). It seems that the host rock is often crushed and reworked by tectonic stresses (Fig. 5). Obsidians in this region have a dark green to black colour, glassy luster and shelly fracture.

3.3. GEOGRAPHICAL LOCATION OF GHIZILJA (BOZGUSH MOUNTAINS, MIYANEH)

The Ghizilja area (N 37° 68' 85" - E 47° 08' 45") is located between Qara-Chaman and Tikmeh Dash towns in the East Azerbaijan province and 90 km east of Tabriz. The closest village to this area is the Imamiyeh village. To reach the obsidian rich perlite quarries in this area one has to move along the old road of Tabriz, after moving through Bostanabad and Tikmehdash, use the exit at the village of Qizilja on the north side of the road before the Qar-e Chaman reaches the Imamiyeh village. Then from c.5 km of Imamiyeh perlite quarry, after 6.5 km, we finally reach the Ghizilja perlite quarry. Both ranges are easily accessible by using rides (Fig.1, 2.2).

Figure 3. Obsidian formation outcrop and its foot and hang walls (view to South)

Figure 4. The location of Obsidian level into Tuff-Agglomerate member (view to South)

Figure 5. A mesoscopic view of the crushed Obsidian particles at Tajaraq (view to South)

3.4. GEOLOGY OF THE SITE (GHIZILJA)

Based on structural zoning of Iran, this region in located in western Alborz of Azerbaijan structural zone (Nabavi, 1976), and generally all of the rock outcrops and lithologies observed in it are of Pliocene age volcanic lavas and pyroclastic units. In visited zones, the perlite is in actual layers compatible with the layering of lava and pyroclastic units in the form of layers between 1 cm to 2 m thickness with grey, brown and black colours and the perlitic structure is common. In addition, the so called thunder eggs derived from devitrification, can be found. The quarries are currently semi-active (Fig. 2.2).

In the Imamiyeh quarry, with 670126, 4176104 to 683871, 4173333 coordinates (UTM-WGS-1984 / N38Zone system): obsidian rich perlite layer are observable as concordant intercalation with their porphyry texture volcanic and pyroclastic host rocks.

The same status are observable in obsidian rich perlite Ghizilja quarry in 685785, 4173624 coordinates. In c. 100 m distance of the quarry (at 685735, 4173672 coordinates) a place with concentrations of ancient pottery is observable.

3.5. STUDIED SAMPLES AND ANALYTICAL METHODS

The samples of this study were gathered on a survey from surface obsidian outcrops. A total of 18 samples were selected from several sets of rocks and 10 samples were analyzed. Of these 10 samples, eight samples belong to the Tajaraq deposit near Miyaneh and two samples were selected from the Ghizilja deposit (Shahriyar Perlite quarry) near Bostanabad. (Fig. 6) Up to now only small homogenous obsidian specimens have been collected, with a maximum diameter of c. 5 cm. Larger samples were fractured substantively tectonically or by perlitization. Therefore it is not clear at the moment, if large and homogenous obsidian nodules of good quality occur in the area, which is essential if this raw material should have been used in Prehistory for tool making.

Figure 6: Selected samples from Tajaraq, Miyeneh, and Ghizilja, Bostanabad (MA-TJ- 001, MA-TJ- 002, MA-TJ- 003, MA-TJ- 004, MA-TJ- 007, MA-TJ- 008, MA-TJ- 012, MA-TJ- 014; Finding place of the samples, Tajaraq village, Miyaneh city, East Azerbaijan BS-GHZ-001 ،BS-GHZ-003; Finding place of the samples, Ghizilja/Shahryar perlite quarry, Bostanabad, East Azerbaijan)

For the measurements a portable ED-XRF device (Thermo Scientific Niton XL3t 950-HE GOLDD+ Serial nr. 89086 from the Eurasia Department of the German Archaeological Institute, Berlin) was used, equipped with an Ag anode at max. 50 kV, silicon drift detector. Technical parameters: TestAllGeo-mode with filter settings 90/90/60/125 seconds, total measuring time 360 seconds, aperture 8 mm. This setting gives best results for ceramics, stones, slags and other material with high silica content and not too bad results for light elements also. Sodium cannot be detected with this device, but most elements from magnesia onwards, which have higher atomic weights. Factory calibration was used and the oxides were normalized to 100 wt% (without Na_2O). To ensure reliable data, measurements of international certified standard reference material (NIST2780, NIST2709a, Till4 and others) were used during the sessions. The standard deviation and the variability according to the standards is in a low and normal range, that ensures comparability with published datasets. Some of the most reliable element concentrations in obsidian that can be obtained using portable ED-XRF are Rb, Sr, Y, Zr and Nb, if the concentrations are above the detection limit (Darabi and Glascock, 2013). Sample thickness plays an important role and several elements are difficult to be detected in low quantities, when the samples or artefacts are too thin (as documented for the device used in this study by test measurements of the Eurasia Department; also for other difficulties using pXRF on obsidian and further references c.f.: Ferguson 2012).

Table I. pXRF results of elemental analysis of the samples from Tajaraq, Miyaneh, and Ghizilja Bostanabad (oxides normalized to 100 wt%, without Na2O)

Samples No	Location	SiO_2	TiO_2	Al_2O_3	Fe_2O_3	MnO	MgO	CaO	K_2O
MA TJ2016 - 001	NTV*	79,04	0,07	13,25	1,64	0,08	0,93	0,46	4,51
MA TJ2016 003	NTV	80,53	0,07	12,63	1,64	0,07	0,11	0,43	4,48
MA TJ2016 002	NTV	75,9	0,3	14,04	2,43	0,11	0	1,16	6,01
MA TJ2016 004	NTV	79,81	0,08	11,67	1,7	0,08	0,67	0,5	5,45
MA TJ2016 007	NTV	80,34	0,07	10,99	1,72	0,08	0,72	0,46	5,59
MA TJ2016 008	NTV	78,68	0,07	12,48	1,73	0,08	0,9	0,56	5,45
MA TJ2016 012	NTV	73,18	0,39	15,23	2,84	0,1	1,26	1,61	5,36
MA TJ2016 014	NTV	74,01	0,38	15,2	2,86	0,08	0,56	1,06	5,8
BS GHZ 2016 001	SPM**	82,7	0,13	10,88	0,77	0,06	0,65	0,01	3,72
BS GHZ 2016 003	SPM**	83,41	0,14	10,28	0,72	0,06	0,29	1,1	3,92

***NTV: NEAR TAJARAQ VILLAGE **SPM: SHAHRIAR PERLITE MINE**

3.6. RESULTS

The chemical analysis clearly shows that the samples of the two sources have a peculiar composition that is different from other obsidian groups previously known (Tab. I-II and Fig. 7). These new groups are introduced and proposed as the new group of Tajaraq Obsidian (MA TJ – Miyaneh Tajaraq Obsidian Source) and are referred to as Tajaraq A and Tajaraq B, while from Ghizilja the analysed samples seem to form one homogenous group.

3.6.1. DISPERSION CHART ANALYSIS – ZIRCONIUM AND RUBIDIUM (ZR/RB)

The zirconium and rubidium relation (Fig. 8) shows that the above mentioned three groups are clearly distinguishable. Group Tajaraq A is very dense because the samples were comparably fresh and from a small scale geological horizon. Group Tajaraq B is more variable. The other two samples belong to the Ghizilja perlite quarry of Bostanabad (BS GHZ).

3.6.2. DISPERSION CHART ANALYSIS: RUBIDIUM AND STRONTIUM (RB/SR)

In the diagram of Rb/Sr the samples of the three sites plot again in three distinct areas (Fig. 9) and therefore they can be separated geochemically quite easy.

Table II. pXRF results of elemental analysis of the samples from Tajaraq, Miyaneh, and Ghizilja Bostanabad (trace elements in ppm)

Sample No	Loction	Zn	As	Rb	Sr	Y	Zr	Nb	Sn	Sb	Ba
MA TJ2016 001	NTV*	55	22	270	2	45	290	66	7	12	185
MA TJ2016 003	NTV	55	23	275	2	45	295	69	7	9	131
MA TJ2016 002	NTV	48	10	215	101	35	611	62	8	13	477
MA TJ2016 004	NTV	52	21	257	4	41	271	62	7	12	165
MA TJ2016 007	NTV	53	20	254	5	41	266	61	9	13	188
MA TJ2016 008	NTV	53	21	261	4	42	272	62	8	11	172
MA TJ2016 012	NTV	55	10	203	135	34	627	64	7	11	388
MA TJ2016 014	NTV	57	12	237	74	40	718	73	7	11	380
BS GHZ 2016 001	SPM**	24	9	92	121	9	77	12	13	26	1126
BS GHZ 2016 003	SPM**	26	8	124	126	10	77	13	11	22	1109

***NTV: NEAR TAJARAQ VILLAGE **SPM: SHAHRIAR PERLITE MINE**

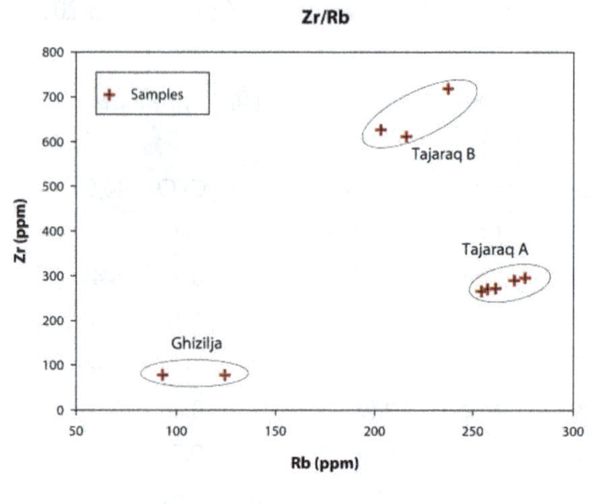

Figure 7. Scatterplot of Zr versus Rb for obsidian samples from Tajaraq and Ghizilja obsidian sources (pXRF).

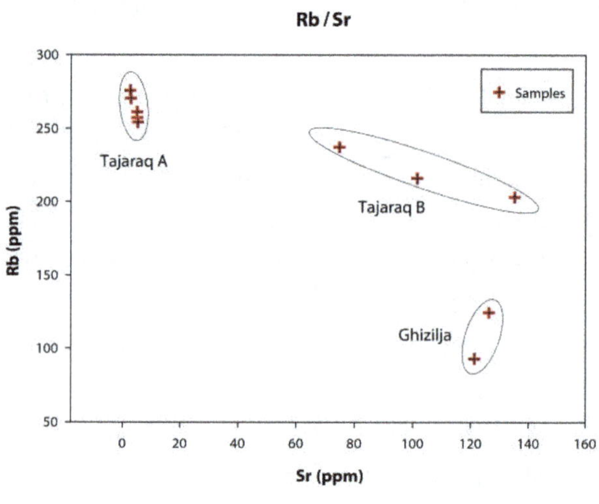

Figure 8. Scatterplot of Rb versus Sr for obsidian samples from Tajaraq and Ghizilja obsidian sources (pXRF).

4. DISCUSSION AND CONCLUSION

The present study introduces new obsidian sources in the northwest of Iran. The research has been carried out with a focus on locating the origins and resources of obsidian procurement in the northwest of Iran, in order to rethink and reconstruct the regional and supra-regional trade and exchange networks in future. The project clearly identified the three groups of geochemically different obsidians named Tajaraq A, Tajaraq B, and Ghizilja. Due to the fact that Tajaraq obsidian is of a higher quality than the Ghizilja ones, it seems likely that the samples of Tajaraq obsidians have had the ability to be used for tool-making in the past, while the samples of Ghizilja, Bostanabad are too fragile and perlitic in structure.

Hence, as the two groups of Tajaraq A and Tajaraq B have the ability to be used for ancient tools in all probability, they can be introduced as candidates for obsidian mining in prehistoric times in the northwest of Iran. The proposed hypothesis is actually still at a very early stage and future scientific studies and field research have to follow. Comparing the new results with prehistoric sites in the cultural areas of Miyaneh and Bostanabad, it becomes obvious that the Tajaraq B obsidian overlaps in some trace elements with published data Anatolian sources (Darabi and Glascock, 2013) (Fig. 10). If this overlap could be found also by comparing other elements and their combination and if it will be confirmed by other methods in future, it could lead to a complete review of all previous obsidian analysis from Iran. Several samples that were up to now thought to be from Anatolia could come from source B of Tajaraq in reality. This is a serious and peculiar hypothesis, which means at first more data have to collected at the geological outcrops and especially by analyzing archaeological finds from well stratified context.

Although the biplots Zr-Rb, Sr-Rb may be on a local scale discriminative they are not necessary condition for differentiation between peripheral sources e.g. Iranian with those from Anatolian or Aegean. For example, in the Aegean for Melos source Sr=~120, Rb=~112 ppm (Liritzis, 2007) which is similar to NW Iranian. This must be noted, in addition to Anatolian sources. Although it has been noted here for the Tajaraq B obsidian which overlaps in some trace elements with published data from Nemrut Dağ, and also with other Anatolian sources, it is too premature to pinpoint the question of provenance. Thus, in a future provenance project major and trace elements should be subjected to Cluster, PCA etc analysis. (Liritzis & Zacharias, 2013).

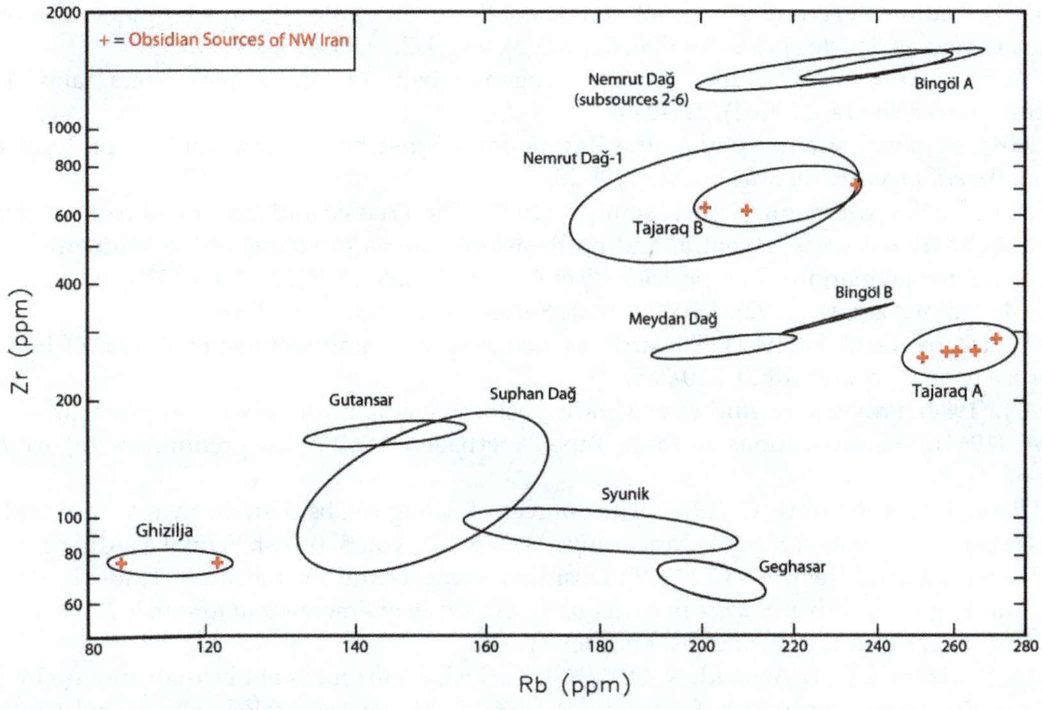

Figure 9. Log scatterplot of Rb versus Zr for obsidian sources of Turkey and Armenia (modified after Darabi and Glascock, 2013) and Tajaraq A, B and Ghizilja (NW Iran, pXRF).

SUGGESTIONS AND THE WAY FORWARD

The next important step is certainly the investigation of ancient sites from the Neolithic to the Iron Age, especially in the eastern part of Lake Urmia and close to the cities of Miyaneh and Bostanabad, so that it can be proven that the samples of Tajaraq obsidian and other comparable sources in this region have been used for the manufacture of artefacts in Prehistory. As there have been many investigations and excavations in the areas of Miyaneh and Bostanabad in the recent years, the systematic and minute examination of the obsidian finds from these sites will be a huge part of the project. Then all these findings of obsidian have to be analysed, first with pXRF and for detailed studies selections of the whole could be measured by laboratory methods. Another important part is the fieldwork and surveying around the obsidian outcrops themselves, for the identification of possible traces of ancient mining and processing, besides the first steps in the chaîne opératoire of obsidian manufacture. In a close circle around the deposits, settlements can be expected, that were specialized in obsidian mining and the first steps of raw material treatment, before the valuable matter was excangend and transported in the vicinity. This study opened a new horizon to research in NW-Iran around the Sahand, Sabalan and Bozgush Mountains and provided a sound base for future studies in the field of obsidian provenance.

ACKNOWLEDGEMENTS

The present article is a part of the results of the research project entitled "Exploring and Identifying the Obsidian Resources and Mines in the Miyaneh (Bozgush and Sabalan Mountains) and Sarab of East Azarbaijan province and its adaptation to the ancient sites of east of Urmia lake", which with was realized at Tabriz Islamic Art University, under the contracts no. 11148 and 1155. Therefore, the authors thank this institute for providing the facilities and funding for this research. The German Archaeological Institute, Teheran Branch and Eurasia Department Berlin, supported the research substantially in cooperation with the Tabriz Islamic Art University.

REFERENCES

Abdi, K. (2004). Obsidian in Iran from the Epipalaeolithic period to the Bronze Age. *Persiens antike Pracht*, 148-153.

Abedi, A. (2015). A Review of Obsidian Studies in Iran, Provenance the Source and Prehistoric Obsidian Artifacts, Researches and Questions. *Journal of Research on Archaeometry*, *1*(1), 55-85.

Aghanabati, S. A., (2004). Geology of Iran, GSI Publication, Tehran, 592pp (in Persian).

Alavi, M. (1991). Sedimentary and structural characteristics of the Paleo-Tethys remnants in northeastern Iran. *Geological Society of America Bulletin*, *103*(8), 983-992.

Alavi, M. (1994). Tectonics of the Zagros orogenic belt of Iran: new data and interpretations. *Tectonophysics*, *229*(3-4), 211-238.

Alavi, M. (2004). Regional stratigraphy of the Zagros fold-thrust belt of Iran and its proforeland evolution. *American journal of Science*, *304*(1), 1-20.

Alavi, M., Vaziri, H., Seyed-Emami, K., & Lasemi, Y. (1997). The Triassic and associated rocks of the Nakhlak and Aghdarband areas in central and northeastern Iran as remnants of the southern Turanian active continental margin. *Geological Society of America Bulletin*, *109*(12), 1563-1575.

Behrouzi, A., & Amini Azar, R. (1992). 1:100000 scale Sarab quadrangle, GSI, Tehran.

Berberian, M., & King, G. C. P. (1981). Towards a paleogeography and tectonic evolution of Iran. *Canadian journal of earth sciences*, *18*(2), 210-265.

Blackman, M. J. (1984). Provenance studies of Middle Eastern obsidian from sites in highland Iran.

Burney, C. A. (1964). The excavations at Yanik Tepe, Azerbaijan, 1962: third preliminary report. *Iraq*, *26*(1), 54-61.

Cann, J. R., Dixon, J. E. & Renfrew, C. (1968). The Sources of Saliagos Obsidian. In Evans, J. D., and Renfrew, C. (Eds.), *Excavations at Saliagos Near Antiparos*: 105-107. vol. 5. British School at Athens.

Cann, J. R., Dixon, J. E. and Renfrew, C. (1969). Obsidian Analysis and the Obsidian Trade. In Brothwell, D. R., and Higgs, E. (Eds.), *Science in Archaeology: A Survey of Progress and Research, Revised and Expanded Edition*: 578-591. Praeger Publishers, New York.

Chataigner, C., Poidevin, J. L., & Arnaud, N. O. (1998). Turkish occurrences of obsidian and use by prehistoric peoples in the Near East from 14,000 to 6000 BP. *Journal of Volcanology and Geothermal Research*, *85*(1), 517-537.

Chataigner, C., & Gratuze, B. (2014)a. New data on the exploitation of obsidian in the Southern Caucasus (Armenia, Georgia) and eastern Turkey, Part 1: Source characterization. *Archaeometry*, *56*(1), 25-47.

Chataigner, C., & Gratuze, B. (2014)b. New data on the exploitation of obsidian in the Southern Caucasus (Armenia, Georgia) and eastern Turkey, Part 2: Obsidian procurement from the Upper Palaeolithic to the Late Bronze Age. *Archaeometry*, *56*(1), 48-69.

Dehghani, G. A., & Makris, J. (1983). The gravity field and crustal structure of Iran. In: Geodynamic project of Iran (Geotraverces), Geol. Surv. Iran. Rep. No. 51: 51-68.

Dixon, J. E. (1976). Obsidian characterization studies in the Mediterranean and Near East. *Advances in obsidian glass studies: archaeological and geochemical perspectives*, 288-333.

Dixon, J., Cann, J. and Renfrew, C. (1968). Obsidian and the Origins of Trade. *Scientific American* 218(3): 38-46.

Frahm, E. E. (2010). *The Bronze-Age obsidian industry at Tell Mozan (ancient Urkesh), Syria: redeveloping electron microprobe analysis for 21st-century sourcing research and the implications for obsidian use and exchange in northern Mesopotamia after the Neolithic*. University of Minnesota.

Ghorabi, S., Glascock, M. D., Khademi, F., Rezaie, A., & Feizkhah, M. (2008). A geochemical investigation of obsidian artifacts from sites in northwestern Iran. *IAOS Bulletin, 39*, 7-10.

Glascock, M. D., Braswell, G. and Cobean, R. H. (1998). A Systematic Approach to Obsidian Source Characterization. In Shackley, M. S. (Ed.) *Archaeological Obsidian Studies: Method and Theory*: 15-65. Society for Archaeological Sciences.

Darabi, H., & Glascock, M. D. (2013). The source of obsidian artefacts found at East Chia Sabz, Western Iran. *Journal of Archaeological Science, 40*(10), 3804-3809.

Düring, B. S., & Gratuze, B. (2013). Obsidian exchange networks in Prehistoric Anatolia: New data from the Black Sea region. *Paléorient*, 173-182.

Ferguson, J. R. (2012) X-Ray fluorescence of obsidian: Approaches to calibration and the analysis of small samples. In Shugar, A. N. & Jennifer L. Mass, J. L. (Eds.), Handheld XRF for Art and Archaeology. University Press, Leuven, 401-422.

Gourgaud, A. (1998). Géologie de L'obsidienne. *In L'obsidienne au Proche et Moyen-Orient: Du Volcan à l'Outil*, In Cauvin, M. C., Gourgaud, A., Gratauze, B., Arnaud, N., Poupeau, G., Poidevin, J. L. and Chataigner, C. (Eds.): 15-29. British Archaeological Reports. Maison de l'Orient Méditerranéen, Archaeopress, Oxford.

Khademi Nadooshan, F., Philips, S. C., & Safari, M. (2007). WDXRF spectroscopy of obsidian tools in the northwest of Iran. *International Association for Obsidian Studies Bulletin, 37*, 3-6.

Liritzis, I. (2002). Revival of obsidian studies. *Mediterranean Archaeology & Archaeometry*, 2(2), 79-82.

Liritzis, I (2007) Assessment of Aegean obsidian sources by a portable ED-XRF analyzer (grouping, provenance and accuracy). In: Proceedings of PanHellenic Archaeometry Conference (Facorellis et al., eds) Archaeopress, BAR International Series, 399-406.

Liritzis, I., & Zacharias, N. (2011). Portable XRF of archaeological artifacts: current research, potentials and limitations. In *X-ray fluorescence spectrometry (XRF) in geoarchaeology*, pp. 109-142. Springer New York.

Liritzis, I., & Stevenson, C. M. (Eds.). (2012). *Obsidian and Ancient Manufactured Glasses*. New Mexico Press.

Mahdavi, A., & Bovington, C. (1972). Neutron activation analysis of some obsidian samples from geological and archaeological sites. *Iran*, 148-151.

Moayyed, M. & Moazzen, M. (2002). A new view to Paleo- Tethys suture zone in Iran, 6th Iranian Geology congress, Shahid Bahonar Kerman University, 716-717.

Moayyed, M., 2002, A review on the development of Neo-Tethys and its relationship with Tertiary magmatism in Urmia-Dokhtar and Western Alborz-Azarbaijan, , 6th Iranian Geology congress, Shahid Bahonar Kerman University, p 374-378.

Moayyed, M., Javanmardi, A. R., Hosseinzadeh, Q. (2001). Skarnification and alteration in SheivarDagh intrusive contact margin, 20th Geology symposium of Iran, GSI, 47-48.

Nabavi, M. H. (1976). *Geology of Iran, GSI*, Tehran.

Nadooshan, F. K., Abedi, A., Glascock, M. D., Eskandari, N., & Khazaee, M. (2013). Provenance of prehistoric obsidian artefacts from Kul Tepe, northwestern Iran using X-ray fluorescence (XRF) analysis. *Journal of Archaeological Science, 40*(4), 1956-1965.

Nadooshan, F. K., Ayvatwand, M., Deghanifar, H., Glascock, M. D., & Colby Phillips, S. (2010). Report on the Chogabon site, a new source of obsidian artifacts in west-central Iran. *IAOS Bulletin, 42*, 9-12.

Niknami, K. A., Amirkhiz, A. C., & Glascock, M. D. (2010). Provenance studies of Chalcolithic obsidian artefacts from near Lake Urmia, northwestern Iran using WDXRF analysis. *Archaeometry, 52*(1), 19-30.

Potts, P. J., & West, M. (Eds.). (2008). *Portable X-ray fluorescence spectrometry: Capabilities for in situ analysis*. Royal Society of Chemistry.

Reedy, C. L. (2008). *Thin-Section Petrography of Stone and Ceramic Materials*. London, Archetype.

Renfrew, C. (1969). Trade and culture process in European prehistory. *Current Anthropology, 10*(2/3), 151-169.

Renfrew, C. (1977). The later obsidian of Deh Luran–the evidence of Chagha Sefid. *Studies in the Archaeological History of the Deh Luran Plain*, 289-311.

Renfrew, C., & Dixon, J. (1976). Obsidian in western Asia: a review. *Problems in economic and social archaeology*, 137-150.

Renfrew, C., Dixon, J. E., & Cann, J. R. (1966, December). Obsidian and early cultural contact in the Near East. In *Proceedings of the Prehistoric Society* (Vol. 32, pp. 30-72). Cambridge University Press.

Renfrew, C., Dixon, J. E., & Cann, J. R. (1969, February). Further analysis of Near Eastern obsidians. In *Proceedings of the Prehistoric Society* (Vol. 34, pp. 319-331). Cambridge University Press.

Shahabpour, J. (2005). Tectonic evolution of the orogenic belt in the region located between Kerman and Neyriz. *Journal of Asian Earth Sciences*, *24*(4), 405-417.

Williams-Thorpe, O. (1995). Obsidian in the Mediterranean and the Near East: a provenancing success story. *Archaeometry*, *37*(2), 217-248.

Wright, G. A. (1969). *Obsidian analyses and prehistoric near eastern trade: 7500 to 3500 BC*. University of Michigan. Museum of Anthropology.

12

THE COMMON ATTRIBUTES BETWEEN THE BALTIC THUNDER GOD *PERKŪNAS* AND HIS ANTIQUE EQUIVALENTS *JUPITER* AND *ZEUS*

Vytautas Tumėnas

The Lithuanian Institute of History, dept. of Ethnology (Vilnius, Lithuania)

Corresponding author: Vytautas Tumėnas (vytautui.vytui@gmail.com)

ABSTRACT

The problem of regional uniqueness and intercultural relations of traditional images of Thunder-god as mythological celestial, cosmogonic, astronomic-calendaric and atmospheric being remains relevant to this day. Perkūnas image, his representations and attributes share certain similarities in different European cultures but they are still not investigated from visual point of view.

This semiological investigation is mainly based on a comparative and interdisciplinary analysis of visual and narrative representations of the Baltic and Antique Thunder-gods. It aims to reveal the intercultural contextuality of the symbolic elements of images of Baltic *Perkūnas* and to demonstrate their similarities with the attributes of supreme Antique deities *Zeus* and *Jupiter*. A diachronic intercultural analysis of local, national or regional representations of Baltic Thunder-god helps avoid a localized ethno-centrism in explaining images of European deities as mere elements of a regional culture and will shed new light on their broader archetypal basis. It aims to bring some controversial, unique and fragmented interpretations of Baltic Thunder-god symbolism into the light of a wider transcultural historical context.

The author draws from a wide range of comparative data: from Lithuanian, Prussian, Eastern and Western European Christian, and other classical sources. This complex overview is primarily based on medieval and folk art images, artefacts and architecture. Folklore, language and other ethnographic material and mythology-related data are also used.

Such a comparative and interdisciplinary attitude to the European Thunder gods' attributes, drawing on anthropology, art history and folklore approached from a Baltic perspective, will help to establish new insights into the deeper understanding of celestial symbolism implicated in similarities of thunder god's attributes and congeniality of these mythical representations tradition till our days.

KEYWORDS: Baltic Thunder-god, Perkunas of Kernave, Jupiter, Zeus, Videvutis' flag, eight-pointed star, trident, axe, spiral.

1. INTRODUCTION

A detailed look at the particular symbolic elements of the Baltic Thunder-god helps us to formulate new insights about the essential features of this mythical being, its intercultural affinities and local uniqueness. Furthermore, closer analysis of the similar and common elements of symbolism of the thunder gods of Antiquity will help to outline their historical influence.

The attention must be paid to a comparison particular visual symbols and attributes of *Perkūnas* and *Jupiter* and *Zeus*: the symbols of thunder and water, their motion means and links with a calendar.

Previous investigations in the Baltic cosmological, atmospheric and calendar mythology of *Perkūnas* (Lithuanian, Latvian, Old Prussian) was based on historical records and folklore material, with reference to the related Slavic *Perun* and Germanic and Nordic *Thor,* and *Donar* folklore narratives (Brückner, 1904; Balys, 1939: 3-326; Gimbutas, 1973; Greimas, 1990; Lowmianski, 1986; Vėlius, 1987; Laurinkienė, 1996; Ivanov, Toporov, 1974; Kowalik, 2004; Rosik, 2000).

Though the importance of the Baltic *Perkūnas* and Slavic *Perun* in the mythology of Eastern European cultures is significant, the questions about Ancient Roman analogues of *Perkūnas'* visual representations and his folkloric affinities (Długossius, 1711; Sibley, 2009: 264-269) remain very actual. The 15th-century historian J. Długosz (Długossius) was one of the first authors to note the similarities between *Perkūnas* and *Jupiter*. The details of several historical visual images of Baltic god *Perkūnas* still are not precisely analysed from iconographical and comparative point of view.

2. PERKŪNAS AND THE CALENDAR

The Baltic *Perkūnas/Perkons* is one of the best known deities in ancient texts and was a popular mythical entity in folklore. The ethnoastronomical data has several references clearly linking Thunder-god with specific festive dates and days of the week.

The oldest data denoting the link of astronomic calculations with the Sun and *Perkūnas* comes from the temple of the 14-15th c. on Birutė Hill in Palanga. An idol of *Perkūnas* was erected there. Later it was transferred to Vilnius, the capital of Lithuania. The paleoastronomic temple was mainly intended to observe and honour the sun and moon festive positions of solstitions and equinoxes (Klimka, 1989:73-85), and especially of the April 23rd (Žulkus, 1999: 41-47). In Latvian tradition this is the day of *Usiņš* who is a rider and owner of a pair of horses that draw the solar chariot. For Lithuanians this is the day of folkloric mythic person *Joris* and also Christian saint *šv. Jurgis* (*St. George*).

Analogically in Ancient Greece, April 23rd was dedicated to the Thunder-god *Zeus Georgius* (farmer). The Romans offered libations to Jupiter on this day as part of the *Vinalia urbana* or *Vinalia priora.* The Lithuanians on *Jurginės* festival paid respect to domestic animals: the cows were decorated with wreaths and led from the barn to the fields. This time is also associated with the first thunder of the year, which "awakens the earth" and stimulates it to blossom. This day is also known as *Jorė* (the name for the first spring greens) and folk songs invoke lonely *Joris* or *Jurja,* entreating him to thaw and unlock the earth, to release dew, and to marry. Seeking a rose for a wife, he is willing to break the garden fence, to flood the land with water and at least to pluck a flower (Misevičienė, 1972: 291, Nr. 425-426). This narrative image has strong connotations of *Perkūnas* wedding and fertile relations with Sun and earth.

The Thursday was associated with *Perkūnas* (Laurinkienė, 1996). Similarly Thursday was likewise dedicated to *Jupiter* in Roman cultures (*Iovis dies* in Latin, *joves* in old Portuguese, *jueves* in Spanish and *jeudi* in French).

This demonstrates that Lithuanian calendar bear striking similarities to the Greco-Roman calendar traditions linked with *Zeus* and *Jupiter.*

3. THE "TRADITIO LEGIS" TYPE HAND GESTURE OF PERKŪNAS

One of the oldest pieces of evidence testifying to early representations of *Perkunas* is the so-called Videvutis flag (Fig. 1/1-2). The legendary king *Videvutis* lived in the 6th century and established the Prussian state of Balts (Stellae, 1518: 23-31). "The Videvutis' flag", according to Simonus Grunau "Preussische Chronik" (1510–1529) description, depicted the three main Prussian gods - *Potrimppo, Perkuno and Patollo* together with a heraldic pair of white horses beneath them. *Perkūnas,* as the highest god, is at the centre of the image. The Teutons invading the west coast of Lithuania found a wooden shelter beneath an oak tree, where an eternal fire was kept burning by pagan priests. The huge oak has three hollows that contained three idols honouring what might be termed the Baltic pagan Triad. *Perkuno* occupied the most prominent niche: he was depicted as middle aged, with a solemn ruddy face, a black beard, arrows in his hand, and a flaming crown upon his head. The permanently burning fire served to signify him (Grunau, 1875: 77-78).

It is evident that the attire of these gods is close to that of Renaissance style peasants' clothing. It is entirely possible that S. Grunau simply redrew the archaic sample of the flag by adapting the apparel of the characters to the style of the author's time fashion. This refers to the simultaneity between the text and illustration of the flag in S. Grunau's book and his interpretation of pagan gods as an element of then-Prussian peasant culture.

Figure 1. The parallels in representation of the Old Prussian and Lithuanian folkloric Perkūnas (flames on a head and association with horses, and blessing gesture) with the Roman Sun God and Christ in Glory, and St. Peter: 1) Videvutis' flag (medieval Prussia); 2) Perkūnas image from king's Videvutis flag; 3) tympanum The Last Judgment, Elstertrebnitz, 12th c., Saxony; 4) St. Peter, mosaic in St. Mark Basilica, 12-13th c., Venice; 5) the Prussian grave good saddle with horses image; 6) Sol in Chariot, metope from Athena temple, 4th c. BC, Troy VIII, (Altes Museum, Berlin); 7) the Roman Sun-god Sol, silver leaf disc, 3rd c., Pessinus, Bala-Hissar; 8) beehive roof decoration, 19th c., Lithuania (Dundulienė, 1988, ill. 43); monumental pillar Horses of Perkūnas by V. Kašuba, 1938, Kaunas.

The middle figure is shown en face, while the surrounding characters are turned at ¾ angle, and this measure of construction of the hierarchical superiority reflects the strong relation with the context of the time or even older Christian arts tradition. This method of portrayal is quite different from the method of frontal depicting the divine triad in the Roman period (for example see the Capitoline Triad of *Iuppiter*, *Iuno* and *Minerva*).

The most important characteristic of Perkūnas'representation on Videvutis flag contains features of Catholic and Orthodox iconic images of an enthroned Christ, which was one of the first of his images to emerge from early Christianity. In Catholic Europe this is known as *Maiestas Domini* (*Christ in Majesty* or *Christ in Glory*) (for example ; in Orthodox Christianity it is called *Pantokrator* (Greek *Παντοκράτωρ*). Both convey just one of the many names for god in Judaism. *Pantokrator* was used both for *YHWH Sabaoth* (*Lord of Hosts*) and for *El Shaddai* (*God Almighty*) in the Greek translation of the Bible. Latourette (1975: 572) argues that the enthroned Christ - *Pantocrator* iconography is a Christian adaptation of earlier representations of an enthroned *Zeus*, such as the great statue of Zeus at Olympia. The most important here is the hand gesture of "Christ Pantocrator" which is known from early Christian art and has its origins in ancient Rome, where it was known as *Traditio legis* (*Transmission of the Law*). This gesture was directly borrowed with the formulae of depiction of the enthroned Roman Emperor. This type gesture of a vertical palm with three fingers pointed to the sky and two bent downwards, is also peculiar to the iconography of some Christian saints. This gesture of the right palm raised to the chest level is more characteristic of Orthodox *Christ Pantocrator*. This is also peculiar to Catolic and Orthodox representations of St. Peter (for example *St. Peter Enthroned* statue from the 5th or 13th century in St. Peter's Basilica; St. Peter mosaic in St. Mark Basilica, 12-13th c., Venice) (Fig. 1/4).

The *Traditio Legis* type gesture is evident in Romanesque style tympanum *The Last Judgment* of Martinskirche in Elstertrebnitz (12th c., Saxony, Staatliche Kunstammlungen Dresden, SAV 2611). Here a conversion of pagan worshipers of Jupiter into Christianity possibly is depicted (Fig. 1/3). The artistic style and hierarchy of this three partial frontal composition - the turn of lateral figures to the main central person of Christ with uplifted hand in *Traditio Legis* type gesture - this is very similar to the scene of *Videvutis' flag*. The carriage wheel with eight winged cross in the left side is the attribute of "palmer" with halo. A three-leaved trident of ceraunia is also depicted next to him. He prays to the *Christ in Majesty*, who is visually interpreted as a bust of a hero/god on the Roman stepped altar.

The most important characteristic of *Perkūnas'* image on Videvutis flag it is his *Tradicio Legis* type gesture. But, on the other hand, his gesture of the left hand represents a mirror reflection of the right hand gesture characteristic of the *Tradicio Legis* tradition.

In the Baltic and other Indo-European traditions the age of gods and their respective functions related to the expression of their vitality were conventionally listed in succession from their youth and right to the old age. The calendar cycles conventionally commence with the idea of the creation of the world and the youth, and completed with the idea of the old age and death. The moon phases' hierarchy was conventionally described starting with the young-moon phase and completing with the old-moon phase. The famous Hindu triad of *Brahma, Vishnu* and *Shiva* is in a similar manner related to the function of creation, maintenance and destruction. In textual explanation of Baltic Prussian divine Triade: the young god *Patrimpas* is mentioned the first and the god of death - *Patulas* is the last. Therefore, the interpretation of the Prussian gods in Videvutis flag starting from *Patūlas*, shown in the left, does not look logical or characteristic of archaic traditions and differs from S. Grunau's textual description. That leads to a conclusion that the original image of the divine Triad must have been a mirror reflection of the later representation. This suggests mistakes made subsequently by those redrawing the original pictures based on conventional iconography (Antique, Christian or pre-Christian Baltic Prussian). Furthermore, *Perkūnas* hand is unusually expressly leaning diagonally to the right. This unique and strange interpretation of *Traditio Legis* type gesture is undoubtedly local phenomenon.

4. HORSES AND THE HEAD OF CELESTIAL GOD EMANATING FLAMES OR RAYS

The decoration with an image of a pair of horses painted below the Videvutis flag in the illustration of S. Grunau (Fug, 1/1) is closely associated with an authentic necrocult image of a pair of white horses on a saddle found in a shroud of a Prussian burial (Fig. 1/5) (Širouchovas 2011: 281). It means that the image of a pair of white horses is not accidental; it is related to the Prussian tradition of sacred visual culture. In the Baltic tradition *Perkūnas* appears riding the horses. While a pair of horses in the celestial god *Dievas* folklore sometimes is associated with the twin sons of Celestial god *Dievas*.

In Latvian folklore God's twin sons (*Dieva Deli*) saddle the horses and ride them. This mythic poetic image of horse pairs is highly popular in the decorations of roof ridges in the ethnographic architecture of Lithuania Minor. Similarly, in ancient Rome mythology a white horse is associated with Jupiter. In the late Antiquity the iconography of *Jupiter* is sometimes equalised with *Sol*, the god of the Sun. *Sol*, the male Roman god of the Sun is often depicted as riding four horses (*Sol in quadriga*), or with a pair of horses (Fig. 1/6-7).

The head of Perkūnas surrounded with flames in the Videvutis' flag (Fig. 1/2) corresponds to the Lithuanian folklore image of *Perkūnas*, who is shown as a bearded old man with flames on his head (LTR 832/38). Such images of heads in flames without a halo have not been found in Christian art. However, the origins of depicting the head of *Perkūnas* surrounded with rays can be discerned in Roman images of the Sun god *Sol*.

The decorative roof elements in a form of horse pair *lėkiai* in Lithuanian folk architecture corresponds to the images of Sol of the ancient Roman art (Fig. 1/8, 6, 7). Similar analogies may be found even in the modern Lithuanian art: Vytautas Kašuba erected in Kaunas (1938) a monumental column portraying the figure of *Perkūnas* with a pair of horses (Fig. 1/9).

The disclosed contexts of the image of *Perkūnas* imply an assumption that the image of Videvutis flag in the book by S. Grunau may be an adapted interpretation based on earlier authentic sources that are related not only to the local sacred Prussian, but also to the Antique origin of *Jupiter* and *Sol* iconography motifs.

5. THUNDER GOD'S WEAPON OF THUNDERBOLT REPRESENTED AS ZIGZAG LIGHTNING, SPIRAL, TRIDENT, AXE AND FLINT STONE

Another interesting well-known interpretation of Videvutis' flag Perkūnas comes from the work of the 19th century historian T. Narbutas (Narbutt 1835: Fig. 41). He published a rather strange image of *Perkūnas* in which the Thunder-god wields a thunderbolt of four zigzags and a spiral sceptre in his right hand and holds a loaf of bread in his half-raised left hand (Fig 2/1).

There have not been identified in the Lithuanian tradition any direct links between *Perkūnas* and bread. However, he is strongly associated with grindstones and flour milling. The association of *Perkūnas* with bread is clearly reflected in folklore images of thunder where it is caused by *Perkūnas* milling and making flour, cakes, peas or beams (LTR 763/9; 1001/493; 757/148; 828/24). Interestingly, God - *Dievas* (in the Baltic tradition specifically close to *Perkūnas*) in his heavenly realm has not only a carriage, but also stores bread leaven in the tub (LTR 038 (418), LTR 2750(356), LTR 4318(132).

The association between *Perkūnas* and bread may be uncovered analysing the Lithuanian customs. The girls are allowed to participate in the first bread making only having reached their sexual maturity, i.e. after their first periods (Šaknys 1998: 45-46) which in the mythical world outlook are indirectly associated with *Perkūnas* activities. The figurative relation between the thunder roar and menstrual blood is revealed in a Lithuanian folk song about Sun Maiden - *Aušrinė "Aušrinė was celebrating the wedding/ Perkūnas came on his horse through the gates/ Struck the green oak/ The oak's blood was dripping/ The blood sprinkled on my clothes/ The blood sprinkled on my wreath..."* (Rėza 1958, 1: Nr 62).

It is evident that the image of bread in *Perkūnas'* left hand is much closer to Lithuanian folklore tradition. However his thunderbolt in T. Narbutas' depiction is strikingly similar to Roman representations of Jupiter.

The similar double trident, (six pointed) zigzagged thunderbolt in the right hand was characteristic of the image of *Jupiter* as a rider slaying a giant snake in the latest North Antiquity in Germany (Fig. 2/6). The attributes of *Jupiter Keraunos*, who is always represented with a forked or zigzagged thunderbolt in his hand, according to A. Clark, are similar to the horns of rays *kernaims* coming out of the Hebrew God's hand according to "Prophet Habakkuk book" (Clarke 1836: III part, 956/4rd verse). The double trident in *Iovis* right hand is very clear in Roman coin of Elagabalus 219 AD (i23598). The double trident thunderbolt or triple bladed arrow was a popular attribute of Zeus (Fig. 2/4,5). The trident thunderbolt or triple arrow is characteristic of the Etruscan god *Tinia* (Fig. 2/7). Like Zeus and Jupiter, he was the supreme ruler of the sky, storms, and thunder.

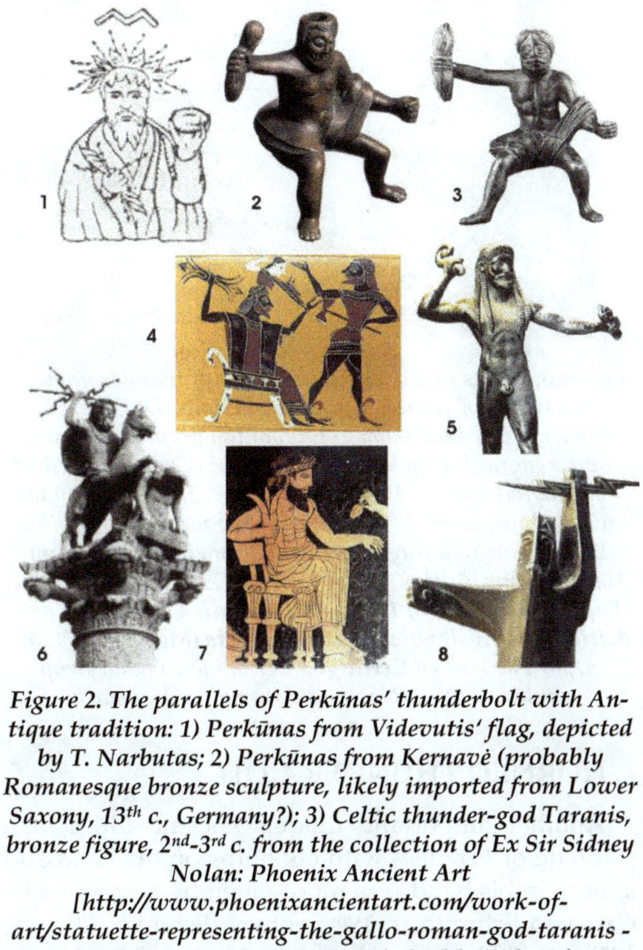

Figure 2. The parallels of Perkūnas' thunderbolt with Antique tradition: 1) Perkūnas from Videvutis' flag, depicted by T. Narbutas; 2) Perkūnas from Kernavė (probably Romanesque bronze sculpture, likely imported from Lower Saxony, 13th c., Germany?); 3) Celtic thunder-god Taranis, bronze figure, 2nd-3rd c. from the collection of Ex Sir Sidney Nolan: Phoenix Ancient Art [http://www.phoenixancientart.com/work-of-art/statuette-representing-the-gallo-roman-god-taranis - accessed 28.04.2016]; 4) Zeus with double trident form thunderbolt in the scene of The birth of Athena, the Greek black figure vase painting, 560 BC (British Museum, London); 5) Greek Zeus hurling lightning, holding a spiral and thunderbolt, archaic bronze statuette (Glyptothec Munich); 6) Roman monument of Iupiter holding zigzag ceraunos and killing Gigant, Archaeologic park in Xanten, Germany; 7) Etruscan thunder-god Tinia with three-pronged (trident-lily form) thunderbolt, vase painting, 420-400 BC; 8) monumental copper sculpture Perkūnas by J. Ruzgas, 1967, Kaunas.

In T. Narbutas' illustration, *Perkūnas* has a zigzag symbol above the head (Fig. 2/1). This corresponds with the insight of R. Wittkower that the zigzag form of the snake was equated with the thunderbolt in ancient times (Wittkower, 1939: 2 (4): 293-325; 309). Likewise, J. S. Hayes suggests an affinity between *Jove's* thunderbolt and the snake in Roman mythology (Hayes 2014: 10).

Most Lithuanian researchers believe that this image is actually the result of T. Narbutas' imagination. Though it is surprising to what extent the depicted attributes of *Perkūnas* are similar to the representations of *Jupiter* and *Zeus* in the Antique tradition. Therefore T. Narbutas' adaptive compilative interpretation has quite unique hybrid features of the Antique and later Baltic cultural elements.

Another divine weapon and archetypal symbol in the hands of Antique thunder-gods was the drill-shaped spiral arrow (Fig. 3/5; 4/1). Together with the trident thunderbolt it is characteristic of *Jupiter Dolichenus*, who is standing on a bull and also has an axe (Fig. 4/1,4) (Nash-Williams 1952). He was usually accompanied by a pair of male figures *Castores*. They are depicted either as the classical *Dioscuri* (i.e. *Castor* and *Pollux*, twin boxers leading horses) or else as *caryatids* (Merlat 1947).

The thunderbolt in the form of a drill-shaped spiral may also be linked to *Iovem Lapidem*, a stone symbol for worshipping *Jupiter* (Aulus 1927: 21; Smith 1873), and *Lapis Manalis*, a sacred rain-stone which was used in prayers, processions and water pouring dedicated to *Jupiter*. A cylindrical rain-stone was prayed to as a personification of *Jupiter Pluvius* in order to bring about rainfall (Bailey 1907: 5-6). Meteorites, fossils may also have fulfilled this role. The flint stone *Lapis Silex* or red onyx *ceraunium* also served as a token of god's axe and representation of *Jupiter*. Italian folklore believed that *ceraunia* were the remains of spent thunderbolts (Dwight 1873: 121; Sibley 2009: 119-121, 125). *Ceraunia* name was given to the Stone Age weapons (axes, arrows and spears) and was believed to be leftover matter from divine thunderbolts. In Denmark and Britain, fossilized belemnites, sea urchins and stone axes were similarly regarded as thunderbolt remains and were placed in tombs and dwellings (Sibley 2009: 26). The axe was an important symbolic attribute of *Perun* in Slavic cultures (Darkevich 1961: 94-102).

Similarly in Lithuanian folklore *Perkūnas* is believed to have another prominent attribute, i.e. belemnites, referred to as *Perkūnas' bullet* (*Perkūnkulkė*), and the stone axes of the Stone Age origin is called *Perkūnas's axe* (*Perkūno kirvis)*. The parallels with Roman traditions are evident in the 16th century account by the historian M. Strijkowski that the Lithuanian Grand Duke Gediminas built an idol for Perkūnas (*Perkun, Piorun*) made from a huge flint stone in Vilnius Castle in the 14th century. The priests striking the flint-stones in their hands created a forever lasting fire from them. This fire of oak wood was burned day and night in worship of Perkūnas (Stryjkowski 1846: 4).

In this context another retold story about the worship of miraculous hammer made of metal in Lithuania of the 15th c. becomes important. The Jesuit chronicler Jerome of Prague (1369-1440) had told about how this hammer was forged by the blacksmith *Televelis* and used by Zodiac signs in liberation of the *Sun* (Piccolomineus 1571: 418). This hammer worship is similar to the adoration of the double hammer by the Lappis and Saamis (Fig. 3/2, 5). This artefact is comparable to the thunderbolt of *Jupiter Dolichenus* in a form of hammer or axe.

The worship of the hammer of *Televelis* corresponds with the tradition of the double-edges axes/hammer's worship related to the Ruler of Thunder, and known not only in Antique arts but also in other European cultures (Baltic, German, Saami and Slavic).

A spiral or wave and fire form attributes are another common feature of Thunder-gods. The medieval bronze sculpture of so-called "Perkūnas from Kernavė", discovered in the 19th century in the environs of the ancient Lithuanian capital, holds a weapon of this form in his hand (Fig.2/2). According to the hypothesis of Russian archaeologist A. Darkevich (1963: 221-223), it is Romanesque candle stick from Lower Saxony, depicting one of four Biblical mythological characters holding the four rivers of Paradise. He also supposed this sculptural image derived from the Antique iconography of Jupiter. Therefore, his insight about the enthroned *Jupiter* iconography present in a piece of medieval Christian decorative art seems to be appropriate, because that could be acceptable for the pre-Christian Lithuanian mentality. This figurine's similarity with the image of *Perkūnas* might have prompted its import to Kernavė.

The arguments of the archaeologist did not refer to close historic analogues; however, nobody ever even attempted to challenge his assumptions. On the other hand very similar is 2nd-3rd AD bronze figure of "Gallo-Roman God Taranis" from the private collection of Ex Sir Sidney Nolan (Fig. 2/3). This fact supports presumption about the much earlier origin of "Perkūnas from Kernavė" and his stronger relation with *Jupiter/Taranis* iconography.

The Antique link of spiral thunderbolt with Jupiter, and his typological similarity to *Perkūnas* were intuitively reflected in the monumental sculpture of "Perkūnas" created in Kaunas in late 20th c. by Juozas Ruzgas who was not seriously interested in Antique symbolism. Perkūnas is holding lightning in his left hand and a spiral roll may be seen in the palm of his right hand (Fig. 2/8).
purely intuitively conveyed the archetype iconographic features of the God of Thunder that specifically corresponds to the Antique tradition.

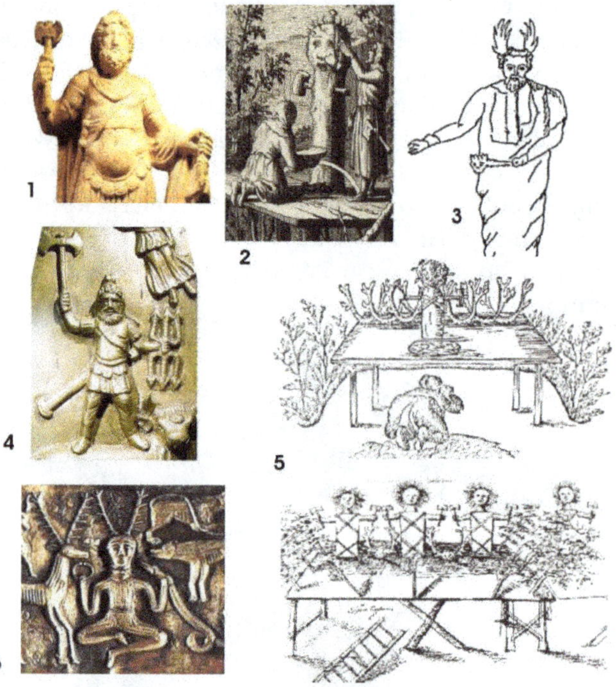

Figure 3. Horns and axes as attributes of thunder-gods: 1) The statue of Jupiter Optimus Maximus Dolichenus, Museum Carnuntinum; 2) Lapponian divinity Thoron, copper engraving by Bernard Picart in 1726 (as described by Schefferus in 1674) (Moubach, 1729: 310); 3) Perkūnas with a horned head (Shmith, (1863), Sweden); 4) Jupiter Dolichenus in a fragment of votive metal plaque from Heddernheim, 4th c. (Römermuseum Osterburken); 5) The Lapponian altars of 17th c. with installed deer horns and deities holding double axes or hammers (Malker, 1971: 56-57; 6) The horned Celtic god Cernunnos, Gundestrup cauldron, 1st c. (National Museum of Denmark, Copenhagen).

6. HORNED THUNDER-GOD

Another important unique ancient Lithuanian statuette of *Perkūnas* with elk horns on the head and a mace in his hand was represented by archaeologist Carl von Schmith in 19th century (Schmith, 2006: 4, 101) (Fig. 3/3). An analogy for such iconography can be seen in the image ascribed to *Cernunnos* – a Celtic deity, ruler of wild animals (Fig. 3/6). (Here the links with the semantic field of *Perkūnas* and *Jupiter* might be also discerned in the similarity of the name of *Cernunnos* with *Perkūnas* and a Latin *quercus* (a rock) and *ceraunios, craunia*, or a Slavic *kremen* (a flint stone).

The association between the horned elk and thunder-god (who is the ruler of rains) and may be unfolded appealing to the relict of old Lithuanian believe in swimming elk help in protection against floods: the Christian legends from Zapyškis tells that an elk with the holy picture was released to swim from Vilnius dawn the river Neris to Nemunas, in order to protect people from an anger of rivers (Kviklys, 1966: 271).

The two-sided elk horns, hammers/axes, and sun images decorating frontal altars of Thunder-god was known in Finland three centuries ago (Manker 1971) (Fig. 3/2,5). Here we see the symbolic link of horns and hammer/axe with Thunder-god. Possibly such altars represent the link between Thunder-god and Sun-god, because the association of the sun movement with running reindeer is well known in Nordic folklore.

The symbolic association of deer with the sun is evident in Lithuanian folklore also. An Advent-Christmas folk song "Here comes a nine horned deer" ("Atbėga elnias devynragis") speaks about a miracle of a rose (a symbol of Sun) burst into blossom on the Christmas morning, and about a deer with a flame burning and blacksmiths hammering on his horns (LMTA MIES, Nr. KF 3503). This discloses and represents the relation between metalsmithery, hammer and celestial bodies. The metalsmiths working on the horns of the deer are asked to make a golden cup, what is again related to the symbolism of the Sun.

So we can find a lot of analogies of a deer/elk horns link with the Sun and Thunder-god's hammering in local and neighbouring traditions.

7. CHARIOT WHEEL, EIGHT-POINTED CROSS AND PENTACLE AS SYMBOLS OF THUNDER-GOD

Quite obviously, the form of a six-winged cross/star matches the geometry of the double three-forked lightning of Jupiter.

Based on Slavic archaeological data, the reconstruction of the ancient temple of the Slavic deity *Perun* in Novgorod region was made by V. Sedov (1953). Its topographic design consists of a sacrificial fire places erected on a strictly geometrical eight-pointed cross axes (Fig. 4/6), which resembles the so-called *Pentacle of Jupiter* and the *Key of Solomon* in the Kabbalah tradition (Fig. 4/8, 7).

This type of construction, based on the eight-pointed leaf star also has similarities with geometric representations of *Perkūnas*. The interpretation of eight-pointed leaf star as symbol of sun is popular in contemporary studies on Latvian folk design (Celms 2008: 153-158). Comparative material from European Medieval culture reveals this symbol as being peculiar to alchemy. This kind of star sign is also peculiar to the Jewish tradition where it is known as *The Flower of Life* (Fig. 4/9). It also features prominently in ancient Roman and Greek traditions. The geometrical form of the *Pentacle of Jupiter* may be observed in the symbol of a wheel of *Jupiter's* chariot (Fig. 4/1-3; 1/3). This means that the eight or six-pointed star/cross and *Jupiter's* chariot wheel corresponds with the attributes of Baltic *Perkūnas/Perkons* and Slavic *Perun*. *Jupiter* is depicted as riding a *quadriga*; similarly *Perkūnas* is a celestial charioteer riding through the sky in the Baltic mythology. Thunder is the consequence of his journey through the sky. According to folk belief, it thundered when *Perkunas* was grinding wheat for bread using the two circular stone wheels of his chariot. Folkloric images of *Perkūnas* riding a chariot are popular in modern Lithuanian folk art: it is visually interpreted by the famous Lithuanian folk sculptor of the second part of 20th century - Ipolitas Užkurnys (Fig. IV/4). It is worth noting that neither folk artist had much knowledge of Antique art at the time.

Figure 4. Eight or six pointed cross, chariot wheel or pentacle as an attributes of Thunder-gods: 1) Jupiter, 3rd c., Antikensam-mlung, Kassel, Germany; 2) Jupiter riding a chariot and slaying the giants on the top of Jupiter column, Ludwigsburg; Baden-Württemberg; 3) The enthroned Jupiter column with wheel symbol, Germany; 4) Perkūnas, wooden sculpture by I. Užkurnys, 1971; 5) Wooden towel horse with an eight pointed star patterns, 19th c., Lithuania; 6) hypothetical Perun temple near Novgorod, 1st milenium, Russia; 7) Pentacles from the Greek Key of Solomon (Harley MS. 15th. C., 5596, Geomancy: 31); 8) Jupiter Pentacle of Kabbalah; 9) Flower of Life sign in Kabbalah.

8. CONCLUSIONS

The Baltic images of Perkūnas have a range of the similar specific elements known in the Antique culture.

The interface of the April the 23rd and a Thursday of the Lithuanian traditional calendar with the field of symbolism of the Thunder-god corresponds to the Greco-Roman traditions of the holidays dedicated to *Zeus* and *Jupiter*.

The most important depicted attributes of the Baltic thunder-god *Perkūnas* are connected with lightning (*Perkūnas' bullets* and *Perkūnas' axes*). Similarly the lightning of *Zeus* and *Jupiter* often is represented by a double trident zigzag, spiral bullet or double axe.

The range of the similar specific elements known in the Antique culture would include an idol for Perkūnas built by the King Gediminas of a huge piece of flint stone that is very similar to the *ceraunia* of Jupiter; and the *Traditio Legis* type gesture of *Perkūnas* and his central position in the tripartite hierarchical composition of "Videvutis flag", that conforms the Roman divine Triad scene.

The figure of *Perkūnas* in T. Narbutas's picture is holding a six-pointed zigzag lightning and a spiral bullet very characteristic of the rulers of thunder in the Antique cultures. It is also assumed that "Perkūnas from Kernavė" sitting and holding spiral in his hand is much more closer to *Jupiter* iconography and Celtic art than it was thought earlier.

The image of *Perkūnas'* head decorated with elk's horns presented by Swedish archaeologist C. Von Schmith reminds the post-Antique iconography of the Celtic *Cernunnos*. The ancient Lithuanian adoration of the hammer which was made by *Televelis* for salvation of the Sun is an analogy of the quite archetypal worship of double-edged axes/hammers that is related to the Ruler of Thunder. This fact was known not only in Antique art, but also in Baltic, German, Saami and Slavic cultures.

The Baltic representation of *Perkūnas* as a celestial rider and charioteer with white horses and with the head surrounded by flames shares many similarities with the iconography of Antique Thunder-gods and Sun-god. The modern interpretations of an eight-winged star symbolism in the Baltic art are very much in line with the Antique tradition where the star pattern was an attribute of Thunder-god linked with the wheel of his chariot. The forms of the decorative roof elements *lėkiai* correspond to the images of the God of Sun *Sol* in the ancient Roman art. The Antique analogies are abundant in the images of *Perkūnas* in Lithuanian folk art, and even in the modern art *Perkūnas* representations as well.

The entirety of the observations suggests an assumption of a much closer interactions between the Antique art and the Baltic tradition - both authentic and reconstructed or compiled.

REFERENCES

LMTA MIES – Dept. of Ethnomusicology of The Institute of Lithuanian Musicology, Lithuanian Academy of Music and Theatre.

LTR - The Institute of Lithuanian Literature and Folklore, Folklore Archyve.

Aulus, G. (1927) *The Attic Nights* (Translated by John C. Rolfe), London, Harvard University Press, vol 1: 21.

Bailey, C. (1907) *The Religion of Ancient Rome*, London: Archibald Constable & Co Ltd.

Balys, J. (1939) Griaustinis ir velnias Baltoskandinavijos kraštų tautosakoje. *Tautosakos darbai,* vol. 6: 3-236, Kaunas.

Bertram, L. (1974) *Classical Mythology and Arthurian Romance – A Study of the Sources of Crestien de Troies' "Yvain" and Other Arthurian Romances,* Geneve, Slatkine Reprints: 64-66.

Brückner, A. (1904) *Starożytna Litwa. Ludy i bogi. Szkice historyczne i mitologiczne*, Warszawa, Księgarnia Naukowa.

Celms, V. (2008) *Latvju raksts un zīmes*, Rīga, Folkloras Informācijas Centrs.

Clarke, A. (1836) *The Holy Bible Containig the Old and New Testaments: the Text Printed from the Most Correct Copies of the Present Authorized Translation Including Marginal Readings and Parallel Texts. With a Comentary and Critical Notes. Designed as a Help to the Better Understanding of the Sacred Writings*, Baltimore, John J. Harrod, agent for the book company of the Methodist Protestant Churche.

Darkevich, V.P. (1963) O tak nazyvajemom "idole Perkuna" iz Kernova. *Sovetskaya arxeologia,* No. 3: 221-223.

Darkevich, B.P. (1961) Topor kak symvol Peruna v drevnerusskom jazychestve. Sovetskaya arxeologia, No.4: 94-102.

Długossius, I. (1711) *Ioannis Dłvgossi sev Longini Canonici Qvondam Cracoviensis Historiae Polonicae... Liber XIII et vltimvs*, Lipsk, Svmptibvs Io. Lvdov. Gleditschii & Mavritii Georgii Weidmanni. Pars II saeculi XV (AD 997).

Dwight, M. A. (1949) Grecian and Roman Mythology, intr. T. Lewis, New Yor, Chicago, A. S. Barnes & co.

Gimbutas, M. (1973) Perkūnas: Perun the Thunder God of the Balts and the Slavs, *The Journal of Indo European Studies,* No 1 (4).

Greimas, A. J. (1990) *Tautos atminties beieškant: Apie dievus ir žmones*, Chicago, A. Mackaus knygų leidimo fondas.

Grunau, S. (1875) *Preussische Chronik: Im auftrage des Vereins für die Geschichte der Provinz Preussen*, herausgegeben von Dr. M. Perlbach, Band 1, Leipzig, Verlag von Duncker & Humblot.

Harley MS. (15th c.) 5596, Geomancy (manuscript, British Library).

Hayes, J. S. (2014) Jupiter's Legacy: The Symbol of the Eagle and Thunderbolt in Antiquity and Their Appropriationby Revolutionary America and Nazi Germany, *Vassar College Digital Window @Vassar, Senior Capstone Projects*, Paper 26: 1-39. [http://digitalwindow.vassar.edu/cgi/viewcontent.cgi?article=1260&context=senior_capstone - accesed 03.01.2016].

Ivanov, V.V., Toporov, V.N. (1974) Issledovanija v oblasti slovianskih drevnostej, Moskva, Nauka.

Klimka L. (1989) Birutės kalnas-astronominių stebėjimų vieta. In *Lietuvos pajūrio žemės viduramžiais*. Vilnius, Mokslas: 73-85.

Kowalik, A. (2004) *Kosmologia dawnych Slowian: Prolegomena do teologii politycznej dawnych Słowian*, Krakow, Nomos.

Kviklys B. (1966) Mūsų Lietuva, Boston, Lietuvių enciklopedijos leidykla, Vol. 3.

Latourette, K.S (1975) A History of Christianity Volume 2: Reformation to the Present (AD 1500 - AD 1975).

Laurinkienė, N. (1996) *Senovės lietuvių dievas Perkūnas: kalboje, tautosakoje, istoriniuose šaltiniuose*, Vilnius, Lietuvių literatūros ir tautosakos institutas.

Łowmiański, H. (1986) *Religia slowian i jej upadek (w. VI - XII)*, Warszawa, Państwowe wydawnictwo naukowe.

Manker, E. (1971) *Samefolkets könst*, Halmstad:Askild & Kärnekull.

Merlat, P. (1947) Jupiter Dolichenus, Sérapis et Isis. *Revue archéologique*, 6e série, vol. 27, (January-June): 15-19.

Misevičienė, V. (1972) *Lietuvių liaudies dainų katalogas: Darbo dainos. Kalendorinių apeigų dainos*, Vilnius, Vaga.

Moubach, A. (1729) *Naaukeurige beschryving der uitwendige godtsdienst-plichten, kerk-zeden en gewoontens van alle volkeren der waereldt. Deel 4.* Hermanus Uytwerf, Amsterdam/ Jan Daniel Beman, Rotterdam/ Isaak van der Kloot, Den Haag.

Narbutt, T. (1835) *Dzeje narodu litewskiego*, Wilno, Nakładem i drukem A. Marcinkowskiego, Vol. 1.

Nash-Williams, V. E. (1952) Iuppiter Dolichenus. *Greece & Rome*, Vol. 21, No 62: 72-77.

Piccolomineus, A. S. (1571) *Opera quae extr omnia...*, Basileae; (Vėlius, N. (ed.) (1996) *Baltų religijos ir mitologijos šaltiniai, vol. 1: Nuo seniausių laikų iki XV amžiaus pabaigos,* Vilnius, Mokslo ir enciklopedijų leidykla: 588-597.

Rėza, L. (1958) *Lietuvių liaudies dainos*, Vilnius, Valstybinė grožinės literatūros leidykls, Vol.1.

Rosik, S. (2000) *Interpretacja chreścijańska religini pogańskich Słowian w świetle kronik niemieckich XI-XII wieku (Thietmar, Adam z Bremy, Helmold)*, Wroclaw, Wydawnictwo Uńiversitetu Wrocławskiego.

Sedov, V. (1953) Drevnerusskoje yazycheskoje sviatylishche v Peryni. *Kratkie soobshchenia Instituta istorii materialnoj kultury*, vol. 50: 92-103.

Sibley, J. T. (2009) *The Divine Thunderbolt - Missile of the Gods*, USA, Xlibris Corporation.

Smith, W. (1873) *A Dictionary of Greek and Roman biography and mythology*, London, John Murray, printed by Spottiswoode and Co.

Stellae, E. (1518) *Erasmi Stellae Libonothani De Borvssiae Antiqvitatibvs Libri Duo*, Germaniae, Basileam.

Stryjkowski, M. (1846) *Kronika polska, litewska, źmódzka i wszystkiéj Rusi Macieja Stryjkowskiego. Wydanie nowe, będące dokładném powtórzeniem wydania pierowtnego królewieckiego z roku 1582, poprzedzone wiadomością o życiu i pismach Stryjkowskiego przez Mikolaja Malinowskiego, oraz rozprawą o latopiscach ruskich przez Daniłowicza, pomnożone przedrukiem dzieł pomniejszych Stryjkowskiego według pierwotnych wydań*, Warszawa, Nakład Gustawa Leona Glücksberga, Księgarza, Vol 1.

Šaknys, Ž. (1996) *Jaunimo brandos apeigos Lietuvoje XIX a. pabaigoje-XX a. pirmojoje pusėje*, Vilnius: Pradai.

Širouchovas, R. (2011) Nauji prūsų X-XIII a. kapinynų tyrimai vakarų baltų kultūros kontekste. *Lituanistica*, vol. 57, No. 3(85): 276-304.

Vėlius, N. (1987) *Chtoniškasis lietuvių mitologijos pasaulis: folklorinio velnio analizė,* Vilnius, Vaga.

Von Schmith, C. (1863/2006) *Necrolituanica*, Griškaitė, R., Katilius, A., Kazakevičius, V. (eds.), Vilnius, Versus Aureus.

Wittkower, R. (1939) Eagle and Serpent. A Study in the Migration of Symbols. *Journal of the Warburg Institute*, 2 (4): 293-325.

Žulkus, V. (1999) Palangiškiai pagonys. In Žulkus V. (ed.) *Palangos istorija*, Klaipėda, Libra Memelensis: 41-47.

13

THE EFFECTS OF USING ISLAMIC HISTORIOGRAPHY IN ARCHAEOLOGICAL STUDIES: THE CASE OF SASANIAN ROCK RELIEFS

Arvin Maghsoudlou, Seyyed Rasool Mousavi Haji

Faculty of Art and Architecture, University of Mazandaran, Babolsar, Iran

Corresponding author: Arvin Maghsoudlou (arvinmaq@gmail.com)

ABSTRACT

Islamic historiography has long been identified as a secondary source (behind material culture) to study late antiquity and Medieval period in the Near East and the Eastern Mediterranean cultures. But since recently, as the rate of archaeological findings in the region started to decelerate, the need to revisit these texts as primary sources of study arose. Moreover, the ability of Islamic history books to provide data on subjective aspects of the past societies, the sort of data which is probably not reflected through material culture solely, have also caused a growing interest in these evidence.

This study explores examples of Muslim historiography regarding the events depicted in Sasanian rock reliefs (224-651 A.D), and tries to show the effects of using Islamic histories in archaeological research particularly by addressing three main issues; First to show how accurate the data exploited from Islamic historiography could be, second, to what extent are Islamic texts capable of providing additional data to what material culture offers, and lastly, how these two sources of evidence (Material and texts) could be tested against each other to reveal validity of one another.

Moreover, with a careful scrutiny on the Islamic texts and rock reliefs, this study suggests that a methodical study of both textual and material data simultaneously could offer new insights into the political history of Sasanians.

KEYWORDS: Islamic historiography, Muslim historians, Historical archaeology, Sasanian rock reliefs

1. INTRODUCTION

There are 35 Sasanian rock reliefs discovered until today. Except for one, which is located in Afghanistan (Rage Bibi), all the other reliefs are located inside the political borders of today Iran. These reliefs are very significant in the study of the Sasanians because they encompass accurate data on Sasanian art, culture and religious and political ideologies. These reliefs also have been seen as the only strictly Iranian source to study Sasanian history. Amongst the sources that could potentially help get a much better understanding of these reliefs are the texts written by Muslim historians. These important texts which have already given us vast understandings on Sasanian history, often contain narratives which are most likely translations of the original Pahlavi texts written by Sasanian authors. Moreover, as both the Sasanian Empire and early Islamic dynasties included lands in the Eastern Mediterranean, Muslim narratives are also comprise important information about the history of this region.

Due to the lack of the evidence or the fact that the existing sources have not addressed the cognitive matters of the ancient Iranian societies, many questions on intellectual history of Iran in late antiquity are unanswered. Although, the number of archaeological findings in Iran is still growing, but the rate of excavations has fallen considerably and based on experience, the chances of discovering sources directly comprise the subjective data are very limited. Also, because the territories of the Sasanian Empire included lands and cultures of the Eastern Mediterranean, the study of the Sasanian rock reliefs could potentially disclose subjective aspects of the Eastern Mediterranean history and archaeology in late antiquity. Textual sources have been identified as the perfect pieces of evidence to study the ideas through history. Thus, it seems convincing for an archaeologist to revisit the Islamic textual sources which, compared to their significance have been overlooked. Historical archaeology represents practical methods to extract valuable data from historical narratives while avoiding the possible drawbacks that unsystematic usage of these sources could have on historical studies.

In this research, by choosing Sasanian rock reliefs as examples of the archaeological evidence and a selection of prominent Islamic history books as our textual data, we seek to address three main issues; First, in order to aid archaeological studies, how reliable Islamic histories could be? Second, to prove their important role in archaeological studies, in what extent are these texts capable of providing additional data, which are not reachable via material culture? And lastly, to present a more practical method for employing Islamic historiography, we aim to show how it could be possible to test the textual evidence against the material culture to prove or disprove their credibility.

In addition, we also try to show that if textual and material data were to be employed together, a broader perspective would open to archaeological studies.

The aim of this study is to show how accredited and helpful are the Islamic history books in studying the late antique Persian World and the Eastern Mediterranean. It is important to consider that we do not intend to enter the ongoing debate over the real identity of the figures in the reliefs. For our purposes, and to draw our conclusions the real identity of each figure is relatively inconsequential.

1.1 Sasanian Rock Reliefs

Sasanians (224-651 A.D) ruled a vast territory stretched from The Eastern Mediterranean to the Central Asia. Sasanian reliefs which are particularly concentrated in the region of Fars (southwestern Iran) constitute undeniable evidence of the grandeur of Iran under Sasanian (Classen 2011: 29). These reliefs yield accurate linguistic, historical, social and religious information and often they include trilingual, bilingual and monolingual inscriptions in Middle Persian, Parthian and Greek (Davaran 2010: 57). The great majority of Sasanian rock reliefs carved during the first century of Sasanian rule- between A.D. 224 and 309 (Grossman 2008: 1077-1078). Reliefs of Ardashir I, Shapur I, Bahram II, Shapur III and Khosrow II are the most important of these governmental designs.

In choosing this medium for their glorification the Sasanian rulers were perpetuating an ancient Near Eastern tradition, the origin of which is undoubtedly to be identified in the Proto-historic and Early Dynastic stelae of Mesopotamia. It was under the Akkadians (c. 2334-c. 2154 B.C) that such memorial stelae first reached monumental proportions and it was evidently in imitation of these that the first great rock sculptures were carved (Ibid: 1078). This tradition lived on through the later centuries, as Darius the great (r. 522-486 B.C), the Achaemenid ruler depicted a historical relief at Bistun. Ardashir who overthrown the Parthians (247 B.C-224 A.D) and founded the Sasanians (224-651 A.D), commemorate this event in his first carving at Firuzabad. This carving is often compared with the earlier reliefs of the Parthians. (Ibid)

The subjects of these reliefs often contain political or religious concepts. For example, one common concept of Sasanian rock reliefs is investiture. In these reliefs, the God (Usually Ahura Mazda) is bestowing the kingship to the Sasanian king. These reliefs are witnesses of how Sasanian kings sought to establish their legitimacy. Throughout the years, much research has been conducted to the rock reliefs, but there has been never-ending debates over both the identity of the figures, and the subject of the scenes. Josef Wiesehofer extends this dilemma to a third issue, as he puts it, "There have been disagreement about the purport of these works. Is there any unified objective for all the themes, or are some of them to be interpreted as idealized testimonies of historical events, others as royal figureheads with generally accepted truths?" (Wiesehofer 2001: 160)

In this research we have brought examples of Sasanian rock reliefs from Ardashir I (r. 224-241 A.D), Shapur I (r. 241-272 A.D), Bahram II (r. 276-293 A.D), Narseh (r. 293-303 A.D), and Shapur III (r. 383-388 A.D).

1.2 Textual Historical Archaeology

An important boundary in the field of archaeology runs between disciplines studying periods without writing and those studying the periods of human history which writing was invented. This boundary separates prehistoric archaeology from historical archaeology (Andren 1998: 1). In other words, the most prominent privilege of historical archaeology is the employment of texts and historical sources. Material and documentary resources represent independent lines of evidence (Leone & Potter 1988). Because historical archaeology uses textual and material evidence together, it is quite variable in its form and content and always have the freedom to define what counts as evidence and to weigh different kinds of evidence in constructing their accounts. (Hall, Silliman 2009: 42)

The question of the role of texts in archaeological work has been perceived in very different ways. Michel de Bouard (1975) believes that the starting point for archaeology is always questions formulated in history, And Jes Wienberg (1988) claims that there is no decisive difference between artifact and text, since both are at once remains from the past. Historical archaeologists have formed a sustained debate over the contributions of material evidence and textual evidence, both their proportional importance and which should dominate. Some have used material culture to confirm or test literary data and others have used textual evidence as commentary on material data (Hall. Silliman 2009: 42 & Broodbank 1993: 68). Yet other scholars have sought to use both kinds of evidence to construct a full and integrated account of lifeways, ethnicities, or even important events. (Hall, Silliman 2009: 42). Historical and archaeological evidence could be viewed as complementary features. Archaeology is able to explain aspects of a past society which have not been reflected through texts. These aspects might have been perceived as incontrovertible or unimportant through the eyes of the elite (Which writers were a part of it). The reverse is also true, Textual evidence are able to explain issues which are unattainable through archaeology. This would be due to the inability of the material culture to describe subjective matters. Moreover, while material data demonstrate information on everyday life and the working class, the literary data could be a source to study the elite and noble. Regardless of the methods that a historical archaeologist chooses in order to employ texts and material culture in the study, it is very likely to face dissonance between the story a textual narrative tells and that of a material object. Hall suggests that careful attention to the differences between these two might reveal valuable data on lives and practices that have been historically invisible heretofore (Hall 1999). Galloway believes that this dissonances must first be recognized as arising from the separate production processes for the two forms of evidence (Galloway 2009: 43)

Inquiry of literary data should be with great care. Because historical texts may be accurate, distorted, fictional or a mixture. A historical archaeologist should always be prepared to face each of these variants and as Davies (2011: 332) noted "all ancient historiographical narratives must be treated a priori as evidence of what the authors believed, wished or imaginatively reconstructed, but not as an accurate recollection of what actually transpired".

1.3 Islamic Historiography

By Islamic historiography we mean the history books which have been written in the Islamic period of the Near East, North Africa and the Eastern Mediterranean, either in Arabic or Persian. The Islamic conquests of the early seventh century ushered in a quiet exceptional period of cultural synthesis and experimentations. In the course of this synthesis, Arabic established itself as the administrative and literary language of the Islamic Near East, and forms of Arabic oral culture (poetry and storytelling) were given literary forms such as historiography (Robinson and Crone 2003: 18). One should also consider the role of the Near Eastern pre-Islamic traditions in accelerating these breakthroughs. Apparently Sasanian historiography was translated from Pahlavi into Arabic. Although none of the Pahlavi originals nor any of these translations is extant, it seems from Hamza al-Isfahani`s introduction to his *Tarikh sini muluk al-ard Wa`l-anbiya* that several Arabic versions were available to him when he composed his history in 961 A.D. (Marlow 2002: 72-73). Gibb believes that the ordering of history by the reigns of rulers seems to have been a pre-Islamic Persian historiographical tradition, imported into Arabic via translations of

Sasanian historical works (Gibb 1982: 117). These facts lead us to one probable conclusion; that the Islamic narratives about Sasanians, are very likely translations of the original Pahlavi histories written in the pre-Islam Iran. Later in this article, this hypotheses will help reach one of the objectives of the research.

There are various considerations to take when reading Islamic historiography, and regarding the present paper, we should recognize a few of them. For one, Robinson and Crone (2003: 18) believe that the early Islamic historians followed the model engineered by the people of hadith and they collected narratives rather than composing them. This would explain why Islamic historical texts have so many contradictory reports on crucial religious and political matters. Noth (1973) first presented this thesis. Likewise, he believes that early Muslim historians were collectors and not composers.

One other consideration of a great importance is the mixture of facts and fictions in Islamic historiography. Robinson points out that the Islamic historiography should be categorized as narrative history, as tradition and techniques of storytelling are frequently put to use in this method of history-telling (Robinson 2003: 13). Meisami puts it this way that "Medieval historian `s primary interest lay less in recording the facts of history than in the construction of a meaningful narrative" (Meisami 1999: 3). Although we do not own any concrete criteria for dividing facts from fictions in a historical narrative, but there are some methods to extract factual data from Islamic historiography. The most common would be to test texts with material culture. Thus, for example a discovered archaeological object could be used to verify the validity of a particular narrative.

One should consider that these texts are mediums in which authors have expressed ideas. Therefore, the credit for these evidence are not limited to the facts which could be extracted from them. Gennet and Porter believe that "there is no such thing as pure fiction and no such thing as history so rigorous that it abjures the techniques of fiction. The two regimes are not as far apart and not as homogeneous as one might suppose following the convention" (Gennet & Porter 1993: 82). Hexter also noted that "rhetoric in historiography are not merely decorative but have true Noetic value… it affects not merely the outward appearance of history, its delights and seemliness, but its inward character, its essential function, its capacity to convey knowledge of the past as it actually was" (Hexter 1967).

2. MIXTURE OF *FICTION* AND FACT

This issue may have its roots in Persian traditions, as the authors had an interest to link the great kings to fables and give them a mythological facet. The fictions could be seen as a genius product of the imperial authors who intended to give their sovereign a sacred display (Rezaee Raad 2000: 349).

However, the level of this mixture is not the same regarding different periods and rulers. For example the amount of fictions around kings like Khosrow I or Khosrow II is relatively higher than the other Sasanian monarchs. In the following lines, by bringing one example, we will try to test the authenticity of the Islamic historiography.

Equestrian victory relief located at Firuzabad is a memorial artwork regarding the Hormozdgan battle; the defeat of the Parthians and the Foundation of the Sasanian dynasty (224 A.D) (Picture 1).

Picture 1: Equestrian victory relief in Firuzabad

In this relief we could recognize three Sasanian cavalry attacking their Parthian rivals. The first two horsemen assault the rivals with a spear, while the third cavalry have thrown his rival off its horse and is wrestling with him. Archaeologists have identified the figures in this relief. They believe the first duo are Ardashir I (r. 224-241 A.D), and Artabanus V (r. 216 - 224 A.D); the first king of the Sasanians and the last king of the Parthians and the second duo are Shapur I, the oldest son of Ardashir, and the grand Vizier of Parthians. It seems that the whole relief is a summary of important events of the battlefield (Herman 1977).

Most Islamic historians tell a narrative in which, Shapur I is the offspring of Ardashir I and Artabanus V`s daughter (Look at: Dinvari 1992: 69-71; Tabari 1996: 586-589; Ibn Athir 1992: 206-210). In this story, Ardashir who defeated Artabanus would go to bed with Artabanus`s daughter without knowing who she is. Then, when they inform Ardashir of the girl`s real identity, he orders her to be killed. The girl, who at the time was pregnant of Shapur, faithfully escapes death, and the following chain of events continue in the way of other similar tales: She gives birth to Shapur, he grows and becomes an adult and then, they inform Ardashir of his existence, and the king who curiously had no other male offspring would make him his crown prince. But despite this and with reference to the Firuzabad relief we now know that one of the figures depicted in the combat relief is Shapur I the eldest son of Ardashir I.

Based on this, it would be rather troubling to accept that Shapur was born after the Hormozdgan battle.

Tabari was amongst the historians who told the story above and this was written in his volume II of *Tarikh al-Rusul wa al-Muluk* (1996). But in the first volume of the same book (Volume I: 583-584) we will find not only an apparent instance of contradictory reports in Islamic historiography, but unlike the later story, it seems that this one is analogous to the real events: "And Artabanus came, and the armies queued to start the battle, and Shapur, son of Ardashir moved toward Artabanus, he got involved in the combat, and Darbandaz, Artabanus`s vizier, was killed by Shapur, and then Ardashir attacked Artabanus and he killed him, and many of Artabanus`s troops were killed and the others escaped". When we compare this story to the reliefs, it turns out it would be very close to the accepted historical facts about this certain event. The relief in Firuzabad seems to be the image of this narrative. It also fully denies the tale which Tabari himself tells further in his book. We will revisit this relief from a new perspective further in this article.

3. ADDITIONAL DATA

Tayob (1999: 209) has shown that a methodical reading of the Islamic historiography would disclose data on aspects which are not reflected in other sources of historical information (e.g. Material culture). In this condition, texts could be seen as complementary sources to the archaeological data.

An example of this role, in this essay, is the investiture relief of Narseh in Naqshe Rostam. Archaeologists believe that unlike all the other Zoroastrian Sasanian kings who were assuming the kingship from Ahura Mazda, Narseh (r. 293-303 A.D) in this relief, depicted Anahita (Mousavi Haji and Mehrafarin 2009) as the deity who is bestowing the kingship to him (Picture 2).

Picture 2: investiture relief of Narseh in Naqshe Rostam

The question will immediately arise that on what ideological or religious basis Narseh did this design? A narrative from Al-Tha`alibi (2005: 242) could bear explanation: "Narseh had never gone to fire temple and when they asked him on this matter, he replied: praying the true god leaves me no time to worship the fire". Certainly it would be very hard to accept this narrative in this form as a historical fact, but this text, which is probably a translation of an earlier Pahlavi narrative, could demonstrate Narseh`s different religious beliefs.

One other example of the unique nature of data derived from works of Muslim historians, is the case of Bahram II (r. 276-293 A.D) reliefs. One of the unique features of Bahram II reliefs is that Mowbadan Mowbad (high priest of Sasanians), Kartir, is present in almost all of his designs. For example, he is depicted between the king and his wife in Sar Mashhad relief (Picture 3). The occasional presence of Kartir in Bahram`s reliefs raises questions about the quality of the relationship between Bahram II and his high priest. We now know that Kartir was a powerful and inspiring figure in Bahram II reign, and for example, it is believed that executing Mani was under his advice. But is there any signs of this relationship in the Islamic sources? Al-Muqaddasi (1982: 512-513) brings a narrative in his book which more resembles a fable than history, but it could bear some distorted reality; "He (Bahram II) was an angry and rough man and he did not care for his people and he humiliated them. Eventually people turned to Mowbadan Mowbad. He told them: at tomorrow morning, no one comes out of their house and no one goes to him, even if you see him standing at the door. He also ordered servants not to serve him; and if he calls for someone, they were advised not to answer him nor to obey his orders. They did so. Bahram spent his days sitting on the throne with the same temper. He did not see any of his servants and slaves and he looked at the council of vizier and authors and he did not find anyone there. He called his confidante, but heard no answer. He called the slaves, they did not answer too. He got scared and was wondering what was going on in his court. He was in his thoughts when Mowbadan Mowbad came to him. He was delighted to see him and asked about this. Mowbadan Mowbad said: you know that you are a king who is not being obeyed, your people will not take your orders unless with kindness and peace. Bahram learned, and he abandoned angriness and became benevolent and soft." (Al-Tha`alibi 2005: 239-241)

Although this narrative is probably not historically authentic, but with a closer look, it turns out to be a very important text. If we suppose that this text is an altered translation from the original Pahlavi histories, then it was probably what the Sasanian court wanted to exhibit, just like what was the intentions behind making those rock reliefs; Bahram`s court wanted to show that the king has the support of the most powerful Mowbad of the empire. This was possibly a two way trend in which Bahram was gaining religious legitimacy and Kartir, an important role in the decision making. With this picture, it is plausible to think that every rock relief was just a part of a bigger propagandistic package, which copies of official imperial stories (Which we find in Islamic historiography) were also part of it.

Picture 3: Kartir, Bahram II and his wife in Sar Mashahad

This also is applicable to the case of Firuzabad relief. The perfect analogy between the story that the relief exhibits with the one which Tabari brings in his second Volume of Tarikh *al-Rusul wa al-Muluk,* could have one plausible explanation; that the original source which Tabari referred to in his book was probably an state narrative from the Sasanian court which together with the rock relief, were meant to transmit the same idea; the state approved account of Hormozdgan battle.

4. EMPLOYING TEXTS TO CONFIRM ARCHAEOLOGICAL HYPOTHESES

Textual data can serve as a gauge of the reliability of the information that we extract from material culture. We will try to study this theory in detail with two examples from Sasanian rock reliefs.

Picture 4: Ardashir I and Shapur I in Salamas

The first one is the relief of Ardashir I and Shapur I in Salmas (Canepa 2013) (Picture 4). Archaeologists believe that in this relief, Ardashir I is depicted with his son and successor, Shapur I (r. 241-272 A.D), while both are bestowing the kingship to the king of Armenia (Mousavi and Sarfaraz 2016). This relief is politically important because it is showing that Ardashir have associated kingship with his son. To confirm this theory, we should look for evidence in textual sources. Even though the texts are not very clear on this matter, but they provide us with enough evidence: "Then he (Ardashir) returned to Al-Mada`in and sent his son, Shapur to other territories, Shapur was always victorious and he made kings obey him" (Ibn Khaldun 1984: Vol 1: 193). Al-Masudi describes how Shapur became king: "(Ardashir) ruled for 10 years and a couple of months, then he lost his interest in kingship and bestowed it to his son; Shapur" (Al-Masudi 1995: 93). Al-Ya`qubi also describes the last days of Ardashir rule: " So he (Ardashir) went to Khurasan and captured a number of cities there and after suppressing cities he chose his son, Shapur, as the next king and crowned him and called him Shah (king). Ardashir died after 14 years as a ruler" (Al-Ya`qubi 1992, Vol 1: 195). The second example is Shapur II (r. 309-379 A.D) and Shapur III Shapur III (r. 383-388 A.D). rock relief in Taq Bostan (Picture 5).

Picture 5: Shapur II and Shapur III rock relief in Taq Bostan

This relief, which is constructed in the reign of Shapur III, shows Shapur III with his father Shapur II and contains Pahlavi inscriptions which are still readable and leaves no doubt about the identity of the figures. In this unique relief the two kings are standing and facing each other, and both of them have put their hands on their long swords. After the death of Shapur II, his son, Shapur III, did not succeed him, but it was Shapur II`s brother, Ardashir II who became king. But Ardashir reign was short, and he was dismissed by Sasanian nobles and then Shapur III took the throne. Some archaeologists created hypotheses to justify the intention of Shapur III to design this unparalleled relief. Edith Porada believes that Shapur III depicted himself beside Shapur II to prove his legitimation to take the throne (Porada 1965) and (Mousavi Haji and Sarfaraz 2016). Islamic historiography provides supporting evidence: "When Ardashir (II) became king, and he settled his rule, he turned from nobles and killed many of them. Therefore, people dismissed him from the kingship in his fourth year at the throne" (Ibn Athir 1992, Vol 4: 260-261). And Shapur III became king, "He was son of Shapur II, son of Hormoz, son of Narseh. People were happy that the kingship of his father was returned to his rightful heir. He was kind to people, he ordered his agents to be nice to people." (Tabari 1996, Vol 2, 607).

Here again like what we suggested earlier about the reliefs of Bahram II and Ardashir I, if one carefully observe the text, it would seem analogous with its related rock relief. This was most probably what the court of Shapur III was trying to advertise in the state propaganda; "The kingship of Shapur II was returned to his "rightful heir", Shapur III.

5. CONCLUSION

In this article we sought to show how a methodical investigation of Islamic historiography could further our knowledge of the Sasanian Iran. In particular, we addressed three main issues regarding the effects of employing Islamic texts in archaeological studies:

- Generally, it is a challenging job to approve or reject the validity of Islamic histories, as fictions are common features of Islamic historiography, and there are no concrete criteria to separate the fictions from facts. But as we have shown in this study with a careful reading of these narratives and testing them against other sources of evidence, one would be able to prove or disprove their reliability.
- As this study suggests, Islamic history books are capable of providing additional data to what material culture offers. These additional data are mostly dealing with subjective and ideological aspects which are likely unattainable through artifacts. Consequently, employing Islamic texts in future studies could potentially extend our knowledge of the cultural and intellectual history of late antique and early Medieval Iran.
- As it has been suggested in historical archaeology, different sorts of evidence could be tested against each other to prove or disprove the credibility of one another. The Islamic historical sources are not exceptions in this manner and by bringing examples of Sasanian rock reliefs, we have shown that it could be possible to prove archaeological hypotheses with the aid of the Islamic historical narratives. Definitely, the reverse is also true and material culture could be used to verify historical hypotheses raised from the textual sources.

This study illustrated that the data extracted from Islamic historiography could be seen as archaeological evidence and therefore, employed in the archaeological studies in the region (Near East and Eastern Mediterranean). But like all other textual sources, there are certain considerations to take when reading an Islamic history book. And because these considerations could be very diverse in character in the case of Islamic historiography, extracting the needed information from these sources should be with great care.

Moreover, we tried to demonstrate that if the Islamic texts and Sasanian rock reliefs were to be looked at the same time, it would bring a new dimension in studying the political intentions of the Sasanian court. However, in this way it is necessary to fully understand how Muslim historians had gathered their histories.

Although it is advisable to employ Islamic historiography in future archaeological and historical studies of the late antique and Medieval Near East and Eastern Mediterranean, but in order to improve the prospects of employing Islamic texts in the archaeological studies, we urgently need fresh in-depth studies on the texts themselves to further our knowledge about the structure of the texts and the exact methods by which the Muslim writers gathered the historical information.

ACKNOWLEDGMENTS

I thank the anonymous referees for constructive comments.

REFERENCES

Andren, A. and n, A.A. (1998) *Between artifacts and texts: Historical archaeology in global perspective*. Plenum Publishing Co.,N.Y, United States.

Broodbank, C. (1993) *Documentary archaeology in the new world*. Edited by Mary Carolyn C. Beaudry and Francoise Audouze. Cambridge University Press, United Kingdom.

Canepa, M.P. (2013) *The Two eyes of the earth: Art and ritual of Kingship between Rome and Sasanian Iran*. University of California Press, United States.

Classen, A. (ed.) (2011) *Handbook of medieval studies: Terms - methods - trends*. Walter de Gruyter & Co, Berlin, Germany.

Davaran, F. (2010) *Continuity in Iranian identity: Resilience of a cultural heritage*. Routledge, London, United Kingdom.

Davies, P.R. (2011) 'Between text and archaeology 1', *Dead Sea Discoveries*, vol 18(3), pp. 316–338.

De Bouard, M. (1975) *Manuel D'archeologie Medievale de la Fouille a L'histoire*. Société d'édition d'enseignement supérieur, Paris, France.

Dīnawarī, Ā. Ḥanīfah (2004) *al-Akhbar al-Tiwal, Translated from Arabic to Persian by Mohammad Mehdi Damghani*. Nashre Ney, Tehran, Iran.

Edith, P. (1965) *The art of ancient Iran: Pre-Islamic cultures*. Crown Publishers, United States.

Galloway, P. (2009) *Historical archaeology*. Edited by Martin Martin and Stephen W Silliman. John Wiley & Sons, NY, United States.

Genette, G. and Porter, C. (1993) *Fiction & diction: Gaerard Genette: Translated by Catherine Porter*. Cornell University Press, United States.

Gibb, H.A.R. (1982) *Studies on the Civilization of Islam*. Princeton University Press, Princeton, United States.

Grossman, S.I. (2008) *The Cambridge history of Iran: V. 3: Seleucid, Parthian and Sasanian periods: Pt. 1*. Edited by Ehsan Yarshater. Camridge University Press, United Kingdom.

Hall, M. and Silliman, S.W. (eds.) (2009) *Historical Archaeology*. John Wiley & Sons, United States.

Herrmann, G. (1977) *The Iranian Revival*. Edited by Georgina Hermann.: Oxford University Press, Cambridge, United Kingdom

Hexter, J.H. (1967) 'The rhetoric of history', *History and Theory*, vol 6(1), p. 3.

Ibn Athir, A. (1992) *Al-Kāmil fī al-tārīkh, Translated from Arabic to Persian by Abbas Khalili, Abolghasem Halat*. Elmi, Tehran, Iran.

Ibn Khaldūn, A. ar-R. ibn M. (1984) *Tarikh, Translated from Arabic to Persian by Abdolmohammad Ayati*. Motale`at Farhangi, Tehran, Iran

Lendering, J. (no date) *Sasanian rock reliefs*. Available at: http://www.livius.org/sao-sd/sassanids/sassanid-reliefs.html (Accessed: 11 January 2016).

Leone, M.P. and Potter, P.B. (eds.) (1989) *The recovery of meaning: Historical archaeology in the eastern United States*. Smithsonian Books, United States.

M. ibn A. Al- (1982) *Ahasan al-Taqasim Fi Ma'rifat al-Aqalim, Translated from Arabic to Persian by Ali Monzavi*. Mo`alefan va Motarjeman, Tehran, Iran.

Marlow, L. and Morgan, D. (2002) *Hierarchy and egalitarianism in Islamic thought*. Cambridge University Press, Cambridge, United Kingdom.

Mas'udi, A. ibn al-Ḥusayn ibn Al- (1995) *Muruj adh-dhahab wa ma'adin al-jawhar, Translated from Arabic to Persian by Abolghasem Payandeh*. Elmi va Farhangi, Tehran, Iran.

Meisami, J.S.S. (1999) *Persian historiography to the end of the twelfth century*. Edinburgh University Press, Edinburgh, UK.

Mousavi Haji, S.R. and Mehafarin, R. (2009) 'The lady represented in Narseh's relief: Shapurdokhtak or Anahita?', *The International Journal of Humanities*, vol 16(2), pp. 75–85.

Mousavi Haji, S.R. and Sarfraz, A.K. (2016) Sasanian Rock Reliefs. SAMT, Tehran, Iran

Noth, A. (1973) 'Zum Verhaltnis von Kalifaler Zentralgewalt und Provinzen in Umayyadischer Zeit: Die "Sulh"-"Anwa"-Traditionen fur Agypten und den Iraq', *Die Welt des Islams*, vol 14(1/4), p. 150.

Rezaee Raad, M. (2000) *The Foundations of Political Thought In The Mazdaik Wisdom*. Persian Language edn. Iran: Tarh-e No.

Robinson, C.F. and Crone, P. (2003) *Islamic historiography*. Cambridge: Cambridge University Press.

Tabari, A.J.M. Al- (1996) *Ta'rikh al-rusul wa-l-muluk, Translated from Arabic to Persian by Abolghasem Payandeh*. Asatir, Tehran, Iran.

Tayob, A.I. (1999) 'Ṭabarī on the companions of the prophet: Moral and political contours in Islamic historical writing', *Journal of the American Oriental Society*, vol 119(2), p. 203.

Tha'ālibī, A.M. Al- (2005) *Ghurar akhbar muluk al-furs, Translated from Arabic to Persian by Mahmoud Hedayat*. Asatir, Tehran, Iran.

Wienberg, J. (1988) 'Metaforisk arkæologi og tingenes sprog', *Meta*, vol 1-2, pp. 30–57.

Wiesehofer, J. (2001) *Ancient Persia*. I. B.Tauris & Company, London, UK.

Ya'qubi, A. ibn A.Y. al- (1992) *Ta'rikh ibn Wadih, Translated from Arabic to Persian by Mohammad Ibrahim Ayati*. Elmi va Farhangi, Tehran, Iran.

14

NEITHER MINOANISED NOR MYCENAEANISED: KARPATHOS IN THE BRONZE AGE

Maria Mina[1], Manolis Stefanakis[2]

[1]*Hellenic Open University, Patras, Greece & University of Cyprus, 1 Panepistimiou Avenue*

2109 Aglantzia, Nicosia, Cyprus

[2]*Department of Mediterranean Studies, University of the Aegean, Rhodes, Greece*

Corresponding author: stefanakis@rhodes.aegean.gr

ABSTRACT

Karpathos forms one of the islands of the Dodecanese, situated in the southeast Aegean along the string of islands between Rhodes and Crete. It is argued in this paper that Karpathos can provide useful insights into the processes conventionally termed as 'Minoanisation' and 'Mycenaeanisation'. In the first part of the paper, we outline recent approaches to Minoanisation and Mycenaeanisation, followed in the second part by a presentation of the available data that indicate external cultural influence. In the concluding section, it is proposed that the terms Minoanisation and Mycenaeanisation cannot fully account for the processes unfolding in Bronze Age Karpathos. Our investigation of the available evidence shows that Minoan cultural influence on the island did not obliterate local traditions, nor was it fully replaced by the adoption of Mycenaean cultural practices in the final phase of the Late Bronze Age. It is proposed that the amalgamation of local, Minoan and Mycenaean cultural traits that characterised Karpathos in Late Minoan/Late Helladic III, can best be explained as a phenomenon of hybridisation, which underpinned a distinct cultural identity.

KEYWORDS: Minoanisation, Mycenaeanisation, Crete, southeast Aegean, colonisation, acculturation, hybridisation

1. INTRODUCTION

The terms Minoanisation and Mycenaeanisation have been widely employed to describe and explain the cultural affinities attested at a number of sites with material forms and practices originating on Crete and the southern mainland. In recent years, models that have been put forward for the explanation of Minoanisation, such as Davis' 'Western String' (Davis, 1979; Cherry and Davis, 1982), Wiener's 'Versailles effect' (Wiener, 1990; 2007; 2013), and Branigan's colony classifications (Branigan 1981; 1984) have come under scrutiny by a number of scholars. It is not within the scope of this paper to present a detailed account of past perspectives; rather, in the first part of the paper, we aim to outline recent approaches to the concepts of Minoanisation and Mycenaeanisation, which we consider relevant for the discussion of the available evidence from Bronze Age Karpathos.

Despite recent nuanced approaches to Minoanisation and Mycenaeanisation, as discussed later on, both terms in effect refer to forms of acculturation, whereby communities changed as a result of the external cultural influences exerted on them. Such a radical transformation should in fact mean a change of material culture and practices in their totality as they were being replaced by newly introduced ones. Unless we are referring to an intrusive foreign colony or community, then we would have difficulty pinning down cases of complete cultural reforms in the Bronze Age Aegean. Considering the axiomatic inferences of both terms with regard to acculturation, one wonders whether we should seek the use of more neutral definitions when discussing phenomena traditionally recognised as cases of Minoanisation and Mycenaeanisation; introducing terms, such as 'Minoan-influenced' or 'Crete-influenced' and 'Mycenaean-influenced' or 'mainland-influenced' respectively, may describe more accurately phenomena that do not conform to the criteria of an invasive colony.

Recent developments in theoretical archaeology have placed Minoanisation and Mycenaeanisation under scrutiny. In the last decades, the term 'acculturation', that has been traditionally employed in archaeology as a top-down approach to explain cultural transformation, has been criticised for its colonialist roots and its oversimplified explanation of cultural contact (Knapp, 2008: 54). In line with the critical review of the term acculturation, recent discourse in Aegean archaeology has deconstructed the concept of Minoanisation by exposing its imperialist origins and the central place it holds in the construction of European, national and regional identities (Hamilakis, 2002; 2006). It is now widely accepted that the term presents limitations and pitfalls both at the level of identification and interpretation. Even the associated term 'Minoan thalassocracy' is considered problematic because of its heavy imperialist load, which inhibits us from considering less than idyllic aspects of Minoanisation, including the exploitation of local communities by Cretan emigrants, their own urgency to escape maltreatment on Crete, or the emulation of Cretan customs aimed at undermining established social inequalities at a local level (Broodbank, 2004: 50-51). Tempting as it may be to do away altogether with the term Minoanisation, Broodbank (2004) warns us against it as it may generate more problems than the flaws we seek to remedy; alternatively, it is proposed by the same author that a heuristic use of the term, to refer to material culture and practices originating on Crete, creates a common ground for understanding, while avoiding generalisations of the past.

How then can we identify Minoanisation in the archaeological record? A useful definition of the phenomenon has been proposed by Broodbank, who describes it as "a modern term of sometimes deceptive convenience for a heterogeneous range of ancient material cultural traits and practices that indicate the adoption in places beyond Crete, through whatever means, of ways of doing things that originated directly or indirectly within that island" (Broodbank, 2004: 46). Practices originating on Crete may be manifested in a variety of ways, including artefact styles, production and consumption modes of material culture, cooking habits, writing and weight systems, weaving, wall-painting, architecture and use of space, funerary and ritual practices (Broodbank, 2004: 46). On this premise, it is acknowledged that there are indeed distinct cultural traits that can be tied to Crete, but in no way should we assume cultural homogeneity across the island, or an associated ethnically unified group of people (Broodbank, 2004: 51). For the purposes of this paper, therefore, the term Minoan refers to material forms and practices that derive from Crete, while acknowledging the cultural heterogeneity that characterised the island in the Bronze Age.

Intersection of two cultures is now understood as dynamic and unpredictable, involving power relations and resistance between communities (Knapp, 2008: 54-55). With reference to Minoanisation, acknowledging the active role played by agents implies that communities outside Crete were equally involved in the adoption and transmission of Minoan material forms and practices, which goes some way towards explaining the diversity of the phenomenon in question. Recently, Berg and Knappett have stressed the complexity that characterised the process of Minoanisation and the active role that sites outside Crete played in the development of the phenomenon across the Aegean (Berg, 2007: 169; Knappett, 2016: 203). Moreover, it has been proposed that the evident differential levels of Cretan influence were the result of the negotiation of various social segments of communities regarding the type and the degree to which they incorporated Minoan cultural traits (Berg, 2007: 170).

Recent approaches have also shifted the emphasis from the criteria that constitute Minoanisation, to the processes it entailed. Nikolakopoulou and Knappett, in an attempt to bridge the 'colonisation' and 'acculturation' models proposed in the past, have argued that we can benefit from both, as the first one acknowledges human mobility, while the other allows for the continuation of local traditions at Minoanised sites at a different pace and to varying degrees (Nikolakopoulou and Knappett, 2016: 104). For Nikolakopoulou and Knappett (2016: 104), mobility needs to be acknowledged as a factor behind the adoption of Minoan traits. Going beyond the presence of Minoanised artefacts, it is argued that production techniques are fundamental to detecting population mobility as the transmission of technical skills presupposes interaction among the arriving craftspeople and local communities (Broodbank, 2004: 60-62; Nikolakopoulou and Knappett, 2016: 105). Migration of craftspeople and intimate interaction with the local population are vital in the process of acquiring new skills and actually prove more effective in the transmission of technical knowledge than other modes of technology transfer (Frankel, 2000: 168). Wear pattern analysis can also be particularly telling about the adoption of innovative production practices, as demonstrated in the case of Bronze Age Cyprus where, further to the use of Anatolian type of spindle-whorls on the island, traces of wear point to similar motor habits to those performed in western Anatolia (Frankel, 2000: 172).

An alternative avenue for exploring population mobility in prehistory is the study of human physical remains of southern Aegean groups, which could encompass existing burial evidence, analyses of known skeletal material in the region, and hopefully new data recovered from burials in the future (Broodbank, 2004: 68-69). In addition, palaeodemography can allow us to assess patterns of possible population inflow, as for example in the case of the increase of farmsteads exhibiting Minoanising traits attested on Kythera and Karpathos, which contrasts to evidence known from islands further removed from Crete (Broodbank, 2004: 69; Melas, 1985; 1988a). Finally, the extent of consumption of Minoan material forms and related practices, as well as the association of Minoanising traits and the operation of trade networks, can provide insights into the degree and ways in which cultural transmission took place (Broodbank, 2004: 60-62).

Regarding Mycenaeanisation, Knappett has recently suggested that, similar to Minoanisation, it should also be considered as a series of processes that was manifested at varying degrees (Knappett, 2016: 203). As for Minoanisation, Knappett has argued that agents and their mobility played a central role in the spread of technical knowledge and skills across the Aegean (Knappett, 2016: 203-204), as illustrated by the study of J. Cutler (2016) on female textile workers producing fine fabrics intended for elite groups. On a scale that supersedes that of individuals, religious institutions must have also been involved in the process of Minoanisation and Mycenaeanisation, although artefacts and practices are likely to have taken on a distinct local character (Knappett, 2016: 204). We can conclude, therefore, that recent approaches to Minoanisation and Mycenaeanisation stress the distinct and variable combinations of adopted traits locally, which is accounted for by the dynamic choices made by the communities involved (Knappett, 2016: 204).

Concepts that are particularly useful for understanding direct or indirect cultural contact, that Minoanisation and Mycenaeanisation refer to, include transformation, assimilation and hybridisation. In the case where the initial material forms and practices developed into new widespread types, then we can argue for a process of acculturation and transformation, a process which is not symmetrical in the transmission of traits between cultures (Frankel, 2000: 182-183), whereas the loss of identity of the newcomers is recognised as an indication of assimilation. The term 'hybridisation' has been defined in archaeology as referring "(1) to the practices in which cultural differences are either naturalised or neutralised when distinct cultures meet and mix, (2) to the visible manifestation of difference, in terms of both material culture and identity, as a consequence of incorporating foreign elements" (Knapp, 2013: 268). The concept of hybridisation, pertaining to social, material or cultural mixing, which does not imply the imposition of a superior or 'pure' culture, can prove particularly useful for explaining cultural interaction, while acknowledging the active role played by social agents (Knapp, 2008: 59-60). This way we are in a better place to understand innovations in a variety of contexts, that were adopted or adapted to established practices, and how their mixing generated new forms and meanings of the objects involved (Knapp, 2008: 61). The argument for hybridisation has been put forward with reference to the migration of Anatolian migrants to Cyprus in the Bronze Age that, in the process of maintaining or adapting to the indigenous culture, generated new and distinct material culture forms (Knapp, 2008: 106). However, as a point of caution, we need to bear in mind that although bi-directional negotiation in the contact between cultures needs to be recognised, we should not assume that all areas of social or economic life were drawn into hybridisation processes, nor should we attribute apparent developments to both cultural traditions indiscriminately (Mina, 2014: 230).

2. THE EVIDENCE FROM BRONZE AGE KARPATHOS

In the present paper, we discuss together the processes of Minoanisation and Mycenaeanisation in order to explore cultural dynamics in the later Middle Bronze Age (hereafter MBA) and Late Bronze Age (hereafter LBA) in the southeast Aegean. We are aware, however, of the diverse historical circumstances at play during the Minoan and Mycenaean floruit, and of the varying degrees to which political, economic and institutional forces shaped the networks of cultural connectivity in the southeast Aegean. The discussion that follows, therefore, is intentionally Karpatho-centric in addressing specifically the ways in which local communities entered a dialectic relationship with off-island cultures, which resulted in a distinct identity.

Figure 1: View of Saria from the sea (Photograph by S. Phillips).

What picture then does the available evidence from Bronze Age Karpathos afford us regarding the processes of Minoanisation and Mycenaeanisation in the southeast Aegean? The earliest Minoan evidence on Karpathos dates as early as Middle Minoan (hereafter MM) II. In particular, by the later Middle Bronze Age, Karpathos and Saria (Figure 1), the small island to its north, exhibit traits of Minoan influence (Davis, 2001: 70) and are conventionally quoted in the bibliography as cases of Minoanisation along with Trianda on Rhodes and Kythera in the western Aegean, among others. In the paragraphs that follow, the available evidence is organised according to broad categories that have traditionally been defined as criteria for Minoanisation and Mycenaeanisation: occupation pattern and architecture, material culture and consumption practices, technological production, ideological norms and practices, and trade network connectivity.

2.1. *Occupation pattern and architecture*

In the MBA, the available evidence suggests a shift from the earlier settlement pattern of the Neolithic and the Early Bronze Age (hereafter EBA) in the form of short-lived open-air sites, hamlets or farmsteads, which were situated on promontories inland or near the coast (Melas, 1985: 156, 158). In the early MBA, a new settlement pattern emerged which reveals an abrupt increase of sites, a preference for new locations, coupled with the presence of Minoan pottery (wheelmade, conical cups, rounded bowls and basins, goblets and kylikes, craters and amphoroid craters, jugs and ewers, hole-mouthed jars, tripod cooking pots), predominantly locally made, with some imports, as diagnosed on the grounds of typology and the visual examination of clay (Melas, 1985: 91-136, 159). The case is illustrated by the fact that of the 25 settlement sites of MBA–LBA 1 date, 21 appear to be new, whereas the remaining four may have continued from the earlier period, thus presenting some maintenance of local tradition (Melas, 1985: 159). The newly founded settlements of isolated farmhouses or small communities, made up of dispersed farmhouses, conform to the pattern typical of that of Crete at the time, exhibiting a preference for elevated and well sheltered locations near the coast with a beach (for example Vonies [Figure 2], Melas, 2009; Melas, 1985: 159; Zervaki, 2006: 18-19). Moreover, of the 41 sites securely or possibly dated to MBA–LBA 1, 39 have produced definite or probable Minoan pottery on typological grounds (Melas, 1985: 159). The foundation of new sites, the change of preferred location, together with the presence of Minoan material culture forms, have led Melas to argue for a case of gradual Minoanisation, instigated by the arrival of Cretan population on the island. In fact, the abandonment of earlier promontory or high-hill inland sites is consistent, according to Melas, with the needs of Cretan merchants who used Kasos, Karpathos and Saria as necessary stopovers for their ventures to the east (Melas, 1985: 160).

Melas' argument for Minoanisation is further bolstered by evidence from Pigadia (Figure 2) in the south, which has been interpreted as a harbour town of considerable size, enjoying some level of prosperity resulting from its involvement in maritime trade. The prominent place held by Pigadia, in a landscape dotted by hamlets and farmsteads, has been recognised as an indication for proto-urbanism which developed with the impetus of trade and industrial activities, such as ceramic and textile production, partly attributed to the arrival of Cretan settlers (Melas, 1985: 161, 162). Evidence of architectural remains at Manolakakis' Land in Pigadia also exhibits Crete-derived traits, such as the presence of red-wall plaster, which is further associated with a deposit of household debris containing Minoan pottery, such as conical cups and fragments of tripod vessels and hole-mouthed jars (Melas, 1985: 29; Davis, 2001: 71; Zervaki, 2003: 60).

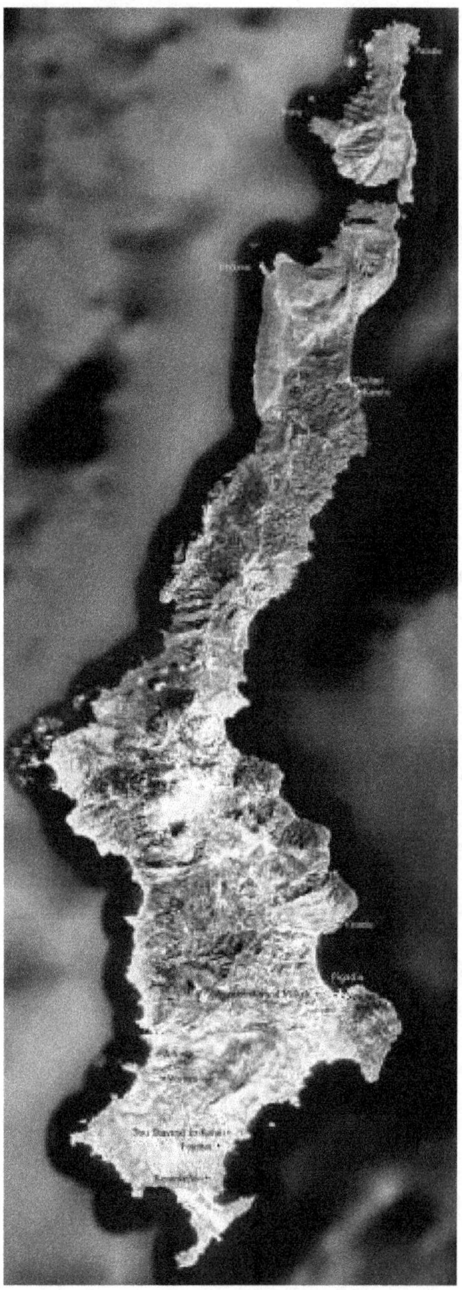

Figure 2. Satellite map of Karpathos and Saria with sites mentioned in the text (Source: Google Earth, Image Landsat/Copernicus, Data SIO, NOAA, U.S. Navy, NGA GEBCO).

Evidence dating to the later part of the LBA, indicates a shift from Minoan to a more prevalent Mycenaean cultural influence on Karpathos, although it needs to be stressed that the mainland-derived tradition formed part of the island's material culture along with Minoan and local material culture traits. The shift to predominant Mycenaean cultural influence is illustrated by six sites dating to Late Minoan (hereafter LM)/Late Helladic (hereafter LH) III which have produced Mycenaean rather than Minoan finds. They also present a drastic contrast to the earlier pattern of occupation as they are now situated on rugged promontory sites, two of which (Pigadia Acropolis, Arkasa Paliokastro; Figure 2) preserve an acropolis and remains of 'Cyclopean' walls (Hope Simpson and Lazenby, 1962: 161; Melas, 1985: 162-163). Pigadia continues to be occupied, as suggested by evidence of Mycenaean LH IIIA and IIIB date recovered from the site of Xenona (Figure 2), and a fortified citadel may have been situated at the site of the Classical acropolis of Poseidion (Hope Simpson and Lazenby, 1970: 68-69; Melas 1985: 30). A second centre of the same period must have operated at Arkasa in the south, along with sites that must have been occupied by communities using the tombs known from Vonies, Tou Stavrou to Kefali at Afiartis, and Diafani, Avlona and Makello at Pilai in the north (Figure 2; Zervaki, 2006: 25).

Habitation evidence for the later part of the LBA suggests a shift from a dispersed settlement pattern to nucleation, most probably associated with a new need for security, but it may also be linked to a population increase (Melas, 1985: 163). The trend for urbanisation of the earlier period also intensified and the decrease of the number of settlements may be symptomatic of political centralisation (Melas, 1985: 163) at a time when the cultural homogeneity of the southeast Aegean may be attributed to political unity under the control of Rhodes (Melas, 1988a: 118).

2.2. Material culture and consumption practices

Evidence from Karpathos indicates novel material culture forms already in the MBA, along the continuation of indigenous ceramic production of utilitarian forms in plain ware. Among the newly introduced material culture we need to include imported objects from Crete diagnosed on grounds of their typology and visual inspection of the clay, such as one crater, a number of stirrup jars and ritual vessels most likely to have come from Palaikastro (LM/LHIIIA1, IIIA2), and a piriform jar from Farmakokefalo (LM/LH IIIA2) (Melas 1985: 176-177,

Table 1). Furthermore, technical innovations are apparent in ceramic production resulting from the introduction of the wheel, and the improvement of manufacture methods with carefully made and adequately baked vessels through the particular choice of clay and the attainment of appropriate firing conditions (Melas 1985: 91). Other ceramic types suggest local production with parallels from east Crete, namely jugs, goblets and kylikes (LM/LH IIIA1), cups, bowls, craters, amphoroid craters, and jugs (LM/LH IIIA2) (Melas, 1985: 176-177, Table 1). The new ceramic varieties (imported and imitated) imply a change in the consumption practices relating to cooking and serving, as well as the adoption of new ritual norms employing particular vessels, modes of dress and adornment through the use of textiles, metal jewellery or weapons, also associated with particular types of social performance, as discussed later in the text.

Pottery, particularly emblematic of Minoan culture, has been recovered from Karpathos, such as conical cups, which were predominantly locally made in the periods LM/LH IIIA2 and IIIA2/IIIB, with a few imported examples diagnosed on a typological basis (cups, craters, piriform jars, stirrup jars) dated to phases IIIA1/2 and IIIA2 (Melas, 1985: 176-177, Table 1). The wheelmade vessels intended for domestic use (mainly conical cups of various types) in fact account for the greatest part of the pottery found on the island (Melas, 1985: 92, 176-177, fig. 45, Table 1). Excavations at the settlement Fournoi, in the Afiartis area, brought to light a dwelling occupied during the MM II–LM I period, which produced utilitarian pottery, but also a considerable proportion of imported Protopalatial ceramic types identified on typological grounds (MM IIB–IIIA jars, cups, cooking vessels), including two Kamares ware sherds (Melas, 2009: 61-63, 68-70; for shapes and decoration see Zachariadou, 1984: 276-277, 279-281, figs. 11-15). Other evidence comes from a number of MM–LM I pottery deposits that were unearthed in Pigadia at the Tsekou, Manolakaki and Sevdali plots in the form of red plaster fragments, a deposit of domestic debris containing Minoan pottery and a rounded cup (Melas, 1985: 29-30; Zervaki, 2003: 59 with references). In particular, the Tsekou plot yielded imports, including kylikes and kyathoi that on typological grounds could have come from Rhodes or Palaikastro, and locally made vessels exhibiting influences of LM and LH ceramic tradition of major centres (Zervaki, 2003: 64, 65).

In 1999, test pits cut by the 4th Ephoreia in the north edge of the bay of Pigadia also produced pottery that parallels varieties from Crete of MMIII/LM I date, as well as numerous conical cups (Davis, 2001: 71; Zervaki, 2003: 60). Furthermore, excavations of the MM II–LM I dwelling at Kontokephalo, termed "Minoan villa" by Melas, has revealed a considerable quantity of Minoanising local pottery of mainly LM IA date, including a great number of cups (shallow straight-sided, deep incurving, shallow rounded) (Melas and Karantzali, 2000: 287-288). Specifically, the Minoanising local pottery varieties include utilitarian vessels with light buff self-slip and rare decoration, such as cups, a hole-mouthed jar, an oval-mouthed vessel, tripod cooking vessels, shallow cooking trays and deep basins (Melas and Karantzali, 2000: 288). Vessels believed to represent imports on the basis of their typology, comprised cups or deep bowls decorated with spirals or semi-circular motifs pendant from the rim (Melas and Karantzali, 2000: 287). The distribution of Minoan-type pottery is not restricted to the south, as sites in the north of Karpathos and on the island of Saria have also yielded sherds of Minoan cups, alongside plain ware (Melas, 1985: 45). Other forms of material culture that point to the influence of Crete-derived traditions include Minoan variety loomweights recovered from sites near the coast (Davis, 2001: 71). Pigadia has also provided evidence for Minoan practices, such as wall-painting (Manolakakis'plot) and the processing of murex shells for the production of dye (Tsekou plot) (Melas, 1985: 161; Zervaki, 2003: 60).

In the final phase of the LBA, pottery recovered especially from Rhodes, Kos, as well as Karpathos, indicates the introduction of Mycenaean types, which suggests cultural influence originating from the mainland in the southeast Aegean. In particular, the LM/LH III A1 phase marks the period of Mycenaean infiltration of the south Aegean islands, corroborated by Mycenaean pottery from Rhodes (Trianda settlement), Kos (Eleona and Langada cemeteries) and Karpathos (Anemomiloi Makeli chamber tomb), indicating the importation of vessels from the mainland (Argolid) and the co-presence of Minoan and Mycenaean traditions (Mountjoy, 1993: 169). In the LM/LH III A2 phase, there was a marked Mycenaean expansion in the Aegean islands which is attested by an increase of imported and locally made Mycenaean pottery, illustrated on Karpathos by the abundant presence of Mycenaean pottery in the Anemomiloi Makeli chamber tomb (Mountjoy, 1993: 171). Evidence dating to the LM/LH III A2–B1 period reveals the coexistence of Minoan and Mycenaean imports (Melas, 1985: 162), at the same time that production of locally made varieties continued. Among the possible imports, diagnosed on typological grounds, we can include bowls from Palaikastro, piriform jars from Palaikastro and the Argolid, goblets and kylikes from the Argolid, whereas local ceramic production is represented by cups, craters or stirrup jars (Melas 1985: 176-177, Table 1). A house floor exposed at the Tsekou plot in Pigadia produced a large quantity of pottery of LM/LH III date, some of which may have been imported from either Crete or the mainland, exhibiting affinities both with vessels from Rhodes and Palaikastro on Crete (Zervaki, 2003: 64). The assemblage also includes locally made utilitarian pottery which suggests that, although the local household maintained contact with major centres of the time and imported and imitated fine ware, they nevertheless chose to cook in their own local vessels (Zervaki, 2003: 65). Mycenaean sherds are also attested in the north of the island at the site of Vrykous (Figure 3) (Hope Simpson and Lazenby, 1962: 161). Evidence dating to the LM/LH IIIB phase, shows a decrease in the distribution and numbers of Mycenaean pottery on islands of the southeast Aegean, suggesting a continuing but decreased Mycenaean presence in the region (Mountjoy, 1993: 173).

Figure 3: View of Vrykous (Photograph by S. Phillips).

Mycenaean pottery, co-occurring with the Minoan and local varieties on Karpathos, also comes from tombs. The pottery contained in a chamber tomb at the site Makeli near Pigadia, dated to the LBA IIIA phases 1 and the transitional 1/2, presents an intriguing pattern of shifting cultural influence; vessels of the III A1 phase, some of which were intended for domestic use, bear indisputable Minoan traits (Charitonidis, 1963: no. 1, Table 12β, 13α; no. 31, Table 19ε left; nos. 88, 89, Table 26ζ; no. 95, Table 26ς), whereas those dated to the III A1/2 phase (Charitonidis, 1963: no. 21, Table 17α, γ, ε; no. 29, Table 19δ; no. 30, Table 19β, ε left; no. 31, Table 19ε, 26η) exhibit close affinities to pottery from Rhodes, suggesting they may have been imported from there (Figure 4; Charitonidis, 1963: 33-36, 43-46, 49-51, 66, 67, 75). In the north, in the fertile plateau of Avlona (Figure 5), fragmentary vases and sherds, dating to LM/LH III A2 and LH III B1, were recovered from a chamber tomb during road works (Platon and Karantzali, 2003: 189). The typological traits of the pottery found at Avlona suggest that products of Minoan and Helladic workshops arrived in equal amounts on Karpathos during the later part of fourteenth and the early part of the thirteenth centuries BC, owing to the key position the island held at the intersection of sea routes of the eastern Mediterranean (Platon and Karantzali, 2003: 200).

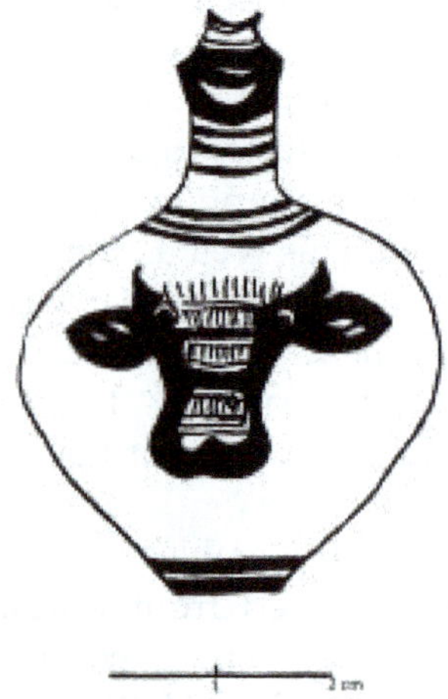

Figure 4: LH III A 1 beaked jug decorated with bucranium (drawn by M. Mina, after Charitonidis, 1963: no. 22, fig. 5).

Figure 5: View of the Avlona plateau (Photograph by S. Phillips).

LBA metal objects known from Karpathos also demonstrate close cultural affinities to their counterparts from Crete, which replaced the prevalent Anatolian and Levantine traditions of the earlier metal implements (Melas, 1985: 148-153). The assemblage of metal finds includes four swords (nos. 39, C102, C101, 1273), five spearheads (nos. 25, 37, 38, C105), a knife (no. 40) and a razor (no. C103) (Melas, 1985: 148-153). The swords parallel MM II-III examples from Mallia, Kakovatos Tholos B, Arkalokhori, Knossos, Farmakokephalo in Siteia, the spearheads parallel counterparts from Knossos and Mochlos, and the knife resembles examples from east Crete and Mallia (Melas, 1985: 151-153 with references).

The presence of weaponry (spearheads, a sword and a knife) in the chamber tomb at Anemomiloi Makeli would suggest the existence of local armed groups that may have resisted or negotiated the imposition of Mycenaean power (Charitonidis, 1963: nos. 98-105, 68-70, 75). Alternatively, the presence of weapons has been interpreted as an indication of a newcoming class of warriors, or as evidence for an associated palatial context (Zervaki, 2006: 32).

2.3. *Technological production*

It has been convincingly argued that Minoanisation entailed the adoption of technical skills that formed an integral part of Cretan cultural traditions (Nikolakopoulou and Knappett, 2016: 103). Interestingly, communities in the Dodecanese appear to have continued their local pottery traditions in the Bronze Age alongside the adoption of new, Crete-derived traits (Nikolakopoulou and Knappett, 2016: 109). This pattern is especially apparent during the Neopalatial period, which saw (1) an increase in the number of imports from Crete and imitation of pottery on a local scale, (2) the adoption of Minoan consumption practices, and (3) the use of Minoan traits and skills in pottery production (Nikolakopoulou and Knappett, 2016: 109). We should envisage that in the initial phase of ceramic technology transfer in the MBA, close contact among craftspeople was necessary (Nikolakopoulou and Knappett, 2016: 109). Such a scenario would imply that we need to recognise the geographical mobility of people across the south Aegean, but also the operation of social mobility that enabled the successful integration of craftspeople in local communities, essential for the transfer of skills (Nikolakopoulou and Knappett, 2016: 111). Technical identity, therefore, has been suggested as playing a vital role in the process of Minoanisation during the Neopalatial period in the wider southern Aegean (Nikolakopoulou and Knappett, 2016: 114-115).

Apart from the imitation of Cretan ceramic varieties and the adoption of the associated technical skills in local production, another phenomenon developed which underpinned the distinct cultural signature of Karpathos. This was achieved through the assimilation of both Minoan and subsequent Mycenaean cultural influences in ceramic production in phases III A2 (Charitonidis, 1963: no. 25, Table 17β, 46-47) and III A2/III B (six kylikes on high foot; Charitonidis, 1963: no. 35, Table 20α, no. 37, Table 20γ, 52, 53) (Charitonidis, 1963: 75; Davis, 2001: 70). This assimilation was manifested in two ways: (a) through the introduction of Minoan or Mycenaean formal and technical elements in locally made pottery, and (b) as a fusion of Minoan, Mycenaean and local traits evident in pottery production. Although it is not possible to date to detect local workshops operating on the island, the ceramic products themselves suggest that local potters assimilated both Minoan and Mycenaean stylistic innovations (Platon and Karantzali, 2003: 200). The assimilation of external cultural influence in local pottery production is betrayed by the crude composition of the clay and style of decoration on otherwise Minoan-type vessels included in the Vonies chamber tomb (Zachariadou, 1984: 294). Other ceramic finds of the same tomb exhibit Minoan influence (Figure 6; Zachariadou, 1984: LBA III A1 utilitarian vessel no. 22, fig. 4 and miniature stirrup jar no. 9, fig. 1), followed by a tradition in LBA III A1/2 and 2 phases that combined both Minoan and Mycenaean elements, the latter showing a close affinity to counterparts known from nearby Rhodes (Figure 7; Zachariadou, 1984: kylix no. 33, fig. 3; no. 46, fig. 3; miniature stirrup jars no. 12, figs. 5, 11; no. 32, figs. 5, 13; pithoid amphora with three handles no. 45, fig. 10; crater no. 24, fig. 8; 251, 253, 256, 257, 263-265, 267-268, 273-275, 276, 279, 282, 286, 293). The Mycenaean cultural influence exerted on Karpathos is evident in the stylistic traits that characterise local pottery which conforms to the classification for mainland ceramic tradition devised by Furumark (Charitonidis, 1963: 32-33, 75; Zachariadou, 1984: 250; Mountjoy, 1993: 169, 171, 173). Nevertheless, the introduction of mainland-derived cultural influence did not replace wholly earlier ceramic traditions; the existence of vessels combining Minoan and Mycenaean traditions would imply that a form of local Mycenaean-style pottery developed in the later part of the LBA that had assimilated traits of both varieties (Zachariadou, 1984: 293). Pottery from the chamber tomb at Anemomiloi Makeli also preserves traits typically associated with LM and LH potters (cup no. 70), suggesting that we are witnessing the development of a distinct local type of pottery in the LBA IIIA 1/2 and 2 phases (Charitonidis, 1963: 75; characteristic examples mentioned above; Zachariadou, 1984: 284).

Figure 6: LM III A1 two-handle amphora with spout (drawn by M. Mina, after Zachariadou, 1984: 256, no. 22 [Π6867], fig. 4).

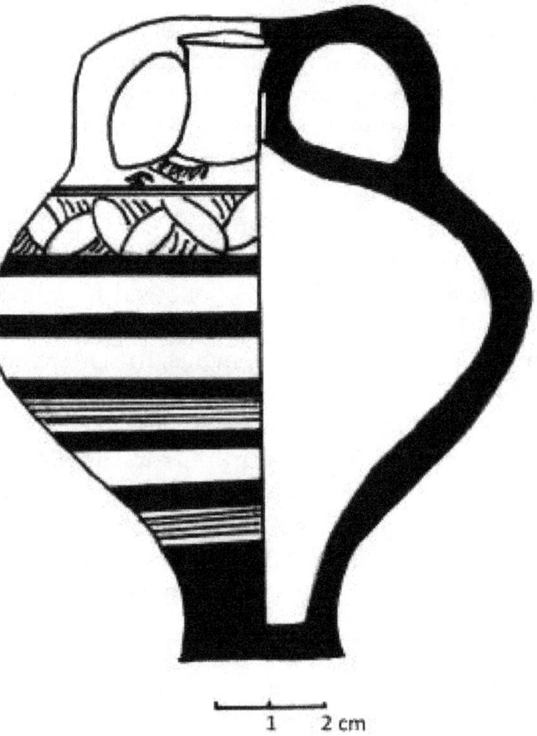

Figure 7: LM/LH III A1/2 miniature stirrup jar (drawn by M. Mina, after Zachariadou, 1984: 257, no. 32 [Π6877], fig. 5).

Textile production also suggests the influence of Crete-derived cultural tradition (at the production and possibly consumption level), as indicated by Minoan-type loomweights recovered from sites near the coast (Davis, 2001: 71). The use of Cretan-style discoid loomweights with a flattened or grooved top on LBA Karpathos suggests that the associated technical knowledge may have in fact been acquired through contact with communities already familiar with the use of the Cretan type loomweight, although direct contact should not be dismissed, at least in the earliest period (Cutler, 2016: 175). Once the necessary skills were acquired, they could then be passed on through vertical transmission from one generation to the next, eventually forming part of the local technological tradition (Cutler, 2016: 175).

2.4. Ideological norms and practices

Evidence for ritual practices from Karpathos that attest to a cultural influence from Crete or the mainland takes three forms: (a) artefacts associated with symbolic behaviour, (b) funerary architecture, and (c) mortuary rites.

Artefacts found on Karpathos that are associated with ritual behaviour include the Kamares ware sherds (Melas 2009: 68, fig. 11), the rhyta (nos. 1268, 1269), composite vessels (nos. C97, 48) and a bird vase (no. 36), the use of which must be associated with domestic and religious activities (Melas, 1985: 131-134). The imported Kamares ware sherds recovered from Fournoi settlement have led Melas to argue that perhaps they indicate the practice of Minoan worship activities which would also be consistent with the presence of rock-shelters in the surrounding area, on the west side of the small plateau (Melas, 2009: 64). The LBA rhyta, the composite vessels and the bird-vase from Karpathos, find close parallels to specimens known from Crete (Melas, 1985: 131-134). The above mentioned artefacts do conform to the general picture of Minoan cultural influence exerted on Karpathos in the LBA, although more light could be shed on the associated practices if more contextual evidence for use and deposition was available. To date, we have secure evidence only for part of the composite vessel (no. 48) and the fragment belonging to a bird-vase (no. 36) that were recovered from the Anemomiloi Makeli cemetery (Melas, 1985: 28, 52). The other composite vessel (no. C97) was unearthed from a rubbish pit of domestic type, and the two rhyta possibly came from a tomb at Kambi in the Diafani area (Melas, 1985: 29, 43, 52). The available evidence, therefore, is not sufficient to support an argument for the adoption of ritual activities performed in a way similar to that on Crete.

A new element that was introduced in the second half of the LBA is the use of chamber tombs, which first appeared during the LH II B–LH III A1 period, and continued until the LH IIIB period (Georgiadis, 2003: 47; 2015: 88). These tombs featured one chamber with a dromos and they housed multiple burials. They present, therefore, architectural features and burial customs that are consistent with the Mycenaean funerary tradition (Georgiadis, 2015: 88). Chamber tombs are known to date from seven sites across the island (Afiartis area Stavrou to Kefali, Pigadia area Diakonis' Hotel plot, Vonies, Anemomiloi Makeli area, south of the Acropolis hill at the Tsaousopoulos house, Diafani area at Kambi, further north at Avlona) (Paton, 1889: 333; Charitonidis, 1963; Zachariadou, 1984; Georgiadis, 2003: 47; Zervaki, 2006: 25). The array of grave goods contained in the burials include imported (diagnosed on typological grounds) and locally made pottery, as well as metal implements, all of which reveal a Minoan and Mycenaean influence in terms not only of consumption practices, but also of funerary norms (Paton, 1887: 449; Dawkins, 1902-03: 201; Hope Simpson and Lazenby, 1962: 161; Melas, 1985: 43-44).

The funerary practices carried out in these chamber tombs show familiarity with the Mycenaean traditions as exemplified by the use of communal burials and the dispersal of the bones inside the tomb.

Such practices may also be indicative of a form of social organisation that conforms to Mycenaean patterns that promoted the importance of family or kin connections (Zachariadou, 1984: 249), and suggest that Karpathos formed an integral part of the changes that characterised the southeast Aegean at that time (Georgiadis, 2003: 48; Georgiadis, 2015: 88). Regarding social reproduction, the wealth contained in the chamber tombs and the presence of pouring vessels and weaponry suggest social differentiation and the emergence of a ruling class of landowners that came to power through the control of trade and industrial production, consistent with Mycenaean norms (Melas, 1985: 163).

Evidence also reveals the fusion of Mycenaean, Minoan and Anatolian elements of mortuary behaviour within the same context. An eloquent example is presented by the chamber tomb at Vonies in the south, dating to the transitional LM/LH III A1/2–III B, which was accidentally found in 1978 during road works (Zachariadou, 1984: 249; Melas 1985: 39; for a conjectural ground plan and section see Melas 1985: 207, fig. 16). The tomb was roughly elliptical in plan with incurving walls, and the chamber, which was facing north, measured an area of around 4,5 square metres and a height of 1,5 metres (Melas 1985: 39). The chamber tomb included an interment with its offerings in a larnax (variation of type FS 1; dating to EM-LM III; common on Crete; parallels known from Pyrgos, Sphoungaras, Pachyammos), indicating the adoption of funerary customs from Crete (Zachariadou, 1984: 280, 249) in an otherwise Mycenaean context. If the ash layer containing bones and sherds in the same chamber tomb belonged to a cremation, we would then have evidence for a funeral rite of central Anatolian origin, coexisting with differential customs in the same tomb (Georgiadis, 2003: 48).

2.5. *Trade network connectivity*

Can Minoan and Mycenaean cultural influence evident on Karpathos be accounted for as a result of the island's involvement in trade networks of the eastern Mediterranean? We believe that we need to acknowledge the position of Kasos, Karpathos and Saria as significant nodes in the trade network that linked Crete and the mainland through the Dodecanese to Anatolia, and ultimately to Cyprus and the Levant in the MBA and LBA periods (Charitonidis, 1963; Melas, 1985: 164; Platon and Karantzali, 2003: 202; Niemeier, 2009: 17). The position of coastal settlements on Karpathos, combined with evidence for material culture forms and practices deriving from Crete or the mainland, indicate an outward-looking orientation (albeit partial) of the island from the MBA. The architectural remains of Minoan type, together with imported pottery from Crete, that were revealed in the north edge of the bay of Pigadia, led Zervaki to argue that, further to the settlement identified by Hope Simpson and Lazenby south of Eparcheio, a second coastal settlement existed during LM I at Vrontis that maintained close contact with Crete and its palatial centres (Platon and Karantzali, 2003: 201; Zervaki, 2003: 59; 2006: 20-21). A port (or ports) in the south would have operated as an intermediary stop along the eastern trade route (Zervaki, 2003: 59; 2006: 20-21). It has further been supported that the Dodecanese, with the possible inclusion of Karpathos and Kasos, was an area that was under the control of Ahhiyawa (i.e. Mycenae), either as possessions or with some sort of colonial status (Hope Simpson, 2003: 236; Niemeier, 2009: 17). The participation of Karpathos in maritime networks would have entailed direct or indirect contact with Crete and the mainland. This interaction would have partly been supported through bilateral population movement, most likely on a modest scale, and would have included seafarers, merchants, but also craftspeople.

The lack of important centres on Crete during the LH IIIC may explain the decline of Karpathos in that period, as the limited interaction between Crete and the eastern Mediterranean meant that it ceased being an important node on the eastern trade network (Zervaki, 2006: 33; Georgiadis, 2015: 88). The association between declining maritime activities in nearby areas and the subsequent marginalisation of Karpathos suggests that seafaring may have contributed considerably to the island's connectivity with the rest of the Aegean in terms of traded or exchanged goods, population mobility and the transfer of skills.

3. CONCLUSION: CULTURAL INTERFACE AND HYBRIDISATION

An inherent element in the terms Minoanisation and Mycenaeanisation is the notion that an action emanates from Minoan or Mycenaean culture proper, which impacts drastically on other communities. Linguistically the use of the suffix -ise (-isation for the noun) in fact denotes the meaning 'to become, to make or to cause' something to happen, which in our case would refer to the cultural transformation of communities outside Crete and the mainland through the process of acculturation. It may be argued, therefore, that the terms in themselves are already flawed in presupposing a one-way process of cultural interaction. As already discussed in recent discourse, we now need to acknowledge that negotiation between communities, or their individual segments, played a vital role in the integration or rejection of novel material forms and social practices. Considering a series of questions can elucidate further the processes of cultural contact between communities: (a) who was involved in the contact?, (b) how was the contact played out?, and (c) what were the consequences of the contact? The answer to the last question can illuminate whether the available evidence is consistent with acculturation and transformation (as implied by the terms Minoanisation and Mycenaeanisation), assimilation of newcomers (whereby the arriving population became fully integrated), or hybridisation, which resulted in the formation of new identities through the amalgamation of foreign (Minoan and/or Mycenaean) and local elements.

Let us now turn our attention to Bronze Age Karpathos and address the issue of who might have participated in the cultural contact between local and off-island communities. Was the contact direct or indirect? Should we envisage population mobility from Crete or the mainland? If so, who might these immigrants be and why did they move to Karpathos? Did all local communities, or all their segments, interact with the newcomers? For Melas, the phenomenon of urbanism, as well as a series of technological advances, are signs of cultural transformation (i.e. Minoanisation), which resulted from the 'Minoan penetration of static and inferior cultures' that served the Cretans' economic interests through the establishment of exchange networks (Melas, 1988a: 118). It has been postulated that the 'proto-urban' settlement of Pigadia, which exhibits Minoan traits, was the effect of acculturation of local communities by the newcomers, at the same time that Cretan immigrants maintained their cultural identity through the continuous influx of population from Crete, and locals reproduced Minoan culture through the 'Versailles effect' (Melas, 1988b: 54). Despite the idea of cultural superiority, which in fact contradicts his own critique of the colonial package associated with the concepts of Minoan colonialism and thalassocracy, Melas does acknowledge the active role played by segments of the local communities in imitating or manipulating the "culturally superior" Minoan culture in their attempts to undermine local established elites (Melas, 2009: 71). Melas and Karantzali do accept, therefore, the presence of Cretan population on Karpathos, although they attribute Minoanising material culture predominantly to aggrandising behaviour of the locals through imitation of Minoan practices (Melas and Karantzali, 2000: 290).

Recent ancient DNA research has provided evidence for genetic admixture in the prehistoric Aegean that would have been fostered by population mobility. The study carried out by Lazarides and colleagues (Lazaridis et al., 2017) has revealed that the genetic fingerprint of prehistoric Aegean population resulted from migration episodes and genetic admixture. Analysis of 19 ancient individuals, including Minoans from Crete and Mycenaeans from mainland Greece, has shown that the 'northern' and 'eastern' ancestry detected in Aegean prehistoric population is absent from Neolithic samples of the same region, suggesting that genetic admixture took place in the period between the fourth to second millennium BC, that is sometime in the second half of the Final Neolithic and the LBA (Lazaridis et al., 2017).

In order to shed light on the cultural identity of communities or individuals, however, we need to turn to archaeological evidence which can elucidate the extent to which the physical contact between population groups may or may have not resulted in cultural 'admixtures'. With reference to evidence from Bronze Age Karpathos, we would argue that the archaeological record does indicate cultural influence deriving from Crete and the mainland at different times, to varying degrees and in different domains. This is particularly apparent in the shift of occupation pattern which may be partly accounted for by off-island population mobility, but also by local communities' initiative to join the maritime network. The initial introduction of Minoan and Mycenaean elements may have resulted from small-scale population movement mainly from Crete, and later from the mainland, but also from indirect exposure to Mycenaean culture through islands, such as Crete and Rhodes. The impetus behind population mobility may have been related to seafaring activities, as Karpathos could have provided supplies and safety along the maritime route to Anatolia, Cyprus and the Levant. At the same time, the locals' involvement in the same maritime network must have also been responsible for the transfer of new material culture forms and practices. It is important to remember, however, that not all communities (or all their members) were equally affected by cultural interaction, as some population continued to live in small farming inland settlements that may have in fact changed little from the earlier Neolithic or EBA predecessors whose economic survival did not rely on maritime connections.

Returning to the earliest phase of systematic direct contact, the newly arriving population most likely did not include whole dislocated communities; rather it must have been composed of individuals and single families, among which were included seafarers, possibly as distinct from tradespeople, but also craftspeople, such as potters. These first groups may have been responsible for the systematic exposure of local communities to novel material forms, consumption practices and technological skills. It is in this context of interaction that technical identity, as suggested by Nikolakopoulou and Knappett (2016: 111, 114-115), would have emerged as a key factor underpinning cultural, social and economic roles in local communities, and the transfer of new skills. Nevertheless, the newly acquired technical knowledge and tastes for objects did not obliterate the indigenous tradition for the production of local shapes and wares that pertained to the mundane aspects of life associated with culinary practices. The perseverance of local traditions would suggest that we are not seeing the foundation of organised colonies on Karpathos, as newly arrived communities would have introduced a wholesale transfer of material culture and practices.

After the initial impact of direct cultural interaction, the continuing involvement of Karpathos in maritime trade, supported by foreign groups and local communities, may account for the maintenance and renewed introduction of Cretan and mainland-derived traits. The participation of Karpathos in the Mycenaean network of palatial centres is supported by evidence for people's mobility. The Pylos Linear B tablets include a mention to a priestess, known as *ka-ra-wi-po-ro*, i.e. the *Keybearer*, in connection with her personal name, *ka-pa-ti-ja*, which denotes ethnic designation, meaning from Karpathos (Melas, 1985: 180; Palaima, 2007: 199; Boloti, 2014: 245). Such evidence is consistent with the Mycenaean material culture and practices present on Karpathos and Rhodes (Palaima, 2007: 199), but also indicates that peoples' mobility was bidirectional and was not restricted to the domains of seafaring or technological production, nor was it gender exclusive. The establishment of a particularly distinct combination of off-island and local traits apparent in material culture forms and funerary practices in the later part of the LBA, would suggest that people arriving on Karpathos became fully assimilated and integrated by local communities.

How was the contact between communities played out? In the initial phase we should envisage the coexistence of newcoming and local population in the same settlements, or at least the maintenance of regular interaction between members of different communities. The transmission of technological skills and knowledge evident in pottery production would require the intimate contact between the craftsperson and an apprentice which may have taken place locally or even elsewhere as the operation of a maritime network would have entailed a bidirectional population mobility, albeit to varying degrees. It has been suggested that the use of the potter's wheel for the production of the iconic conical cups, amply present on Karpathos, would have required a close and long-term contact between Cretan and off-island communities (Knappett and Hilditch, 2015: 107). A direct or indirect cultural contact between communities is also implied by the adoption of similar consumption practices, such as pouring and the serving of liquids and foodstuffs, the use of weaponry, modes of attire in life and/or death (as suggested by metal implements and jewellery deposited in tombs), or mortuary rituals. With reference to the conical cups in particular, it has been proposed that their adoption marks not only the introduction of wheel-turned pottery, but also of culturally Minoan consumption practices (Knappett and Hilditch, 2015: 101, 107). Furthermore, the performance of activities associated with combat or hunting, or even styles of dress, may signify the emergence of distinct social identities at a local level that embraced, at least symbolically, a Mycenaean way of life. It is important to remind ourselves, however, that not all individuals or social groups would have adopted, in a secular or ritual context, the newly introduced material culture and practices.

Karpathos, however, does not exhibit a straightforward adoption of Mycenaean culture in the final part of the LBA. Although mainland-derived influence became prevalent, it did not obliterate the earlier Minoan or local traditions. The eclecticism evident in funerary norms, as exemplified by the chamber tomb at Vonies which combined practices derived from Crete, and possibly Anatolia, in an otherwise mainland context of funerary practice (Zachariadou, 1984: 294; Georgiadis, 2003: 48), suggests that a new distinct local identity was generated. The metaphorical cherry-picking exercised by local communities suggests that they were active in choosing to adopt, resist or adjust foreign elements to their indigenous traditions. The same point is supported by the survival of older material culture forms alongside new ones, especially evident in pottery production. We cannot be certain what the criteria for adopting new elements were, or for what reason, but the construction of social identities and performance of social roles in a public context may have held a central place in the process. This would be consistent, for example, with the use of imported fine vessels for pouring and serving, whereas local varieties were used for food-processing and cooking (Zervaki, 2003: 65). The production of textiles and the employment of metal weapons and jewellery also created a conspicuous appearance witnessed publicly in life (although this still waits to be proven), and no doubt in death. More importantly, the integration of foreign material vocabulary and novel ways of doing things within local traditions did not simply imitate Minoan or Mycenaean identities; instead it underpinned a distinct local identity founded on the amalgamation of foreign and local cultural traits.

Crucially, what were the consequences of the cultural dynamics described above? The eclectic adoption of traits and their fusion with continuing local traditions resulted in the unique cultural signature of Bronze Age Karpathos. The development of a local identity, through the selective adoption or rejection of material culture forms and practices deriving from Crete or the mainland, suggests that local communities were not passive receivers of foreign elements. Karpathos, therefore, beyond certain traits shared with their counterpart communities on Crete or the mainland, defies strict classification as either Minoanised or Mycenaeanised. We are justified in arguing, therefore, that Bronze Age Karpathos can be identified as an example of cultural hybridisation which exhibited an idiosyncratic cultural identity through the incorporation of intrusive elements that was dynamic in the sense that the intensity of its cultural components (local, Minoan, Mycenaean) shifted diachronically. In a situation of acculturation (i.e. Minoanisation or Mycenaeanisation in a strict sense of the terms), we should be able to detect a widespread adoption of new material culture forms and practices replacing older ones, which is clearly not the case. The survival of new and old, and the fusion of foreign and local, would suggest that Karpathos constituted a locus of cultural interface. The distinct local identity, that was shaped through cultural interaction, differs from those attested on various parts of Crete or the mainland and is, therefore, neither 'Minoan' nor 'Mycenaean', but other.

ACKNOWLEDGMENTS

This article has benefitted from the comments of two anonymous reviewers. Photographs no 1, 3 and 5 are courtesy of Simon Phillips.

REFERENCES

Berg, I. (2007) *Negotiating Island Identities: The Active Use of Pottery in the Middle and Late Bronze Age Cyclades* (Gorgias Dissertations 31, Classics 5). Piscataway, NJ, Gorgias Press.

Boloti, T. (2014) e-ri-ta's dress: contribution to the study of the Mycenaean priestesses' attire. In *Prehistoric, Ancient Near Eastern and Aegean Textiles and Dress: An Interdisciplinary Anthology* (Ancient Textiles Series Vol. 18), M. Harlow, C. Michel, and M.-L. Nosch (eds.), Oxford and Philadelphia, Oxbow Books, pp. 245-270.

Branigan, K. (1981) Minoan colonialism. *Annual of the British School at Athens*, Vol. 76, pp. 23-33.

Branigan, K. (1984) Minoan community colonies in the Aegean? In *The Minoan Thalassocracy: Myth and Reality, Proceedings of the Third International Symposium at the Swedish Institute in Athens, 31 May-5 June, 1982* (Acta Instituti Atheniensis Regni Sueciae, series 4°, Vol. 32), R. Hägg, and N. Marinatos (eds.), Stockholm, Svenska Institutet i Athen, pp. 49-54.

Broodbank, C. (2004) Minoanisation. *The Cambridge Classical Journal*, Vol. 50, pp. 46-91.

Charitonidis, S. (1963) Thalamoides taphos Karpathou. *Archaiologikon Deltion*, Vol. 1961/62, No. 17 A, pp. 32-76.

Cherry, J. F. and Davis, J. L. (1982) The Cyclades and the Greek mainland in LC I: the evidence of the Pottery. *American Journal of Archaeology*, Vol. 86, pp. 333-341.

Cutler, J. (2016) Fashioning identity: weaving technology, dress and cultural change in the Middle and Late Bronze Age Southern Aegean. In *Beyond Thalassocracies: Understanding Processes of Minoanisation and Mycenaeanisation in the Aegean*, E. Gorogioanni, P. Pavúk, and L. Girella (eds.), Oxford, Oxbow Books, pp. 172-185.

Davis, J. L. (1979) Minos and Dexithea: Crete and the Cyclades in the later Bronze Age. In *Papers in Cycladic Prehistory*, J. L. Davis, and J. F. Cherry (eds.), Los Angeles, Institute of Archaeology, University of California, pp. 143-157.

Davis, J. L. (2001) Review of Aegean prehistory I: the islands of the Aegean. In *Aegean Prehistory: A Review* (American Journal of Archaeology Supplement 1, Archaeological Institute of America), T. Cullen (ed.), Boston, Archaeological Institute of America, pp. 19-76.

Dawkins, R. M. (1902–3) Notes from Karpathos. *Annual of the British School at Athens*, Vol. 9, pp. 176-210.

Frankel, D. (2000) Migration and ethnicity in prehistoric Cyprus: technology as *habitus*. *European Journal of Archaeology*, Vol. 3, pp. 167-187.

Georgiadis, M. (2003) The burial landscape of Late Bronze Age III Karpathos. In *SOMA 2002, Symposium on Mediterranean Archaeology, Proceedings of the Sixth Annual Meeting of Postgraduate Researchers, University of Glasgow, Department of Archaeology, 15–17 February*, 2002 (BAR International Series 1142), A. Brysbaert, A. N. de Bruijn, E. Gibson, A. Michael, and M. Monaghan (eds.), Oxford, Archaeopress, pp. 45-52.

Georgiadis, M. (2015) The Bronze Age on Karpathos and Kythera. In *Aegis: Essays in Mediterranean Archaeology Presented to Matti Egon by the Scholars of the Greek Archaeological Committee*, Z. Theodoropoulou, and E. Doniert (eds.), Oxford, Archaeopress Publishing Ltd, 85-91.

Hamilakis, Y. (2002) What future for the "Minoan" past? Rethinking Minoan archaeology. In *Labyrinth Revisited: Rethinking 'Minoan' Archaeology*, Y. Hamilakis (ed.), Oxford, Oxbow Books, pp. 2-28.

Hamilakis, Y. (2006) The colonial, the national, and the local: legacies of the 'Minoan' past. In *Archaeology and European Modernity: Producing and Consuming the "Minoans"* (Creta Antica 7), Y. Hamilakis, and N. Momigliano (eds.), Padova, Bottega d'Erasmo, pp. 145-162.

Hope-Simpson, R. and Lazenby, J. F. (1962) Notes from the Dodecanese I. *Annual of the British School at Athens*, Vol. 57, pp. 154-169.

Hope-Simpson, R. and Lazenby, J. F. 1970. Notes from the Dodecanese II. *Annual of the British School at Athens*, Vol. 65, pp. 47-77.

Knapp, A. B. (2008) *Prehistoric and Protohistoric Cyprus: Identity, Insularity, and Connectivity*. Oxford, Oxford University Press.

Knapp, A. B. (2013) *The Archaeology of Cyprus: From Earliest Prehistory Through the Bronze Age*. Cambridge, Cambridge University Press.

Knappett, C. (2016) Minoanisation and Mycenaeanisation: a commentary. In *Beyond Thalassocracies: Understanding Processes of Minoanisation and Mycenaeanisation in the Aegean*, E. Gorogioanni, P., Pavúk, and L. Girella (eds.), Oxford, Oxbow Books, pp. 202-206.

Knappett, C. and Hilditch, J. (2015) Colonial cups? The Minoan plain handleless cup as icon and index. In *Plain and Simple, The Evolution and Significance of Plain Pottery Traditions in the Second Millennium BC Near East and East Mediterranean*, C. Glatz, London, Routledge, pp. 91-113.

Lazaridis, I., Mittnik, A., Patterson, N., Mallick, S., Rohland, N., Pfrengle, S., Furtwängler, A., Peltzer, A., Posth, C., Vasilakis, A., McGeorge, P. J. P., Konsolaki-Yannopoulou, E., Korres, G., Martlew, H., Michalodimitrakis, M., Özsait, M., Özsait, N., Papathanasiou, A., Richards, M., Roodenberg, A. S., Tzedakis, Y., Arnott, R., Fernandes, D. M., Hughey, J. R. , Lotakis, D. M., Navas, P. A., Maniatis, Y., Stamatoyannopoulos, J. A., Stewardson, K., Stockhammer, P., Pinhasi, R., Reich, D., Krause, J. and Stamatoyannopoulos, G. (2017). "Genetic origins of the Minoans and Mycenaeans". *Nature* 548, pp. 214–218. Available at: 10.1038/nature23310

Melas, E. M. (1985) *The Islands of Karpathos, Saros, and Kasos in the Neolithic and Bronze Age*. Göteborg, P. Åströms Förlag.

Melas, E. M. (1988a) The Dodecanese and W. Anatolia in prehistory: interrelationships, ethnicity and political geography. *Anatolian Studies*, Vol. 38, pp. 109-120.

Melas, E. M. (1988b) Minoans overseas: alternative models of interpretation. In *Annales d' archéologie égéenne de l' Universitè de Liège, Aegaeum* 2, R. Laffineur (ed.), Liège, Université de l'Etat à Liège, Histoire de l'art et archéologie de la Grèce antique, pp. 45-70.

Melas, E. M. 2009. The Afiartis Project: excavations at the Minoan settlement of Fournoi, Karpathos (2001–2004) – a preliminary report. In *The Minoans in the Central, Eastern and Northern Aegean – New Evidence, Acts of a Minoan Seminar, 22–23 January 2005 in collaboration with the Danish Institute at Athens and the German Archaeological Institute at Athens* (Monographs of the Danish Institute at Athens Book 8), C. F. Macdonald, E. Hallager, and W.-D Niemeier, Athens, The Danish Institute at Athens, pp. 59-72.

Melas, M. and Karantzali, E. (2000) Anaskaphi Minoikis 'vilas' stin Karpatho 1992–1994. In *Pepragmena tou H' Diethnous Synedriou Kretologikon Spoudon, Herakleio, Sept. 1995, A2. Proistoriki kai Arcaia Elliniki Periodos*, Herakleion, Etaireia Kretikon Istorikon Meleton, pp. 281-296.(in Greek)

Mina, M. (2014) Forging identities: metallurgical technology and embodied experiences in the Philia period. In *Structure, Measurement and Meaning: Insights into the Prehistory of Cyprus: Studies in Honour of David Frankel* (Studies in Mediterranean Archaeology, Vol. CXLIII), J. M. Webb (ed.), Uppsala, Åströms förlag, pp. 229-243.

Mountjoy, P. A. (1993) *Mycenaean Pottery: An Introduction*. Oxford, Oxford University Committee for Archaeology; Oxbow Books.

Niemeier, W.-D. (2009) 'Minoanisation' *versus* 'Minoan Thalassocracy' – an introduction. In *The Minoans in the Central, Eastern and Northern Aegean – New Evidence, Acts of a Minoan Seminar, 22–23 January 2005 in collaboration with the Danish Institute at Athens and the German Archaeological Institute at Athens* (Monographs of the Danish Institute at Athens Book 8), C. F., Macdonald, E. Hallager, and W.-D. Niemeier, Athens, The Danish Institute at Athens, pp. 11-29.

Nikolakopoulou, I. and Knappett, C. (2016) Mobilities in the Neopalatial southern Aegean: the case of Minoanisation. In *Human Mobility and Technological Transfer in the Prehistoric Mediterranean* (British School at Athens Studies in Greek Antiquity 1), E. Kiriatzi, and C. Knappett (eds.), Cambridge, Cambridge University Press, pp. 102-115.

Palaima, T. G. (2007) *Ilios, Tros* and *Tlos*: Continuing Problems with *to-ro, to-ro-o, to-ro-wo, to-ro-ja , wi-ro* and *a-si-wi-ja / a-si-wi-jo*. In *ΣΤΕΦΑΝΟΣ ΑΡΙΣΤΕΙΟΣ, Festschrift für Stefan Hiller zum 65, F.* Lang, C., Reinholdt, and J. Weilhartner (eds.), Geburtstag, Vienna, Phoibos, pp. 197-204.

Paton, W. R. (1887) Vases from Calymnos and Carpathos. *Journal of Hellenic Studies*, pp. 446-460.

Paton, W. R. (1889) Mycenaean tombs in Carpathos. *The Classical Review*, Vol. 3, p. 333.

Platon, L. and Karantzali, E. (2003) Nees endixeis gia tin istoria tis Minoikis parousias stin Karpatho. *Karpathiaka*, A', pp. 71-84.

Wiener, M. H. (1990) The isles of Crete? The Minoan Thalassocracy revisited. In *Thera and the Aegean World III. Proceedings of the Third International Congress, Santorini, Greece, 6–9 September, 1989,* D. A. Hardy (ed.), London, Thera & the Aegean World, pp. 128-161.

Wiener, M. H. (2007) Times change: the current state of the debate in Old World chronology. In *The Synchronisation of Civilisations in the Eastern Mediterranean in the Second Millennium B.C. – III*, M. Bietak, and E. Czerny (eds.), Vienna, Verlag der Österreichischen Akademie der Wissenschaften, pp. 25-47.

Wiener, M. H. (2013) Realities of power: the Minoan thalassocracy in historical perspective. In *AMILLA: The Quest for Excellence Studies Presented to Guenter Kopcke in Celebration of His 75th Birthday*, R. B. Koehl, Pennsylvania, INSTAP Academic Press, pp. 149-173.

Zachariadou, O. (1984) Thalamoides taphos stin Arkasa Karpathou. *Arcaiologikon Deltion*, Vol. 33 (1978*), A-Meletes*, pp. 249-294. (in Greek)

Zervaki, F. (2003) I egkatastasi sta Pigadia Karpathou kata tin Ysteri Epochi tou Chalkou: mia proti proseggisi. *Karpathiaka*, Vol. A', pp. 55-69.

Zervaki, F. (2006) I Karpathos kata ti Neolithiki periodo kai tin Epochi tou Chalkou, mesa apo ta ekthemata tou Mouseiou Karpathou. *Karpathiaka,* Vol. B', pp. 13-49 (in Greek)

15

AN OVERVIEW OF THE ECONOMIC STATUS OF THE SAFAVID ERA ON THE BASIS OF SILVER COINS, CASE STUDY: SHAH ABBAS II AND SULTAN HUSSEIN

Hassan Kohansal Vajargah

Department of History, University of Guilan, Rasht, Iran.
(kohansal@guilan.ac.ir)

ABSTRACT

Safavid era is one of the important periods in the history of Iran at the Islamic period. In the Safavid period, trade and particularly foreign trade was highly developed due to the established security on the roads. Silk was one of the goods that received attention in foreign trade cycle. As a result, a great number of merchants traveled to Iran in this period, and this led to an economic boom in this period. In the Safavid era, gold, silver, and copper coins were minted, but silver coins were used in trade exchanges. In this study, the total of 13 silver coins belonging to the mid and late Safavid era (Shah Abbas II, Shah Sultan Hussein) was analyzed using PIXE method. This study is an attempt to figure out the economic situation of the Safavid period. The amount of silver used in the coins pertaining to Shah Abbas II represents a good grade of the coins belonging to the king. In the reign of Sultan Hussein, coins were of very high grade despite the undesired political and social conditions of the country.

KEYWORDS: Safavid, coin, Shah Abbas II, Shah Sultan Hussein, PIXE

1. INTRODUCTION

Utilizing PIXE technique to study ancient coins is one of the prevailing methods for finding the chemical composition of ancient metals (Smith, 2005, 258-264). Elemental analysis of coins provides valuable information on metallurgy of minting time,metal sources, changes in monetary system, political and economic conditions (Tripathy, 2010). Ancient coins are often struck with a well- controlled alloy by a known mint with a date of issue and for most of them references can be found in ancient documents dealing about their typology and metrology (Ben Abdelouahed, 2010). The Safavid was an Iranian and Shiite dynasty who dominated in the years 1501-1722. Shah Ismail I, crowned in 1501 in Tabriz, is the founder of the Safavid dynasty and the last Safavid king is Shah Sultan Hussein who was defeated by the Afghans in 1722 and, thereby, the Safavid dynasty was abolished in practice (Asef, 1978: 20; Savory, 1984: 32). Safavid period is one of the most important historical periods of Iran because an Iranian concentered empire could rule the whole land of Iran at that time after the passage of nine hundred years from the destruction of the Sassanid empire. In the Safavid era, gold, silver, bronze, and copper coins were minted; however, silver and bronze coins were used in trade exchanges and gold coins were usually used in festivals and ceremonies (Tavernier, 1957: 806). The names and titles of kings and date and place of coinage were written on the Safavid coins and most titles were written in the form of Persian poetry from Shah Abbas II onwards. The heyday of economic boom of this dynasty pertained to Shah Abbas I when trade enormously flourished in this period. At the time of this king, silver money was plentifully found in Iran because Armenian merchants who took Iran's silk and other goods to Europe brought back some silver in addition to foreign goods. This amount of silver was consumed for minting. However, the Armenians took back gold coins from foreign countries into Iran and refused to sell them. Therefore, the amount of silver coins was reduced, as well (Falsafi, 1966: 260). At the beginning of the Safavid era, coins were not as diverse and valuable as those of the next times because of the economic and business conditions of that time. For example, half-Shahi, one-Shahi and two-Shahi coins were common at the time of Shah Ismail I and 20-Shahi coin also came into existence for the first time from the reign of Shah Tahmasb. At the time of Mohammad Khodabande, Mohammadi coins equivalent to two Shahis and three-shahi coin were minted. At the time of Shah Abbas I, gold and silver coins known as Abbasi and equivalent to four Shahis and 200 dinars, were minted for the first time. When it comes to Shah Abbas II, a wider variety of coins were minted and 10-Shahi and 5-Abbasi coins were also minted. The weight of Abbasi coins was gradually reduced in later periods (Albuquerque, 1923: 106) and Abbasid gold coinage was stopped in the late Safavid era (Chardin, 1966: 383-384). There were several mints in the Safavid period and the Safavid kings embarked on minting coins in each city in order to stabilize their political and military power. It is possible to review the political situation of the periods by investigating the name of these mints.

2. POLITICAL AND ECONOMIC SITUATION IN THE ERA OF SAFAVID SHAH ABBAS II AND SHAH SULTAN HUSSEIN

Shah Abbas II was the seventh king of the Safavid dynasty in Iran. He reigned from 1642 to 1666. At his time, culture and economy were booming again. In this period, silk trade was still flourishing, some concessions were assigned to French merchants in this period, and their businesses were created in Isfahan and Bandar Abbas (Ravandi, 1985: 155-167). During this period, trade relations with Europe were largely peaceful. He paid nonstop attention to public affairs and severely acted against corruption and irregularities in political and bureaucratic organizations and generally reformed the political situation of the Safavid era (Roemer, 1974)

Shah Sultan Hussein was the last king of the Safavid dynasty who ruled from 1694 to 1722. End of his reign marked the collapse of the Safavid lasting dynasty. Corruption of the government agency, vigilantes' placement in governmental positions, marauding cities rulers, huge lavish spending by the king, back-breaking taxes, foreign trade collapse, the king's neglect of civil and military affairs, and the like were among the direct reasons for the collapse of the Safavid dynasty within the kingdom of Shah Sultan Hussein (Panahi Soleimani, 1995: 59).

3. MATERIAL AND METHODS

3.1 Preparation of samples

The silver coins in this research have been selected, which had been found in the archaeological excavations and kept in private collections. After choosing, they have been classified. The coins belonging to Safavi Kings Shah Abbas II and were minted in a Tabriz and Ardebil and Sultan Hussein were minted in a Nakhchivan, Tbilisi, Esfahan, Yerevan, Mashhad. the silver coins were submitted to the PIXE for spectroscopy to study elemental composition.

3.2 Experimental setup

A 2 MeV proton beam with a current of 2-3 nA from AEOI, Van de Graff accelerator was used to bombard the coins. A multipurpose scattering chamber with 12 in. the beam size at the target position was 0.5 in 0.5 mm in diameter. The beam direction and the characteristic X-rays emitted from the samples were detected by an ORTEC Si (Li) detector (FWHM 170 eV at 5.9 keV) at 45°. Each target was run for 2 mm approximately. The GUPIX software was employed to analyze the obtained spectra. The vacuum obtained inside the experimental chamber was of the order of 10^{-5}Torr. The detector signal was shaped and amplified and finally, through a pulse height analysis, the energy spectrum was store and displayed in a multichannel analyzer. Standard Merck Art 2700 were used for calibration (Masjedi *et al*, 2013). 13 coins belonging to Safavid Period (Shah Abbas II, Shah Sultan Hussein) were collected for our analysis (Fig 1). The results of this study are shown in Table 1.

1

2

3

4

Table 1: Percentage concentration of present elements in analyses coins

sample	Cl	Ca	Si	S	Fe	Cu	Ag	Au	Pb	King	Mint
1	0.63	0.62	1	0.28	0.05	0.48	96.73	0.11	0.34	Sultan Hussein I	Nakhchivan
2	83	0.37	0	-	-	1.94	86.76	0.12	0.57	Sultan Hussein I	Esfahan?
3	0.45	0.45	1	0.42	-	1.1	96.29	0.15	0.57	Sultan Hussein I	Tbilisi
4	0.48	0.47	1.3	-	0.12	8.32	88.45	0.52	0.36	Sultan Hussein I	Esfahan
5	0.66	1.38	3.4	0.44	7.65	1.50	85.12	0.40	0.20	Sultan Hussein I	Esfahan
6	0.69	1.32	3.8	0.46	7.58	1.57	83.66	0.11	0.33	Sultan Hussein I	Yerevan
7	0.44	0.92	1	-	0.11	0.56	96.96	0.44	0.92	Sultan Hussein I	Mashhad
8	0.53	0/8	2.6	-	0.28	1.41	93.78	0.12	0.43	Sultan Hussein I	Nakhchivan
9	0.55	0/6	2.2	-	0.27	1.40	94.2	0.10	0.37	Sultan Hussein I	Nakhchivan
10	0.53	0.76	0.4	-	0.04	0.66	97.2	0.25	0.19	Sultan Hussein I	Mashhad
11	1.34	0.83	-	-	-	15.63	80.56	0.81	0.83	Abbas II	Tabriz
12	1.73	1.16	5.1	0.54	1.44	3.73	81.38	0.83	1.32	Abbas II	Ardebil
13	2.54	0.72	-	-	-	11.61	83.24	0.83	1.06	Abbas II	Tabriz

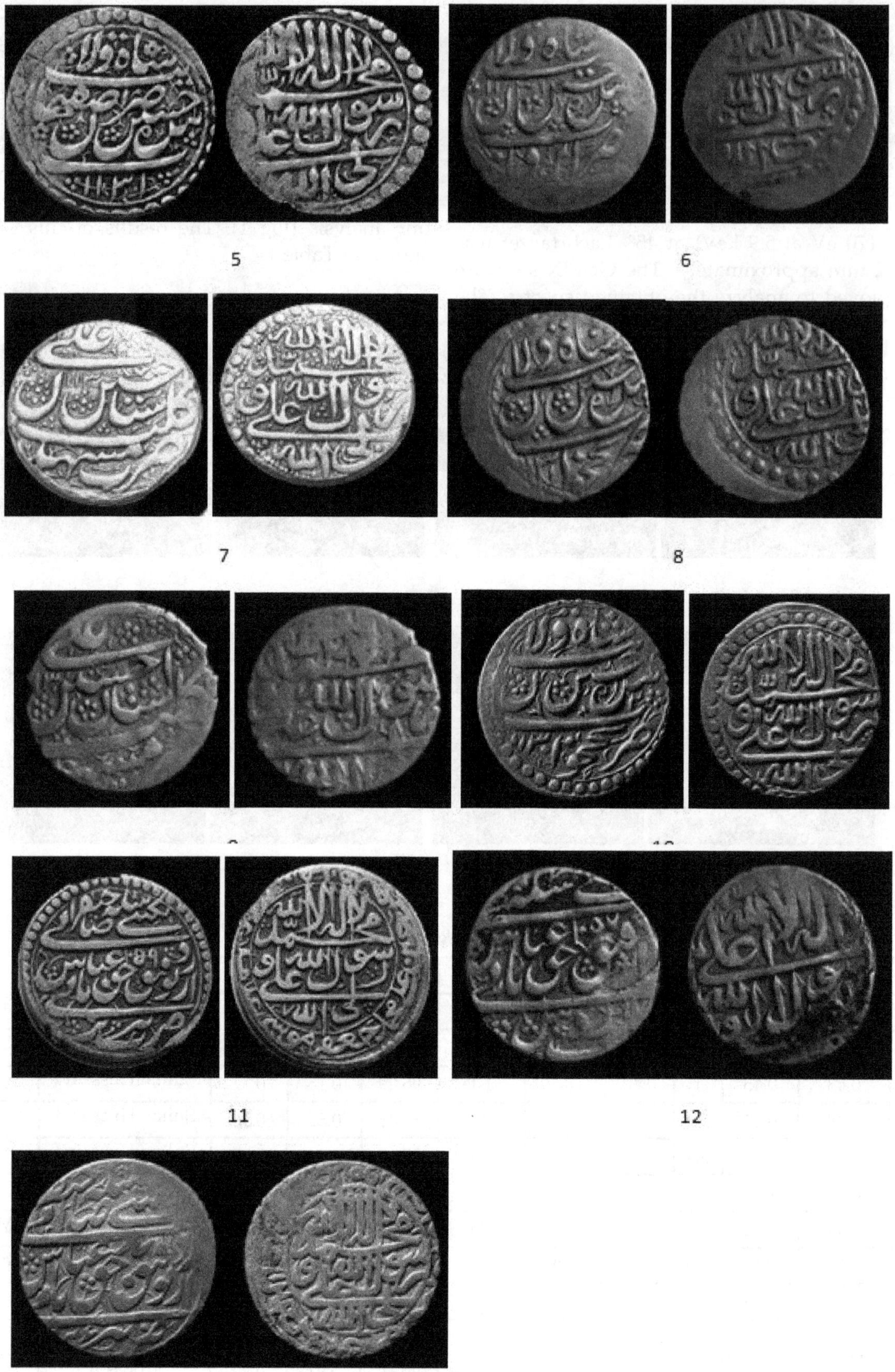

Fig 1: Both sides of silver coins used in the study.

4. RESULTS AND DISCUSSION

In this study, 13 silver coins belonging to the Safavid kings was studied using PIXE method. In these coins, the elements Ag, Pb, Au, Cu, Fe, S, Si, Ca, and Cl were identified. Among the total number off the coins, the number of 3 coins belonged to Shah Abbas II that has been minted in Tabriz and Ardebil from 1647 to 1649; and 10 coins also belonged to the Safavid Shah Sultan Hussein that have been minted in Nakhchivan, Yerevan, Tbilisi, Mashhad, and Isfahan's mints from 1717 to 1718. It is noteworthy that the silver concentration in coins pertaining to Shah Abbas II is between 80.56 and 83.24 percent (Figure 1). This shows the presence of a good grade and reflects the economic boom in this period. In these coins, there is a copper concentration of 3.73 to 15.63 percent, which is a high amount and has been added intentionally to the coins according to economic requirements (Tripathy, 2010). In addition, the existence of lead in the coins numbered 12 and 13 shows that lead and zinc ores have been used in making these coins (Uzonyi, 2000). Given that gold concentration can be a sign that silver ore has been used (Meyers, 1975), the percentage of gold in the coins belonging to Shah Abbas II shows that an ore has been used in making these coins (Figure 3). In the coins belonging to Sultan Hussein's period, there was a silver concentration of 93.78 to 97.2 percent in Nakhchivan, Tbilisi, Mashhad's mints (Figure 2), which represents the very high grade of these coins. In addition, there was a silver concentration of83.66 to 88.45 percent (Figure 2) in Isfahan and Yerevan's mints. According to the written sources of the Safavid period, social unrests and civil strife, significant decline in foreign trade, corruption have dominated the society during the kingdom of Shah Sultan Hussein and the country has not been placed in a desired situation. However, the results of analysis on the coins minted in the last years of his kingdom represent the desired grade of the coins. Since the cities where the coins were minted were important and key cities, this can be the sign of Shah Sultan Hussein's attempt towards the improvement of trade and economic situation. On the other hand, the high grade of these coins can indicate the rich silver resources in this period. Low levels of lead in the coins of Shah Sultan Hussein Safavid represent the good refining process of silver (Tripathy, 2010). The figure of gold percentage shows that the ore used in the coins numbered 4, 5, and 7 is different from that of the other coins (Fig. 4).

5. CONCLUSION

These coins had been minted in the mints active in Safavid period. According to the written sources within the kingdom of Shah Abbas II, the country has still enjoyed an acceptable socio-political situation and trade has been booming. However, in the era of Sultan Hussein, the country has been involved in social and political turmoil and it eventually fell apart by Afghans' invasion.

However, the results of analysis on the coins minted in the last years of his kingdom represent the desired grade of the coins. Since the cities where the coins were minted were important and key cities, this can be the sign of Shah Sultan Hussein's attempt towards the improvement of trade and economic situation. On the other hand, the high grade of these coins can indicate the rich silver resources in this period. Low levels of lead in the coins of Shah Sultan Hussein Safavid represent the good refining process of silver (Tripathy, 2010). The figure of gold percentage shows that the ore used in the coins numbered 4, 5, and 7 is different from that of the other coins (Figure 4). On the other hand, analysis of the coins represents a very high grade of the coins belinging to the kingdom of Sultan Hussein. This is very interesting in that the silver coins, based on which trade has been basically done, enjoyed a suitable grade despite the military and political unrests in the country. More interestingly, the coins minted in Nakhchivan, Yerevan, Tbilisi, Mashhad, and Isfahan's enjoy greater purity compared the coins minted during the kingdom of Shah Abbas II. It can be argued that the Safavids even have not stopped their efforts improve the economic situation of the country when the dynasty has been on the brink of collapse.

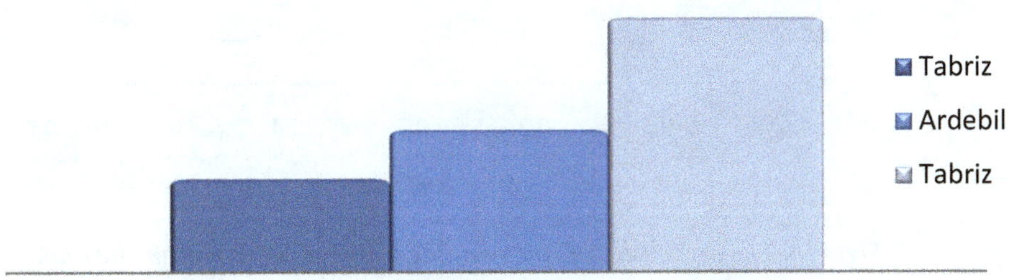

Chart 1: The percentage of Ag in the the coins of Shah Abbas II.

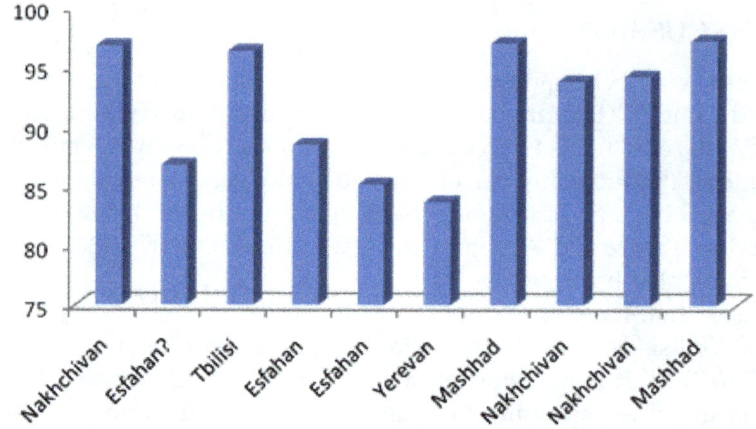

Figure 2: Mints location w.r.t. silver percentage in the coins of Sultan Hussein.

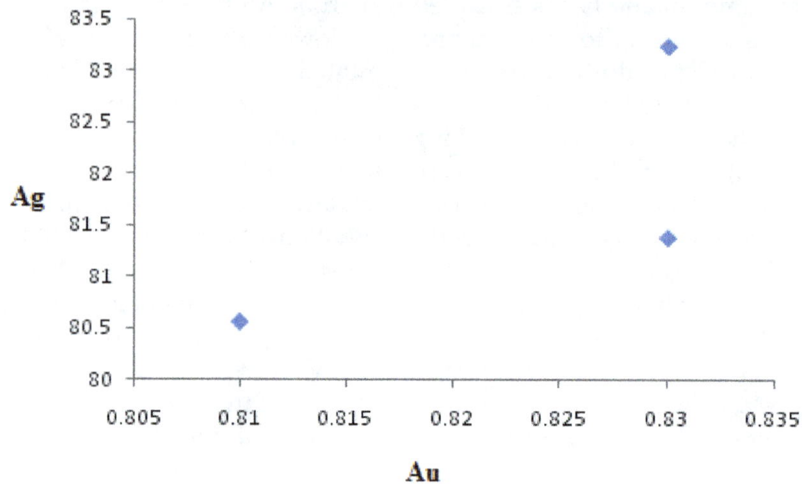

Figure 3: The percentage of Au/Ag in the Coins of Shah Abbas II

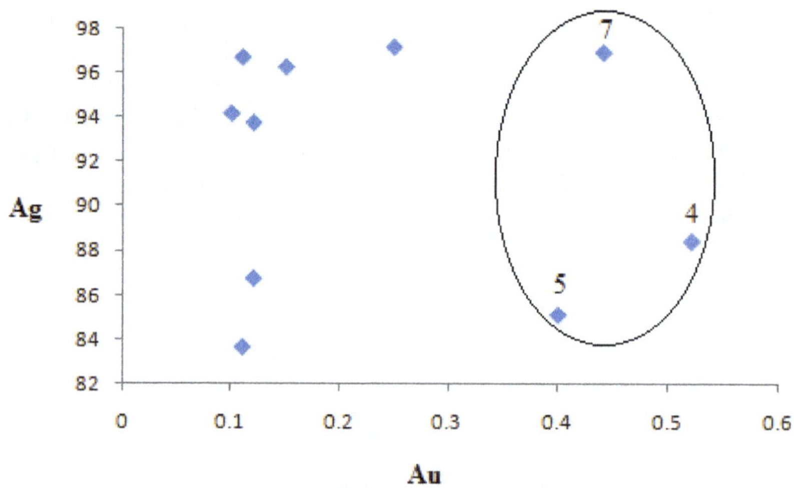

Figure 4: The percentage of Au/Ag in the Coins of Shah Sultan Hussein.

REFERENCES

Albuquerque, Affonso de. (1923) *Commentarios do grande Affonso de Albuquerque*, Coimbra : Imprensa da Universidade.

Asef, Mohamad Hashem. (1978) *Rostam Al-Tavarikh*, edited by Mohamad Moshiri.Tehran: Amir Kabir publication (In Persian).

Ben Abdeluahed, H., Gharbi. F,. Roumie. M., Baccouche. S., Ben Romdhane, K. Nsouli, B. Trabelsi, A. (2010) PIXE analysis Of medieval silver coins, *Materials Characterization* 61, pp. 59- 64.

Chardin, Jean. (1966) *Safarnameye Chardin*. Vol 4. Tranlsleted by Mohamad Abbasi. Tehran: Amir Kabir Publication (In Persian).

Falsafi, Nasrolah. (1966) *Zendegi Shah Abbas I*. Tehran: University of Tehran Publication (In Persian).

Masjedi, P., Khademi, F., Hajivaliei, M., Neyestani, J., and Mosavi Kouhpar, M. (2013) Elemental analysis of silver coins of Seljuk's' of Rome by PIXE: A case study. *Mediterranean Archaeology & Archaeometry*, Vol. 13, No 2, pp. 181-187.

Meyers, P.,Van Zelst, L., Sayre, E.V. (1975) Major and Trace Elements in Sasanian Silver, Archaeological Chemistry, Advances in Chemistry Series, 138, *American Chemical Society*, pp. 22–23.

Panahi Semnani, Mohamad Ahmad. (1995) *Shah Sultan Hussein Safavi Tragedy-e Natavani Hokomat*. Tehran: Ketabe Nemoneh Publication (In Persian).

Ravandi, Morteza. (1985) *Tarikhe Ejtemaie Iran*. Vol 5. Tehran: Moalef Publication (In Persian).

Roemer, H. R. (1974) Das fruhsafawidische Esfahan als historische Forschungsaufgabe, ZDMGCXXIV, pp. 306-310.

Savory, Roger M. (1984) *Iran Dar Asre Safavi*. Translated by Kambiz Azizi. Tehran: Nashre Sahar (In Persian).

Smith, Z. (2005) Recent development of material analysis with PIXE, *Nuclear Instrument and Methods in Physics Research B*(240), pp. 258-264.

Tavernier, Jean-Baptiste. (1957) *Safarnameye Tavernier (Tavernier Journey)*. Translated by Abou Torab Nouri. Esfahan: Sanaii (In Persian).

Tripathy, B.B., Rautry, TR., Nayak, SS., Rautray, AC. (2010) Elemental analysis of silver coins by PIXE technique, *Applied Radiation and Isotopes*, Vol 68, pp. 454-458.

Uzonyi., I.Bugoi., R.Sasianu., A.Kiss, A. Z.Constantinescu., B. (2000) Characterization of Dyrrhachium silver coins by micro-PIXE method, *Nuclear Instruments and Methods in Physics Research* Section B, Vol. 161, pp. 748-752.

16

HISTORICAL GRANARIES AT TAŞKALE (TURKEY) UNDER RISK: A GEOTECHNICAL ANALYSIS

Mustafa Korkanç[1], İsmail İnce[2], M. Ergün Hatır[3] and M. Bahadır Tosunlar[3]

[1]*Niğde Ömer Halisdemir University, Geological Engineering Department, Turkey*
[2]*Selçuk University, Geological Engineering Department, Turkey*
[3]*Selçuk University, Architecture Department, Turkey*

ABSTRACT

Granaries are bioclimatic conservation structures with various forms using in different countries. In the past, granaries have been an important structure in both the storage and conservation of products (such as like wheat, barley, oats). According to the historical documents, the Taşkale village includes the studied granaries have been using as a settlement area since the Byzantine period. Recently, rockfalls have observed on the walls of the northeastern parts of these historical granaries. The geological and geotechnical features of the rock units used in these areas were determined to understand such problems. In the field, the rocks with different colours and textural characteristics have taken into account and sampling has carried out from three different levels. Laboratory studies were conducted for determining the mineralogical, chemical, petrographic and geomechanical properties. The granaries in the region carved in the fossiliferous reefal limestones and clayey-sandy limestones. These limestone levels are more sensitive to atmospheric conditions than the overlaying travertine. The aim of the study is to provide geotechnical data to use in the conservation processes of the ancient Taşkale granaries.

KEYWORDS: Granary, rockfall, capillary zone, Taşkale, central Anatolia, geological, analysis

1. INTRODUCTION

A horreum (plural: horrea) was a type of public warehouse used during the Roman period. Although the Latin term is often used to refer granaries, the Roman horrea were used to store many other types of consumables; the giant Horrea Galbae in Rome were used not only to store grain but also olive oil, wine, foodstuffs, clothing and even marble (Richardson, 1992). The oldest granaries date back to 9500 BC and are located in the Pre-Pottery Neolithic A settlements in the Jordan Valley. First examples were generally located between other buildings. However by ~8500 BC, they were moved inside houses, and by 7500 BC storage occurred in special rooms. The first granaries were builded as 3 x 3 m on the outside and had suspended floors that protected the grain from rodents and insects and provided air circulation (Kuijt and Finlayson, 2009). Thus, granaries are bioclimatic conservation structures particularly have been used in the last 2000 years in different countries across Europe and Asia. Their natural ventilation does not require energy consumption (Ecim-Djuric and Topisirovic, 2010; Saá et al., 2011).

The surrounding region of the Taşkale granaries includes cave settlements (e.g. Manazan caves) dated back to 2-3. centuries B.C., however the region used as a settlement since the Roman period and have been been using as a village since the Seljukid period (Tapur, 2009; Asrav, 2015). The architectural structure of the studied wall including the granaries has a space used as a chapel during the Early Christianity period; however, later on, it started to be used as a mosque that called 'Taş Cami' (Stone Mosque) (Asrav, 2015). This indicates a religious continuity in the same place occupied by the different societies with different religions. Due to this long history, the granaries and the surrounding areas are under conservation as an archeological site (Tapur, 2009).

Although, there are some studies about the geology of the study area (e.g., Akarsu, 1960; Bilgiç, 2009; Blumenthal, 1956; Demirtaşlı, 1976; Demirtaşlı et al., 1973; Gökten, 1976; Koçyiğit, 1976; Pampal, 1987) there is no study that was carried on the geotechnical features of the Taşkale granaries and rock structures in the area. The historical rural landscape of Taşkale village studied by Asrav (2015). The study area is located in the Karaman region in south-central Anatolia region. In the Taşkale granary area, three lithological levels that represent different colours and engineering characteristics were investigated. Our study represents that the lower, middle and upper levels of the rock unit where the granaries carved show markedly different lithological facies. Especially the lower and middle levels of fossiliferous reefal limestone in the region represent weak engineering properties. As a result of these structural discontinuities and lithological variations, it is expected that rockfalls will threat these ancient granaries if the necessary measures not taken to understand the stability problems in such areas (Fig. 1). It is worth mentioning the earlier (3rd millennium BC) granary facilities which appeared in abundance in the early stage of the Ninevite 5 period. These storage facilities were of grid structure with reed mat floors used as grain silos (Badra, 2015).

Figure 1. Panoramic view of the granaries carved in limestone and rockfalls area.

2. MATERIALS AND METHODS

2.1. *The characteristics of Taşkale granaries*

The surface of the rock formation was used also for the living environment as rock-cut houses. In order to build them, the surface was carved living place-sized and the front facade was closed by the masonry wall. These rock-cut houses were built attached to each other. They had flat roof, thus a circulation pattern on the roof was created. Some of the houses had their own granary carved on the top of their houses. They could reach these granaries by passing among the roofs (Asrav, 2015; Tapur, 2009).

In the Taşkale region, a part of the rock formations has been used through centuries as granaries with the aim of storing the cereal products. The main rock formation containing these granaries is 40 m in height and 165 m in width. There are 251 stone granaries. The depth of them changes from 5 to 10 meters and the storage capacity changes from 5 to 60 tons (Fig. 2) (Tapur, 2009).

Grains must be kept away from moisture as long as possible to preserve it in good conditions and prevent mold growth. Newly harvested grains brought into a granary tend to contain excess moisture, which encourages mold growth leading to fermentation and heating, both of which are undesirable and affect the quality. Fermentation generally spoils grain and may cause chemical changes that create poisonous mycotoxins (Kuijt and Finlayson, 2009). The cereal products can be stored in these rooms for many years and according to the statistics of Soil Products Office in Turkey, the wheat is being floured in the amount of 5% in 50 years (Asrav, 2015; Tapur, 2009).

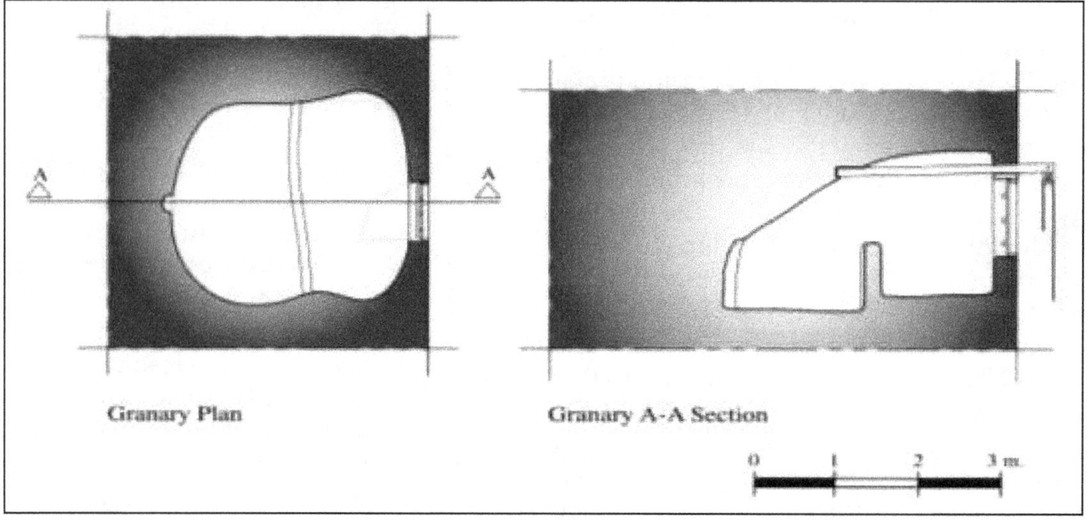

Figure 2. View of granary plan and granary cross section view.

2.2. *In situ and laboratory studies*

This study was conducted in two stages, namely in-situ and laboratory studies. In this study, infrared thermography study, surface moisture measurement and Schmidt rebound number measurements were taken from non-destructive (NDT) experiments in the granaries and stone mosque areas. Then 3 representative blocks were sampled according to the lithological change in the area where the granaries were opened (Fig. 3). To determine the mineralogical, petrographic chemical and geomechanical properties of the samples, thin sections, and powder, core and piece samples were prepared in the laboratory.

The rock mass where the Taşkale granaries area was carved in consists of fossiliferous reefal limestone and clayey-sandy limestone. Younger travertines are found on the limestones with an unconformity. The reefal and clayey-sandy limestones are light yellow in color and the nearby areas were investigated in three different facies separated in terms of texture, composition and lithology (Table 1). The rock mass of the granaries have weak rock properties and contains fossils fragments (0.5 to 4.5 cm in diameter).

Table 1. Sample location and remarks of studied samples.

Sample code	Sample location	Sample type	Remarks
T1	The bottom of the granaries	Fresh	Massive, coarse rock and fossil fragments, soft, weak and fractured
T2	Upper parts of the T1 level	Fresh	Yellow, high porous and soft, coarse rock fragments
T3	Upper levels of the granaries region	Fresh	Light gray, with small cavity melting, fine-grained massive and voids are filled with coarse secondary calcite

Figure 3. View of granaries area and lithological boundary.

In this study, detailed observations and measurements were conducted for determining the discontinuity effects of the joints according to the line survey method (ISRM, 2007) in granaries, stone mosque walls and other underground rock structures are placed. During the studies made for this scope, the orientation, number of sets, spacing, continuity, aperture, filling, roughness of the joints and the weathering effects on joint surfaces have been described in some detail.

Preservation of stone structure material is a sensitive and complex problem (Pinto and Rodrigues, 2008). Detecting the damaged sections of the structures (internal voids, joint, heat leaks, etc.) is critical for the sustainable preservation of the monuments (Binda et al., 2007; Grinzato et al., 2004; Martinho et al., 2014). Problems in determining the damages in the stones of the monuments are the preservation requirements, and the lack of samples to be used in the laboratory studies (Jo and Lee, 2014; Martinho et al., 2014). Non destrcustive techniques (NDT) are applicable in the rapid determination of the structural status of the structural elements without taking samples from the respective structure. Through these mapping of the areas of degradation in the respective structure becomes possible (Pinto and Rodrigues 2008; Martinho et al. 2014). A single analytic method often remains inadequate for the preservation studies. Assessment of the monuments by way of joint assessment of different test methods increases the reliability of the test techniques (Lim and Cao, 2013; Svahn, 2006). Therefore, in situ measurements were performed by non-destructive methods by making use of infrared thermography, surface humidity meter, and Schmidt hammer. Schmidt hammer type-L was used for the determination of rock hardness in the study area and laboratory. The Schmidt hammer test was performed according to ISRM (2007). The relative moisture values were determined using a Trotec T660 device.

NDT data have been obtained from the area of investigation divided into grids of 100×100 cm at the location of granaries and the stone mosque, and where 49 measurement stations were established at the specified spots at these grids. These measurements were performed under the weather conditions of 21.1 °C temperature, and 33.2% relative humidity.

Major element contents were determined by chemical analysis using XRF method on the same samples. As a result of the investigation of these prepared thin sections with the use of point counter in polarizing microscope, petrographic properties of the samples were determined. The main mineralogical composition, texture, void and crystal size, and the secondary mineral contents of the samples have been identified.

In order to determine the geomechanical properties of the stones, core samples (samples diameter=5.47 mm) were prepared from block samples with a laboratory core drilling machine. Samples length is 13.5-14.0 cm. Most of the specimens had length to diameter ratios of 2.5. On the samples taken from various levels of the granaries area, were taken based on the suggested methods by the International Society for Rock Mechanics (ISRM, 2007) and Turkish Standards TS 699 (2009), dry and saturated unit weight, water absorption, effective porosity, capillary water absorption, slake durability index, and uniaxial compressive strength values, the P-wave velocity and in-situ Schmidt rebound number measurements.

3. RESULTS

3.1. *Climate and common weathering processes in the Taşkale region*

The study area has an average elevation of 998 m above sea level. The Taşkale region has a continental climate, where summers are hot and dry while winters are cold with moderate snowfalls and springs are rainy. The meteorological records of the Karaman station for the period 1950 and 2015 are given in Table 2. The maximum rain is recorded May and January, and the minimum rain in September (Table 2). The use of the meteorological records of Karaman region on the temperature-precipitation graph recommended by Fookes et al. (1971) reveals that very slight weathering (both physical and chemical) is expected in the study area (Fig. 4). This is in good agreement with the field observations. No air pollution problem exists around the granary area because it is located in a rural region.

Table 2. Sample location and remarks of studied samples.

Month	Temperature (°C)			Precipitation (average, mm)	Rainy days (average)	Average sunrise time (h)
	Average	Maximum	Minimum			
January	0.5	5.5	-3.8	42.2	10.2	3.3
February	1.8	7.1	-2.8	35.9	9.6	4.4
March	6.1	12.4	0.4	36.3	9.3	6.3
April	11.4	18.0	4.9	36.9	8.2	8.6
May	16.2	23.1	8.7	44.8	8.4	10.0
June	20.4	27.7	12.3	36.4	5.0	12.6
July	23.6	31.1	15.0	21.3	1.5	12.5
August	23.0	31.0	14.4	4.4	1.0	12.1
September	18.6	27.1	10.2	4.1	1.9	10.2
October	12.7	20.5	5.6	7.3	6.1	7.6
November	6.7	13.6	1. 1	28.3	6.7	5.3
December	2.6	7.6	-1.8	33.0	9.9	3.3
Annual	12.0	18.8	5.4	330.9	5.8	8.0

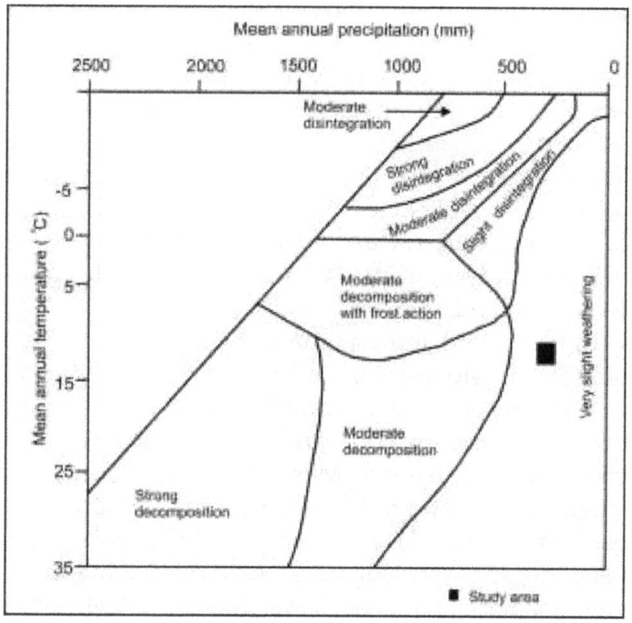

Figure 4. Relationship between climate and type of weathering for the Karaman region (modified from Fookes et al., 1971).

3.2. *Geological setting of the study area*

The middle-upper Miocene Kıraman Formation in the study area unconformably overlies pre-Miocene basement rocks and consists of alternating beds of yellow, brown mudstone, light grey marl, grey-grizzly, thickly bedded limestone and conglomerate (Bilgiç, 2009). The Kıraman Formation is gradationally conformable with the middle-upper Miocene Mut Formation. The Mut Formation is composed of yellow, light grey, cream, thickly bedded or massive, abundant fossiliferous reefal limestone and clayey-sandy limestone (Demirtaşlı et al., 1973; Gökten, 1976; Pampal, 1987). The Taşkale granaries were opened in this formation. The upper Miocene-Pliocene İnsuyu Formation consists of lacustrine clastic and carbonates and unconformably rests on the Mut Formation (Bilgiç, 2009). Quaternary aged alluvium and alluvial fan deposits comprise the upper part of the units and unconformably overlie the previous formations (Figure 5).

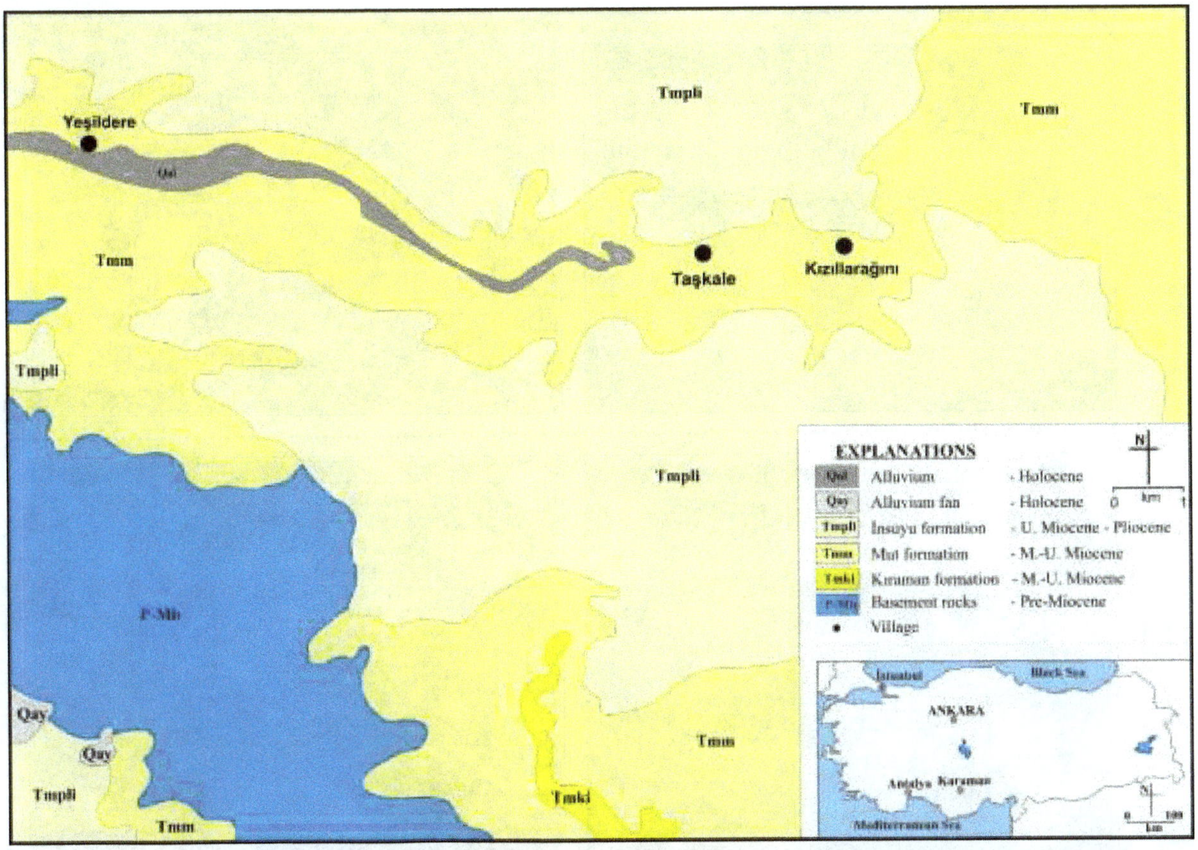

Figure 5. Geological map of the study area (modified from Bilgiç, 2009).

3.3. *Mineralogical characteristics*

XRF analysis showed partly differentiation in three distinct groups. First group contain T1 samples taken from at the bottom of the sample, and second group contain T2 sample that were taken from the granaries areas. T3 sample were taken from at the top of the granaries area. In the field, samples T1 and T2 located in the lower levels where the rock structures were found have relatively close in composition. SiO_2 contents of the T1 and T2 samples are higher; MgO and Fe_2O_3 are higher from T2 and T3 samples. CaO and LOI contents of the T2 and T3 samples are same and higher than T1 samples (Table 3).

Table 3. Chemical composition of the samples.

Major element Oxide (%)	SiO_2	Al_2O_3	Fe_2O_3	MgO	CaO	Na_2O	K2O	TiO_2	P_2O_5	MnO	Cr_2O_3	LOI	Sum
T1	9.37	1.94	1.41	2.98	41.89	0.10	0.39	0.89	0.06	<0.01	0.025	41.0	100.05
T2	1.91	0.43	0.56	0.91	55.57	<0.01	0.08	<0.01	0.07	<0.01	<0.002	40.0	99.53
T3	0.34	0.06	0.08	0.24	57.65	<0.01	<0.01	<0.01	0.02	<0.01	<0.002	41.2	99,59

3.4. *Petrographical characteristics of samples*

According to the polarizing microscopic investigation of the sample-T1, it contains 40% fossils, 27% micrite, 27% clay, 4% iron oxide and 2% void (Figure 6- a, d). This sample was termed as biomicrite based on Folk (1962) classification. Clasts range in size from 0.1-10 mm. As seen in thin section, framework grains in the sample-T2 compose about 50% of the total rock with a grain size of 0.05-0.25 mm (Figure 6- e). The composition of the sample-T2 is made up of fossils (50%), micrite (21%), clay (19%), intraclast (4%), iron oxide (4%) and void (2%) (Figure 6- b, e). The rock was defined as biomicrite according to the classification of Folk (1962). T3 samples were completely composed of calcite. The void ratio of the stone is 5%. Pores T3 samples showed fine grained micritic characteristics, in most of the samples pores are filled with coarse grained secondary calcites. The rock smaple-T3 has 5% of void and it was petrographically named as biolithite (Folk, 1962) (Figs 6- c, f).

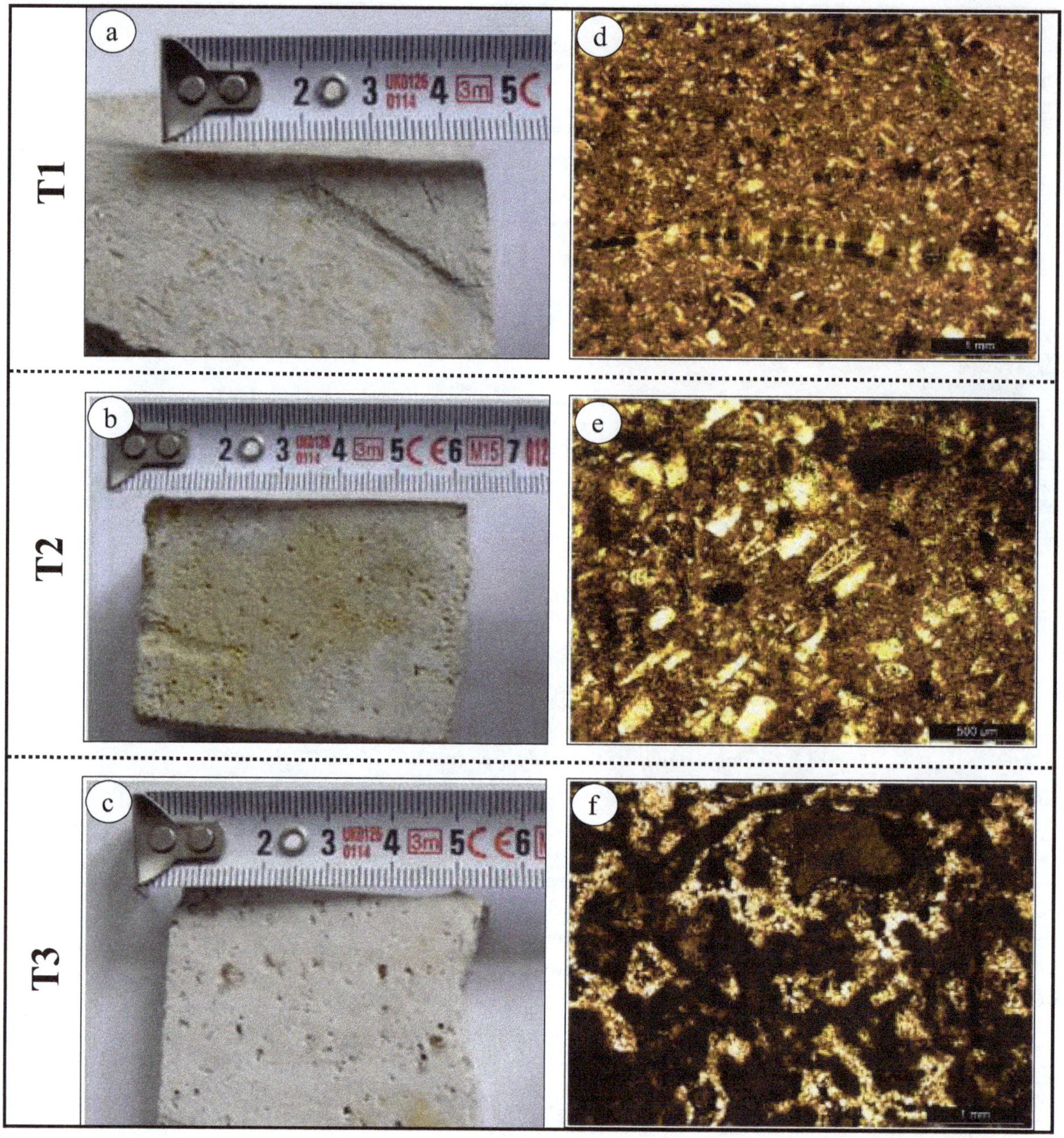

Figure 6. Macroscopic (a-c) and microscopic (d-f, cross nicols) images of the rock samples

3.5. *Structural characteristics of the Taşkale granaries*

Starting from the south granaries section, walls opened to the granary were examined individually in detail, in terms of joint system and the surficial decomposition. Vertical joint surfaces developed in the walls have coarse roughness, very wide aperture and joints were often observed to be unfilled (Fig. 7) (Table 4). As seen in the basis of measurements taken from the granaries areas of fracture-joints are not very regular and approximately E-W direction compression is observed. Stability problems in these fractures were observed (Fig. 7).

Table 4. Discontinuity properties of the granary walls according to ISRM 2007 (*Values in the parentheses obtained from the study area).

Properties	T1 section	T2 section	T3 section
Number of sets	2 and more joints	2 and more joints	3 and more joints
Spacing	(2.5-7.2 m) Very-extremely wide	(3.0-8 m) Very-extremely wide	(3.80-8.20 m) Very-extremely wide
Continuity	(> 12 m) High-very high	(> 15 m) High-very high	(> 16 m) High-very high
Aperture	(1-3 cm) Very wide	(1.2-3.2 cm) Very wide	(2.5-4.3 cm) Very wide
Filling	Unfilled	Unfilled	Unfilled
Roughness	(IV) Rough, undulating	(IV) Rough, undulating	(IV) Rough, undulating
Weathering	(II) Slightly	(II) Slightly	(I) Fresh
Orientation	N45E/20SE, N75E/15SE, N30E/80SW, N50E/32SE	N70E/45SW, N45E/55SE, N40W/36SW, N60E/47NW	N85E/40NW, N35W/45NE, N60W/21NE, N52W/32NE

Figure 7. View of rockfall and potential rockfall area and open joint.

3.6. *Physico-mechanical properties*

Physico-mechanical properties data obtained from the experiments are shown in Table 5. The average lowest values with respect to the representative samples having relatively different textural features taken from the segment where the granaries was opened level from T1 and T2 samples taken from the levels showing the void, clay and fossils content is relatively high (Table 5).

The highest values of the effective porosity were obtained from the samples T1 and T2, the lowest values were obtained from the samples T3 (Table 5). Changes in the values of the rock porosity significantly effect their mechanical properties in addition to physical properties of the rock. Increased porosity also provides a low intensity to the rock, and be effective on the rock's sound and heat conductivity (Goodman, 1989). Porosity values of the samples having high clay and fossils content are relatively high values (Table 5).

Table 5. Some physico-mechanical properties of the studied samples (S.D. = Standard deviation).

Physicomechanical properties	Test number	T1 (mean ±S.D.)	T2 (mean ±S.D.)	T3 (mean ±S.D.)
Dry unit weight (kN/m^3)	5	17.59±0.34	16.33±0.71	24.15±0.18
Saturated unit weight (kN/m^3)	5	20.40±0.13	18.92±0.46	24.56±0.14
Water absorption (%)	5	15.99±0.40	15.92±2.45	1.72±0.13
Effective porosity (%)	5	28.65±0.62	26.36±2.93	4.23±0.33
Uniaxial comp. strength (MPa)	5	5.88±0.06	8.37±0.06	30.81±1.51
Sonic velocity (m/s)	3	1770±21.62	2507±42.43	2913±44.45
Slake durability-4 cycle (%)	2	78.55±0.28	86.90±0.26	98.96±0.02
Capillary water absorption (kg/m^{2}h$^{0.5}$)	3	3.35±0.33	7.72±0.53	0.31±0.04
Schmidt rebound number	10	18.8±3.20	22.5±3.23	38.6±1.82

The highest values of the average capillary water absorption (C) were obtained from the same sample T1 and T2, the lowest values were obtained from the sample T3 (Table 5). The higher the capillary water absorption and porosity, the worse are the negative consequences. Petrographic features, such as type, size, distribution and position of mineral components, homogeneity, and the size, shape and system of interconnected pores in the stone are also important (Tomašić et al., 2011). T1 and T2 samples are "highly absorbing", T3 samples are "slightly absorbing" rock class according to Snethlage (2005).

Particularly to determine the resistance against fragmentation and weakening as a result of wetting and drying of the tuff, marl and clay bearing weak rocks, the dispersion in water against the slake durability index test has been performed using two cycles with the methods proposed by Franklin and Chandra (1972) and ISRM (2007). Some studies (Campos et al., 1983; Dick et al., 1994; Gökceoğlu et al., 2000) were conducted based on number of cycles greater than 2 (3 or 4) in the slake durability test and researchers recommended that 4-cycle slake durability test would be suitable particularly for clay-bearing rocks, such as mudstone, shale, marl, claystone etc. Similarly, in this study 4-cycle slake durability test were performed. Investigated samples are located in the class of "medium (T1, T2) -very high (T3) degree of stable" rock in terms of slake durability index as a result of 4-cycles, according to Gamble (1971).

The average lowest P-wave velocity values were obtained from T1 samples having higher void and fossil content, the highest values were obtained from T2 and T3 samples having relatively higher geomechanical properties (Tablo 5). In terms of P-wave velocity, the samples are located at "rock having very low - low seismic velocity" group according to NBG (1985).

In-situ Schmidt rebound number measurements were made by using L-type hammer on the fresh and weathered smooth surfaces. Very low rebound values were obtained particularly in the lower parts of the underground rock structures where the humidity is high and in the upper parts (T1 and T2 sampling area) relatively higher rebound values were obtained (Table 5). The Schmidt rebound number values obtained as a result of the Schmidt rebound number measurements at different levels in the field, samples take place in "solid soil-soft-hard" rock class according to De Beer (1967).

Taşkale granaries structures were opened is quite low resistance (T1 and T2) level (Figure 1 and Figure 3). The highest average values were obtained from the samples T3 having low porosity, relatively high rate of unit weight (Table 5). Low resistance of the samples caused by, unit weight, and higher level of decomposition and porosity values is considered to be effective. Investigated samples are located in the "low- medium resistance" rock class according to ISRM (1981) "very low-low resistance" rock class according to Deer and Miller (1966).

3.7. *Assessment of the data obtained by NDT methods*

First of all, humidity and surface Schmidt rebound number measurements were taken from these stations via surface humidity meter and Schmidt hammer. As a consequence of the measurements, a significant correlation has been determined between the humidity found within the rock and the values of Schmidt rebound number (Figure 8). While the humidity values increase from stations M-1 up to M-18 Schmidt rebound number values decrease from stations S-1 up to S-18 (Figure 8). This situation is suggested to arise from the capillary water coming from the ground. While the humidity values between the stations M-19 and M-37 remain at average level, Schmidt rebound number values decrease from stations S-19 up to S-37 (Fig. 8). This situation is suggested to arise from the porous and weak endurance provided by the fossil limestone being observed at the region. It may be viewed also in the thermal image displaying the surface heat distribution. While the humidity values decrease between the stations M-38 and M-43, Schmidt rebound number reaches its peak values (Fig. 8). This situation is also suggested to arise due to the unit with less pores and high endurance. While the humidity values increase in between the stations M-44 and M-46 (Fig. 8), Schmidt rebound number decrease within the same range. This situation is suggested to arise not only due to the area in question is located inside the entrance groove, but also due to the lithologically lower endurance, clay content, lack of any porous section thereat. Since this area receives insufficient sunlight, and due to its clay content, humidity is kept within the area, and its Schmidt rebound number decreases accordingly. While the humidity values decrease between the stations M-47 and M-49 (Fig. 8), Schmidt rebound number increase from stations S-47 up to S-49. This situation is suggested to arise not only due to the direct sunshine received by the area in question, but also due to its composition of lithology with lithological higher endurance.

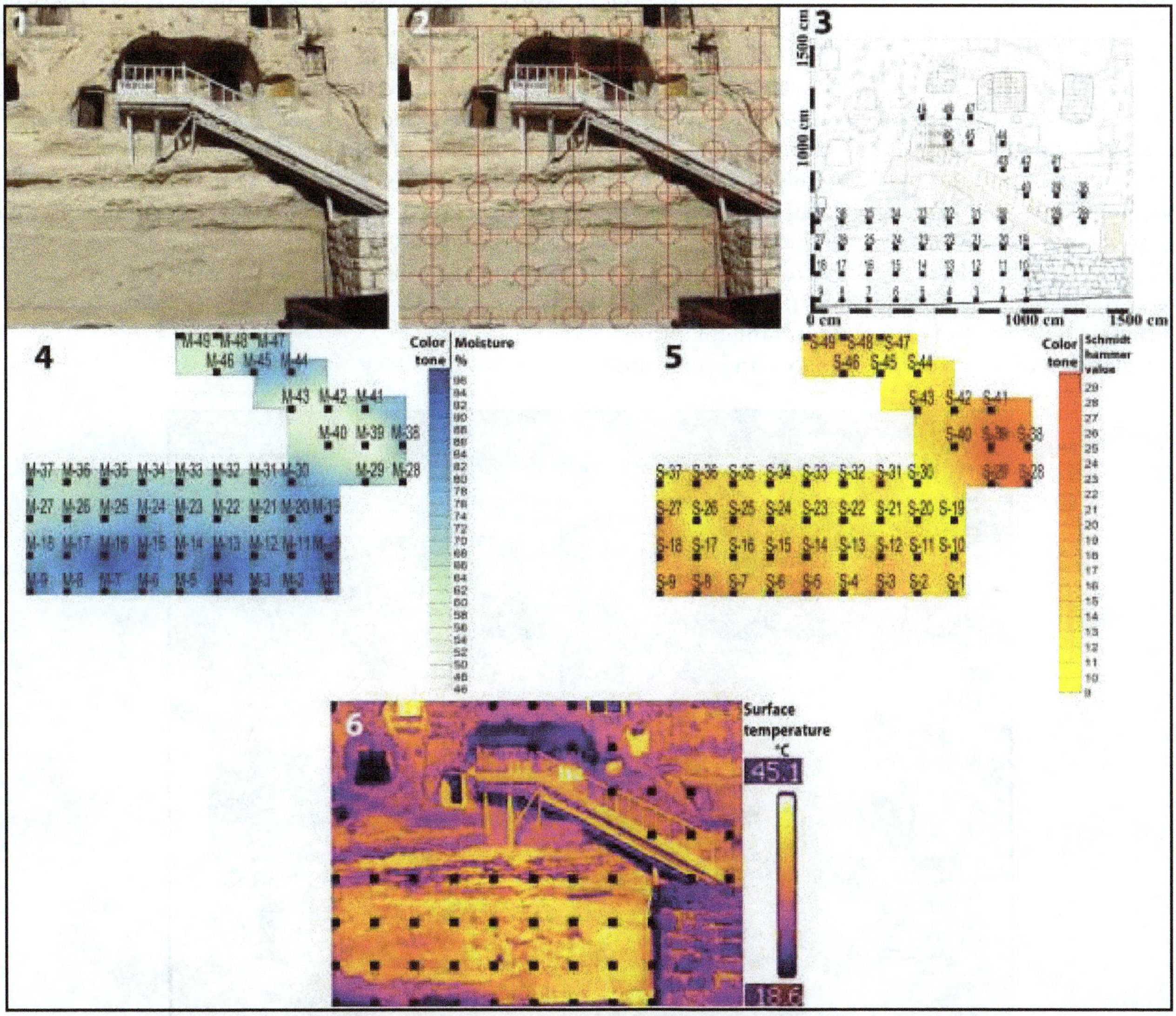

Figure 8. Non-destructive tests values of the granaries and the stone mosque area.

4. DISCUSSION: GEOLOGICAL HAZARDS AND SUGGESTIONS

Since the discontinuities can contribute to instability, an investigation is required for assessing the geological hazards around the Taşkale granaries to ensure both the stability of the stone monument and the safety of residence.

Some studies have been attempted to consider the protection and preservation of historic sites and monuments with regard to geological problems associated with the slope stability, and have been reported in the literature (Choi et al., 2009). Many researchers have studied on the rockfalls around historic sites (e.g., castles (Topal et al., 2007), towns (Sofianos et al., 1988), pedestrian roads built on subvertical cliff (Aversa et al., 1997).

A natural monument undergoes several decay processes due to the exposure to aggressive environmental conditions that threaten its durability and preservation (Charola, 2000; El-Gohary, 2012). Moisture, whose presence may be due to rain, condensation or capillary rise (Sandrolini and Franzoni, 2007; Snethlage, 2005), plays a key role in the degradation of porous materials (Korkanç, 2013; Korkanç et al., 2015; López-Doncel et al., 2013; Lourenço et al., 2006; Rirsch and Zhang, 2010; Vařilová et al., 2011; Wedekind et al., 2011), being directly or indirectly responsible for several decay processes Sandrolini and Franzoni (2006), such as freeze-thaw cycles, soluble salts crystallization cycles, biological growth, chemical attack by acid rain, wind erosion Nardi (1987), lithological properties and discontinuities (El-Gohary, 2017; Korkanç et al., 2015).

In the study area, the capillary water level is usually below the granaries level. According to the investigations in all the walls open to Taşkale granaries and other underground cavities, it is observed that the joints are open, superficial abrasion losses occurred on fracture surfaces are increasing as a result of the moisturizing effect, and the joint openings are also increasing with time (Fig. 9).

These kinds of studies are important for protection, stability of such historical places and for handing down them to the next generations. Alongside the expansion of current cracks, and the formation of new cracks are opened, particularly at levels in strength loss occurs due to capillary moistening and surface losses in the argillaceous limestone, which are found within the capillary zone under the section of the granaries. That is why rockfalls occurred in the crack positioned approximately parallel and vertical to the wall at the northeastern section of the granaries. Entrances of most of the granaries were damaged due to rockfalls. These entrances were then restored by making use of the fallen rocks. There are still risk of rockfalls at the southern section of this crack (Figs 1, 7 and 9). It is thought that, the weight of the huge travertine mass positioned approximately horizontal above this section may play a part in the activation of these cracks. Since there are settlements and roads in this section, a rockfall likely to happen in this section may cause losses of life and traffic problems, it is therefore suggested to have the settlements in this region evacuated (Fig. 9).

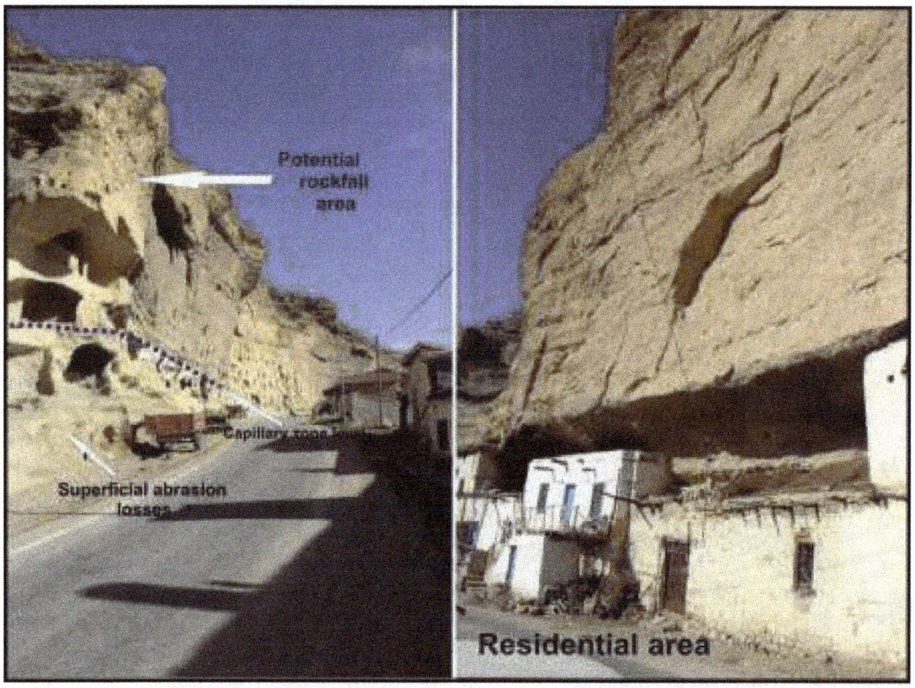

Figure 9. View of potential rockfall and residential area

5. CONCLUSIONS

In this study, the rocks where underground rock structures were placed show markedly different characteristics for their lower and upper levels in terms of color and textural properties. There are carved underground rock structures especially in the middle part of the region. Clayey-sandy limestones and fossiliferous reefal limestones in the lower part of the rock structures have high porosity, low unit weight and low strength values and are more sensitive than the travertines of the upper parts against atmospheric conditions. According to the NDT measurements, a significant correlation have been determined between the humidity and Schmidt rebound values.

On the walls of the northeastern parts of the granaries, rockfalls were observed due to the low strength rocks, due to the negative effects of atmospheric conditions on the joints on this side of granaries. The falling risk of large blocks that became free with discontinuities in the granaries, nearby parts must be determined, and studies must be carried out to support them before they create any life-threatening emergency.

ACKNOWLEDGEMENTS

The authors are grateful to Assis. Prof. Dr. Alper GÜRBÜZ for his comments and suggestions.

REFERENCES

Akarsu, İ. (1960) Mut bölgesinin jeolojisi. *MTA Dergisi,* vol. 54, pp. 36-45.

Asrav, E. Ç. (2015) *Place and community driven conservation and empowerment in historic rural landscapes: Principles and strategies for Taşkale Village, Turkey.* Unpublished Ph.D. Dissertation, Middle East Technical University, Turkey.

Aversa. S., Urciuoli, G., Candela, M. and Nocilla, N. (1997) Stability of the vertical cliff overhaning via Krupp in Capri. *Geotechnical engineering for the preservation of monuments and historic sites,* Balkema, Rotterdam, pp. 139-144.

Bilgiç, T. (2009) *1:100. 000 scaled Geological Maps and Explanations. Sheet Karaman N31 no. 129.* Ankara, Turkey General Directorate of Mineral research and Exploration.

Badra, N. (2015) Storing grains during Ninevite 5 period in the Khabour basin: ways and methods used. *Scientific Culture,* Vol. 1, No. 1, pp. 9-15

Binda, L., Lualdi, M. and Saisi, A. (2007) Non-destructive testing techniques applied for diagnostic investigation: Syracuse Cathedral in Sicily, Italy. *International Journal of Architectural Heritage,* Vol. 1, pp. 380-402.

Blumenthal, M. (1956) Karaman-Konya havzası güneybatısında Toros kenar silsileleri ve şistradyolarit formasyonunun stratigrafisi meselesi. *MTA Enstitusu Dergisi,* Vol. 48, pp. 1-36.

Campos, J. O., Paraguassu, A. B., Dobereiner, L., Soarez, L. and Frazao, E.B. (1983) The geotechnical behaviour of Brazilian sedimentary rocks. *International Symposium Geotechnical Engineering of Hard Soils-Soft Rocks,* Balkema, Athens, pp. 69-84.

Charola, A.E. (2000) Salts in the Deterioration of Porous Materials: An Overview. *Journal of the American Institute for Conservation,* Vol. 39, pp. 327-343.

Choi, Y., Lee ,J.Y., Lee, J. and Park, H.D. (2009) Engineering geological investigation into rockfall problem: A case study of the Seated Seokgayeorae Image carved on a rock face at the UNESCO World Heritage site in Korea. *Geosciences Journal,* Vol. 13, pp.69-78.

De Beer, J. (1967) Subjective classification of the hardness of rocks and the associated shear strength. *Proceedings of 4th reg. cong. Afr. soil mechanical found engineering,* Capetown, pp. 396-398.

Deere, D. U. and Miller, R. (1966) Engineering classification and index properties for intact rock. Technical Report No. AFWL-TR-65-116, Air Force Weapon Laboratory, Kirkland Air Force Base, New Mexico

Demirtaşlı, E. (1976) Toros kuşağının petrol potansiyeli. *Türkiye III Petrol Kongresi,* Ankara, pp. 55-63.

Demirtaşlı, E., Bilgin, A., Erenler, F., Işıklar, S., Sanlı, D., Selim, M. and Turhan, N. (1973) Bolkardağlarının Jeolojisi. *Cumhuriyetin 50. Yılı Yerbilimleri Kongresi,* pp. 42-67.

Dick, J.C., Shakoor, A. and Wells, N. (1994) A geological approach toward developing a mudrock-durability classification system. *Canadian Geotechnical Journal,* Vol. 31, pp. 17-27.

Ecim-Djuric, O. and Topisirovic, G. (2010) Energy efficiency optimization of combined ventilation systems in livestock buildings. *Energy and Building,* Vol. 42, pp. 1165-1171.

El-Gohary, M. (2012) The contrivance of new mud bricks for restoring and preserving the Edfa Ancıent Granary-Sohag, Egypt. *International Journal of Conservation Science,* Vol. 3, pp. 67-78.

El-Gohary, M. (2017) Environmental impacts: Weathering factors, mechanism and forms affected the stone decaying in Petra. *Journal of African Earth Sciences,* Vol. 135, pp. 204-212.

Folk, R.L. (1962) Spectral subdivision of limestone types. In *Classification of carbonate rocks,* Ham, W. E. (ed) Tulsa, Oklhoma, pp. 62-84.

Fookes, P.G., Dearman, W.R. and Franklin, J.A. (1971) Some engineering aspects of rock weathering with field examples from Dartmoor and elsewhere. *Quarterly Journal of Engineering Geology and Hydrogeology,* Vol. 4, pp. 139-185.

Franklin, J. and Chandra, R. (1972) The slake-durability test. *International Journal of Rock Mechanics and Mining Sciences,* Vol. 9, pp. 325-341.

Gamble, J.C. (1971) *Durability-plasticity classification of shales and other argillaceous rocks*. Unpublished Ph.D. Dissertation, University of Illinois at Urbana-Champaign, USA.

Goodman, R.E. (1989) *Introduction to rock mechanics vol 2*. New York, Wiley.

Gökceoğlu, C., Ulusay, R. and Sönmez, H. (2000) Factors affecting the durability of selected weak and clay-bearing rocks from Turkey, with particular emphasis on the influence of the number of drying and wetting cycles. *Engineering Geology*, Vol. 57, pp. 215-237.

Gökten, E. (1976) Silifke yöresinin temel kaya birimleri ve Miyosen stratigrafisi. *Türkiye Jeoloji Kurumu Bülteni*, Vol. 19, pp. 117-126.

Grinzato, E., Marinetti, S., Bison, P., Concas, M. and Fais, S. (2004) Comparison of ultrasonic velocity and IR thermography for the characterisation of stones. *Infrared Physics Technology*, Vol. 46, pp. 63-68.

ISRM (1981) *Rock characterization, testing & monitoring: ISRM suggested methods*. Brown, E.T. (ed), United Kingdom, Oxford and New York.

ISRM (2007) *The Complete ISRM Suggested Methods for Rock Characterization, Testing and Monitoring: 1974-2006*. Ulusay, R. and Hudson, J. (eds.), Ankara, ISRM Turkish National Group.

Jo, Y. and Lee, C. (2014) Quantitative modeling and mapping of blistering zone of the Magoksa Temple stone pagoda (13th century, Republic of Korea) by graduated heating thermography. *Infrared Physics Technology*, Vol. 65, pp. 43-50.

Koçyiğit, A. (1976) Karaman—Ermenek (Konya) bölgesinde ofiyolitli melanj ve diğer oluşuklar. *Türkiye Jeoloji Kurumu Bülteni*, Vol. 19, pp. 103-116.

Korkanç, M. (2013) Deterioration of different stones used in historical buildings within Nigde province, Cappadocia. *Construction and Building Materials*, Vol. 48, pp. 789-803.

Korkanç, M., Tuğrul, A., Savran, A. and Özgür, F.Z. (2015) Structural–geological problems in Gümüşler archeological site and monastery. *Environmental Earth Sciences*, Vol. 73, pp. 4525-4540.

Kuijt, I. and Finlayson, B. (2009) Evidence for food storage and predomestication granaries 11,000 years ago in the Jordan Valley. *Proceedings of the National Academy of Sciences*, Vol. 106, pp. 10966-10970.

Lim, M. K. and Cao, H. (2013) Combining multiple NDT methods to improve testing effectiveness. *Construction and Building Materials*, Vol. 38, pp. 1310-1315.

López-Doncel, R., Wedekind, W., Dohrmann, R. and Siegesmund, S. (2013) Moisture expansion associated to secondary porosity: an example of the Loseros Tuff of Guanajuato, Mexico. *Environmental Earth Sciences*, Vol. 69, pp. 1189-1201.

Lourenço, P.B., Luso, E. and Almeida, M.G. (2006) Defects and moisture problems in buildings from historical city centres: a case study in Portugal. *Building and Environment*, Vol. 41, pp. 223-234.

Martinho, E., Dionísio, A., Almeida, F., Mendes, M. and Grangeia, C. (2014) Integrated geophysical approach for stone decay diagnosis in cultural heritage. *Construction and Building Materials*, Vol. 52, pp. 345-352.

Nardi, R. (1987) Consolidation of a mud brick wall using simple techniques and materials. In: Proceedings of 8th Triennial Meeting, Sydney, Australia

NBG (1985) Engineering Geology and Rock Engineering. *Handbook No. 2*

Pampal, S. (1987) Ayrancı havzasında metamorfik bolkar grubu ve Tersiyer oluşukları. *Gazi Üniversitesi Mühendislik-Mimarlık Fakültesi Dergisi*,Vol. 2, No. 2, pp. 99-116.

Pinto, A. F. and Rodrigues, J. D. (2008) Stone consolidation: the role of treatment procedures. *Journal of Cultural Heritage*, Vol. 9, pp. 38-53.

Richardson, J. L. (1992) *A new topographical dictionary of ancient Rome*. London, JHU Press.

Rirsch, E. and Zhang, Z. (2010) Rising damp in masonry walls and the importance of mortar properties. *Construction and Building Materials*, Vol. 24, pp. 1815-1820.

Saá, C., Míguez, J., Morán, J., Vilán, J., Lago, M. and Comesaña, R. (2011) The influence of slotted floors on the bioclimatic traditional Galician agricultural dry-store structure (hórreo). *Energy and Buildings*, Vol. 43, pp. 3491-3496.

Sandrolini, F. and Franzoni, E. (2006) An operative protocol for reliable measurements of moisture in porous materials of ancient buildings. *Building and Environment*, Vol. 41, pp. 1372-1380.

Sandrolini, F. and Franzoni, E. (2007) Repair Systems for the Restoration of Ancient Buildings - Dampness Rise Problem. Bauinstandsetzen und Baudenkmalpflege, Vol. 13, No. 3, pp. 161-172.

Snethlage, R. (2005) *Leitfaden Steinkonservierung*. Stuttgart, Fraunhofer IRB.

Sofianos, A., Constantinidis, C., Christodoulias, J. and Anagnostopoulos, A. (1988) Rockfall analysis at the ancient region of Argos. *In: The engineering geology of ancient works, monuments and historical sites.*

Preservation and protection. Proceedings of an international symposium. Athens, 19-23 September 1988, pp 213-216.

Svahn, H. (2006) *Non-destructive field tests in stone conservation.* Stockholm, Riksantikvarieämbetet.

Tapur, T. (2009) The geography of Taşkale settlement Atatürk's ancestry homeland. *Selçuk Üniversitesi Türkiyat Araştırmaları Dergisi,* Vol. 1, pp. 265-292.

Tomašić, I., Lukić, D., Peček, N. and Kršinić, A. (2011) Dynamics of capillary water absorption in natural stone. *Bulletin of Engineering Geology and the Environment,* Vol. 70, pp. 673-680.

Topal, T., Akin, M. and Ozden, U. A. (2007) Assessment of rockfall hazard around Afyon Castle, Turkey. *Environmental Geology,* Vol. 53, pp. 191-200.

TS 699 (2009) *Natural building stones-Methods of inspection and laboratory testing,* Ankara, Turkish Standards Institution.

Vařilová, Z., Přikryl, R. and Cílek, V. (2011) Pravčice Rock Arch (Bohemian Switzerland National Park, Czech Republic) deterioration due to natural and anthropogenic weathering. *Environmental Earth Sciences,* Vol. 63, pp. 1861-1878.

Wedekind, W., Ruedrich, J. and Siegesmund, S. (2011) Natural building stones of Mexico–Tenochtitlán: their use, weathering and rock properties at the Templo Mayor, Palace Heras Soto and the Metropolitan Cathedral. *Environmental Earth Sciences,* Vol. 63, pp. 1787-1798.

17

FINITE ELEMENT ANALYSES FOR SEISMIC PERFORMANCE ASSESSMENT OF HISTORICAL MASONRY BUILDINGS: THE CASE OF OMAR TOSON PALACE (CAIRO, EGYPT)

Osama Amer[1], Bassam Saad[1], Ahmed Karim[2]

[1]*Department of Conservation, Faculty of Archaeology, Cairo University, Egypt*
[2] *Department of Civil Engineering, Faculty of Engineering, Misr University for science and technology, Egypt*
Corresponding author: osama_amer@cu.edu.eg

ABSTRACT

This paper presents experimental and numerical investigation of a historical masonry building, Omar Toson palace, subjected to static and earthquake loading in order to assess its structural behaviour and seismic vulnerability with respect to its actual state of conservation. The static behaviour and the dynamic properties of the Palace have been evaluated using the finite element modelling technique, taking into consideration all the geometrical and material nonlinearities, in order to investigate the seismic behaviour of the structure by means of nonlinear analysis. A macro-modelling approach has been used based on the concepts of homogenisated material and smeared cracking and crushing constitutive law. The calculations took the values for external loads, earthquake and displacement into consideration. A full 3D non-linear time-history analysis of the entire structure has been done in order to correctly assess the seismic vulnerability of the palace. The numerical analysis has given a valuable picture of possible damage evolution and provides a basic understanding of the structural performance under seismic loads that can support the selection of possible retrofitting measures.

KEYWORDS: Historical buildings; Seismic vulnerability; Nonlinear analysis; finite element method; Time history analysis; Omar Toson palace.

1. INTRODUCTION

The present scientific research discusses the structural behaviour and the seismic vulnerability of the Omar Toson palace, located in Shubra al-kheyma, Egypt. The conservation and the restoration of ancient buildings belonging to the culture heritage and preserving their main architectural features is a very sensitive problem (Betti et al., 2010; Barbieri et al., 2013, Elyamani and Roca, 2018 a, b, c). The assessment of the vulnerability of the historical unreinforced masonry building (HURM) is an essential prerequisite to its seismic risk assessment (Vicente et al., 2013; Asteris et al., 2014). In order to correctly assess and improve the durability of HURM buildings, it is particularly important to understand its structural behaviour under several load conditions with respect to its original characteristics, the most probable causes of damage, the existing damage products, and the changes occurred over the time.

While the structural behaviour of a new masonry construction is a relatively simple task due to the presence of standard codes and available literature (Betti et al., 2011), the predication of the structural response of historical buildings is a more challenging task. In brief, historical buildings are by definition unique buildings and its typological characteristics do not allow us to refer to simplified standard structural scheme because of the uncertainties that affect the structural behaviour (Betti, M., Vignoli, A., 2008) and the mechanical properties of the material lead to a widely non-linear behaviour whose prediction can be very tricky (Giordano et al., 2002). Furthermore, the seismic behaviour of old masonry structures depends on many factors such as geometry of the structure, to be defined by proper surveys; stiffness of the floors (diaphragm effect); connection between orthogonal walls and structural and non-structural elements (Barbieri et al., 2013) and the peculiar properties of masonry structures (low tensile strength and lack of box behaviour) (Lourenço et al., 2001). In particular the key point of masonry behaviour is the mechanical properties of its components and the interfaces between these materials. Additionally, in the non-linear range, masonry behaviour is usually hard to be predicted, because of the combined material performance depends on the properties and failure mechanisms of each constituting material. Masonry non-linear failure mechanisms involve compressive failure of bricks and mortar, tensile and shear failure at the mortar-brick interface where loss of cohesion and frictional slip are resulted. Nevertheless, the non-linear behaviour of masonry buildings is not only attributable to material properties, but it is also attributable to the interaction between the different structural members, i.e. masonry walls, steel or timber beams and columns, timber floors, and their connections (Vera, 2012). The previous considerations enlighten the need of scientific methodology for modelling and analysis of the seismic vulnerability of historic masonry buildings.

The seismic vulnerability assessment of historical masonry buildings is an essential prerequisite to correctly understand its structural performance, extensive damage and possibly to collapse as explained in the works of (Lagomarsino, 1999; Magenes, 2000; Kappos et al., 2002; Mele et al., 2003; Lagomarsino and Podestà, 2004; Lourenço et al.,2007; Betti and Vignoli, 2008; Petrovc and Kilar, 2013; Preciado, 2015; Cakir et al., 2015). In order to correctly assess the structure behaviour and seismic vulnerability of Omar Toson palace different levels of approaches were carried out; the evaluation of the structural performance of the palace mainly depended on the interpretation of various mechanical and physical testing and the structural analysis calculations. The numerical modelling of the palace using FEM was adopted for Linear and Non-linear analyses of static and seismic loads. Various issues concerning the URM building behaviour had to be assessed; the present study concentrates on three of these issues: (i) the construction materials properties, (ii) the structural system of the building, and (iii) numerical modelling and analysis of the palace using FEM under static and seismic loads. Firstly, the construction materials properties affecting the behaviour of Omar Toson palace have been investigated through mechanical and physical testes including, bricks, stones, mortars, and woods using standard experimental tests. Secondly, the structural system of the palace have been investigated; the exact geometry of the structure is acquired; measured drawings were prepared; the structural deficiencies were determined; and finally a 3D model of the structure was assembled together to achieve this goal. Finally, the static and seismic response of the palace had been evaluated using the finite element modelling technique, where the nonlinear behaviour of masonry has been taken into account by proper constitutive assumptions. The calculations took the values for external loads, earthquake and displacement into consideration. 3D nonlinear static and dynamic analyses of the overall structure have been done in order to correctly assess the structural behaviour and seismic vulnerability of the palace. The main information which obtained from the linear analyses of the palace is the interaction, and in particular the stress resultant distribution, among its structural elements in the two principal directions.

2. CASE STUDY

2.1. *Architectural characteristics and materials properties*

Omar Toson place is located in Shubra al-kheyma district, south of Cairo, which was constructed sometime after 1869 A.D during the Ottoman's period in Egypt. The geometry of the palace has been completely acquired and organized within a CAD system. The positions of openings and the variation of the thickness of the palace with respect to that quoted have been carefully recorded. The CAD model served as a basis for the mesh generation needed for further FEM analysis.

The palace is a rectangular masonry construction consists of a basement and two floors. Basement is consists of long rectangular corridors with semi-circular brick masonry vaults based on brick masonry pillars. The upper floors consist of a major corridor, several rooms used for receive visitors, living rooms and a large room which was used as a library (Fig. 1-H). The rigid basement roof, of semi-circular brick-masonry vaults, making load bearing walls are totally braced till the roof of ground level (Fig. 1-F), and the flat wooden roof of two upper floors make the rest of height of these walls are partially braced (Fig. 1-G). The roofs of upper floors are simple flat wooden roof. The whole building was constructed by load bearing wall system. The masonry wall thickness ranges between 0.70 m and 1.20 m. The load bearing walls are variable between solid and multi-leaf type; the internal filling is composed of heterogeneous material (the remainder brick tied by a poor mortar). Brick masonry walls used in the construction of the small rooms on the upper floor and the vaulted roof in the basement were observed; these walls have thickness of 0.40 m. The main dimensions of the palace were a maximum length of about 86.50 m, a maximum width of 38.75 m and a maximum height of about 23.30 m (Fig. 2, 3 and 4). However, despite these differences, the construction was mostly made of irregular limestone masonry with thick lime mortar joints. Laboratory tests have been carried out on limestone, red-bricks, and timber to define its physical and mechanical properties.

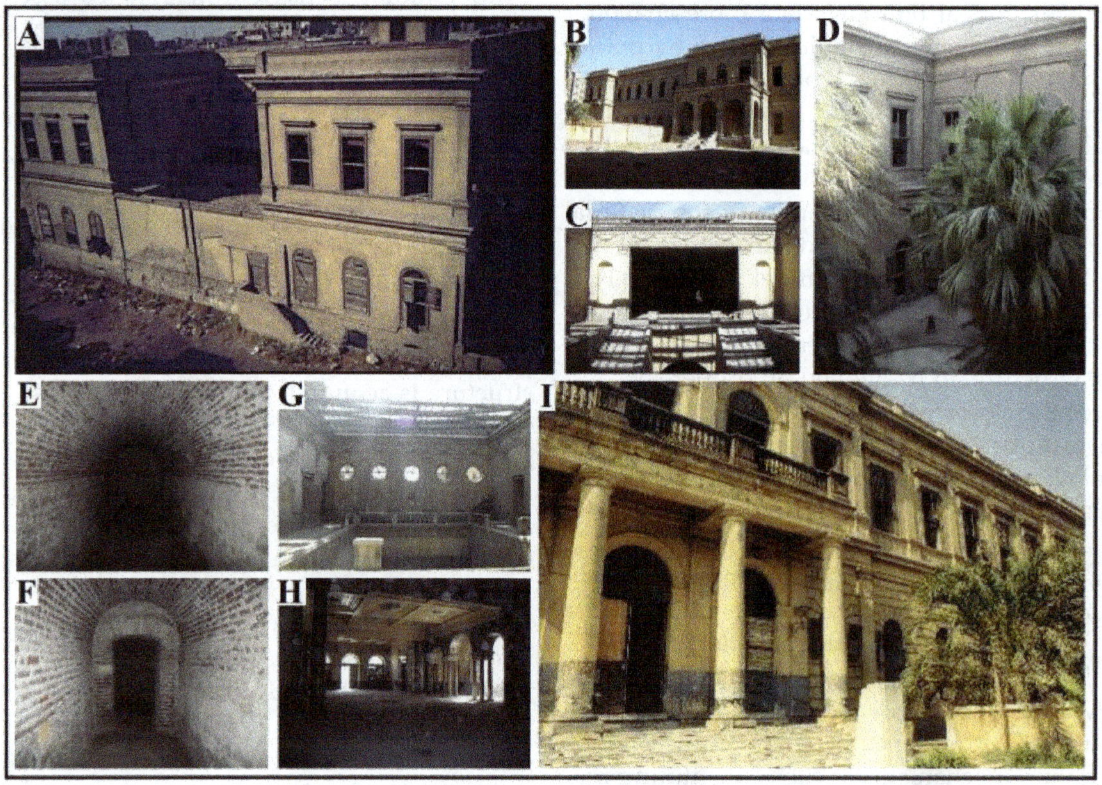

Fig. 1. General views of Omar Toson palace showing: A) North-eastern façade, B) South-eastern façade, C) Stairs to the second floor , D) the internal courtyard , E) long rectangular corridors in basement, F) semi-circular brick masonry vaults, G) damaged roofs in the second floor , H) major corridor in the second floor I) south-eastern (main) façade

In order to obtain basic material parameters which define load bearing capacity, (compressive strength and modulus of elasticity) compression tests were performed. These tests were done on main construction materials to determine the elastic, inelastic and strength parameters required for the present finite element modelling. The specimens were taken from various locations of the Omar Toson palace and tested under standard uniaxial compression test, the specimens were centrally positioned in the testing machine and the applied load was uniformly distributed. In addition, the load increased continuously. The obtained results from the experimental program are reported in Table 1, 2.

Simple calculations, based on the relation between the compressive strength of masonry and the compressive strength of its single components (units and mortar), were used in accordance with the Eurocode 6, CEN (CEN, 2003) to predict the compressive strength fc of masonry walls. The fc value was obtained as follows:

$$f_c = K f_{cu}^{\ 0.7} f_m^{\ 0.3} \tag{1}$$

Where f_{cu} is the characteristic compressive strength of masonry unite, f_m is the characteristic compressive strength of mortar, and K is a constant depending on the quality of the masonry units. K factor ranges between 0.40-0.60. These equations can be used where the thickness of the mortar joints, both horizontally and vertically, is between 8 and 15mm. According to (Abdel-Aty, 2004), in the case of stone masonry, the value of K factor can be estimated as 0.5; and for mortar joint width of 1 cm, the fc can be approximated to:

$$f_c = 0.35 f_{cu} \tag{2}$$

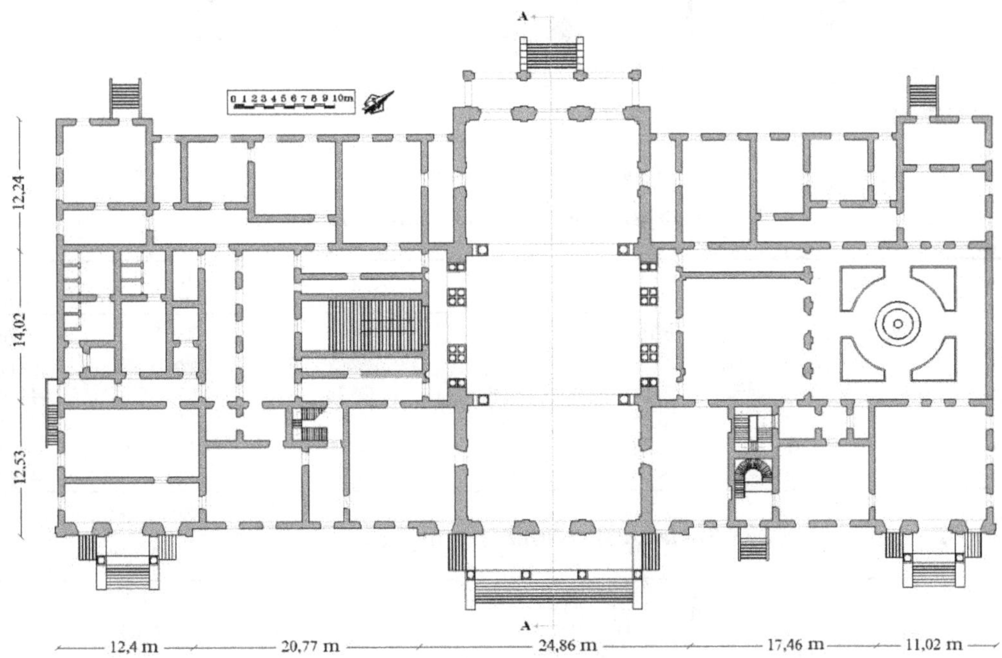

Fig. 2. Ground floor layout

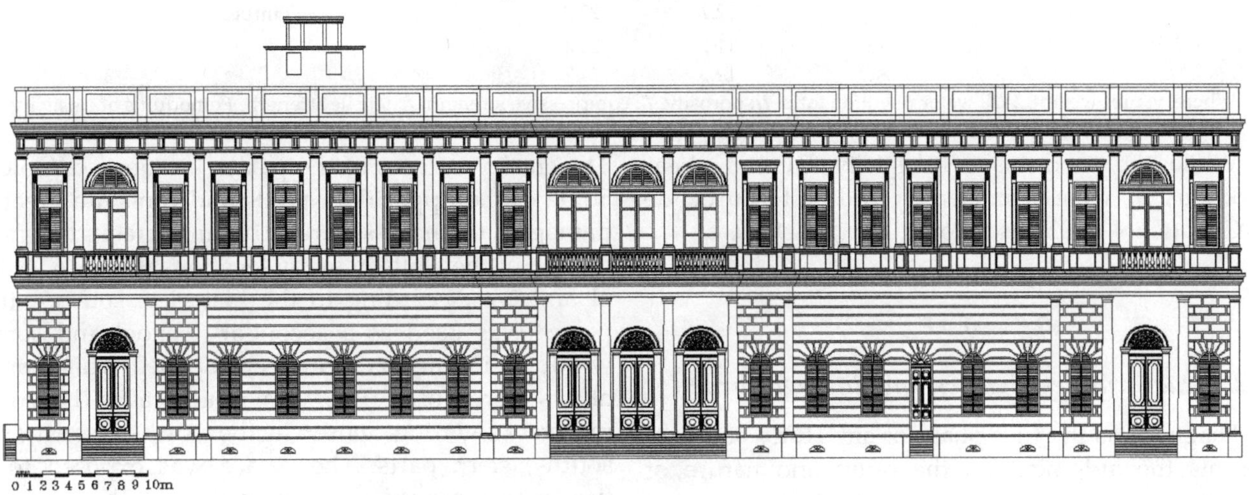

Fig. 3. North-western elevation of Omar Toson palace

Fig. 4. South-western elevation

Table 1. Experiments results for stone and bricks

S. No		γ (kN/m³)	W. A %	η %	f_c N/mm²	f_t N/mm²	E N/mm²
stone	1	22.13	6.16	4.6	36.14	2.9	5526.14
	2	20.20	5.07	3.3	28.57	2.2	5311.32
	3	19.02	2.03	1.8	26.14	1.9	4480.87
Bricks	1	21.03	18,95	11.4	6.51	2.9	3634.46
	2	19.41	12.54	10.5	4.45	2.7	3602.73
	3	19.68	18.80	11.2	8.20	2.8	4729.95

Table 2. Experiments results for timber

S. No		Weight per unit Volume (kN/m³)	W. Ab %	f_c N/mm² Parallel to grain	f_c N/mm² Perpendicular to grain	f_t N/mm² (in fibre direction)	E N/mm²
Timber	1	7.8	12.1	25.3	44.6	**Timber**	1
	2	6.3	11.7	22.4	48.4		2
	3	7.6	12.3	24.7	43.2		3

Where, γ: unit weight, *WA*: water retention ratio, η: porosity, f_c: compressive strength, f_t: tensile strength, *E*: modulus of elasticity

While the modulus of elasticity E_m and shear modulus G_m were estimated, according to Eurocode 6, CEN (CEN, 2003), as follows:

$$E_m = 1000 f_c \quad (3)$$

$$G_m = 0.4 E_m \quad (4)$$

2.2. *Structural deficiencies and damage survey*

Diagnosis is the first phase of any study and represents the judgment on the cause and nature of damage, cracks, decay and the other phenomena that have affected a building. Safety evaluation is the subsequent judgment on the capacity of the structure to resist specific actions such as loads, earthquakes, etc., and the potential risk involved (Croci, G., 2000). The cracks patterns of the palace are quite complex. Some of the upper floor walls and roofs are greatly damaged; there are several structural cracks through the top of the walls in many locations (Fig. 5-A, B, C, H and G). According to the historical sources, the palace was used as a secondary school and some windows in various sizes were opened while some others were closed (Fig. 1-A); which cause the existing cracks getting denser in the north-western and south-eastern parts. The palace was exposed to a fire, which caused the destruction of the wooden roof of the south-western area of the upper floor. Moreover, the weathering factors have decreased the compressive strength of the stones. Similarly, the current mortar used in the joints bonding the stones is extremely cracked and the stones are practically held on under gravity. Major cracks are observable on the north-western and south-western façades and on the corresponding internal masonry walls. In contrast, the north-eastern and the south-eastern facades are substantially in a good state of preservation. Fig. 5-A shows cracks on the north-western facade which are concentrated on the central part that is the most damaged area. Fig. 5-G shows cracks on the internal wall parallel to the south-western facades. Fig 5-D, H, J show the main cracks in the internal walls on the first floor, while Fig 5-C reports details of the cracks present at the basement in the eastern area of the palace. The ground floor tiles are have sever settlement in many location that reach in some parts to about 12cm depression (Fig. 5-F). The internal walls have high dampness and covered with efflorescence salts. It is noteworthy to underline that, it is possible to observe that the damage does not affect the whole palace, but mainly the western and southern parts of the building that can slight to moderate impact on the structural stability of different elements in the building.

3. STRUCTURAL ANALYSIS METHODOLOGY

As already discussed in the introduction, the seismic behaviour of old masonry structures is particularly difficult to be investigated, It depends on many factors such as material properties, to be characterized by direct inspection, geometry of the structure, to be defined by proper surveys; stiffness of the floors (diaphragm effect) and connection between orthogonal walls and structural and non-structural elements (Barbieri et al., 2013).

The assessment methodology in the present study is mainly the achievement of an adequate knowledge of structural behaviour. A preliminary in situ survey of the palace was made to obtain basic information on the geometry, the structural details and any irregularities. The paper approaches the numerical problem using the FE technique to assess the seismic vulnerability of the palace. In order to assess the seismic vulnerability of the structure 3D static and dynamic analyses of the whole structure have been done taking into account the masonry nonlinear behaviour.

The numerical model has been prepared according to the geometrical information gathered from the historical documents and by the measurement of the actual conditions of the structure with focusing on the variations in the wall thickness, in the geometrical and structural irregularities and on the wall connections. Finally, the major openings in the building have been reproduced as it shown in (Fig. 6). The 3D numerical model was developed, using the F.E. ANSYS software package. According to (Betti et al., 2011), the nonlinear behaviour of the masonry elements was reproduced assuming a Mohr-Coulomb type failure criterion with tension cut-off type behaviour, a Drucker-Prager (DP) perfectly plastic material criterion has been joined with the Willam and Warnke (WW) failure surface.

Table 3 reports values assumed for both linear and non-linear characterization of masonry materials. According to (Lourenco P.B, 2002; Senthivel & Lourenço, 2009; Asteris & Giannopoulos, 2012; Betti M., Galano L., Vignoli A., 2015), macro-modeling approach was used (Fig. 7), masonry is considered as a homogeneous anisotropic continuum, stone, mortar joints and interfaces are globally represented by single continuous elements (Masonry as an one-phase material).

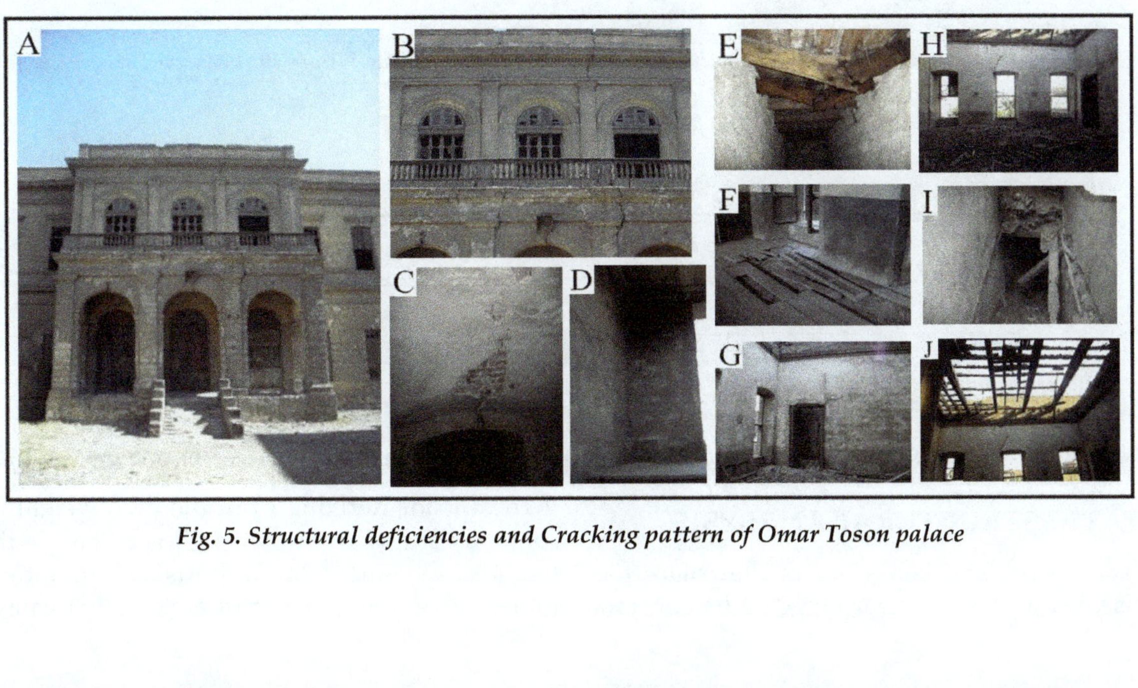

Fig. 5. Structural deficiencies and Cracking pattern of Omar Toson palace

The behaviour of the masonry wall is replicated by use of Solid65 elements (three-dimensional eight noded isoparametric elements) and its stiffness is modified by the crack and crushing development; Shell143 elements (isoparametric two-dimensional element with four nodal points) have been used to model the vaults in basement. After meshing, the final 3D model consisted of 22,887 joints and 75,952 elements that correspond to 73,512 degrees of freedom (Fig. 6). All the variations in wall thickness, geometrical irregularities and wall connections were taken into account, and the deterioration and damage states of the structural elements have been considered in the modelling phase. In both the static and dynamic analyses the models have been subjected to the vertical loads deriving from the masonry own weight and from the roof loads. The whole palace was analysed under the following load cases: static load case, modal analysis case (in order to determine the fundamental participation factors and natural frequencies for the palace which will be used for the dynamic analysis), and time-history case to evaluate the seismic behaviour and resulting internal stresses under the dynamic actions.

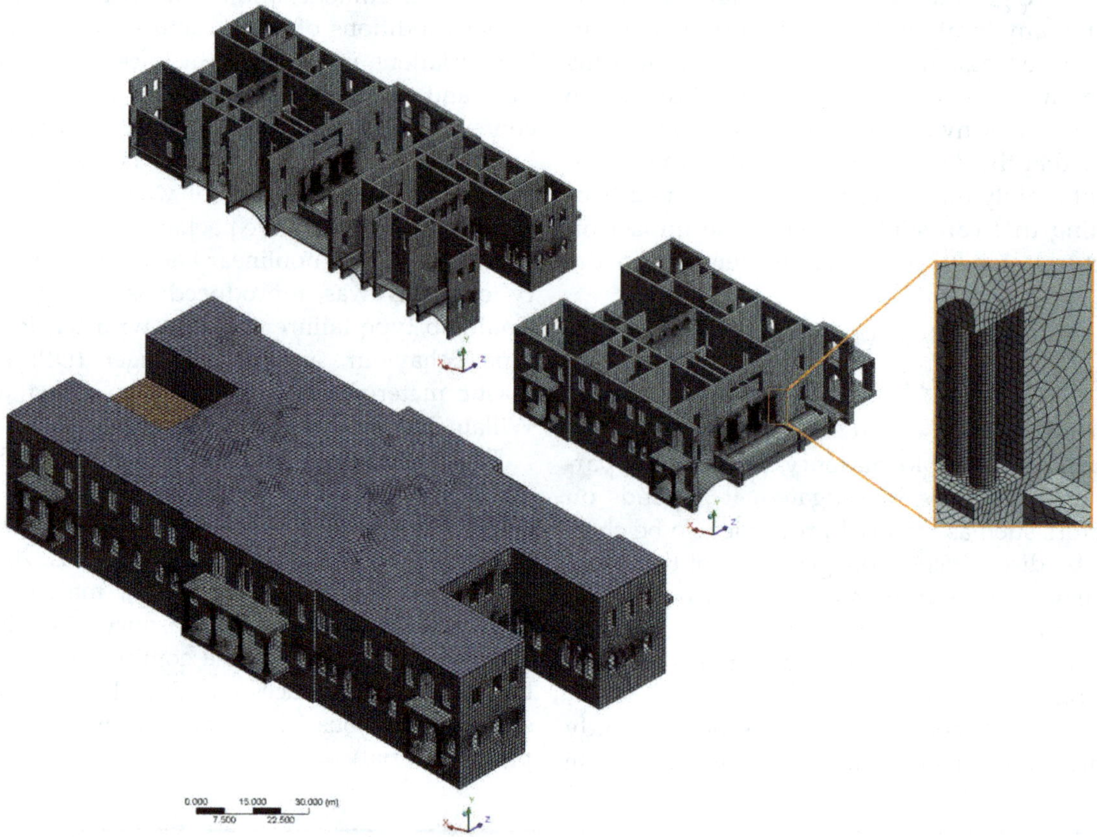

Fig. 6. Geometrical model and finite element discretization of the Palace in its current state

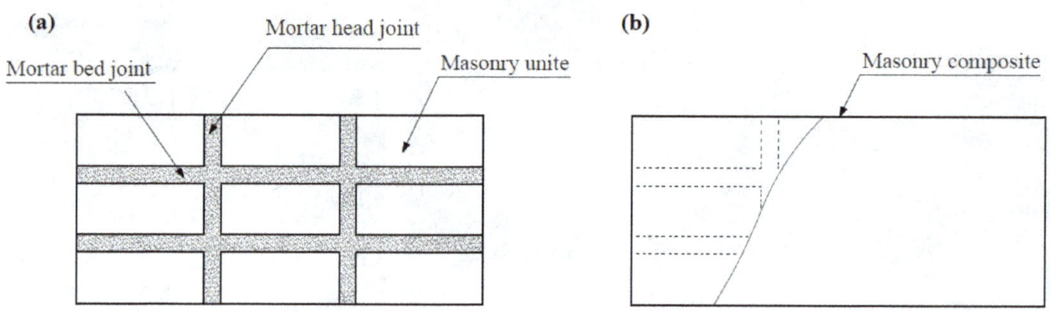

Fig. 7. Macro-modelling strategy for masonry structures. (A) masonry sample, (B) macro-modelling technique

4. STATIC STRUCTURAL ANALYSIS

The static structural behaviour of the palace has been analysed in the nonlinear range under constant vertical loads deriving from the own weight of masonry walls and from the roof loads, beside the differential settlement of supports in order to determine the various forces and actions that caused the structural deficiencies in the whole structure. The main goals in the static analysis is to solve the equilibrium conditions, compatibility and to analyse the structure reactions, stresses, strains and displacements when it is subjected to its own weight to identify the weak points of potential failure. Results of the static analyses on the 3D palace model are reported in Fig. 8 and 9.

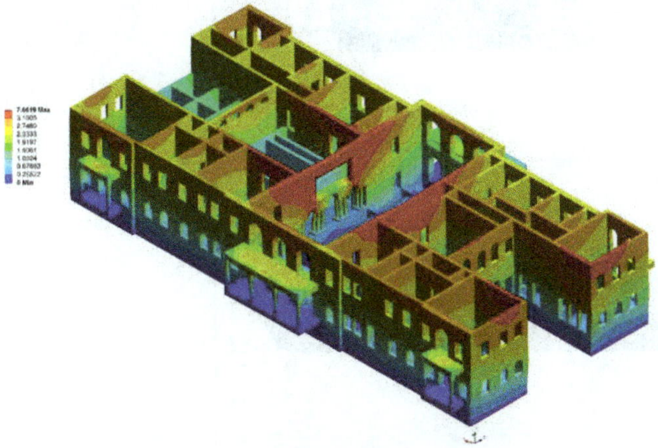

Fig. 8. Vertical displacement (mm)

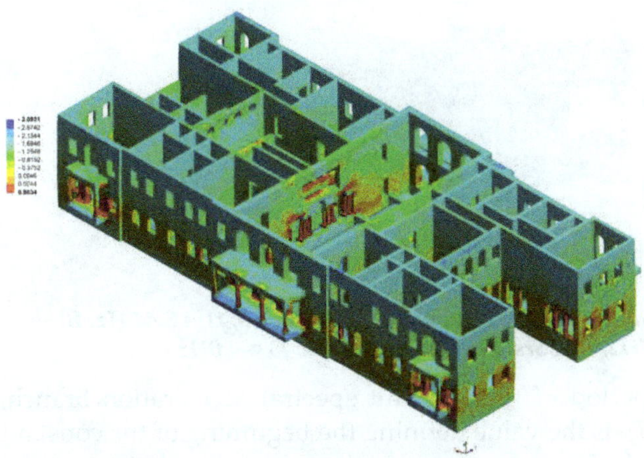

Fig. 9. Vertical stress state σ_y (N/mm²): global view

The obtained results (deformed shape and stress distribution) give realistic values. The total weight of the entire palace is 269427 KN, The structure is almost everywhere compressed and only in a few points the analysis detects the presence of tensile stresses, the maximum value of tensile stress appears on the top surface of the main walls, due to the timber roof loads but this is mainly a local numerical effect depending on the punctual connection between beam and solid elements. The maximum value of compressive stresses ranged from (1.5) to (2.0) N/mm2. These results confirm that the palace is adequate to withstand vertical static loads in a very safe and stable way; this is a quite common result for historical masonry structures because its structural system (bearing wall system) is perfectly able to transfer vertical compressive static loads.

5. MODAL ANALYSIS

The 3D model was investigated for the modal eigenvalue analysis, to determine their modal natural frequencies and the fundamental participation factors. The first 100 modal shapes of the palace have been evaluated with the aim to assure that the total effective modal mass of the model is at least 90% of the actual mass. It has been found that the 90% of the total mass is accounted for by using the first 71 modes.

The first mode of vibration acts along the weakest transversal direction (Z-direction) involving a rotation about X-direction (Fig. 10-A). This mode has a participating mass ratio of about 36.76%. The second mode involves translation in longitudinal direction with out-of-plane deformation of the orthogonal elements, with a participating mass ratio of about 31.37% (Fig. 10-B). The first frequency (Z-direction) is about 5.4% more than the second one (X direction); although this difference is relatively low, it could be evidences a tendency of the building to be more deformable in direction Z that is parallel to the shorter side. While the third modal shape displays torsional deformations (Fig. 10-C).

The remained modes are less important, due to the lower mass contribution and basically excite the structure in various torsional modes. The distribution of the modal shapes demonstrates that the palace displays low transversal and torsional stiffness, with significant out-of-plane deformations of the orthogonal structural elements. Table 4 reports the natural frequencies and effective masses for the first 10 vibration modes in the transversal, longitudinal and vertical direction.

6. SEISMIC ANALYSIS

Historical unreinforced masonry buildings are perfectly able to transfer vertical compressive static loads and its own weight in a very safe and stable way; it mainly consists of vertical load-bearing elements designed primarily to resist in-plane compressive forces, while they are rather sensitive, from a structural point of view, and not adequate to withstand horizontal loads deriving from seismic actions. The high seismic vulnerability of this type of building is due to both the specific mechanical properties of masonry materials (highly non-linear behaviour and very small tensile strength) and the particular configuration of the buildings itself that are characterized by an open plan layout often with perimeter slender walls (Tzamtzis and Asteris, 2004; Betti and Vignoli, 2008; Betti and Vignoli, 2011).

As already stated in the premise, the analysis of the seismic behaviour of the URM buildings is a quite difficult task. So that it is necessary to start from the assessment of the seismic performance of URM buildings, the determination of mechanical and physical properties of construction materials, the characterization of the most vulnerable elements of the structure, and the identification of the possible mechanisms of failure.

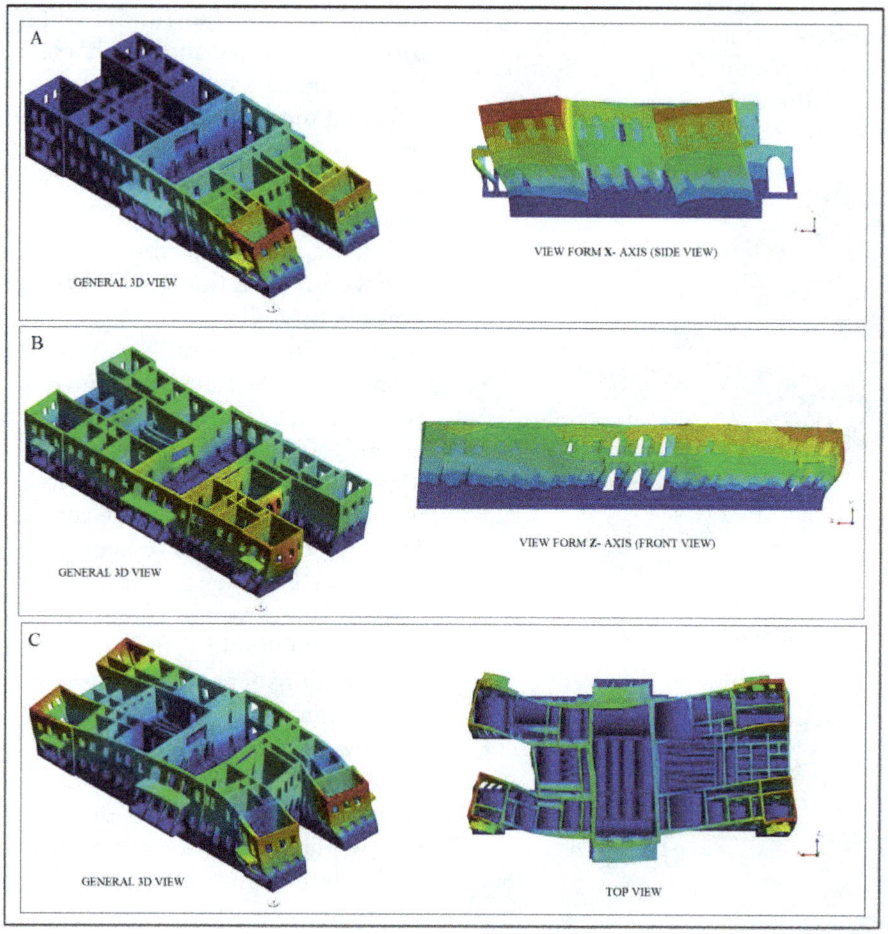

Fig. 10. The three primarily modes of vibration of the palace: A) Rotational about X-direction; f1 = 3.44 Hz, B) Translation in longitudinal direction; f2 = 3.87Hz, C) Torsional deformations; f3 = 4.0Hz

The seismic loads have been evaluated according to the Egyptian code (ECP, 2012). For the case study the response spectrum has been assumed with a soil type B. The following expressions have been used to evaluate the elastic response spectrum:

$$0 \le T \le T_B \quad \Rightarrow S_e(T) = a_g.\gamma_t.S.\left[1 + \frac{T}{T_B}(2.5_\eta - 1)\right]$$

$$T_B \le T \le T_C \quad \Rightarrow S_e(T) = 2.5\,.a_g\,.\gamma_t.S\,.\eta$$

$$T_C \le T \le T_D \quad \Rightarrow S_e(T) = 2.5\,.a_g\,.\gamma_t.S\,.\eta.\left[\frac{T_C}{T}\right] \tag{5}$$

$$T_B \le T \le 4_{sec.} \quad \Rightarrow S_e(T) = a_g\,.\gamma_t.S\,.\eta.\left[\frac{T_C\,.T_D}{T^2}\right]$$

In Eq. (5), *Se(T)* is the elastic response spectrum; *T* is the fundamental period of vibration of the building for lateral motion in the direction considered; T_B is the lower limit of the period of the constant spectral acceleration branch; T_C is the upper limit of the period of the constant spectral acceleration branch; T_D is the value defining the beginning of the constant displacement response range; a_g is the design ground acceleration for the reference return period; γ is the importance factor of the building; η is the design damping correction factor for the horizontal elastic response spectrum where a reference value of $\eta = 1$ corresponds to a normal 5% viscous damping ratio, according to (ECP, 2012). The peak ground acceleration (PGA) for the reference return period is denoted by a_g and for the case study it is equal to 0.12g according to the ECP. *S* is a factor depending on the ground type that in this case (soil type B) is assumed equal to 1.35.

Although nonlinear TH analysis is very time consuming, it is an accurate and reliable analysis to predict all possible failure mechanisms due to seismic actions, as a result of its capability to evidence both

Table 3. Elastic parameters, Yield criterion and Failure surface of main element

	Walls	Columns	Vaults
E_m (Young's modulus)	1460 N/mm²	1500 N/mm²	1900 N/mm²
v (Poisson's ratio)	0.2	0.2	0.2
γ_m (Specific weight)	2300 kg/m³	2400 kg/m³	1600 kg/m³
c (Cohesion)	0.1 N/mm²	0.1 N/mm²	0.1 N/mm²
η (Flow angle)	15°	15°	15°
φ (Friction angle)	38°	38°	38°
f_c (Uniaxial compressive strength)	8.67 N/mm²	9.47 N/mm²	9.32 N/mm²
f_t (Uniaxial tensile strength)	0.86 N/mm²	0.94 N/mm²	0.93 N/mm²
β_c (shear transfer coefficient across close crack)	0.75	0.75	0.75
β_t (shear transfer coefficient across open crack)	0.15	0.15	0.15

in-plane and out-of-plane, local and global failure mechanisms of the structures. In this paper, a TH analysis was performed to assess the seismic vulnerability of Omart Toson palace. In the current analysis the vertical loads combined with seismic horizontal actions along the transversal and longitudinal directions are considered.

Nonlinear dynamic analysis was carried out using an artificial accelerogram compatible with the elastic response spectrum of the Egyptian codes (ECP). The corresponding acceleration history applied at the basis of the building, having a total duration of 15 sec., is visualized in Fig. 11. The seismic behaviour of the palace, the seismic horizontal actions along the transversal (Z) and longitudinal (X) directions are considered. The TH analysis results show that the most critical direction is the transversal direction, the damage is mainly concentrated in the structural elements in the south- western parts exhibit major problems of stability, due to excessive damage and consequent exhaustion of the material strength. This result was expected due to the remarkable out-of-plane deformations of the orthogonal structural elements in the transversal direction. The main façade shows diagonal and vertical cracks, the most damage is concentrated in the openings and near the springers of the arches. The unsafe horizontal stresses of the TH analysis have reached the most of the cracks in the palace structure. The maximum lateral displacements in transversal direction reached from 21 to 34mm. In Fig. 12 a and b the displacements' time histories in transversal and longitudinal direction of the considered control points shown, respectively. While Fig. 13 reports the obtained base shear and *Fig. 14* plots the base shears vs. the displacement of the considered control points in both transversal and longitudinal direction. While Fig. 15 a and b report the principle stresses distribution under the time history cases in transversal and longitudinal direction respectively. As expected, the Top point (located on the top of the main façade) presented largest displacements. With the exclusion of the initial transitory, the base shear oscillates at the principal frequency corresponding to the first fundamental frequency of the structure, the same at which the displacement of the considered points oscillates, and at the frequency of the second vibration mode of the structure. Therefore, while the displacement is dominated by the first modal shape, the base shear is also conditioned by the effects of the higher modes.

Table 4. Natural frequencies and mass participation ratio for transversal, longitudinal and vertical direction

Mode no.	F (Hz)	Z- D (transversal) Meff (%)	X-D (longitudinal) Meff (%)	Y-D (Vertical) Meff (%)
1	3.44744	36.76	0.127	0.00
2	3.87416	0.35	31.37	0.002
3	4.00956	29.57	21.45	0.010
4	4.08532	14.26	0.022	0.000
5	4.57087	1.02	0.636	0.003
6	4.89072	0.29	2.504	0.000
7	5.15817	2.16	0.736	2.031
8	5.22415	0.00	4.729	0.014
9	5.3887	2.02	3.112	0.074
10	5.71642	0.00	0.127	0.003

Depending on the non-linear behaviour of the palace synthesized by the relationship between the base shear, that is the resultant of the horizontal forces, and the displacement of the considered control points of the building, the palace showed different capacities regarding the direction of the seismic loads. The location of hinges in the longitudinal direction obtained by the nonlinear TH analysis were clearly less damage than those obtained in the transversal direction. Besides, lower capacity was noticed in the transversal direction than that found in the longitudinal one, as the absolute maximum resisted load in the longitudinal direction was 0.218g, while in the transversal direction the absolute maximum resisted load was 0.1418g, which relatively was 11.7% and 39.2% less than those resisted in +X and –X, respectively.

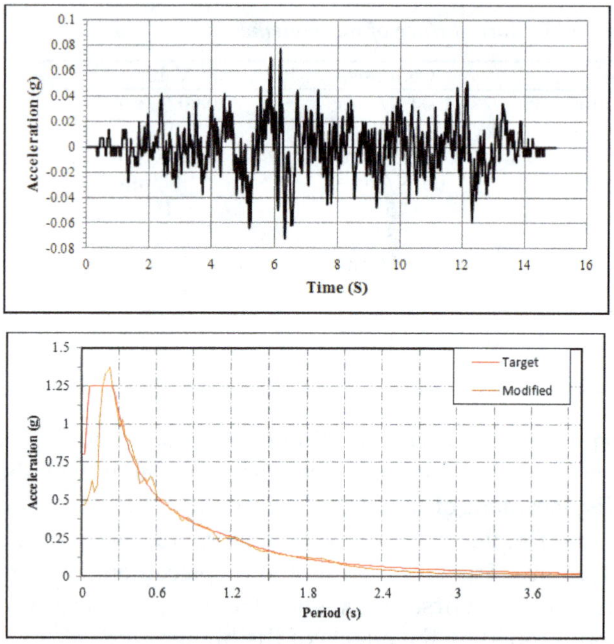

Fig. 11. Acceleration history artificially generated: A) accelerogram; B) Comparison between artificial time history and return period

In the transversal direction, the observed collapse mechanism for the seismic analysis was the overturning of the main facades. The damage concentrated around the openings and the springers of the arches as well as the top and the bases of the columns.

7. CONCLUSIONS AND RECOMMENDATIONS

The present paper contains the results of laboratory testing and numerical investigation to investigate the structural behaviour and seismic vulnerability of an important historical uninformed masonry structure, Omar Toson Palace in Egypt, in order to evaluate its structural performance and deficiencies under earthquake loading. The importance of considering the exact nonlinear and three dimensional behaviour of the masonry structure is shown, in order to determine all the structural deficiencies of the palace under seismic loads. For this purpose, 3D FE static and dynamic with time integration analysis of the overall structure have been done in order to correctly assess the structural behaviour and seismic vulnerability of the palace. The numerical model has been prepared according to the geometrical information gathered from the historical documents and by the measurement of the actual conditions of the structure.

The static structural behaviour of the palace has been analysed under constant vertical loads deriving from the own weight of masonry walls and from the roof loads. The static analysis shows that the structure is almost everywhere compressed and only in a few points the analysis detects the presence of tensile stresses.

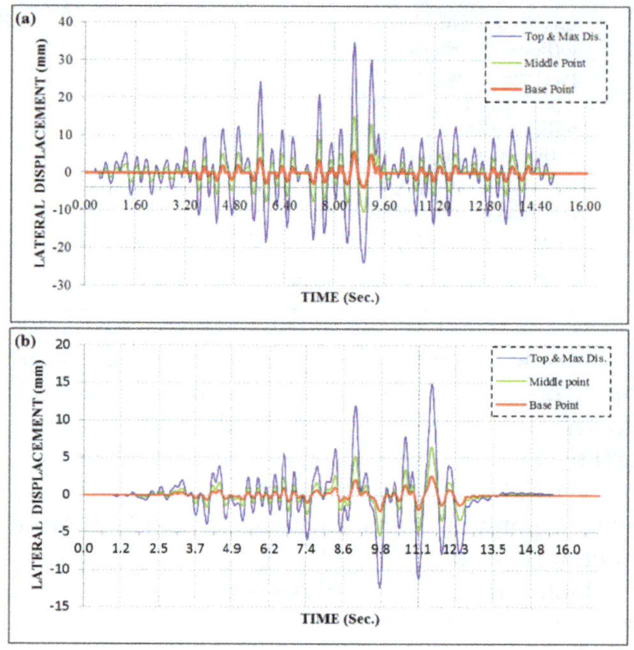

Fig. 12. Time histories of the displacements of the considered control points in (a) transversal and (b) longitudinal direction

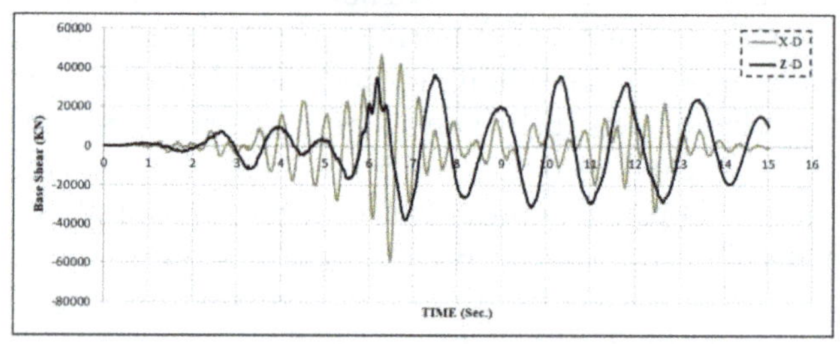

Fig. 13. Time histories of the obtained base shear in transversal and longitudinal direction

The seismic analysis has been evaluated according to the Egyptian codes (ECP-2008); the RS has been assumed with a soil type B and an artificial accelerogram compatible with the seismicity of the palace site have been used to performer the TH analysis. The non-linear seismic analysis prove that the seismic resistance of the palace in the transversal direction is lower than that in the longitudinal direction. This is due to the fact that in the weakest/shorter transversal direction, the orthogonal elements is highly exhibited to out-of-plane deformation due to applied horizontal seismic loads acting in ±Z direction results these elements tend to overturning about X direction. The most tension unsafe zones obtained by the present models are in the currently cracked sections. According to the analysis results, the dynamic behaviour of the palace is very sensitive to the structure damage and vulnerable to seismic actions.

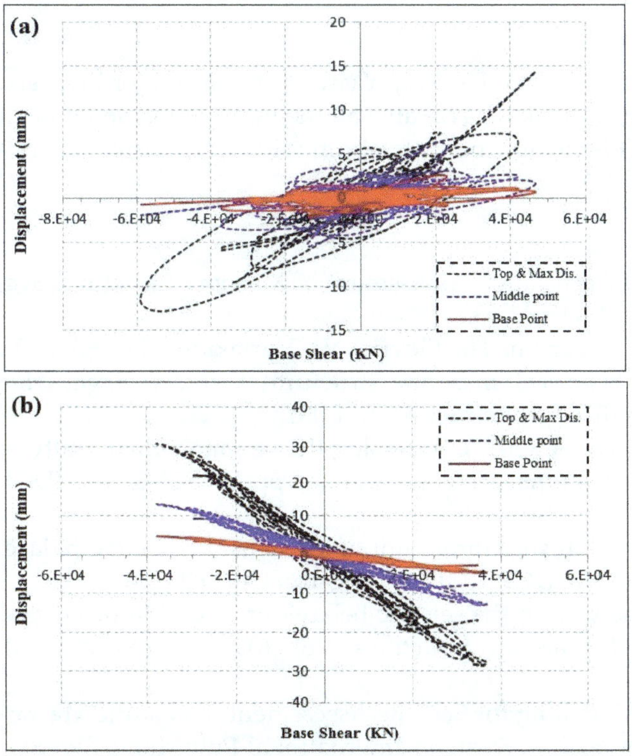

Fig. 14. Base shear vs. displacement curves of the considered control points in (a) transversal, (b) longitudinal direction

Therefore, scientific intervention methodology is necessary to be performed to reach a certain level of structural safety and to achieve successful conservation processes taking into account all criteria and requirements regarding preservation of the architectural value of the building.

The performed study underlines the importance of the nonlinear three-dimensional dynamic analysis in the evaluation of the actual seismic performance of a masonry structure in order to investigate all possible failure mechanisms under seismic loading. Besides, the examination of the final deformed configuration and stresses distribution helps to understand the global behaviour of the structural elements. As well as the accurate seismic assessment allows identifying essential and appropriate intervention strategies to increase the seismic capacity of the historic masonry structures. Additionally, the macro-element technique for modelling the nonlinear response of masonry structures is particularly efficient and suitable for the seismic performance investigation. The paper also proves that the nonlinear behaviour of masonry structures and the number of integration points both in-plane and in the thickness directions plays an important role for the accuracy of the results.

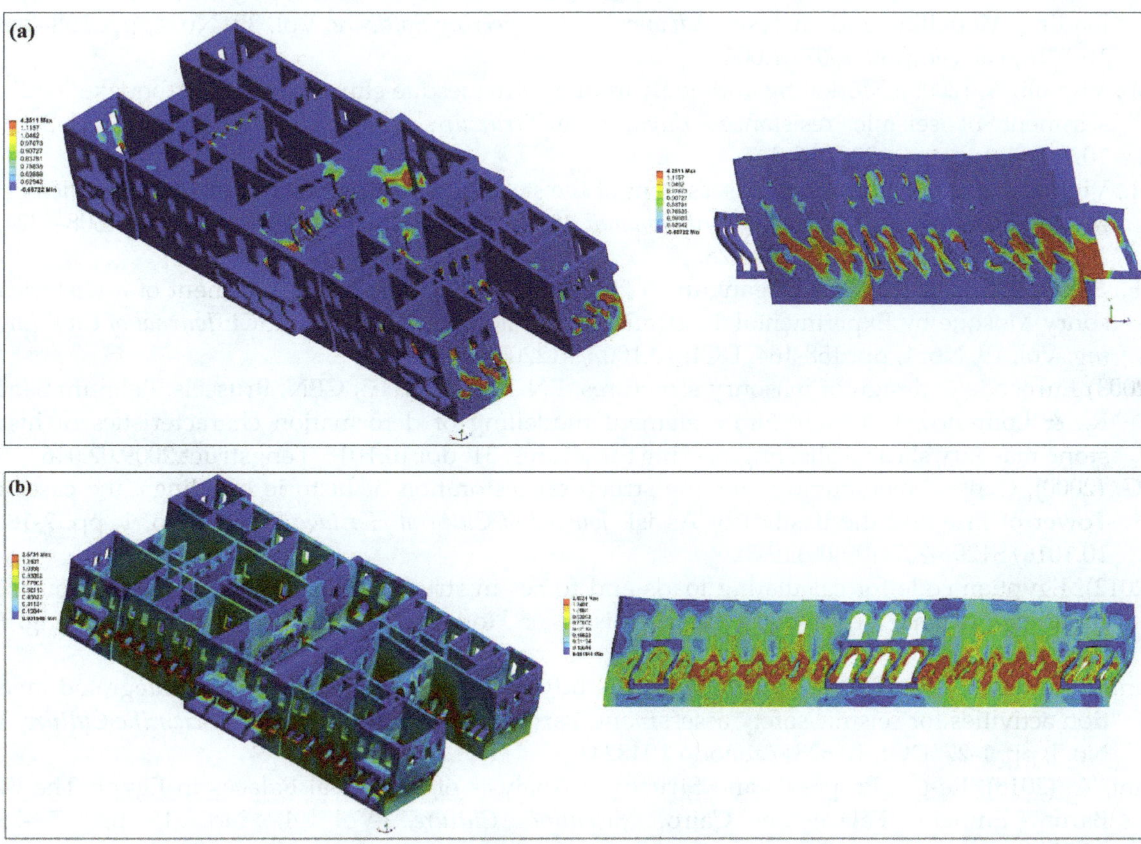

Fig. 15. Deformed configuration and principal stress distribution due to the artificial earthquake accelerogram in (a) transversal, (b) longitudinal direction (N/mm2)

ACKNOWLEDGEMENTS

The first author, O. Amer, would like to express his gratitude to Dr. Eng. Yasser Yehia Amin for his assistance during the present numerical modelling work and for making available all the information and data at his disposal. Special thank goes also to Eng. Mohamed El-Feel for the enthusiasm with which he collaborated in developing this study.

REFERENCES

Asteris, P., & Giannopoulos, I. (2012). Vulnerability and Restoration Assessment of Masonry Structural Systems. *Electronic Journal of Structural Engineering*, 12(1), 82-93.

Asteris, P.G., Chronopoulos, M.P., Chrysostomou, C.Z., Varum, H., Plevris, V., Kyriakides, N., Silva, V. (2014). Seismic vulnerability assessment of historical masonry structural systems. *Engineering Structures*, Vol. 62, No. 63, pp. 118-134, DOI:10.1016/j.engstruct.2014.01.031.

Barbieri, G., Biolzi, L., Bocciarelli, M., Fregonese, L., Frigeri, A. (2013). Assessing the seismic vulnerability of a historical building. *Engineering Structures*, Vol. 57, pp. 523–535, DOI: 10.1016/j.engstruct.2013.09.045.

Betti, M., Bartoli, G., Orlando, M. (2010). Evaluation study on structural fault of a renaissance Italian palace. *Engineering Structures*, Vol. 32, No. 7, pp. 1801–1813, DOI: 10.1016/j.engstruct.2010.03.001.

Betti, M., Galano, L., Vignoli, A. (2014). Comparative analysis on the seismic behaviour of unreinforced masonry buildings with flexible diaphragms. *Engineering Structures*, Vol. 61, pp. 195–208, DOI: 10.1016/j.engstruct.2013.12.038.

Betti, M., Galano, L., Vignoli, A. (2015). Finite Element Modelling for Seismic Assessment of Historic Masonry Buildings. In: *Earthquakes and Their Impact on Society*. Springer International Publishing, Switzerland, pp. 377-415, DOI: 10.1007/978-3-319-21753-6_14.

Betti, M., Orlando, M., Vignoli, A. (2011). Static behaviour of an Italian Medieval Castle: Damage assessment by numerical modelling. *Computers & Structures*, Vol. 89, No. 21-22, pp. 1956–1970, DOI: 10.1016/j.compstruc.2011.05.022.

Betti, M., Vignoli, A. (2008). Assessment of seismic resistance of a basilica-type church under earthquake loading: Modelling and analysis. *Advances in Engineering Software*, Vol. 39, No. 4, pp. 258–283 DOI: 10.1016/j.advengsoft.2007.01.004.

Betti, M., Vignoli, A. (2008). Modelling and analysis of a Romanesque church under earthquake loading: assessment of seismic resistance. *Engineering Structures*, Vol. 30, No. 2, pp. 352–367, DOI: 10.1016/j.engstruct.2007.03.027.

Betti, M., Vignoli, A. (2011). Numerical assessment of the static and seismic behaviour of the basilica of Santa Maria all'Impruneta (Italy). *Construction and Building Materials*, Vol. 25, No. 12, pp. 4308-4324, DOI: 10.1016/j.conbuildmat.2010.12.028.

Cakir, F., Seker, B. S., Durmus, A., Dogangun, A., Uysal, H. (2015). Seismic Assessment of a Historical Masonry Mosque by Experimental Tests and Finite Element Analyses. *KSCE Journal of Civil Engineering*, Vol. 19, No. 1, pp. 158-164, DOI: 10.1007/s12205-014-0468-4.

CEN (2003) Eurocode 6: design of masonry structures. EN 1996-1-1:2003, CEN, Brussels, Belgium Senthivel, R., & Lourenço, P. (2009). Finite element modelling of deformation characteristics of historical stone masonry shear walls. Engineering Structures, 31. doi:10.1016/j.engstruct.2009.02.046

Croci, G. (2000). General methodology for the structural restoration of historic buildings: the cases of the Tower of Pisa and the Basilica of Assisi. *Journal of Cultural Heritage*, Vol. 1, No. 1, pp. 7-18, DOI: 10.1016/S1296-2074(99)00119-3.

ECP. (2012). Egyptian code for calculating loads and forces in structural work and masonry. Housing and Building National Research Center, Ministry of Housing, Utilities and Urban Planning, Cairo, Egypt.

Elyamani, A. and Roca, P. (2018a). A review on the study of historical structures using integrated investigation activities for seismic safety assessment. Part I: dynamic investigation, *Scientific Culture*, Vol. 4, No. l, pp. 1-27. DOI: 10.5281/zenodo.1048241

Elyamani, A. (2018). Re-use Proposals and Structural Analysis of Historical Palaces in Egypt: The Case of Baron Empain Palace in Cairo. *Scientific Culture*, Vol. 4, No. l, pp. 53-73.DOI: 10.5281/zenodo.1048245

Elyamani, A. and Roca, P. (2018b). A review on the study of historical structures using integrated investigation activities for seismic safety assessment. Part II: model updating and seismic analysis, *Scientific Culture*, Vol. 4, No. 1, pp. 29-51. DOI: 10.5281/zenodo.1048243

Giordano, A., Mele, E., De Luca, A. (2002). Modelling of historical masonry structures: comparison of different approaches through a case study. *Engineering Structures*, Vol. 24, No. 8, pp. 1057–1069, DOI: 10.1016/S0141-0296(02)00033-0.

Kappos, A., Penelis, G., Drakopoulos, C. (2002). Evaluation of simplified models for lateral load analysis of unreinforced masonry buildings. *Journal of Structural Engineering* - asce, Vol. 128, No. 7, pp. 890–897, DOI: 10.1061/(ASCE)0733-9445(2002)128:7(890).

Lagomarsino, S. (1999). Damage survey of ancient churches: the Umbria-Marche experience. Proc. Int. workshop on *Measures of seismic damage to masonry buildings*, Balkema, Rotterdam.

Lagomarsino, S., Podestà, S. (2004) Seismic vulnerability of ancient churches: I. damage assessment and emergency planning. *Earthquake Spectra,* Vol. 20, No. 2, pp. 377–394, DOI: 10.1193/1.1737735.

Lourenco, P.B. (2002) Computations on historic masonry structures. *Progress in Structural Engineering and Materials*, Vol. 4, No. 3, pp. 301-319.

Lourenço, P.B., Mendes, N., Ramos, L.F., Oliveira, D.V. (2001). On the Analysis of Masonry Structures without box behavior. *International Journal of Architectural Heritage*, Vol. 5, No. 4-5, pp. 369-382, DOI: 10.1080/15583058.2010.528824.

Lourenço, P.B., Roque, J.A. (2006). Simplified indexes for the seismic vulnerability of ancient masonry buildings. *Construction and Building Materials*, Vol. 20, No. 4, pp. 200–208, DOI: 10.1016/j.engfailanal.2013.02.014.

Magenes, G. (2000). A method for pushover analysis in seismic assessment of masonry buildings. Proc., 12th world conference on earthquake engineering, New Zealand Society for Earthquake Engineering, Auckland, New Zealand.

Mele, E., De Luca, A., Giordano, A. (2003). Modelling and analysis of a basilica under earthquake loading. *Journal of Cultural Heritage*, Vol. 4, No. 4, pp. 355–367, DOI: 10.1016/j.culher.2003.03.002.

Milania, G., Lourenço, P. B., Trallia, A. (2007). 3D homogenized limit analysis of masonry buildings under horizontal loads. *Engineering Structures*, Vol. 29, pp. 3134–3148, DOI: 10.1016/j.engstruct.2007.03.003.

Petrovc,ˇicˇ S., Kilar, V. (2013). Seismic failure mode interaction for the equivalent frame modeling of unreinforced masonry structures. *Engineering Structures*, Vol. 54, pp. 9–22, DOI: 10.1016/j.engstruct.2013.03.050.

Preciado, A. (2015). Seismic vulnerability and failure modes simulation of ancient masonry towers by validated virtual finite element models. *Engineering Failure Analysis*, Vol. 57, pp. 72–87, DOI: 10.1016/j.engfailanal.2015.07.030.

Tzamtzis, A.D., Asteris, P.G. (2004). FE Analysis of Complex Discontinuous and Jointed Structural Systems (Part 1: Presentation of the Method - A State-of-the-Art Review). *Electronic Journal of Structural Engineering*, Vol. 1, pp. 75-92.

Vera, C. (2012). *Damage identification of unreinforced masonry structures based on vibration response*. Ph.D. thesis. Department of Civil and Environmental Engineering, The University of Auckland, New Zealand.

Vicente, R., Ayala, D., Ferreira, T.M., Varum, H., Costa, A., da Silva, J.A.R.M., Lagomarsino, S. (2013). Seismic Vulnerability and Risk Assessment of Historic Masonry Buildings. In: *Structural Rehabilitation of Old Buildings*. Springer-Verlag, Berlin, Heidelberg, Germany, pp. 307 - 348, DOI: 10.1007/978-3-642-39686-1_11.

Permissions

All chapters in this book were first published in MAA, by University of the Aegean; hereby published with permission under the Creative Commons Attribution License or equivalent. Every chapter published in this book has been scrutinized by our experts. Their significance has been extensively debated. The topics covered herein carry significant findings which will fuel the growth of the discipline. They may even be implemented as practical applications or may be referred to as a beginning point for another development.

The contributors of this book come from diverse backgrounds, making this book a truly international effort. This book will bring forth new frontiers with its revolutionizing research information and detailed analysis of the nascent developments around the world.

We would like to thank all the contributing authors for lending their expertise to make the book truly unique. They have played a crucial role in the development of this book. Without their invaluable contributions this book wouldn't have been possible. They have made vital efforts to compile up to date information on the varied aspects of this subject to make this book a valuable addition to the collection of many professionals and students.

This book was conceptualized with the vision of imparting up-to-date information and advanced data in this field. To ensure the same, a matchless editorial board was set up. Every individual on the board went through rigorous rounds of assessment to prove their worth. After which they invested a large part of their time researching and compiling the most relevant data for our readers.

The editorial board has been involved in producing this book since its inception. They have spent rigorous hours researching and exploring the diverse topics which have resulted in the successful publishing of this book. They have passed on their knowledge of decades through this book. To expedite this challenging task, the publisher supported the team at every step. A small team of assistant editors was also appointed to further simplify the editing procedure and attain best results for the readers.

Apart from the editorial board, the designing team has also invested a significant amount of their time in understanding the subject and creating the most relevant covers. They scrutinized every image to scout for the most suitable representation of the subject and create an appropriate cover for the book.

The publishing team has been an ardent support to the editorial, designing and production team. Their endless efforts to recruit the best for this project, has resulted in the accomplishment of this book. They are a veteran in the field of academics and their pool of knowledge is as vast as their experience in printing. Their expertise and guidance has proved useful at every step. Their uncompromising quality standards have made this book an exceptional effort. Their encouragement from time to time has been an inspiration for everyone.

The publisher and the editorial board hope that this book will prove to be a valuable piece of knowledge for researchers, students, practitioners and scholars across the globe.

List of Contributors

William C. Mahaney
Quaternary Surveys, 26 Thornhill Ave., Thornhill, Ontario, Canada, L4J 1J4, and Department of Geography, York University, 4700 Keele St., Toronto, Ontario, Canada, M3J 1P3

I. V. Florinsky
Institute of Mathematical Problems of Biology, Russian Academy of Sciences, Pushchino, Moscow Region, 142290, Russia

Michelangelo Messina
University of Catania, Department of Humanities, Piazza Dante, 32, 95124, Catania (Italy)

Lucia Arcifa
University of Catania, Department of Educational Sciences, Via Biblioteca, 4, 95124, Catania (Italy)

Germana Barone, Claudio Finocchiaro and Paolo Mazzoleni
University of Catania, Department of Biological, Geological and Environmental Sciences, C.so Italia, 57, 95129 Catania (Italy)

G. Sabatino, M. Di Bella, S. Quartieri, G. Marcianò, A. Tripodo and D. Romano
Dipartimento di Scienze Matematiche e Informatiche, Scienze Fisiche e Scienze della Terra, University of Messina, Viale G. d'Alcontres 31, 98166 S. Agata, Messina

A. Giuliano
Museo Regionale di Messina, Viale della Libertà 465, 98121 Messina

F. Italiano
Istituto Nazionale di Geofisica e Vulcanologia, Sez. Palermo, Via Ugo La Malfa, 153, 90146 Palermo, Italy

Mohammad Nassar
The University of Jordan, Faculty of Arts and Design, Amman, Jordan

B. AbuHelaleh
Petra College for Tourism and Archaeology, Al Hussein Bin Talal University, 71110 Ma'an, Jordan

S. Bourke
NEAF, SOPHI, A14, University of Sydney, Sydney, Australia

U. Thun Hohenstein
University of Ferrara, Department of Humanities, Corso Ercole I d'Este 32 - 44121 Ferrara, Italy

S. Papamarinopoulos
Faculty of Geology, University of Patras, GR 26504, Rio Patras, Greece

P. Preka-Papadema and K. Gazeas
Section of Astrophysics, Astronomy and Mechanics, Faculty of Physics, National and Kapodistrian University of Athens, University Campus, GR 15784, Athens, Greece

P. Nastos
Laboratory of Climatology and Atmospheric Environment, Faculty of Geology & Geoenvironment, National and Kapodistrian University of Athens, University Campus, GR 15784, Athens, Greece

K. G. Kiriakopoulos
Laboratory of Mineralogy and Petrology, Faculty of Geology & Geoenvironment, National and Kapodistrian University of Athens, University Campus, GR 15784, Athens, Greece

W. C. Mahaney
Quaternary Surveys, 26 Thornhill Ave, Thornhill, Ontario, Canada, L4J1J4 and Department of Geography, York University, 4700 Keele St., N. York, Ontario, Canada, M3J 1P3

A. Sampson
University of the Aegean, Laboratory of Environmental Archaeology, Rhodes, Greece

J. K. Kozlowski
Jaggiellonian University, Krakow, Poland

M. Kaczanowska
The Polish Academy of Arts and Sciences, Krakow, Poland

G. Barone, P. Mazzoleni and S. Raneri
Department of Biological, Geological and Environmental Sciences, University of Catania, C.so Italia 57, 95129 Catania, Italy

G. Spagnolo and A. Santostefano
Department of Ancient and Modern Civilizations, University of Messina, Polo Universitario Annunziata, 98168 Messina, Italy

Akbar Abedi, Mehdi Razani and Masoud Bagherzadeh Kasiri
Archaeometry Department, Tabriz Islamic Art University, 51385/4567, Tabriz, IRAN

Bahram Vosough
Geology Department, Payam-e Noor University, Tabriz, IRAN

Daniel Steiniger
Deutsches Archäologisches Institut, Eurasien Abteilung, Berlin, GERMANY

Ghader Ebrahimi
Archaeology Department, Mohagegh Ardabili University, Ardabil, IRAN

Vytautas Tumėnas
The Lithuanian Institute of History, dept. of Ethnology (Vilnius, Lithuania)

Arvin Maghsoudlou and Seyyed Rasool Mousavi Haji
Faculty of Art and Architecture, University of Mazandaran, Babolsar, Iran

Maria Mina and Manolis Stefanakis
Hellenic Open University, Patras, Greece & University of Cyprus, 1 Panepistimiou Avenue 2109 Aglantzia, Nicosia, Cyprus

Hassan Kohansal Vajargah
Department of History, University of Guilan, Rasht, Iran

Index

CPSIA information can be obtained
at www.ICGtesting.com
Printed in the USA
LVHW061112030222
710136LV00005B/106

9 781639 892600